DATE DUE

DE 16 '04			
FE 1 1 '10			

DEMCO 38-296

ECONOMICS

An Introduction to Traditional and Radical Views

SIXTH EDITION

E. K. Hunt
University of Utah

Howard J. Sherman
University of California, Riverside

1817

HARPER & ROW, PUBLISHERS, New York
Grand Rapids, Philadelphia, St. Louis, San Francisco,
London, Singapore, Sydney, Tokyo

To Barbara and Linda

Project Editor: Lester A. Sheinis
Art Direction/Cover Coordinator: Heather A. Ziegler
Cover Design: Edward Smith Design, Inc.
Text Art: Accurate Art, Inc.
Production: Beth Maglione
Compositor: TAPSCO, Inc.
Printer/Binder: R. R. Donnelley & Sons Co.
Cover Printer: New England Book Components

ECONOMICS
An Introduction to Traditional and Radical Views, Sixth Edition

Library of Congress Cataloging-in-Publication Data

Hunt, E. K.
    Economics: an introduction to traditional and radical views/
E. K. Hunt, Howard J. Sherman.—6th ed.
        p. cm.
    Includes bibliographical references.
    ISBN 0-06-043002-8
    1. Economics. I. Sherman, Howard J. II. Title.
HB171.5.H83 1990
330—dc20   89-20020
                                                          CIP

89 90 91 92 9 8 7 6 5 4 3 2 1

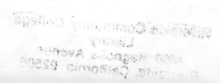

Contents

PART TWO   PRICES AND POVERTY: AN INTRODUCTION TO MICROECONOMICS

Chapter 15   Market Allocation of Resources: Efficiency Versus Fairness   219

Chapter 16   Prices and Income: The Neoclassical Theory   236

Chapter 17   Income Distribution: The Neoclassical Theory   254

Chapter 45   Market Socialism and Perestroika   671

Chapter 46   Socialism, Democracy, and Glasnost   682

Preface

In Part One of this book we introduce economics by way of a history of the great economists (some of them wild and wonderful). We present their ideas within the context of the institutions of their times, so we sketch an economic history as well as a history of economic thought.

There is no easier and more pleasant way of learning economics than to follow the evolution of the main ideas of the great thinkers in the field. This approach will also impress upon the reader, as nothing else could, that there are at least two (and usually more) views on every subject in economics.

It is interesting to see how our modern economic institutions slowly evolved from feudal times. The usual textbooks start off cold from the present. We believe it is much more meaningful to witness all of the curious zigzags and the fighting that occurred in the development of our present institutions. How our economic ideas and institutions developed in the past gives us a key to understanding the present and, we hope, the future.

The history of economic ideas and the history of economic institutions are not totally independent of one another. In reality, they are very closely related, each affecting the other at all times. Thus, we shall see that the specific problems and interests of various groups gave rise to very specific economic ideologies and that these ideologies served as an excuse for the status quo or as a call for drastic change. For example, we shall see in the first few chapters that the dominant ideology in the medieval period fully supported the feudal economic system as just and correct and eternal. Eventually, however, the contrary ideas of the new groups of merchants and industrialists were reflected in new economic ideologies, which then helped overturn the old restrictive feudal order.

TEACHING ECONOMIC THEORY

The traditional approach to teaching economic theory concentrates on explaining how the consumer may maximize his or her satisfaction from spending, how the businessperson may maximize profits, and how the government may aid private business to maximize growth. This approach is often dull and mechanical. We include these usual and somewhat mechanical subjects, but to a lesser degree, focusing on the more exciting present-day social and political issues. In fact, ours is more a political economics textbook than a purely economics textbook.

Thus, in Part Two we discuss the traditional microeconomic problems of the individual consumer and the individual business firm. We also investigate often neglected problems—for example, poverty, racism, sexual discrimination, monopoly power, unequal education opportunities, and tax loopholes.

Similarly, in Part Three we discuss the usual macroeconomic problems of the economy as a whole, including the basic questions of inflation and unemployment. In addition, we examine such problems as pollution and waste, population, war spending, the less developed countries, and imperialism.

OBJECTIVITY

Some traditional economists will complain that we do not present the conservative or traditional views completely enough. We do try, especially in the historical presentations of Part One, to state both the traditional and radical views as impartially as possible. Of course, no one is impartial, so we undoubtedly state the radical view somewhat more effectively. In Parts Two and Three we again state the traditional views first, before giving the radical view, but our sympathy with the radical view will be quite apparent.

Some radical economists who have read this book have complained of the opposite. They have said that we sound too impartial between the conservative and radical views, especially in their historical presentation. We do indeed present both views as fully as possible.

A COMPARATIVE APPROACH

In Part Four we take the reader on an excursion through some of the countries that call themselves socialist, particularly the Soviet Union. Various chapters examine their historical development, current institutions, and current problems. Their development and institutions are compared with those of the Western capitalist countries. This is done not merely to give us an idea of what the rest of the world looks like. It is also important because the comparisons bring out more clearly many of the features of the Western capitalist countries. For example, in studying the market process of the United States, it is very interesting and helpful to compare it with the planned nonmarket economics of Eastern Europe.

SOME OTHER SPECIAL FEATURES

The usual elementary economics text is filled with graphs and mathematics. We have used graphs only where necessary to illustrate a point, but we have always explained them first in ordinary English and have kept the graphs as simple as possible.

For the convenience of students, summaries are provided at the end of each chapter. *Warning:* No summary can explain a chapter; it may merely remind you of the most important points. *Another warning:* No summary can be very accurate because it is too short to include all the necessary qualifications.

For instructors accustomed to standard textbooks, we have presented most theory in its usual order and covered the usual topics. In a few places, however, that is not so. For example, international trade is sometimes placed in the microeconomics section, even though the discussion must always contain many macroeconomic observations. Because we have found that the macroeconomic issues in international trade are the most interesting, we have emphasized them and put the discussion of that subject under macroeconomics. (It is independent enough of the surrounding chapters that it can be used at another point in the course.) Also, we have omitted production functions, a traditional topic, because we approach the subject differently and believe recent theory has shown this approach to be based on indefensible assumptions.

HOW TO USE THIS BOOK

This book has been designed so that it may be used as the main text for a one-year course, but with plentiful use of supplements. Many good collections of readings are available. It may also be used for a one-semester or one-quarter course if one wishes to cover the material rather lightly or emphasize particular areas.

Most instructors prefer to teach macroeconomics before microeconomics. That is understandable because microeconomic theory is usually especially dull and lifeless as treated in most texts. This book is so arranged that instructors may, if they wish, teach macroeconomics first, even though it comes second.

After some heated discussion between the authors, we decided to put microeconomics first. For one, we believe our microeconomics section is much more interesting than the average. We go through the usual supply and demand graphs, though as simply as possible. But the section also emphasizes views on poverty, government behavior, and racial and sexual discrimination—all of which, we believe, the reader will find interesting. We also present the usual graphs on monopoly theory, but give a great deal more attention than most books to the history and facts of monopoly in the United States. We believe the material on income distribution and monopoly is particularly important in understanding the later macro material on waste and cyclical unemployment in the United States. (But, again, we emphasize that instructors could conceivably teach Part Three ahead of Part Two if they so desire.)

Finally, the book may be used in special ways in one-quarter or one-semester courses emphasizing only one aspect of economics. First, in a macroeconomics course we suggest that Part One, on history, be assigned to be read lightly in the first few weeks. (The chapter on Keynes could be emphasized.) Then jump to Part Three, on macroeconomics, which is lengthy and will give the students plenty of meat, although a supplement could certainly be used as well.

Second, in a course on microeconomics we would again suggest beginning with Part One so that the student sees how microeconomics developed through the history of thought (particularly emphasizing the chapters on the neoclassical economists and on Marx). Part Two will then follow naturally. Since Part Two is fairly short, you may have time for the comparative material of Part Four, which examines several microproblems in the context of economic planning. You should also have time to include a supplement.

Third, some courses emphasize history and institutions and deemphasize theory. We believe our book is better suited for such a course than any other complete textbook available. All of Part One could be emphasized. In Part Two the chapters on price and value theory could be omitted. On the other hand, the chapters on the labor movement, monopoly power, government, and discrimination are mainly institutional. In Part Three, the chapters on national income accounting and income determination could be omitted. The other chapters in Part Three are mainly institutional, although certain sections and appendices might be omitted. In Part Four all of the chapters are heavily historical and institutional.

SUGGESTED READINGS

Three journals contain numerous very useful and very interesting articles on every subject mentioned in this book. One is the *Review of Radical Political Economics* (Union for Radical Political Economics, Department of Economics, University of California, Riverside, Calif. 92521). The second is *Monthly Review* (122 West 27th Street, New York, N.Y. 10001). The third is *Dollars and Sense* (342 Somerville Avenue, Somerville, Mass. 02143).

Other suggested readings on specialized topics are included at the end of appropriate chapters.

ACKNOWLEDGMENTS

We are profoundly grateful to those whose teaching or direct help made this book possible: Professors Sidney Coontz, William Davisson, Douglas Dowd, Robert Edminster, David Felix, John Gurley, J. W. Hanks, Kiyotoshi Iwamoto, Robert Lekachman, Lawrence Nabors, Andreas Papandreou, Lynn Turgeon, Benjamin Ward, Thomas Weisskopf, and Stephen Worland. Extensive research help, for which we express our thanks, was furnished by Maryanna Boynton, Faris Bingaradi, Brian Bock, William Harnett, Kathleen Pulling, and Michael Sheehan.

We also wish to thank various publishers for giving us permission to use certain materials from our previous books: Hunt, *Property and Prophets* (Harper & Row, 1978); Sherman, *Elementary Aggregate Economics* (Appleton, 1966); Sherman, *The Soviet Economy* (Little, Brown, 1969); Sherman, *Profit Rates in the United States* (Cornell University Press, 1968); Sherman, *Radical Political Economy* (Basic Books, 1972); and Sherman, *Stagflation* (Harper & Row, 1976).

For later editions we gratefully acknowledge the extensive but constructive criticism of many reviewers, including professors Fikret Ceylhun, Norris Clement, James Cypher, Richard Edwards, Reza Ghorashi, Kenneth Harrison, Clint Jencks, Ross La Roe, Victor Lippit, John Pool, Larry Sawyers, Eric Schutz, Dick Shirey, Jim Starkey, Howard Wachtel, Rick Wolff, and Michael Yates.

We warmly appreciate the typing and clerical help of Shirlee Pigeon and Sandy Schauer.

For the future we invite any useful ideas for improvements in the book. Please write to us and we will take your suggestions very seriously.

E. K. Hunt
Howard J. Sherman

Introduction

This book presents throughout two different views of economics: the traditional, conservative view versus the critical, liberal or radical view. It may surprise you to learn that there is no single *truth* in economics but, rather, two or more conflicting approaches to it. That, however, is the sad fact in economics and in all the other social sciences. In the study of society there is no important point that is noncontroversial; on every important issue there is a range of opinions from the most conservative to the most radical. Certainly, there are some facts on which most economists agree, and there are some tools that most economists use, but we differ over what the important problems are, how to approach them, and how to interpret the findings.

One basic area of disagreement concerns the possibility of change. Radicals contend that society can and should be drastically changed. Conservatives contend that nothing can ever change because our behavior is rooted in an unchanging human nature.

TRADITIONAL VIEWS OF HUMAN NATURE

The traditional or conservative economists, like Wowsy, assume that people are born with certain ideas—such as eating people or holding slaves or being a competitive capitalist—and that there is no way to change those ideas. Since these ideas are held by everyone, our behavior is determined by these ideas and cannot be changed. Where do they come from? Some conservatives say God gives us our ideas. Others claim that certain ways of living are just "natural" and obvious, so everyone naturally knows they are best. Others, like Freud, simply say we are born with innate, inherited drives—for example, all men are aggressive and domineering, while all women are passive and like to be dominated.

Similarly, conservatives in the South before the Civil War said that slavery was natural, that blacks were happy only as slaves, and that whites were natural slave owners. The clergy added that slavery was divinely ordained by God, that keeping slaves so that they would be happy—and whipping them occasionally for their own good—was the Christian white man's burden.

In the Middle Ages, conservative religious leaders and social thinkers held that serfdom was natural and reflected human nature. The serfs were happy working for landlords because that was a serf's nature. The landlords were happy directing serfs, judging them, and even executing them (but only when necessary) because that was a landlord's nature. Thomas Aquinas contended that some prices are normal and natural and that it is a sin to buy or sell at more or less than those prices. Chapter 1 will explore medieval economic views more fully.

During the Industrial Revolution, a school of economists known as the classical school preached that capitalism is natural and eternal, earlier economic systems being "unnatural." They claimed that it is the natural proclivity of every person to be greedy, to compete relentlessly, and to calculate rationally every purchase and every other economic activity. These views are further explored in Chapter 4 of this book.

Finally, most traditional economists of today (called neoclassical economists) take as given at birth all the preferences of individual consumers. They seem to think that we are born with a certain order of preferences for Cadillacs or TV sets. In Chapter 8 we shall see that these natural consumer preferences constitute the heart of their economics.

THE CRITICAL VIEW OF HUMAN NATURE

By contrast with conservatives, critical economists believe that all ideas and preferences—such as our desire for Cadillacs—are shaped by the society in which we live. Consumers are influenced not only by obvious means like advertising but also by more subtle and pervasive means, like family upbringing, religion, education, and the mass media. Similarly, it is no coincidence that the dominant view or ideology under slavery supports slavery, that under serfdom supports serfdom, and that under capitalism supports capitalism. Social scientists are human beings like everyone else and thus have their own ideas and preconceptions shaped by society.

Critical economists contend that, since our ideology is determined by our social environment, a change in our socioeconomic structure will eventually change the dominant ideology. For example, before the Civil War most Southerners (including their social scientists) declared that slavery was natural and good; but after 100 years of capitalist socioeconomic institutions, most Southerners (including their social scientists) declared that capitalism is natural and good. We conclude that dominant ideas are not given by human nature, but are shaped by socioeconomic relations and can be changed by changes in the underlying relationships. There is thus hope for a completely new and better society with new and better views by most people.

This does not mean that ideas are unimportant in the process of social change. The ideas of at least a large number of people must change before a revolutionary social change is possible. The point is only that our ideological views are not God-given and do not change at random. New views—such as the revolutionary ideology of liberty, equality, and fraternity—appeared and caused the French and American revolutions only because they reflected underlying social conflicts. The needs of most people (farmers, workers, and industrialists) came into conflict with the old socioeconomic relationships (the French feudal monarchy or British colonialism). These conflicts caused social thinkers, such as Voltaire and Tom Paine, to present new ideologies. The new ideologies spread because they reflected most people's needs and desires. This led to political revolutions, which changed socioeconomic structures. The new structures reinforced the new ideas and made their ideological conquest complete. This circular process is charted in the figure below.

Economic forces are defined here to include all the labor that workers do, the tools and machinery with which they work, the use of known natural resources, and the use of the available level of technology. *Economic relations* are the relations among people engaged in economic activity—for example, the relations between slaves and slave owners, between workers and capitalists, or between debtors and creditors. In Chapter 6 we shall find that Karl Marx said that economic forces and relations, defined in this

Ideas and Economics

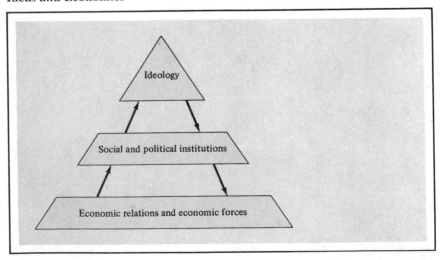

broad manner, form the *base,* or foundations, of society; on this base is built a *superstructure* consisting of institutions and ideologies. The social and political *institutions* include the family, government, organized religions, all the laws, the educational system, and the media of communication. *Ideologies* include philosophy, much of the social sciences, religion, and all folk customs and biases (such as white or male supremacy).

In any nonrevolutionary period, all the elements of this system reinforce each other. Suppose the economic forces consist of a fairly low level of technology on isolated agricultural estates and the economic relations are those of feudalism, of landlords ruling over serfs. The political institutions reflect feudal relations in a hierarchy of power reaching up to the largest landlord, the king. The ideology reflects this hierarchy, claiming that the whole system—especially the king—is divinely ordained. In this way the ideology reinforces the existing institutions, which reinforce the existing economic relations.

In the rare revolutionary situations, conflicts (which are always present to some extent) suddenly become very evident among the elements of the system. For example, over a long period in feudal Europe, commerce and industry slowly replaced agricultural economic activity. As a result, a new economic class of capitalists and merchants appeared. There was conflict because the old feudal lords had control of the political institutions and did not want to surrender any power to the upstart capitalists. Eventually, these conflicts led to revolutionary new ideologies, new institutions, and new relations.

DIFFERENCES BETWEEN TRADITIONAL AND CRITICAL VIEWS

Traditional, conservative views have mainly been stated by the schools of economics known as classical and neoclassical. Critical, liberal to radical views come mainly from the followers of Karl Marx, Thorstein Veblen, and John Maynard Keynes. In Part One of this book, we shall explore these different views of economics in detail as they developed. In Parts Two and Three we will contrast their views on each of the main issues of economics. Here we merely give the reader an appetizer, a brief glimpse of things to come.

Briefly, the main differences between the traditional and critical views are:

1. Traditional economics begins with the assumption of fixed human nature with given desires and preferences. Critical economics shows how different economic systems have evolved and how these have changed people's ideas and preferences.
2. Traditional economics is most concerned about how the economy reaches an equilibrium or static situation. Critical economics thinks

it is unrealistic to say that our dynamic economy is ever in equilibrium, so it concentrates on change and historical evolution.

3. Traditional economics sees economics as a purely technical subject about people's preferences and scarce objects with economic laws that are the same everywhere. Critical economics believes that the economy must be seen as a set of human relations, so each economic system has different human relations and different economic laws in each system.

4. Traditional economics sees the economy as purely harmonious with everyone benefiting from it. Critical economics sees the economic system as characterized by conflicts between groups, differing amounts of power (such as between the poor and the big corporations), and in some systems oppression or exploitation of one person by another (for example, under slavery).

5. More specifically, traditional economists find very little environmental destruction, very little discrimination against women or minorities, very little monopoly power exerted by the giant corporations, and they find that most unemployment is voluntary. Critical economists, on the contrary, are extremely concerned about widespread environmental destruction, extensive discrimination against women and minorities, the enormous power of the giant corporations, and the human misery caused by massive involuntary unemployment in recessions or depressions.

This thumbnail sketch has laid out the issues that divide traditional and radical economists. Before we examine the evolution of economic ideas in the modern world, it is worth a brief look backward in time at earlier economies and how they worked.

PRIMITIVE ECONOMIES

As an example of the various economies that have existed, let us examine the so-called *primitive* type. One British archaeologist (Childe) lists the characteristics of most areas of human settlement in our first half-million years or so as follows: (1) very small communities; (2) communities that are quite isolated and self-sufficient, with little or no trade; (3) no writing; (4) a homogeneous group of people; (5) no full-time specialists; (6) an economic unit that is the family or extended family of kinsmen; (7) personal and status hereditary relationships rather than economic ones; and (8) few or no political institutions. There is one still-existing primitive community where even today "there is no private property in productive goods, and whatever the hunting band manages to kill is shared out among the members of the group." (Nash, p. 3). In general, the most primitive societies have no market exchange, no money, and no economic competition in the modern sense. It is true that even the most primitive peoples known to anthropologists usually own their weapons, tools, and ornaments as individual private property; but the basic means of production at this stage are the hunting groups, and these are owned collectively.

The point cannot be overstressed that in primitive societies people are not hired for jobs, they are not paid money, and purely economic relations do not prevail in any area (nor is force used in most cases). Rather, "men work together because they are related to each other, or have social obligations to one another." (Forde and Douglas, p. 17). Furthermore, work is done collectively, and the results are shared collectively. Or, as another anthropologist writes, "with qualifications such as the special shares locally awarded for special contributions to the group endeavor—the principle remains . . . 'goods collectively produced are distributed through the collectivity.' " (Sahlins, p. 142).

The striking thing about such primitive societies from our present view is that everyone is on about the same plane of economic and political power. There is no ruling class, such as the ancient Roman or Greek or Egyptian slave owners, and no ruled class, such as the slaves in those societies. How did some collectivist, primitive societies evolve into class-divided societies, as in Greece, Rome, and Egypt?

THE TRANSITION TO CLASS SOCIETY

When "civilization" became established in the Middle East in the Bronze and Iron ages, it was marked by large communities, taxes, public works, writing, use of mathematics and astronomy, internal and foreign trade, full-time specialists such as farmers and metallurgists, political organization beyond family or kinship, a privileged ruling class, and an exploited class of workers, whether slaves or feudal serfs or peasants paying tribute. The key revolution, however, is the earlier transformation from hunting and gathering food to animal herding and agriculture.

How did the agricultural revolution occur, and how did it end the primitive classless societies of these areas and bring about class rule? We know there was a slow expansion of technical knowledge and improvement of tools over hundreds of thousands of years. Then, in a few particularly fertile areas—perhaps more or less independently in China, Mesopotamia, Egypt, Mexico, and Peru—people discovered how to tame and breed animals and how to grow the most edible plants. This "revolution" did not occur in a momentary flash of insight to some individual. Rather, it seems to have been a very gradual process over thousands of years.

Both in ancient Mesopotamia and in the Aztec areas of Mexico, first, communities became more permanently settled, intensively collected food, and hunted in a smaller given area than previously (see Adams, pp. 39–43). Second, the New Stone Age saw better tools being produced, including improved bows, drills, digging tools, and even boats and nets. Third, some crop—wheat, for example—that was already growing in the area might be moved to different areas as desired, protected by such means as the removal of any weeds, and eventually selected so as to obtain the desired food characteristics. Similarly, hunters of goats or cows might begin to follow one particular herd, protect it against its other enemies, and finally feed and shelter it at times. All these changes could take thousands of years.

Once the pastoral-agricultural revolution is well under way, several important changes occur as a direct result. Obviously the level of productivity per worker increases. The first consequence of this fact is a much higher population density; herding and agriculture can support many people per square mile, whereas hunting and gathering require several square miles per person. At the same time, agriculture means that the population must settle in one place rather than move here and there around the country. Such large, settled agglomerations mean the founding of permanent villages and, eventually, towns and cities in the most favored places.

There is enough economic surplus above immediate needs so the economy may support various specialists, such as carpenters, shoemakers, and the like. Specialization, in turn, calls for exchange of products between individuals and between groups. Moreover, the higher productivity makes wealth available in the form of cattle and gold as well as consumer durables. Then the specialization and exchange slowly destroy the collective use and possession of property, so that some individuals come to own more wealth than others.

With this increase of private property and larger, more permanently located groups of people, there is a need for a broader and stronger political structure to replace the family unit. At first, in both possession of private property and control of political power, the families or clans retain the semblance of unity and direction. Individuals slowly accumulate private property as there is more of it; so, too, do individuals slowly accumulate more political power as politics grows more complex.

A war chief may be elected from time to time as a result of small tribal conflicts; the post is likely to become lifelong or even hereditary as larger armies come into being. The area and intensity of wars increase because wars for economic motives are used by advanced agricultural societies for obtaining cattle or slaves. Most often, the large-scale introduction of slavery seems to follow as the effect of a war of conquest. Yet such wars seem to occur only as the effect of new technology high enough to be profitable to keep a slave (because he or she can produce a surplus). Slavery and wars of conquest are thus intertwined as cause and effect at a certain level of economic evolution.

To oversimplify a bit, better technology following the agricultural revolution led to higher productivity per worker. The higher productivity, in turn, meant that a society could for the first time "afford" to have some nonworking individuals (such as slave owners, landlords, priests, full-time warriors). Conversely, until product per worker passed the point at which one worker could just keep himself or herself alive, there could have been no surplus left for the ruling classes. Before that point, slavery or serfdom could not pay; hence prisoners were simply killed or eaten.

A similar increase of power might have accrued to those in charge of public works. A director of irrigation for a small tribe might have been appointed for a short time in one season; a director of irrigation for a large agricultural area along the Nile might have been given more power for a longer period. Thus, in Egypt the government separated from and rose above family or clan for two different reasons: (1) to carry through public projects, including irrigation and warfare, and (2) to guard private property, including slaves (and to prevent slave revolt).

TYPES OF ECONOMIES

There have been many different types of economy in the world. We have examined in detail the *primitive* type, in which people worked in collective groups and shared the fruits of their labors. Another type is the *slave* economy, in which one class, the slaves, does all the work. The class of slave owners legally owns both the slaves and their whole product. They give the slaves barely enough to live on, keeping the surplus for themselves.

Still another economic system is *feudalism*, varieties of which appeared at different times in Europe, Asia, and Africa. Under feudalism, serfs are bound to the land of an estate. Serfs owe to the landlord—by tradition, but also by force if necessary—150–200 days a year of service on the landlord's land. Yet serfs are better off than slaves, since they are not owned in body by the landlord and may work their own tiny plots of land when they finish their chores on the landlord's land. In Chapters 1 and 2 we discuss the transition from feudalism to capitalism in western Europe.

Most of this book discusses *capitalism*, the system existing at present in the United States. In this system, capitalists are the class of people who own all factories and equipment. Capitalists employ workers, paying them a wage. Workers are not forced to work by physical coercion, as are slaves and serfs, but are "free" to work for a capitalist or not to work and hence to starve. Capitalists own the entire product beyond wages and material costs; they produce only if they expect to make a profit.

Part Four of this book discusses socialist economies. *Socialism* means ownership and control of the economy by the entire working population. Production is carried on for the benefit of society. Many countries, such as Cuba, the Soviet Union, and China, claim to have socialist economies.

SUGGESTED READINGS

A full statement of the theory of history and society sketched in this Introduction has been given by Howard J. Sherman and James L. Wood,

Sociology: Traditional and Radical Perspectives (New York: Harper & Row, 1989). The best overall book on economic history is *Studies in the Development of Capitalism*, by Maurice Dobb (New York: International Publishers, 1946). A comprehensive history of economic theories from a critical view is *History of Economic Thought, A Critical Perspective*, 2d ed., by E. K. Hunt (New York: Harper & Row, 1990).

REFERENCES

Adams, Robert. *The Evolution of Urban Society.* Chicago: Aldine, 1965.

Childe, V. Gordon. *Social Evolution.* London: Watts, 1951.

Forde, Darryll, and Mary Douglas. "Primitive Economics." In *Tribal and Peasant Economies.* Edited by George Dalton. Garden City, N.Y.: Natural History Press, 1967.

Nash, Manning. "The Organization of Economic Life." In *Tribal and Peasant Economies.* Edited by George Dalton. Garden City, N.Y.: Natural History Press, 1967.

Quinn, Mike. *On the Drumhead.* San Francisco: The Pacific Publishing Foundation, 1948.

Sahlins, Marshall. "On the Sociology of Primitive Exchange." In *The Relevance of Models for Social Anthropology.* Edited by Michael Barton. New York: Praeger, 1965.

PART One

PROPERTY AND PROPHETS

The Evolution of Economic
Institutions and Ideologies

Chapter
1

The Ideology of Precapitalist Europe

Human beings must exist in societies in order to survive. Unlike some species of animals, whose individual members can exist fairly adequately in relative isolation, human beings are not equipped by nature with the physical prowess to provide the material requisites of life by themselves. Humans survive and indeed prosper because by living in groups they have learned to subdivide tasks and use tools. It was this division of labor and the accumulation of more and better tools (or capital) that made possible the impressive increases in humankind's control over nature, or increases in our potential to produce the material necessities of life.

This division of labor also resulted, of necessity, in a differentiation of the roles that the different members of a society occupy. This differentiation was probably purely functional in earliest times; that is, when productivity was low, all members of society lived near the subsistence level, and social class, or hierarchical differentiation, was absent. Increasingly elaborate divisions of tasks, combined with more sophisticated tools, however, led to higher productivity, which made possible an escape from the drudgery of everyday toil for at least a small part of society.

A small leisure class could be supported because with higher per capita productivity the labor of a smaller number of people could support the entire society at its customary standard of living or at an even higher standard. When this occurred, societies began to differentiate among their members according to social class. This hierarchical class differentiation was generally economic in nature. Those who worked were usually assigned to the lowest classes; those who escaped the burdens of ordinary labor were of higher class standing. Although these higher-class people were no longer directly connected with the production of everyday necessities, they often performed rites, rituals, or extensive duties, some of which were undoubtedly beneficial to society.

Such a system would not have been able to exist for long if the majority of its members did not share common feelings about the proper way of conducting economic and social affairs. These common feelings and values, which generally stemmed from a common world view, or system of metaphysics, justified both the division of productive tasks and the class differentiation that existed. These common feelings and values were expressed in ideologies.

An *ideology*, as the term is used in this book, refers to ideas and beliefs that tend to provide moral justification for a society's social and economic relationships. Most members of a society internalize the ideology and thus believe that their functional role as well as those of others is morally correct and that the method by which society divides its produce is fair. This common belief gives society its cohesiveness and viability. Lack of it creates turmoil and strife—and ultimately revolution, if the differences are deep enough.

This book is concerned primarily with our present economic system, capitalism. We sketch the broad outlines of the evolution of this system. In doing so, we focus on conflicts and social antagonisms and examine the ideologies with which the capitalist system attempted to mitigate these conflicts and to promote social cohesiveness. By way of background we begin with the economic systems and ideologies of precapitalist Europe.

ANCIENT GREEK AND ROMAN SLAVERY

In ancient Greece and Rome as many as 80 percent of the people were slaves. The slaves did all the manual work and even much of the clerical, bureaucratic, and artistic work of these societies. They were given just enough food and clothing for bare subsistence. The slave owners owned and utilized the entire surplus produced by the slaves above their own subsistence. Most of the economy was agricultural, aside from a few cities where the central government was located. On each agricultural plantation the slave owner was king and lived in splendid luxury—though he might also have a villa in Athens or Rome. In addition to his wife, who was treated as a valuable piece of property, he sexually exploited his slave women.

What sort of economic ideology existed? There were a few treatises, especially in the Roman period, on the best ways to plant crops, the best agricultural implements to use, and the best ways to supervise, control, and punish slaves. In addition, there were a large number of justifications of slavery. Even such brilliant philosophers as Plato and Aristotle argued that slavery was "natural," was the only possible system, and would exist forever; they argued that some men and women were born to be slaves and were inherently inferior, while others were born superior and were meant to be slave owners. Plato and Aristotle were not apologists; this was the dominant ideology and they simply took it for granted.

Slavery had many limitations, although it did result in many great public works and the advance of science and culture. One limitation was the fact that slaves could not be given complex or delicate machinery of any sort; they would break it up and would often use it for weapons to revolt. Moreover, agricultural organization had to be very simple, usually limited to one crop tilled with crude implements. As a result, much land was totally ruined and the agricultural product limited. Another effect of slavery was the view that all work was demeaning. Because this attitude spread even to invention, the Roman period saw little technological advance and the economy stagnated.

Its economic weaknesses—and accompanying political and social weaknesses—made the Roman Empire vulnerable to attack by the primitive Germanic and Slav tribes. The empire collapsed in the West, and out of the chaos eventually arose the system of feudalism. The kings of the feudal states were mostly former chiefs of the primitive tribes that invaded the area.

FEUDALISM

The decline of the western part of the old Roman Empire left Europe without the laws and protection the empire had provided. The vacuum was filled by the creation of a feudal hierarchy. In this hierarchy, the serf, or peasant, was protected by the lord of the manor, who, in turn, owed allegiance to and was protected by a higher overlord. And so the system went, ending eventually with the king. The strong protected the weak, but they exacted a high price. In return for payments of money, food, labor or military allegiance, overlords granted the fief, or feudum—a hereditary right to use land—to their vassals. At the bottom was the serf, a peasant who tilled the land. The vast majority of the population raised crops for food or clothing or tended sheep for wool and clothing. (See Claphan and Power for a more complete discussion of these matters.)

Custom and tradition are the keys to understanding medieval relationships. In place of laws as we know them today, the custom of the manor governed. There was no strong central authority in the Middle Ages that could have enforced a system of laws. The entire medieval organization was based on a system of mutual obligations and services up and down the hierarchy. Possession or use of the land obligated one to certain customary services or payments in return for protection. The lord was as obligated to protect the serf as the serf was to turn over a portion of the crop to or perform extensive labor for the lord.

Customs were broken, of course; no system always operates in fact as it is designed to operate in theory. One should not, however, underestimate the strength of custom and tradition in determining the lives and ideas of medieval people. Disputes between serfs were decided in the lord's court according to both the special circumstances of each case and the general customs of the manor for such cases. Of course, a dispute between a serf and a lord would usually be decided by the lord in his own favor. Even in this circumstance, however, especially in England, an overlord would impose sanctions or punishments on a lord who, as his vassal, had persistently violated the customs in his treatment of serfs. This rule by the custom of the manor stands in sharp contrast to the legal and judicial system of capitalism. The capitalist system is based on the enforcement of contracts and universally binding laws, which are softened only rarely by the possible mitigating circumstances and customs that often swayed the lord's judgment in medieval times.

The extent to which the lords could enforce their "rights" varied greatly from time to time and from place to place. It was the strengthening of these obligations and the nobleman's ability to enforce them through a long hierarchy of vassals and over a wide area that eventually led to the emergence of the modern nation-states. This process occurred during the period of transition from feudalism to capitalism. Throughout most of the Middle Ages, however, many of these claims were very weak because political control was fragmented.

The basic economic institution of medieval rural life was the manor, which contained within it two separate and distinct classes: noblemen, or lords of the manors, and serfs (from the Latin word *servus*, "slave"). Serfs were not really slaves however. Unlike slaves, who were simply property to be bought and sold at will, serfs could not be parted from either their families or their land. If their lord transferred possession of the manor to another nobleman, the serfs simply had another lord. In varying degrees, however, obligations were placed upon the serfs that were sometimes very onerous and from which there was often no escape. Usually, they were far from being "free."

The lord lived off the labor of the serfs who farmed his fields and paid taxes in kind and money according to the custom of the manor. Similarly, the lord gave protection, supervision, and administration of justice according to the custom of the manor. It must be added that although the system did rest on reciprocal obligations, the concentration of economic and political power in the hands of the lord led to a system in which, by any standard, the serf was exploited in the extreme.

The Catholic church was by far the largest owner of land during the Middle Ages. Although bishops and abbots occupied much the same place as counts and dukes in the feudal hierarchy, there was one important difference between religious and secular lords. Dukes and counts might shift their loyalty from one overlord to another, depending on the circumstances and the balance of power involved, but bishops and abbots always had (in principle at least) a primary loyalty to the church in Rome. This was also an age during which the religious teaching of the church had a very strong and pervasive influence throughout western Europe. These factors combined to make the church the closest thing to a strong central government throughout this period.

Thus the manor might be secular or religious (many times secular lords had religious overlords and vice versa), but the essential relationships between lord and serfs were not significantly affected by this distinction. There is little evidence that serfs were treated any less harshly by religious lords than by secular ones. The religious lords and the secular nobility were the joint ruling classes; they controlled the land and the power that went with it. In return for very onerous appropriations of the serf's labor, produce, and money, the nobility provided military protection and the church provided spiritual aid.

In addition to manors, medieval Europe had many towns, which were important centers of manufacturing. Manufactured goods were sold to manors and, sometimes, traded in long-distance commerce. The dominant economic institutions in the towns were the guilds—craft, professional, and trade associations that had existed as far back as the Roman Empire. If anyone wanted to produce or sell any good or service, it was necessary to join a guild.

The guilds were as involved with social and religious questions as with economic ones. They regulated their members' conduct in all their activities: personal, social, religious, and economic. Although the guilds did regulate very carefully the production and sale of commodities, they were less concerned with making profits than with saving their members' souls. Salvation demanded that the individual lead an orderly life based on church teachings and custom. Thus the guilds exerted a powerful influence as conservators of the status quo in the medieval towns.

THE CHRISTIAN PATERNALIST ETHIC

The feudal lords, secular as well as religious, needed an ideology that would reflect and justify the feudal status quo. This ideology, which provided the moral cement holding feudal Europe together and protecting its rulers, was the medieval version of the Judeo-Christian tradition. This tradition evolved a moral code sometimes called the Christian corporate ethic, reflecting the fact that all of society was considered a single entity or corporation. To emphasize another feature of it, the Judeo Christian moral code, as interpreted in the medieval period, will be called the *Christian paternalist ethic* in this book. It can be understood most easily by comparing society with a family. Those with positions of power and wealth can be likened to the father or keeper of the family. They have strong paternalistic obligations toward the common people—the poor or, in our analogy, the children. The common person, however, is expected to accept his or her place in society and to be willingly subordinate to the leadership of the wealthy and the powerful in much the same way that a child accepts the authority of his or her father.

The Old Testament Jews quite literally regarded themselves as the children of one God (see Gray, Chap. 2). This relationship meant that all Jews were brothers; the Mosaic law was intended to maintain this feeling of membership in one big family. This brotherhood was one of grown children who acknowledged their mutual obligations, even though they no longer shared possessions.

From the confused mass of duties and regulations governing the early Jews, the most salient feature is the large number of provisions made for the prevention and relief of poverty. Their humane treatment of debtors was also notable. Each Jew was to be his brother's keeper; indeed, his obligations extended to caring for his neighbor's animals should they wander his way (Deut. 22:1–4). The first duty of all, however, and particularly of the wealthy, was to care for the poor. "Thou shalt open thine hand wide unto my brother, to the poor, and to the needy, in the land" (ibid. 15:7–11). An important element in this paternalistic code was the sanction against taking a worker's tools as a means of satisfying a debt: "No man shall take the nether or the upper millstone to pledge; for he taketh a man's life to pledge" (ibid. 24:6). The same point was made elsewhere in the Old Testament: "He that taketh away his neighbor's living slayeth him" (Eccles. 34:22).

All Jews did not, of course, live up to these lofty professions. Great extremes of wealth and poverty existed that would have been impossible had the Mosaic law been strictly observed. Many of the prophets, who were often radical champions of the poor, eloquently denounced the rich for their abuse of their wealth, for their wicked, slothful luxury, and for their general unrighteousness. The important point is not that they failed to live up to the code but that the moral code of this small tribe left so important an imprint on much of the subsequent history.

The teachings of Christ in the New Testament carry on part of the Mosaic tradition relevant to economic ideology. He taught the necessity of being concerned with the welfare of one's brother, the importance of charity and almsgiving, and the evil of selfish acquisitiveness and covetousness. His emphasis on the special responsibilities and obligations of the rich is even more pronounced than that of the earlier Jewish writers. In fact, on the basis of a reading of the Gospel of Luke, one might conclude that Christ condemned the rich simply because they were rich and praised the poor simply because they were poor: "Woe unto you that are rich! . . . Woe unto you that are full! for ye shall hunger. Woe unto you that laugh now! for ye shall mourn and weep" (quoted in Gray, p. 41). However, on examining the other gospels, it must be concluded that this is probably Luke speaking, not Christ. Luke must be seen as the radical "leveller among the apostles" (ibid., p. 42).

In the other gospels there are warnings that wealth may be a stumbling block in getting to heaven, but there is no condemnation of wealth as such. The most important passages in this regard deal with the wealthy young man who wants to know what he must do to attain eternal life (Matt. 19:

16–26, etc.). Christ's first answer amounts to nothing more than a brief statement of the Ten Commandments. It is only after being pressed further that Christ goes beyond the binding, universal moral requirements to a counsel of perfection. "If thou wilt be perfect" (ibid. 19) begins the statement in which he tells the young man to sell whatever he has and give to the poor.

The Christian paternalist ethic, with its parental obligations of the wealthy toward the poor, was developed more specifically and elaborately by most of the Christian fathers. The writings of Clement of Alexandria are a reasonably good reflection of the traditional attitudes of the early church. He emphasized the dangers of greed, love of material things, and acquisition of wealth. Those who had wealth were under a special obligation to treat it as a gift from God and to use it wisely in the promotion of the general well-being of others.

Clement's *The Rich Man's Salvation* was written in order to free the rich of the "unfounded despair" they might have acquired from reading passages in the gospels like those found in Luke. Clement began by asserting that, contrary to anything one might find in Luke, "it is no great or enviable thing to be simply without riches." Those who were poor would not for that reason alone find God's blessedness. In order to seek salvation, the rich man need not renounce his wealth but need merely "banish from the soul its opinions about riches, its attachment to them, its excessive desire, its morbid excitement over them, its anxious cares, the thorns of our earthly existence which choke the seed of the true life" (quoted in Gray, p. 48).

Not the possession of wealth but the way in which it was used was important to Clement. The wealthy were given the responsibility of administering their wealth, on God's behalf, to alleviate the suffering and promote the general welfare of their brothers. In decreeing that the hungry should be fed and the naked clothed, God certainly had not willed a situation in which no one could carry out these commandments for lack of sufficient material prerequisites. It followed, thus, that God had willed that some men should have wealth but had given them the important functions of paternalistically caring for the well-being of the rest of society.

In a similar vein, Ambrose wrote that "riches themselves are not blamable" as long as they are used righteously. In order to use wealth righteously, "we ought to be of mutual help one to the other, and to vie with each other in doing duties, to lay all advantages . . . before all, and . . . to bring help one to the other" (quoted in ibid., p. 49).

The list of Christian fathers who wrote lengthy passages to the same effect could be expanded greatly. Suffice it to say that by the early feudal period the Christian paternalist ethic was thoroughly entrenched in western European culture. Greed, avarice, materialistic self-seeking, the desire to accumulate wealth—all such individualistic and materialistic motives— were sharply condemned. The acquisitive, individualistic person was considered the very antithesis of the good man, who concerned himself with the well-being of all his brothers. The wealthy man had the potential to do either great good or great evil with his wealth and power, and the worst evil resulted when wealth was used either exclusively for self-gratification or as a means of continually acquiring more wealth and power for its own sake. The righteously wealthy were those who realized that their wealth and power were God's gift, that they were morally obligated to act as paternalistic stewards, and that they were to administrate their worldly affairs in order to promote the welfare of all.

THE ANTICAPITALIST NATURE OF FEUDAL IDEOLOGY

The philosophical and religious assumptions on which medieval people acted were extensions of the Christian paternalist ethic. The many particular additions to the ethic were profoundly conservative in purpose and content. Both the continuity in and conservative modifications of this ethic can be seen in the writings of Thomas Aquinas, the preeminent spokesman of the Middle Ages.

Tradition was upheld in his insistence that private property could be justified morally only because it was a necessary condition for almsgiving. The rich, he asserted, must always be "ready to distribute, . . . [and] willing to communicate" (quoted in ibid., p. 57). Aquinas believed, with the earlier fathers, that "the rich man, if he does not give alms, is a thief" (ibid.). The rich man held wealth and power for God and for all society. He administered his wealth for God and for the common good of mankind. Wealth that was not properly used and administered could no longer be religiously and morally justified, in which case the wealthy man was to be considered a common thief.

Aquinas's and, indeed, most of the medieval church fathers' profoundly conservative addition to the Christian paternalist ethic was their insistence that the economic and social relationships of the medieval manorial system reflected a natural and eternal ordering of these relationships—indeed, that these relationships were ordained by God. They stressed the importance of a division of labor and effort, with different tasks assigned to the different classes, and insisted that the social and economic distinctions between the classes were necessary to accommodate this specialization.

If one occupied the position of a lord, secular or religious, it was necessary to have an abundance of material wealth in order to do well the tasks providence had assigned. Of course, it took little wealth to perform the tasks expected of a serf. It was every person's duty to labor unquestioningly at the task providence had assigned, to accept the station into which one was born, and to accept the rights of others to have and do the things appropriate to their stations in life. Thus the Christian paternalist ethic could be, and was, used to defend as natural and just the great inequities and intense exploitation that flowed from the concentration of wealth and power in the hands of the Church and nobility.

Any account of medieval social and economic thought must also stress the great disdain with which people viewed trade and commerce and the commercial spirit. The medieval way of life was based on custom and tradition; its viability depended on the acceptance by the members of society of that tradition and their place within it. Where the capitalist commercial ethic prevails, greed, selfishness, covetousness, and the desire to better oneself materially or socially are accepted by most people as innate qualities. Yet they were uniformly denounced and reviled in the Middle Ages. The serfs (and sometimes the lower nobility) tended to be dissatisfied with the traditions and customs of medieval society and thus threatened the stability of the feudal system. It is not surprising, therefore, to find pervasive moral sanctions designed to repress or to mitigate the effects of these motives.

One of the most important of such sanctions, repeated over and over throughout this period, was the insistence that it was the moral duty of merchants and traders to transact all trade or exchanges at the just price. This notion illustrates the role played by paternalistic social control in the feudal era. A *just price* was one that would compensate the seller for his efforts in transporting the good and in finding the buyer at a rate that was just sufficient to maintain the seller at his *customary* or *traditional* station in life. Prices above the just price would, of course, lead to profits, which would be accumulated as material wealth.

It was the lust for wealth that the Christian paternalist ethic consistently condemned. The doctrine of the just price was intended as a curb on such acquisitive and socially disruptive behavior. Then as now, accumulation of material wealth was a passport to greater power and upward social mobility. This social mobility was eventually to prove totally destructive to the medieval system because it put an end to the status relationships that were the backbone of medieval society.

Another example of this condemnation of acquisitive behavior was the prohibition of usury, or the lending of money at interest. A "bill against usury" passed in England reflected the attitudes of most of the people of those times. It read in part,

> But forasmuch as usury is by the word of God utterly prohibited, as a vice most odious and detestable . . . which thing, by no godly teachings and persuasions can sink in to the hearts of divers greedy, uncharitable and covetous persons of this Realm . . . be it enacted . . . that . . . no person or persons of what Estate, degree, quality or condition so ever he or they be, by any corrupt, colorable or deceitful conveyance, sleight or engine, or by any way or mean, shall lend, give, set out, deliver or forbear any sum or sums of money . . . to or for any manner of usury, increase, lucre, gain or interest to be had, received or hoped for, over and above the sum or sums so lent . . . as also of the usury . . . upon pain of imprisonment. (Quoted in Huberman, p. 39)

The church believed usury was the worst sort of acquisitive behavior because most loans on which interest was charged were granted to poor farmers or peasants after a bad crop or some other tragedy had befallen them. Thus, interest was a gain made at the expense of one's brother at a time when he was most in need of help and charity. Of course, the Christian ethic strongly condemned such rapacious exploitation of a needy brother.

Many historians have pointed out that bishops and abbots as well as dukes, counts, and kings often flagrantly violated these sanctions. They themselves granted loans at interest, even while they were punishing others for doing so. We are more interested, however, in the values and motives of the period than in the bending or breaking of the rules. The values of the feudal system stand in stark, antithetical contrast to those that were shortly to prevail under a capitalist system. The desire to maximize monetary gain, accumulate material wealth, and advance oneself socially and economically through acquisitive behavior was to become the dominant motive force in the capitalist system.

The sins that were most strongly denounced within the context of the Christian paternalist ethic were to become the behavioral assumptions on which the capitalist market economy was to be based. It is obvious that such a radical change would render the Christian ethic, at least in its medieval version, inadequate as the basis of a moral justification of the new capitalist system. The ethic would have to be modified drastically or rejected completely in order to elaborate a defense for the new system. Attempts to do both are explored in later chapters.

SUMMARY

Economic systems organize human effort to transform the resources given in nature into usable articles, or economic goods. Ideologies are systems of ideas and beliefs that are used to provide moral justification for the economic and social relationships within an economic system.

The Christian paternalist ethic was used to justify the feudal economy and its attendant social and economic relationships. This ideology contained elements that were antithetical to the functioning of a capitalist market system. In later chapters we examine the ways in which men attempted to substitute new ideologies for the older Christian paternalist ethic or to modify this ethic in such a way that it could be used to provide a moral justification of a capitalist market economic system.

REFERENCES

Claphan, J. H., and Eileen E. Powers, eds. *The Agrarian Life of the Middle Ages.* 2d ed. London: Cambridge University Press, 1966.

Gray, Alexander. *The Socialist Tradition.* London: Longmans, 1963.

Holy Bible. Cleveland, Ohio: World Publishing Company, n.d. Deuteronomy. Ecclesiastes. Luke. Mark. Matthew.

Huberman, Leo. *Man's Worldly Goods.* New York: Monthly Review Press, 1961.

Chapter
2

The Transition to Early Capitalism and the Beginnings of the Mercantilist View

Medieval society was an agrarian society. The social hierarchy was based on individuals' ties to the land, and the entire social system on an agricultural base. Yet, ironically, increases in agricultural productivity gave the original impetus to a series of profound changes. These changes, occurring over several centuries, resulted in the dissolution of medieval feudalism and the beginnings of capitalism. Before we examine this transition to capitalism, however, we should define the essential features of a capitalist economy.

DEFINITION OF CAPITALISM

If an individual could be transported through space and time to England of the late eighteenth century, Japan in the early twentieth century, and the contemporary United States, and could compare what she or he saw, chances are that the many striking differences among these three societies would seem to be much more significant than any similarities that were observed. Yet despite vast, numerous differences, the underlying economic system in each of these three societies is essentially the same. Each has a capitalist economy. It is clearly very important to be able to identify the essential features of a capitalist economy if one is to understand the economic similarity of these culturally diverse social systems and to understand the evolution of the capitalist economic system.

Capitalism is defined by three essential features that are always present in a capitalist economy. First is the ubiquity of monetary exchange. For the vast majority of people in capitalism, one can get the things one wants

11

and needs only if one has money with which to buy these things in the market. Second, capitalism always has at least four clearly identifiable socioeconomic classes: the class of wealthy capitalists, the class of small businesspeople and independent professionals, the class of working people, and the class of destitute persons who live by various welfare programs or by theft, prostitution, or whatever means are available. Third, in a capitalist economy the pursuit of profits determines what will be produced, how and where it will be produced, and by whom and for whom it will be produced.

The first feature of capitalism—the ubiquity of market exchange—renders most human economic interdependencies cold and impersonal. Each person must rely on the productive efforts of a great many people, and many people, in turn, rely on any given individual to perform his or her productive functions. This interdependency is not experienced as a real human connection among people, however. It is experienced only as a dependence of each individual on money with which to buy commodities in the market.

The second feature—the class structure of capitalism—requires a separation of ownership and control of productive resources (natural resources, tools, machines, factories, etc.) from the working people who use these productive resources to create the commodities that satisfy society's needs and wants. The capitalist class is comprised of individuals with sufficient ownership of productive resources that the income from this ownership (in the form of interest, stock dividends, rent, and profit) will sustain them at their customary standard of living independently of how productively or unproductively they spend their lives. The working class has no significant access to or ownership of productive resources. Individuals in this class must sell control of their power to labor (i.e., get a job) as their only means to escape sinking to the destitute class.

Between the capitalist class and the working class is a middle class of small businesspeople and independent professionals. Individuals in this class own and control some productive resources and receive monetary returns from this ownership. Their ownership is not, however, sufficient, as it is for capitalists, to exempt them from working. Small businesspeople and independent professionals must also work in order to get by. Finally, the lowest class in every capitalist society is the destitute class that lacks any significant ownership and, for a wide variety of reasons, cannot sell their power to labor. In any capitalist society, income from ownership and the wages of workers are considered to be the only socially respectable sources of income. The destitute class must depend on the somewhat "less than respectable" sources of income, such as welfare, charity, or the fruits of quasilegal or illegal activities in order to get by. The stigma that attaches to members of this class, motivates all propertyless individuals to try very hard to secure employment even if working conditions and wages are poor.

The third feature—the allocation of resources through the quest for profits—follows from the nature of the socioeconomic classes of capitalism.

All productive resources are owned and controlled by the capitalist and middle classes, with the capitalists controlling big businesses and the middle class controlling many small businesses. Nearly all of the creative, productive endeavor in a capitalist society is done by wage earners who are hired by these businesses. The motivation for hiring the worker is a simple one: If the worker creates more value for the business than he or she costs the business in wages, then the worker will be hired because he or she will contribute to the capitalist's profits. This is, in general, the only reason for hiring a worker to engage in productive activity in a capitalist society. Therefore, what workers will produce what commodities is not determined by any evaluation of human, social, or individual needs, but soley by the criterion of what is profitable to the capitalist. There is no reason to suppose that the two criteria of social needs and profitability will always be in conflict with each other, nor is there any reason to suppose the two criteria will be always in harmony. When the two conflict, profit, not human needs, determines production in capitalism.

The capitalist system is drastically different from the feudal system of medieval Europe. In this chapter we examine some of the most important changes that occurred in the period that saw the dissolution of feudalism and the slow, gradual evolution of the essential institutions of capitalism.

CHANGES IN TECHNOLOGY

The most important technological advance in the Middle Ages was the replacement of the two-field system of crop rotation with the three-field system. Although there is evidence that the three-field system was introduced into Europe as early as the eighth century, its use was probably not widespread until around the eleventh century.

Yearly sowing of the same land would deplete the land and eventually make it unusable. Consequently, in the two-field system half of the land was always allowed to lie fallow in order to recover from the previous year's planting.

With the three-field system, arable land was divided into three equal fields. Rye or winter wheat would be planted in the fall in the first field; oats, beans, or peas would be planted in the spring in the second; and the third would lie fallow. In each subsequent year there was a rotation of these positions. Any given piece of land would have a spring planting one year, a fall planting the next year, and none the third year.

A dramatic increase in agricultural output resulted from this seemingly simple change in agricultural technology. With the same amount of arable land, the three-field system could increase the amount under cultivation at any particular time by as much as 50 percent (White, pp. 71–72).

The three-field system led to other important changes. Spring sowing of oats and other fodder crops enabled the people to support more horses, which began to replace oxen as the principal source of power in agriculture.

Horses were much faster than oxen, and consequently the region under cultivation could be extended. An increase in the area under cultivation enabled the countryside to support more concentrated population centers. Transportation of people, commodities, and equipment was much more efficient with horses. Greater efficiency was also attained in plowing: A team of oxen required three people to do the plowing; a horse-drawn plow could be operated by one person. The costs of transporting agricultural products were substantially reduced in the thirteenth century when the four-wheeled wagon with a pivoted front axle replaced the two-wheeled cart.

These improvements in agriculture and transportation contributed to two important and far-reaching changes. First, they made possible a rapid increase in population growth. The best historical estimates are that the population of Europe doubled between 1000 and 1300 (Miskimin, p. 20). Second, closely related to the expansion of population was a rapid increase in urban concentration. Before the year 1000, most of Europe, except for a few Mediterranean trade centers, consisted of only manors, villages, and a few small towns. By 1300, there were many thriving cities and larger towns.

The growth of towns and cities led to a growth of rural-urban specialization. With urban workers severing all ties to the soil, specialization increased and this, in turn, increased the output of manufactured goods. Interregional, long-distance trade and commerce was another very important result of this increased specialization.

THE INCREASE IN LONG-DISTANCE TRADE

Many historians have argued that the spread of trade and commerce was the single most important force leading to the disintegration of medieval society. The importance of trade cannot be doubted, but it must be emphasized that this trade did not arise by accident or by factors completely external to the European economy, such as increased contact with the Arabs. On the contrary, it was shown in the previous section that this upsurge in trade was prepared for by the internal economic evolution of Europe itself. The growth of agricultural productivity meant that a surplus of food and handicrafts was available for local and international markets. The improvements in power and transportation meant that it was possible and profitable to concentrate industry in towns, to produce on a mass scale, and to sell the goods over a widespread, long-distance market. Thus the basic agricultural and industrial developments were necessary prerequisites for the spread of trade and commerce, which in turn further encouraged industry and town expansion.

The expansion of trade, particularly long-distance trade in the early period, led to the establishment of commercial and industrial towns that serviced this trade. And the growth of these cities and towns, as well as their increased domination by merchant capitalists, led to important changes in both industry and agriculture. Each of these areas of change, particularly the latter, brought about a weakening and ultimately a complete dissolving of the traditional ties that held together the feudal economic and social structure.

From the earliest part of the medieval period, some long-distance trade had been carried on throughout many parts of Europe. This trade was very important in southern Europe, on the Mediterranean and Adriatic seas, and in northern Europe, on the North and Baltic seas. Between these two centers of commercialism, however, the feudal manorial system in most of the rest of Europe was relatively unaffected by commerce and trade until the later Middle Ages.

From about the eleventh century onward, the Christian Crusades gave impetus to a marked expansion of commerce. Yet the Crusades themselves cannot be viewed as an accidental or external factor to European development. The Crusades were not undertaken for religious reasons, nor were they the result of Turkish molestation of pilgrims, for the Turks continued the Moslem policy of tolerance. Developments on the Moslem side did lead to increased attacks on Byzantium, but the West would normally have sent only token aid since it had no great love for Byzantium. The basic reasons for the Crusades may be seen in the internal developments of France, where they had their most powerful backing. France had been growing stronger, it had more trade relations with and interest in the East, and it needed an outlet for social unrest at home. Additional propaganda for the Crusades came from the oligarchy of Venice, which wanted to expand its own Eastern trade and influence.

The development of trade with the Arabs—and with the Vikings in the North—led to increased production for export and to the great trade fairs that flourished from the twelfth through the late fourteenth centuries. Held annually in the principal European trading cities, these fairs usually lasted one to several weeks. Northern European merchants exchanged their grain, fish, wool, cloth, timber, pitch, tar, salt, and iron for the spices, silks, brocades, wines, fruits, and gold and silver that were the dominant items in southern European commerce. (For a more complete discussion of the rise of trade and commerce, see Dillard, pp. 3–178).

By the fifteenth century the fairs were being replaced by commercial cities where year-round markets thrived. The trade and commerce of these cities were incompatible with restrictive feudal customs and traditions. Generally the cities were successful in gaining independence from the church and feudal lords. Within these commercial centers there arose complex systems of currency exchange, debt-clearing, and credit facilities, and modern business instruments like bills of exchange came into widespread use. New systems of commercial law developed. Unlike the system of paternalistic adjudication based on custom and tradition that prevailed in the manor, the commercial law was fixed by precise code. Hence it became the basis of the modern capitalistic law of contracts, negotiable instruments, agency sales, and auctions.

In the manorial handicraft industry, the producer (the master craftsman) was also the seller. The industries that burgeoned in the new cities, however, were primarily export industries—that is, the producer was distant from the final buyer. Craftsmen sold their goods wholesale to merchants, who, in turn, transported and resold them. Another important difference was that the manorial craftsman was also generally a farmer. The new city craftsman gave up farming and became devoted to a craft, with which money could be obtained to satisfy other needs.

THE PUTTING-OUT SYSTEM AND THE BIRTH OF CAPITALIST INDUSTRY

As trade and commerce thrived and expanded, the need for more manufactured goods and greater reliability of supply led to increasing control of the productive process by the merchant-capitalist. By the sixteenth century the handicraft type of industry, in which the craftsman owned his workshop, tools, and raw materials and functioned as an independent, small-scale entrepreneur, had been largely replaced in the exporting industries by the *putting-out system*. In the earliest period of the putting-out system, the merchant-capitalist would furnish an independent craftsman with raw materials and pay the latter a fee to work the materials into finished products. In his way the capitalist owned the product throughout all stages of production, although the work was done in independent workshops. In the later period of the putting-out system, the merchant-capitalist owned the tools and machinery and often the building in which the production took place. The merchant-capitalist hired the workers to use the tools, furnished them with the raw materials, and took the finished products.

The worker no longer sold a finished product to the merchant. Rather, the worker sold only the worker's own labor power. The textile industries were among the first in which the putting-out system developed. Weavers, spinners, fullers, and dyers found themselves in a situation where their employment, and hence their ability to support themselves and their families, depended on the merchant-capitalists, who had to sell what the workers produced at a price that was high enough to pay wages and other costs and still make a profit.

Capitalists' control was, then, extended into the process of production. At the same time, a labor force was created that owned little or no capital and had nothing to sell but its labor power. These two features mark the appearance of the economic system of capitalism. Some writers and historians have defined capitalism as existing when trade, commerce, and the commercial spirit expanded and became more important in Europe. Trade and commerce, however, had existed throughout the feudal era. Yet as long as feudal tradition remained the organizing principle in production, trade and commerce were really outside the social and economic system. The market and the search for money profits replaced custom and tradition in determining who would perform what task, how that task would be performed, and whether a given worker could find work to support himself. When this occurred, the capitalist system was created (Dobb, chap. 4).

Capitalism became dominant with the extension to most lines of production of the relationship that existed between capitalists and workers in the sixteenth-century export industries. For such a system to evolve, the economic self-sufficiency of the feudal manor had to be broken down and manorial customs and traditions undermined or destroyed. Agriculture had to become a capitalistic venture in which workers would sell their labor power to capitalists, and capitalists would buy labor only if they expected to make a profit in the process.

A capitalist textile industry existed in Flanders in the thirteenth century. When for various reasons its prosperity began to decline, the wealth and poverty it had created led, starting around 1280, to a long series of violent class wars that almost completely destroyed the industry. In the fourteenth century a capitalist industry flourished in Florence. There as in Flanders, adverse business conditions led to tensions between a poverty-stricken working class and their affluent capitalist employers. The results of these class antagonisms significantly worsened the precipitous decline in the Florentine textile industry, as it had earlier in Flanders.

In the fifteenth century England dominated the world textile market. Its capitalist textile industry solved the problem of class conflict by ruralizing the industry. Whereas the earlier capitalist textile industries of Flanders and Florence had been centered in the densely populated cities, where the workers were thrown together and organized resistance was easy to initiate, the English fulling mills were scattered about the countryside. This meant that the workers were isolated from all but a small handful of other workers, and effective organized resistance did not develop.

The later system, however, in which wealthy owners of capital employed propertyless craftsmen, was usually a phenomenon of the city rather than of the countryside. From the beginning, these capitalistic enterprises sought monopolistic positions from which to exploit the demand for their products. The rise of livery guilds, or associations of merchant-capitalist employers, created a host of barriers to protect their position. Different types of apprenticeships, with special privileges and exemptions for the sons of the wealthy, excessively high membership fees, and other barriers, prevented ambitious poorer craftsmen from competing with or entering the new capitalist class. Indeed, these barriers generally resulted in the transformation of poorer craftsmen and their sons into a new urban working class that lived exclusively by selling its labor power.

THE DECLINE OF THE MANORIAL SYSTEM

Before a complete system of capitalism could emerge, however, the force of capitalist market relations had to invade the rural manor, the bastion of feudalism. This was accomplished as a result of the vast increase of population in the new trading cities. Large urban populations depended on the rural countryside for food and much of the raw materials for export industries. These needs fostered a rural-urban specialization and a large flow of trade between the rural manor and the city. The lords of the manors began to depend on the cities for manufactured good and increasingly came to desire luxury goods that merchants could sell to them.

The peasants on the manor also found that they could exchange surpluses for money at the local grain markets; the money could be used by the peasants to purchase commutation of their labor services. Commutation involved the substitution of money rents for the labor services required of the serf. Commutation often resulted in a situation in which the peasant became very nearly an independent small businessman. He might rent the land from the lord, sell the product to cover the rents, and retain the remaining revenues himself. This system gave peasants a higher incentive to produce and thereby increased their surplus marketings, which led to more commutations, more subsequent marketings, and so forth. The cumulative effect was a very gradual breaking down of the traditional ties of the manor and a substitution of the market and the search for profits as the organizing principle of production. By the middle of the fourteenth century, money rents exceeded the value of labor services in many parts of Europe.

Another force that brought the market into the countryside and was closely related to commutation was the alienation of the lords' demesnes. The lords who needed cash to exchange for manufactured goods and luxuries began to rent their own lands to peasant farmers rather than have them farmed directly with labor service obligations. This process led increasingly to a situation in which the lord of the manor was simply a landlord in the modern sense of that term. In fact, he very often became an absentee landlord, as many lords chose to move to the cities or were away fighting battles.

The breakup of the manorial system, however, stemmed more directly from a series of catastrophes in the late fourteenth and fifteenth centuries. The Hundred Years' War between France and England (1337–1453) created general disorder and unrest in those countries. The Black Death was even more devastating. On the eve of the plague of 1348–1349, England's population stood at 4 million. By the early fifteenth century, after the effects of the wars and the plague, England had a population of a scant 2.5 million. This was fairly typical of trends in other European countries. The depopulation led to a desperate labor shortage, and wages for all types of labor rose abruptly. Land, now relatively more plentiful, began to rent for less.

These facts led the feudal nobility to attempt to revoke the commutations they had granted and to reestablish the labor service obligations of the serfs and peasants (peasants were former serfs who had attained some degree of independence and freedom from feudal restrictions). They found, however, that the clock could not be turned back. The market had been extended into the countryside, and with it had come greater freedom, independence, and prosperity for the peasants. They bitterly resisted efforts to reinstate the old obligations, and their resistance did not go unchallenged.

The result was the famous peasant revolts that broke out all over Europe from the late fourteenth through the early sixteenth centuries. These rebellions were extreme in their cruelty and ferocity. A contemporary French writer described a band of peasants who killed a "knight and putting him on a broach, roasted him over a fire in the sight of his wife and children. Ten or twelve of them ravished the wife and then forced her to eat of her husband's flesh. Then they killed her and her children. Wherever these ungracious people went they destroyed good houses and strong castles" (Gras, p. 108). Rebellious peasants were ultimately slaughtered with equal or greater cruelty and ferocity by the nobility.

England experienced a series of such revolts in the late fourteenth and fifteenth centuries. But the revolts that occurred in Germany in the early sixteenth century were probably the bloodiest of all. The peasant rebellion in 1524–1525 was crushed by the imperial troops of the Holy Roman emperor, who slaughtered peasants by the tens of thousands. Over 100,000 persons probably were killed in Germany alone.

These revolts are mentioned here to illustrate the fact that fundamental changes in the economic and political structure of a social system are often achieved only after traumatic and violent social conflict. Any economic system generates a class or classes whose privileges are dependent on the continuation of that system. Quite naturally, these classes go to great lengths to resist change and to protect their positions. The feudal nobility fought a savage rearguard action against the emerging capitalist market system, but the forces of change ultimately swept them aside. Although the important changes were brought about by aspiring merchants and minor noblemen, the peasants were the pathetic victims of the consequent social upheavals. Ironically, they were usually struggling to protect the status quo.

THE CREATION OF THE WORKING CLASS

The early sixteenth century is a watershed in European history. It marks the vague dividing line between the old, decaying feudal order and the rising capitalist system. After 1500, important social and economic changes began to occur with increasing frequency, each reinforcing the other and together ushering in the system of capitalism. Among the most important of these changes were those creating a working class that was systematically stripped of any control over the production process and forced into a situation in which the sale of its labor power was its only means of survival. The population of western Europe, which had been relatively stagnant for a century and a half, increased by nearly one-third in the sixteenth century and stood at about 70 million in 1600.

The increase in population was accompanied by the enclosure movement, which had begun in England as early as the thirteenth century. The feudal nobility, in ever-increasing need of cash, fenced off or enclosed lands that had formerly been used for communal grazing, using the lands to graze sheep to satisfy the booming English wool and textile industries' demand for wool. The sheep brought good prices, and a minimal amount of labor was needed to herd them.

The enclosure movement reached its peak in the late fifteenth and sixteenth centuries, when in some areas as many as three-fourths to nine-tenths of the tenants were forced out of the countryside and into the cities to try to support themselves. Subsequent waves of enclosure continued until well into the nineteenth century. The enclosures and the increasing population further destroyed the remaining feudal ties, creating a large new labor force—a labor force without land, without any tools or instruments of production, and with only labor power to sell. This migration to the cities meant more labor for the capitalist industries, more men for the armies and navies, more men to colonize new lands, and more potential consumers, or buyers of products.

But the enclosures and the increase in population were by no means the sole source of the new working class. Innumerable peasants, yeomen, and minor nobility were bankrupted by exorbitant increases in monetary rents. Mounting debts that could not be repaid ruined countless others. In the cities and towns the guilds came to be more and more concerned with the income levels of their members. It was obvious to the craftsmen and merchants in the guilds that steps taken to minimize their number would serve to monopolize their crafts and to increase their incomes. Increasing numbers of urban producers came to be denied any means of independent production as the guilds became more exclusive. Thus a considerable portion of the new working class was created within the towns and cities.

Many of the farmers and craftsmen who were thus uprooted and denied access to their former means of production became vagabonds and beggars. Even more attempted to secure a subsistence by squatting on marginal, unused lands where they could grow crops for their own use. Harshly repressive laws were passed against such farming and against being an unemployed vagabond (Dobb, chap. 6). Thus when force, fraud, and starvation were insufficient to create the new working class, criminal statutes and government repression were used.

OTHER FORCES IN THE TRANSITION TO CAPITALISM

Other sources of change were also instrumental in the transition to capitalism. Among these was the intellectual awakening of the sixteenth century, which fostered scientific progress that was promptly put to practical use in navigation. The telescope and the compass enabled men to navigate much more accurately for far greater distances—hence the Age of Exploration. Within a short period, Europeans had charted sea routes to India, Africa, and the Americas. These discoveries had a twofold importance: First, they resulted in a rapid and large flow of precious metals into Europe, and second, they ushered in a period of colonization.

Between 1300 and 1500, European gold and silver production had stagnated. The rapidly expanding capitalist trade and the extension of the market system into city and countryside had led to an acute shortage of money. Because money consisted primarily of gold and silver coin, the need for these metals was critical. Beginning around 1450, this situation was alleviated somewhat when the Portuguese began extracting metals from the African Gold Coast, but the general shortage continued until the middle of the sixteenth century. After that date there occurred such a large inflow of gold and silver from the Americas that Europe experienced the most rapid and long-lasting inflation in history.

During the sixteenth century prices rose in Europe between 150 and 400 percent, depending on the country or region chosen. Prices of manufactured goods rose much more rapidly than either rents or wages. In fact, the disparity between prices and wages continued until late in the seventeenth century. This meant that the landlord class (or feudal nobility) and the working class both suffered, because their incomes rose less rapidly than their expenses. The capitalist class was the great beneficiary of the price revolution. It received larger and larger profits as it paid lower real wages and bought materials that appreciated greatly as it held the materials as inventories.

These larger profits were accumulated as capital. Capital refers to the materials that are necessary for production, trade, and commerce, and consists of all tools, equipment, factories, raw materials, goods in process, means of transporting goods, and money. There are physical means of production in every kind of economic system, but they can become capital only in a social context in which the social relationships exist that are necessary for commodity production and private ownership. Thus capital refers to more than simply physical objects; it refers to a complex set of social relations as well. In our earlier discussion we saw that one of the defining features of the capitalist system is the existence of a class of capitalists who own the capital stock. By virtue of their ownership of this capital they derive their profits. These profits are then reinvested, or used to augment the capital stock. The further accumulation of capital leads to more profits, which leads to more accumulation, and the system continues in an upward spiral.

The term *capitalism* describes this system of profit seeking and accumulation very well. Ownership of capital is the source of profits and hence the source of further accumulation of capital. But this chicken-egg process had to have a beginning. The substantial initial, or primitive, accumulation of capital took place in the period under consideration. The four most important sources of the initial accumulation of capital were (1) the rapidly growing volume of trade and commerce, (2) the putting-out system of industry, (3) the enclosure movement, and (4) the great price inflation. There were several other sources of initial accumulations, some of which were somewhat less respectable and often forgotten—for example, colonial plunder, piracy, and the slave trade.

During the sixteenth and seventeenth centuries the putting-out system was extended until it was common in most types of manufacturing. Although this was not yet the modern type of factory production, the system's increased degree of specialization led to significant increases in productivity. Technical improvements in shipbuilding and navigation also lowered transportation costs. Capitalist production and trade and commerce were thus able to grow very rapidly during this period. The new capitalist class (or middle class or bourgeoisie) slowly but inexorably replaced the nobility as the class that dominated the economic and social system.

The emergence of the new nation-states signaled the beginning of the transition to a new dominant class. The new monarchs usually drew on the bourgeois capitalist class for support in their efforts to defeat feudal rivals and unify the state under one central power. This unification freed the merchants from the feudal maze of different rules, regulations, laws, weights and measures, and moneys; consolidated many markets; and provided military protection for commercial ventures. In return, the monarch relied on the capitalists for much needed sources of revenues.

Although England was nominally unified much earlier, it was not until Henry VII (1485–1509) founded the Tudor line of monarchs that England was unified in fact. Henry VIII (1509–1547) and Elizabeth I (1558–1603) were able to complete the work of nation building only because they had the support of Parliament, which represented the middle classes of the shires and boroughs. In the revolutions of 1648 and 1688, the supremacy of Parliament, or of the bourgeois middle classes, was finally established.

The other important early capitalist nation-states also came into existence during this period. In France, Louis XI (1461–1483) was the first king to unify France effectively since the time of Charlemagne. The marriage in 1469 of Ferdinand of Aragon and Isabella of Castile, and their subsequent defeat of the Moors, led to the unification of Spain. The Dutch republic, the fourth of the important early nation-states, did not win its independence until 1690, when it finally expelled its Spanish oppressors.

By the late sixteenth and early seventeenth centuries, most of the large cities in England, France, Spain, and the Low Countries (Belgium and Holland) had been transformed into thriving capitalist economies dominated by the merchant-capitalists, who controlled not only commerce but also much of the manufacturing. In the modern nation-states, coalitions of monarchs and capitalists had wrested effective power from the feudal nobility in many important areas, especially those related to production and commerce. This period of early capitalism is generally referred to as mercantilism.

MERCANTILISM: FEUDAL PATERNALISM
IN EARLY CAPITALISM

The earliest phase of mercantilism, usually called *bullionism*, originated in the period (discussed earlier) during which Europe was experiencing an acute shortage of gold and silver bullion and hence did not have enough money to service the rapidly expanding volume of trade. Bullionist policies were designed to attract a flow of gold and silver into a country and to keep them there by prohibiting their export. These restrictions lasted from the late Middle Ages into the sixteenth and seventeenth centuries.

Spain, the country into which most of the gold from the Americas flowed, applied bullionist restrictions over the longest period and imposed the most severe penalty for the export of gold and silver—death. Yet the needs of trade were so pressing and such large profits could be made by importing foreign commodities that even in Spain merchant-capitalists succeeded in bribing corrupt officials or smuggling large quantities of bullion out of the country. Spanish bullion rapidly found its way all over Europe and was, to a large extent, responsible for the long period of inflation described above. Spain did not legalize the export of gold and silver until long after the bullionist restrictions had been removed in England and Holland in the middle of the sixteenth century.

After the bullionist period, the mercantilists' desire to maximize the gold and silver within a country took the form of attempts by the government to create a favorable balance of trade. To them a *favorable balance of trade* meant that money payments into the country would be greater than the money flow out of the country. Thus exports of goods as well as such activities as shipping and insuring when performed by compatriots and paid for by foreigners were encouraged, and imports of goods and shipping and insurance charges paid to foreigners were discouraged. A favorable balance of trade would ensure the augmentation of the country's treasure. Even though some gold and silver would be paid out in the process, more would come in than would leave.

One of the most important types of policies designed to increase the value of exports and decrease that of imports was the creation of trade monopolies. A country like England could buy most cheaply (from a backward area, for example) if only one English merchant bargained with the foreigners involved rather than having several competing English merchants bidding the price up in an effort to capture the business. Similarly, English merchants could sell their goods to foreigners for much higher prices if there was only one seller rather than several sellers bidding the price down to attract one another's customers.

The English government could prohibit English merchants from competing in an area where such a monopoly had been established. It was much more difficult, however, to keep out French, Dutch, or Spanish merchants. Various governments attempted to exclude such rival foreign merchants by establishing colonial empires that could be controlled by the mother country to ensure a monopoly of trade. Colonial possessions could thereby furnish cheap raw materials to the mother country and purchase expensive manufactured goods in return.

In addition to the creation of monopolies, all the western European countries (with the exception of Holland) applied extensive regulations to the businesses of exporting and importing. These regulations were probably most comprehensive in England, where exporters who found it difficult to compete with foreigners were given tax refunds or, if that were not enough, subsidized. Export duties were placed on a long list of raw materials to keep them within England. Thus the price English merchant-manufacturers would have to pay for these raw materials would be minimized. Sometimes, when these items were in short supply for British manufacturers, the state would completely prohibit their export. The English prohibited the export of most raw materials and semifinished products, such as sheep, wool, yarn, and worsted, which were used by the textile industry.

Measures aimed at discouraging imports were also widespread. The importation of some commodities was prohibited, and such high duties were placed on other commodities that they were nearly eliminated from trade. Special emphasis was placed on protecting England's principal export industries from foreign competitors attempting to cut into the export industries' domestic markets.

Of course, these restrictions profited some capitalists and harmed others. As would be expected, coalitions of special-interest groups were always working to maintain the restrictions or to extend them into different areas in different ways. Attempts such as the English Navigation Acts of 1651 and 1660 were made to promote the use of both British-made and British-manned ships in both import and export trade. All these regulations of foreign trade and shipping were designed to augment the flow of money into the country while decreasing the outflow. Needless to say, many of the measures also stemmed from appeals and pressures by special-interest groups.

In addition to these restrictions on foreign trade, there was a maze of restrictions and regulations aimed at controlling domestic production. Besides the tax exemptions, subsidies, and other privileges used to encourage larger output by industries that were important exporters, the state also engaged in extensive regulation of production methods and of the quality of produced goods. In France, the regime of Louis XIV codified, centralized, and extended the older decentralized guild controls. Specific techniques of production were made mandatory, and extensive quality-control measures were enacted, with inspectors appointed in Paris charged with enforcing these laws at the local level. Jean Baptiste Colbert, Louis XIV's famous minister and economic advisor, was responsible for the establishment of extensive and minute regulations. In the textile industry, for example, the width of a piece of cloth and the precise number of threads contained within it were rigidly specified by the government.

In England, the Statute of Artificers (1563) effectively transferred to the state the function of the old craft guilds. It led to central control over the training of industrial workers, over conditions of employment, and over allocation of the labor force among different types of occupations. Regulation of wages, of the quality of many goods, and of other details of domestic production was also tried in England during this period.

What was the source of this extensive control of trade, commerce, and domestic production? It might seem at first glance that the state was merely using its powers to promote the special interests of capitalists. This view is reinforced by the fact that most of the important writers of this period who dealt with economic issues were either merchants or employees of merchants. Undoubtedly many of the particular statutes and regulatory measures were backed by special-interest groups that benefited handsomely from them.

However, the rising new middle class of merchant and industrial capitalists were often constrained in their pursuit of profits by the maze of state regulations. Therefore, throughout the period one finds extensive arguments advanced by these capitalists and their spokesmen for greater freedom from state controls. Economic regulation increasingly became anathema to the capitalists and their spokesmen. In fact, the mercantilist period represents an era in which an outdated economic ideology, the medieval version of the Christian corporate ethic, came into increasingly sharp conflict with a new social and economic order with which it was incompatible. Chapter 3 is concerned with this conflict.

SUMMARY

A series of profound changes resulted in the decline of feudalism and the rise of a new market-oriented economy. Perhaps the most important of these changes were the improvements in agricultural technology that occurred between the eleventh century and the end of the thirteenth century. These improvements in farming techniques were the original force that set into motion a centuries-long chain of events that ushered in capitalism.

The rapid growth of population and increase in urban concentration led to a resurgence of long-distance trade. In the cities the putting-out system was created to produce items that were sold in this trade. This practice, in turn, led to an urban-rural specialization that could be accomplished only by the monetization of economic tasks and productive activities. The transformation of feudal social relationships into market cash relations destroyed the social base of feudalism. Attempts to preserve the feudal system resulted in peasant revolts—and their ruthless suppression.

The new capitalist market system was ushered in by the enclosure movement, an intellectual awakening, world exploration, the discovery of large quantities of precious metals, the price inflation of the sixteenth and seventeenth centuries, and the creation of the new nation-states.

In the early stages of capitalism, mercantilist policies resulted in extensive government intervention into market processes, particularly those related to international commerce. These policies were generally aimed at securing high profits for the great merchant trading companies, raising revenues for national governments, and, more generally, bringing a maximum of precious metals into the country concerned.

REFERENCES

Dillard, Dudley. *Economic Development of the North Atlantic Community.* Englewood Cliffs, N.J.: Prentice-Hall, 1967.

Dobb, Maurice H. *Studies in the Development of Capitalism.* London: Routledge & Kegan Paul, 1946.

Gras, N. S. B. *A History of Agriculture in Europe and America.* New York, Appleton, 1940.

Miskimin, Harry A. *The Economy of Early Renaissance Europe, 1300–1460.* Englewood Cliffs, N.J.: Prentice-Hall, 1969.

White, Lynn, Jr. *Medieval Technology and Social Change.* Oxford: Clarendon, 1962.

Chapter 3

The Conflict in Mercantilist Thought

The Christian paternalist ethic, with its condemnation of acquisitive behavior, conflicted with the interests of merchants throughout the feudal
period. As the importance of trade and commerce grew, the intensity of
the conflict grew. There were two principal themes underlying the development of English mercantilism.* "One was the biblical injunction to
promote the general welfare and common good of God's corporate world
and its creatures. The second was the growing propensity to define God's
estate as the civil society in which the Christian resided" (Williams, p.
33). During this period the state began to take over the role of the church
in interpreting and enforcing the Christian paternalist ethic. The basic
issue for the earliest formulators of mercantilist policies was whether the
growing merchant class was to be allowed to pursue its profits recklessly,
regardless of the social and economic consequences of that pursuit. The
Christian ethic demanded that the activities of the merchants be checked
and controlled in the interest of the welfare of the entire community.

THE MEDIEVAL ORIGINS OF MERCANTILIST POLICIES

The first indications of a mercantilistic type of economic policy can be
traced to Edward I (1272–1307), who evicted several foreign economic

---

* We concentrate primarily on English mercantilism in this chapter because industrial capitalism developed first in England and because most of the ideas in the capitalist ideology that
we discuss in Chapter 4 were developed in England.

enterprises from England, established the English wool trade in Antwerp, and made various attempts to control commerce within England. A short time later, Edward III significantly extended these policies of economic control. The long war with France (1333–1360) led him to attempt to mitigate the harsh effects of wartime inflation on the laborers. He did this by fixing wages and prices in a ratio that was more favorable to the laborers. In return for this aid, Edward required all men to work at whatever jobs were available. "As this quid pro quo indicates, mercantilism was grounded in the idea of a mutual, corporate responsibility. God's way was based on such reciprocal respect and obligation, and Jerusalem provided the example to be followed" (ibid., p. 34).

Richard II (1377–1399) extended and systematized his predecessors' policies. The principal problems facing England during his reign were the social and economic conflict that led to the Peasants' Rebellion of 1381 (see Chapter 2) and the necessity of countering foreign competition more effectively. The latter led to the Navigation Act of 1381, which was designed to favor English shippers and traders and to bring gold and silver into England. This money was needed for his program of building England into a "well and rightly governed kingdom" in which greater economic security for all would mitigate the social tensions that existed.

Henry VII (1485–1509) renewed these policies. He commissioned numerous voyages of explorers and adventurers and attempted in various ways to secure legislation and negotiate treaties advantageous to English merchants. At the same time he subjected merchants to many controls and regulations imposed by the Crown, for he believed that the unlimited pursuit of self-interest in the quest for profits was often harmful to general social interests and harmony.

Henry was still balancing feudal and capitalist interests; neither was dominant enough to persuade him to favor one over the other. The rapid growth of mining and wool raising during his reign led to an unfortunate neglect of food production. Moreover, the general excesses of the merchants had alienated both the peasants and the agrarian aristocracy. The merchants seemed to understand these problems and accepted a relationship in which, in return for Crown policies that would benefit them in foreign dealings, they submitted to domestic regulation of manufacturing and commerce.

THE SECULARIZATION OF CHURCH FUNCTIONS

During the reign of Henry VIII, England broke with Roman Catholicism. This event was significant because it marked the final secularization (in England at least) of the functions of the medieval church. Under Henry, "the state in the form of God's monarchy assumed the role and the functions of the old universal church. What Henry had done in his own blunt way was to sanctify the processes of this world," (ibid., p. 36). During his reign, as well as the reigns of Elizabeth I, James I, and Charles I (1558–

1649), there was widespread social unrest. The cause of this unrest was poverty, and the cause of much of the poverty was unemployment.

The enclosure movements (discussed in Chapter 2) were responsible for much of the unemployment. Another factor, however, was the decline in the export of woolens in the second half of the sixteenth century, which created a great deal of unemployment in England's most important manufacturing industry. There were also frequent commercial crises similar to, but without the regularity of, the depression phase of later business cycles. In addition to these factors, seasonal unemployment put many workers out of work for as many as 4 months of the year.

The people could no longer look to the Catholic church for relief from widespread unemployment and poverty. Destruction of the power of the church had eliminated the organized system of charity. The state attempted to assume responsibility for the general welfare of society. In order to do this, "England's leaders undertook a general, coordinated program to reorganize and rationalize . . . industry by establishing specifications of standards of production and marketing" (ibid., p. 40). All these measures were designed to stimulate English trade and alleviate the unemployment problem.

In fact, it appears that the desire to achieve full employment is the unifying theme of most policy measures advocated by mercantilist writers. The mercantilists preferred measures designed to stimulate foreign rather than domestic trade "because they believed it contributed more to employment, to the nation's wealth and to national power. The writers after 1600 stressed the inflationary effect of an excess of exports over imports and the consequent increase in employment which inflation produced" (Grampp, p. 59).

Among the other measures taken to encourage industry during this period was the issuance of patents of monopoly. The first important patent was granted in 1561, during the reign of Elizabeth I. Monopoly rights were given in order to encourage inventions and to establish new industries. These rights were severely abused, as might be expected. Moreover, they led to a complex system of special privileges and patronage and a host of other evils, which outraged most mercantilist writers every bit as much as similar abuses outraged late nineteenth-century American reformers. The evils of monopoly led to the Statute of Monopolies of 1624, which outlawed all monopolies except those that involved genuine inventions or would be instrumental in promoting a favorable balance of payments. Of course these loopholes were large, and abuses continued almost unchecked.

The Statute of Artificers (1563) specified conditions of employment and length of apprenticeships, provided for periodic wage assessments and established maximum rates that could be paid to laborers. The statute is important because it illustrates the fact that the Crown's paternalistic ethic never led to any attempt to elevate the status of the laboring classes. Monarchs of this period felt obliged to protect the working classes but, like their predecessors in the Middle Ages, believed those classes should be kept in their proper place. Maximum wage rates were designed to protect the capitalists, and furthermore, the justices who set these maximums and enforced the statute generally belonged to the employing class themselves. It is probable that these maximums reduced the real wages of laborers because prices generally rose faster than wages during the succeeding years.

Poor laws passed in 1531 and 1536 attempted to deal with the problems of unemployment, poverty, and misery then widespread in England. The first sought to distinguish between "deserving" and "undeserving" poor. Only the deserving poor were allowed to beg. The second decreed that each individual parish throughout England was responsible for its poor and that the parish should, through voluntary contributions, maintain a poor fund. This proved completely inadequate, and the "pauper problem" grew increasingly severe.

Finally, in 1572 the state accepted the principle that the poor would have to be supported by tax funds and enacted a compulsory "poor rate." And in 1576 "houses of correction" for "incorrigible vagrants" were authorized and provisions made for the parish to purchase raw materials to be worked up by the more tractable paupers and vagrants. Between that time and the close of the sixteenth century, several other poor-law statutes were passed.

The Poor Law of 1601 was the Tudor attempt to integrate these laws into one consistent framework. Its main provisions included formal recognition of the right of the poor to receive relief, imposition of compulsory poor rates at the parish level, and provision for differential treatment for various classes of the poor. The aged and the sick could receive help in their homes; pauper children who were too young to be apprenticed in a trade were to be boarded out; the deserving poor and unemployed were to be given work as provided for in the act of 1576; and incorrigible vagrants were to be sent to houses of correction and prisons. (For an extension of this discussion of the poor laws, see Birnie, chaps. 12 and 18.)

From the preceding discussion it is possible to conclude that the period of English mercantilism was characterized by acceptance, in the spirit of the Christian paternalist ethic, of the idea that "the state had an obligation to serve society by accepting and discharging the responsibility for the general welfare" (Williams, p. 41). The various statutes passed during this period "were predicated upon the idea that poverty, instead of being a personal sin, was a function of the economic system" (ibid., p. 44). They acknowledged that those who were the victims of the deficiencies of the economic system should be cared for by those who benefited from the system.

THE RISE OF INDIVIDUALISM

After the civil war of 1648–1660 and the Glorious Revolution of 1688, the English government was dominated by the gentry and the middle-class capitalists. The medieval world view that underlay the Christian paternalist ethic was eclipsed. A fundamental shift in the philosophy of the role of the state in society took place over the next 100 years. In 1776, with the publication of Adam Smith's *The Wealth of Nations*, a new individualistic philosophy—classical liberalism* had definitely gained the ascendancy in England. This individualistic philosophy had existed throughout the mercantilist period, struggling to break the hold of the older paternalist world view. In the end the new classical liberalism prevailed because it—and not the older, essentially medieval world view—reflected the needs of the new capitalist order.

In condemning greed, acquisitive behavior, and the desire to accumulate wealth, the medieval Christian paternalist ethic condemned what had become the capitalist order's dominant motive force. The capitalist market economy, which had been extended by the late eighteenth century to almost every phase of production, demanded self-seeking, acquisitive behavior to function successfully. In this context new theories about human behavior began to emerge. Writers began to assert that selfish, egoistic motives were the primary if not the only ones that moved people to action.

This interpretation of humankind's behavior is expressed in the writings of many important thinkers of the period. Many philosophers and social theorists began to assert that every human act was related to self-preservation and hence was egoistic in the most fundamental sense. The English nobleman Sir Robert Filmer was greatly alarmed by the large number of people who spoke of "the natural freedom of mankind, a new, plausible and dangerous opinion" with anarchistic implications (McDonald, p. 29). Thomas Hobbes's *Leviathan*, published in 1651, trenchantly articulated a widely held opinion—that all human motives stem from a desire for whatever promotes the "vital motion" of the human organism. Hobbes believed that everyone's motives, even compassion, were merely so many disguised species of self-interest: "Grief for the calamity of another is *pity*, and ariseth from the imagination that the like calamity may befall himself; and therefore is called . . . *compassion*, and . . . fellow-feeling" (quoted in Girvete, pp. 28–29).

Except for the few special interest groups that benefited from the extensive restrictions and regulations of commerce and manufacturing during this period, most capitalists felt constrained and inhibited by state regulations in their quest for profits. The individualistic and egoistic doctrines were eagerly embraced by such people. This view began to dominate economic thinking, even among the mercantilists. One careful history asserts that "most of the mercantilist . . . policy assumed that self-interest governs individual conduct" (Grampp, p. 69).

The majority of mercantilist writers were either capitalists or employees

---

* We use the adjective classical to differentiate the traditional liberal world view from what is called liberalism in the twentieth century. This distinction is clarified further in Chapter 4.

of the great capitalist trading companies. It was quite natural for them to perceive the motives of the capitalists as universal. From the capitalists' views of the nature of humans, and their need to be free from the extensive economic restrictions that inhibited them in the conduct of their everyday business, grew the philosophy of individualism that provided the basis of classical liberalism. Against the well-ordered, paternalistic view Europe had inherited from the feudal society, they asserted "the view that the human person ought to be independent, self-directing, autonomous, free— ought to be, that is, an individual, a unit distinguished from the social mass rather than submerged in it" (McDonald, p. 16).

PROTESTANTISM AND THE INDIVIDUALIST ETHIC

One of the most important examples of this individualistic and middle-class philosophy was the Protestant theology that emerged from the Reformation. The new middle-class capitalists wanted to be free not only from economic restrictions that encumbered manufacturing and commerce but also from the moral opprobrium the Catholic church had heaped upon their motives and activities. Protestantism not only freed them from religious condemnation but eventually made virtues of the selfish, egoistic, and acquisitive motives the medieval church had so despised. (The classic studies of the relationship between Protestantism and Capitalism are Weber's and Tawney's.)

The principal originators of the Protestant movement were quite close to the Catholic position on such questions as usury and the just price. On most social issues they were deeply conservative. During the German peasant revolt of 1524, Luther wrote a virulent pamphlet, *Against the Murdering Hordes of Peasants,* in which he said princes should "knock down, strangle and stab . . . Such wonderful times are these that a prince can merit heaven better with bloodshed than another with prayer." His advice contributed to the general atmosphere in which the slaughter of over 100,000 peasants was carried out with an air of religious righteousness.

Yet despite the conservatism of the founders of Protestantism, this religious outlook contributed to the growing influence of the new individualistic philosophy. The basic tenet of Protestantism, which laid the groundwork for religious attitudes that were to sanction middle-class business practices, was the doctrine that human beings were justified by faith rather than by works. The Catholic church had taught that humans were justified by *works,* which generally meant ceremonies and rituals. In the Catholic view no one could be justified on merit alone. "Justification by works . . . did not mean that an individual could save himself: it meant that he could be saved through the Church. Hence the power of the clergy. Compulsory confession, the imposition of penance on the whole population . . . together with the possibility of withholding absolution, gave the priests a terrifying power" (Hill, p. 43). These powers also created a situation in which the medieval doctrines of the Catholic church were not easily abandoned and in which the individual was still subordinated to society (as represented by the church).

The Protestant doctrine of justification by faith asserted that motives were more important than specific acts or rituals. Faith was "nothing else but the truth of the heart" (ibid.). Each person had to search his or her own heart to discover if acts stemmed from a pure heart and faith in God. Each man and woman had to judge for himself and herself. This individualistic reliance on each person's private conscience appealed strongly to the new middle-class artisans and small merchants. "When the businessman of sixteenth and seventeenth century Geneva, Amsterdam or London looked into his inmost heart, he found that God had planted there a deep respect for the principle of private property . . . Such men felt quite genuinely and strongly that their economic practices, though they might conflict with the traditional law of the old church, were not offensive to God. On the contrary: they glorified God" (ibid., pp. 46–47).

It was through this insistence on the individual's own interpretation of God's will that the "Puritans tried to spiritualize [the new] economic processes" and eventually came to believe that "God instituted the market and exchange" (ibid., p. 49). It was only a matter of time before the Protestants expounded dogma that they expected everyone to accept. But the new dogma was radically different from medieval doctrines. The new doctrines stressed the necessity of doing well at one's earthly calling as the best way to please God, and emphasized diligence and hard work.

The older Christian distrust of riches was "translated" into a condemnation of extravagance and needless dissipation of wealth. Thus the Protestant ethic stressed the importance of asceticism and abstemious frugality. A theologian who has studied the connection between religion and capitalism sums up the relationship in this way: "The religious value set upon constant, systematic, efficient work in one's calling as the readiest means of securing the certainty of salvation and of glorifying God became a most powerful agency in economic expansion. The rigid limitations of consumption on the one hand and the methodical intensification of production on the other could have but one result—the accumulation of capital" (Fullerton, p. 19). Thus, although neither Calvin nor Luther was a spokesman for the new middle-class capitalist, within the context of the new religious individualism the capitalists found a religion in which, over time, "profits . . . [came to be] looked upon as willed by God, as a mark of his favor and a proof of success in one's calling" (ibid., p. 18).

THE ECONOMIC POLICIES OF INDIVIDUALISM

Throughout the mercantilist period this new individualism led to innumerable protests against the subordination of economic affairs to the will of the state. From the middle of the seventeenth century, almost all mercantilist writers condemned state-granted monopolies and other forms of protection and favoritism in the internal economy (as opposed to international commerce). Many believed that in a competitive market that pitted buyer against buyer, seller against seller, and buyer against seller, society would benefit most greatly if the price were left free to fluctuate and find its proper (market-equilibrating) level. One of the earliest mercantilist writers of importance, John Hales, argued that agricultural productivity could best be improved if husbandmen were allowed to

> have more profit by it than they have, and liberty to sell it at all times, and to all places, as freely as men may do their other things. But then no doubt, the price of corn would rise, specially at the first more than at length; yet that price would evoke every man to set plough in the ground, to husband waste grounds, yes to turn the lands which be enclosed from pasture to arable land; for every man will gladder follow that wherein they see the more profit and gains, and thereby must need ensure both plenty of corn, and also much treasure should be brought into this realm by occasion thereof; and besides that plenty of other victuals increased among us. (Quoted in Grampp, p. 78)

This belief—that restrictions on production and trade within a nation were harmful to the interests of everyone concerned—became increasingly widespread in the late seventeenth and early eighteenth centuries. Numerous statements of this view can be found in the works of such writers as Malynes, Petty, North, Law, and Child. Of these men, perhaps Sir Dudley North (1641–1691) was the earliest clear spokesman for the individualistic ethic that was to become the basis for classical liberalism. North believed that all men were motivated primarily by self-interest and should be left alone to compete in a free market if the public welfare were to be maximized. He argued that whenever merchants or capitalists advocated special laws to regulate production or commerce, "they usually esteem the immediate interest of their own to be the common Measure of Good and Evil. And there are many, who to gain a little in their own Trades, care not how much others suffer; and each man strives that all others may be forced in their dealings to act subserviently for his Profit, but under the cover of the Publick" (quoted in Lekachman, p. 185). The public welfare would best be served, North believed, if most of the restrictive laws that bestowed special privileges were entirely removed.

In 1714 Bernard Mandeville published *The Fable of the Bees: or Private Vices, Publick Benefits,* in which he put forth the seemingly strange paradox that the vices most despised in the older moral code, if practiced by all, would result in the greatest public good. Selfishness, greed, and acquisitive behavior, he maintained, all tended to contribute to industriousness and a thriving economy. The answer to the paradox was, of course, that what had been vices in the eyes of the medieval moralists were the very motive forces that propelled the new capitalist system. And in the view of the new religious, moral, and economic philosophies of the capitalist period these motives were no longer vices.

The capitalists had struggled throughout the mercantilist period to free themselves from all restrictions in their quest for profits. These restrictions had resulted from the paternalistic laws that were the remnants of the feudal version of the Christian paternalist ethic. Such an ethic simply was not compatible with the new economic system that functioned on the basis of strict contractual obligations between people rather than on traditional personal ties. Merchants and capitalists who invested large sums in market ventures could not depend on the forces of custom to protect their investments.

Profit seeking could be effective only in a society based on the protection of property rights and the enforcement of impersonal contractual commitments between individuals. The new ideology that was firmly taking root in the late seventeenth and eighteenth centuries justified these motives and relationships between individuals. It is to a consideration of this new individualistic philosophy of classical liberalism that we turn in Chapter 4.

SUMMARY

There is a basic continuity between medieval and mercantilist social thought. State intervention in economic processes was originally justified in terms of the medieval Christian notion that those to whom God had given power were obligated to use this power to promote the general welfare and common good of all society. In early capitalism the state began to assume many of the roles formerly held by the church.

The Christian paternalist ethic, however, had thoroughly condemned the acquisitive behavior that was to become the dominant motive force of the new capitalist system. It was therefore necessary to create a new philosophical and ideological point of view that morally justified individualization, greed, and profit seeking.

Protestantism and the new philosophies of individualism furnished the bases for the new ideology. The economic writings of the later mercantilists reflected the new individualism. The new point of view emphasized the need for greater freedom for capitalists to seek profits and hence the need for less government intervention in the market. Thus the presence of two fundamentally different general points of view in mercantilist writings created an intellectual conflict that was not resolved until the classical liberal philosophy, including classical economics, effectively ferreted out all remnants of the medieval Christian paternalist ethic.

REFERENCES

Birnie, Arthur. *An Economic History of the British Isles*. London: Methuen, 1936.

Fullerton, Kemper. "Calvinism and Capitalism; an Explanation of the Weber Thesis." In *Protestantism and Capitalism: The Weber Thesis and Its Critics*. Edited by Robert W. Green. Lexington, Mass.. Heath, 1959.

Girvetz, Harry K. *The Evolution of Liberalism.* New York: Colliers, 1963.

Grampp, William D. *Economic Liberalism.* Vol. 1. New York: Random House, 1965.

Hill, Christopher. "Protestantism and the Rise of Capitalism." In *The Rise of Capitalism.* Edited by D. S. Landes. New York: Macmillan, 1966.

Lekachman, Robert, ed. *The Varieties of Economics.* Vol. 1. New York: Meridian, 1962.

McDonald, Lee Cameron. *Western Political Theory: The Modern Age.* New York: Harcourt Brace Jovanovich, 1962.

Tawney, Richard H. *Religion and the Rise of Capitalism.* New York: Mentor Books, 1954.

Weber, Max. *The Protestant Ethic and the Spirit of Capitalism.* New York: Scribner's, 1958.

Williams, William Appleman. *The Contours of American History.* New York: Quadrangle, 1966.

Chapter
4

Classical Liberalism and the Triumph of Industrial Capitalism

A single theme runs through the works of the later mercantilist writers (considered in the latter part of Chapter 3) that distinguished them from the later classical liberal writers. They argued for a minimum of internal restriction and regulation, but they favored an active government policy designed to further England's commerce in the international trading markets. The classical liberals, however, advocated free trade internationally as well as domestically. In this chapter we examine the changes in England's commercial position that encouraged its economists to favor free trade.

THE INDUSTRIAL REVOLUTION

Between 1700 and 1770 the foreign markets for English goods grew much faster than did England's domestic markets. During the period 1700–1750, output of domestic industries increased by 7 percent, while that of export industries increased by 76 percent. For the period of 1750–1770, the figures are 7 percent and 80 percent, respectively. This rapidly increasing foreign demand for English manufactures was the single most important cause of the most fundamental transformation of human life in history: the Industrial Revolution.

Eighteenth-century England was an economy with a well-developed market and one in which the traditional anticapitalist and antimarket biases in attitudes and ideology had been greatly weakened. In this England, larger outputs of manufactured goods produced at lower prices meant ever-increasing profits. Thus profit seeking was the motive that, stimulated by increasing foreign demand, accounted for the virtual explosion of technological innovations that occurred in the late eighteenth and early nineteenth centuries, radically transforming all England and eventually most of the world.

The textile industry was the most important in the early Industrial Revolution. In 1700 the woolen industry had persuaded the government to ban the import of Indian-made "calicoes" (cotton) and thus had secured a protected home market for domestic producers. As outlined earlier, rising foreign demand spurred mechanization of the industry.

More specifically, an imbalance between the spinning and weaving processes led to many of the innovations. The spinning wheel was not as productive as the hand loom, especially after the 1730s, when the flying shuttle was invented and the weaving process was speeded up considerably. This imbalance led to three inventions that reversed it: the spinning jenny, developed in the 1760s, with which one person could spin several threads simultaneously; the water frame, invented in 1768, which improved spinning by using both rollers and spindles in the process; and the mule, developed in the 1780s, which combined features of the other two and permitted the application of steam power. These new inventions could be used most economically in factories located near sources of water power (and later steam power). Richard Arkwright, who claimed to be the inventor of the water frame, raised sufficient capital to put a great many factories into operation, each employing anywhere from 150 to 600 people. Others followed his example, and textile manufacturing in England was rapidly transformed from a cottage to a factory industry.

The iron industry was also very important in the early drive to mechanized factory production. In the early eighteenth century England's iron industry was quite inconsequential. Charcoal was still used for smelting, as it had been since prehistoric times. By this time, however, the forests surrounding the iron mines were almost completely depleted. England was forced to import pig iron from its colonies, as well as from Sweden, Germany, and Spain. In 1709, Abraham Darby developed a process for making coke from coal for use in the smelting process.

Despite the relative abundance of coal near the iron mines, it was not until the latter part of the eighteenth century (when military demands on the arms and munitions industries were very great) that the iron industry began using coke extensively. This increased demand led to the development of the puddling process, which eliminated the excess carbon left by the coke. A whole series of innovations followed, including the rolling mill, the blast furnace, the steam hammer, and metal-turning lathes. All these inventions led to a very rapid expansion of the iron- and coal-mining industries, which permitted the increasingly widespread use of machines made of iron in a great variety of industries.

Entrepreneurs in many other industries saw the possibilities for larger profits if they could increase output and lower costs. In this period there was a "veritable outburst of inventive activity":

During the second half of the eighteenth century, interest in technical innovations became unusually intensive. For a hundred years prior to 1760, the
number of patents issued during each decade had reached 102 only once, and
had otherwise fluctuated between a low of 22 (1700–1709) and a high of 92
(1750–1759). During the following thirty-year period (1760–1789), the average number of patents issued increased from 205 in the 1760s to 294 in the
1770s and 477 in the 1780s. (Bendix, p. 27)

Undoubtedly the most important of these innovations was the development of the steam engine. Industrial steam engines had been introduced
in the early 1700s, but mechanical difficulties had limited their use to the
pumping of water in mines. In 1769 James Watt designed an engine with
such accurate specifications that the straight thrust of a piston could be
translated into rotary motion. A Birmingham manufacturer named Boulton
formed a partnership with Watt, and with Boulton's financial resources
they were able to go into large-scale production of steam engines. By the
turn of the century steam was rapidly replacing water as the chief source
of power in manufacturing. The development of steam power led to profound economic and social changes.

> With this new great event, the invention of the steam engine, the final and
> most decisive stage of the industrial revolution opened. By liberating it from
> its last shackles, steam enabled the immense and rapid development of large-
> scale industry to take place. For the use of steam was not, like that of water,
> dependent on geographical position and local resources. Whenever coal could
> be brought at a reasonable price a steam engine could be erected. England
> had plenty of coal, and by the end of the eighteenth century it was already
> applied to many different uses, while a network of waterways, made on purpose,
> enabled it to be carried everywhere very cheaply; the whole country became
> a privileged land, suitable above all others for the growth of industry. Factories
> were now no longer bound to the valleys, where they had grown up in solitude
> by the side of rapid-flowing streams. It became possible to bring them nearer
> the markets where their raw materials were bought and their finished products
> sold, and nearer the centers of population where their labor was recruited.
> They sprang up near one another and thus, huddled together, gave rise to
> those huge black industrial cities which the steam engine surrounded with a
> perpetual cloud of smoke. (Mantoux, pp. 344–345)

The growth in the major manufacturing cities was truly spectacular.
For example, the population of Manchester rose from 17,000 in 1760 to
237,000 in 1831 and 400,000 in 1851. Output of manufactured goods
approximately doubled in the second half of the eighteenth century and
grew even more rapidly in the early nineteenth century. By 1801 nearly
30 percent of the English work force was employed in manufacturing and
mining; by 1831 this figure had risen to more than 40 percent. Thus the
Industrial Revolution transformed England into a country of large urban
manufacturing centers, where the factory system was dominant. The result
was a very rapid growth of productivity that vaulted England into the
position of the greatest economic and political power of the nineteenth

century. The effects of the Industrial Revolution on the lives of the English people are discussed in Chapter 5.

THE RISE OF CLASSICAL LIBERALISM

It was during this period of industrialization that the individualistic world view of classical liberalism became the dominant ideology of capitalism. Many of the ideas of classical liberalism had taken root and even gained wide acceptance in the mercantilist period, but it was in the late eighteenth and nineteenth centuries that classical liberalism most completely dominated social, political, and economic thought in England. The Christian paternalist ethic was still advanced in the writings of many of the nobility and their allies as well as many socialists, but in this era these expressions were, by and large, dissident minority views.

The Psychological Creed

Classical liberalism's psychological creed was based on four assumptions about human nature. People were believed to be egoistic, coldly calculating, essentially inert, and atomistic. (See Chapter 3 for a discussion of the egoistic theory of human nature.) The egoism argued by Hobbes furnished the basis for this view, and in the works of later liberals, especially Jeremy Bentham, it was blended with psychological hedonism: the view that all actions are motivated by the desire to achieve pleasure and avoid pain.

"Nature," Bentham wrote, "has placed mankind under the governance of two sovereign masters, *pain* and *pleasure*. . . . They govern us in all we do, in all we say, in all we think" (Bentham, p. 341). Pleasures differed in intensity, Bentham believed, but there were no qualitative differences. He argued that "quantity of pleasure being equal, pushpin is as good as poetry." This theory of human motivation as purely selfish is found in the writings of many of the most eminent thinkers of the period, including John Locke, Bernard Mandeville, David Hartley, Abraham Tucker, and Adam Smith. Smith's ideas are examined in some detail later in this chapter.

The rational intellect played a significant role in the classical liberal's scheme of things. Although all motives stemmed from pursuit of pleasure and avoidance of pain, the decisions people made about what pleasures or pains to seek or avoid were based on a cool, dispassionate, and rational assessment of the situation. Reason would dictate that all alternatives in a situation be weighed in order to choose that which would maximize pleasure or minimize pain. It is this emphasis on the importance of rational measurement of pleasures and pains (with a corresponding deemphasis of caprice, instinct, habit, custom, or convention) that forms the calculating, intellectual side of the classical liberal's theory of psychology.

The view that individuals were essentially inert stemmed from the notion that pleasure or the avoidance of pain were people's only motives.

If people could see no activities leading to pleasurable conclusions or feared no pain, then they would be inert, motionless, or, in simpler terms, just plain lazy. Any kind of exertion or work was viewed as painful and therefore would not be undertaken without the promise of greater pleasure or the avoidance of greater pain. "Aversion," wrote Bentham, "is the emotion— the only emotion—which labor, taken by itself, is qualified to produce: of any such emotion as *love* or *desire, ease,* which is the *negative* or *absence* of *labor*—ease not labor—is the object" (quoted in Girvetz, p. 38).

The practical outcome of this doctrine (or perhaps the reason for it) was the widespread belief of the time that laborers were incurably lazy. Thus only a large reward or the fear of starvation and deprivation could force them to work. The Reverend Joseph Townsend put this view very succinctly: "Hunger is not only peaceable, silent and unremitted pressure, but, as the most natural motive to industry and labor, it calls forth the most powerful exertions." Townsend believed that "only the experience of hunger would goad them [laborers] to labor" (Bendix, p. 74).

This view differed radically from the older, paternalistic ethic that had led to the passage of the Elizabethan Poor Relief Act of 1601. The pater- nalistic concern for the poor had lasted for two centuries and had culmi- nated in 1795 in the *Speenhamland system,* which guaranteed everyone, able-bodied or not, working or not, a minimal subsistence to be paid by public taxes. It was against this system that the classical liberals railed. They eventually succeeded in passing the Poor Law of 1834, the object of which, according to Dicey, "was in reality to save the property of hard- working men from destruction by putting an end to the monstrous system under which laggards who would not toil for their support lived at the expense of their industrious neighbors" (Dicey, p. 203).

Classical liberals were persuaded, however, that the "higher ranks" of individuals were motivated by ambition. This differentiation of people into different ranks betrayed an implicit elitism in their individualistic doc- trines. In order to ensure ample effort on the part of the "elite," the classical liberals believed the state should put the highest priority on the protection of private property. Although the argument began "as an argument for guaranteeing to the worker the fruits of his toil, it has become one of the chief apologies for the institution of private property in general" (Girvetz, p. 50).

The last of the four tenets was atomism, which held that the individual was a more fundamental reality than the group or society. "Priority . . . [was] . . . assigned to the ultimate components out of which an aggregate or whole . . . [was] composed; they constituted the fundamental reality" (ibid., p. 41). With this notion the classical liberals rejected the concept, implicit in the Christian paternalist ethic, that society was like a family and that the whole and the relationships that made up the whole were more important than any individual. The liberals' individualistic beliefs were inconsistent with the personal and human ties envisioned in the Christian paternalist ethic. The group was no more than the additive total of the individuals that constituted it. They believed that restrictions placed on the individual by society were generally evil and should be tolerated only when an even worse evil would result without them.

This atomistic psychology can be contrasted with a more socially oriented psychology that would lead to the conclusion that most of the characteristics, habits, ways of perceiving and thinking about life processes, and general personality patterns of the individual are significantly influenced, if not determined, by the social institutions and relationships of which he or she is a part. Atomistic psychology, however, sees the makeup of the individual as somehow independently given. It therefore regards social institutions as both tools for and the handiwork of these individuals. In this view society exists only because it is useful, and if it were not for this usefulness each individual could go his or her own way, discarding society much as he or she would discard a tool that no longer served its purpose.

The Economic Creed

Several explanations are necessary for an understanding of why the classical liberals thought society so useful. For example, they talked about the "natural gregariousness of men," the need for collective security, and the economic benefits of the division of labor, which society makes possible. The latter was the foundation of the economic creed of classical liberalism, and the creed was crucial to classical liberalism because this philosophy contained what appears to be two contradictory or conflicting assumptions.

On the one hand, the assumption of the individual's innate egoism had led Hobbes to assert that, in the absence of restraints, people's selfish motives would lead to a "natural state" of war, with each individual pitted against all others. In this state of nature, Hobbes believed, the life of a person was "solitary, poor, nasty, brutish, and short." The only escape from brutal combat was the establishment of some source of absolute power—a central government—to which each individual submitted in return for protection from all other individuals (Hobbes, pp. 192–205).

On the other hand, one of the cardinal tenets of classical liberalism was that individuals (or, more particularly, businessmen) should be free to give vent to their egoistic drives with a minimum of control or restraint imposed by society. This apparent contradiction was bridged by the liberal economic creed, which asserted that if the competitiveness and rivalry of unrestrained egoism existed in a capitalist market setting, then this competition would benefit the individuals involved and all society as well. This view was put forth in the most profound single intellectual achievement of classical liberalism: Adam Smith's *The Wealth of Nations*, published in 1776.

Smith believed that "every individual . . . [is] continually exerting himself to find out the most advantageous employment for whatever capital he can command" (Smith, p. 421). Those without capital were always searching for the employment at which the monetary return for their labor would be maximized. If both capitalists and laborers were left alone, self-interest would guide them to use their capital and labor where they were most productive. The search for profits would ensure that what was produced would be what people wanted most and were willing to pay for. Thus Smith and classical liberals in general were opposed to having some authority or law determine what should be produced: "It is not from the benevolence of the butcher, the brewer, or the baker, that we expect our dinner, but from their regard to their own interest" (ibid., p. 14). Producers of various goods must compete in the market for the dollars of consumers. The producer who offered a better-quality product would attract more consumers. Self-interest would, therefore, lead to constant improvement of the quality of the product. The producer could also increase profits by cutting the cost of production to a minimum.

Thus a *free market*, in which producers competed for consumers' money in an egoistic quest for more profits, would guarantee the direction of capital and labor to their most productive uses and ensure production of the goods consumers wanted and needed most (as measured by their ability and willingness to pay for them). Moreover, the market would lead to a constant striving to improve the quality of products and to organize production in the most efficient and least costly manner possible. All these beneficial actions would stem directly from the competition of egoistical individuals, each pursuing his or her self-interest.

What a far cry from the "solitary, poor, nasty, brutish" world Hobbes thought would result from human competitiveness. The wonderful social institution that could make all this possible was the free and unrestrained market, the forces of supply and demand. The market, Smith believed, would act as an "invisible hand," channeling selfish, egoistic motives into mutually consistent and complementary activities that would best promote the welfare of all society. And the greatest beauty of it was the complete lack of any need for paternalistic guidance, direction, or restrictions. Freedom from coercion in a capitalist market economy was compatible with a natural orderliness in which the welfare of each, as well as the welfare of all society (which was, after all, only the aggregate of the individuals that constituted it), would be maximized. In Smith's words, each producer

intends only his own security; and by directing that industry in such a manner as its produce may be of the greatest value, he intends only his own gain, and he is in this, as in many other cases, led by an invisible hand to promote an end which was no part of his intention. Nor is it always the worse for the society that it was not a part of it. By pursuing his own interest he frequently promotes that of society more effectually than when he really intends to promote it. I have never known much good done by those who affected to trade for the public good. It is an affectation, indeed, not very common among merchants, and very few words need be employed in dissuading them from it. (Ibid., p. 423)

With this statement it is evident that Smith had a philosophy totally antithetical to the paternalism of the Christian paternalist ethic. The Christian notion of the rich promoting the security and well-being of the poor through paternalistic control and almsgiving contrasts sharply with Smith's picture of a capitalist who is concerned only with "his own advantage, indeed, and not that of the society. . . . But the study of his own advantage naturally, or rather necessarily leads them to prefer that employment which is most advantageous to the society" (ibid., p. 421).

Not only would the free and unfettered market channel productive energies and resources into their most valuable uses, but it would also lead to continual economic progress. Economic well-being depended on the capacity of an economy to produce. Productive capacity depended, in turn, on accumulation of capital and division of labor. When one man produced everything he needed for himself and his family, production was very inefficient. But if men subdivided tasks, each producing only the commodity for which his own abilities best suited him, productivity increased. For such a subdivision of tasks a market was necessary in order to exchange goods. In the market each person could get all the items he needed but did not produce.

This increase in productivity could be extended further if the production of each commodity were broken down into many steps or stages. Each person would then work on only one stage of the production of one commodity. To achieve a division of labor of this degree, it was necessary to have many specialized tools and other equipment. It was also necessary that all the stages of production for a particular commodity be brought together and coordinated, as, for example, in a factory. Thus an increasingly fine division of labor required accumulation of capital in the form of tools, equipment, factories, and money. This capital would also provide wages to maintain workers during the period of production before their coordinated efforts were brought to fruition and sold on the market.

The source of this capital accumulation was, of course, the profits of production. As long as demand was brisk and more could be sold than was being produced, capitalists would invest their profits in order to expand their capital, which would lead to an increasingly intricate division of labor. The increased division of labor would lead to greater productivity, higher wages, higher profits, more capital accumulation, and so forth, in a neverending, upward-moving escalator of social progress. The process would be brought to a halt only when there was no longer sufficient demand for the products to warrant further accumulation and more extensive division of labor. Government regulation of economic affairs, or any restriction on the freedom of market behavior, could only decrease the extent of demand and bring the beneficial process of capital accumulation to a halt before it would have ended otherwise. So here again there was no room for paternalistic government meddling in economic affairs.

The Theory of Population

Thomas Robert Malthus's population theory was an important and integral part of classical liberal economic and social doctrines. He believed most human beings were driven by an insatiable desire for sexual pleasure and that consequently natural rates of human reproduction, *when unchecked*, would lead to geometric increases in population—that is, the population would increase each generation at the ratio of 1, 2, 4, 8, 16, and so forth. But food production, at the very best, increases at an arithmetic rate— that is, with each generation it can increase only at a rate such as 1, 2, 3, 4, 5, and so on.

Obviously, something would have to hold the population in check. The food supply could not support a population that was growing at a geometric rate. Malthus believed there were two general kinds of checks that limited population growth: preventive checks and positive checks. Preventive checks reduced the birthrate, whereas positive checks increased the death rate.

Moral restraint, vice, and birth control were the primary preventive checks. Moral restraint was the means by which the higher ranks of humans limited their family size in order not to dissipate their wealth among larger and larger numbers of heirs. For the lower ranks of humans, vice and birth control were the preventive checks; but they were grossly insufficient to curb the vast numbers of the poor.

Famine, misery, plague, and war were the positive checks. The fact that preventive checks did not succeed in limiting the numbers of lower-class people made these positive checks inevitable. Finally, if the positive checks were somehow overcome, the growing population would press upon the food supply until starvation—the ultimate and unavoidable check— succeeded in holding the population down.

Before starvation set in, Malthus advised that steps be taken to help the positive checks do their work:

> It is an evident truth that, whatever may be the rate of increase in the means of subsistence, the increase in population must be limited by it, at least after the food has once been divided into the smallest shares that will support life. All the children born, beyond what would be required to keep up the population to this level, must necessarily perish, unless room be made for them by the deaths of grown persons. . . . To act consistently therefore, we should facilitate, instead of foolishly and vainly endeavouring to impede, the operation of nature in producing this mortality; and if we dread the too frequent visitation of the horrid form of famine, we should sedulously encourage the other forms of destruction, which we compel nature to use. Instead of recommending clean-liness to the poor, we should encourage contrary habits. In our towns we should make the streets narrower, crowd more people into the houses, and court the return of the plague. In the country, we should build our villages near stagnant pools, and particularly encourage settlements in all marshy and unwholesome situations. But above all, we should reprobate specific remedies for ravaging diseases; and those benevolent, but much mistaken men, who have thought

they were doing a service to mankind by projecting schemes for the total extirpation of particular disorders. If by these and similar means the annual mortality were increased . . . we might probably every one of us marry at the age of puberty, and yet few be absolutely starved. (Malthus, pp. 179–180)

The masses, in Malthus's opinion, were incapable of exercising moral restraint, which was the only real remedy for the population problem. They were therefore doomed to live perpetually at a bare subsistence level. If all income and wealth were distributed among them, it would be totally dissipated within one generation because of profligate behavior and population growth, and they would be as poor and destitute as ever.

Paternalistic attempts to aid the poor were thus doomed to failure. Furthermore, they were a positive evil because they drained wealth and income from the higher (more moral) ranks of human beings. These higher-class individuals were responsible, either in person or by supporting others, for all the great achievements of society. Art, music, philosophy, literature, and the other splendid cultural attainments of Western civilization owed their existence to the good taste and generosity of the higher classes of men. Taking money from them would dry up the source of such achievement; using the money to alleviate the conditions of the poor was a futile, foredoomed exercise.

It is obvious that the Malthusian population theory and the liberal economic theories led to the same conclusion: Paternalistic government should avoid any attempt to intervene in the economy on behalf of the poor. Malthusian views—that poverty is the fault of the poor, who have too many babies, and that nothing can be done to end poverty—are still held by many people today.

The Political Creed

The economic and population doctrines of classical liberalism gave rise quite naturally to a political creed that rejected the state, or government, as an evil to be tolerated only when it was the sole means of avoiding a worse evil. Much of this antipathy stemmed directly from the many corrupt, despotic, capricious, and tyrannical actions of several European kings, as well as from the actions of the English Parliament, which was notoriously unrepresentative and often despotic. The liberal creed was not put forward as an objection against particular governments, however, but against governments in general. Thomas Paine reflected the sentiment of classical liberals when he wrote: "Society in every state is a blessing, but government, even in its best state, is but a necessary evil; in its worst state an intolerable one" (quoted in Girvetz, p. 66).

What were the functions that classical liberals thought should be given to governments? In *The Wealth of Nations* Adam Smith listed three: protection of the country against foreign invaders, protection of citizens against "injustices" suffered at the hands of other citizens, and the "duty . . . of erecting and maintaining those public institutions and those public works, which, though they may be in the highest degree advantageous to a great society, are, however, of such a nature, that the profit could never repay the expense to any individual or small number of individuals, and which it therefore cannot be expected that any individual or small number of individuals should erect and maintain" (Smith, p. 681).

This list is very general, and almost any kind of government action could be justified under one of these three functions. In order to understand the specific functions the liberals believed government should have, it is necessary to deal first with an objection that is frequently raised when the writings of Adam Smith are said to comprise part of an ideology justifying capitalism. It is often pointed out not only that Smith was not a spokesman for the capitalists of his day but also that many of his passages show that he was in general suspicious and distrustful of capitalists. This contention is certainly true. Nevertheless capitalists used the arguments put forward by Smith to justify their attempts to eliminate the last vestiges of paternalistic government when these stood in the way of their quest for profits. It was Smith's rationale that enabled them to quiet their consciences when their actions created widespread hardship and suffering. After all, they were only following his advice and pursuing their own profits; and this was the way they should act if they wished to be of the greatest service to society.

Finally, most classical liberals interpreted Smith's theory of the three general governmental functions in a way that showed they were not hesitant about endorsing a paternalistic government when they, the capitalists, were the beneficiaries of paternalism. Thus "the original doctrine of laissez-faire . . . passed, for the most part, from the care of intellectuals like Adam Smith . . . into the custodianship of businessmen and industrialists and their hired spokesmen" (Girvetz, p. 81).

First, the requirement that the government protect the country from external threats was often extended in the late nineteenth century to a protection or even enlargement of foreign markets through armed coercion. Second, protection of citizens against "injustices" committed by other citizens was usually defined to mean protection of private property, enforcement of contracts, and preservation of internal order. Protection of private property, especially ownership of factories and capital equipment, is of course tantamount to protection of the sine qua non of capitalism. It was their ownership of the means of production that gave the capitalists their economic and political power. Giving the government the function of protecting property relations meant giving the government the job of protecting the source of power of the economically and politically dominant class: the capitalists.

Contract enforcement was also essential for the successful functioning of capitalism. The complex division of labor and the necessity of complex organization and coordination in production, as well as the colossal capital investments necessary in many commercial ventures, meant that capitalists had to be able to depend on people to meet contractual commitments. The medieval notion that custom and the special circumstances of a case defined an individual's obligations was just not compatible with capitalism. Therefore the duty to enforce contracts amounted to governmental coercion of a type necessary for capitalism to function.

The preservation of internal order was (and is) always necessary. In the late eighteenth and early nineteenth centuries, however, it often meant brutally crushing labor union movements or the English Chartist movement, which capitalists considered threats to their profit-making activities.

Finally, the function of "erecting and maintaining those public institutions and those of public works" that were in the public interest generally was interpreted to mean the creation and maintenance of institutions that fostered profitable production and exchange. These included the provision of a stable and uniform currency, standard weights and measures, and the physical means necessary for conducting business. Roads, canals, harbors, railroads, the postal services, and other forms of communication were among the prerequisites of business. Although these were often privately owned, most capitalist governments were extensively involved in their erection and maintenance either through financial subsidies to private businesses or through the government's direct undertaking of these projects.

Thus it may be concluded that the classical liberals' philosophy of laissez-faire was opposed to government interference in economic affairs only if such interference were harmful to the interests of capitalists. They welcomed and even fought for any paternalistic interferences in economic affairs that stabilized business or made larger profits possible.

CLASSICAL LIBERALISM AND INDUSTRIALIZATION

The Industrial Revolution and the triumph of the classical liberal capitalist ideology occurred together during the late eighteenth and early nineteenth centuries. Liberalism was the philosophy of the new industrial capitalism, and the new liberal ideas created a political and intellectual atmosphere in eighteenth-century England that fostered the growth of the factory system.

In its medieval version the Christian paternalist ethic had led to a pervasive system of restrictions on the behavior of capitalists during the mercantilist period. Capitalists and their spokesmen opposed most of these restrictions with a new individualistic philosophy that advocated greater freedom for the capitalist to seek profits in a market free of encumbrances and restrictions. It is not surprising that the triumph of this philosophy should coincide with the greatest achievement of the capitalist class: the Industrial Revolution. The Industrial Revolution vaulted the capitalist class into a position of economic and political dominance, and this fact goes far toward explaining the triumph of classical liberalism as the ideology of the new age of industrial capitalism.

SUMMARY

The pressure of rapidly increasing demand and the prospect of larger profits led to a "veritable outburst of inventive activity" in the late eighteenth and early nineteenth centuries. This period of widespread innovation—the Industrial Revolution—transformed England (and later western Europe and North America) into urban societies dominated by great manufacturing cities in which large numbers of workers were subjected to the dehumanizing discipline of factory production.

During this period the classical liberal ideology of capitalism came to dominate social and economic thinking. The new ideology pictured individuals as egoistic, coldly calculating, lazy, and generally independent of the society of which they were a part. Adam Smith's analysis of the market as an "invisible hand" that channeled egoistic drives into the most socially useful activities supported a doctrine of laissez-faire. The only functions this philosophy assigned to the government were those that would support and encourage profit-making activities.

Finally, the Malthusian theory of population taught that social action designed to mitigate the suffering of the poor was not only useless but even had socially deleterious effects. Acceptance of this view necessitated complete abandonment of the Christian paternalist ethic.

REFERENCES

Bendix, Reinhard. *Work and Authority in Industry*. New York: Harper & Row, Torchbooks, 1963.

Bentham, Jeremy. "An Introduction to the Principles of Morals and Legislation." In *Ethical Theories*. Edited by A. I. Meiden. Englewood Cliffs, N.J.: Prentice-Hall, 1955.

Dicey, Albert V. *Law and Public Opinion in England*. 2d ed. London: Macmillan, 1926.

Girvetz, Harry K. *The Evolution of Liberalism*. New York: Colliers, 1963.

Hobbes. *Leviathan*. Reprinted in *Ethical Theories*. Edited by A. I. Meiden. Englewood Cliffs, N.J.: Prentice-Hall, 1955.

Malthus, Thomas Robert. *Essay on the Principle of Population*. Vol. 2. New York: Dutton, 1961.

Mantoux, Paul. *The Industrial Revolution in the Eighteenth Century*. New York: Harcourt Brace Jovanovich, 1927.

Robbins, Lionel. *The Theory of Economic Policy in English Classical Political Economy*. London: Macmillan, 1953.

Samuels, Warren J. *The Classical Theory of Economic Policy*. New York: World Publishing, 1966.

Smith, Adam. *The Wealth of Nations*. New York: Modern Library, 1937.

Chapter
5

Socialist Protest Amid
the Industrial Revolution

The Industrial Revolution brought about increases in human productivity without precedent in history. The widespread construction of factories and extensive use of machinery represented the mechanical basis of this increase. In order to channel the economy's productive capacity into the creation of capital goods, however, it was necessary to devote a relatively much smaller part of this capacity to the manufacture of consumer goods. Capital goods had to be purchased at a social cost of mass deprivation.

THE SOCIAL COSTS OF THE INDUSTRIAL REVOLUTION

Historically, in all cases in which society has had to force a bare subsistence existence on some of its members it has always been those with the least economic and political power who have made the sacrifices. So it was in the Industrial Revolution in England. The working class lived near the subsistence level in 1750, and their standard of living (measured in terms of the purchasing power of wages) deteriorated during the second half of the eighteenth century. The trend of working-class living standards in the first several decades of the nineteenth century is a subject of dispute among historians. Many eminent scholars find sufficient evidence to argue that the living standard failed to increase, or even decreased, so one can conclude that any increase during this period was slight at best.

Throughout the period of the Industrial Revolution, there is no doubt that the standard of living of the poor fell precipitously in relative terms. A detailed analysis shows that "relatively the poor grew poorer, simply because the country, and its rich and middle class, so obviously grew wealthier. The very moment when the poor were at the end of their tether . . . was the moment when the middle class dripped with excess capital, to be wildly invested in railways and spent on the bulging opulent household furnishings displayed at the Great Exhibition of 1851, and on palatial municipal constructions . . . in the smoky northern cities" (Hobsbawm, p. 72). There can be no doubt about which class paid the social costs in terms of the sacrificed consumption that was necessary for industrialization.

Yet decreased consumption was by no means the only, and perhaps not even the worst, of the hardships forced upon the laboring class by the Industrial Revolution. The new factory system completely destroyed the laborers' traditional way of life, throwing them into a nightmare world with which they were completely unprepared to cope. They lost the pride of workmanship and close personal relationships that had existed in handicraft industries. Under the new system their only relationships with their employers was through the impersonal market, or *cash nexus*. They lost direct access to the means of production and were reduced to mere sellers of labor power totally dependent on market conditions for their livelihoods.

Perhaps worse still was the monotonous, mechanical regularity imposed on the worker by the factory system. In preindustrial Europe the worker's tasks were not so specialized. The worker went from one task to another, and the work was interrupted by variations in the seasons or the weather. When the worker felt like resting or playing or changing the pace of the work routine, there was a certain amount of freedom to do so. Factory employment brought the tyranny of the clock. Production was mechanized. Absolute regularity was necessary to coordinate the complex interaction of processes and to maximize the use of new, expensive machinery. The pace of work was no longer decided by the worker but by the machine.

The machine, which had formerly been an appendage to the worker, was now the focal point of the productive process. The worker became a mere appendage to the cold, implacable, pace-setting machine. During the late eighteenth and early nineteenth centuries, in a spontaneous revolt against the new factory system, bands of workers smashed and destroyed machines and factories, which they blamed for their plight. These revolts, called the Luddite revolts, ended in 1813 when large numbers of workers were hanged or deported for their activities.

The extensive division of labor in the factory made much of the work so routine and simple that untrained women and children could do it as well as men, and because in many cases entire families had to work in order to earn enough to eat, women and children were employed widely. Many factory owners preferred women and children because they could be reduced to a state of passive obedience more easily than men. The widespread ideology in this period that the only good woman is a submissive woman was a great help to their employers.

Children were bound to factories by indentures of apprenticeship for 7 years, or until they were 21 years old. In these cases almost nothing was given the children in return for long hours of work under the most horrendous conditions. Poor-law authorities could indenture the children of paupers. This led to "regular bargains . . . [where] children . . . were dealt with as mere merchandise . . . between the spinners on the one hand and the Poor Law authorities on the other. Lots of fifty, eighty or a hundred children were supplied and sent like cattle to the factory, where they remained imprisoned for many years" (Mantoux, pp. 410–411).

These children endured the cruelest servitude. They were totally isolated from anyone who might take pity on them and were thus at the mercy of the capitalists or their hired managers, whose main concern was the challenge of competitive factories. The children's workday was from 14 to 18 hours, or until they dropped from complete exhaustion. The foremen were paid according to how much the children produced and therefore pushed them mercilessly. In most factories the children had hardly more than 20 minutes a day for their main (and often only) meal. "Accidents were very common, especially toward the end of the overlong day, when the exhausted children almost fell asleep at their work. The tale never ended of fingers cut off and limbs crushed in the wheels" (ibid., p. 413). The children were disciplined in such savage and brutal ways that a recitation of the methods used would appear completely incredible to the reader of today.

Women were mistreated almost as badly. Work in a factory was long, arduous, and monotonous. Discipline was harsh. Many times the price of factory employment was submission to the sexual advances of employers and foremen (ibid., p. 416). Women in the mines toiled from 14 to 16 hours a day, stripped naked to the waist, working with men and doing the work of men. There were reports of women who came out of the mines to bear children and were back in the mines within days after the birth. Many accounts have been written of the fantastically cruel and dehumanizing working conditions for women during this period. Of course, workingmen were not much better off than the women or their children. Industrialization was stern, harsh, and cruel in the extreme for men as well as for women and children.

Another important consideration in assessing the living standard of the working class during the period of capitalist industrialization was the rapid urbanization that took place at that time. In 1750, only two cities in Britain had populations over 50,000. In 1850, there were 29. By the latter date nearly one person in three lived in a city with more than 50,000 inhabitants. Conditions in the cities of this period were terrible:

And what cities! It was not merely that smoke hung over them and filth impregnated them, that the elementary public services—water-supply, sanitation, street-cleaning, open spaces, etc.—could not keep pace with the mass migration of men into the cities, thus producing, especially after 1830, epidemics of cholera, typhoid and an appalling constant toll of the two great groups of nineteenth-century urban killers—air pollution and water pollution, or respiratory and intestinal disease. . . . The new city populations . . . [were] pressed into overcrowded and bleak slums, whose very sight froze the heart of the observer. "Civilization works its miracles" wrote the great French liberal de

Tocqueville of Manchester, "and civilized man is turned back almost into a savage." (Hobsbawm, pp. 67–68)

Included in these slums was a district of Glasgow that, according to a report of a government commissioner, housed

> a fluctuating population of between 15,000 and 30,000 persons. This district is composed of many narrow streets and square courts and in the middle of each court there is a dunghill. Although the outward appearance of these places was revolting, I was nevertheless quite unprepared for the filth and misery that were to be found inside. In some bedrooms we visited at night, we found a whole mass of humanity stretched on the floor. There were often 15 to 20 men and women huddled together, some being clothed and others naked. There was hardly any furniture there and the only thing which gave these holes the appearance of a dwelling was fire burning on the hearth. Thieving and prostitution are the main sources of income of these people. (Engels, p. 46)

The total destruction of the laborers' traditional way of life and the harsh discipline of the new factory system, combined with deplorable living conditions in the cities, generated social, economic, and political unrest. Chain reactions of social upheaval, riots, and rebellion occurred in the years 1811–1813, 1815–1817, 1819, 1826, 1829–1835, 1838–1842, 1843–1844, and 1846–1848. In many areas these were purely spontaneous and primarily economic in character. In 1816 one rioter from the Fens exclaimed: "Here I am between Earth and Sky, so help me God. I would sooner lose my life than go home as I am. Bread I want and bread I will have" (Hobsbawm, p. 74). In 1845 an American named Colman reported that the working people of Manchester were "wretched, defrauded, oppressed, crushed human nature lying in bleeding fragments all over the face of society" (ibid., p. 75).

There can be no doubt that industrial capitalism was erected on the base of the wretched suffering of a laboring class denied access to the fruits of the rapidly expanding economy and subjected to the most degrading of excesses in order to increase the capitalists' profits. The basic cause of the great evils of this period was "the absolute and uncontrolled power of the capitalist. In this, the heroic age of great undertakings, it was acknowledged, admitted and even proclaimed with brutal candor. It was the employer's own business, he did as he chose and did not consider that any other justification of his conduct was necessary. He owed his employees wages and once those were paid the men had no further claim on him." (Mantoux, p. 417)

LIBERAL SOCIAL LEGISLATION

From the time that factory production was first introduced into the textile industries, workers tried to band together to protect their interests collectively. In 1787, during a period of high unemployment, the Glasgow muslin manufacturers attempted to lower the piece rates they were paying. The workers resisted collectively, refusing to work below a certain minimum rate. The struggle led to open rioting and shooting, but the workers proved to have a strong and well-disciplined group, and they built a strong union. In 1792, a union of weavers forced a collective agreement upon Bolton and Bury Manufacturers.

Labor organizations spread rapidly in the 1790s. As a result of this and the concurrent growth of social and economic discontent, the upper classes became very uneasy. The memory of the French Revolution was fresh in their minds, and they feared the power of the united workers. The result was the Combination Act of 1799, which outlawed any combination of workers whose purpose was to obtain higher wages, shorter hours, or the introduction of any regulation constraining the free action of their employers. Proponents couched their arguments in terms of the necessity of free competition and the evils of monopoly—cardinal tenets of classical liberalism—but did not mention combinations of employers or monopolistic practices of capitalists. The effects of this legislation have been summarized as follows:

> The Combination Laws were considered as absolutely necessary to prevent ruinous extortions of workmen, which, if not thus restrained, would destroy the whole of the trade, manufactures, commerce and agriculture of the nation. . . . So thoroughly was this false notion entertained, that whenever men were prosecuted to conviction for having combined to regulate their wages or the hours of working, however heavy the sentence passed upon them was, and however rigorously it was inflicted, not the slightest feeling of compassion was manifested by anybody for the unfortunate sufferers. Justice was entirely out of the question: They could seldom obtain a hearing before a magistrate, never without impatience or insult. . . . An accurate account . . . of proceedings, or hearings before magistrates, trials at sessions and in the Court of King's Bench, the gross injustice, the foul invective, and terrible punishments inflicted would not, after a few years have passed away, be credited to any but the best evidence. (Ibid., p. 449)

Another cause for which the classical liberals campaigned vigorously was the abolition of the Speenhamland system of poor relief that had come into existence in 1795. This system was (continuing in the tradition of the Elizabethan Statute of Artificers) the result of the Christian paternalist ethic. It held that unfortunates would be entitled to a certain minimum living standard whether employed or not. To be sure, the system had serious drawbacks: It actually depressed wages below the relief level in many cases (with the parish taxes making up the difference) and severely limited labor mobility at a time when greater mobility was needed.

The important issue, however, is not the deficiencies of the Speenhamland system but rather the type of legislation the liberals enacted in its place when they succeeded in abolishing it in 1834. The view of the classical liberals was that workers should accept any job the market offered, regardless of the conditions or pay involved. Any person who would not or could not do so should be given just enough to prevent physical starvation. His dole should be substantially lower than the lowest wage offered in the market, and his general situation should stigmatize him sufficiently to motivate him to seek gainful employment. Thus the new law

> was an engine of degradation and oppression more than a means of material relief. There have been few more inhuman statutes than the Poor Law Act of 1834, which made all relief "less eligible" than the lowest wage outside, confined it to the jail-like workhouse, forcibly separated husbands, wives and children in order to punish the poor for their destitution, and discourage them from the dangerous temptation of procreating further paupers. (Hobsbawm, pp. 69–70)

SOCIALISM WITHIN THE CLASSICAL LIBERAL TRADITION

Socialism had it origins in England in the late eighteenth and early nineteenth century. It was a protest against the inequality of capitalism and the social evils resulting from this inequality. This inequality, in the opinion of all socialists from the earliest times to the present, resulted inevitably from the institution of private property in the means of production. Hence socialism's most cardinal tenet is that social justice requires the abolition of private ownership of capital. Socialists have never accepted unanimously any particular social philosophy or body of doctrines. On nearly any given issue one can find differences of opinion among socialists. The essential and defining feature of socialism, and the one idea that all socialists accept, is that private ownership of capital necessarily involves inequality and a host of other evils and that such ownership must be abolished if we are ever to achieve a just society.

Although there are today many schools of socialism, if we go back to the early 1800s we find that socialists can be divided into two groups, each having a distinctly different general social philosophy. The two traditions can be labeled *classical liberal individualistic socialism* and *cooperative socialism*. As we saw in Chapter 4, as well as the preceding section of this chapter, classical liberalism most generally functioned as an ideology justifying the new capitalist order and its many economically oppressive laws. In order for classical liberalism to function in this manner, however, people had to accept without question the institution of private ownership of capital.

There were many classical liberals who did not accept the institution. Particularly influential among these liberals was Thomas Hodgskin (1787–1869), who for most of his life received a naval disability pension that enabled him to devote most of his time to writing. In 1825 Hodgskin wrote a book entitled *Labour Defended Against the Claims of Capital,* in which he attempted to refute the principal intellectual justification for the private ownership of capital—the argument that capital is productive.

Hodgskin's refutation of the notion that capital was productive showed that the production usually attributed to capital was actually the production of interdependent workers. If we observe, for example, a fisherman catching fish with the aid of a net, then it appears to the conservative defender of capitalism that part of the fish are caught by the labor of the fisherman and part are caught by aid of the net. Therefore, it appears that the net is productive and that the capitalist owner of the net *deserves* a profit due to the productivity of his net. The real productivity, said Hodgskin, is that of interdependent workers. The fisherman was able to catch so many fish because other *workers* are making nets. The fish are caught through the joint labors of *both* the fisherman *and* the net makers. But since at the point at which the catch takes place the net-making laborers are not present then it may appear that their share of the productive endeavor of fishing is actually performed by the product they have created—the net. Thus, while in capitalism it may appear that a worker (e.g., a fisherman) depends on the productivity of capital (e.g., the net) and hence depends on the capitalists (e.g., the capitalist owner of the net), this appearance is false. The worker depends solely on the co-existing labor being performed by other workers. Hodgskin concluded that the productive

> effects usually attributed to a stock of commodities are caused by co-existing labour, and that it is by the command the capitalist possesses over the *labour of some men*, not by possessing a stock of commodities, that he is enabled to *support* and consequently employ other labourers. (Hodgskin, pp. 51–52)

Hodgskin argued that labor is interdependent in all societies. But only in capitalist economies does private ownership of the means of production transform this universal interdependence into "capital." Then, the strange theory that things "produce" obscures the true essence of what capital really is. "Capital is a sort of cabalistic word, like Church or State, or any other of those general terms which are invented by those who fleece the rest of mankind to conceal the hand that shears them" (ibid., p. 60).

With the exception of rejecting private ownership of capital by capitalists who do not produce, Hodgskin accepted all of the tenets of classical liberalism. It is not surprising, therefore, that his intellectual defense of economic greed and the unrestrained operation of the free market was nearly identical to that of the classical liberals. He was the first advocate of what today we call free market socialism. He took Adam Smith's notion of the invisible hand a giant step beyond the conservative classical liberals.

Hodgskin's arguments that capital is not productive and that private ownership of capital is the source of the worst inequities of capitalism remains the basis for the advocacy of market socialism to this day. Most market socialists, like Hodgskin, accept the tenets of classical liberalism and believe that a competitive market will indeed function like a benevolent invisible hand *if and only if* social ownership of the means of production is substituted for private ownership of these means.

WILLIAM THOMPSON AND THE REJECTION OF CLASSICAL LIBERALISM

Most socialists, however, have rejected many of the individualistic tenets of classical liberalism as well as the notion that the market should allocate resources in a socialist society. Perhaps the most influential of the early socialists in this regard was William Thompson. Writing in the 1820s, he agreed with Hodgskin that if one had to live in a competitive market society, then market socialism was certainly preferable to capitalism. He argued, however, that the individualistic pursuit of wealth within a competitive market, whether that market be in a capitalist or a socialist society, led inevitably to five evils. These evils were "inherent in the *very principle* of competition" (Thompson, p. 258).

The first evil of competitive, market socialism was that every "labourer, artisan and trader [saw] a competitor, a rival in every other." Moreover, each saw "a second competition, a second rivalship between . . . [his or her profession] and the public" (ibid., p. 259). Hence, the "principle of selfishness necessarily . . . [dominated] in all ordinary affairs of life" (ibid., p. 257). For example, under competitive, market socialism, it would be "in the interest of all medical men that diseases should exist and prevail, or their trade would be decreased ten, or one hundred, fold" (ibid., p. 259).

The second evil inherent in the individualistic pursuit of wealth even in a market socialist economy was the systematic oppression of women. This oppression was an evil in itself, and it also led to enormous economic waste. The individualistic pursuit of wealth, Thompson believed, was compatible only with individual nuclear families. Within an individual family "all the little items of domestic drudgery" must be "done at stated hours." Women could be relieved of this drudgery if "numbers of families adjoining each other . . . [formed] a common fund for preparing their food and educating their children" (ibid., p. 260).

The third evil of market competition—whether capitalistic or socialistic—was the economic instability caused by the anarchy of the market. Although socialism would eliminate the capriciousness of the luxurious tastes of the capitalists as a source of crises and depressions, as long as the competitive market allocated resources, economic instability, unemployment, waste, and social suffering would result (ibid., pp. 261–263).

The fourth evil of competitive, market socialism was that it would not eliminate many of the insecurities of capitalism—insecurities that came from reliance on the market. The selfishness and egoism fostered by a competitive market society would create a situation in which there would be "no adequate . . . resource for malformation, sickness, or old age, or for numerous accidents incident to human life" (ibid., p. 263).

The fifth evil of market competition was that it retarded the advance and dissemination of knowledge by making the acquisition of knowledge subsidiary to greed and personal gain. "Concealment, therefore, of what

is new or excellent from competitors, must accompany individual competition . . . because the strongest personal interest is by it opposed to the
principle of benevolence" (ibid., p. 267).

Thus, Thompson concluded that while competitive, market socialism
would be a dramatic improvement over capitalism, the reliance on the
market would still involve numerous social evils. The best form of society,
he argued, would be a planned cooperative socialist society. Such a society
would consist of mutually coordinated, self-governing, cooperative communities, each having from 500 to 2000 members.

In such communities, people could freely obtain the necessities of life
from a common store. Children would be cared for communally and sleep
in common dormitories, while adults would live in small apartments. There
would be common kitchen facilities for everyone. There would be no sexual
division of labor—cooking, child rearing, and other forms of women's
drudgery would be shared by everyone on a rotational basis. All persons
would become skilled in a variety of occupations and would regularly al-
ternate employments in order to eliminate the monotony of work. Every
adult member of each community would participate regularly in the necessary coordinating or governing bodies. The finest education would be
freely available to everyone. Absolute political, intellectual, and religious
freedom would be guaranteed. Finally, all wealth would be communally
controlled and shared so that no invidious distinctions could result from
the distribution of material wealth. (ibid., pp. 269–367) Thompson's view
of a cooperative, socialist community reflected, in general, the views of
most of the people in the Owenite movement of his era (discussed in the
next section). Throughout the history of that movement, he was its most
influential spokesman after Robert Owen. Thompson's description of a
planned, cooperative, socialist society was one of the earliest and the most
fully elaborated in the history of socialist ideas.

THE PATERNALISTIC SOCIALISM OF ROBERT OWEN

The most important of the early organizers of a socialist movement to
transform capitalism was Robert Owen. Born in 1771, Owen served as a
draper's apprentice from the age of 10. At 20 he was the manager of a
large mill. Wise business decisions and good luck soon resulted in the
acquisition of a considerable fortune. Owen was a perfect example of a
benevolent autocrat. His factory at New Lanark became known throughout
all England because he insisted on decent working conditions, livable wages,
and education for working-class children. His workers received "affec-
tionate tutelage" from him, and he thought of himself as their trustee and
steward.

The paternalistic attitude did not interfere with Owen's very strict
organizational discipline in his factory. Owen described one of his methods
of maintaining discipline:

that which I found to be the most efficient check upon inferior conduct was the contrivance of a silent monitor for each one employed in the establishment. This consisted of a four-sided piece of wood, about two inches long and one broad, each side colored—one side black, another blue, the third yellow, and the fourth white, tapered at the top, and finished with wire eyes, to hang upon a hook with either side to show front. One of these was suspended in a conspicuous place near to each of the persons employed, and the color at the front told the conduct of the individual during the preceding day, to four degrees of comparison. Bad, denoted by black and No. 4; indifferent by blue, and No. 3; good by yellow, and No. 2; and excellent by white, and No. 1. Then books of character were provided, for each department, in which the name of each one employed in it was inserted in the front of succeeding columns, which sufficed to mark by the number of daily conduct, day by day, for two months; and these books were changed six times a year, and were preserved; by which arrangement I had the conduct of each registered to four degrees of comparison during every day of the week, Sundays excepted, for every year they remained in my employment. (Beer, p. 111)

So in his life and deeds, Owen, like other capitalists of his era, strove to maximize his profits. He believed his competitors' harsh treatment of their workers was stupid and shortsighted, and he based his life on the assumption that the Christian paternalist ethic was compatible with the capitalistic system, at least at the factory level. In his own words, "My time, from early to late, and my mind, were continually occupied in devising measures and directing their execution, to improve the condition of the people, and to advance at the same time the works and the machinery as a manufacturing establishment" (ibid., p. 112).

Although Owen's life and actions did not differentiate him from many of the conservative Tory radicals of his time, some of his ideas did. He did not believe that any society in which one class was elevated to a position of power and used this power to exploit the lower classes could ultimately become a truly good society. Private ownership of the means of production (factories, machinery, tools) was the social institution by which one small class in the existing economic system gained immense power over the mass of farmers and workers. The profit motive was the force that drove this small class to use its power to exploit the workers and farmers in order to gain profits.

Owen believed that in an ideal society the people could most effectively control nature because they would reap the greatest collective benefit if they cooperated. This cooperation should take the form of self-governing industrial and agricultural communities. In such communities, private ownership of the means of production would be abolished and the selfish quest for profits eliminated. He maintained that only when such a society was established would it be true that

one portion of mankind will not, as now, be trained and placed to oppress, by force or fraud, another portion, to the great disadvantage of both; neither will one portion be trained in idleness, to live in luxury on the industry of those whom they oppress, while the latter are made to labor daily and to live in poverty. Nor yet will some be trained to force falsehood into the human mind and be paid extravagantly for so doing while other parties are prevented from teaching the truth, or severely punished if they make the attempt. (Owen, pp. 47–48)

There was something in these writings that differed very radically from his description of the way in which he ran his own factory at New Lanark. In the ideal society, for Owen, the paternalism of the traditional Christian ethic would be expressed as a brotherhood of equals, a considerable shift from the parent-child type of subordination expressed in the medieval and Tory radical versions of the Christian paternalist ethic.

The feudal version of that ethic had accepted a hierarchical society. In this version those at the top lived lavishly (by the standard of the day, at least), and they did so by exploiting those at the bottom. Chaucer's parson's description of the medieval view is apt: "God has ordained that some folk should be more high in estate and degree and some folk more low, and that everyone should be served in his estate and his degree" (Hammond and Hammond, p. 215). This traditional feudal ethic seemed to most capitalists to be incompatible with the capitalist order, and it was gradually replaced by the new individualist philosophy of classical liberalism.

Classical liberalism, however, was a two-edged sword. Although this ideology was used to justify the new capitalist order (see Chapter 1), its individualistic assumptions were very radical. If the old feudal aristocracy had no inherent superiority over the middle class and if any member of the middle class was to be freed of the old restraints, and if individuals should be the best judge of their own affairs, then how could one stop short of asserting the same rights and advantages for the lowest classes? The ideal that each individual ought, in some abstract way, to be considered as important as any other individual was radical indeed.

If individualism seemed to imply equality in theory, it certainly did not lead to it in practice. The rugged battle for more profits led not only to the social misery described earlier but also to a new class division of society that was sharply defined and as exploitative in nature as the medieval class structure. Membership in the higher class of the new system depended not on genealogy but on ownership. Capitalists derived their income and their power from ownership of the means of production.

Socialism, then, was a protest against the inequality of capitalism and the social evils resulting from that inequality. The inequality itself, in the opinion of socialists from the earliest times to the present, resulted inevitably from the institution of private property in the means of production. Hence, socialism asserted as its most cardinal tenet the idea that social justice demanded the abolition of private ownership of capital.

Intellectually, socialism was a wedding of the liberal notion of the equality of all human beings to the notion inherent in the traditional Christian paternalist ethic that every man should be his brother's keeper. Incorporating the egalitarian elements of classical liberalism into the traditional Christian ethic made this a utopian ethic, in comparison with which existing society was criticized. Without this egalitarian element the Christian ethic served well as an ideological justification of the hierarchical class system of the Middle Ages and was sometimes used to defend the capitalist system, particularly in the late nineteenth and twentieth centuries.

OTHER IMPORTANT PRE-MARXIST SOCIALISTS

When Owen asserted that in the ideal society private property and acquisitive profit seeking would be eliminated, he became part of a socialist tradition that was already firmly established. One of the first voices of socialist protest against capitalist property relations was that of Gerrard Winstanley (1609–1652), a cloth merchant who had been bankrupted in the depression of 1643. He blamed his own misfortune as well as that of others on the "cheating art of buying and selling" (quoted in McDonald, p. 63). In 1649 he led a strange band of followers from London to Saint George's Hill, Surrey. There they occupied unused crown lands, which they cultivated in common and, in general, shared in a communal existence.

In the same year Winstanley published *The True Levellers Standard Advanced*, in which he rebuked "the powers of England" and "the powers of the world" for their failure to realize that "the great creator . . . made the Earth a common treasury for beasts and man." He asserted that all who derived their incomes in part or in full from property ownership were violating God's commandment "Thou shalt not steal." "You pharaohs, you have rich clothing and full bellies, you have your honors and your ease; but know the day of judgment is begun and that it will reach you ere long. The poor people you oppress shall be the saviours of the land" (ibid., p. 63).

Babeuf

Throughout the eighteenth and nineteenth centuries, a large number of writers argued that private property was the source of the inequities and exploitation that existed in the capitalist economy. In this chapter we can mention only a few of the better known among them. One of the most interesting was the Frenchman Gracchus Babeuf (1760–1797). Babeuf argued that nature had made all persons equal in rights and needs. Therefore the inequalities of wealth and power that had developed should be redressed by society. Unfortunately, most societies did the opposite: They set up a coercive mechanism to protect the interests of the property holders and the wealthy. For Babeuf the presence of inequality meant, of necessity, the presence of injustice. Capitalist commerce existed, he said, "for the purpose of pumping the sweat and blood of more or less everybody, in order to form lakes of gold for the benefit of the few" (Gray, p. 105). The workers who created the wealth of society received the least in return; and unless private property were eliminated the inequalities in society could never be redressed.

Babeuf led the extreme left wing of the French revolutionary movement. After the fall of Robespierre he masterminded a conspiracy to destroy the French government and replace it with one dedicated to equality and brotherhood. The plot was betrayed and its leaders were arrested. Babeuf and his lieutenant, Darthe, were executed on February 24, 1797.

Babeuf is important in the socialist tradition because he was the first to advance the notion that if an egalitarian socialist state is to be achieved, the existing government must be toppled by force. The issue of whether socialism can be achieved peacefully has divided socialists since Babeuf's time. Babeuf also believed that if his revolt were successful, a period of dictatorship would be necessary during the transition from capitalism to a communist democracy to extirpate the surviving remnants of the capitalist system. Thus in several important ways Babeuf was a precursor of the twentieth-century Russian Bolsheviks.

Godwin

Other important ideas in the socialist critique of capitalism can be seen in the writings of the Englishman William Godwin (1756–1836). While the classical liberals were bemoaning the natural laziness and depravity of the lower classes, Godwin argued that the defects of the working class were attributable to corrupt and unjust social institutions. The capitalist society, in Godwin's opinion, made fraud and robbery inevitable: "If every man could with perfect facility obtain the necessities of life . . . temptation would lose its power" (quoted in ibid., p. 119). Men could not always obtain the necessities because the laws of private property created such great inequality in society. Justice demanded that capitalist property relations be abolished and that property belonged to that person whom it would benefit most:

> To whom does any article of property, suppose a loaf of bread, justly belong? To him who most wants it, or to whom the possession of it will be most beneficial. Here are six men famished with hunger, and the loaf is, absolutely considered, capable of satisfying the cravings of them all. Who is it that has a reasonable claim to benefit by the qualities with which the loaf is endowed? They are all brothers perhaps, and the law of primogeniture bestows it exclusively to the eldest. But does justice confirm this reward? The laws of different countries dispose of property in a thousand different ways; but there can be but one way which is most conformable to reason. (Quoted in ibid., p. 131)

That one way, of course, must be based on equality of all human beings. To whom could the poor turn to correct the injustices of the system? In Godwin's opinion it most certainly would not be the government. With economic power went political power. The rich were "directly or indirectly the legislators of the state; and of consequence are perpetually reducing oppression into a system." The law, then, is the means by which the rich oppress the poor, for "legislation is in almost every country grossly the favorer of the rich against the poor."

These two ideas of Godwin's were to be voiced again and again by nineteenth-century socialists: (1) Capitalist social and economic institutions, particularly private property relations, were the causes of the evils and suffering within the system; and (2) government in a capitalist system would never redress these evils because it was controlled by the capitalist class. Godwin, however, had an answer to this seemingly impossible situation. He believed human reason would save society. Once people become educated about the evils of the situation, they would reason together and arrive at the only rational solution. As Godwin saw it, this solution entailed the abolition of government, the abolition of laws, and the abolition of private property. For this radical social transformation Godwin believed socialists could rely primarily on education and reason. Most subsequent socialists argued that education and reason alone were insufficient. Education, they believed, should be only a part of the larger objective of creating a mass socialist movement. The importance of education and intellectual persuasion in attaining socialist ends has remained a much-debated issue to this day.

Saint-Simon

Other important socialist ideas were advanced by Henri de Saint-Simon (1760–1825), who was actually closer to the Tory radicals than the socialists in many ways. He came from an impoverished family of nobility, and his writings show an aristocrat's disdain for the antisocial egoism of the rich capitalists.

He also condemned the idle rich who lived off the labor of the poor but contributed nothing to society's well-being:

> Suppose that France preserves all the men of genius that she possesses in the sciences, fine arts and professions, but has the misfortune to lose in the same day Monsieur the King's brother [and all of the other members of the royal household] . . . Suppose that France loses at the same time all of the great officers of the royal household, all the ministers . . . all the councillors of state, all the chief magistrates, marshals, cardinals, archbishops, bishops, vicars-general and cannons, all the prefects and subprefects, all the civil servants, and judges, and, in addition, ten thousand of the richest proprietors who live in the style of nobles. This mischance would certainly distress the French, because they are kind-hearted, and could not see with indifference the sudden disappearance of such a large number of their compatriots. But this loss of thirty thousand individuals . . . would result in no political evil for the state. (Markham, ed., pp. 72–73)

Saint-Simon was the first to emphasize the efficiency of huge industrial undertakings and argued that the government should actively intervene in production, distribution, and commerce in the interest of promoting the welfare of the masses. He sanctioned both private property and its privileges as long as they were used to promote the welfare of the masses.

Many of his followers were more radical. They wrote endless pamphlets and books exposing abuses of capitalism, attacking private property and inheritance, denouncing exploitation, and advocating government ownership and control of economic production in the interest of the general welfare. It was from Saint-Simon and his followers that socialism inherited the idea of the necessity of government administration of production and distribution in a socialist economy.

Fourier

There were many other important socialists in the first half of the nineteenth century. The Frenchman Charles Fourier popularized the idea of cooperatives (or *phalanxes*, as he called them). He attempted to change society by encouraging the formation of phalanxes. His failure proved to many socialists that capitalism could not be reformed by the mere setting of examples. He was also one of the first socialists to predict that competition among capitalists would lead inevitably to monopoly:

> Among the influences tending to restrict man's industrial rights, I will mention a formation of privileged corporations which, monopolizing a given branch of industry, arbitrarily close the doors of labour against whomsoever they please. . . . Extremes meet, and the greater the extent to which anarchical competition is carried, the nearer the approach to *universal monopoly*, which is the opposite excess . . . Monopolies . . . operating in conjunction with the great landed interest, will reduce the middle and labouring classes to a state of commercial vassalage . . . The small operators will be reduced to the position of mere agents, working for the mercantile coalition. (Quoted in Coontz, p. 54)

Fourier believed that in a capitalist economy only one-third of the people really did socially useful work. The other two-thirds were directed by the corruption and distortion caused by the market system into useless occupations or were useless, wealthy parasites. He divided these wastes into four categories:

> First Waste: Useless or destructive labour. (1) the army (2) the idle rich (3) ne'er-do-wells (4) sharpers (5) prostitutes (6) magistrates (7) police (8) lawyers (9) philosophical cranks (10) bureaucrats (11) spies (12) priests and clergymen.
>
> Second Waste: Misdirected work, since society makes it repellent, and not a vehicle of man's personality, attractive to him. (a) Deflection of the passions into greed and morbidity, instead of being utilized as society's motors. (b) Scale of production too small to utilize labour properly. (c) No co-operation. (d) No control of production. (e) No adjustment of supply to demand, except by the mechanism of the "blind" market. (f) The family: this economic and educational unit is absurdly small.
>
> Third Waste: Commerce dominated by middlemen. It takes a hundred

men to do what society, with warehouses, distributed according to need, could do with one. A hundred men sit at counters, wasting hours waiting for someone to enter, a hundred people write inventories, etc., competitively. These hundred wasted merchants eat without producing.

Fourth Waste: Wage labour in indirect servitude; cost of class antagonisms. Since class interests are opposed, the costs of keeping men divided are greater than the gains in making them co-operate. (Quoted in ibid., p. 55)

Most socialists agreed that capitalism was irrational and wasteful and led to extreme inequalities, and hence was unjust and immoral. They disagreed, however, on the tactics they should use to achieve socialism. Many famous socialists, such as Louis Blanc (1811–1882), believed that the government could be used as an instrument of reform and that socialism could be achieved through gradual, peaceful, piecemeal reform. Others, such as Auguste Blanchqui (1805–1881), a pupil of Babeuf, based his ideas on the assumption that capitalism involved a constant class war between capitalists and workers. He believed that as long as capitalists occupied the position of power that ownership of capital gave them, they would exploit the workers, and the government and laws would be weapons used in this exploitation. He therefore saw no hope of achieving socialism through gradual political reform. Revolution was, for him, the only answer.

Proudhon

Pierre Joseph Proudhon (1809–1865), in his well-known book *What Is Property?*, answered the question posed in the title with a slogan that made him famous: "Property is theft." He believed property was "the mother of tyranny." The primary purpose of the state was the enforcement of property rights. Because property rights were simply sets of special privileges for the few and general restrictions and prohibitions for the masses, they involved coercion, of necessity, in their establishment and continued enforcement. Hence the primary function of the state was to coerce.

"Every state is a tyranny," declared Proudhon. The state was the coercive arm of the ruling class, and Proudhon advocated resistance rather than servitude: "Whoever lays a hand on me to govern me is a usurper and a tyrant. I declare him to be my enemy." There could be no justice until property relations were abolished and the state was made unnecessary:

To be governed is to be watched over, inspected, spied on, directed, legislated, regimented, closed in, indoctrinated, preached at, controlled, assessed, evaluated, censored, commanded; all by creatures that have neither the right, nor wisdom, nor virtue . . . To be governed means that at every move, operation, or transaction one is noted, registered, entered in a census, taxed, stamped, priced, assessed, patented, licensed, authorized, recommended, admonished, prevented, reformed, set right, corrected. Government means to be subjected to tribute, trained, ransomed, exploited, monopolized, extorted, pressured, mystified, robbed; all in the name of public utility and the general good. Then, at the first sign of resistance or word of complaint, one is repressed, fined, despised, vexed, pursued, hustled, beaten up, garroted, imprisoned, shot, machine-gunned, judged, sentenced, deported, sacrificed, sold, betrayed, and to cap it all ridiculed, mocked, outraged, and dishonored. That is government, that is its justice and its morality! . . . O human personality! How can it be that you have cowered in such subjection for sixty centuries? (Quoted in Guerin, pp. 15–16)

Property rights were not only the source of tyranny and coercion, but also the source of economic inequality. Whereas the amount of labor expended determined how much was produced in a capitalist society, ownership of property determined how that produce was divided. It was divided in such a way that those who produced received almost nothing of what they produced, whereas those who owned property used the laws of private ownership to "legally steal" from the workers. Proudhon's ideal state rejected not only capitalist property relations but industrialization as well. Like Thomas Jefferson, Proudhon envisioned a golden age of small-scale agriculture and handicraft production, in which each farmer and worker owned his or her own capital and no one lived through property ownership alone. The list could be continued, but we have included most of the important pre-Marxist socialist ideas and have introduced some of the most famous socialist thinkers. Unquestionably the most influential socialist thinker was Karl Marx, and it is to a summary of his ideas that we turn in Chapter 6.

SUMMARY

The workers bore the cost of industrialization. The new factory system reduced most of them to poor, unhealthy, dehumanized wretches. Classical liberalism was generally not only impervious to their plight but even taught that the desire to improve the conditions of the poor was quixotic and doomed to failure.

There were, however, a few exceptions among the classical liberals, the most outstanding of whom was Thomas Hodgskin. Hodgskin argued that capital was unproductive and the profits represented an unfair, coercive extraction of a parasitic elite from the produce of the producers, the working people. He believed that the invisible hand of the competitive market system could function effectively only in a market socialist economy.

William Thompson argued that market competition—even under its very best form, market socialism—contained several inherent evils that could be eliminated only in a planned, cooperative, socialist economy. Robert Owen was a wealthy capitalist who espoused and helped build a movement for cooperative socialism. The ideas of several other socialists were briefly discussed in this chapter. All of them protested the inequities of capitalism. They believed that by eliminating the capitalists' method of robbing workers—private ownership of capital—they could create an industrial society in which every man and woman was treated with dignity and in which the fruits of production were reasonably and equitably divided.

REFERENCES

Beer, M., ed., *Life of Robert Owen*. New York: Knopf, 1920.

Coontz, Sydney H. *Productive Labor and Effective Demand*. New York: Augustus M. Kelley, 1966.

Engels, Friedrich. *The Condition of the Working Class in England in 1844*. New York: Macmillan, 1958.

Gray, Alexander. *The Socialist Tradition*. London: Longmans, 1963.

Guerin, Daniel. *Anarchism*. New York: Monthly Review Press, 1970.

Hammond, J. L., and Barbara Hammond. *The Rise of Modern Industry*. New York: Harper & Row, Torchbooks, 1969.

Hobsbawm, E. J. *Industry and Empire: An Economic History of Britain Since 1750*. London: Weidenfeld & Nicolson, 1968.

Hodgskin, Thomas. *Labour Defended Against the Claims of Capital*. London: Labour Publishing, 1922.

McDonald, Lee Cameron. *Western Political Theory: The Modern Age*. New York: Harcourt Brace Jovanovich, 1962.

Mantoux, Paul. *The Industrial Revolution in the Eighteenth Century*. New York: Harcourt Brace Jovanovich, 1927.

Markham, F. M. H., ed. *Henri Comte de Saint-Simon, Selected Writings*. Oxford: Blackwell, 1952.

Owen, Robert. "The Book of the New Moral World." Reprinted in part in *Communism, Fascism, and Democracy*. Edited by Carl Cohen. New York: Random House, 1962.

Thompson, William. *An Inquiry into the Principles of the Distribution of Wealth Most Conducive to Human Happiness*. London: Wm. S. Orr & Co., 1850. First published in 1824.

Chapter
6

Marx's Conception of Capitalism

Karl Marx (1818–1883) has been the most influential of all socialists. His writings have had, and continue to have, a profound impact not only on socialist thought but also on policy decisions that affect a large percentage of the world's population. Although he worked in close collaboration with Friedrich Engels (1820–1895) and was unquestionably deeply influenced by Engels, Marx was the intellectual leader in most matters of political economy, so no attempt is made in this chapter to distinguish Engels's separate contributions.

HISTORICAL MATERIALISM

Marx believed that most of the late eighteenth- and early nineteenth-century socialists were humanitarians who were rightly indignant about the harsh exploitation that accompanied early capitalism. Despite his admiration for many of them, he gave to them the derisive label "utopian socialists." He believed most of them to be quixotic utopians who hoped to transform society by appealing to the rationality and moral sensibilities of the educated class. In Marx's view, educated men were usually members of the upper classes, and thus they owed their position, prosperity, and superior knowledge and education to the privileges inherent in the capitalist system. Therefore they would generally do everything within their power to preserve that system. The few heretics and humanitarians among them would certainly never constitute the power base from which a transition from capitalism to socialism could be effected. Yet Marx had an undying faith that such a social and economic transition would occur. This faith was not the result of his belief in the rationality and humanity of men but rather was based on an analysis of capitalism. He concluded that internal contradictions and antagonisms within the capitalist system would eventually destroy it.

Marx based his study of capitalist society on a historical approach that has been called *historical materialism.* When he looked at the mass of ideas, laws, religious beliefs, mores, moral codes, and economic and social institutions that were present in all social systems, he tried to simplify the complex cause-and-effect relationships among these many facets of social systems. Such a simplification, he believed, would enable him to focus his attention on the relationships that were most fundamental in determining a social system's overall direction of movement and change.

He believed that although all social institutions and intellectual traditions were reciprocally related in a complex web of cause-and-effect relationships (each affecting and, in turn, affected by the others), a society's economic base, or mode of production, exerted the most powerful influence in determining the other social institutions as well as social and religious thought. The mode of production consisted of two elements: (1) the forces of production and (2) the relations of production. The forces of production included tools, factories, equipment, production skills, the level of knowledge of the labor force, natural resources, and the general level of technology. The relations of production were the social relationships among humans, particularly the relationship of each class of humans to the means of production. These relations included the ownership of productive facilities and the division of the fruits of productive activity. The whole economic system, or mode of production, was referred to by Marx as the base, or substructure of society. The religions, ethics, laws, mores, and political institutions of society he called the superstructure.

Although the mode of production and the superstructure interacted reciprocally as both cause and effect, the mode of production was the base on which the superstructure was built. Therefore, the line of causation running from this economic base to the superstructure was much more powerful and important than the reverse line of causation. To argue that Marx believed the economic base determined, completely and rigidly, every aspect of the superstructure is grossly inaccurate (although it is often done). He did assert, however, that the mode of production was the most important single aspect in determining not only the present social superstructure but also the direction of social change.

When he referred to the relations of production, Marx meant the class structure of society, the most important single aspect of the mode of production. The antagonisms between social classes were, for Marx, the propelling force in history. "The history of all hitherto existing society is the history of class struggles," he proclaimed (Marx and Engels, p. 13). The importance of the mode of production and the class antagonisms it engendered have been summarized by Marx in a famous passage:

In the social production which men carry on they enter into definite relations that are indispensable and independent of their will; these relations of production correspond to a definite stage of development of their material powers of production. The sum total of these relations of production constitutes the economic structure of society—the real foundation, on which rise legal and political superstructures and to which correspond definite forms of social consciousness. The mode of production in material life determines the general character of the social, political, and spiritual process of life. It is not the consciousness of men that determines their existence, but, on the contrary, their social existence determines their consciousness.

At a certain stage of their development, the material forces of production in society come into conflict with the existing relations of production, or— what is but a legal expression for the same thing—with the property relations within which they had been at work before. From forms of development of the forces of production the relations turn into their fetters. Then comes the period of social revolution. With the change of economic foundation the entire immense superstructure is more or less rapidly transformed. In considering such transformation a distinction should always be made between the material transformation of the economic conditions of production which can be determined with the precision of natural science and the legal, political, religious, aesthetic, or philosophic—in short ideological forms in which men become conscious of this conflict and fight it out. (Marx, 1970, pp. 20–21)

Marx identified four separate economic systems, or modes of produc tion, through which the European civilization had evolved: (1) primitive communal, (2) slave, (3) feudal, and (4) capitalist. In any one of these economic systems there was a unique mode of production that included forces of production as well as a particular class structure, or relations of production. Increasing demands for more production inevitably led to changes in the forces of production; yet the relationships of production, or class positions, remained fixed and were fiercely defended. Therefore there were conflicts, tensions, and contradictions between the changing forces of production and the fixed social relations (and vested interests) of production. These conflicts and contradictions grew in intensity and importance until a series of violent social eruptions destroyed the old system and created a new system. The new system would have new class relationships compatible (for a time at least) with the changed forces of production.

In each mode of production the contradictions that developed between the forces of production and the relations of production showed themselves in the form of a class struggle. The struggle raged between the class that controlled the means of production and received most of the benefit and privilege of the system (such as the Roman slaveholders) and the much larger class they controlled and exploited (such as the Roman slaves). In all economic systems prior to capitalism, this class struggle had destroyed one system only to create a new system based on exploitation of the masses by a new ruling class, and hence the beginning of a new class struggle. Capitalism, however, was, in Marx's opinion, the last mode of production that would be based on the existence of antagonistic classes. The capitalist class, which ruled by virtue of ownership of the means of production, would be overthrown by the proletariat, or working class, which would establish a classless society in which the means of production were owned in common by all.

Before we can understand Marx's views on the ways in which capitalism tended to create the seeds of socialism, however, we must understand his conception of capitalism. Capitalism is an economic system in which resources are allocated by, and income distribution is determined within, the market. Marx called this a "commodity-producing society." In addition to this, capitalism is characterized by a particular class structure. In the next section we discuss the market, and in the following section the class structure of capitalism.

THE MARKET

The most conspicuous aspect of capitalism is the pervasive or ubiquitous functioning of the market. In any society, human beings are interdependent, each relying upon and requiring innumerable things, services, and activities from many others. In capitalism, nearly all human social and economic interdependencies are mediated by the market. This means that in capitalism, every thing, service, or activity that I need from another I must buy in the market. Similarly, if I perform or act for others, it is only in response to their buying things, services, or activities from me in the market.

When one stops to consider any one of the thousands of things necessary to sustain daily life, one becomes aware of how extensive and complex human social interdependence is. For example, we may begin our day by eating a bowl of cereal. For that cereal we depend upon farm workers who plant and harvest the grain, transportation workers who take it to mills, production workers in mills who transform it into the cereal we eat, transportation workers who transport it to grocery stores, and clerks who sell it to us. But that is only the beginning. The farm workers (as well as all of the other workers in the process) use machinery and tools that must be constantly produced by thousands of other workers. These latter workers, in turn, require materials, partly finished goods, tools, and machinery produced by still other workers.

From this example we see that even the simplest act of consumption or production involves interdependencies among tens or even hundreds of thousands of productive individuals. Thus, above all else, an act of consumption or an act of production is a *social* act. It is social because it requires the cooperation and social coordination of countless productive activities on the part of other people.

This merely reflects the fact that in all societies people must *socially* transform the natural environment in order to make it livable. This social transformation of the environment *is* production. For Marx, three facts about production were true in every society: First, production did, of course, require a natural environment to transform. Human beings could not exist in a vacuum.

Second, nature itself contributed nothing toward its own transformation—it simply was the "stuff" being transformed in production. Only human labor transformed nature. Marx's views contrast sharply with the conservative ideology of capitalism, which claims that nature and tools both contribute to production and that landlords and capitalists are entitled to rewards commensurate with the contributions of nature and tools. For Marx, the fact that we exist in a natural environment that can be transformed in such a way that it fulfills our needs, however, had nothing whatsoever to do with the fact that landlords own the natural environment. Likewise, tools, which certainly must be used in production, were themselves in existence, he insisted, only because working people had produced them, and not because of the peculiarities of ownership. Thus, labor was the *only* human cause or source of production.

Third, any individual laborer or producer was, Marx argued, very nearly helpless alone. Production was a social activity where the production of one laborer depended upon the simultaneous or previous production of many other laborers. These three facts were true in every socioeconomic system, including capitalism.

What distinguished capitalism was that productive activity was not directly or immediately social. An individual producer had no direct social relation to (and generally had no knowledge of) either the workers upon whom his own production depended or those who depended upon his production. He bought what he needed in the market and produced for sale in the market. Therefore, the labor of the workers upon whom he depended confronted him *not* as the activity of particular people but as the market prices of the commodities they had produced. Likewise, the people who depended upon his labor did not know him as an individual. They knew nothing of the peculiar characteristics of him as a person or of his labor. His labor existed for them only as the selling price of the commodity he had produced.

In capitalism, then, labor was not directly social. It became social only when it appeared as the price of a commodity that was exchanged. The prices of commodities and the buying and selling of commodities at these prices constituted the *indirect* social relations of interdependent laborers. Thus, in capitalism the social interdependence of workers appeared, in the form of commodity prices, to be a set of relations among things (commodities) rather than a set of relations among workers. In capitalism, Marx wrote,

> articles of utility become commodities only because they are products of the labour of private individuals or groups of individuals who carry on their work independently of each other. The sum total of the labour of all these private individuals forms the aggregate labour of society. Since the producers do not come into social contact with each other until they exchange their products,

the specific social character of each producer's labour does not show itself except in the act of exchange. In other words, the labour of the individual asserts itself as a part of the labour of society, only by means of the relations which the act of exchange establishes directly between the products, and indirectly, through them, between the producers. To the latter, therefore, the relations connecting the labour of one individual with that of the rest appear, not as direct social relations between individuals at work, but as . . . social relations between things. (Marx, 1961, Vol. 1, pp. 72–73)

The common belief that the exchange of commodities is merely a set of relations among *things*, rather than social relations among *human individuals*, makes a fetish of things, so Marx called this belief the "fetishism of commodities." Marxist economics focuses on the human relations directly involved in market exchange, as well as other social and productive relations that form the necessary economic foundation for the kind of exchange that characterizes capitalism.

The prices of commodities, for Marx, had no inherent relation to the physical characteristics of the commodities. Wheat, for example, had certain physical characteristics when it was produced for the use of the producer and those directly associated with him or her in a precapitalist society with no markets and no prices. Wheat had exactly the same physical characteristics when it was produced, in capitalism, only for sale at some price in the market where its users had no direct social relation with its producers. Since prices had no inherent connection to the physical characteristic or useful qualities of things, prices could only be mental abstractions that were socially attached to things in order to coordinate the interdependence of producers. The social coordination or allocation of productive labor, in capitalism, depended entirely on prices and buying and selling. Therefore, prices were abstractions whereby capitalism rendered private labor into social labor through market exchange. As such, prices represented this social labor. But they appeared to be attributes of commodities rather than attributes of people. These views were the foundation of Marx's labor theory of value, which we discuss in the next chapter.

Whether social labor is allocated to the production of food, shelter, clothing, and other necessities or to yachts, mansions, pornography, hydrogen bombs, and nerve gas depends upon whether sellers of commodities (who are generally capitalists) can find buyers who are able and willing to pay the price that makes production of those various commodities profitable. Marx and his disciples have put considerable stress on the fact that the search for profits, and not inherent human or social needs, allocates and directs labor in capitalism. No matter how useful or beneficial some particular productive activity may be, it will generally not be undertaken if it does not yield profit to a capitalist. Likewise, the most useless, or even socially harmful, activities will be undertaken if they yield a profit for a capitalist.

Already in our discussion of the market, however, we have found it necessary to introduce the other defining feature in Marx's conception of capitalism, the distinction between workers who produce and capitalists who, through their search for profit, direct and control (and hence socially allocate) productive workers.

Marx's first defining feature of capitalism was that the market coordinated and allocated social labor by mediating all productive relationships among workers in such a way that *the social nature of labor appeared as the prices of commodities.* This allocation was effected through the search for profits. To understand Marx's views on the nature and role of profits we must understand his second defining feature of capitalism, its peculiar *class structure.*

THE CLASS STRUCTURE OF CAPITALISM

Marx believed that in every historical setting and within every cultural or national boundary in which capitalism had existed, it had been characterized by the existence of four classes of people: the class of capitalists, the class of small shopkeepers and independent craftsmen or professional people, the class of workers, and a poverty-stricken class that generally owned little or no property and whose members for a variety of reasons could not work. In some settings capitalism had had other classes as well. In the period of early capitalism, for example, by the side of these four classes were peasants and nobility, the remaining vestiges of the two main classes characteristic of feudalism. But the above-mentioned four classes were always characteristic of capitalism, and together they constituted its second defining feature. We shall briefly discuss Marx's view of each of these four classes.

Of the four, the working class and the capitalist class were by far the most important. In most capitalist settings, and always in well-developed capitalist economies, the working class constituted the absolute majority of the population and created or produced nearly all of the commodities. The capitalist class had the bulk of economic and political power in a capitalist society. We therefore discuss these two classes first.

A capitalist class could not exist without a class of wage laborers. Working for wages, or wage labor, characterized the working class in capitalism. Wage labor came into existence in the sixteenth to eighteenth centuries when large numbers of peasants were pushed off the land by landlords who took over the peasant's land and the formerly common lands. Peasants were thus forced to migrate to the cities, where they found a commercial market-oriented economy. The peasants could no longer sell the commodities they produced in order to acquire the commodities necessary to sustain their lives because they had no access to the land or to means of production.

But workers in the city had to buy commodities in order to live, and they could not buy commodities without selling something first so as to acquire money for purchases. Such workers had but one salable thing—a body or capacity to produce. A worker could not sell his or her body once and for all, or we would have had a slave economy and not a capitalist economy. In capitalism, workers recurringly sold control over their capacity to work, or labor power, for definite periods of time only. For example, they "hired out" by the hour, the day, or the week. The wage was the price workers received for selling control of themselves for this period of time. Therefore, the defining characteristic of the working class of capitalism was that it was comprised of wage laborers who had to sell their labor power as a commodity in order to survive.

The class that owned the means of production, of course, was the capitalist class. Exactly the same historical forces that created the wage laborer created the capitalist. The enclosure movements and the other forms of the primitive accumulation of capital that we discussed in Chapter 2 deprived the working class of any access to the means of production while simultaneously putting these means into the hands of the capitalist class. Therefore, the creation of the wage labor class was also necessarily the creation of the capitalist class.

Because of their ownership, capitalists needed to do nothing productive. They were free to do almost anything they chose. A few of them might simply choose to engage in productive endeavors. Yet such endeavor had absolutely nothing to do with their role as capitalists. They could cease such endeavor at will and still remain capitalists. Thus, for example, the Rockefeller family has produced governors, bank presidents, a vice-president of the United States, and so forth. Any one of them was also free at any time, without jeopardizing the family's status as capitalists, to become a functionless playboy.

The capitalist class owned the materials necessary for production. They then bought labor power as a commodity on the market. They directed the laborers, whose labor power they had purchased, to produce. The laborers produced commodities having some given magnitude of value. These commodities were owned by the capitalists, of course, who then sold the commodities. The value that the laborers had produced was generally sufficient for the capitalist to pay the laborers their wage, to pay for raw materials used, to pay for the wear and tear of the machines and tools used, or to acquire new machines and tools, and to leave a surplus for the capitalist. Capitalists received the surplus purely as a result of their ownership of property.

Not all of this surplus, however, was profit. The capitalist might have borrowed funds to augment his capital, or he might have rented the land on which his factory was constructed. For the capitalist, the interest he paid on his debt and the rent he paid on the land were both expenses which he deducted, along with his other expenses, from the value his laborers had created in order to arrive at his profit. The persons who received this interest and rent were also, in Marx's view, receiving income purely from ownership. Thus, the surplus value created by workers, in excess of the value of their own wages and the materials and tools used up in production, went to profit, interest, and rent. All three of these latter forms of income were derived from ownership. Therefore they were all capitalist income. Ownership of money, land, or tools and machinery could thus all become capital under the right circumstances, and the return from owning capital could take the form of interest, rent, or profit.

The capitalist class comprised those people whose ownership was so significant that it brought them sufficient income to live in luxury and to have great economic and political power without ever having to engage in any form of socially useful toil.

In every capitalist economy there was another social class that stood between the capitalists and the wage laborers. This was the class of small shopkeepers, independent craftsmen, and professionals or other independent proprietors. This class had features resembling both capitalists and workers. They owned their own means of production and did much (and sometimes all) of the work in creating or selling their commodities. Most frequently they themselves, like wage laborers, had to work, but they also, like capitalists, hired wage laborers to assist them. Included in this class would be most doctors, lawyers, independent accountants, barbers, and many owners of such small businesses as hamburger stands, dry cleaners, repair garages, small retail shops, and the like. This class has always been much smaller than the working class and much larger than the capitalist class. In some circumstances the interests of this class might be very close to those of the capitalist class, whereas in other circumstances their interests might be closer to those of the working class.

Finally, the last class in capitalism was the poorest class. It included people who received little or no income from either owning or working. Included in this class were two distinctly different groups. First, there were those who could not work for a variety of reasons, such as mental, physical, or emotional handicaps or problems; people who were too young or too old to work and had no one to support them; and people such as single parents of very small children whose necessary activities left no time for wage labor. The second group included people who were able and willing to work but for whom capitalism did not provide enough jobs. Throughout the history of capitalism there have always been millions of such involuntarily unemployed people. They have generally performed two very important economic functions. First, they have weakened the bargaining power of employed laborers in their wage negotiations, since if employed workers demanded too much, they could easily be replaced. Second, capitalism has always been an unstable economy. It has experienced alternative periods of prosperity and depression. The involuntarily unemployed have constituted a reserve of workers who could be used in times of prosperity when the economy was growing and needed more workers and could be discarded when recession or depression set in and fewer workers were needed. Thus, the size of this lowest or poorest class in capitalism has always varied in accordance with general business conditions.

After examining the sources of income among all four classes, Marx concluded that interest, rent, and profit were not the only forms taken by the surplus created by the working class. Taxes also came from this surplus. Whether the taxes were collected from wage earners or from the recipients of interest, rent, and profits, they represented a claim on the product of labor and were hence a part of the surplus value created by but not received by workers. Thus we see that two of the classes in capitalism—the highest and the lowest—did not contribute to the production of commodities but lived off the surplus created by wage laborers.

Within the context of Marx's theory, it is interesting to note that whenever workers become angry or frustrated by their support of unproductive consumers, it is, of course, much more conducive to the peace and stability of capitalism if all of their anger and frustration is turned against those living in dire poverty—the unemployed and unemployable—rather than against those living in extravagant luxury—the capitalists. It is not surprising that conservatives generally protest the parasitic nature of the very poor and the powerless, while critics who have been influenced by Marx protest the parasitic nature of the wealthy and the powerful. In Marx's view, however, both classes were integral parts of capitalism and would continue to exist as long as capitalism existed.

Thus the market allocation of productive labor and natural resources, together with the four-level class structure of capitalism, constituted the main defining features of capitalism for Marx. In discussing this class structure, however, we have used the concepts of private property and capital, concepts which Marx understood somewhat differently than do most of us. We shall therefore discuss them at somewhat greater length.

MARX'S VIEW OF PRIVATE PROPERTY

It is difficult to find a general definition that will cover all property rights, in all societies, in all times. One thing, however, is clear. A property right is *not* simply or even primarily a relation between an isolated individual and a material thing. An isolated individual could use any material object in any way he or she chose, subject only to the laws of physics, chemistry, and human anatomy. He or she would have absolutely no need for, and no conception of, property rights. Property rights are essential social relations between people. But not all social relations are property rights.

An adequate general definition of property rights is, of necessity, fairly vague and complex. The best definition, in our opinion, is as follows: *Within a particular social or cultural setting* (e.g., a modern nation-state) *property rights represent a set of social relations that defines privileges and corresponding sanctions. The privileges and sanctions are related to objects* (whether material or not). *The privileges and sanctions are coercively established and coercively maintained by an agency of coercion that is widely believed to "rightly" or "properly" use coercive force* (such as the police).

For most of us, private property simply means private ownership of our personal means of consumption. We have the exclusive privilege of using and disposing of our own food, clothing, and assorted personal effects (though generally *not* of the dwelling in which we reside). Others cannot have this privilege with our personal effects. They face coercive sanctions. If they try to use or dispose of our personal effects, their action constitutes theft and they face coercion from the police, one of our institutionalized agencies whose use of coercion (within defined limits) is generally deemed proper.

Private ownership of the means of consumption strikes most of us as a reasonable and useful social convention. It would seem difficult for a society to function if certain items, such as food and clothing, were not allocated in such a manner as to give particular individuals the right to use and dispose of particular means of consumption, at least where that consumption is primarily a private matter. Defenders of private property generally use the means of personal consumption to illustrate that private property is "natural," "inevitable," and "just." Marx's concern, however, was not so much with private ownership of the means of consumption as with private ownership of the means of production.

Marx insisted that all production was social. Yet there were two different ways in which it was social. First, in handicraft production, a single or at most a few producers working together created a finished product. Even in the case of a single producer, there was an economic or productive dependence on other producers who had to provide the individual producer with materials on which to work as well as equipment, machines, and tools with which to work. Defenders of private ownership of the means of production have generally used examples of handicraft production to construct their defense. In such production, the individual's social dependence was similar to that involved in private consumption; that is, others produced both the necessary means of consumption and production. Thus, when handicraft production alone was considered, the same rationale would defend private ownership of both productive and consumptive goods.

Marx felt that it was ironic that handicraft production was frequently used as the basis for defending capitalist private ownership of the means of production. He argued that it was such historical processes as the enclosure movement and increased indebtedness, among other things, that had made independent handicraft production *impossible for the vast majority of workers* and, in so doing, had simultaneously created a supply of unemployed wage workers. In other words, the necessary condition for capitalism's historical creation was that the form of production that was used to defend capitalist ownership had to become inaccessible to most producers and therefore had to become relatively unimportant to the whole capitalist economy.

There were, of course, still a few independent handicraft producers in most capitalist economies of Marx's time (as there are today). They constituted a small part of the class of independent small shopkeepers, producers, and professionals that stood somewhere between the capitalist class and the working class. Obviously, this first form of productive inter-dependence, characteristic of handicraft production, was neither the most important form nor the characteristic form in a capitalist economy.

The second form of productive interdependence, then, was the one most characteristic of capitalism. This interdependence reflected the form of social production that inevitably went with a capitalist economy and was, historically, the outcome of the Industrial Revolution, discussed in Chapter 4. This form of productive interdependence was characteristic of factory and industrial production. In industrial production, no single worker or small group of workers produced a finished commodity. There was an elaborate division of labor in which each individual repetitiously performed a single task or a few tasks and only the coordinated effort of hundreds (and even, in some cases, tens of thousands) of individuals resulted in the production of a particular commodity. Such industrial production generally involved massive factories or work places, as well as very expensive and elaborate machines and tools.

Thus, industrial production, which was the form social productive in-terdependencies generally took in a capitalist economy, made it utterly impossible for the vast majority of working people to own individually as private property the means necessary for them to produce. In capitalism most production was totally social. It was social in the same way that han-dicraft production was social; that is, workers in a factory depended upon other workers to produce the materials on which they worked and the tools with which they worked. But it was also social in a new way: Any production process now involved the coordinated endeavors of hundreds or even thousands of workers working with complex, expensive machinery.

In this situation what then constituted the nature of private ownership of the means of production? Marx was aware that in the case of private ownership of the means of individual consumption—or private ownership of the means of individual, independent handicraft production—such ownership meant the privilege or right to use and dispose of the things owned. In industrial corporations, however, the ownership of stock (which constituted ownership of shares of the means of production) conferred this right to only a few of the biggest and most powerful owners. Even then, this right generally consisted only in naming powerful managers to oversee, direct, and control the use of these means of production by work-ing people who did not own them. The common privilege of all ownership of stocks for every owner, from the smallest to the largest, was the right or privilege to take a proportionate share (depending on the amount of stock owned) of the surplus value created by workers. Ownership of the industrial means of production, in capitalism, thus had only one inherent or common privilege for all owners: to reap where they had not sown, to receive a part of the value of commodities produced without having to take any part whatsoever in the production of these commodities.

Thus Marx argued that capitalism had resulted in a

transformation of the actually functioning capitalist into a mere manager, administrator of other people's capital, and of the owner of capital into a mere owner, a mere money-capitalist. Even if the dividends which they receive include the interest and the profit of enterprise, i.e. the total profit (for the salary of the manager is, or should be, simply the wage of a specific type of skilled labour, whose price is regulated in the labour-market like that of any other labour), this total profit is henceforth received only in the form of interest, i.e. as mere compensation for owning capital that now is entirely divorced from its function in the actual process of reproduction just as this function in the person of the manager is divorced from ownership of capital. Profit thus appears . . . as a mere appropriation of the surplus-labour of others. (Marx, 1961, Vol. 3, p. 427)

During Marx's time (and, indeed, right up to the present) the dominant economic ideology of capitalism justified colossal incomes from ownership as being the fruits of high moral character. In capitalism, the ideologists argued, workers earned wages because of, or in payment for, the strain of producing. On the other hand, because it has always been extraordinarily difficult (very nearly impossible) for a noncapitalist to save enough to become a capitalist, the ideologists argued that whenever anyone did become a capitalist they must have undergone strain and sacrifices that were much more severe than the mere strain of productively creating things that were socially needed. Therefore, their profit, rent, and interest were earned because of, or in payment for, the strains and sacrifices of their abstinence.

There were many arguments by which Marx refuted the ideologists' apologetic views on profit. Here we shall mention only three of them.

First, the abstinence and strain that were necessary for one to become a capitalist involved no contribution to society. For example, if a person saved all his life in order to buy a factory, he saved only for himself. He had not, in so doing, done any of the work necessary to construct the factory. All the work had been done by working people. Rather, the extent of his stress and strain merely reflected the fact that in any class-divided society there had to be significant barriers to entrance into the ruling class. If it had been relatively easy for anyone to become a capitalist, then everyone would have become a capitalist; there would have been no workers; nothing would have been produced and everyone would have starved. There had been in history, and were in Marx's time, numerous socioeconomic systems that operated effectively without the abstinence of capitalists, in fact, without capitalists at all. But there had never been, and there never would be, a society without working people creating needed products.

Second, if sacrifice and abstinence could justify capitalists' income, then they could similarly justify the wealth, power, and income of any ruling class in any society. For example, in the American South prior to the Civil War, the economic system was one of commercial slavery. Slaves were very expensive, and most southern whites did not own slaves. Slave owners, of course, enjoyed great wealth and lavish incomes from the surplus their slaves produced over the costs of their maintainence. For a non-slave owner to become a slave owner was very difficult. It required extreme strain and abstinence. It is therefore clear that according to this ideology the surplus that these owners extracted from the sweat and toil of their slaves was merely the just reward for the owners' strain and abstinence.

Third, the majority of capitalists inherited their ownership of capital. Not only did they not strain and abstain, most of them lived lives of indolent luxury. And for those who had not inherited their wealth, most had become capitalists not because they had produced and abstained, but through some combination of ruthlessness, shrewdness, chicanery, and luck. Marx detailed the piracy, slave trading, and colonial plundering in the early process of building capitalist fortunes.

When confronted with these criticisms, defenders of capitalist ideology had two responses. The first response was that regardless of how a capitalist acquired his fortune, he abstained when he did not fritter the whole thing away. He could have consumed so incredibly profligately and luxuriously that he would soon have had none of his inherited fortune left. In fact, a few capitalists actually did this, and every capitalist constantly had the choice of, on the one hand, abstaining from such extreme profligacy and luxury in order that he or all of his descendents might live in ordinary profligacy and luxury or, on the other hand, recklessly throwing his entire fortune away. In fact, in order for a capitalist family to remain in the ruling class, generation after generation, the members of the family had to "abstain" to that degree just as they had to abstain from committing suicide before they had had any offspring to inherit their wealth. Such abstinence, in the ideology of capitalism, remained a moral justification for the large incomes of capitalists.

The second response to critics was that abstinence alone did not morally justify ruling-class income, but only abstinence that led to or perpetuated the ownership of nonhuman objects as capital. Thus the defenders of capitalism argued that abstinence in the acquiring of slaves did not justify property income because slave owning was inherently immoral, whereas the owner of capital did society a great service because capital was productive. The capitalist used his capital productively and thereby contributed to everyone's well-being.

Before we can understand all of Marx's critique of the ideology of capitalism, however, we must understand his conception of the nature of capital.

MARX'S VIEW OF CAPITAL

The standard ideology of capitalism was based on the notion that capital was one of the three factors of production—land, labor, and capital—that were necessary for production in every society. These factors were said to account for all production. Above all, the ideology held that the three were complementary and not alternatives or competitors. All production required the cooperation of all three. Without labor, no production was possible; without land, no production was possible; and without capital, no production was possible. Ideologists concluded that all three factors had to cooperate peacefully and harmoniously.

But the ideology went on to insist that all three factors of production were merely collections of three different kinds of commodities. Land, labor, and capital were names for three different sorts of commodities that are bought and sold in the market. Since commodities did not cooperate peacefully and harmoniously, it was obvious that the ideologists meant that the owners of the commodities must cooperate peacefully and harmoniously.

Next, the ideologists argued that entrepreneurs went into the market and bought certain quantities of each of the three commodity factors of production. The entrepreneur then combined these factors in a production process that yielded output in the form of commodities having certain value. He sold these commodities on the market. If everything functioned properly, then two very interesting "facts" could be observed to result from the process. First, one could precisely ascertain the productive contribution of each of the factors: land, labor, and capital. Second, the price that the entrepreneur paid for each of these commodities—wages being the price of labor, rent being the price of land, and profit (or interest) being the price of capital—turned out to be exactly equal to the value of the productive contribution of each factor; that is, each factor was returned just what it had contributed to production. Hence there could not possibly be any economic exploitation. It is clear why the ideologists of capitalism held that harmony and not conflict is the natural social state of capitalism. This conservative ideology can still be found in many conservative economics textbooks on microeconomic theory.

Capital, in this ideology, was merely a commodity like the other factors of production. It produced for society and received a reward based on its productivity. If one doubted the productivity of capital, argued the ideologist, then one could try making steel without a blast furnace, or digging a trench without a shovel, or tightening a screw without a screwdriver, or, in general, producing without tools. Capital was identified as commodities that were tools (or other means of producing). And because tools were indispensable, they argued that capital was indispensable.

Marx immediately saw several difficulties with this analysis. Human beings had always used tools. Yet capitalism, capital, and profit were social categories that did not even exist as such in some societies. In fact, capitalism, capital, and profit had actually existed for only a few hundred years.

Obviously, land did not yield rent and tools did not yield profit simply because they entered into the production process. They had been used in societies that did not even have rent or profit. Clearly tools were not, per se, capital. Moreover, since one could own both land and tools and yet receive no rent or profit, it was equally clear that ownership of land or tools does not necessarily or automatically mean capitalistically owned land that yields rent or capital that yields profit. The problem of identifying the nature of capital remained unsolved within the context of capitalist ideology.

In Marx's opinion, the key to resolving these inconsistencies was to realize that land, labor, and capital were not, in the same sense, factors of production. Moreover, tools and land, simply purchased as commodities, required other social conditions before they could become profit-yielding capital and rent-yielding land.

The production process, Marx insisted, presupposed that human beings lived in an environment they could transform. Production was this trans- formation of nature by human beings. Although land, as this environment, was certainly necessary, to say that nature "produced" something was to engage in a kind of confusion (Marx called it fetishism) where human qualities were attributed to nonhuman things. It was the equivalent of saying that nature transformed itself expressly for human use.

Just as saying that land, as an inanimate object, could produce anything by itself was a confusion (or a form of fetishism), so was the notion that tools produced anything by themselves. A tool undertook no activity. It was an object produced by human labor. The producer of the tool had in mind, of course, that the tool would be used in further production. But the tool, as such, did not produce anything. Only people produced things— usually by using tools.

The statement that tools were absolutely necessary for modern pro- duction was true. It did not mean that tools engaged in production, how- ever. It meant, rather, that production was social and that producers were interdependent. The carpenter, for example, depended upon the working people who produced hammers, nails, saws, and lumber. After the car- penter had built a house, the procapitalist ideologist would insist that a hammer, some nails, a saw, and some lumber—together with a carpenter— built the house. Contrary to this ideology, Marx argued that human beings had socially built the house by dividing the work in such a manner that some had produced the hammers, others nails, others saws, others lumber, and still others had brought all of these human exertions together by per- forming the last step (carpentering) in this social production process.

In fact, capital was not simply a commodity that produced. Capital was a word that was attached to tools only when a very specific set of social relations existed. Capital, then, did not refer to tools per se, or to tools sold as commodities per se, but to tools sold as commodities and used in a specific way within the context of a specific set of social relations.

Capital existed, then, only when three conditions were met: (1) Tools were produced as commodities. (2) These commodities were owned by a social class other than the class that productively used them. (3) The class that used the tools to produce received the permission to do so only on the condition that they did not receive ownership of the product that they produced; instead, these producers had to accept a wage having less value than the value of the commodities they produced. The difference, or extra value, went to owners in the form of interest, rent, or profit.

Capital, then, was the capacity of capitalists to place themselves between every human productive interdependency and to extract a return for allowing this interdependent production process to proceed. Between the carpenter who had to use a hammer, a saw, nails, and lumber and the producers of these items he required stood several capitalists. The worker-producer of nails produced nails for a capitalist, not for a carpenter. The same held true for the hammer, saw, and lumber worker-producers. But the carpenter did not receive these items directly from the capitalists involved. A capitalist owning the construction company bought them from the other capitalists.

In all human productive interdependencies one laborer required the labor of others and others required his labor. In capitalism, however, laborers never dealt with each other. Every interdependency of labor found actual expression in, or actually took effect through, financial dealings among capitalists. The interdependence of labor became, in capitalism, an absolute dependence of any particular laborer on a capitalist. At every point where one worker needed another worker stood a capitalist who demanded his share, in the form of profit, interest, or rent, before he would permit the process to go on.

Thus capitalism was a society in which labor became social by taking the form of the price of a commodity and in which every social interdependency of labor took the form of commodities owned by nonlaborers who extracted a concession for allowing producers to produce. In such a society and *only* in such a society did tools become capital that yielded profit.

Thus, for Marx, the historically specific social relations whereby the owners of the means of production exploited workers within a capitalist system were totally obscured when the procapitalist ideologists argued that rent and profit simply resulted from the physical nature of land and tools, which rendered them indispensable to production. Marx argued that this was a "complete mystification of the capitalist mode of production." The capitalism of the ideologists was "an enchanted, perverted, topsy-turvy world in which Monsieur le Capital and Madame La Terre do their ghost-walking as social characters and at the same time directly as mere things" (Marx, 1961, Vol. 3, p. 809).

By contrast, Marx's definition of capital stressed its historical specificity:

One thing . . . is clear—Nature does not produce on the one side owners of money or commodities [means of production], and on the other men possessing nothing but their own labour-power. This relation has no natural basis, neither is its social basis one that is common to all historical periods. It is clearly the result of a past historical development, the product of many economic revolutions, of the extinction of a whole series of older forms of social production. (Ibid., Vol. 1, p. 169)

Capital is not a thing, but rather a definite social production relation, belonging to a definite historical formation of society, which is manifested in a thing and lends this thing a specific social character. . . . It is the means of production monopolized by a certain section of society, confronting living labour-power as products and working conditions rendered independent of this very labour-power. (Ibid., Vol. 3, pp. 794–795)

Capital was the social relation that defined the two most important classes of the capitalist mode of production. It did not exist on a significant scale prior to capitalism and it would not exist after capitalism had been overthrown.

SUMMARY

In Marx's historical materialism, the mode of production was the most significant aspect of any social system. The capitalist mode of production was one in which the market allocated labor and resources. It was made up of four classes: capitalists, small and independent shopkeepers and professionals, workers, and poor people with few if any sources of income. The most important classes were the capitalists and the workers. The capitalists' power was based upon private ownership of capital. Property ownership was a social relation involving privileges and sanctions coercively created and coercively maintained. Capital could not be identified as simply tools and machinery. Rather, capital involved ownership of tools and machines within the context of the social and economic relations between capitalists and laborers, whereby laborers received as wages only a part of the value they produced and capitalists demanded the remaining surplus as a necessary condition for permitting laborers to produce.

REFERENCES

Marx, Karl. *Capital.* 3 vols. Moscow: Foreign Languages Publishing House, 1961.

———. *Critique of Political Economy.* New York: New World Paperbacks, 1970.

——— and Friedrich Engels. "The Communist Manifesto." In *Essential Works of Marxism.* Edited by Arthur P. Mendel. New York: Bantam, 1965.

Chapter 7

Marx's Social and Economic Theory

Marx's conception of the nature of capitalism, which was described in the preceding chapter, furnished the intellectual foundation for his theories of how capitalism functioned. Many of Marx's economic arguments cannot be fully comprehended unless one first understands this overview of the nature of capitalism as a socioeconomic system. Likewise, many of Marx's economic theories are difficult to separate entirely from his moral critique of capitalism. We therefore begin this chapter with a discussion of that critique as it was spelled out in Marx's theory of alienation. After that we consider various aspects of his economic theory of how capitalism functions.

ALIENATION

Capitalism, in Marx's view, simultaneously increased society's capacity to produce while systematically rendering this increased productive capacity less serviceable in fulfilling some of the most basic of human needs. More production certainly made possible a more adequate fulfillment of the basic needs for food, shelter, and clothing. Because of the extreme inequalities in the distribution of wealth and income, however, millions of workers in the capitalist system of Marx's time suffered from extreme material poverty and deprivation.

Most of the socialists whose ideas we discussed in Chapter 5 based their moral critique of capitalism on a condemnation of the misery caused by this widespread poverty and inequality. Many interpreters of Marx's ideas have erroneously asserted that this was also the primary basis of Marx's moral critique. When Marx argued that the continued development of capitalism would only sharpen and increase the misery of workers, these interpreters have imagined him to have been arguing that the poverty and material deprivation of workers would grow worse. The fact that the purchasing power of workers' wages has generally risen during the century since Marx's death is therefore widely cited as a refutation of Marx's economic theory.

These interpreters have, however, misunderstood the primary basis of Marx's moral critique of capitalism. Although Marx was appalled by the inequities of capitalism and the material deprivation and suffering of the working class, he was well aware that with the increasing productivity of the capitalist system it would become possible for workers to win higher wages in their struggles with capitalists. If they did win such increases, Marx wrote, then

> a larger part of their own surplus . . . comes back to . . . [workers] in the shape of means of payment, so that they can extend the circle of their enjoyments; can make some additions to their consumption-fund of clothes, furniture, etc., and can lay by small reserve-funds of money. But just as little as better clothing, food, and treatment, and a larger peculium, do away with the exploitation of the slave, so little do they set aside that of the wage-workers. (Marx, 1961, Vol. 1, p. 618)

The most fundamental evil of capitalism was not, Marx insisted, the material deprivation of workers. Rather, it was to be found in the fact that capitalism systematically prevented individuals from achieving their potential as human beings. It diminished their capacity to give and receive love and it thwarted the development of their biological, emotional, aesthetic, and intellectual potential. In other words, capitalism severely crippled human beings by preventing their development.

This crippling effect could not, moreover, be overcome within a capitalist system. The forces that increased social productivity could only be utilized in capitalism through the very methods that degraded workers. This was because the technological improvements were always introduced for one purpose and only one purpose: to increase profit. Profit was the source of capitalists' wealth; profit could only be increased by extending and solidifying the control of the capitalists over the work process. Yet it was the control of capital over nearly all processes of human creativity that was the source of the degradation of workers in capitalism. Marx concluded that the "accumulation of wealth at one pole is, therefore, at the same time accumulation of misery, agony of toil, slavery, ignorance, brutality, [and] mental degradation at the opposite pole" (ibid., p. 646).

The social nature of the work process was, for Marx, extremely important. It was through social cooperation in transforming nature into useful things that human beings achieved their sociality and developed their potential as individual human beings. If that production were a cooperative venture among social equals, it would develop bonds of affection, love, and mutual affirmation among people. Moreover, such creative endeavor was the source of human aesthetic development. It is significant that when ancient people spoke of the "arts" they were referring to various productive skills. Moreover, the creation and use of tools have always been involved in the advancement of human knowledge and scientific understanding.

The production process, however, had exactly the opposite set of effects on workers in a capitalist system. In feudalism the exploitative class structure had severely limited human development. Yet because these exploitative social relations were also personal and paternalistic, not all of the human developmental potential of the work process was stunted or thwarted. Work in feudalism was more than merely a means of making a livable wage for the worker while he created wealth for his overlord. This changed with capitalism, when, in Marx's opinion:

> the bourgeoisie, wherever it has got the upper hand, has put an end to all feudal patriarchal, idyllic relations. It has pitilessly torn asunder the motley feudal ties that bound man to his "natural superiors," and has left remaining no other nexus between man and man than naked self-interest, than callous "cash payment." It has drowned the most heavenly ecstasies of religious fervor, of chivalrous enthusiasm, of philistine sentimentalism, in the icy water of egotistical calculation. It has resolved personal worth into exchange value. (Marx and Engels, p. 15)

In a capitalist society the market separated and isolated "exchange value," or money price, from the qualities that shaped a person's relations with things as well as with other human beings. This was especially true in the work process. To the capitalist, wages were merely another expense of production to be added to the costs of raw materials and machinery in the profit calculation. Labor became a mere commodity to be bought if a profit could be made on the purchase. Whether the laborer could sell his or her labor power was completely beyond his or her control. It depended on the cold and totally impersonal conditions of the market. The product of this labor was likewise totally outside of the laborer's life, being the property of the capitalist.

Marx used the term *alienation* to describe the condition of individuals in this situation. They felt alienated or divorced from their work, from their institutional and cultural environment, and from their fellow humans. The conditions of work, the object produced, and indeed the very possibility of working were determined by the numerically small class of capitalists and their profit calculations, not by human need or aspirations. The effects of this alienation can best be summarized in Marx's own words:

> What, then, constitutes the alienation of labour? First, the fact that labour is external to the worker, i.e., it does not belong to his essential being; that in his work, therefore, he does not affirm himself but denies himself, does not feel content but unhappy, does not develop freely his physical and mental energy but mortifies his body and ruins his mind. The worker therefore only feels himself outside his work, and in his work feels outside himself. He is at home when he is not working, and when he is working he is not at home. His

labour is therefore not voluntary but coerced; it is *forced labour.* It is therefore not the satisfaction of a need; it is merely a *means* to satisfy needs external to it. Its alien character emerges clearly in the fact that as soon as no physical or other compulsion exists, labour is shunned like the plague. External labour, labour in which man alienates himself, is a labour of self-sacrifice, or mortification. Lastly, the external character of labour for the worker appears in the fact that it is not his own, but someone else's, that it does not belong to him, that in it he belongs, not to himself, but to another . . . As a result, therefore, man (the worker) no longer feels himself to be freely active in any but his animal functions—eating, drinking, procreating, or at most in his dwelling and in dressing up, etc.; and in his human functions he no longer feels himself to be anything but an animal. What is animal becomes human and what is human becomes animal. (Marx, 1959, p. 69)

It was this degradation and total dehumanization of the working class, thwarting man's personal development and making an alien market commodity of man's life-sustaining activities, that Marx most thoroughly condemned in the capitalist system. His moral critique thus went far beyond those of most of his socialist precursors.

His faith in the possibility of a better future for the working class, however, was not based on the hope that ever-increasing numbers of people would share his moral indignation and therefore attempt to reform the system. Rather, he believed the capitalist mode of production and the class conflict inherent in it would lead to the destruction of capitalism. Capitalism, like all previous modes of production in which class conflicts were present, would destroy itself. In order to understand the basis for his faith, it is necessary to examine his economic theory, in which he attempted to analyze the "laws of motion" of capitalism.

THE LABOR THEORY OF VALUE AND SURPLUS VALUE

Because for Marx the capitalist mode of production was based on the opposition of labor and capital, he began by analyzing the capital-labor relationship. This relationship was essentially one of exchange. The worker sold his or her labor power to the capitalist for money, with which the worker bought the necessities of life. Thus this exchange relation was obviously merely a special case of the general problem of exchange values within a capitalist market economy. Marx therefore began volume I of *Capital* with a section entitled "Commodities," in which he defined *commodities* as objects that are usually intended for exchange rather than for the direct personal use of the producer. He then attempted to analyze the basic determinant of the exchange value of commodities. In other words, he analyzed the ratio in which commodities could be exchanged for other commodities, as opposed to use value, which was a measure of the usefulness of commodities to their possessor.

Like Adam Smith, David Ricardo, and most of the pre-Marxist classical economists, Marx believed the exchange value of a commodity was determined by the amount of labor time necessary for its production. His theory is therefore usually called the *labor theory of value*. He recognized that laborers differed in abilities, training, and motivation, but he believed skilled labor could be calculated as a multiple of unskilled labor. Thus all labor time could be reduced to a common denominator.

He also realized that labor time expended in the production of a useless commodity (one for which there was no demand) would not create a commodity with an exchange value equal to the labor time embodied in it. The desire of capitalists to maximize their profits would, however, prevent the production of objects for which there was no demand. Capitalists would produce only commodities for which market demand would permit the realization of at least their costs of production. Market demand would determine not only what commodities were produced but also the relative quantities in which they were produced.

Marx began by describing how the capitalist buys the means of production and the labor power. Then when the laborers complete the production process, the capitalist sells the commodities for more money. Thus the amount of money at the end of the production process is greater than that at the start. This difference is what Marx called *surplus value*. He considered it the source of capitalist profits.

Surplus value originated in the fact that capitalists bought one commodity—labor power—and sold a different commodity—that which labor produced in the production process. Profits were made because the value of labor power was less than the value of the commodities produced with the labor power. The value of labor power was "determined, as in the case of every other commodity, by the labor time necessary" for its maintenance and reproduction, which meant that "the value of labor power . . . [was] the value of the means of subsistence necessary for the maintenance of the laborer at a socially defined standard of living" (Marx, 1961, Vol. 1, pp. 170–171). The fact was that the average length of the working day exceeded the time necessary for a laborer to produce the value equivalent of his or her subsistence wage, which enabled the capitalist to appropriate the surplus produced over and above this subsistence. Marx called this process the *exploitation* of workers by capitalists. If the worker works for 8 hours but uses only 6 hours to produce the value of his or her wage goods, then that worker is exploited because he or she works 2 surplus hours for the capitalist.

THE ACCUMULATION OF CAPITAL

Ownership of capital enabled the capitalist to gain profit. Most of these profits were reinvested in order to increase capital and hence increase future profits, which could then be plowed back into more capital, and so forth. This was the process of capital accumulation: Capital led to profits, which led to more capital. When and how did the process originate? Many classical economists and liberals, particularly the English economist Nassau Senior (1790–1864), had answered this question in a way favorable to the capitalist, arguing that through hard, diligent work and abstemious behavior a modest saving program was begun, which enabled the capitalist to accumulate slowly the fortunes many nineteenth-century capitalists owned. Laborers, on the contrary, rather than devoting themselves to working and living abstemiously, had profligately squandered their earnings.

Marx accused these defenders of the capitalist system of being totally ignorant of history. In a famous passage, which gives the flavor of some of his most colorful writing, Marx described the process of "primitive accumulation" by which the fortunes were originally made:

> This primitive accumulation plays in Political Economy about the same part as original sin in theology. Adam bit the apple, and thereupon sin fell on the human race. Its origin is supposed to be explained when it is told as an anecdote of the past. In times long gone by there were two sorts of people; one the diligent, intelligent, and above all, frugal elite; the other, lazy rascals, spending their substance, and more, in riotous living. . . . Thus it came to pass that the former sort accumulated wealth, and the latter sort had nothing to sell except their own skins. And from this original sin dates the poverty of the great majority that, despite all its labour, has up to now nothing to sell but itself, and the wealth of the few that increases constantly although they have long ceased to work. Such insipid childishness is every day preached to us in the defence of property. . . . As soon as the question of property crops up, it becomes a sacred duty to proclaim the intellectual food of the infant as the one thing fit for all ages and for all stages of development. In actual history it is notorious that conquest, enslavement, robbery, murder, briefly force, play the great part. . . . The methods of primitive accumulation are anything but idyllic. (Ibid., pp. 713–714)

Marx listed the important forms of primitive accumulation as the enclosure movement and the dislocation of the feudal agrarian population, the great price inflation, monopolies of trade, colonies, "the extirpation, enslavement and entombment in mines of the aboriginal population, the beginning of the conquest and looting of the East Indies, [and] the turning of Africa into a warren for the commercial hunting of black skins" (ibid., p. 751).

Once this initial accumulation of capital had taken place, the drive to acquire more capital became the moving force of the capitalist system. The capitalist's social standing and prestige as well as his economic and political power depended on the size of capital he controlled. He could not stand still; he was beset on every side by fierce competition. The system demanded that he accumulate and grow more powerful in order to outdo his competitors, or else his competitors would force him to the wall and take over his capital. Competitors were constantly developing new and better methods of production. Only by accumulating new and better capital equipment could this challenge be met. Thus Marx believed the capitalist

> shares with the miser the passion for wealth as wealth. But that which in the miser is a mere idiosyncrasy, is in the capitalist the effect of the social mechanism of which he is but one of the wheels. Moreover, the development of capitalist production makes it constantly necessary to keep increasing the amount of capital laid out in a given industrial undertaking, and competition makes the imminent laws of capitalist production to be felt by each individual capitalist as external coercive laws. It compels him to keep constantly extending his capital, in order to preserve it, but extend it he cannot except by means of progressive accumulation. (Ibid., p. 592)

SECTORAL IMBALANCES AND ECONOMIC CRISES

It was this ceaseless drive to accumulate more capital that created many of the contradictions to capitalist development. The capitalist would begin with the acquisition of more machines and tools of the types that were currently being used. This would require a proportional increase in the number of workers employed in order to operate the new equipment. But the capitalist had been able to keep the wage rate at the subsistence level only because there existed what Marx called an "industrial reserve army" of unemployed labor, which was living below the subsistence level and striving to take jobs that would pay a mere subsistence wage. Therefore, capitalists usually had no problem in keeping wage rates down. As the industrial expansion took place, however, the increasing demand for labor soon depleted the ranks of the reserve. When this happened, the capitalist began to find that he had to pay higher wages to get enough labor.

The individual capitalist took the wage level as given and beyond his power to change, so he attempted to make the best of the situation. The most profitable course of action seemed to be changing the techniques of production by introducing new labor-saving machinery so that each laborer would then be working with more capital, and output per laborer would be increased. This labor-saving investment would enable the capitalist to expand output with the same or an even smaller work force. When all or most of the capitalists, acting individually, did this, the problem of high wages was temporarily alleviated as the reserve army was replenished by workers who had been displaced by the new productive techniques, introducing new problems and contradictions.

Labor-saving expansion permitted increases in total production without increasing the wages paid to workers. Therefore, while new goods were flooding the market, workers' wages were being restricted, with the result that consumer demand was limited. As Marx put it, the workers were still producing more profits in the form of goods, but the capitalists could not "realize" the profits by selling these goods in the market because of lack of consumer demand.

In order to clarify this process further, Marx divided the capitalist economy into two sectors, one producing consumer goods and the other producing capital goods. Lack of consumer demand meant that capitalists in the consumption goods sector would find that they could not sell their entire output and thus would lower their expectations of profits and would certainly *not* want to add to their productive facilities. They would therefore cancel any plans to add to their already excessively large capital stock. These decisions would, of course, significantly reduce the demand for capital goods, which would result in a decrease in production in the capital goods sector. Unlike the naïve underconsumptionist theories of the earlier socialists, Marx's view held that the first obvious sign of a depression might thus appear in the capital goods sector.

The actual decrease in capital goods production would mean that some workers in that sector would be fired, which would lower total wages, decrease national income, and reduce consumer demand. Thus there would be a cutback in consumer goods production, and layoffs of workers would spread to those industries. Wages and incomes would then be further reduced, causing a glut, or surfeit, of consumer goods. The entire process of successive repercussions in both sectors would then be one of economic collapse.

The resulting depression would more than restore the reserve army of unemployed and push labor's standard of living back to or below the subsistence level. Marx, however, was not a "stagnationist"—that is, he did not believe capitalism would suffer one long depression or that mass unemployment at high levels would last forever. During the depression, workers' wages would fall, but not as rapidly as the output of goods. Thus eventually supply would be lower than consumer demand, and therefore recovery would occur. Marx believed that capitalism does grow, but jerkily, in cycles of boom and bust, with periodic high levels of unemployment for the workers.

ECONOMIC CONCENTRATION

Concentration of wealth and economic power in the hands of fewer and fewer capitalists was another important consequence of capital accumulation. This concentration was the result of two forces. First, competition among capitalists tended to create a situation in which the strong either crushed or absorbed the weak. "Here competition rages in direct proportion to the number, and in inverse proportion to the magnitudes, of the antagonistic capitals. It always ends in the ruin of many small capitalists, whose capitals partly pass into the hands of their conquerors, partly vanish" (ibid., p. 626).

Second, as technology improved there was "an increase in the minimum amount of . . . capital necessary to carry on a business under its normal conditions." In order to remain competitive, a firm would constantly have

to increase the productivity of its laborers. The "productiveness of labor
. . . depended] on the scale of production" (ibid., p. 626). Thus changing
technology as well as competition among capitalists created an inexorable
movement of the capitalist system toward larger and larger firms owned
by fewer and fewer capitalists. In this way the gulf between the small class
of wealthy capitalists and the great majority of society, the proletariat,
would continually widen.

THE IMMISERIZATION OF THE PROLETARIAT

At the same time that this increasing concentration of capital was taking
place, the misery of the proletariat grew constantly worse. In his famous
"doctrine of increasing misery" (immiserization), Marx argued that the
conditions of labor would worsen relative to the affluence of the capitalists
until the laborers could stand no more—and revolution became inevitable.
Because Marx's doctrine of immiserization is very often misrepresented,
we quote his own writings on this point:

> Within the capitalist system all methods for raising the social productiveness
> of labour are brought about at the cost of the individual labourer; all means
> for the development of production transform themselves into means of dom-
> ination over, and exploitation of, the producers; they mutilate the labourer
> into a fragment of a man, degrade him to the level of an appendage of a machine,
> destroy every remnant of charm in his work and turn it into hated toil; they
> estrange from him the intellectual potentialities of the labour-process in the
> same proportion as science is incorporated in it as an independent power; they
> distort the conditions under which he works, subject him during the labour-
> process to a despotism the more hateful for its meanness; they transform his
> life time into working time, and drag his wife and children beneath the wheels
> of the Juggernaut of capital. But all methods for the production of surplus-
> value are at the same time methods of accumulation; and every extension of
> accumulation becomes again a means for the development of those methods.
> It follows therefore that in proportion as capital accumulates, the lot of the
> labourer, be his payment high or low, must grow worse. The law . . . establishes
> an accumulation of misery, corresponding with accumulation of capital. Ac-
> cumulation of wealth at one pole is, therefore, at the same time accumulation
> of misery, agony of toil, slavery, ignorance, brutality [and] mental degradation
> at the opposite pole. (Ibid., p. 646)

It should be noted that Marx asserted that laborers would become
worse off even if their wages increased. There were two reasons for this.
First, Marx believed that even if workers' wages increased, they would
not increase by as much as capitalists' profits increased. The worker would
therefore become continuously worse off relative to the capitalist. Second,
Marx correctly foresaw that as the capitalist system progressed, there was
to be an increasingly minute division of labor.

A finer division of labor makes the worker's activities less varied, and
the job becomes more repetitious and tedious. Marx agreed with Adam

Smith, who had stated that "the man whose whole life is spent in performing a few simple operations . . . generally becomes as stupid and ignorant as it is possible for a human creature to become" (Smith, p. 80). Forced into a condition of stupor and increasingly severely alienated, "the lot of the labourer, *be his payment high or low*, must grow worse" (Marx, 1961, Vol. 1, p. 645).

THE CAPITALIST STATE

Marx rejected the notion that socialism could be created through gradual, piecemeal reforms undertaken by the state. By *the state* Marx meant something more than simply any government: "We may speak of a state where a special public power of coercion exists which, in the form of an armed organization, stands over and above the population" (Hook, p. 256).

Many socialists believed the state was (or could be) an impartial arbiter in the affairs of society, and they had faith in moral and intellectual appeals to the state. Marx rejected this idea. "Political power," he declared in the *Communist Manifesto*, "is merely the organized power of one class for oppressing another." During each period of history, or for each mode of production, the state is the coercive instrument of the ruling class.

Friedrich Engels summarized the Marxist argument:

> Former society, moving in class antagonisms, had need of the state, that is, an organization of the exploiting class at each period for the maintenance of external conditions of production; that is, therefore, for the forcible holding down of the exploited class in the conditions of oppression (slavery, villeinage or serfdom, wage labor) determined by the existing mode of production. The state was the official representative of society as a whole, its embodiment in a visible corporation; but it was this only in so far as it was the state of that class which itself, in its epoch, represented society as a whole; in ancient times, the state of the slave-owning citizens; in the Middle Ages, of the feudal nobility; in our epoch, of the bourgeosie. (Engels, p. 295)

Thus the state is simply a dictatorship of the ruling class over the remainder of society.

In the capitalist system a dictatorship has two functions. First, it has the traditional function of enforcing the dictatorship of the capitalists over the rest of society. The state achieves this primarily by enforcing property rights, the source of the capitalists' economic power. It also serves in innumerable other ways—for example, jailing or harassing critics of capitalism, fighting wars to extend capitalists' markets, and providing roads, railroads, canals, postal service, and hundreds of other prerequisites for profitable commerce. Second, the government acts as the arbiter of rivalries among capitalists. Each capitalist is interested only in his own profits, and therefore it is inevitable that the interests of capitalists will clash. If not resolved, many of these clashes would threaten the very existence of the system. Thus the government intervenes, and in doing so it protects the viability of the capitalist system. This is why it is sometimes possible to observe the government acting in a way that is contrary to the interests of some of the capitalists. But the government never acts in a way that is contrary to the interests of *all* capitalists as a class.

For these reasons Marx rejected the notion that socialists could rely on the government for help in bringing about the transition from capitalism to socialism. The establishment of socialism, in Marx's opinion, would require a revolution.

THE SOCIALIST REVOLUTION

In his overall view of capitalism Marx saw the process of capital accumulation as inevitably involving several steps. Business cycles or crises would occur regularly and with increasing severity as the capitalist economy developed. There would be a long-run tendency for the rate of profit to fall, and this would exacerbate the other problems of capitalism. Industrial power would become increasingly concentrated in fewer and fewer giant monopolistic and oligopolistic firms, and wealth would become concentrated in the hands of fewer and fewer capitalists. The plight of the laborer would steadily deteriorate.

Given these increasingly bad conditions, the system could not be perpetuated. Eventually life under capitalism would become so intolerable that workers would revolt, overthrow the whole system, and create a more rational socialist economy:

> Along with the constantly diminishing number of magnates of capital, who usurp and monopolize all advantages of this process of transformation, grows the mass of misery, oppression, slavery, degradation, exploitation; but with this too grows the revolt of the working-class, a class always increasing in numbers, and disciplined, united, organized by the very mechanism of the process of capitalist production itself. The monopoly of capital becomes a fetter upon the mode of production, which has sprung up and flourished along with, and under it. Centralization of the means of production and socialization of labour at last reach a point where they become incompatible with their capitalist integument. This integument is burst asunder. The knell of capitalist private property sounds. The expropriators are expropriated. (Marx, 1961, Vol. 1, p. 763)

In subsequent chapters we shall examine the defenses of capitalism offered in opposition to Marx, as well as the further development of socialist thought after Marx.

SUMMARY

Karl Marx, the most influential of all socialists, based his economic analysis on a theory of history called historical materialism. Most social and political institutions, he believed, were significantly shaped by the economic base of society: the mode of production. Over time, conflicts developed between the forces of production and the relations of production. The working out of these conflicts was the most important element in the historical evolution of society.

Marx's economic writings were aimed at understanding the conflicts between the class system (or private property system) of capitalism and the methods of production and commodity exchange under capitalism and its replacement by a classless, socialist society.

REFERENCES

Engels, Friedrich. "Anti-Duhring." In *Handbook of Marxism*. New York: Random House, 1935.

Hook, Sidney. *Towards the Understanding of Karl Marx*. New York: Day, 1933.

Marx, Karl. *Capital*. Vol 1. Moscow: Foreign Languages Publishing House, 1961.

———. *Economic and Philosophic Manuscripts of 1844*. Moscow: Progress Publishers, 1959.

———, and Friedrich Engels. "The Communist Manifesto." In *Essential Works of Marxism*. Edited by Arthur P. Mendel. New York: Bantam, 1965.

Smith, Adam. *The Wealth of Nations*. Edited by Andrew Skinner. London: Penguin Books, 1970.

Chapter
8

The Rise of Corporate Capitalism and Its Ideological Defenses

The period from the mid-1840s to 1873 (the year that marked the beginning of the Long Depression in Europe) has been called the golden age of competitive capitalism (Dillard, p. 363). These were years of rapid economic expansion throughout most of Europe. Industrialization was getting under way in the United States and continental Europe. The new capital goods necessary for industrialization were, to a large extent, imported from England. Between 1840 and 1860 England experienced an expansion of exports that was more rapid than ever before or since. Capital goods increased from 11 percent of English exports to 22 percent, and exports of coal, iron, and steel also rose sharply.

Between 1830 and 1850, England experienced a railroad-building boom in which some 6000 miles of railroads were constructed. This railroad building created a strong demand for iron, and iron production doubled between the mid-1830s and the mid-1840s. During the next 30 years the increases in industrial production were also very impressive. Between 1850 and 1880 the production of pig iron increased from 2,250,000 to 7,750,000 tons per year; steel production went from 49,000 to 1,440,000 tons; and coal increased by 300 percent, to 147,000,000 tons. The Bessemer converter (in the 1850s), the open-hearth furnace (in the 1860s), and the basic process (in the 1870s) completely revolutionized the steel industry, making large-scale production of high-quality steel possible at much lower costs. The capital goods industries also prospered in the second half of the nineteenth century. Production of machines, ships, chemicals, and other important capital goods employed twice as many workers in 1881 as in 1851.

THE CONCENTRATION OF CORPORATE POWER

Just as competitive capitalism seemed to be achieving its greatest successes, the forces Marx had predicted would lead to the concentration of capital began to show themselves. Improvements in technology were such that larger-sized plants were necessary to take advantage of more efficient methods of production. Competition became so aggressive and destructive that small competitors were eliminated. Large competitors, facing mutual destruction, often combined in cartels, trusts, or mergers in order to ensure their mutual survival. In the United States this competition was particularly intense. (It is described in greater detail in Chapter 9.)

A factor that Marx had nearly overlooked, the revolutionary changes in transportation and communication, led to ever-widening markets that could be efficiently supplied by single companies or corporations. The joint stock company, or corporation, became an effective means by which a single business organization could gain control over vast amounts of capital. A large, well-organized money market evolved in Europe and North America that successfully channeled the smaller capital holdings of many thousands of individuals and small businesses into the hands of large corporations.

In the late nineteenth-century world of giant corporations, in which articles were mass produced for nationwide or worldwide markets, price competition (and indeed sometimes any kind of competition) proved so destructive that it was abandoned almost completely in the large and important industries. There was an inexorable trend toward monopoly power accruing to a few corporations. Many business giants entered into voluntary combinations in which each firm remained somewhat autonomous (e.g., cartels and pools). Other combinations used a financial enterprise such as a trust or holding company to control the voting stock of the corporations involved. Still others used direct mergers and amalgamations from which a single unified corporation emerged.

The English Case

England, where the classical liberal laissez-faire philosophy had taken root most firmly, was perhaps least affected by this movement to corporate monopolies. Advances in technology led to a steel industry made of very large producers. Nevertheless, the fact that England had very few restrictions on imports prevented the industry from combining into an effectively coordinated group until after the trade restrictions of 1932. However, producers of some heavy steel products, such as ship and boiler plate, were able to create effective monopolies much earlier.

In other industries, amalgamations led to heavy concentrations. English railroads were combined very early into four main companies. Banking was consolidated until five large commercial banks dominated the industry by the time of World War I. In 1896 the five rivals in the cotton sewing-thread industry merged into a single monopoly (J. & P. Coats), which came to dominate the world market for that commodity and regularly made profits of 20 percent or more. The firm of Lever Brothers, through amalgamations, gained dominance over the soap business in England as well as in several other countries. Monopolies or closely coordinated oligopolies came to control the wallpaper, salt, petroleum, and rubber industries. Many other industries were either dominated or strongly influenced by a few large firms.

The German Case

In Germany the classical liberal ideology had never really taken root. During Germany's rapid rise to industrial power during the second half of the nineteenth century, there were neither philosophical nor ideological nor legal barriers to large-scale monopolistic industries. It is therefore not surprising that monopolies and combinations were more widespread in Germany than in any other country in Europe. The cartel was the main type of monopolistic business combination in Germany. There were approximately 16 cartels in 1879; the figure rose to 35 by 1885, to 300 by 1900, to 1000 by 1922, and to 2100 by 1930.

Thus by the early twentieth century monopolistic cartels completely dominated almost all the important sectors of the German capitalist economy. (The legal and philosophical justifications of these monopolistic German cartels are discussed in Chapter 9.)

The American Case

In the United States the Civil War gave a great stimulus to industrialization. The war not only increased the demand for industrially produced commodities but also led to the passage of laws that were beneficial to the newly emerging corporations that were soon to dominate American industry.

In an effort to provide civil and political rights for all Americans, Congress had passed the first Civil Rights Act in 1866. By 1868 the Fourteenth Amendment to the U.S. Constitution had been ratified by the states. The ostensible aim of these laws was to confer citizenship and equal rights on American blacks. The Civil Rights Act declared that citizens "of every race and color" were to have equal rights to make contracts, to sue, and enjoy "full and equal benefit of all laws and proceedings for the security of person and property" (Stampp, p. 136).

Most of the Civil Rights Act was incorporated into the Fourteenth Amendment. The Amendment also included the famous due process clause, which prohibited any state government from depriving "any person of life, liberty, or *property*, without due process of law" (ibid.).

For decades after its ratification the Fourteenth Amendment had no effect at all on the civil rights of American blacks; many of them were thrust into situations worse than slavery. Rather, most court decisions based on the Fourteenth Amendment involved corporations. The courts ruled that corporations were persons and, as such, were protected under the due process clause.

Each time a state government attempted to curb the extravagant excesses of corporations by passing regulatory legislation, the federal courts would invalidate the legislation because it violated the due process clause of the amendment. State governments became powerless before the growing strength of large corporations.

Representative John A. Bingham, who had written the due process clause, later admitted that he had phrased it "word for word and syllable for syllable" to protect the rights of private property and corporations. Representative Roscoe Conkling, who had also helped frame the Amendment, later declared: "At the time the Fourteenth Amendment was ratified, individuals and *joint stock companies* were appealing for congressional and administrative protection against invidious and discriminating state and local taxes. . . . [The Fourteenth Amendment embodies] the Golden Rule, so entrenched as to curb the many who would do to the few as they would not have the few do to them" (ibid.).

With the knowledge that they could go to almost any length in their pursuit of profits without fear of state government controls, the corporations thrived. They grew through internal expansion and, more important, by absorbing their competitors. As the giant corporations flourished, the entire American economy thrived and grew.

By the turn of the century, the United States had become the leading industrial power in the world. By 1913, when the American economy produced over one-third of the world's industrial output—more than double that of its closest competitor, Germany—most of the strategic industries (railroads, meatpacking, banking in the large cities, steel, copper, and aluminum) and important areas of manufacturing were dominated by a relatively small number of immensely powerful corporations.

With the exception of the railroads, most industries in the immediate post-Civil War years had been relatively atomistic by present-day standards. Although accurate statistics are not available for this early period, it has been estimated that the 200 largest nonfinancial enterprises would have controlled a very minor and inconsequential percentage of all business assets. By the end of the 1920s this had grown to 33 percent of all assets (Bain, 1959, pp. 191–192).

The primary cause of this concentration was the wave of combinations and mergers that took place at an unprecedented rate during the last quarter of the nineteenth century. This merger movement was the outgrowth of the particularly severe competition that had ravaged and destroyed scores of businesses. During this period many people began to question seriously the liberal notion of the invisible hand. It seemed to them that unrestrained individualism had led to unrestrained warfare.

> As growing giant businesses locked horns, railroad against railroad, steel mill against steel mill, each sought to assure the coverage of its fixed expenses by gaining for itself as much of the market as it could. The outcome was the steady growth of cutthroat competition among massive producers. . . . On the Railroads for example, constant rate-wars were fought in the 1870s. In the oil fields, the coal fields, among the steel and copper producers, similar price-wars repeatedly broke out as producers sought to capture the markets. (Heilbroner, p. 120)

The outcome of such competition was the destruction or absorption of small competitors. Eventually only giants remained, and at this point further competition was immensely destructive to all competitors. The merger movement represented the means whereby the surviving firms could escape this competition.

> The scope of the merger movement was so great that by 1904 it had basically altered the structure of American industry. By the beginning of that year there were over three hundred large industrial combinations with a combined capitalization in excess of $7,000,000,000. They controlled more than two-fifths of the manufacturing capital of the country and had affected about four-fifths of important American industries. (Bain, 1951, p. 619)

THE CONCENTRATION OF INCOME

Accompanying this concentration of industry was an equally striking concentration of income in the hands of a small percentage of the population. Although no accurate statistics for the early part of the period exist, it seems reasonably certain that the degree of concentration increased substantially between 1870 and 1929. By 1929 just 5 percent of the population received 34 percent of personal disposable income in the United States. The degree of concentration had probably reached this extreme as early as 1913. By the end of the 1920s, the highest one-fifth of "families and unattached individuals" were receiving more than 50 percent of all personal income.

REEMERGENCE OF THE CLASSICAL LIBERAL IDEOLOGY

With this immense concentration of economic power in the hands of a small number of giant firms and a small percentage of the population, it would seem that the classical liberal ideology of capitalism would have been abandoned. The economic creed of classical liberalism, as developed by Adam Smith and refined by such well-known classical economists as David Ricardo, Nassau Senior, and J. B. Say, was based on an analysis of an economy composed of many small enterprises. In such an economy no individual enterprise could exercise a significant influence on the market price or on the total amount sold in the market. The actions of any firm were dictated to it by consumer tastes, as registered in the marketplace, and by the competition of innumerable other small firms, each vying for the consumer's dollars.

As wide as the gulf between classical economic theory and late nineteenth-century economic reality seems to have been, the economic creed of classical liberalism did not fall by the wayside in this later period. Rather, it was combined with Benthamite utilitarianism (which was already implicit in Adam Smith's normative model of the invisible hand) and refurbished within an elaborate and esoteric framework of algebra and calculus. This resurgence of the classical liberal economic creed was accomplished by a new school of economic thinkers known as *neoclassical* economists.

THE NEOCLASSICAL THEORY OF UTILITY AND CONSUMPTION

During the early 1870s, at precisely the time when the drive toward the economic concentration of corporate capitalism was taking place, three very famous economics texts were published. William Stanley Jevons's *The Theory of Political Economy* and Karl Menger's *Grundsätze der Volkswirtschaftslehre* both appeared in 1871, and three years later Léon Walras's *Eléments d'économie politique pure* was published. Although there were many differences among the analyses of these men, the similarities in both approach and content of these books were striking.

Their theories pictured an economy composed of large numbers of small producers and consumers, each having insufficient power to influence the market significantly. The business firms hired or bought factors of production; they utilized the factors in the production process in such a way that their profits were maximized. Prices of the final products and factors of production were taken as given and beyond their control. The firms could control only the productive process chosen and the amount produced.

Households likewise sold their land and capital, as well as their labor, at prices determined in the market and used the receipts (their incomes) to buy goods and services. Consumers apportioned their income among the various commodities they wished to purchase in a way that maximized the utility they received from these commodities.

Commodities were the ultimate source of pleasure or utility, and the utility they yielded was assumed to be quantifiable. Jevons wrote, "A unit of pleasure or pain is difficult even to conceive; but it is the amount of these feelings which is continually prompting us to buying and selling, borrowing and lending, laboring and resting, producing and consuming; *and it is from the quantitative effects of the feelings that we must estimate their comparative amounts*" (Jevons, p. 11).

Walras was less ambiguous in arguing that utility was quantifiable: "I shall, therefore, assume the existence of a standard measure of intensity of wants or intensive utility, which is applicable not only to similar units of the same kind of wealth but also to different units of various kinds of wealth" (Walras, p. 117).

These economists, having presumably quantifiable magnitudes with which to work, next set up general mathematical formulas purporting to show a functional relationship between the utility a consumer received and the amounts of the various commodities he or she consumed. The problem then was to show how the consumer could get the maximum utility, given his or her income and the commodity prices prevailing in the market.

Consumers maximized utility when the increase in utility derived from the last unit consumed, expressed as a ratio over the price of that commodity, was an equal proportion for all commodities. In other words, the last dollar spent on a commodity should yield the same increase in the utility derived by the consumer as the last dollar spent on any other commodity. Jevons explained the same thing in a different way, stating that the consumer maximized utility because he or she "procures such quantities of commodities that the final degrees of utility of any pair of commodities are inversely as the ratios of exchange [prices] of the commodities" (Jevons, p. 139).

Suppose there were a free market in which consumers could freely exchange their incomes for commodities. They would be led by their self-interest to maximize utility. Therefore it was concluded that consumers distributed their income among purchases of commodities in such a way that the welfare of all would be maximized, given the existing distribution of wealth and income.

THE NEOCLASSICAL THEORY OF PRODUCTION

In neoclassical production theory the analysis of the business firm was perfectly symmetrical with the analysis of consumer behavior. In order to maximize profits, the firm would operate at its highest efficiency and hence produce at the lowest possible cost. It purchased factors of production (such as labor) until the amount added to production by the last unit of each factor of production, expressed as a ratio over the price of the factor, was an equal proportion for all factors. The last dollar spent on each factor should yield the same increase in production from all factors. In a free market, firms would always attempt to maximize efficiency in order to maximize profits. Therefore this condition would always hold. Thus the factors of production would all be used in such a way that no possible reorganization of production (given the existing technology) could result in a more efficient use of the factors of production.

Neoclassical economists also believed that if an economy were characterized by a free market with many small competitive firms, then each commodity would be produced in such quantities and with such methods that it would be impossible to shift resources from the production of one commodity to the production of a different one without diminishing that total value of what was produced in the market economy.

LAISSEZ-FAIRE

Thus the neoclassical economists gave a very elaborate and esoteric analytic defense of Adam Smith's notion of the invisible hand of market competition and the economic policy of laissez-faire. They showed that, in a competitive market economy made up of innumerable small producers and consumers, the market would guide the consumers in such a way that they would end up with an optimal mix of commodities, *given their original income and wealth.* Factors of production would be used in the most efficient way possible. Moreover, commodities would be produced in amounts that would maximize the value of society's production. This optimal result depended, however, on a minimum of interference by government in the processes of the free market.

They recognized that this result was optimal if one accepted the existing distribution of income. Some (particularly the American economist John Bates Clark) tried to defend the distribution of income that obtained in a free-market economy. They argued that the principles of profit maximization would lead to a situation in which each category of productive factors would be paid an amount equal to the value of its marginal contribution to the productive process. This seemed to them a model of distributive justice, with each unit of the productive factors being paid an amount equal to what it produced. Critics were quick to point out, however, that units of productive factors were not people (at least as far as land, natural resources, and capital were concerned). In order for such a system to be fair, these critics insisted, an equitable distribution of ownership of the factors of production would be necessary.

Nevertheless, the neoclassical economists did succeed in erecting an impressive intellectual defense of the classical liberal policy of laissez-faire. They did it by creating a giant chasm between economic theory and economic reality, however. From the 1870s until today, many economists in the neoclassical tradition have abandoned any real concern with existing economic institutions and problems. Instead, many of them have retired to the rarefied stratosphere of mathematical model building, constructing endless variations on esoteric trivia.

SUBSEQUENT MODIFICATIONS OF NEOCLASSICAL THEORY

Some economists in the second and third generations of neoclassical analysis recognized the need to make the theory more realistic. The economic system was *not* characterized by "perfect competition"; it had flaws. The principal admitted weaknesses were as follows: (1) Some buyers and sellers *were* large enough to affect prices; moreover, the economics of large-scale production seemed to render this inevitable. (2) Some commodities should be "consumed socially," and their production and sale might never be profitable in a laissez-faire capitalist economy, even though they might be deemed highly desirable by most citizens (e.g., roads, schools, or armies). (3) The costs to the producer of a commodity (such as automobiles) might differ significantly from the social costs (such as smog) of producing that commodity. In such a case it was possible that for society as a whole the costs of production might exceed the benefits of production for the commodity, even though the producer still profited from making and selling it. For example, consider the poisoning of the water and air by producers making profits but doing little or nothing about the evil, even though its side effects could endanger human life itself. (4) An unrestrained free-market capitalist system appeared to be quite unstable, being subject to recurring depressions that incurred enormous social waste. The free-market, capitalist economy always resulted in massive inequalities of income, with those at the bottom of the income distribution being unable to live even at a subsistence standard, while those at the top enjoyed colossal incomes, often hundreds of times higher than an ordinary person would spend on consumption.

It was generally agreed that such flaws did exist and did disrupt the otherwise beneficial workings of the capitalist system, but they could be corrected only by some amount of government intervention in the market system. Government antitrust actions, it was argued, could force giant firms to act as if they were competitive, and something called "workable competition" could be achieved. Roads, schools, armies, and other socially consumed commodities could be provided by the government. Extensive systems of special taxes and subsidies could be used to equate private and social costs in cases where they differed. It was also believed (especially after the 1930s), that through wise use of fiscal and monetary policy the government could eliminate the instability of the system. (This last point is discussed in more detail in Chapter 12.) Finally, through taxes and welfare programs government could mitigate the unacceptable extremes of the income distribution.

The flaws in the system were thus seen as minor and ephemeral. An enlightened government could correct them and free the invisible hand once again to create the best of all possible worlds. There did develop, however, an inability to agree on the extent and significance of the flaws. Those who believe them to be fairly widespread and quite significant have, during the course of the twentieth century, become known as *liberals*. They have sometimes advocated fairly extensive government intervention in the economic system, but most have continued to use neoclassical economic theory as an ideology to defend the private-ownership, capitalist market economic system.

Economists who see the flaws as minor and unimportant continue to advocate a minimum of government intervention in the market economy. Despite the fact that the laissez-faire policies advocated by these economists have been much closer to those advocated by the nineteenth-century classical liberals, they have become known in the twentieth century as *conservatives*. Both liberals and conservatives, as we have described them here, have used neoclassical economic theory to justify the capitalist system.

LAISSEZ-FAIRE AND THE SOCIAL DARWINISTS

Before we leave the topic of late nineteenth- and early twentieth-century advocates of laissez-faire capitalism, a brief discussion of social Darwinism is necessary. *Social Darwinists* believed the government should allow capitalists to compete freely in the marketplace with a minimum of government restrictions and, in general, favored as little government intervention as possible in all spheres of life. Therefore many people have imagined their defense of laissez-faire capitalism to be similar to that of the neoclassical economists. This is not so. Their policy recommendations were based on a substantially different theoretical framework.

The social Darwinists took Darwin's theory of evolution and extended it to a theory of social evolution (in a manner that Darwin himself strongly disapproved of, it may be added). Competition, they believed, was a teleological process in which each succeeding generation was superior to the preceding one. This upward progress was made possible because those least fit to survive did not succeed in maintaining themselves and procreating. Greater ability to survive was equated with a biological as well as a moral superiority.

Herbert Spencer (1820–1903), the father of social Darwinism, based his evolutionary as well as his moral theory on what he called the *law of conduct and consequence*. He believed survival of the human species could be ensured only if society distributed its benefits in proportion to a person's merit, measured by his or her power to be self-sustaining. One ought to reap the benefits or suffer the evil results of one's own actions. Thus the people most adapted to their environment would prosper, and those least adapted would be weeded out—provided that the laws of conduct and consequence were observed. If the government, wishing to mitigate inequalities of wealth and income in society, took "from him who . . . [had] prospered to give to him who . . . [had] not, it [violated] its duty towards the one to do more than its duty towards the other" (quoted in Fine, p. 38). This type of action slowed social progress and could, if carried to excess, destroy the human species. Survival and progress could be ensured only if the weak were weeded out and destroyed by the impersonal forces of social evolution.

In Spencer's opinion, "the poverty of the incapable, the distresses that come upon the imprudent, the starvation of the idle and those shoulderings aside of the weak by the strong . . . are the decrees of a large, far-seeing benevolence" (ibid., p. 38). Spencer categorically opposed any action by the government that interfered with trade, commerce, production, or the distribution of wealth or income. He rejected welfare payments of any kind, attempts to decrease the economic insecurity of workers, and government provision of schools, parks, or libraries as detrimental to human progress. His laissez-faire was thus much more extreme than that of the classical economists or most of the conservative neoclassical economists.

Social Darwinists accepted the large monopolistic and oligopolistic industries as the beneficient result of evolution. Neoclassical economists, if they did not simply define away or ignore the concentrations of economic power, believed government should attempt to create a more competitive and atomistic market situation. In this very important respect the two theories were thus quite antagonistic.

LAISSEZ-FAIRE AND THE IDEOLOGY OF BUSINESSMEN

Most businessmen, however, were not very concerned with intellectual inconsistency. They feared radical and socialist reformers who wanted to use the government as a means of achieving greater equality, and they welcomed any theory that concluded that the government should not intervene in the economic process. Even though they themselves used the government to promote their own interests (through special tariffs, tax concessions, land grants, and a host of other special privileges), they relied on laissez-faire arguments when threatened with any social reform that might erode their status, wealth, or income. Thus in the ordinary businessman's ideology of the late nineteenth and early twentieth centuries there was a general attempt to combine neoclassical economics and social Darwinism.

In this ideology the accumulation of wealth was considered de facto proof of evolutionary superiority, whereas poverty was believed to be evidence of evolutionary inferiority. Success, asserted writer Benjamin Woods, was "nothing more or less than doing thoroughly what others did indifferently." Andrew Carnegie equated success with "honest work, ability and concentration"; another businessman argued that "wealth has always been the natural sequence to industry, temperance, and perseverance, and it will always so continue." At the same time, S. C. T. Dodd, solicitor for Standard Oil, maintained that poverty existed "because nature or the devil has made some men weak and imbecile and others lazy and worthless, and neither man nor God can do much for one who will do nothing for himself." (These quotations are cited in Fine, p. 98.)

The beneficial results of competition in neoclassical economic theory seemed to reinforce reliance on the "survival of the fittest" in the "struggle for survival." "Competition in economics," asserted Richard R. Bowker, "is the same as the law of . . . 'natural selection' in nature" (ibid., p. 100).

Although some businessmen and their spokesmen were trying to perpetuate the laissez-faire conclusions of the classical liberal ideology of capitalism, many defenders of the capitalist system believed that in the new age of mass production (with gigantic concentrations of wealth and power in the hands of so few corporations and capitalists) the older, individualistic, laissez-faire ideology was no longer appropriate. The late nineteenth century witnessed a rebirth of the older paternalistic ethic. In the next section we examine a new ideology of capitalism that was based, in many essential respects, on a new version of the Christian paternalist ethic.

A NEW CHRISTIAN PATERNALIST ETHIC

The distance separating the neoclassical liberal ideology of capitalism and economic reality impressed itself on the minds of many academicians and businessmen. The result was a new ideology for the new age of corporate capitalism. Just as the new industrial and financial entrepreneurs came to resemble the feudal robber barons, so the new ideology resembled the feudal version of the Christian paternalist ethic. It emphasized the natural superiority of a small elite, the new industrial and financial magnates, and the paternalistic functions of that elite in caring for the masses.

The new ideology reflected the fact that many of the wealthy capitalists of the era were becoming something of folk heroes among the general public. The last two decades of the nineteenth century and the first three of the twentieth were an age during which the businessman became the most admired social type. The success of businessmen was viewed as de facto proof that they possessed virtues superior to those of the ordinary person. This version of success was the theme of the biographies of William Makepeace Thackeray and the novels of Horatio Alger. These men and other writers created a cult of success that viewed the increase of industrial concentration as proof of Darwinian superiority on the part of the industrialists, glorified the self-made individual, and kept the Horatio Alger rags-to-riches myth constantly in the public mind.

The veneration of businessmen, added to the strong rejection of destructive competition by both businessmen and the general public, led to a new conservative version of the Christian paternalist ethic, which resembled the philosophy of the Tory radicals of the late eighteenth and early nineteenth centuries. The unfortunate plight of the poor received prominent mention in the new writings. This problem, as well as that of economic instability, could best be solved, according to the new ideology, by encouraging cooperation among the leaders of the giant corporations. Competition was viewed as antisocial. Through cooperation business cycles could be eliminated and the plight of the poor improved.

This new version of the Christian paternalist ethic received the support of Pope Leo XIII (1810–1903). Between 1878 and 1901 the pope sought to analyze the problems of corporate capitalism and to suggest remedies in a series of encyclicals. In *Rerum novarum* (1891) he argued that "a remedy must be found . . . for the misery and wretchedness which press so heavily at this moment on the large majority of the very poor." He continued with a condemnation of unrestrained laissez-faire competition:

> Working men have been given over, isolated and defenseless, to the callousness of employers and the greed of unrestrained competition. The evil has been increased by rapacious usury . . . still practiced by avaricious and grasping men. And to this must be added the custom of working by contract, and the concentration of so many branches of trade in the hands of a few individuals, so that a small number of very rich men have been able to lay upon the masses of the poor a yoke little better than slavery itself. (Quoted in Fusfeld, p. 86)

This passage, which sounds so socialist in tone and content, was followed by a strong condemnation of socialism and a defense of private property. The pope hoped the problems could be corrected by rejection of competition and a return to the Christian virtues of love and brotherhood, with the leaders of business and industry leading the way to a new Christian paternalism within the context of a private property capitalist system.

The German Version

The new paternalistic ideology was probably strongest in Germany, where classical liberalism had never gained a good hold and industrial concentration was most pronounced. A famous German economist, Gustave Schmoller, expressed the very widely held view that

> the proper kind of cartelization creates more or less a system of justice and equity. . . . The directors of the cartels are educators who wish to bring about the triumph of wide interests of a branch of industry over the egoistic interests of the individual. . . . The cartel system is like a co-operative or merchant's association, an important element in the education of commercial and technical officials who want to make money but who have also learned to put themselves in the service of general interests and to administer the property of others in a loyal and honorable fashion. (Quoted in Pinson, p. 236)

Cartels were also widely justified as means of eliminating economic crises. A German court decision, one of several that formed the legal justification of the cartel system in that country, stated, "Indeed the formation of syndicates and cartels . . . has repeatedly been considered a device especially useful for the economy as a whole since they can prevent uneconomic overproduction and ensuing catastrophe" (quoted in Dillard, p. 396).

The American Version

In the United States, as mentioned earlier, the new ideology thrived in an atmosphere that venerated the successful businessman and was extremely weary of destructive competition. The view of many American industrial and financial magnates was expressed by Andrew Carnegie, one of the most successful of the magnates:

> Not evil, but good, has come to the race from the accumulation of wealth by those who have the ability and energy that produce it. . . . We have the true antidote for the temporary unequal distribution of wealth, the reconciliation of the rich and the poor—a reign of harmony—another ideal, differing, indeed, from that of the Communist in requiring only further evolution of existing conditions, not the total overthrow of our civilization. . . . Under its sway we shall have an ideal state, in which the surplus wealth of the few will become in the best sense, the property of the many, because administered for the common good, this wealth passing through the hands of the few can be made a more potent force for the elevation of our race than if it were distributed in sums to the people themselves. (Carnegie, pp. 3, 5, 6)

Carnegie argued, and many businessmen and their spokesmen agreed, that the millionaire would be "a trustee for the poor, entrusted for a season with a great part of the increased wealth of the community, but administering it for the community far better than it could or would have done for itself (Kennedy, p. xii).

The Right Reverend William Lawrence gave the new elitist view the sanction of religion. "In the long run, it is only to the man of morality that wealth comes. . . . Godliness is in league with riches." Railroad president George F. Baer had the same idea in mind when he tried to assure railroad workers that "the rights and the interests of the laboring man will be protected and cared for, not by the labor agitators, but by the Christian men to whom God, in his infinite wisdom, has given control of the property interests of the country" (ibid.).

SIMON PATTEN'S ECONOMIC BASIS FOR THE NEW ETHIC

Perhaps the most influential academic spokesman for the new corporate ideology was Dr. Simon N. Patten, professor of economics at the University of Pennsylvania from 1888 to 1917 and one of the founders of the American Economic Association (see Hunt, 1970, pp. 38–55). In keeping with the paternalistic element of the new ideology, Patten denounced the poverty and economic exploitation of his era. The following passage could almost have been written by a Marxist of that era:

> There have flowed then, side by side, two streams of life, one bearing the working poor, who perpetuate themselves through qualities generated by the stress and mutual dependence of the primitive world, and the other bearing aristocracies, who dominate by means of the laws and traditions giving them control of the social surplus. (Patten, 1907, p. 39)

In the same vein, 15 years later, he wrote:

> The glow of Fifth Avenue is but the reflection of a distant hell into which
> unwilling victims are cast. Some resource is misused, some town degraded, to
> create the flow of funds on which our magnates thrive. From Pennsylvania,
> rich in resources, trains go loaded and come back empty. For the better half
> no return is made except in literary tomes designed to convince the recipients
> that exploitation is not robbery. . . . But Nature revolts! Never does the rising
> sun see children yanked from bed to increase the great Strauss dividends, nor
> the veteran cripples of the steel mill tramping in their beggar garb, but that
> it shrivels, reddens, and would strike but for the sight of happier regions beyond.
> (Ibid., 1922, p. 226)

This poverty and exploitation were, in Patten's opinion, the last vestiges
of an earlier age characterized by scarcity. In the economy of scarcity
capitalists competed aggressively with each other, with the result that laborers as well as the general public suffered. The fierce competition of the
robber barons, however, had marked a watershed in history. The merger
movement that followed this competition was the beginning of a new era,
an era of plenty rather than scarcity. Capitalists were becoming socialized.
They were putting the public welfare ahead of their pursuit of profits, and
in doing this they eschewed competition, recognizing that the public welfare could best be promoted by cooperation. (Of course we have seen that
capitalists cooperated with each other mostly to squeeze more profit from
the public.)

Evidence that the conditions of economic prosperity at the turn of the
century were socializing capitalists could be seen in the fact that "hospitals
. . . [were] established, schools . . . [were] made free, colleges . . . [were]
endowed, museums, libraries, and art galleries . . . [received] liberal support, church funds . . . [grew] and missions . . . [were] formed at home
and abroad." (ibid., 1902, p. 170). On almost every policy issue of his
day, Patten took a strongly proindustrial capitalist position. He viewed the
late nineteenth-century captains of industry as a paternally beneficent
elite:

> The growth of large-scale capitalism has resulted in the elimination of the
> unsocial capitalist and the increasing control of each industry by the socialized
> groups. . . . At bottom altruistic sentiment is the feeling of a capitalist expressing
> itself in sympathy for the laborer. This desire of upper class men to improve
> the conditions of lower classes is a radically different phenomenon from the
> pressure exerted by the lower classes for their own betterment. The lower
> class movement stands for the control of the state by themselves in their own
> interests. The upper class movement directs itself against the bad environmental
> conditions preventing the expression of character. (Patten, 1924, p. 292)

He believed competition should be discouraged by taxing competitive
firms and exempting trusts and monopolies from these taxes. This would
benefit all society by eliminating the extensive waste created by competition. In *The Stability of Prices* he argued that competition was largely
responsible for the economic instability of the late nineteenth century.
When the movement toward trusts and monopolies had been completed,

production would be controlled and planned in such a way that this instability would be eliminated.

Patten's paternalistic ideology was, like the liberal ideology of capitalism, ultimately a plea for a minimum of government interference with the actions of businessmen. The government was to interfere in the economy only by encouraging trusts and monopolies and discouraging competition. In Patten's scheme all important social and economic reforms were to be carried out voluntarily by the socialized capitalists in a system of cooperative corporate collectivism.

THE NEW PATERNALISM AND THE NEW DEAL

Patten's version of the new ideology of corporate capitalism was to be very important historically. When the Great Depression of the 1930s struck, two of Patten's students and devotees, Rexford Guy Tugwell and Frances Perkins, had influential positions as members of Roosevelt's original cabinet. (For a more complete discussion of the material covered in this section, see Hunt, 1971, pp. 180–192). Tugwell had asserted that Patten's views "were the greatest single influence on my thought. Neither Veblen nor Dewey found their orientation to the future as completely and instinctively as did Patten. The magnificence of his conceptions and the basic rightness of his vision become clearer as time passes. I am eternally grateful to him" (quoted in Gruchy, p. 408). Perkins believed her former teacher to be "one of the greatest men America has ever produced" (quoted in Schlesinger, 1965, p. 229).

Through these two former students Patten exerted a considerable influence on the economic policies of the early phase of the New Deal. His ideas helped create the intellectual basis of the National Industrial Recovery Act of 1933 (ibid., p. 98). Patten was not, of course, the only source of these ideas. During World War I, the War Industries Board had generated enthusiasm for corporate collectivism. Throughout the 1920s, trade associations prospered and the doctrine of business self-government gained many adherents in the business world. In 1922, Franklin Roosevelt was president of one such association: the American Construction Council. However, Patten's teachings were unquestionably influential. His protégés, Tugwell and Perkins, were both instrumental in the actual framing of the National Industrial Recovery Act (NIRA).

The NIRA proclaimed the intent of Congress "to promote the organization of industry for the purpose of cooperative action among trade groups" (quoted in ibid., pp. 98–99). The bill contained sections providing for codes of fair competition that permitted and even encouraged cooperative price fixing and market sharing and for virtually complete exemption from antitrust laws. Section 7A was designed to promote labor organization but was so diluted that very often it promoted the formation of company unions. "If it [the NIRA] worked, Tugwell thought, each industry would end with a government of its own under which it could promote its fundamental purpose ('production rather than competition'). The NIRA could have been administered, Tugwell later wrote, so that a 'great collectivism' would have channeled American energy into a disciplined national effort to establish a secure basis for well-being" (quoted in ibid., p. 108).

In explaining the bill to the National Association of Manufacturers, General Hugh S. Johnson, the first head of the National Recovery Administration (NRA), declared that "NRA is exactly what industry organized in trade associations makes it." He further asserted that before the NRA the trade associations had about as much effectiveness as an "Old Ladies' Knitting Society; now I am talking to a cluster of formerly emasculated trade associations about a law which proposes for the first time to give them power" (quoted in ibid., p. 110).

Most of the economics literature that appeared in 1934 recognized that the early New Deal reforms had not significantly extended government control over business. On the contrary, it had given voluntary trade associations the support of the government in forcing the controls of trade associations on all industry (see Rogin, pp. 338, 346, 349–355).

This experiment in business self-government proved disastrous. The distinguished historian Arthur M. Schlesinger, Jr., has assessed the success of this phase of the early New Deal. With Schlesinger we concur:

> And the result of business self-government? Restriction on production, chiseling of labor and of 7A, squeezing out of small business, savage personal criticism of the President, and the general tendency to trample down everyone in the rush for profits. Experience was teaching Roosevelt what instinct and doctrine had taught Jefferson and Jackson; that to reform capitalism you must fight the capitalists tooth and nail. (Schlesinger, 1959, pp. 30–31)

The early New Deal philosophy underlying the NIRA was very quickly abandoned. The NIRA was declared unconstitutional by the Supreme Court. The new paternalistic ideology of capitalism, however, was to receive more elaborate statements after World War II.

SUMMARY

In the late nineteenth century capitalism was characterized by the growth of giant corporations. Control of most of the important industries became more and more concentrated. Accompanying this concentration of industry was an equally striking concentration of income in the hands of a small percentage of the population.

In view of these facts it would seem that the classical liberal ideology (which depended on an analysis of an economy based on many small, relatively powerless enterprises) would have had to be abandoned. The gulf that separated the theory from reality had widened into a giant chasm. But the idea that the market economy channeled acquisitive profit seeking into socially benevolent practices was simply too elegant an apologia for un-restrained profit-making activity. The classical liberal ideology of capitalism was thus even more assiduously disseminated in a new school of neoclassical economics.

An elaborate deductive theory permitted the neoclassical economists to defend the classical policy prescription of laissez-faire. Conservative neoclassical economists assigned to the government only the tasks that would directly or indirectly promote business profits. Liberal neoclassical economists also believed the government should enter a limited number of other areas in which the operation of the free market did not maximize the social welfare. Whether in the hands of the conservative or the liberal faction, neoclassical economics remained essentially an ideological defense for the status quo.

Social Darwinist ideology and the ideology of most businessmen de-fended many of the neoclassical economists' conclusions. They did so, however, on entirely different grounds. They accepted the fact that cor-porate power, personal wealth, and personal income were highly concen-trated. This, they believed, was evidence of the evolutionary superiority of the wealthy and, as such, was socially beneficial.

During this period, however, many ideologists of capitalism rejected classical liberalism because of its unrealistic assumptions. These thinkers created a new version of the Christian paternalist ethic that pictured cap-italists as beneficent, fatherly protectors of the public welfare. This new ethic was to become particularly influential in the social and economic legislation of the early New Deal in the 1930s.

REFERENCES

Bain, Joe S. *Industrial Organization.* New York: Wiley, 1959.

———. "Industrial Concentration and Anti-Trust Policy." In *Growth of the American Economy,* 2d ed. Edited by Harold F. Williamson. Englewood Cliffs, N.J.: Prentice-Hall, 1951.

Carnegie, Andrew. "Wealth." In: Kennedy, Gail, ed. *Democracy and the Gospel of Wealth.*

Dillard, Dudley. *Economic Development of the North Atlantic Community.* Engle-wood Cliffs, N.J.: Prentice-Hall, 1967.

Fine, Sidney. *Laissez Faire and the General Welfare State.* Ann Arbor: University of Michigan Press, 1964.

Fusfeld, Daniel R. *The Age of the Economist.* Glenview, Ill.: Scott, Foresman, 1966.

Gruchy, Allan G. *Modern Economic Thought: The American Contribution.* New York: Augustus M. Kelley, 1967.

Heilbroner, Robert L. *The Making of Economic Society.* Englewood Cliffs, N.J.: Prentice-Hall, 1962.

Hunt, E. K. "A Neglected Aspect of the Economic Ideology of the Early New Deal." *Review of Social Economy*, September 1971.

———. "Simon N. Patten's Contribution to Economics." *Journal of Economic Issues*, December 1970.

Jevons, William Stanley. *The Theory of Political Economy*. 1st ed. London: Macmillan, 1871.

Kennedy, Gail, ed. *Democracy and the Gospel of Wealth*. Lexington, Mass.: Raytheon/Heath, 1949.

Menger, Karl. *Grundsätze der Volkswirtschaftslehre*. Translated as *Principles of Economics*. New York: Free Press, 1950.

Patten, Simon Nelson. *Mud Hollow*. Philadelphia: Dorrance, 1922.

———. *The New Basis of Civilization*. New York: Macmillan, 1907.

———. "The Reconstruction of Economic Theory." Reprinted in *Simon Nelson Patten, Essays in Economic Theory*. Edited by Rexford Guy Tugwell. New York: Knopf, 1924.

———. *The Theory of Prosperity*. New York: Macmillan, 1902.

Pinson, Koppel S. *Modern Germany: Its History and Civilization*. New York: Macmillan, 1954.

Rogin, Leo. "The New Deal: A Survey of Literature." *Quarterly Journal of Economics*, May 1935.

Schlesinger, Arthur M., Jr. "The Broad Accomplishments of the New Deal." In *The New Deal: Revolution*. Edited by Edwin C. Rozwenc. Lexington, Mass.: Raytheon/Heath, 1959.

———. *The Coming of the New Deal*. Boston: Houghton Mifflin, 1965.

Stampp, Kenneth M. *The Era of Reconstruction, 1865–1877*. New York: Random House, Vintage Books, 1967.

U.S. Department of Commerce. *Historical Statistics of the United States*. Washington, D.C.: GPO, 1961.

Walras, Leon. *Elements d'économie politique pure*. Translated as *Elements of Pure Economics*. Homewood, Ill.: Irwin, 1957.

Chapter
9

The Consolidation of Monopoly Power and the Writings of Veblen

The process of industrialization in the United States after the Civil War involved, in its initial stages, a competition among industrial and financial capitalists that was unique in its ferocity. From 1860 until the early 1880s the strongest and shrewdest businessmen built great empires with the fruits of economic conquest. The great improvements in transportation that occurred during this period, the rise of standardization in parts and finished products, and the increased efficiency in large-scale mass production created the possibility of nationwide markets. The stakes in the economic struggle were very large, and the participants neither asked for quarter nor received any.

COMPETITION AS INDUSTRIAL WARFARE

Examples of the industrial warfare of the time have filled many books (see, e.g., Josephson). In the oil industry, for example, John D. Rockefeller and Henry M. Flagler shipped so much oil that they were able to demand large concessions from the railroads. With this cost advantage they could undersell competitors. Their company, which was incorporated in 1870 under the name of Standard Oil Company of Ohio, was able to force many competitors to the wall and thus achieve regional monopolies, at which point the price could be substantially increased without fear of competition. After securing large rebates on transport costs, Standard Oil's share in the petroleum industry quickly increased from 10 to 20 percent. But the company did not stop there. Next it succeeded in forcing the railroads to give it rebates on its *competitors'* shipments as well as "all data relating to shipper, buyer, product, price and terms of payment," a scheme that "provided Rockefeller and his associates with rebates on all their own shipments, rebates on all shipments by their competitors, and in addition a complete spy system on their competitors" (Dillard, p. 410). With this power Rockefeller was able to smash most of his competitors. By 1879, only 9 years after incorporation, Standard Oil controlled between 90 and 95 percent of the nation's output of refined petroleum. A sympathetic biographer of Rockefeller has written, "Of all the devices for the extinction of competition, this was the cruelest and most deadly yet conceived by any group of American industrialists" (Nevins, p. 325).

Competition among the railroad magnates was particularly intense. Rate wars were common, forcing weaker competitors out of business and giving stronger competitors monopoly power over large regions. The battles sometimes got so brutal that locomotives were crashed into each other and track was destroyed. The railroads also extorted money from towns along proposed railroad lines. A member of the California Constitutional Convention of 1878 described the technique:

> They start out their railroad track and survey their line near a thriving village. They go to the most prominent citizens of that village and say, "If you will give us so many thousand dollars we will run through here; if you do not we will run by." And in every instance where the subsidy was not granted this course was taken and the effect was just as they said, to kill off the little town. (Josephson, pp. 84–85)

According to the same report, the railroad "blackmailed Los Angeles County for $230,000 as a condition of doing that which the law compelled them to do." The railroads also manipulated connections with politicians to get government handouts of public lands. It is estimated that these giveaways amounted to 158,293,000 acres—a greater land area than that of some whole countries. The railroads were certainly not in favor of a laissez-faire policy in practice.

The great entrepreneurs of that age were definitely not men of estimable social conscience. Many founded their fortunes on the Civil War. When shortages of supplies became desperate, they received high prices for selling to the army "shoddy blankets, so many doctored horses, and useless rifles, [and] . . . stores of sickening beef." In order to eliminate their competitors, they did not hesitate to use hired thugs, kidnapping, and dynamite. Likewise, they stopped at nothing as they milked the public of millions of dollars through stock frauds, schemes, and swindles. Some of these actions were legal and some were not, but the dominant mood of these capitalist entrepreneurs was expressed by Cornelius Vanderbilt, who, when cautioned about the questionable legality of a desired course of action, exclaimed, "What do I care about the law? Hain't I got the power?" Much the same idea was expressed by William Vanderbilt during a public outcry against one of his policy decisions: "The public be damned. I am working for my stockholders." (Quotations in this paragraph are from Josephson, pp. 67, 72.)

BUSINESS COLLUSION AND GOVERNMENT REGULATION

After a few years of this type of competition, however, most of the remaining business firms were battle-tested giants. Continuing such competition would have been ruinous for all. So, whereas competition was the road to large profits before 1880, after that date it became obvious that cooperative collusion would be more beneficial for the remaining firms. In that way they could exercise monopolistic power for their mutual benefit. Thus, pools, trusts, and mergers (described in Chapter 8) were the consequence of the earlier competition. Increasingly as the turn of the century neared, the neoclassical vision of many small competing firms diverged from the reality of massive corporations acting cooperatively to maximize their joint profits.

With the rise of big corporations there was a parallel growth of grassroots popular opposition to these companies and their blatant disregard for the public welfare. This popular antagonism became so widespread and intense that in the presidential campaign of 1888 both the Democrats and Republicans advocated federal laws to curb the abuses of big corporations.

After the 1888 election, both parties became extremely reluctant to take any such action. Many of the most important Republicans controlled the very corporations they had promised to curb, and the Democrats were only slightly less involved with big business. Only when public pressure reached incredible heights did Congress respond, in December 1889, by passing the Sherman Anti-Trust Act. The act, an obvious concession to aroused public opinion, passed both houses of Congress with only a single dissenting vote. But the wording of the law was so weak and vague that it appeared to be designed to ensure that it would be ineffective. Another proposal, which recommended meaningful punishment of firms that violated the law, was overwhelmingly defeated.

The law proscribed "every contract, combination in the form of a trust or otherwise, or conspiracy, in restraint of trade or commerce among the several states or with foreign nations." It also declared that any person who attempted "to monopolize, or combine or conspire with any other person . . . to monopolize any part of the trade or commerce among the several states, or with foreign nations" was guilty of a misdemeanor.

The primary effect of the Sherman Act over the next few decades was to weaken labor unions. What had begun as a concession to the public's hatred of abuses by big business became an antilabor law. This effect followed because the courts ruled that many union strikes constituted constraints of trade. On this basis the government arrested numerous union leaders and broke up many unions.

While President McKinley was in office there were only five cases initiated under the Sherman Act, despite the fact that 146 major industrial combinations were formed between 1899 and 1901 alone. One of these was the massive United States Steel Corporation. In 1901 U.S. Steel controlled or acquired 785 plants worth $1,370,000,000, which would be many times that amount in today's dollars.

Staggeringly high profits, graft, corruption, and discriminatory practices on the part of the nation's railroads led to the establishment of the first federal government regulatory agency. The Interstate Commerce Act of 1887 established the Interstate Commerce Commission (ICC), which was designed to regulate the railroads in order to protect the public interest.

Competition among the railroads had been so destructive that the railroads themselves were the leading advocates of extended federal regulation. A few years after the passage of the Interstate Commerce Act, U.S. Attorney General Olney wrote a letter to a railroad president that read, in part, "The [ICC] . . . is, or can be made, of great use to the railroads. It satisfies the popular clamor for a government supervision of railroads, at the same time that supervision is almost entirely nominal. Further, the older such a commission gets to be, the more inclined it will be found to take the business and railroad view of things" (quoted in McConnell, p. 197).

The attorney general's prediction has certainly been borne out by the facts. In the years since the establishment of the ICC, many other federal regulatory agencies have been established. The Federal Communications Commission (FCC), the Civil Aeronautics Board (CAB), and the Securities and Exchange Commission (SEC) were among the federal agencies that joined the ICC as "protectors" of the public interest. Most serious students of government regulation would agree that "the outstanding political fact about the . . . regulatory commissions is that they have in general become promoters and protectors of the industries they have been established to regulate" (ibid., p. 199). The agencies help the industries make extraordinary profits at the expense of the public.

Many oligopolistic industries seemed unable to cooperate and act collectively as a monopoly. There is a considerable body of evidence indicating that these industries turned to the government and to federal regulatory agencies as a means of achieving this monopolistic coordination (see Kolko). Regulatory agencies have generally performed this function very effectively.

The collusive behavior of the oligopolistic businesses seemed to go unnoticed by neoclassical economists. They continued to frame their analyses in terms of innumerable small, competing business firms. In their advocacy of laissez-faire policies, they failed to see that it was primarily big business that supported active government intervention.

Neoclassical economists also continued to accept the classical economists' view that as long as free competition prevails, the economy will tend toward full utilization of its productive capacity, and full employment will be more or less continuous. During the second half of the nineteenth century, however, economic depressions became more frequent and more severe. During the first half of the nineteenth century, the United States had had two economic crises (in 1819 and 1837), and England had had four (in 1815, 1825, 1836, and 1847). During the second half of the century, the number increased to five in the United States (1854, 1857, 1873, 1884, and 1893), and six in England (in 1857, 1866, 1873, 1882, 1890, and 1900). Thus, the neoclassical economic ideology was as poor a reflection of economic performances as it was of industrial concentration.

CHANGES IN THE STRUCTURE OF CAPITALISM

During the late nineteenth and early twentieth centuries, capitalism underwent an important and fundamental transformation. Although the foundations of the system—the laws of private property, the basic class structure, and the processes of commodity production and allocation through the market—remained unchanged, the process of capital accumulation became institutionalized in the large corporation. In the earlier stages of capitalist development, individual capitalists had played a central role in the accumulation process. The process from their standpoint had depended on organizational skills, cunning, business acumen, ruthlessness, and no small amount of luck. From the standpoint of society, however, the fortune of any particular capitalist was irrelevant—accumulation was an inexorable, ceaseless, spiraling process that had momentum and patterns of development that were quite independent of the actions of any particular capitalist.

The late nineteenth century saw the accumulation process rationalized, regularized, and institutionalized in the form of the large corporation. "Taylorism" and scientific management replaced the older, more individualistic mode of capital accumulation. A new managerial class became increasingly important. Ownership of the means of production remained the principal source of economic, social, and political power in capitalism. The new managerial class was primarily composed, at least in its highest echelons, of important and powerful owners of capital. The managerial class was clearly and decisively subordinated to the entire capitalist class.

Among the consequences of this institutional transformation were two changes of particular importance. The first was the internationalization of capital. We discuss this in Chapter 11. The second was a change in the structure of the capitalist class. Although the social, political, and economic dominance of the capitalist class remained unchanged, the institutionalization of the accumulation process permitted the majority of capitalists to perpetuate their status merely through passive absentee ownership. The majority of capitalists became a pure rentier class, while a minority engaged in managerial functions (in both the economy and the polity) and acted as a kind of executive committee to protect the interests of the entire capitalist class. This committee performed its function by "managing the

managers" of the new corporate structure; meanwhile, the remaining capitalists simply enjoyed lavish incomes derived from ownership alone.

These changes in economic organization and activities were reflected
in diverse ways in the realm of economic theory. But the economic writings
that most completely reflected and described the institutional and cultural
transformation of this period were those of Thorstein Veblen (1857–1929).
Veblen was probably the most significant, original, and profound social
theorist in American history.

Veblen taught at the University of Chicago and at Stanford University,
and was mistreated at both institutions, particularly the latter. He wrote
prolifically, publishing ten important books and innumerable articles and
reviews in journals and periodicals. His great genius and unusual writing
style make all of his works enormously enjoyable and intellectually valuable.

THE ANTAGONISTIC DICHOTOMY OF CAPITALISM

Veblen believed that there were two generally antagonistic clusters of
behavioral traits, which were manifested in different historical eras through
the social institutions and modes of behavior peculiar to those eras. Central
to one of the clusters was Veblen's notion of the "instinct of workmanship."
Central to the other cluster was his notion of the instinct to "exploit," or
the "predatory instinct." Associated with workmanship were traits that
Veblen referred to as the "parental instinct" and the "instinct of idle cu
riosity." These traits were responsible for the advances that had been made
in productivity and in the expansion of human mastery over nature. They
were also responsible for the degree to which the human needs for affection,
cooperation, and creativity were fulfilled. Associated with exploit, or the
predatory instinct, were human conflict, subjugation, and sexual, racial,
and class exploitation. Social institutions and habitual behavior often tended
to hide the true nature of exploitation and predatory behavior behind facades that Veblen referred to as "sportsmanship" and "ceremonialism."

The antithesis between these two sets of behavioral traits, and the
social institutions through which they were manifested, was the central
focal point of Veblen's social theory. Veblen was primarily interested in
analyzing the capitalist system of his era within the context of this social
theory. Just as Marx in the mid-nineteenth century had taken England as
the prototype of capitalist society, Veblen, writing during the last decade
of the nineteenth and first quarter of the twentieth centuries, took the
United States as the prototype. The central question for him was how these
two antagonistic clusters of behavioral traits were manifested in and through
the institutions of capitalism.

The question could be approached from several vantage points; Veblen
used at least three. From a social psychological point of view, he distinguished individuals and classes whose behavior was dominated by the propensity to exploit, or the predatory instinct, from those whose behavior

was dominated by the instinct of workmanship, the parental bent, and the development of idle curiosity. From the standpoint of economics, Veblen saw the same dichotomy between the forces that he referred to as "business"—which he defined as grubbing for profit—and the forces that he referred to as "industry"—which he defined as production of socially useful commodities. From the standpoint of sociology, the dichotomy was manifested in the differences between the "ceremonialism" and "sportsmanship" characteristic of the "leisure class" and the more creative and cooperative behavior characteristic of the "common man."

Each of these three levels of analysis tended to merge with the other two, for Veblen was in fact analyzing a society that was mainly constituted of two major classes. One class was the capitalists, whom he variously referred to as the "vested interest," the "absentee owners," the "leisure class," or the "captains of industry." The other class was the productive or working class, whom he variously referred to as the "engineers," the "workmen," and the "common man."

PRIVATE PROPERTY, CLASS-DIVIDED SOCIETY, AND CAPITALISM

At the foundation of this class structure was the institution of private property. In the earliest stages of human society, low productivity made a predominance of the instinct of workmanship a social prerequisite for survival. During this period, "the habits of life of the race were still perforce of a peaceful and industrial character, rather than contentious and destructive" (Veblen, 1964B, p. 86). During this early period, "before a predacious life became possible" and while society was still dominated by the instinct of workmanship, "efficiency [or] serviceability commends itself, and inefficiency or futility is odious" (ibid., pp. 87, 89). In this type of society, property was social and not private.

Only after production became substantially more efficient and technical knowledge and tools were socially accumulated did predatory exploitation become possible. Invidious distinctions among different members of society became possible only at that point. With greater productivity, it became possible to live by brute seizure and predatory exploitation. "But seizure and forcible retention very shortly gain the legitimation of usage, and the resultant tenure becomes inviolable through habitation" (ibid., p. 43). In other words, private property came into existence.

Private property had its origins in brute coercive force and was perpetuated both by force and by institutional and ideological legitimization. Class-divided societies inevitably came with the development of private property: "Where this tenure by prowess prevails, the population falls into two economic classes: those engaged in industrial employments, and those engaged in such nonindustrial pursuits as war, government, sports, and religious observances" (ibid.).

Private property and the predatory instinct led to the predatory, class-divided societies of the slave and feudal eras. Capitalism was the outgrowth of feudalism in western Europe. Whereas the predatory instinct totally dominated society in slavery and feudalism, in capitalism there had occurred an important, profound growth of the instinct of workmanship. Capitalism—or as Veblen sometimes referred to capitalism, "the régime of absentee ownership and hired labor"—had begun as a "quasi-peaceable" society in which the forces of workmanship had originally developed very rapidly. With the passage of time, however, the forces of workmanship and the predatory forces of exploitation had become locked in a struggle. This antagonism was expressed by Veblen as a conflict between "business" and "industry," or between "salesmanship" and "workmanship."

These two social forces were embodied in entirely different classes of people in capitalism. "The interest and attention of the two typical . . . classes . . . part company and enter on a course of progressive differentiation along two divergent lines." (ibid., 1964C, pp. 187–188). The first class embodied the instinct of workmanship or industry:

> The workman, laborers, operatives, technologists—whatever term may best designate that general category of human material through which the community's technological proficiency functions directly to an industrial effect—those who have to work, whereby they get their livelihood and their interest as well as the discipline of their workday life converges, in effect, on a technological apprehension of material facts. (Ibid., p. 188)

The second class embodied the predatory instinct, the business viewpoint, and salesmanship:

> These owners, investors, masters, employers, undertakers, businessmen, have to do with the negotiating of advantageous bargains. . . . The training afforded by these occupations and requisite to their effectual pursuit runs in terms of pecuniary management and insight, pecuniary gain, price, price-cost, price-profit, and price-loss; . . . that is to say in terms of the self-regarding propensities and sentiments. (Ibid., pp. 189–190)

While the essence of success for laborers involved workmanship or productive creativity, the essence of success for owners and businessmen involved exploitative advantage over others. Profit making, or business, created behavior that was totally removed from industry or workmanship. Increasingly, owners had less and less to do in the direction of production, which became entrusted to a "professional class of 'efficiency engineers' " (ibid., p. 22). But the concern of this new managerial class of efficiency engineers was never with productivity itself or with serviceability to the community at large. "The work of the efficiency engineers . . . [is] always done in the service of business . . . in terms of price and profits" (ibid., p. 224).

The nature of the control of business over industry was described by Veblen in one term: "sabotage." Business sabotaged industry for the sake of profit. Sabotage was defined as "a conscientious withdrawal of efficiency." For business owners, "a reasonable profit always means, in effect, the largest obtainable profit" (ibid., 1965A, pp. 1, 13). The problem in capitalism was that large-scale industry and the forces of workmanship were always increasing the quantity of output that could be produced with a given quantity of resources and workers. But given the existing, extremely unequal distribution of income, this added output could only be sold if prices were reduced substantially. Generally, the necessary price reductions were so great that selling a larger quantity at lower prices was less profitable than selling a lesser quantity at higher prices. Therefore, in modern capitalism

> [there] is an ever increasing withdrawal of efficiency. The industrial plant is increasingly running idle or half idle, running increasingly short of its productive capacity. Workmen are being laid off. . . . And all the while these people are in great need of all sorts of goods and services which these idle plants and idle workmen are fit to produce. But for reasons of business expediency it is impossible to let these idle plants and idle workmen go to work—that is to say for reasons of insufficient profit to the business men interested, or in other words, for the reasons of insufficient income to the vested interests. (Ibid., 1965A, p. 12)

The normal state of modern capitalism, Veblen believed, was one of recurring depressions: "It may, therefore, be said, on the basis of this view, that chronic depression, more or less pronounced, is normal to business under the fully developed regimen of the machine industry" (ibid., 1965B, p. 234). Moreover, throughout the business cycle and at all times, capitalism necessarily involved a continuous class struggle between owners and workers:

> In the negotiations between owners and workmen there is little use for the ordinary blandishments of salesmanship. . . . And the bargaining between them therefore settles down without much circumlocution into a competitive use of unemployment, privation, restriction of work and output, strikes, shutdowns and lockouts, espionage, maneuvers, pickets, and similar maneuvers of mutual derangement, with a large recourse to menacing language and threats of mutual sabotage. The colloquial word for it is "labor troubles." The business relations between the two parties are of the nature of hostilities, suspended or active, conducted in terms of mutual sabotage; which will on occasion shift from the footing of such obstruction and disallowance as is wholly within the law and custom of business, from the footing of legitimate sabotage in the way of passive resistance and withholding of efficiency, to that illegitimate phase of sabotage that runs into violent offenses against person and property. The negotiations . . . have come to be spoken of habitually in terms of conflict, armed forces, and warlike strategy. It is a conflict of hostile forces which is conducted on the avowed strategic principle that either party stands to gain at the cost of the other. (Ibid., 1964A, p. 406–407)

GOVERNMENT AND THE CLASS STRUGGLE

The ultimate power in the capitalist system was in the hands of the owners because they controlled the government, which was the institutionally legitimized means of physical coercion in any society. As such, the government existed to protect the existing social order and class structure. This meant that in capitalist society the primary duty of government was the enforcement of private property laws and the protection of the privileges associated with ownership. Veblen repeatedly insisted that

> modern politics is business politics. . . . This is true both of foreign and domestic policy. Legislation, police surveillance, the administration of justice, the military and diplomatic service, all are chiefly concerned with business relations, pecuniary interests, and they have little more than an incidental bearing on other human interests. (Ibid., 1965B, p. 269)

The first principle of a capitalist government was that the "natural freedom of the individual must not traverse the prescriptive rights of property. Property rights . . . have the indefeasibility which attaches to natural rights." The principal freedom of capitalism was the freedom to buy and sell. The laissez-faire philosophy dictated that "so long as there is no overt attempt on life . . . or the liberty to buy and sell, the law cannot intervene, unless it be in a precautionary way to prevent prospective violation of . . . property rights." Above all else, therefore, a "constitutional government is a business government." (These quotations from Veblen 1965B, pp. 272, 278, 285.)

Thus, in the ceaseless class struggle between workers and absentee owners, the owners have nearly always prevailed. Government, as the institutionally legitimized means of physical coercion, was firmly in their hands. Since workers greatly outnumbered owners, the maintenance of the owners' supremacy—that is, the maintenance of the existing class structure of capitalism—depended on the absentee owner being in control of the government. At any point in the class struggle when the workers of a particular industry appeared to be getting the upper hand, the government was called in.

Whenever the prerogatives of private property were threatened in any way, the property-owning class responded by force of arms. Property rights were the basis of this class's power and of its "free income," and it would protect them at any cost: "And it is well known, and also it is right and good by law and custom, that when recourse is had to arms the common man pays the cost. He pays it in lost labor, anxiety, privation, blood, and wounds" (Veblen, 1964B, p. 413).

CAPITALIST IMPERIALISM

During the last quarter of the nineteenth century and the early twentieth century, aggressive, imperialist expansion was one of the dominant features of industrial capitalism. In Chapter 11 we discuss some economic theories of imperialism. Veblen also wrote extensively on this topic. He believed that the quest for profits knew no national boundaries. The absentee owners of business saw rich possibilities for profits in different areas of the world if those areas could be brought under the domination of capitalist countries or domestic governments that approved of foreigners extracting profits from their countries. The absentee owners' success in getting the population to believe that everyone's interest was identical to the corporations' interest extended into the realm of patriotism. Patriotism was a nationalist sentiment that could be used to gain support for the government's aggressive, imperialist policies on behalf of business interests. "Imperialism is dynastic politics under a new name," Veblen wrote, "carried on for the benefit of absentee owners" (Veblen, 1964A, p. 35). He was convinced that there was "a growing need for such national aids to business." Continuous economic expansion was necessary to maintain high profits.

But the profits that imperialism brought to the absentee owners were not, in Veblen's opinion, its most important feature. Imperialism was a conservative social force of the utmost social importance. With the development of the techniques of machine production, human productivity had expanded rapidly during the capitalist era. The natural concomitant of the growth of productivity was the growth of the instinct of workmanship and its related social traits. As workmanship and its attendant traits became dominant in the culture, the social basis of absentee ownership and predatory business practices became endangered. The ethos of workmanship stressed cooperation rather than competition, individual equality and independence rather than pervasive relations of subordination and superordination, logical social interrelationships rather than ceremonial role playing, and peaceable rather than predatory dispositions generally. Thus the traits associated with workmanship were subversive to the very foundation of the existing class structure. The absentee owners had to find some means to counteract the subversive effects of workmanship, cooperation, individual independence, and the quest for a peaceable brotherhood.

For this important task the absentee owners turned to imperialism. This social role of imperialism was so central to Veblen's view of the functioning of capitalism that we quote him at length:

> The largest and most promising factor of cultural discipline—most promising as a corrective of iconoclastic vagaries—over which business principles rule is national politics. . . . Business interests urge an aggressive national policy and business men direct it. Such a policy is warlike as well as patriotic. The direct cultural value of a warlike business policy is unequivocal. It makes for a conservative animus on the part of the populace. During war time, . . . under martial law, civil rights are in abeyance; and the more warfare and armament the more abeyance. Military training is a training in ceremonial precedence, arbitrary command, and unquestioning obedience. A military organization is essentially a servile organization. Insubordination is the deadly sin. The more consistent and the more comprehensive this military training, the more effectually will the members of the community be trained into habits of subordination and away from the growing propensity to make light of personal authority that is the chief infirmity of democracy. This applies first and most decidedly, of course, to the soldiery, but it applies only in a less degree to the rest of the

population. They learn to think in warlike terms of rank, authority, and subordination, and so grow progressively more patient of encroachments upon their civil rights. . . . The disciplinary effects of warlike pursuits . . . direct the popular interest to other noble, institutionally less hazardous matters than the unequal distribution of wealth or creature comforts. Warlike and patriotic preoccupations fortify the barbarian virtues of subordination and prescriptive authority. Habituation to a warlike, predatory scheme of life is the strongest disciplinary factor that can be brought to counteract the vulgarization of modern life wrought by peaceful industry and the machine process, and to rehabilitate the decaying sense of status and differential dignity. Warfare, with the stress on a military organization, has always proved an effective school in barbarian methods of thought.

In this direction, evidently, lies the hope of a corrective for "social unrest" and similar disorders of civilized life. There can, indeed, be no serious question but that a consistent return to the ancient virtues of allegiance, piety, servility, graded dignity, class prerogative, and prescriptive authority would greatly conduce to popular content and to the facile management of affairs. Such is the promise held out by a strenous national policy. (Ibid., 1965B, pp. 391–393)

THE SOCIAL MORES OF PECUNIARY CULTURE

Where the instinct of workmanship held sway, the social tendency was toward the advancement of knowledge, cooperation, equality, and mutual aid. But the class division of capitalism depended on the continued social prominence of the traits associated with predatory exploit—the admiration of predatory skills, acquiescence in the hierarchy of subordination, and the widespread substitution of myth and ceremony for knowledge. The free and unearned income of the absentee owners ultimately depended on the cultural and social domination of the mores of the predatory or (what in capitalism amounted to the same thing) the pecuniary or business aspects of the culture.

When the predatory instinct dominated society, the prevailing mores were those of the leisure class, which constituted the ruling element of society. Veblen believed that "the emergence of a leisure class coincides with the beginning of ownership. . . . They are but different aspects of the same general facts of social structure." In all class-divided societies there had always been a fundamentally significant differentiation between the occupations of the leisure class and those of the common people. "Under this ancient distinction," he wrote, "the worthy employments are those which may be classed as exploit; unworthy are those necessary everyday employments into which no appreciable element of exploit enters" (ibid., 1965, pp. 22, 8).

Under capitalism there came to be a hierarchy of occupations ranging from the most honorific—absentee ownership—to the most vulgar and repulsive—creative labor.

Employments fall into a hierarchical gradation of reputability. Those which have to do immediately with ownership on a large scale are the most reputable. . . . Next to these in good repute come those employments that are immediately subservient to ownership and financering, such as banking and law. Banking employments also carry a suggestion of large ownership, and this fact is doubtless accountable for a share of the prestige that attaches to the business. The profession of law does not imply large ownership; but since no taint of usefulness, for other than competitive purpose, attaches to the lawyer's trade, it grades high in the conventional scheme. The lawyer is exclusively occupied with the details of predatory fraud either in achieving or in checkmating chicane, and success in the profession is therefore accepted as marking a large endowment of that barbarian astuteness which has always commanded men's respect and fear. . . . Manual labour, or even the work of directing mechanical processes, is of course on a precarious footing as regards respectability. (Ibid., pp. 231–232)

But wealthy absentee owners usually lived in large cities and spent most of their time with lawyers, accountants, stockbrokers, and other advisers, buying and selling stocks and bonds, manipulating financial deals, and generally engineering schemes of sabotage and fraud. Therefore, whereas the predatory virtues in more barbarian cultures were so obvious and immediate as to easily incite the admiration of the populace, the predatory virtues in a capitalist society were largely hidden from view and could not so readily incite admiration. Therefore, capitalists had to conspicuously display their prowess.

Most of *The Theory of the Leisure Class* was devoted to a detailed description of how the leisure class displayed its predatory prowess through conspicuous consumption and the conspicuous use of leisure. For Veblen, conspicuous consumption often coincided with conspicuous waste. The housing of the rich, for example, "is more ornate, more conspicuously wasteful in its architecture and decoration, than the dwelling houses of the congregation" (ibid., p. 120). It was always necessary for the rich to have expensive, ornate, and largely useless—but above all, expensive—paraphernalia prominently displayed. For the wealthy, the more useless and expensive a thing was, the more it was prized as an article of conspicuous consumption. Anything that was useful and affordable to common people was thought to be vulgar and tasteless.

The beauty and elaborate dressing and display of one's wife were essential for a substantial citizen of good taste. Innumerable servants were indicators that a wife had to do none of the vulgar work of an ordinary housewife and that she was herself primarily an ostentatious trophy of beauty and uselessness that added to the esteem of her husband. Villas on the sea, yachts, and elaborate mountain chateaus, all of which were rarely used but prominently visible, were essential for respectability.

Veblen had much more in mind in describing the conspicuous consumption of the rich than merely giving an amusing anecdotal account. Pecuniary culture was above all else a culture of invidious distinction.

When an individual's personal worth was measured primarily in a pecuniary system of invidious distinction, one of the most powerful forces in society was emulation, which was the most important guarantor of social, economic, and political conservatism.

If the majority of working people came to realize that capitalists contributed nothing to the production process, that the capitalists' business and pecuniary activities were the cause of depressions and other malfunctions in the industrial system, that the disproportionately large share of wealth and income going to the capitalists caused the impoverishment of the majority of society, that the degradation of the work process was the result of the prevailing predatory ethos of capitalists—if the workers came to realize these facts, then they would surely free the industrial system from the oppressive and archaic fetters of the laws, governments, and institutions of the pecuniary business culture. There would be a revolutionary overthrow of capitalism.

The capitalists relied on two principal means of cultural discipline and social control. The first, as we have seen, was patriotism, nationalism, militarism, and imperialism. The second means of emotionally and ideologically controlling the population was through emulative consumption (or "consumerism," as this phenomenon later came to be called). The importance of this phenomenon in Veblen's total theory was so great that we quote him at length:

> A certain standard of wealth . . . and of prowess . . . is a necessary condition of reputability, and anything in excess of this normal amount is meritorious.
>
> Those members of the community who fall short of this somewhat indefinite, normal degree of prowess or property suffer in the esteem of their fellowmen; and consequently they suffer also in their own esteem, since the usual basis of self-respect is the respect accorded by one's neighbours. Only individuals with an aberrant temperament can in the long run retain their self-esteem in the face of the disesteem of their fellows. . . .
>
> So soon as the possession of property becomes the basis of popular esteem, therefore, it becomes also a requisite to that complacency which we call self-respect. In any community . . . it is necessary, in order to have this own peace of mind, that an individual should possess as large a portion of goods as others with whom he is accustomed to class himself; and it is extremely gratifying to possess something more than others. But as fast as a person makes new acquisitions, and becomes accustomed to the resulting new standard of wealth, the new standard forthwith ceases to afford appreciably greater satisfaction than the earlier standard did. The tendency in any case is constantly to make the present pecuniary standard the point of departure for a fresh increase of wealth; and this in turn gives rise to a new standard of sufficiency and a new pecuniary classification of one's self as compared with one's neighbours. So far as concerns the present question, the end sought by accumulation is to rank high in comparison with the rest of the community in point of pecuniary strength. So long as the comparison is distinctly unfavourable to himself, the normal average individual will live in chronic dissatisfaction with his present lot; and when he has reached what may be called the normal pecuniary standard of the community, or of his class in the community, this chronic dissatisfaction will give

place to a restless straining to place a wider and ever-widening pecuniary interval between himself and this average standard. The invidious comparison can never become so favourable to the individual making it that he would not gladly rate himself still higher relative to his competitors in the struggle for pecuniary reputability. (Ibid., pp. 30–32)

When people were caught on this treadmill of emulative consumption, or consumerism, they led a life of "chronic dissatisfaction," regardless of the amount of income they received. The misery of workers, in Veblen's view, arose predominantly from material deprivation only in that part of the working class that lived in abject poverty. For the remainder of the working class, the misery was caused by both the social degradation of labor and the "chronic dissatisfaction" associated with emulative consumption. The misery of the materially advantaged workers was spiritual. But Veblen insisted that this misery "is . . . none the less real and cogent for its being of a spiritual kind. Indeed it is all the more substantial and irremediable on that account" (ibid., 1964C, p. 95).

It seemed irremediable because the workers' response to the misery furthered and perpetuated the misery, the reaction being to believe that they would be happy if they acquired more and consumed more. So the workers went into debt, depended more and more heavily on moving up in their jobs and securing more income, and ultimately were convinced that their only possibility for transcending their chronic dissatisfaction was to please their employers and never do or say anything disruptive or radical.

But such a treadmill was endless. The harder one tried to overcome one's chronic dissatisfaction and misery, the more dissatisfied and miserable one became. In a system of invidious social ranking and conspicuous consumption, workers rarely blamed the "system," the "vested interest," or the "absentee owners" for their plight. They generally blamed themselves, resulting in a further decline in self-esteem and self-confidence and a tighter clinging to the values of pecuniary culture.

Veblen hoped that the more secure elements of the working class, in whom the instinct of workmanship was most highly developed, might someday transform capitalism. He envisioned a better society in which absentee ownership would be a thing of the past, in which there would no longer be a business class to subvert industry, and in which production would reflect the needs of all people rather than being controlled solely by the profits, and greed, of a tiny minority. But his social theory showed that capitalism systematically created an overwhelming conservative prejudice in most people and that, therefore, this transformation of capitalism would certainly be a profoundly difficult task.

SUMMARY

In the late nineteenth century the potential profits made possible by mass production and nationwide markets led to intense industrial warfare. Through the crushing of competitors and not infrequently the swindling of the general public, a handful of giant corporations came to dominate the American economy.

The passage of the Sherman Act and the establishment of various government regulatory agencies were ostensibly aimed at controlling these giant corporations. In practice, however, government tended to aid these giants in consolidating and stabilizing their massive empires.

Thorstein Veblen's writings best reflect and describe the effects of this collusion of government and big business on the welfare of the general public. Veblen stressed the distinction between industry (which produces needed articles for human well-being) and business (which produces profits for the wealthy absentee owners by sabotaging industry). He analyzed imperialism, militarism, and the general "chronic misery" caused by emulative consumption in an acquisitive, competitive, capitalist society. The profundity of many of Veblen's insights is unmatched in American intellectual history.

REFERENCES

Dillard, Dudley. *Economic Development of the North Atlantic Community.* Englewood Cliffs, N.J.: Prentice-Hall, 1967.

Josephson, Matthew. *The Robber Barons.* New York: Harcourt Brace Jovanovich, Harvest Books, 1962.

Kolko, Gabriel. *The Triumph of Conservatism.* New York: Free Press, 1963.

McConnell, Grant. "Self-Regulation, the Politics of Business." In *Economics: Mainstream Readings and Radical Critiques.* Edited by D. Mermelstein. New York: Random House, 1970.

Nevins, Allan. *John D. Rockefeller, The Heroic Age of American Enterprise.* Vol 1. New York: Scribner's, 1940.

Veblen, Thorstein. *Absentee Ownership and Business Enterprise in Recent Times.* New York: Augustus M. Kelley, 1964A.

———. "The Beginnings of Ownership." In *Essays in Our Changing Order.* New York: Augustus M. Kelley, 1964B.

———. "The Instinct of Workmanship and the Irksomeness of Labor." In *Essays in Our Changing Order.* New York: Augustus M. Kelley, 1964C.

———. *The Engineers and the Price System.* New York: Augustus M. Kelley, 1965A.

———. *The Theory of Business Enterprise.* New York: Augustus M. Kelley, 1965B.

———. *The Theory of the Leisure Class.* New York: Augustus M. Kelley, 1965C.

Chapter
10

Economic Prosperity and Evolutionary Socialism

In the late nineteenth and early twentieth centuries, the socialist analysis of capitalism was profoundly affected by two developments: (1) the economic and political gains made by the working class and (2) the imperialistic carving up of the economically less developed areas of the world by the major capitalist powers. These developments split the socialist movement into two camps. Some became convinced that governmental power could be peacefully acquired by socialists and used to promote economic and social reforms that would result in gradual evolution to socialism. The more militant socialists, however, continued to accept the Marxist view of the class nature of capitalist governments and to insist on the necessity of revolution. This chapter considers the economic and political gains of the working class and the resultant conservative reformist tendency in the socialist movement. Imperialism and revolutionary socialism are discussed in Chapter 11.

THE ECONOMIC AND POLITICAL GAINS
OF THE WORKING CLASS

During the second half of the nineteenth century, the real income of workers rose throughout the capitalist world. In England the average real wage increased rapidly throughout the 1860s and early 1870s. By 1875 it was 40 percent higher than it had been in 1862. After 10 years in which wages sagged, they again rose sharply between 1885 and 1900. By 1900, the average real wage was 33 percent higher than in 1875 and 84 percent higher than in 1850. Most of the gains in real wages can be attributed to the advent of mass production techniques that permitted the prices of many commodities consumed by laborers to be lowered. As a result of new methods of producing and labor's greater purchasing power, there was a fundamental change in patterns of consumption. Workers began to eat more meats, fruits, and sweets. Mass-produced shoes and clothing, furniture, newspapers, bicycles, and other new products came within the reach of many. Unquestionably, the average worker's lot improved substantially during the period.

It should be mentioned, however, that averages can be misleading. Two late nineteenth-century social surveys revealed that about 40 percent of the working class in London and York still lived in abject poverty. The fact that this could be so after a half-century of rapid increases in average real wages gives an indication of the truly pitiful conditions that must have existed in the early nineteenth century.

Similar gains were being made in western Europe and the United States during this period, and in most of these countries economic gains were accompanied by political gains. Most of the industrialized capitalist countries had nearly complete male suffrage by the early twentieth century. Political parties were created that were devoted to furthering the cause of workingmen. The most successful of these was the German Social Democratic party, formed at a meeting in Gotha in 1875 between the followers of Marx, led by Wilhelm Leibknecht and August Bebel, and the followers of Ferdinand Lassalle. The program adopted in this first party congress was known as the *Gotha Programme.* It represented a compromise that was bitterly attacked by Marx.

Marx believed his followers had made too many concessions to the Lassallian outlook, which conceived of the government as a neutral instrument to be used by workers to achieve socialism through peaceful reform. Excessive concern with reformism could, he believed, divert workers from their task of overthrowing capitalism. The conflict between the revolutionary socialists and the reformers was to remain important in the Social Democratic party for the next 40 years. Ultimately Marx's misgivings proved prophetic, however, and the reformists became dominant in the party.

In 1874 the two socialist groups polled 340,000 votes. In the election of 1877 the newly formed party received more than 500,000 votes and had 12 representatives elected to the Reichstag. This show of strength frightened Bismarck, and in 1878 a series of infamous antisocialist laws was passed. Many of the more militant socialist leaders were exiled, and the Social Democratic party was prohibited from holding meetings or publishing newspapers.

In spite of this repression the party continued to grow. It received 549,000 votes in 1884 and 763,000 in 1887. By 1890 the Social Democratic party polled 1,427,000 votes and had become the largest single party in the Reich. The repression had not worked; the antisocialist laws were abandoned.

In both England and Germany, as well as several other western European countries, it appeared to many socialists that the capitalist system had provided the workers with an escalator on which they could steadily and peacefully advance in both economic well-being and political power.

THE FABIAN SOCIALISTS

In England, despite the brilliant achievements of individual Marxists like William Morris, the socialist movement was largely non-Marxist; the Fabian Society was the primary influence on English socialism, and it rejected Marx's analysis completely. In their economic analysis the Fabians used orthodox neoclassical utility theory. They believed labor received an amount equal to what it produced, and capitalists and landlords received the value of what was produced with their capital and land. The chief cause of the injustice was not that labor's surplus value was appropriated by capitalists but rather that all the income from ownership accrued to a tiny percentage of the population. The only way to achieve an equitable society would be to divide the income from ownership equally, and this could be done only through government ownership of the means of production.

On the issue of the nature and role of the government, the Fabians differed radically from Marx. For Marx, the government was an instrument of coercion controlled and used by the ruling class to perpetuate the privileges inherent in the capitalist system. The Fabians believed that in a parliamentary democracy based on universal suffrage the state was a neutral agency that could be freely used by the majority to reform the social and economic system. Because the working class was the majority in a capitalist economy, they were confident that, step by step, piecemeal reforms would strip away the privileges of the owning class and result in socialism achieved by peaceful evolution rather than violent revolution.

The most influential of the Fabians were George Bernard Shaw, Sidney and Beatrice Webb, and Graham Wallas. For many years Shaw was the principal draftsman of Fabian publications and was widely known as the society's most lucid and forceful spokesman. The worst evil of capitalism was in Shaw's opinion, the enormous inequality of wealth and income that prevailed in every capitalist country. The cause of the most egregious inequality was the income that accrued from ownership of land and capital. Such unearned incomes, which Shaw combined under the label of "rents," created extremes of incredible wealth and power for a tiny minority while the majority of those who created the wealth lived in poverty. He also believed the capitalist system suffered from periods of chronic underproduction and incurred enormous wastes by devoting productive capacity to the creation of mountains of useless consumption goods for the rich. By expropriating these rents and eliminating the wastes and inefficiencies of capitalism, a socialist government could easily provide economic security and an ample livelihood for everyone.

The only ultimately just distribution of income was absolute equality. To achieve this, it would be necessary to sever any connection between productive services rendered and monetary remuneration. This, in turn, would require a reliance on noneconomic, or social, incentives to accomplish the necessary productive tasks. Shaw envisioned this equality not as an immediate possibility but only as a long-run goal.

Perhaps the least attractive aspect of Shaw's socialism was his extreme elitist bias. He had little faith in democracy. Rather, he believed an efficient and just organization of society required that policymaking and administrative tasks be handled by experts. According to one eminent historian of socialism, Shaw "was apt to admire dictators, if only they would give the experts a free hand" (Cole, Vol. III, p. 211).

Shaw's elitism was shown most clearly in his defense of British imperialism. He believed that

> no group or nation had any right to stand in the way of the full development in the interest of the whole world of any productive resource of which it stood possessed, and that accordingly higher civilizations had a complete right to work their will upon backward peoples and to override national or sectional claims, provided only that by doing so they increased the total wealth of the human race. (Ibid., p. 219)

In view of these opinions, Shaw's leadership of the pro-imperialist faction of the Fabian Society is easily understandable (see Chapter 11).

Among the general public Shaw was probably the most influential of the Fabians. Within the Fabian Society itself, however, the most influential theoreticians were Sidney and Beatrice Webb. The Webbs were probably the most serious scholars in the Fabian Society and undoubtedly among the most prolific writers in the history of socialism.

One of their first and most influential books, *Industrial Democracy*, rejected the notion that workers had neither the desire nor the capability to run their enterprises. Rather, industrial democracy under socialism was envisioned as a scheme in which industry was controlled by professional managers, who in turn were to be made accountable to the general population through supervision by a democratically elected parliament, local governments, and consumers' cooperatives.

They rejected the idea that socialism would involve ownership of all industry by the national government. Ownership should reside both in national government and in any of a variety of smaller local or regional administrative units. The scope of an enterprise's activities and the portion of the population affected by these activities should, they believed, determine the nature of social ownership of any particular business firm.

In *A Constitution for the Socialist Commonwealth of Great Britain* they proposed the creation of two separate, democratically elected parliaments. One was to handle political affairs and the other to preside over social and economic affairs. In addition, they advocated a system of local governments based on local units with fixed geographic boundaries. These local governments, however, were to be combined in various ways to form administrative units to supervise and control different economic and social services. The particular size, shape, and location of these administrative units would depend on the nature of the service involved.

In general, it may be said that the Webbs wrote a great deal about the nature of the socialist society they would have liked to have seen created at some future time but very little about specific tactics for transforming existing society into that future socialist system. They believed labor unions should confine their activities to representing the economic interests of their members in the collective bargaining process and should not act as insurgents. In fact, they seemed to see little hope for political change coming from a broadly based movement of workers. Rather, they assumed that an intellectual appeal might ultimately change the general public's opinions in a manner that would lead to the election of members of Parliament who were sympathetic to socialist ideas.

The Fabian Society gradually succeeded in gaining influence in the parliamentary Labour party. By 1918 the Labour party had adopted a socialist program that reflected the Fabian Society's views and attitudes. By the 1920s the Labour party had formed a government, and the cause of socialism via the voting booth seemed to many to be on the road to triumph.

The Fabians had never wanted to be a mass-membership society. They were a small, select group, and most of their efforts were devoted to educating the middle class to accept socialism. They published innumerable tracts exposing the poverty and injustice they found in early twentieth-century England. Remedies for these evils would be forthcoming through paternalistic government actions and programs, they believed, once the government was made truly democratic and the people were made aware of these conditions.

However debatable their certainty that socialism could be achieved through education, it is undeniable that the Fabians offered an impressive group of teachers. Some of the most brilliant of the English intellectual elite were members of the society, including, in addition to the Webbs and Shaw, H. G. Wells, Sydney Olivier, and Graham Wallas. With such sponsorship the Fabians' reformist, evolutionary socialism became eminently respectable. One could espouse socialism and still remain completely secure in a comfortable middle-class niche in English capitalistic society.

THE GERMAN REVISIONISTS

The German counterparts of the English Fabians were the Revisionists. At the turn of the century the Social Democratic party was nominally a Marxist party. A large portion of the membership argued, however, that the course of history had proved Marx wrong on many issues, and that a "revision" of Marx's ideas was necessary to make them relevant to German economic and social life. The most famous of the Revisionists was Eduard Bernstein, who presented a detailed critique of Marxist ideas in his best-known work, *Evolutionary Socialism*, published in 1899. Bernstein maintained that capitalism was not approaching any kind of crisis or collapse and, indeed, had never been more viable. Marx was also wrong, Bernstein declared, in predicting the concentration of all industries in the hands of a few giant firms. He argued that enterprises of all sizes thrived and would continue to do so (despite the fact that corporate concentration and the cartel movement were more extreme in Germany than in any other capitalist country). Even if large trusts did dominate the economy, Bernstein insisted, there would be a "splitting up of shares," making petty capitalists of a very large percentage of the population, including many workers. He believed the economy had already gone far in this direction: "The number of members of the possessing classes is today not smaller but larger. The enormous increase of social wealth is not accompanied by a decreasing number of large capitalists, but by an increasing number of capitalists of all degrees" (Bernstein, p. xii).

Furthermore, even workers who received no profits, rents, interest, or dividends were rapidly becoming much better off. Improvements in the general standard of living and the democratization of the government had made revolution not only highly unlikely but also morally undesirable. The hopes of the working class lay more "in a steady advance than in the possibilities offered by a catastrophic crash" (ibid., p. xiv).

Bernstein's book contained much more than the simple substitution of "peaceful evolution" for "revolution": It was, in fact, a direct attack on nearly all of the intellectual foundations of Marxism. Capitalism was not, he asserted, characterized by two polarized, conflicting classes. Class struggle could hardly be the moving force of history when class distinctions were rapidly breaking down and frequently nonexistent. Workers were far from being a homogeneous mass, he argued, and therefore "the feeling of solidarity between groups of workers . . . is only very moderate in amount" (ibid., p. 120). Instead of two fundamentally antagonistic classes, Bernstein saw a multiplicity of interest groups that were often in conflict but even more often united in a collective "community."

From his rejection of the class nature of capitalist society, it follows that Bernstein had to reject Marx's theory of historical materialism. He argued that as society developed, economic forces were coming to be less and less important and ideological and ethical forces becoming increasingly significant:

> Modern society is much richer than earlier societies in ideologies which are not determined by economics and by nature operating as an economic force. Science, the arts, a whole series of social relations are nowadays much less dependent on economics than formerly they were; or let us say, in order to leave no room for misunderstanding, the point of economic development that has now been reached leaves the ideological, and especially the ethical, factors

greater scope for independent activity than used to be the case. Consequently, the interdependence of cause and effect between technological, economic evolution and the evolution of other social tendencies is becoming continually more indirect; and accordingly the necessities of the former are losing much of their power to dictate the form of the latter. (Quoted in Cole, p. 280)

He similarly rejected Marx's theory of surplus value. Marx had asserted that surplus value was created in the process of production by living labor alone. Bernstein simply dismissed this theory by stating that surplus value "can only be grasped as a concrete fact by thinking of the whole economy of society" (Bernstein, p. 38). This, he believed, was a most damning criticism of Marx because the theory of surplus value was seen as the scientific basis for Marx's socialism. Henceforth, Bernstein averred, socialism would have to be based on ethical and not scientific foundations.

Perhaps the most fundamental difference between Marx and Bernstein was their difference concerning the nature of government in a capitalist society. Marx had asserted (and Bernstein's contemporary Marxist adversaries continued to assert) that capitalist governments were primarily instruments of class rule. Capitalists maintained their economic status and privileges through capitalistic property relations. They used their wealth, in turn, to control the political process in order to ensure the continuation of governments that were, above all else, committed to the defense of these property relations.

Bernstein dismissed the Marxist view of capitalist government as "political atavism." The Marxist notion may have once been valid, but contemporary extensions of suffrage had, he believed, invalidated it. Universal suffrage could make all people equally powerful in selecting the government and could thereby destroy class conflict by making each individual an "equal partner" in the community. "The right to vote," he wrote, "in a democracy makes its members virtually partners in the community, and this virtual partnership must in the end lead to real partnership" (ibid., p. 144).

Thus Bernstein, like the Fabians, rejected the notion that the government in a capitalist society had an inherent class bias. In a capitalist democracy each worker was seen as an equal partner with each capitalist, and they could all be induced, through moral appeals, to use peaceful political means to promote the general interests of the entire community.

THE FATE OF EVOLUTIONARY SOCIALISM

Throughout the period from the publication of *Evolutionary Socialism* until the outbreak of World War I, Bernstein's ideas evoked intense controversy in the Social Democratic party and also throughout the entire worldwide socialist movement. The issue at stake was of the utmost significance.

The Fabians and the Revisionists argued that persistence in legislating reforms would ultimately achieve socialism. No single reform would, by itself, threaten the capitalist structure, but eventually the cumulative effect of many reforms would be the peaceful abdication of the capitalist class.

Marxists continued to believe, however, that as soon as any reforms seriously threatened the privileges and prerogatives of property rights, the capitalist class would resort to intimidation, repression, and ultimately abolition of the democratic rights of workers rather than seeing their economic power and social status eroded. When this happened, the working class would have to be prepared for revolution. If it were not, all of its hard-won concessions and advances would be lost.

By the beginning of World War I, it was obvious that the conservatives in the socialist movement had won at least a temporary victory over the revolutionaries. Capitalism in both England and Germany had passed through a period of prosperity in which the plight of workers had improved and a general feeling of optimism prevailed. In England the Fabian philosophy had come to dominate the Labour party, and in Germany the Revisionists had gained control of the Social Democratic party.

The subsequent history of those two parties was to illustrate the basic weakness of socialism that relied entirely on legislative reforms. Even though many party leaders continued to propound socialist ideas for some time, it was found that the pressure to attain an electoral majority continually forced party policies toward greater conservatism. In the 1950s both parties officially announced that they had given up the quest for social ownership of the means of production, distribution, and exchange. They asserted that ameliorative legislation to improve the living standards of the poor was all that remained to achieve a good and just society.

SUMMARY

In the late nineteenth and early twentieth centuries, improved working conditions, living standards, and political rights led to a split in the socialist movement. While the Marxist revolutionary socialists continued to affirm the necessity of a socialist revolution, a new school of reformist, evolutionary socialists argued that socialism could be achieved through gradual, peaceful legislative reforms.

In England, reformist socialism found its ablest leaders in George Bernard Shaw, Sidney and Beatrice Webb, and the other members of the Fabian Society. In Germany, it was Eduard Bernstein and the Revisionists who led the movement toward reformism. Both of these parties were ultimately pushed, by the pressures of achieving electoral majorities, to abandon the most fundamental tenet of socialism—socialization of the means of production.

REFERENCES

Bernstein, Eduard. *Evolutionary Socialism.* New York: Schocken Books, 1961. First published 1899.

Cole, G. D. H. *A History of Socialist Thought.* Vol. III, pt. 1. London: Macmillan, 1956.

Chapter
11

Imperialism and Revolutionary Socialism

The idea that a democratic government in a capitalist country could be used to effect a gradual and peaceful transition from capitalism to socialism led to a controversy that split the European socialist movement. However, the issue of imperialism was of equal if not greater significance in precipitating this division among socialists. During the late nineteenth and early twentieth centuries, European economic imperialism was most intensive. The nature and importance of an appropriate socialist response to imperialism were issues that created profound divisions among socialists—divisions that persist to this day.

EUROPEAN IMPERIALISM

India was one of the earliest and most dramatic cases of European imperialism. The East India Company had traded extensively in India for 150 years before the conquest of Bengal in 1757. During this period India was relatively advanced economically. Its methods of production and its industrial and commercial organization could definitely be compared with those prevailing in western Europe. In fact, India had been manufacturing and exporting the finest muslins and luxurious fabrics since the time when most western Europeans were backward primitive peoples.

After the conquest of Bengal, however, the East India Company became the ruling power in much of India, and the trade of the previous 150 years turned to harsh exploitation. It has been estimated that between 1757 and 1815 the British took between £500 million and £1000 million of wealth out of India. The incredible magnitude of this sum can be appreciated when compared with the £36 million that represented the total capital investment of all the joint stock companies operating in India (Baran, p. 145).

The policy of the East India Company in the last decades of the eighteenth century and in the early nineteenth century reflected two objectives. First, in the short run the myriad of greedy officials sought personal fortunes overnight: "These officials were absolute, irresponsible and rapacious, and they emptied the private hoards. Their only thought was to wring some hundreds of thousands of pounds out of the natives as quickly as possible, and hurry home to display their wealth. Enormous fortunes were thus rapidly accumulated at Calcutta, while thirty millions of human beings were reduced to the extremity of wretchedness" (Adams, quoted in ibid., p. 146).

A British observer described this ruthless quest for wealth in similar terms: "No Mahratta raid ever devastated a countryside with the thoroughness with which both the Company [East India Company] and, above all, the Company's servants in their individual capacities, sucked dry the plain of Bengal. In fact, in their blind rage for enrichment they took more from the Bengali peasants than those peasants could furnish and live. And the peasants duly died" (Strachey, p. 296).

The second was a long-run goal: to discourage or eliminate Indian manufacturers and make India dependent on British industries by forcing the Indians to concentrate on raw materials and export them to supply the textile looms and other British manufacturers. The policy was brutally, methodically—and successfully—executed.

> The total effect of this was that the British administration of India systematically destroyed all the fibres and foundations of Indian economy and substituted for it the parasitic landowner and moneylender. Its commercial policy destroyed the Indian artisan and created the infamous slums of the Indian cities filled with millions of starving and diseased paupers. Its economic policy broke down whatever beginnings there were of an indigenous industrial development and promoted the proliferations of speculators, petty businessmen, agents, and sharks of all descriptions eking out a sterile and precarious livelihood in the meshes of a decaying society. (Baran, p. 149)

It was only later, however, after the period of extensive railroad construction beginning in 1857, that the British thoroughly penetrated the interior of India. British investors who sank money into these railroads were guaranteed a 5 percent return by the government, which enforced a provision that if profits fell below 5 percent the Indian people would be taxed to make up the difference. Thus Indians were taxed to ensure that British investors would have adequate transport for further economic exploitation of the Indian interior.

Despite such harsh measures, the age of European imperialism really did not get under way on a broad, pervasive front until the last quarter of the nineteenth century. Between 1775 and 1875 the European countries had lost about as much colonial territory as they had won. The opinion was widely held that colonies were expensive luxuries.

All this changed suddenly and drastically after 1875. By 1900 Great Britain had grabbed 4,500,000 square miles, which she added to her empire; France had gobbled up 3,500,000; Germany, 1,000,000; Belgium, 900,000; Russia, 500,000; Italy, 185,000; and the United States, 125,000. Imperialism ran rampant as one-fourth of the world's population was subjugated and put under European and American domination.

Imperialism in Africa

By 1800 the Europeans had hardly penetrated beyond the coastal areas of Africa. By the early twentieth century, after a 100-year orgy of land grabbing and empire building, they controlled over 10 million square miles, or about 93 percent of the continent. In that gigantic plunder, various European powers sought to acquire the abundant minerals and agricultural commodities of the "dark continent."

The brutality of the European exploitation of Africa was perhaps most severe in the Belgian Congo. Belgian King Leopold II had sent H. M. Stanley into central Africa in 1879. Serving a private, profit-seeking company headed by Leopold and some of his associates, Stanley had a network of trading posts constructed and also duped native chiefs into signing "treaties" that established a commercial empire stretching over 900,000 square miles. Leopold set himself up as sovereign ruler of the Congo Free State and proceeded to exploit the natural and human resources of the area for the profits of his company.

The exploitation was ruthless. Natives were forced through outright physical coercion to gather rubber from the wild rubber trees and ivory from the elephants. Leopold confiscated all land that was not directly cultivated by the natives and placed it under "government ownership." Atrocities of the worst sort were committed to force the natives to submit to a very burdensome tax system that included taxes payable in rubber and ivory as well as in labor obligations.

By the twentieth century the Congo had also become a rich source of diamonds, uranium, copper, palm oil, palm kernels, and coconuts. In general, it can be said that the Congo was one of the most profitable of European imperialistic exploits as well as one of the most scandalous.

The British grabbed the most populous and also the richest holdings in Africa. In 1870 Cecil Rhodes went to South Africa for his health. Within two years his genius for organizing and controlling joint stock companies and his ability to corner the market on diamonds had made him a millionaire. In later years, the British South Africa Company, which Rhodes headed, came to control South Africa completely. Although it was a private, profit-seeking company, it had all the power of government, including the authority (given in its charter of 1889) to "make treaties, promulgate laws, preserve the peace, maintain a police force, and acquire new concessions."

The expansionist policies of the British South Africa Company led to the Boer War (1899–1902), which crushed the Dutch republics (the Orange Free State and the Transvaal republic) and gave Britain complete control over all South Africa. South Africa proved to be a rich mining region. But the legacy of British and Dutch imperialism is most vividly seen today in the suppression of the blacks, who constitute the vast majority of the population.

The other instances of imperialism in Africa are no less deserving of study. It must suffice in this short account, however, to mention that on the eve of World War I France held about 40 percent of Africa (much of it within the Sahara desert), England controlled 30 percent, and roughly 23 percent was divided among Germany, Belgium, Portugal, and Spain.

Imperialism in Asia

The results of the British takeover of India were evident by the turn of the twentieth century. In 1901 the per capita income was less than $10 per year, over two-thirds of the population were badly undernourished, and most native Indian manufacturing had been either ruined or taken over by the British. Nearly 90 percent of the population struggled to subsist in villages where the average holding was only 5 acres and farming techniques were primitive. Much of the meager produce was paid out in taxes, rents, and profits that accrued to the British. Famine, disease, and misery were rife. In 1891 the average Indian lived less than 26 years and usually died in misery.

Much of the rest of Asia was also subjugated during this period. In 1878 the British overran Afghanistan and placed it under the Indian government, and in 1907 Persia was divided between Russia and Britain.

In 1858 the French had used the murder of a Spanish missionary as the rationalization for invading Annam, a tributary state of China. They soon established a French colony in what is now Vietnam. With this toehold the French succeeded, through war and intrigue, in bringing all the territory of Indochina under their domination by 1887.

The Malay Peninsula and the Malay Archipelago (which stretches for nearly 3000 miles) were also carved up. The British grabbed Singapore and the Malay States, the northern part of Borneo, and south New Guinea. Another part of New Guinea was taken by the Germans, and most of the remaining islands (an area comprising about 735,000 square miles) went to the Dutch.

AMERICAN IMPERIALISM

Throughout much of the nineteenth century American imperialism channeled all its energies into conquering the continent and exterminating the native American Indian population. The Samoa Islands were America's first overseas imperialist acquisition. In 1878 the natives of Pago Pago granted the Americans the right to use their harbor. Eleven years later, the islands had been conquered and divided between the United States and Germany.

Similarly, Pearl Harbor became a U.S. naval station in 1887. In a very short time American capitalists controlled most of Hawaii's sugar production. The tiny minority of white Americans soon revolted against Queen Liliuokalani's rule and, with the help of U.S. Marines, subjugated the native population. In 1898 Hawaii was officially annexed by the United States.

It was also in 1898 that the United States used the convenient sinking of the battleship *Maine* as an excuse to declare war on Spain and "liberate" the Cubans from Spanish oppression. Recognizing that it was no match for the United States, the Spanish government accepted every American demand, but the United States declared war anyway as a "measure of atonement" for the *Maine*. The American victory gave it Puerto Rico, Guam, and the Philippine Islands outright, and the newly "independent" Cubans soon found American capitalists taking over most of their agriculture and commerce. Cuban independence had been restricted by a provision that the United States could intervene at its own discretion into Cuba's internal affairs "for the protection of life, property and individual liberty," a slogan that has been used to justify imperialism more than a few times. American troops invaded Cuba in 1906, 1911, and 1917 before secure control was finally established.

The Filipinos, who had been fighting for their independence from Spain, discovered the American brand to be no better than Spanish domination. President McKinley had decided that Americans were obligated "to educate the Filipinos and uplift and Christianize them," but the Filipinos, who had been Roman Catholics for centuries, resisted American "Christianization." It took 60,000 American troops, as well as endless atrocities and concentration camps, before the Filipinos were finally "uplifted" and "educated."

In 1901, when the republic of Colombia refused to sell a strip of land (on which the Panama Canal was to be constructed) to the United States, President Roosevelt took action. A Panamanian insurrection was organized with American approval and help. United States warships were strategically placed to prevent Colombian troops from moving in to suppress the rebellion. The revolt started on November 3, 1903; on November 6, the United States extended diplomatic recognition to the "new nation"; on November 18, the United States had the Canal Zone on much more favorable terms than it had originally offered.

In 1904 President Roosevelt announced that the United States believed in the principle of self-determination for nations that acted "with reasonable efficiency and decency in social and political matters." He added, however, that "chronic wrongdoing, or any impotence which results in a general loosening of the ties of civilized society, may in America, as elsewhere, ultimately require intervention by some civilized nation" (quoted in Fite and Reese, p. 472).

In 1909 U.S. Marines invaded Nicaragua to overthrow José Santos Zelaya, who threatened American economic concessions there. American troops were back in Nicaragua in 1912. In 1915 American Marines invaded Haiti, and in 1916 American troops overwhelmed the Dominican Republic and established a military government there.

By World War I the United States had seized or otherwise controlled Samoa, Midway Island, Hawaii, Puerto Rico, Guam, the Philippines, the island of Tutuila, Cuba, Santo Domingo, Haiti, Nicaragua, and the Panama Canal Zone.

IMPERIALISM AND EVOLUTIONARY SOCIALISM

The Boer War jolted British public opinion and resulted in strong conflicts among many radicals and socialists. On the one hand, it produced an abundance of jingoist sentiment and imperialist ideology that influenced some socialists; on the other hand, J. A. Hobson's *Imperialism: A Study* caustically ridiculed this sentiment and ideology and advanced a theory of imperialism that was to have a profound influence on Marxists and many non-Marxist socialists.

Imperialism, according to Hobson, was a struggle for political and economic domination of areas of the world occupied by "lower races." Its "economic taproot" was the necessity for advanced capitalist countries to find markets for goods and capital produced domestically but for which there was inadequate domestic demand. Evoking traditions of nationalism and militarism, it could "appeal to the lust of quantitative acquisitiveness and of forceful domination surviving in a nation from early centuries of animal struggle for existence" (Hobson, p. 368).

The basic cause of the deficiency in domestic demand was, Hobson believed, a severely inequitable distribution of income that resulted in a distorted allocation of resources, which led, in turn, to the quest for foreign markets. Hobson argued that the imperialist tendencies of the late nineteenth and early twentieth centuries could be reversed only by reform radical enough to effect a more equitable distribution of income. He summarized his position succinctly in the following passage:

> There is no necessity to open up new foreign markets; the home markets are capable of indefinite expansion. Whatever is produced in England can be consumed in England, provided that the "income," or power to demand commodities, is properly distributed. This only appears untrue because of the unnatural and unwholesome specialization to which this country has been subjected, based upon a bad distribution of economic resources, which has induced an overgrowth of certain manufacturing trades for the express purpose of ef-

fecting foreign sales. If the industrial revolution had taken place in an England founded upon equal access by all classes to land, education, and legislation, specialization in manufactures would not have gone so far . . . ; foreign trade would have been less important though more steady; the standard of life for all portions of the population would have been high, and the present rate of national consumption would probably have given full, constant, remunerative employment to a far larger quantity of private and public capital than is now being employed. (Ibid., pp. 88–89)

The issue of whether publicly to denounce English imperialism bitterly divided the Fabians. Sydney Olivier's insistence that the society's executive committee issue a pronouncement condemning the Boer War in particular and imperialism in general was rejected by one vote, but the committee agreed to the demand that the issue be put to a general vote.

Led by George Bernard Shaw, the pro-imperialist faction argued that small, backward nations could not manage their own affairs and should not be considered as nations at all, and that the advanced European nations thus had a duty to police and manage the internal affairs of these backward peoples for their own welfare. The debate was bitter. Finally, 45 percent of the membership voted to condemn English imperialism, and 55 percent opted to approve of or ignore imperialism. Immediately, 18 members of the society, including several of its most prominent personalities, handed in their resignations.

The sentiments of the German Revisionists were similar to those of the Fabians, the majority either approving of European imperialism or not considering it a proper issue on which to take a stand. Bernstein, for example, wrote, "Only a conditional right of savages to the land occupied by them can be recognized. The higher civilization ultimately can claim a higher right" (Bernstein, p. xii). Orthodox Marxists, however, were virtually unanimous in condemning imperialism, which they analyzed as only the latest stage in the historical development of capitalism: Capitalists were forced by the mounting contradictions of the economic system to turn frantically to economic exploitation of more backward areas.

ROSA LUXEMBURG'S ANALYSIS OF IMPERIALISM

Rosa Luxemburg was one of the most important political leaders and exponents of orthodox Marxism. Her book *The Accumulation of Capital* contained a description and analysis of imperialism that was to exert a strong influence on subsequent generations of socialists.

Luxemburg began her analysis by a review of Marx's analysis of the process of *capitalist commodity production*, discussed in Chapter 7, the process in which capitalists started with some given amount of money and purchased one commodity—labor power—and then sold a different commodity—that produced by labor in the production process. From the sales of the products of labor, they received a greater value than they laid out in expenses for raw materials, goods in process, and labor; that is, they received surplus value, or profits. The money they received in sales, however, had to be spent by purchasers of their commodities.

These purchasers of their commodities could be the laborers spending their wages for the means of subsistence, or other capitalists buying the raw materials and goods in process necessary for production. But we have already said that in order for surplus value to exist the proceeds from sales of commodities must exceed wages and expenditures on raw materials and goods in process. Part of the difference might be made up by capitalists' expenditures on consumption. Luxemburg observed, however, that capitalists' consumption expenditures typically make up only a small part of the surplus value they receive.

Another part of the deficiency in expenditures could be made up by capitalists purchasing capital goods that were not necessary to maintain the current level of production but were desired so that future production could be expanded. But the desire to expand production would have to be predicated on the expectation of greater demand for consumption goods, and it was the insufficiency of this demand for consumption goods that represented the crux of the problem. Capitalists would accumulate capital goods not for their own sake but only in the expectation that this accumulation would increase their profits. The inescapable conclusion, for Luxemburg, was that from within the internal sphere of a capitalist economy the expenditures of capitalists and workers could not for any lengthy period be sufficient to permit continuous realization of the surplus value generated from expanding commodity production.

Yet capitalism had been more or less continually expanding for well over a century, and Luxemburg sought to discover the source of the necessary additional expenditures that made this expansion possible. This source she found in the historical tendency of the capitalist mode of production to continually expand into noncapitalist areas, bring these areas under its control, and incorporate them within the domain of capitalist relations. The expenditures of these noncapitalist areas in the purchase of commodities produced in capitalist areas would represent the additional necessary demand:

> From the aspect both of realizing the surplus value and of procuring the material elements of constant capital, international trade is a prime necessity for the historical existence of capitalism—an international trade which under actual conditions is essentially an exchange between capitalistic and noncapitalistic modes. (Luxemburg, p. 359)

Luxemburg therefore believed that "imperialism is the political expression of the accumulation of capital in its competitive struggle for what remains still open of the non-capitalist environment." The continuous diminution of the size of the unexploited noncapitalist areas of the world had led to a situation in which "imperialism grows in lawlessness and violence, both in aggression against the noncapitalist world and in ever more serious conflicts among the competing capitalist countries" (ibid., p. 446).

Within this theoretical framework Luxemburg wrote penetrating and insightful descriptions of the way in which the development of capitalism necessitated the growth of nationalism, militarism, and racism. In her analysis of military spending, for example, she understood the dual function such spending served in protecting capitalist empires around the world while providing the necessary stimulation of aggregate demand at home.

> The multitude of individual and insignificant demands for a whole range of commodities . . . is now replaced by a comprehensive and homogeneous demand of the state. And the satisfaction of this demand presupposes a big industry of the highest order. It requires the most favorable conditions for the production of surplus value and for accumulation. In the form of government contracts for army supplies the scattered purchasing power of the consumers is concentrated in large quantities and, free of the vagaries and subjective fluctuations of personal consumption, it achieves an almost automatic regularity and rhythmic growth. Capital itself ultimately controls this automatic and rhythmic movement of militarist production through the legislature and a press whose function is to mould so-called "public opinion." That is why this particular province of capitalist accumulation at first seems capable of infinite expansion. All other attempts to expand markets and set up operational bases for capital largely depend on historical, social and political factors beyond the control of capital, whereas production for militarism represents a province whose regular and progressive expansion seems primarily determined by capital itself.
>
> In this way capital turns historical necessity into a virtue. (Ibid., p. 466)

This passage was written in 1913. This level of clear understanding of the role of military expenditures was not widely achieved among economists until about a half-century later, when the forces Luxemburg was describing had developed well beyond what they had been on the eve of World War I.

Despite such brilliant insights, Luxemburg's analysis of imperialism rested on a faulty theoretical structure. Noncapitalist consumers are not automatically a source of increased demand. If products are to be sold to them, products must also be purchased from them—otherwise they would have no foreign currency with which to make the purchases. The net result on aggregate demand from this buying and selling cannot be determined in advance. Moreover, in less developed countries capitalist investments are soon yielding surplus value of their own. This tends to worsen rather than solve the problem of adequate demand.

Luxemberg's problem was that she focused on the wrong problem—underconsumption. The real driving force of imperialism was the search for profitable investment outlets to which the advanced capitalist countries could export capital. These deficiencies in the Marxist analysis of imperialism were corrected by Lenin.

LENIN'S ANALYSIS OF IMPERIALISM

The most famous and influential socialist analysis was contained in Lenin's pamphlet *Imperialism: The Highest Stage of Capitalism*, published in 1916. Lenin attempted "to show, as briefly and as popularly as possible, the principal economic characteristics of imperialism" (Lenin, p. 1). The most important was that in the imperialistic phase of capitalist development the capitalist economies were thoroughly dominated by monopolies, a development Marx had correctly foreseen. By monopolies Lenin did not mean industries consisting of only one firm (the modern economic definition of monopoly); rather, he referred to industries dominated by trusts, cartels, combinations, or a few large firms.

Drawing heavily on the German experience, Lenin argued that the development of monopolies was closely related to important changes in the banking system. Banks had assumed a position of central importance in the drive toward cartelization and had come to exercise considerable control over many of the most important industrial cartels. This control was so extensive that Lenin spoke of the imperialistic phase of capitalism as the age of "finance capital."

Banks were able to mobilize huge sums of money for investment, but persistent downward pressures on domestic profit rates dictated that investment outlets be sought outside the home country. Lenin, unlike Hobson, did not believe the necessity to export commodities was the most important economic cause of imperialism. Rather, it was the necessity to export capital. Backward areas offered a large and inexpensive labor force and lucrative investment prospects.

In the imperialist phase of capitalism the various governments fought to gain access to privileged and protected markets for the combines and cartels within their own political boundaries. At the same time, these national combines and cartels sought to partition the world markets through international cartels. Deep-seated rivalry and competition, however, were more important than opportunistic short-run collaborations. Persistent national conflicts and wars were the inevitable result. In Lenin's words:

> The epoch of the newest capitalism shows us that certain relations are being established between capitalist combines, *based* on the economic division of the world; while parallel with this and in connection with it, certain relations are being established between political alliances, between states, on the basis of the territorial division of the world, of the struggle for colonies, of the "struggle for economic territory." (Ibid., p. 69)

Such a situation was, Lenin believed, inherently unstable. Imperialism would lead to wars among the advanced capitalist countries and to rebellions and revolutions in the exploited areas. As long as the capitalist system could support its imperialistic thrust, however, it would prolong its existence by providing outlets for excess investment funds. The extra profits that imperialism secured for the home country meant that the wages paid its workers could be raised. Thus, because it shared in the spoils, labor would be at least temporarily sapped of its revolutionary potential and controlled by right-wing labor leaders, "justly called social imperialists" (ibid., p. 99).

If imperialism expanded the domain of capitalism and in doing so prolonged the system's existence, the tensions and conflicts it engendered were, Lenin believed, more severe than those of the competitive capitalism about which Marx wrote. Capitalism was still doomed, and socialism was still the wave of the future.

SUMMARY

The late nineteenth and early twentieth centuries witnessed the imperialistic carving up of most of the world's economically underdeveloped areas. The inhabitants of these areas were harshly and cruelly exploited for the profits of large corporations in the advanced capitalist countries.

The issue of imperialism split the evolutionary socialist movement. Many of the reform socialists, such as George Bernard Shaw and Eduard Bernstein, were strongly pro-imperialist. Others, among them J. A. Hobson, were strongly anti-imperialist. Hobson's analysis of imperialism stressed the maldistribution of wealth and income as the causes of this socioeconomic phenomenon. He advocated reforms to redistribute income and wealth within the capitalist framework.

Virtually all Marxist socialists opposed imperialism. Rosa Luxemburg saw the root problem as inadequate aggregate demand. Although her theoretical framework had some weaknesses, she had brilliant insights into the nature of imperialism, nationalism, racism, and militarism. Her weaknesses were corrected in Lenin's *Imperialism: The Highest Stage of Capitalism.* He stressed the importance of investment outlets and the capitalists' need to export capital. His analysis has remained the most influential Marxist critique of imperialism.

REFERENCES

Adams, Brooks. "The Law of Civilization and Decay, An Essay on History." In: Paul A. Baran, *The Political Economy of Growth.* New York: Monthly Review Press, 1962.

Baran, Paul A. *The Political Economy of Growth.* New York: Monthly Review Press, 1962.

Bernstein, Eduard. *Evolutionary Socialism.* New York: Schocken Books, 1961. First published 1899.

Fite, G. C., and J. E. Reese. *An Economic History of the United States.* 2d ed. Boston: Houghton Mifflin, 1965.

Hobson, J. A. *Imperialism: A Study.* London: Allen & Unwin, 1938. First published 1902.

Lenin, V. I. *Imperialism: The Highest Stage of Capitalism.* London: Lawrence & Wishart, 1939.

Luxemburg, Rosa. *The Accumulation of Wealth.* New York: Monthly Review Press, 1964.

Strachey, John. "Famine in Bengal." In *The Varieties of Economics.* Vol. 1. Edited by Robert Lekachman. New York: Meridian, 1962.

Chapter
12

Keynesian Economics and the Great Depression

Although the period from the Civil War to 1900 was one of rapid economic expansion in the United States, these accomplishments were dwarfed by the growth that occurred between 1900 and 1929. The following figures show the percentage increase in manufacturing production in several key industries between 1899 and 1927.

Chemicals, etc.	239%
Leather and products	321
Textiles and products	449
Food products	551
Machinery	562
Paper and printing	614
Steel and products	780
Transportation and equipment	969

It has been estimated that U.S. wealth (the market values of all economic assets) reached $86 billion by 1900; in 1929, it stood at $361 billion (data in Huberman, p. 254).

This spectacular growth gave the United States a huge edge over all other countries in manufacturing output. The American prosperity of the 1920s was based on high and rising levels of output—though there were recessions in 1923 and 1927. The gross national product, the value of all goods and services produced, increased by 62 percent from 1914 to 1929.

Only 3.2 percent of the labor force was unemployed in 1929, and labor productivity rose during that decade at least as fast as wages. Between 1921 and 1929, total automobile registrations increased from less than 11 million to more than 26 million; consumers spent tens of millions of dollars on radios, refrigerators, and other electric appliances that had not been available before. American manufacturing seemed to most people a permanent cornucopia destined to create affluence for all.

This leadership in manufacturing was associated with financial leadership in the world economy. The American economic empire began to rival that of England. By 1930 American businessmen owned large investments around the world. The following figures give the values of these investments in 1930.

Canada	$3,942,000,000
Europe	4,929,000,000
Mexico and Central America	1,000,000,000
South America	3,042,000,000
West Indies	1,233,000,000
Africa	118,000,000
Asia	1,023,000,000
Oceania	419,000,000

THE GREAT DEPRESSION

This era of rapid growth and economic abundance came to a halt on October 24, 1929. On that "Black Thursday" the New York stock market saw security values begin a downward fall that was to destroy all faith in business. Their confidence undermined, businessmen cut back production and investment. This decreased national income and employment, which, in turn, worsened business confidence even more. Before the process came to an end, thousands of corporations had gone bankrupt, millions were unemployed, and one of the worst national catastrophes in history was under way.

Between 1929 and 1932 there were over 85,000 business failures; more than 5,000 banks suspended operations; stock values on the New York Exchange fell from $87 billion to $19 billion; unemployment rose to 12 million, with nearly one-fourth of the population having no means of sustaining themselves; farm income fell by more than half; and manufacturing output decreased by almost 50 percent (Hacker, pp. 300–301).

America had plunged from the world's most prosperous country to one in which tens of millions lived in desperate, abject poverty. Particularly hard hit were the blacks and other minority groups. The proportion of blacks among the unemployed was from 60 to 400 percent higher than the proportion of blacks in the general population (Chandler, pp. 40–41). Certain geographic areas suffered more than others. Congressman George Huddleston of Alabama reported in January 1932:

> We have about 108,000 wage and salary workers in my district. Of that number, it is my belief that not exceeding 8,000 have their normal incomes. At least 25,000 men are altogether without work. Some of them have not had a stroke of work for more than 12 months, maybe 60,000 or 75,000 are working one to five days a week, and practically all have had serious cuts in their wages and many of them do not average over $1.50 a day. (U.S. Congress, p. 239)

Many cities reported that they could give relief payments for only a very short time, often one week, before people were forced to their own devices to subsist. The executive director of the Welfare Council of New York City described the plight of the unemployed:

> When the breadwinner is out of a job he usually exhausts his savings if he has any. Then, if he has an insurance policy, he probably borrows to the limit of its cash value. He borrows from his friends and from his relatives until they can stand the burden no longer. He gets credit from the corner grocery store and the butcher shop, and the landlord forgoes collecting the rent until interest and taxes have to be paid and something has to be done. All of these resources are finally exhausted over a period of time, and it becomes necessary for these people, who have never before been in want, to ask for assistance. The specter of starvation faces millions of people who have never before known what it was to be out of a job for any considerable period of time and who certainly have never known what it was to be absolutely up against it. (Quoted in Chandler, pp. 41–42)

The abject despair of these millions of people is at best suggested by a 1932 report describing the unloading of garbage in the Chicago city garbage dumps: "Around the truck which was unloading garbage and other refuse were about 35 men, women and children. As soon as the truck pulled away from the pile all of them started digging with sticks, some with their hands, grabbing bits of food and vegetables" (quoted in Huberman, p. 260).

What had happened to reduce the output of goods and services so drastically? Natural resources were still as plentiful as ever. The nation still had as many factories, tools, and machines. The people had the same skills and wanted to put them to work. Yet millions of workers and their families begged, borrowed, stole, and lined up for a pittance from charity, while thousands of factories stood idle or operated far below capacity. The explanation lay within the institutions of the capitalist market system. Factories could have been opened and people put to work, but they were not because it was not profitable for businessmen to do this. And in a capitalist economy production decisions are based primarily on the criterion of profits, not on people's needs.

THE ECONOMICS OF KEYNES

The socialist cause gained many enthusiasts in the 1930s. While the capitalist world was suffering what was perhaps its most severe depression, the Soviet economy was experiencing rapid growth. When the depression struck, it was a traumatic shock to many Americans, who had come to believe their country was destined to achieve unparalleled and unending increases in material prosperity.

The capitalist economic system seemed to be on the verge of total collapse. Drastic countermeasures were essential, but before the system could be saved the malady had to be better understood. To that task came one of the most brilliant economists of this century: John Maynard Keynes (1883–1946). In his famous book *The General Theory of Employment, Interest and Money*, Keynes attempted to show what had happened to capitalism so that it could be preserved.

Keynes began his analysis by looking at the process of production. In a given production period a firm produces a certain dollar volume of goods. From the proceeds of the sale of these goods, it pays its costs of production, which include wages, salaries, rent, supplies and raw materials, and interest on borrowed funds. What remains after these costs are paid is profit.

The important point to remember is this: What is a cost of production to the business firm represents income to an individual or another firm. The profit is also income—the income going to the owners of the firm. Because the value of production is exhausted by the costs of production and profits, and all these are income, it follows that the value of what has been produced must be equal to the incomes generated in producing it.

In terms of the entire economy the aggregate picture is the same as that for the individual firm: The value of everything produced in the economy during any period is equal to the total of all incomes received in that period. Therefore, in order for businesses to sell all that they have produced, people must spend in the aggregate all their incomes. If an amount equal to the total income in society is spent on goods and services, then the value of production is realized in sales. In that case profits remain high, and businessmen are willing to produce the same amount or more in the succeeding period.

Keynes called this a *circular flow:* Money flows from business to the public in the form of wages, salaries, rents, interests, and profits; this money then flows back to the businesses when the public buys goods and services from them. *As long as businesses sell all they have produced and make satisfactory profits*, the process continues.

This does not happen automatically, however. When money flows from businesses to the public, some of it does not flow directly back to businesses. The circular flow has leakages. To begin with, all people do not spend all their incomes. A percentage is saved, usually in banks, and therefore withdrawn from the spending stream. This saving may be offset by other people, who borrow money from banks and spend more than their income. Keynes, however, pointed out that at the peak of prosperity saving is usually greater than consumer borrowing: thus there is usually net saving, or a net leakage, from the circular income-expenditure flow.

Keynes also identified two other leakages: (1) People buy goods and services from foreign businesses, but the money spent on these imports cannot be spent on domestically produced goods. (2) The taxes people pay are also withdrawn from the income-expenditure flow.

These three leakages (savings, imports, and taxes) may be offset by three spending injections into the income-expenditure flow: (1) Imports can be offset by exports. They are exactly offset when foreigners buy goods produced in the United States in amounts equal to foreign imports purchased by Americans. (2) The government uses taxes to finance the purchase of goods and services. If it uses all taxes for this purpose and balances the budget, then government expenditures will exactly offset taxes in the spending stream. (3) If businessmen wish to expand their capital, they can finance investment in capital goods by borrowing the funds that were saved. Investment, then, may exactly offset the saving leakage.

If these three injections into the income-expenditure flow are just as large as the three leakages, then spending equals the value of production. Everything that has been produced can be sold, and prosperity reigns.

Keynes, however, believed it was unlikely that the process could continue uninterrupted for very long. Investment, which is necessary to absorb savings, enlarges the capital stock and hence increases the economy's productive capacity. In order to utilize the new productive capacity fully, production and income must increase in the next period. But with the higher income there will be more saving, which necessitates more investment, and this investment is by no means automatically forthcoming.

Keynes saw that individuals with higher incomes saved a higher percentage of their incomes than those with low incomes. He concluded that this pattern would hold for the whole society. As the aggregate income of society increases, total savings increase more than proportionately. In other words, at each new higher level of income a larger percentage of income is saved.

Thus investment would have to increase at a faster rate than income if it were to continually offset saving. Only this rapid increase would permit businesses to sell everything they produced; but the faster investment grows, the more rapid is the increase in productive capacity. Because of this, the economy must invest ever-greater amounts (both absolutely and relatively) in each successive period if the balance is to be maintained. However, according to Keynes, in any mature private enterprise economy the number of profitable investment outlets is limited. Hence, as the process of economic growth continues, the difficulty of finding sufficient investment outlets becomes more and more acute.

If it becomes impossible to find enough investment outlets, then investment falls short of saving and total expenditures for goods and services fall short of the value of those produced. Businesses, unable to sell all they have produced, find that their inventories of unsold goods are increasing. Each business sees only its own problem: that it has produced more than it can sell. It therefore reduces production in the next period. Most businesses, being in the same situation, do the same thing. The results are a large reduction in production, a decrease in employment, and a decline in income. With the decline in income, however, even less will be spent on goods and services in the next period. So businesses find that even at the lower level of production they are unable to sell all they have produced. Again they cut back production, and the downward spiral continues.

Under these circumstances businesses have little or no incentive to expand their capital goods (because excess capacity already exists), and therefore investment falls drastically. Expenditures of all types plummet. As income declines, saving declines more than proportionately. This process continues until the declines in income have reduced saving to the point where it no longer exceeds the reduced level of investment. At this low level of income equilibrium is restored. Leakages from the income-expenditure flow are again equal to the injections into it. The economy is stabilized, but at a level where high unemployment and considerable unused productive capacity exist.

Keynes's analysis was not, in its essentials, drastically different from those offered by Marx (Chapter 7) and Hobson (Chapter 11). The principal cause of a depression was, in the opinion of all three thinkers, the inability of capitalists to find sufficient investment opportunities to offset the increasing levels of saving generated by economic growth. Keynes's unique contribution was to show how the relation of saving to income could lead to a stable but depressed level of income with widespread unemployment.

Marx (and Lenin) had believed the disease incurable under capitalism. Hobson had prescribed measures to equalize the distribution of income and thereby reduce saving as a cure. Could Hobson's prescription work? This probably is not a very meaningful question. In most industrial capitalist countries wealth and economic power determine political power, and those who wield power have never been willing to sacrifice it to save the economic system.

In the United States, for example, of the 300,000 nonfinancial corporations existing in 1925 the largest 200 made considerably more profit than the other 299,800 combined. The wealthiest 5 percent of the population owned virtually all of the stocks and bonds and received more than 30 percent of the income. Needless to say, this 5 percent dominated American politics. In these circumstances speculating about what would happen if the income and wealth were radically redistributed amounts to mere fanciful daydreaming.

Keynes's answer to the problem was more realistic. Government could step in when saving exceeded investment, borrow the excess saving, then spend the money on socially useful projects. These projects would be chosen in order not to increase the economy's productive capacity or decrease the investment opportunities of the future. This government spending would increase the injections into the spending stream and create a full-employment equilibrium. In doing so, it would not add to the capital stock. Therefore, unlike investment spending, it would not make a full-employment level of production more difficult to attain in the next period. Keynes summarized his position thus:

> Ancient Egypt was doubly fortunate, and doubtless owed to this its fabled wealth, in that it possessed *two* activities, namely, pyramid-building as well as the search for precious metals, the fruits of which, since they could not serve the needs of many by being consumed, did not stale with abundance. The Middle Ages built cathedrals and sang dirges. Two pyramids, two masses for the dead, are twice as good as one; but not so two railways from London to York. (Keynes, p. 131)

What types of expenditures ought the government make? Keynes himself had a predilection toward useful public works such as the construction of schools, hospitals, parks, and other public conveniences. He realized, however, that this would probably benefit middle- and lower-income recipients much more than the wealthy. And because the wealthy have political power, they would probably insist on policies that would not redistribute income away from them. He saw that it might be politically necessary to channel this spending into the hands of the large corporations, even though little that was beneficial to society would be accomplished directly. He wrote:

> If the Treasury were to fill old bottles with banknotes, bury them at suitable depths in disused coalmines which are then filled up to the surface with town rubbish, and leave it to private enterprise on well-tried principles of laissez-faire to dig the notes up again . . . there need be no unemployment. . . . It would indeed be more sensible to build houses and the like; but if there are political and practical difficulties in the way of this, the above would be better than nothing. (Ibid., p. 129)

The depression of the 1930s dragged on until the outbreak of World War II. From 1936 (the year Keynes's *General Theory* was published) to 1940, economists hotly debated the merits of his theory and policy prescriptions. When the various governments began to increase armament production rapidly, however, unemployment began to melt away. During the war years, under the stimulus of enormous government expenditures, conditions in most capitalist economies were rapidly transformed from a situation of severe unemployment to one of acute labor shortage.

The American armed forces mobilized 14 million people, who had to be armed, quartered, and fed. Between 1939 and 1944 the output of the manufacturing, mining, and construction industries doubled, and productive capacity increased by 50 percent. The American economy produced 296,000 planes, 5400 cargo ships, 6500 naval vessels, 64,500 landing craft, 86,000 tanks, and 2,500,000 trucks. During the war period the most pressing problem was a *shortage* of labor, as contrasted with the 19 percent unemployment that existed as late as the beginning of 1939 (Hacker, p. 325).

KEYNESIAN ECONOMICS AND IDEOLOGY

Most economists believed this wartime experience had proved the basic correctness of Keynes's ideas. Capitalism could be saved, they proclaimed, by wise use of the government's powers to tax, borrow, and spend money. Capitalism was again a viable social and economic system.

Viability alone was insufficient as an ideology for capitalism, however. The USSR did not have unemployment in the 1930s, and its spectacular rate of growth during this period had proved the viability of the Soviet economic system. This challenge elicited a resurgence of the older neo-classical economic ideology. These older theories were cast in an esoteric and highly elaborate mathematical framework. Typical of the new economists was Paul A. Samuelson, whose book *The Foundations of Economic Analysis* (1947) was among the technically most formidable treatments of economics. In 1947 the American Economic Association awarded him the first John Bates Clark Medal for the most outstanding contribution to economics made by an economist under 40 years of age. The book was also instrumental in securing the Nobel Prize in economics for Samuelson in 1970.

Samuelson has made an even more significant contribution in terms of his influence on the dominant economic ideology of capitalism since the 1940s. His introductory text, *Economics* (1948), has undergone twelve editions, has been translated into almost every major language, and has sold millions of copies. The first edition set out mainly to explain and simplify Keynes's ideas. Each subsequent edition has tended to bring in more of the traditional neoclassical ideology of capitalism. In 1955 Samuelson offered his "grand neoclassical synthesis," an integration of Keynesian with neoclassical economics. The Keynesian theory would provide the knowledge necessary to maintain a full-employment economy, and the market system could operate within this Keynesian framework to allocate resources according to the time-honored principles of the neoclassical ideology. Almost all students of economics in recent years have learned their elementary economics from Samuelson's textbook or from one of the many others that have attempted to follow his approach and content.

THE EFFICACY OF KEYNESIAN ECONOMIC POLICIES

After 1945, Keynesian economics became orthodoxy for both economists and the majority of politicians. Almost 3 million veterans were demobilized in that year. In 1946 another 11 million joined the civilian labor force. Congress and many economists feared a new depression and immediately took steps to apply the new Keynesian ideas. Passage of the Employment

Act of 1946 legally obligated the government to use its taxing, borrowing, and spending powers to maintain full employment. The act declared that "it is the continuing policy and responsibility of the Federal government to use all practicable means . . . for the purpose of creating and maintaining . . . conditions under which there will be afforded useful employment opportunities, including self-employment, for those able, willing, and seeking to work, and to promote maximum employment, production and purchasing power." This was the first time the U.S. government ever acknowledged responsibility for employment, and it is still not really committed to full employment for all people.

Have Keynesian economic policies worked? The answer to this question is very complex. Since World War II there have been no major depressions in the United States, but there have been eight recessions (the modern euphemism for a mild depression). In 1948–1949, a recession lasted for 11 months; in 1953–1954, for 13 months; in 1957–1958, for 9 months; and in 1960–1961, for 9 months. The 1969–1971 recession went on for more than two years. The 1974–1975 recession was more severe than those that preceded it. In 1979 and 1980 there was another recession. After a very brief recovery the recession of 1981–1982 incurred levels of unemployment higher than at any time since the Great Depression of the 1930s.

Because of these recessions, the economy's performance in the 1950s left much to be desired. The real rate of growth of GNP was 2.9 percent, which does not compare very favorably with the 4.7 percent for 1920–1929 or the 3.7 percent for 1879–1919. The brightest spot in the American economy's performance was its growth rate in the 1960s, which averaged around 5 percent. In the 1970s the growth rate fell and the economy experienced mild stagnation together with steadily worsening inflation.

Unemployment for the 1950s and early 1960s averaged 4.5 percent, although it dipped to 3.5 percent in the mid-1960s. Moreover, inflation has been a persistent problem since World War II. From 1945 through 1968 the average annual increase in wholesale prices was 3.8 percent (most of which occurred in the late 1940s); the rate of increase from 1968 to 1970 was nearly 5 percent. The 1969–1971 inflation was accompanied by an economic recession in which unemployment soared to rates in excess of 6 percent. The simultaneous occurrence of both high unemployment and a high rate of inflation led to President Nixon's attempt to freeze wages and prices in late 1971, followed by government control over increases in wages and prices. By the late 1970s inflation rose to levels well in excess of 12 percent. In early 1980 an inflation rate of 18 percent worsened the soaring rate of unemployment that signaled another recession. After the 1981–1982 recession the inflation rate was reduced significantly. From 1982 to 1989 the economy avoided both recession and severe inflation. The "prosperity" of the 1980s was, however, partial, at best. It involved a steadily worsening distribution of income and a persistently high rate of unemployment.

Economists like Samuelson argued that Keynesian policies, reflected in enormous government spending, resulted in the impressive growth performance of the 1960s; but they find the accompanying inflation quite mysterious. Before judging this performance, however, it is necessary to see what the American government substituted for the pyramids of Egypt and the cathedrals of the Middle Ages. In 1960 one observer wrote: "A central aspect of our growth experience of the past two decades is one which few spokesmen for the future candidly discuss. This is the fact that our great boom did not begin until the onset of World War II, and that its continuance since then has consistently been tied to a military rather than to a purely civilian economic demand" (Heilbroner, p. 133). As we enter the 1990s the statement remains as true as ever.

THE WARFARE ECONOMY

In 1940 military-related expenditures were $3.2 billion, or 3.2 percent of GNP. In 1943, at the height of World War II, military spending consumed almost 40 percent of GNP, while profits rose to unprecedented heights. The war provided capitalists with a clear example of how government military spending can end a depression and guarantee large returns to capital.

By 1947 military spending was back to only $9.1 billion, or 3.9 percent of GNP. During the rapid growth of the 1960s, military expenditures grew at approximately the same rate as GNP. If other expenses that are related to militarism but not included in the "defense" budget are taken into account, the total has been close to 15 percent in recent years (Fusfeld, pp. 11, 34–35). The United States has spent and continues to spend more on militarism than any other country—more in absolute terms, relative terms, and per capita.

The result of these enormous expenditures has been growth of the *military-industrial complex* as a necessary adjunct to economic prosperity. Its essential features have been described as follows:

> The warfare state we have constructed over the last two generations has a large clientele. At the top of the pyramid is the so-called military-industrial complex. It comprises, first, the Defense Department of the Federal Government, along with such satellites as the CIA and NASA. The admirals and generals, the space scientists and the intelligence men, like all government bureaucrats, are busily engaged in strengthening their influence. To this end they cultivate congressmen and senators, locate military establishments in politically strategic districts, and provide legislators with special favors. Former military men are drawn into the net of influence through the Army and Navy associations and through veterans' organizations. The military are supported by the industrial side of the complex. These are the large corporations on whom the military depend for the hardware of modern war. Some sell the bulk of their output to the military, like North American Aviation, Lockheed Aircraft, General Dynamics, McDonnell-Douglas, and Thiokol Chemical. Others are important military suppliers but make the bulk of their sales in civilian markets,

such as Western Electric, Sperry Rand, General Electric or IBM. Others, such as Dupont and General Motors, are only occasionally military contractors. (Ibid., p. 13)

The extent to which military production dominates the American economy is indicated by a recent survey showing that the five key military-related industries accounted for 7.9 percent of all employment in New York, 12.3 percent in New Jersey, 13 percent in Texas, 14.6 percent in Massachusetts, 15.7 percent in Maryland, 20.9 percent in Florida, 23.4 percent in Connecticut, 30 percent in Kansas, 31.4 percent in California and 34.8 percent in Washington (ibid., p. 15).

In 1988, the Pentagon awarded $142 billion in prime defense contracts. California received a whopping $23.5 billion, Virginia $10.2 billion, and Texas $9 billion. From California's enormous share to Wyoming's minute $54.6 million, 41 states received defense contracts, averaging $3.5 billion each. By 1988 most of the economies of these 41 states were highly dependent on military expenditures for their general prosperity.

Military expenditures operate in exactly the way Keynes believed pyramid building operated in the ancient Egyptian economy. For generals and most politicians, a tenfold overkill potential is twice as good as a fivefold overkill; two ABM (antiballistic missile) systems are twice as good as one but only half as good as four. And if the public cannot be easily convinced of this, the immense amount of research financed by the military-industrial complex comes to the fore. Weapons and delivery systems are rapidly superseded by new models. Horror stories convince the public that a further escalation of the arms race is necessary and that "obsolete" (and often unused) models must be scrapped.

Military spending keeps the capital goods industry operating near full capacity without raising the economy's productive capacity as rapidly as would be the case if they provided capital goods for industry. Demand does not tend to drop below supply as persistently as it formerly did; military spending increases demand without increasing productivity.

The neglect of these effects of the Keynesian military-induced prosperity is perhaps "the most important abdication of any by the economists." This type of economic theory has led to "an ahistorical, a technical or mechanical, a nonpolitical view of what the economy is and how it works" (Rosen, pp. 83, 85).

Very few Keynesian economists have been willing to come to grips with the implication of militarism as a tool of economic policy.

> The arms economy has been the major Keynesian instrument of our times. But its use has been cloaked as "national interest," its effects have been largely undermined, its international consequences largely deleterious and destabilizing, its importance making for uncritical acceptance and dependence by large segments of the society, its long-run effects hardly glanced at. The arms economy has done much more than distort the use of scarce creative scientific and engineering talent . . . It has forced us to neglect a whole range of urgent social

priorities, the consequences of which threaten the fabric of our society. (Ibid., pp. 86–87).

SUMMARY

The severity of the Great Depression of the 1930s caused many economists to become dissatisfied with the orthodox neoclassical economists' view that unemployment was merely a short-run, ephemeral "adjustment" to a temporary disequilibrium situation. Keynes's new ideas were rapidly accepted by most important economists. World War II proved that massive government intervention in the market economy could create full employment; indeed, Hitler's Germany had already established this in the 1930s.

Since the war the United States has not had a major depression. Most economists agree that massive government spending is largely responsible for this improved performance of American capitalism. Critics have argued, however, that the social price of this prolonged prosperity has been the creation of a military-industrial complex that currently threatens the entire fabric of American society.

If this view is correct, then it is possible to conclude that Keynes's theories enabled the neoclassical ideology to come to grips with the most important economic problem of the 1930s but have obscured if not worsened other problems. Some of these problems and some contemporary ideologies of capitalism are examined in Chapter 13.

REFERENCES

Chandler, Lester V. *America's Greatest Depression.* New York: Harper & Row, 1970.

Fusfeld, Daniel R. "Fascist Democracy in the United States." In *Conference Papers of the Union for Radical Economics.* December 1968.

Hacker, Louis M. *The Course of American Economic Growth and Development.* New York: Wiley, 1970.

Heilbroner, Robert. *The Future as History.* New York: Harper & Row, 1960.

Huberman, Leo. *We the People.* New York: Monthly Review Press, 1964.

Keynes, J. M. *The General Theory of Employment, Interest and Money.* New York: Harcourt Brace Jovanovich, 1936.

Rosen, Sumner M. "Keynes Without Gadflies." In *The Dissenting Academy.* Edited by T. Roszak. New York: Random House, Vintage Books, 1968.

Samuelson, Paul A. *Economics.* New York, McGraw-Hill, 1948.

———. *The Foundations of Economic Analysis.* Cambridge, Mass.: Harvard University Press, 1947.

U.S. Congress, Senate. Hearings before a subcommittee of the Committee on Manufactures, 72d Cong., 1st sess., 1932.

Chapter
13

Contemporary American Capitalism and Its Defenders

In the first quarter century following World War II the American economy experienced five mild recessions, although by historical standards its growth was fairly satisfactory. Gross national product, in constant (1958) dollars, grew from $355 billion in 1950 to $727 billion in 1969. Disposable personal income grew at an equally impressive rate. While the growth rate was slightly below the historical average in the 1950s, it was well above average in the 1960s. The late 1970s and early 1980s was a period of general stagnation in the American economy, reflected in the rise of critical economics. Yet the years between 1983 and 1989 saw renewed growth, so the overall perspective again became one of relative prosperity.

The technological advances of American capitalism were particularly impressive during the 1950s and 1960s. For several decades before World War I, the increases in output per labor-hour in American industry had been about 22 percent per decade. In the quarter century following World War II, output per labor-hour increased by 34–40 percent per decade (Hacker, p. 326). This growth was made possible by huge expenditures on research and development, which had increased from $3.4 billion in 1950 to $12 billion in 1960; fully half of these funds came from the federal government. With the advent of the pervasive use of computers in the 1980s the rapid increase in technological innovation continued at an even accelerated pace.

These improvements in technology and increases in production led to a greater concentration of economic power in the hands of a very small number of corporations. In 1929, the 100 largest manufacturing corporations had legal control (actual control being far greater) of 44 percent

Table 13.1   LARGE MERGERS AND ACQUISITIONS
1966–1968

	1966	1967	1968
Total number of acquisitions	1,746	2,384	4,003
Number of acquired manufacturing and mining companies with more than $10 million in assets	101	169	192
Value of assets of acquired companies with more than $10 million in assets (in billions)	$4.1	$8.2	$12.6
Number of acquisitions made by 200 largest companies	33	67	74
Value of assets of companies acquired by 200 largest companies (in billions)	$2.4	$5.4	$6.9

Table 13.1 is constructed from data of the Federal Trade Commission, derived by Paul Sweezy and Harry Magdoff, in "The Merger Movement: A Study in Power," *The Monthly Review*, June 1969, pp. 1–5.

of the net capital assets of all manufacturing corporations. By 1962, this figure had increased to 58 percent (Means, pp. 9–19).

In 1962 there were 420,000 manufacturing enterprises. A mere five of these enterprises owned 12.3 percent of all manufacturing assets; 20 owned 25 percent of the total. The total assets of the 20 largest firms were approximately as large as those of the 419,000 smallest companies combined. These 20 giants took a whopping 38 percent of all after-tax profits, leaving the smallest 419,980 to divide 62 percent. Furthermore, among the 180,000 corporations involved in manufacturing, the net profits of the five largest were nearly twice as large as those of the 178,000 smallest corporations (Mueller, pp. 111–129).

During the 1960s, the rate of concentration quickened. In every year of that decade there were at least 60 mergers involving the acquisition of companies with over $10 million in assets. Table 13.1 illustrates this trend. From 1968 to 1970 the evidence points to an ever-faster rate of acquisition. The process of increasing economic concentration, which began about 100 years ago, continues unabated today.

Although the rate of mergers and acquisitions slowed somewhat during the 1970s, the size of the corporate giants increased steadily. In 1978, five industrial corporations had total sales of over $229 billion, total assets of over $137 billion, and net profits of nearly $11 billion. The magnitude of these numbers is staggering. Most of us would consider a business to be very big if it received net profits of $1 million. It would take 11,000 businesses, each receiving net profits of $1 million, to equal the profits of these five giants. A mere five industrial corporations employed 2,451,048 workers. Since on average somewhat over two people live on the salary of each worker, these five companies directly controlled the destiny and well-being of about 6 million Americans. Indirectly, through their social, political, and economic power, they have enormous control over all of us (*Fortune*, May 1979, pp. 270–271). During the 1980s the Reagan administration virtually abandoned any concern with industrial concentration and the merger movement again accelerated.

The post-World War II prosperity has not reduced the extremes of inequality in the United States. In the most complete study of the distribution of ownership of wealth ever undertaken (see Lampman), it has been shown that the wealthiest 1.6 percent of the population own over 80 percent of all corporate stock and virtually all state and local government bonds. Moreover, the ownership of these income-yielding assets has become steadily more concentrated since the early 1920s.

The distribution of income reflects the same extreme inequality. Despite the economy's impressive growth over the past decades—and the much-publicized war on poverty of the early 1960s, which proved to be a half-hearted minor skirmish—poverty has remained an acute problem in the United States. In 1986, for example, 32.4 million Americans lived in families that had an annual income of less than $11,203, the officially designated "poverty level" for an average family of four persons (Bureau of the Census, *Statistical Abstract*, 1988, table 713). This "poverty" level is inherently misleading, however. It is so unrealistically low that many families on welfare are not even considered to be poor. For example, in 1977, of the more than 20 million families with incomes before taxes or welfare payments that would have classified them as living in poverty more than two-thirds were removed from the poverty category when welfare payments were included. In other words most of the people who are so poor that they must live on the meager welfare dole are not listed as living in poverty by the government's conservative definition of poverty (Bureau of the Census, *Statistical Abstract*, 1978, p. 468). More realistic definitions of the poverty level for an urban family of four in 1986 have involved calculations showing that at the inflated prices of that year it would require a before-tax income of at least $14,004 for an urban family of four to live at a minimal level of subsistence. Nearly 44 million people lived in families that had less income than this minimal figure (Bureau of the Census, *Statistical Abstract*, 1988, table 713). In 1987 an adequate, comfortable life-style for an urban family of four required an income of about $32,000. Well over one-half of Americans received less than this level of family income. Thus extreme poverty remains the plight of tens of millions of Americans, and more than half of all Americans do not receive sufficient income for an adequate, comfortable life-style.

In stark contrast to this widespread poverty, the wealthiest 5 percent of the American population received over 20 percent of all income. At the top of this 5 percent was the elite 1.6 percent that owns most of the income-yielding stocks and bonds in the United States. The richest of the elite had incomes estimated between $50 million and $500 million per year (the latter amounts to nearly $1,400,000 per day). According to *Forbes* magazine, in 1987 the 400 families with the most wealth ranged in net worth from $225 million to $8.5 billion.

Furthermore, taxes do little, if anything, to reduce the inequities in the distribution of income. It is commonly assumed that the U.S. tax system reduces inequality by taking a higher percentage of the income of the wealthy than is taken from the poor. The personal income tax does tend to reduce income inequalities, but the effect is much smaller than most people imagine. And when economists analyze the total tax burden, they find that taxes actually increase inequality in the distribution of income because sales taxes, excise taxes, property taxes, and social security taxes all take a much larger percentage of the poor person's income than of the rich person's.

One economist, a recognized authority on taxes, has analyzed the total tax burden on incomes along the entire distribution spectrum. He found in a study published in 1964 that families with incomes below $2,000 per year—certainly a level of abject poverty—paid out one-third of their income in taxes. Furthermore, families making between $10,000 and $15,000 paid out a proportion of their income that was nearly one-third lower than that paid by families with incomes below $2,000. Only among the wealthiest 5 percent of families did the total tax bite exceed that exacted from the poorest. The wealthy elite actually paid out, on the average, 36.3 percent of their income for taxes—a mere 3 percent higher than the poorest segment of society paid (Musgrave, p. 192). Although this study was published in 1964 and the income figures changed dramatically in the inflation-plagued 1970s, there has been no evidence that the tax structure is any less regressive today. In fact, most economists argue that it is worse, because the rich benefited much more than any other segment of society from the tax reforms of the Reagan administration.

The rapid economic growth experienced during the quarter century following World War II imparted a conservatism to millions of Americans. They acquiesced in the growing inequalities of wealth and power as long as their income grew slowly but steadily. During the 1970s and early 1980s this began to change. The economy suffered two severe recessions, and in these recessions inflation was combined with high unemployment, and wage earners' purchasing power began to stagnate or decline. With inflation pushing them into higher tax brackets, many participated in the "taxpayer revolts" of the late 1970s. The corporations and the wealthy were successful in dominating these revolts, the consequences being greater inequality. It is estimated, for example, that two-thirds of the benefits from Proposition 13 in California (which, in 1978, decreased and set limits on property taxes) went to large corporations. After his election in 1980, President Reagan succeeded in persuading Congress to enact an income tax reduction together with a number of increases in other taxes, such as Social Security taxes. The net effect of these tax changes has been a significant worsening of the distribution of wealth, income, and power. Therefore, the issue of the believability of conservative capitalist ideologies is becoming more and more important.

CONTEMPORARY CLASSICAL LIBERAL IDEOLOGY

Neoclassical economics was the principal purveyor of the classical liberal ideology of capitalism during the late nineteenth and early twentieth centuries. Since the 1930s neoclassical economics has become more and more complex mathematically, which has enabled modern economists to claim many new theoretical and scientific insights. Its most important assumptions, however, those on which the entire theory rests, are still metaphysical in character. They have not been established on a scientific basis, either empirically or theoretically.

The finest summary of contemporary neoclassical economics is C. E. Ferguson's *The Neoclassical Theory of Production and Distribution.* The mathematical reasoning in this book is so complex that very few people other than professional economists who are thoroughly competent in higher mathematics can understand it. Professor Ferguson is aware, however, of the tenuous nature of many of the assumptions of this ideology, which, like the medieval religious ideology of feudalism, ultimately must be accepted on faith alone. He admits this and asserts his personal faith: "Placing reliance upon neoclassical economic theory is a matter of faith. I personally have the faith; but at present the best I can do to convince others is to invoke the weight of Samuelson's authority" (Ferguson, pp. xvii–xviii).

When the thrust toward esoterica removed classical liberal ideology from the level at which it could be widely understood, however, it also substantially reduced its effectiveness as a popular ideology of capitalism. To promote widespread popular acceptance of the ideology has been the task of numerous organizations. The best-known American organizations that propagate a simplified, more popular version of the classical ideology are the National Association of Manufacturers (NAM), the Foundation for Economic Education, the Committee for Constitutional Government, the U.S. Chamber of Commerce, and the American Enterprise Association.

A congressional committee found that out of $33.4 million spent "to influence legislation" $32.1 million was spent by large corporations. Of this $32.1 million about $27 million went to such organizations as these (Monsen, p. 19). The NAM uses this money to publish a large amount of probusiness propaganda, including "an educational literature series, labor and industrial relations bulletins, news bulletins, a magazine of American affairs, and numerous studies on legislation, education, antitrust laws, tariffs and unions (ibid., p. 19).

The Foundation for Economic Education reviews and distributes books that reflect the classical liberal ideology of capitalism, as well as publishing and distributing, free of charge, a monthly journal, *The Freeman,* which propagates this ideology. The other organizations engage in numerous publishing and promotional activities designed to inculcate the same ideology as widely as possible.

The popularized statement of the classical ideology emphasizes the benefits of the free market. It is argued that the forces of supply and demand in a free market will always lead to results that are preferable to anything that could be achieved by the government or a central planning agency. The NAM, for example, asserts that the proper function of the government is to strengthen and "make more effective the regulation by competition" (National Association of Manufacturers, p. 57). Almost none of its literature, however, suggests a concern with the concentration of corporate power. Rather, the main economic problems are the powers of big labor unions and the "socialistic" welfare measures of the government.

In essence, most of this literature uses a drastically simplified version of some of the classical and neoclassical economists' analyses. It supports the view that any conceivable threat to the operation of the free market, whether real or potential, is an evil to be avoided at any cost. These organizations have had considerable success in propagating this point of view, particularly among small businesspeople. (Big business, however, generally continues to look with favor on government intervention because it usually benefits from such actions.)

After the election of President Reagan in 1980 one heard a great deal about "supply-side" economics. This "new" theory was really just an old ideology given a new name. Supply-side economics represented a renewed popularity of the old classical liberal arguments for a very restricted role for the government. There were no new arguments in supply-side economics—only a new name.

CONTEMPORARY VARIANTS OF THE CLASSICAL LIBERAL IDEOLOGY

Most critics of the classical liberal ideology emphasize its failure to come to grips with the realities of the concentration of immense power in the hands of considerably less than 1 percent of all corporations. Several attempts have been made to construct an ideology that retains the competitive, private enterprise flavor of classical liberalism while recognizing the existence of concentrated corporate power. Two of these will be discussed: the *countervailing power* ideology, associated primarily with the economist John Kenneth Galbraith, and the *people's capitalism* ideology, associated primarily with Professor Massimo Salvadori.

In his famous book *American Capitalism, the Concept of Countervailing Power*, Professor Galbraith recognized the existence of large, special-interest power blocks in the American economy, but argued that they should not be of much concern because "private economic power begets the countervailing power of those who are subject to it" (Galbraith, p. 4). The result of this newly created countervailing power is "the neutralization of one position of power by another."

Thus strong unions neutralize strong business firms in the field of labor relations, and strong buyers' associations neutralize the monopolistic or oligopolistic powers of the strong sellers. The result, then, is a kind of market equilibrium or invisible hand that harmonizes the interests of all. The harmonious whole is now simply made up of a few neutralized giants rather than numerous, atomistically competitive small firms. It should be mentioned that Professor Galbraith has published several books since *American Capitalism, the Concept of Countervailing Power* appeared. Even a cursory reading of these books show that he has altered his opinions fundamentally. Nevertheless, because the ideology of countervailing power has been very influential, and because most of this influence flows from his book, we are justified in associating this ideology with his name.

Another influential attempt to show the innocuous (or even beneficial) nature of corporate concentration was made by Professor Salvadori, who used the slogan "people's capitalism" to characterize what he believed to be the most essential feature of contemporary American capitalism: diffusion of ownership. The widespread diffusion of ownership of corporate stock, as well as other types of assets, means to Salvadori that capitalism is no longer a system where a tiny minority reaps most of the privileges, but one in which the majority are rapidly becoming capitalists and getting a share of the privileges. Salvadori has conveniently summarized his people's capitalism ideology:

> At present in the United States there are nearly half a million corporations; stockholders total about ten million (1959). Their numbers have increased rapidly in the post-war period. Standard Oil of New Jersey, for instance, had about 160,000 stockholders in 1946; twelve years later there were three times as many, close to half a million. As a rule, the larger the corporation the more widely spread the ownership. Large corporations in which a majority of shares are owned by an individual or by a family are fewer and fewer. It is already exceptional for a single individual to own more than four or five percent of the stock of a given corporation. Unincorporated non-farm businesses number about four million; they belong to one or more individuals and this means millions of "capitalists." Nearly four million farmers (three-fourths of the total) are full owners of part owners of the farms they cultivate. Even considering that there is a good deal of overlapping among the three groups (shareholders, individual non-farm owners, farmers) one can say that at least one-fourth to one-third of all American families share the ownership of natural and artificial capital. There are also half a million independent professional people—lawyers, doctors, architects, engineers, accountants, etc.—whose other means of production are not only equipment of one kind or another but also skill and training, and whose income is related to the capital invested in acquiring professional efficiency; they are "capitalists" just as much as owners of natural and artificial capital. Most other families own durable consumer goods (houses, summer cottages, furniture, cars, electrical appliances, etc.), federal, state, and municipal bonds, insurance policies and savings to the extent that they can consider themselves "capitalists." (Salvadori, pp. 70–71)

Thus the large size of corporations does not, for Salvadori, appear to be an issue. Ownership is becoming more equitably distributed because most people are becoming "capitalists," and hence, by implication, none is powerful enough to exploit another. Disciples point out that by 1970 there were approximately 30 million stockholders. In this view the United States is becoming a nation where the majority are capitalists.

Even many defenders of capitalism concede that Salvadori's analysis serves only to obscure the nature of the concentration of economic power in the United States and that it neither eliminates nor justifies this concentration. A. A. Berle, Jr., a distinguished scholar of American capitalism as well as a corporate executive, has written:

> In terms of power, without regard to asset positions, not only do 500 corporations control two-thirds of the non-farm economy, but within each of that 500 a still smaller group has the ultimate decision-making power. That is, I think, the highest concentration of economic power in recorded history . . . Since the United States carries on not quite half of the manufacturing production of the entire world today, these 500 groupings—each with its own little dominating pyramid within it—represents a concentration of power over economies which makes the medieval feudal system look like a Sunday school party. (Berle, p. 97)

Contrary to the tone of this quotation, Berle is not a critic of American capitalism but one of the most important developers of a contemporary corporate, or collective, ideology of capitalism. Other conservatives have admitted that a very small percentage of all the millions of stockholders hold most of the corporate stock.

THE CONTEMPORARY CORPORATE ETHIC AND CAPITALIST IDEOLOGY

The tactics of the late nineteenth-century robber barons led to a widespread rejection of the corporate ideology (discussed in Chapter 8). Their destructive competition and financial wheeling and dealing hardly supported the conclusion that they were becoming socialized stewards of the public welfare. Yet the classical liberal ideology had no real defense for the existing concentration of economic and political power. The Christian paternalist ethic, with its emphasis on the benevolence of the powerful, was still the only successful ideological defense of great inequalities of wealth and power.

It was simply not possible to cast the nineteenth-century capitalist in a kindly, paternalistic role. Some twentieth-century ideologists of capitalism have argued that capitalism has changed so drastically that capitalists have lost their importance in the system and have been replaced by a new class of professional managers. These theories envision this "new class" the professional managers, as the paternalistic stewards of public welfare.

In 1932 A. A. Berle and G. C. Means published an important and influential book, *The Modern Corporation and Private Property*. In it they argued that ownership of most of the colossal corporate giants had become so widely diffused that the owners of stock had lost or were rapidly losing control of these corporations. With no single owner holding more than 1 or 2 percent of the stock and with no effective means of collusion, the owners were left with only the formal voting function when selecting the board of directors. Candidates for whom they could vote were selected by the existing board of directors. Thus the board chose their own replacements and were essentially a self-perpetuating oligarchy. They wielded power but had no necessary connection with the owners of stock. They were not capitalists in the usual sense of the term.

In 1955 Berle wrote another book, *The Twentieth Century Capitalist Revolution,* in which he argued that corporations had developed a quasi-political status. Managers were motivated primarily by the desire to promote the general public interest in their decision making, and any who were not so motivated could be brought into line by public opinion and the threat of government intervention. This view has been widely accepted. Another economist, for example, wrote:

> No longer the agent of proprietorship seeking to maximize return on investment, management sees itself as responsible to stockholders, employees, customers, the general public, and, perhaps most important, the firm as an institution. . . . There is no display of greed or graspingness; there is no attempt to push off onto workers or the community a large part of the social costs of the enterprise. The modern corporation is a soulful corporation. (Kaysen, pp. 313–314)

The corporation was "soulful," of course, because in this economist's opinion its managers were conscientious, paternalistic stewards of society's welfare.

The managerial ideology was spelled out in some detail in a series of lectures delivered by prominent corporate managers at Columbia University in 1956. According to the chairman of General Electric, the lectures were intended "to coax us businessmen out of our offices and into the arena of public thought where our managerial philosophies can be put to the test of examination by men trained in other disciplines" (quoted in Heilbroner, p. 30).

One of the dominant themes in these lectures was that because American capitalism has undergone a transformation the complaints people may once have had against capitalism are no longer justified. Thus the chairman of Sears Roebuck asserted, "The historic complaint that big business, as the producing arm of capitalism, exploited the many for the profit of the few and deprived workers of the products of their own labor had a valid basis in the facts of European capitalism, but lacks substance when applied to American capitalism today" (ibid.).

Another theme was the justification of bigness on the grounds of better efficiency and higher quality. "The American public," asserted the chairman of U.S. Steel, "has gradually become accustomed to larger and larger groups and has become convinced that big production groups are outstanding in reliability and in the quality of their products and services and are necessary to perform America's larger production tasks in research, in production, and in the procurement of raw materials" (ibid., pp. 31–32).

Finally, the business leaders all saw managers as "professionals" who are as much concerned with "customers, share owners, employees, suppliers, educational institutions, charitable activities, government and the general public" as with sales and profits. They believed that managers "all know that special power imposes special responsibilities on those who hold it." Most managers, they asserted, fully accept "their responsibilities for the broader public welfare" (ibid., pp. 32–33).

Since 1942 this corporate managerial ideology has been assiduously disseminated by the Committee for Economic Development (CED). The CED has been one of the most effective institutional purveyors of pro-business propaganda. It readily accepted big business and also "the fact that government was big and was constantly growing bigger and that there was no returning to a simpler, happier past in this respect. It believed that the question was not how much the government should do, but what it should do" (Schriftgiesser, p. 224). Government should not only accept all the duties assigned to it by the classical liberal ideology but also follow Keynesian policies to ensure stable full employment. Further, government should cooperate with corporate management in resolving conflicts and maintaining the tranquil, stable atmosphere within which management can effectively perform its public-spirited, paternalistic function of promoting the public welfare (Monsen, pp. 25–29).

Big business and big government are accepted by this ideology as not only inevitable but also necessary for maximum efficiency. Big labor unions are also accepted as long as they recognize that most of their legitimate interests are in harmony with those of business and management.

Another important propagator of the managerial ideology has been the U.S. Information Agency (USIA), the official government agency charged with the worldwide propagandizing of the "American point of view." The USIA operates on a grand scale. Its Voice of America broadcasts are heard around the world daily in scores of languages, and it publishes dozens of newspapers and magazines, maintains libraries, shows motion pictures, and engages in countless other propaganda operations.

Arthur Larson, who as head of the U.S. Information Agency "was a semiofficial ideologist to the Eisenhower Administration," published a book, *What We Are For,* in which he explained the philosophy of USIA propaganda. In the modern capitalist economy, Larson argued, the government should do only what "needs to be done" and cannot be done "as well" by private businesses. Modern capitalism has a multitude of powerful interest groups, such as big business, big unions, big government, and so forth, that have no major or basic conflicts. Rather, their interests harmonize, and they mutually support each other. Larson assumed both that business managers are motivated primarily by the desire to promote social welfare to meet the "basic political and economic needs of all people" and that businesses operate more efficiently than government. There is therefore a built-in preference for a minimal role for government in the economy (Larson, pp. 16–17).

In our discussion of the contemporary corporate ethic, the reader may have noticed that most of the ideas on which it is based are rather old. The same holds for the contemporary variants of the classical liberal ideology in the previous section of this chapter. The fact is that very little new or innovative thinking has emerged in the conservatism of the 1960s and 1970s. When one combines this fact with the fact that the Vietnam War and the Watergate scandals created widespread suspicion and distrust of the American capitalist government, it would appear that if new variations on our old ideologies are not forthcoming in the next few years, we face the distinct possibility of a grave crisis of authority in the American capitalism of the 1990s.

ANTICOMMUNISM AS CAPITALIST IDEOLOGY

It is reasonable to assume that anyone who is committed to the proposition that capitalism is the best possible economic system would be a critic of communism. At first glance it might therefore seem strange to label anticommunism as an ideology of capitalism. Over the last 50 years, however, anticommunism has become the most powerful and the most pervasive ideology of capitalism.

Anticommunism derives its power from a well-known fact—that human beings who are fearful want and need a scapegoat. Throughout the history of capitalism, conservatives have combatted the critics of capitalism by lumping them into some group that could be pictured in conservative propaganda as menacing and evil. To the degree that this was successful, it had two advantages: it closed people's minds so that the ideas of the critics would not be heeded and it created public acquiescence in the violent suppression of critics by either government or right-wing vigilante groups.

In the late nineteenth and early twentieth centuries, conservatives assiduously propagandized the notion that all social critics were socialists, communists, or anarchists, and that socialists, communists and anarchists were evil people who threatened society and all individuals in society.

Prior to the 1930s, the conservatives had some success in painting anarchists as frightening, evil people and using anarchists as scapegoats. In the infamous "Haymarket Affair" of 1886 thousands of Chicago workers had struck while tens of thousands demonstrated and threatened to strike to win an 8-hour day. In a large demonstration, on May 1, a bomb exploded and killed several people. Conservatives managed to incite mass fear of "anarchists," who were supposedly on the brink of inflicting mass terror in society. In this atmosphere of fear, a jury, packed with businessmen and their clerks, condemned eight socialist labor leaders to death. Four were executed and four were later pardoned by the governor of Illinois, who saw that the trial was merely a legal lynching designed to silence social critics. One Chicago businessman frankly declared:

> No, I don't consider these people to be guilty of any offense but they must be hanged. I am not afraid of anarchy; oh, no, it's the utopian scheme of a few philanthropic cranks who are amiable withal, but I do consider that the labor movement must be crushed! The Knights of Labor will never dare to create discontent again if these men are hanged! (Quoted in Boyer and Morais, pp. 103–104)

Similarly, in the years following World War I, the labor movement was decimated, as labor leaders and social critics were hounded, arrested, beaten and deported in what came to be called the "great red scare."

It was, however, in the 1930s and after that anticommunism really caught on in American life. The Great Depression of the 1930s created massive suffering, economic insecurity, and fear. At the same time the government of the Soviet Union was engaged in a massive forced collectivization of agriculture. In that collectivization, the Soviet Union suffered a severe famine together with a struggle that was tantamount to a massive, rural civil war. Millions of peasants died from the combined effects of the civil war and the famine. At the same time Joseph Stalin imprisoned or killed several thousand of his real or imagined political rivals in the infamous "Moscow Trials" of the 1930s.

Conservative propagandists had a field day in every capitalist country. They greatly exaggerated the number of deaths in the Soviet Union and then assiduously propagated the view that each death that occurred in the famine and the civil war was a victim of communism. Communists were painted as evil fiends who liked to kill for the sake of killing and who hated freedom, democracy and everything of value in contemporary culture. Tens of thousands of stories were carried on the radio and published in books, magazines, and newspapers about the evil atrocities of communists in the Soviet Union.

At the end of World War II, the United States dropped two atomic bombs on Nagasaki and Hiroshima and killed nearly 200,000 people. The awesome destructive power of nuclear weapons, combined with the knowledge that the Soviet Union possessed these weapons, created an atmosphere in the 1950s in which propagandists succeeded in creating an intense and pervasive fear of Soviet communism in nearly every capitalist country.

But fear of another country or even fear of another socioeconomic system is not yet tantamount to an ideology of capitalism. For this it requires sufficient fear and paranoia that propagandists can convince an entire society to think illogically.

In order to understand the illogical nature of anticommunism as an ideology, we must examine some of the ideas of Marx and the communist movements prior to the Russian revolution of 1917. Marx believed that capitalism had drastically increased human productivity and had created the technological foundation upon which a good society could be created. This good society would be a communist society in which workers would not only have economic abundance and security, but would also democratically control the mines, factories, offices, and other workplaces in which they created this abundance. Marx did not believe that freedom and democracy could ever develop to a significant level in a capitalist economy because it required workers to sell control over themselves in their workplaces. This he considered to be "wage slavery." And since most workers spent more of their waking hours in their workplaces than anywhere else, in a capitalist system they were destined to be *un*free and in *un*democratic social institutions most of the time. They might be allowed to vote as between which of two procapitalist political parties governed them, but they would never be allowed to have real freedom and democracy in their workplaces. Marx's vision of communism is of a society built on the productive, technological base of advanced capitalism. In the communist society every worker would always be able to secure his or her share of all the necessities and amenities of life. Even more important, every workplace, as well as all levels of governments, would be freely and democratically controlled by working people.

When the Russian Revolution occurred, the Russian economy was, by and large, a very backward, unproductive, precapitalist economy. The Bolsheviks believed that, contrary to Marx's theory, Russia did not require a capitalist productive base on which to create socialism. They tried to reorganize the economy so drastically that they could skip the capitalist phase of economic development. Immediately following their revolution, the Soviet Union was militarily invaded by most of the countries with powerful, industrial, capitalist economies. These capitalist countries, including the United States, tried to militarily crush the new government. Even after these military invasions had failed to destroy the Soviet government, the capitalist powers continued to attempt to subvert and to destabilize the Soviet economy and government.

Faced with a massive socioeconomic transformation, which was fiercely resisted by millions of peasants, and the implacable hostility of the capitalist governments, the Soviet government resorted to tactics and policies that had never been foreseen by Marx and that were often antithetical to Marx's vision of a communist society.

With these few facts in mind, it is easy to see the illogical nature of anticommunism as an ideology. The illogic comes from defining communism in two very different and utterly incompatible ways and then tacitly assuming both definitions are identical and using whichever definition suits the ideologist's purpose. Specifically, communism was (and still very often is) defined in both of the following ways:

> *First Definition:* Communism is the economic and political system established in the Soviet Union in 1917 and in eastern Europe in the years immediately following World War II. Communism inherently

and by its very nature always has included and always will include each and every evil that has ever been reported in any of these countries during these periods of time. Moveover, Communists always inherently try to conquer and enslave noncommunist countries.

Second Definition: Communism is a philosophy as well as a social and political movement whose adherents (a) sympathize with labor in the struggles between capital and labor; (b) desire and work for a more egalitarian distribution of wealth and income; (c) advocate greater economic security and higher economic well-being of the poor; (d) work for fairness and equity for racial, ethnic or national minorities; (e) work for fairness and equity for women; (f) oppose capitalist imperialism or the economic and political domination of Third World countries by advanced, industrialized, capitalist countries; (g) oppose the pollution and degradation of the environment in the pursuit of profits; and (h) believe that all or at least several of these problems, injustices, and inequities are the direct result of the ordinary, usual functioning of a capitalist economy.

With these two definitions, anticommunism works in this manner: (1) The first definition shows us that any communist is an evil person who is trying to help a foreign enemy conquer us in order to destroy our freedom and democracy and to impose every evil that has ever been reported from the Soviet Union or Eastern Europe. (2) The second definition shows us that nearly any critic of capitalism is a communist. Therefore, (3) any suggestion that capitalism involves problems, inequities, or injustices is really a subterfuge of a domestic spy working for an evil foreign country trying to destroy any and everything of value in our culture. Moreover, (4) every society has a right and a duty to protect itself and we therefore should forcefully silence domestic critics of capitalism and forcefully overthrow any Third World government that adheres to some or most of the beliefs listed in the second definition of capitalism.

Thus, anticommunism makes every attempt to criticize capitalism seem to be a phony facade for a much greater evil and permits a capitalist government to silence critics at home and to overthrow governments not to the liking of business interests in third-world countries.

In the United States anticommunism reached its peak in the phenomenon known as "McCarthyism" in the 1950s. In the most exhaustive and scholarly account of this period, in a book entitled *The Great Fear*, David Caute shows in exhaustive detail how private right-wing, conservative organizations worked hand in hand with the FBI, the CIA, and the U.S. Congress and other government agencies to destroy the careers and lives of tens of thousands of Americans who were critical of capitalism. These governmental agencies and right-wing organizations attacked every occupation and profession that influenced public opinion. Critics of capitalism who worked in government, journalism, radio, television, movies, entertainment, law, and teaching were hunted down, placed on "blacklists", called communists, fired from their jobs, and prevented from getting jobs in any of those influential professions. Tens of thousands had their careers destroyed. Hundreds of thousands, indeed, millions, were frightened and intimidated into silence to retain their jobs. Anticommunist propaganda was so pervasive and so effective that these people got very little sympathy and almost no financial or legal help in their struggle to protect themselves.

In the field of foreign policy, since World War II the United States has overthrown, participated in the overthrow of, or attempted to overthrow the governments of Guatemala, Iran, Brazil, the Dominican Republic, Cuba, Chile, Granada, Vietnam, Laos, Cambodia, and Nicaragua. In the cases of Guatemala, Brazil, the Dominican Republic, Iran, and Chile, American intervention destroyed or helped destroy democracies and to replace them with tyrannical dictatorships. In Argentina, Guatemala, El Salvador, Honduras, Brazil, and Chile, the American government helped right-wing dictatorships perfect techniques, torture, terror, and repression as means of controlling social critics within those countries. In each of these cases, the U.S. Government attempted to win approval for these policies by telling the American people that they were either overthrowing communist governments or protecting existing governments from social critics who were communists. In some cases, such as Cuba, the government was indeed a communist government—although most of the propaganda that was derived from the first definition of communism did not apply to Cuba. In most cases, however, the governments were definitely not communist. For example, in the cases of Guatemala, Iran, the Dominican Republic, and Chile, the U.S. government participated in the overthrowing of governments simply because they were pursuing reforms that were not appreciated by the American business community.

Thus, anticommunism is a powerful ideology of capitalism that compliments all of the other ideologies we have surveyed in this chapter and helps to justify the destruction of domestic criticism and the elimination of foreign governments that are not liked by U.S. corporations.

CRITICISMS OF CONTEMPORARY CAPITALIST IDEOLOGIES

Criticisms of capitalism have often gone hand in hand with criticisms of capitalist ideologies. In the remainder of this chapter criticisms of the ideologies of capitalism are examined. Some of the principal criticisms of contemporary American capitalism are discussed in Chapter 14.

Criticisms of Neoclassical Ideology

Neoclassical economics completely dominated orthodox academic economics in the late nineteenth and early twentieth centuries. From the 1930s on, however, it came increasingly under attack. In 1938 Oscar Lange and Fred M. Taylor published their significant book, *On the Economic Theory of Socialism*. Lange and Taylor accepted the neoclassical argument that a "purely" and "perfectly" competitive economy will lead to an "optimum allocation of resources," but they also showed that such an economy need not be a capitalist one. They demonstrated that a socialist economy, in which the means of production were collectively owned, could also operate (through perfect planning or decentralized decision making) in a state of "optimal economic efficiency." Private ownership had absolutely no formal or theoretical importance in the neoclassical theory. Furthermore, under socialist ownership, they argued, the inequities of income distribution under a capitalist system would disappear.

The conclusion that many people drew from this book was that the neoclassical liberal ideology could be equally well (if not better) used as an ideology of socialism. This was, indeed, a radical undermining of neoclassical economics as an ideology defending capitalism.

The classical liberal ideology was rejected by many, however, because it seemed to present a severely distorted picture of the realities of twentieth-century capitalism. Its basic assumption of pure competition—no buyers or sellers large enough to affect prices—was patently ridiculous. Moreover, it had little or nothing to say about the important problem of pollution of the environment. Economists also established that simple countercyclical policies of the Keynesian variety are insufficient to obviate the problems of capitalism's cyclical instability (Friedman; Baumol, pp. 21–26) and cannot cope with inflation.

The coup de grace came with J. De V. Graaff's tightly reasoned *Theoretical Welfare Economics*. De V. Graaff showed that economists had not really appreciated the long and restrictive list of assumptions necessary for the optimally efficient allocation of resources envisioned in the model of a competitive, free-market capitalism to be realized. He cited 17 such assumptions, many of which were so restrictive and unrealistic that De V. Graaff concluded that "the measure of acceptance . . . [this theory] has won among professional economists would be astonishing were not its pedigree so long and respectable" (De V. Graaff, p. 142).

A few of De V. Graaff's 17 conditions will suffice to illustrate his point. Neoclassical ideology requires that any individual's welfare be identical with his preference ordering. In other words, children, dope addicts, fiends, criminals, and lunatics, as well as all other people, always prefer that which is best for them. Neoclassical theory also requires that neither risk nor uncertainty is ever present. De V. Graaff's book devastatingly attacked the very basis for the economic analysis on which the classical liberal ideology was constructed.

Criticisms of the Managerial Ideology

The managerial ideology has also come under extensive criticism. Many economists (including several in the neoclassical tradition) argue that the scale of American big business cannot be shown to be related to efficiency or better service. Giant corporations are much larger than would be required for maximum productive efficiency. Such examples as the electric power industry's competition with the Tennessee Valley Authority (TVA), the oligopolistic airlines' struggle with small, unscheduled competitors, and the challenge to the American steel industry from foreign competition are used to point out that private profits and monopoly power, not social welfare or social efficiency, are the prime motivations of big business (Adams, pp. 240–248).

Critics also argue that managers have exactly the same motives as owner-capitalists. They cite an extensive study of the behavior of "management-controlled" giant corporations that showed managers to be as profit-oriented as owner-capitalists. The author of the study concluded that "it would appear that the proponents of theories of managerial discretion have expended considerable time and effort in describing a phenomenon of relatively minor importance. The large management-controlled corporations seem to be just as profit-oriented as the large owner-controlled corporation (Larner, p. 258).

Many critics assert that modern managers have no more social conscience or "soul" than the nineteenth-century robber barons. The late Professor Edwin H. Sutherland, once known as the dean of American criminologists and former president of the American Sociological Association, conducted a thorough and scholarly investigation of the extent to which corporate executives were involved in criminal behavior. He took the 70 largest nonfinancial corporations, with only a few additions and deletions (due to special circumstances), and traced their criminal histories through official histories and official records. There were 980 court decisions against these corporations. One corporation had 50 decisions against it, and the average per corporation was 14. Sixty of the corporations had been found guilty of restraining trade, 53 of infringements, 44 of unfair labor practices, 28 of misrepresentation in advertising, 26 of giving illegal rebates, and 43 of a variety of other offenses. There were a total of 307 individual cases of illegal restraint of trade, 97 of illegal misrepresentation, 222 of infringement, 158 of unfair labor practices, 66 of illegal rebates, and 130 of other offenses (Lundberg, pp. 131–132). Not all of those cases were outright criminal cases. Yet 60 percent of the corporations had been found guilty of criminal offenses an average of four times each.

From May 10, 1950, to May 1, 1951, a U.S. Senate Special Committee to Investigate Crime in Interstate Commerce, under the chairmanship of Senator Estes Kefauver, probed the connections of business and organized crime. Senator Kefauver, Democratic vice-presidential candidate in 1956, later wrote a book based on those hearings. Although he emphasized that there was no evidence to link most big corporations with organized crime, he was nevertheless greatly alarmed at the extent of such connections.

> I cannot overemphasize the danger that can lie in the muscling into legitimate fields by hoodlums . . . There was too much evidence before us of unreformed

hoodlums gaining control of a legitimate business; then utilizing all his old mob tricks—strong-arm methods, bombs, even murder—to secure advantages over legitimate businessmen or drives them into emulating or merging with the gangsters. The hoodlums are also clever at concealing ownership of their investments in legitimate fields—sometimes . . . through "trustees" and sometimes by bamboozling respectable businessmen into "fronting" for them. (Kefauver, pp. 139–140)

In 1960 Robert Kennedy, who later became attorney general of the United States, published *The Enemy Within.* He gathered the material for this book while serving as chief counsel of the U.S. Senate Select Committee on Improper Activities in the Labor or Management Field. Kennedy, like Kefauver, stressed the fact that he was not condemning all or even most businessmen. He wrote:

We found that with the present-day emphasis on money and material goods many businessmen were willing to make corrupt "deals" with dishonest union officials in order to gain competitive advantage or to make a few extra dollars . . . We came across more than fifty companies and corporations that had acted improperly—and in many cases illegally—in dealings with labor unions . . . in the companies and corporations to which I am referring the improprieties and illegalities were occasioned solely by a desire for monetary gain. Furthermore we found that we could expect very little assistance from management groups. Disturbing as it may sound, more often the business people with whom we came in contact—and this includes some representatives of our largest corporations—were uncooperative. (Kennedy, p 216)

Kennedy's list of names of offending companies included many of the largest and most powerful corporations in the United States.

Ferdinand Lundberg has described the extent to which corporate leaders and management receive either very light punishment or no punishment at all when they become involved in improprieties or illegalities. Among the many cases he cites is that of

the bribe of $750,000 by four insurance companies that sent Boss Pendergast of Missouri to jail, later to be pardoned by President Truman . . . It was almost ten years before the insurance executives went to jail. There was, too, the case of Federal Judge Martin Manton who was convicted of accepting a bribe of $250,000 from agents of the defendant when he presided over a case charging exorbitant salaries were improperly paid to officers of the American Tobacco Company. While the attorney for the company was disbarred from federal courts, the assistant to the company president (who made the arrangements) was soon thereafter promoted to vice president: a good boy. (Lundberg, p. 135)

In recent years the situation has grown worse. In 1978 more businessmen received jail sentences for illegal business practices than during the previous 89 years. In the January 1980 issue of *Harper's* magazine, there is a two-page table listing 25 of the largest and most powerful corporations in America. In these 25 corporations at least one or more of the top executives had been convicted of a major crime connected to the conduct of the business corporation. In the July 23, 1979 issue of *U.S. News & World Report* an article entitled "Business Criminals" estimated that managerial and other white collar business crime added as much as 15 percent to the retail price of U.S.-manufactured merchandise. In the December 17, 1979 issue of *Fortune*, that conservative, business-oriented periodical published a lengthy article complaining that "too many executives are going to jail." On November 14, 1980, Mr. Herchell Britton, executive vice-president of Burns International Security Services, Inc., delivered a speech in Chicago, Illinois, to a number of top executives from America's most powerful corporations. Among his remarks were the following:

> The security of corporations is seriously threatened by the growing incidence of white collar crime. It is a major national problem. Right now, at this moment while you're listening to me some 60 to 65 percent of the companies you represent are being ripped off. . . . White collar crime, excluding computer and industrial espionage crimes currently costs this country nearly $70 billion a year. . . . The Assistant Director of the FBI's Criminal Investigative Division recently reported that there are almost 16,000 white collar crimes—including 1,100 cases of public corruption—now pending nationwide.

Critics of the managerial ideology do not cite such studies and examples to show all businessmen to be criminals. Obviously most of them are not. The point they wish to make is that the power of monetary incentives and the quest for profits are no less pronounced among managers than among owner-capitalists. In fact, the pressure to acquire ever-increasing profits is so strong on many businessmen and managers that some persistently resort to illegal or improper means. With such pressures, the critics argue, society can ill afford to turn to the managerial class for paternalistic stewardship of the social and economic welfare.

Criticisms of the Anticommunist Ideology

The anticommunist ideology was so powerful during the 1950s, 1960s, and 1970s that it was rarely criticized in the United States. Criticism of this ideology was often equated with communism, which might then subject the critic to loss of career. The only criticism of anticommunism that was safe was a criticism of particular individuals who took their anticommunism too far. Senator Joseph McCarthy, for example, was a powerful, widely admired man as long as he confined his anticommunist attacks to liberal and socialist social critics. In the mid-1950s, however, he turned his attacks to the U.S. Army as well as to many probusiness politicians. At that point, the U.S. Senate censured McCarthy and he was widely condemned by many powerful conservatives. Similarly, Robert Welch, founder of the John Birch Society, was admired and respected as long as he attacked only leftist critics of capitalism. When he argued, however, that former president

Dwight Eisenhower was a conscious, dedicated agent of communism, he was widely condemned. But in the cases of McCarthy and Welch, the conservatives were careful only to criticize their idiosyncrasies as individuals who had pushed anticommunism too far. Almost never was there an attack on the ideology of anticommunism per se during the 1950s and early 1960s.

During the 1970s and 1980s, however, critics of anti-communist ideology began to voice their criticisms. The ideologists had lost some of their power by painting every person they disliked as a communist. President Eisenhower, Albert Einstein, and Martin Luther King, Jr., were among the thousands of noncommunists who had been attacked as being communist. The charge that any social critic was a communist became less and less believable. Moreover, in many industrialized capitalist countries—but not in the United States—the practice of identifying local communists with the Soviet Union became less and less effective and the general public became somewhat more tolerant of local communists. In this changing atmosphere, critics of anticommunism began to express their ideas more freely.

The first criticism of anticommunism is obvious. It is an ideology that attacks every leftist social critic as being a communist when many are not. Two scholars of this ideology have written that "anti-communism has been a dominant theme in the political warfare waged by conservative forces against the entire left, communist and non-communist" (Miliband and Liebman, p. 1).

The second criticism is that this ideology paints Soviet communism as *the* Satanic force of the universe only by intellectual distortion.

> Anti-communism is also grossly selective in its view of Communist regimes, and systematically presents a highly distorted picture of their reality . . . Anti-communism not only understates or ignores altogether the advances that are made, but it also pays very little attention to the conditions in which they have been made. (Ibid., p. 4)

Communist governments have come to power in countries that suffered from economic underdevelopment and foreign exploitation. These governments were ravaged by civil war and/or foreign military intervention before or after the coming to power of their communist government, as in the Soviet Union, China, Korea, Vietnam, Laos, and Cambodia. And, as in Cuba, they were often subjected to economic warfare waged by capitalist countries. While these facts do not excuse any excesses or mistakes these governments may have made, they certainly are relevant to the issue of whether or not these regimes represent the path all communist economies are likely to take. The argument that the Soviet Union is the true Satanic face of communism has turned against the anticommunists in the late 1980s as we have witnessed democratic reforms and relatively free elections there.

Third, critics of this ideology point out that communism has always involved a vision of how an advanced industrialized, capitalist economy could be made more free, more democratic, and more humane. Even if the anticommunist ideologists were accurate in their descriptions of the Soviet Union and Eastern Europe, it would not make this ethical vision of a better society go away.

> Anticommunism . . . uses the experience of Soviet-type regimes as a . . . means . . . of combatting as utopian, absurd, dangerous, and sinister any transformative project which goes beyond the most modest attempts at "piecemeal social engineering." Socialists are well aware by now of the difficulties of every kind which are bound to attend the creation of a cooperative democratic and egalitarian commonwealth. But this does not make them renounce their commitment to it; and the experience of the Soviet regime . . . cannot be taken as of decisive relevance elsewhere, least of all in countries whose economic, social, political, and cultural circumstances are vastly vastly different from those in [the Soviet Union]. (Ibid., pp. 3–4)

Finally, the anticommunist ideology uses a grotesquely inconsistent double standard in evaluating governments. Political and human abuses in communist countries are thoroughly and emphatically condemned. Similar and even far worse abuses by right-wing, procapitalist countries are totally ignored. Most of the right-wing governments that are the most tyrannical and the most criminal in their human rights abuses enjoy the steadfast support of the United States and other capitalist governments.

SUMMARY

Since World War II the concentration of corporate power has become more extreme, and inequalities of income distribution have been reduced very little, if at all. Despite these facts, many contemporary ideologies continue to rely on the classical liberal defense of capitalism. Other ideologists continue to place the corporate ethic at the base of their defense of capitalism. The latter group stresses the "efficient, farsighted policies" of the large corporations, and the "professionalism" as well as "broad, humanistic concerns" of corporate managers. Critics of this point of view argue that corporate managers are motivated by the same force that motivated nineteenth-century capitalists—the quest for maximum profits. Since the 1930s, anticommunism has become an important ideology of capitalism. This ideology identifies any criticism of capitalism with communism and identifies communism as evil incarnate. Critics of this ideology point to its selective distortions of reality, its erroneous identification of all criticism as communism, its irrelevance to the traditional ideals of communism and its double standard of judgments concerning human rights.

REFERENCES

Adams, Walter. "Competition, Monopoly, and Planning." In *American Society, Inc.* Edited by M. Zeitlin. Chicago, Ill.: Markham, 1970.

Baumol, William J. "Pitfalls in Counter-Cyclical Policies: Some Tools and Results." In *The Review of Economics and Statistics,* February 1961.

Berle, A. A., Jr. "Economic Power and the Free Society." In *The Corporation Take-Over.* Edited by Andrew Hacker. Garden City, N.Y.: Doubleday, 1965.

Berle, A. A., Jr., and G. C. Means. *The Modern Corporation and Private Property.* New York: Macmillan, 1932.

Boyer, Richard O., and Herbert M. Morais. *Labor's Untold Story.* New York: United Electrical, Radio and Machine Workers of America. 1965.

Bureau of the Census. *Statistical Abstract of the United States for 1977.* Washington, D.C.: GPO, 1978.

———. *Statistical Abstract of the United States for 1982.* Washington, D.C.: GPO, 1983.

Caute, David. *The Great Fear.* New York: Simon & Schuster, 1978.

De V. Graaff, J. *Theoretical Welfare Economics.* London: Cambridge University Press, 1967.

Federal Reserve Bulletin, August, 1970.

Ferguson, C. E. *The Neoclassical Theory of Production and Distribution.* London: Cambridge University Press, 1969.

Forbes, February 5, 1979.

Forbes, Fall 1983.

Fortune, May 1979.

Friedman, Milton. "The Effects of a Full Employment Policy of Economic Stability: A Formal Analysis." In *Essays in Positive Economics.* Chicago, Ill.: University of Chicago Press, 1953.

Galbraith, John Kenneth. *American Capitalism, the Concepts of Countervailing Power.* Boston: Houghton Mifflin, 1956.

Hacker, Louis M. *The Course of American Economic Growth and Development.* New York: Wiley, 1970.

Heilbroner, Robert L. *The Limits of American Capitalism.* New York: Harper & Row, 1966.

Hunt, E. K. "Religious Parable Versus Economic Logic: An Analysis of the Recent Controversy in Value, Capital and Distribution Theory." *Inter-Mountain Economic Review,* Fall 1971.

———, and Jesse Schwartz. *Critique of the Economic Theory.* Sec. III. London: Penguin, 1972.

Kaysen, Carl. "The Social Significance of the Modern Corporation." *American Economic Review,* May 1957.

Kefauver, Estes. *Crime in America.* Garden City, N.Y.: Doubleday, 1951.

Kennedy, Robert. *The Enemy Within.* New York: Harper & Row, 1960.

Lampman, Robert J. *The Share of Top Wealth-holders in National Wealth 1922–1956.* Princeton, N.J.: Princeton University Press, 1962.

Lange, Oscar, and Fred M. Taylor. *On the Economic Theory of Socialism.* Minneapolis: University of Minnesota Press, 1938.

Larner, Robert J. "The Effect of Management-Control on the Profits of Larger Corporations." In *American Society, Inc.* Edited by M. Zeitlin. Chicago, Ill.: Markham, 1970.

Larson, Arthur. *What We Are For.* New York: Harper & Row, 1959.

Lundberg, F. *The Rich and the Super Rich.* New York: Bantam, 1968.

Means, Gardiner C. "Economic Concentration." In Hearings Before the Subcommittee on Antitrust and Monopoly of the Committee of the Judiciary, United States Senate. Washington, D.C.: GPO, July 1964.

Miliband, Ralph, and Marcel Liebman. "Reflections on Anti-Communism." In *The Uses of Anti-Communism.* Edited by R. Miliband, J. Saville, and M. Liebman. London, The Merlin Press.

Monsen, R. Joseph, Jr. *Modern American Capitalism.* Boston: Houghton Mifflin, 1963.

Mueller, Willard F. "Economic Concentration." In Hearings Before the Subcommittee on Antitrust and Monopoly of the Committee of the Judiciary, United States Senate. Washington, D.C.: GPO, 1964.

Musgrave, B. A. "Estimating the Distribution of the Tax Burden." In *Income and Wealth.* Ser. 10. Cambridge, England: Bowers & Bowers, 1964.

National Association of Manufacturers, Economic Principles Commission. *The American Individual Enterprise System, Its Nature and Future.* New York: McGraw-Hill, 1946.

Salvadori, Massimo. *The Economics of Freedom.* Garden City, N.Y.: Doubleday, 1959.

Schriftgiesser, Karl. *Business Comes of Age.* New York: Harper & Row, 1960.

Sutherland, Edwin H. *White Collar Crime.* New York: Holt, Rinehart and Winston, 1961.

Sweezy, Paul and Magdoff, Harry. "The Merger Movement: A Study in Power." In *The Monthly Review*, June 1969.

Vital Speeches, January 1, 1981.

Chapter 14

Contemporary American Capitalism and Its Radical Critics

Radical criticism of American capitalism was widespread during the depression of the 1930s. During the late 1940s and the early 1950s, however, pervasive repression of dissent, combined with a relatively prosperous economy, effectively stifled most radical criticism (see Cook and Belfrage).

THE CIVIL RIGHTS MOVEMENT

The struggle for equality for blacks in America began in 1619, when the first black slaves were brought to the colonies. Since that time the struggle has been nearly continuous. In the 1950s, however, the blacks' quest for their basic human rights entered a new phase.

On May 17, 1954, in the case of *Brown* v. *Board of Education of Topeka*, the U.S. Supreme Court unanimously concluded "that in the field of public education the doctrine of 'separate but equal' has no place!" and declared that "separate educational facilities are inherently unequal."

In 1954 and 1955, the few black individuals who applied for admission to white schools were rebuffed and very often suffered severe reprisals. It began to appear that the Court decision would have little effect on the patterns of segregation that then existed. In December 1955, however, a black woman in Montgomery, Alabama, refused to give up her bus seat to a white man. She was immediately arrested. Within days the blacks of Montgomery had organized a boycott of the bus company.

After a year of intense and bitter conflict, the protest ended in victory. The 50,000 blacks of Montgomery succeeded in getting the local bus segregation law nullified. The symbolic significance of this victory extended

far beyond the particular issue of bus segregation. Blacks everywhere vi-
cariously shared a new sense of dignity, freedom, and power. They began
to organize actively to fight white racism.

Their attempts were met with fanatical resistance. In September 1957,
Arkansas governor Orville Faubus used armed troops to bar the entrance of
nine black students into Central High School in Little Rock. The federal government interpreted this as a blatant challenge to its authority and sent in
paratroopers to enforce the federal court orders. Many southern communities
chose to close their public schools rather than allow them to be integrated.

In 1957 and 1960 Congress passed civil rights acts designed to extend
voting rights to blacks. The Kennedy administration urged young people,
black and white, to concentrate on a massive registration drive to get
southern blacks on voting lists. Attracting both radical critics of capitalism
and liberal young people who generally did not seriously question the
basic social and economic system of capitalism, a civil rights movement
emerged nationwide. They believed that a massive protest against racism
would open the public's eyes and that an aroused population would demand
new laws that would improve, if not completely cure, the situation.

During this period civil rights activists organized sit-ins at segregated
lunch counters and bus depots, pray-ins at segregated churches, and wade-
ins at segregated beaches. Massive nonviolent demonstrations or nonviolent
civil disobedience would, they hoped, reach the consciences of enough
people to achieve integration.

Despite some successes in terms of new civil rights legislation, disil-
lusionment began to affect large numbers of blacks as well as white civil
rights workers. They began to realize that political enfranchisement had
little effect on the vast economic inequalities that blacks suffered. Of what
use was the vote if a black woman could not secure a job, or if he or she
was paid a salary that kept her family in a condition of poverty and degradation? Whereas in 1950 the average salary earned by a black was 61
percent of that earned by a white, by 1962 it had fallen to 55 percent. In
the face of a massive civil rights movement, the relative economic position
of the blacks had actually deteriorated. Furthermore, in 1950 the rate of
unemployment among blacks had been slightly less than twice as high as
that of whites, but by 1964 it was, significantly, more than twice as high.
In 1947 blacks constituted 18 percent of the poorest segment of the population in America; by 1962 they accounted for 22 percent of this segment.

Many civil rights advocates became convinced that the most significant
barriers to black equality were economic. They turned their attention to
a critical analysis of American capitalism as a means of understanding the
perpetuation, indeed the worsening, of the inequalities suffered by blacks.

THE WAR IN VIETNAM

The other major force that helped spark the resurgence of radical criticism
was the war in Vietnam. Throughout the 1950s the U.S. government consistently fought against fundamental social and political change in less de-

veloped countries. In the guise of "protecting the world from communism" the United States had intervened in the internal affairs of at least a score of countries. In some, like Guatemala and Iran, U.S. agents actually engineered the overthrow of the legitimate governments and replaced them with regimes more to American liking.

Most criticism was muted by the political repression of McCarthyism. The college students of the 1950s, the "silent generation," generally acquiesced in the national mood of anticommunism that provided the justification for political repression at home and extensive intervention in other nations' internal affairs. During the 1950s American intervention in Vietnam attracted little attention. It was merely one of many countries that, it was claimed, were being saved from communism. In the 1960s, however, this was to change drastically. The Vietnam War became a powerful force in regenerating radical criticism of American capitalism. For this reason, a brief examination of the origins of the Vietnam War is useful here.

During the World War II occupation of Vietnam, the French colonial regime collaborated with the Japanese. Toward the end of the war the Japanese locked up the colonial administrators and established a puppet regime under the Annamite emperor Bao Dai. Throughout this period the Americans and the French had supported a resistance movement, the Vietminh, headed by Ho Chi Minh. When Japan surrendered, there was a peaceful transfer of political power to the Vietminh.

The French did not want to lose this part of their colonial empire but realized that they were too weak to inflict a quick military defeat on the new government. On March 6, 1946, they signed an agreement with the Ho Chi Minh government that read in part, "The government of France recognizes the Republic of Vietnam as a free state having its government and its parliament, its army and its finances, forming part of the Indo-Chinese federation and of the French Union" (quoted in Huberman and Sweezy, p. 787). This agreement clearly meant that the Ho Chi Minh government would enjoy status similar to the governments of the members of the British Commonwealth. It legally established Ho Chi Minh's regime as the legitimate government of all Vietnam. Nothing that subsequently occurred changed this essential fact.

The French were confident that they could make a subservient puppet of Ho Chi Minh. They failed completely in this task. Unable to reduce Ho Chi Minh to this role, they brought back Emperor Bao Dai, even though he had voluntarily abdicated his throne, changed his name, and retired to Hong Kong. They "installed" him as "chief of state" and declared the Vietminh to be outlaws. There followed 6 years of intense, bitter warfare. Finally, in 1954, the Vietminh decisively defeated the French. The Geneva Accords of July 1954, which arranged for the French surrender, called for a cease-fire and a temporary separation of opposing forces. Ho Chi Minh's followers were to move north of the 17th parallel, and Emperor Bao Dai's were to move to the south. This arrangement was to end within two years with a national election to choose the leader of Vietnam. Shortly after these negotiations American-backed Ngo Dinh Diem ousted Bao Dai, proclaimed the existence of a "Republic of Vietnam," and appointed himself its first president.

There were no elections. The Americans and Diem simply asserted that there were now two Vietnams. The reason for refusing to have the election was candidly admitted by President Eisenhower in his book *Mandate for Change:*

> I am convinced that the French could not win the war because the internal political situation in Vietnam, weak and confused, badly weakened their military position. I have never talked or corresponded with a person knowledgeable in Indochinese affairs who did not agree that had elections been held as of the time of the fighting, possibly 80 percent of the population would have voted for Communist Ho Chi Minh as their leader rather than chief of state Bao Dai. (Quoted in Huberman and Sweezy, p. 78)

Obviously the substitution of Diem for Bao Dai did not change the situation.

This American-imposed solution was rejected not only by Ho Chi Minh and his followers in the North but also by people in the South. So the war of national liberation, which had been previously fought against the Japanese and the French, was continued against the United States.

Americans were repeatedly told that their government was fighting a war to protect the South Vietnamese from the armed aggression of North Vietnam. The North Vietnamese were pictured as violators of the Geneva agreements, determined to enslave the South Vietnamese.

Critics of American policy challenged this official version of the nature of the war. Their assessment of what was happening in Vietnam received widespread support in academic circles, and college campuses became centers of antiwar sentiment. From the early 1960s, through about 1966, opposition to the war was largely confined to the campuses. During the last years of the decade, however, people from all segments of society actively opposed the war. The antiwar movement had become a mass movement.

Finally, in 1968, U.S. Secretary of Defense Robert S. McNamara, himself becoming disillusioned with the official rationale for the war, ordered the U.S. Department of Defense to prepare an in-depth account of how the United States became involved. In early 1971 the report was completed. The 7000-page document was obtained by the *New York Times*, which paid researchers to determine whether new facts had been brought to light. The Defense Department admitted that (1) the Eisenhower administration had played a "direct role in the ultimate breakdown of the Geneva settlement"; (2) from 1954 onward, the United States engaged in "acts of sabotage and terror warfare against North Vietnam"; (3) the United States "encouraged and abetted the overthrow of President Ngo Dinh Diem" when he was no longer considered to be of use; and (4) for many years before 1965 the U.S. government undertook "the careful preparation of public opinion for the years of open warfare that were to follow."

American involvement increased steadily until by 1968 the United

States had an army of over 500,000 men on Vietnamese soil and was spending nearly $3 billion per month ($100 million per day!) in the attempt to impose a "suitable political solution" on the Vietnamese. American battle casualties rose until hundreds of thousands of Americans were wounded and well over 50,000 Americans were killed.

Young people everywhere began to question the morality of the war. Beginning in 1964, teach-ins protesting the war were mounted on college campuses around the United States. Most organizers and participants were convinced that American involvement in the war was a tragic mistake that would be rectified if the public could be made aware of the facts of the situation.

The antiwar movement grew rapidly. President Johnson's landslide victory in 1964 and his decision not to seek another term in 1968 are often attributed, at least in part, to the powerful, widespread opposition to the war. After a few years of debate, antiwar critics were convinced that most Americans did know the basic facts of Vietnam and wanted a hasty end to the war. Yet the American government, without giving any convincing reasons for its actions, continued to seek military victory.

Critics began to ask whether there was not some deeper motive than simple anticommunist sentiment propelling the American government. In particular, they began to search for an economic motive or rationale for the war. They began seriously to reexamine the older radical theories of capitalist imperialism.

THE WOMEN'S LIBERATION MOVEMENT

The women's movement, like the black movement, did not suddenly spring into being in the 1960s out of thin air. The earliest political activity of a significant number of U.S. women emerged in the 1820s and 1830s, in the abolitionist movement to end slavery. Experience in the abolitionist movement made women aware of their own oppression and gave them the confidence to build a movement of their own, especially because they were ignored or dismissed by some of the abolitionists. The women's movement before the Civil War fought not only for the abolition of slavery, but also for ending laws that made the man the sole controller of all property and all decisions in marriage (even giving men guardianship of the children in event of separation), as well as for gaining the right to vote.

The aftermath of the Civil War gave the vote to blacks—or rather, it gave the formal right to black *men*, but with no mechanism of enforcement in the South. Women, both black and white, were not given the vote. The women's movement fought a long hard battle until women were finally given the vote in 1920. The early movement had concerned itself with a broad range of issues, from poverty and divorce laws to working conditions, but after about 1890 the movement concentrated solely on the narrow issue of voting. By 1920 some 2 million women were members of the leading women's suffrage organizations. Yet when the vote was given, most of these women thought the battle was won—so the women's movement collapsed and did not recover until the late 1960s.

A brief upsurge in the fight for women's rights occurred during World War II, when millions of women were drawn into war work. The symbol of Rosie the Riveter replaced that of Hedda the Housewife. Overnight it became fashionable for women to work in a war factory or a war office, and there was even discussion of child care to help working mothers. Moreover, the two political parties made considerable sympathetic noises in favor of the idea of an equal rights amendment for women in the federal constitution.

Unfortunately for women, the late 1940s and 1950s was a period of general repression on the American scene. People were happy to see the war's end and wanted nothing but simple private lives devoted to money-making, with no discussion or recognition of continuing social problems. Radicals and liberals who advocated any social change were hounded by Senator McCarthy and a huge number of publicity-seeking inquisitors; one of those who made a successful career of "witch-hunting" was Richard Nixon. Women were told to leave their war jobs and return to kitchens, children, and churches (just as Hitler had told German women). The media—and even conservative psychologists—painted a picture in which every woman was a happy housewife surrounded by hordes of smiling children and shiny gadgets.

Yet reality was quite different. Later studies have shown that most women who are nothing but housewives are dreadfully unfulfilled and unhappy. Moreover, even in the 1950s the number of women at work kept increasing, despite all the propaganda. By 1988 more than 4 out of every 10 workers were women—and a majority of all women between 16 and 64 now work. Yet they work in the poorest jobs, such as domestic servant or secretary, and are paid less than men even for the same job. The average full-time woman worker only makes 59 percent of what a full-time male worker is paid. Furthermore, in many areas women who are fully qualified are denied promotions. Only a few of the thousands of corporate executives are women, only 9 percent of full professors are women, in 1987 only 25 of the 535 members of the U.S. House and Senate were women, and no woman has ever been president or vice-president.

In the 1960s women began to protest these conditions. The first result of protest was the Equal Pay Act of 1963. Then, in 1964, a provision for women was added to the Civil Rights Act that prohibited discrimination in employment against minority groups. The addition was made by a southern congressman who wanted to defeat the whole act by amending it to add the ban on sex discrimination, and its final passage was a political miracle. Even after it was passed, the agencies who were responsible for enforcing it treated the sex discrimination ban as a joke and made little attempt to enforce it.

As a result, in 1966 the National Organization of Women was formed.

It is a moderate organization that wishes to see the laws against sex discrimination fully enforced and has worked to get other laws—like the Equal Rights Amendment—passed in order to give women fully equal rights at last.

In the meantime, radical women gained a great deal of experience in the civil rights movement and the antiwar movement. Once again, recognition of the oppression of blacks made women conscious of their own oppression. They therefore began to work to direct the left toward the fight for equality for women as well as for minorities. In this, however, they were rebuffed by many male radicals who were unenlightened on the subject of women. When the subject of women's rights was broached by black women in the civil rights organization called the Student Nonviolent Coordinating Committee, its leader, Stokely Carmichael, was reported to have said, "The only position for women in SNCC is prone." By 1968 many radical women were fed up with most leftist organizations, so they organized their own separate movement.

The women's movement, however, has never been intellectually or politically homogeneous. The National Organization of Women has always been its largest and best-organized component. This group advocates reforms that would not seriously alter the more fundamental economic, social, or political institutions of the United States. It seems implicitly to accept the view that sexism is primarily the result of ignorance and that through education and political pressures applied to the Democratic and Republican parties most of the inequities suffered by women can be eliminated by legislative reform.

The most extreme segment of the women's movement is the separatists. They see all men as the enemy and believe that women's liberation cannot be achieved within a society of both men and women. They advocate a radically new society (or new enclaves in society) composed solely of women—they have a variety of plans or schemes by which to assure conception and biological propagation of the women. They see all oppression as merely so many aspects of "male institutions" and all oppressive behavior as "male behavior" (whether the behavior is on the part of a man or a woman).

Marxist feminists form a third component of the women's movement. They see sexism as resulting from social institutions and systematically inculcated subjective attitudes about women, which in both cases serve to strengthen and perpetuate the capitalist system of power and privilege. All Marxist feminists agree that sexism is related to the class oppression that has existed for many centuries, and that sexism will never be eliminated until all class oppression is eliminated. There were and are, nevertheless, continuing disagreements among Marxists concerning the exact relationships between class struggles—in slavery, feudalism, capitalism, and other class-divided societies—and the psychological attitudes and prejudices relating to sexist discrimination.

Some Marxist feminists—probably a minority, but including several influential writers—stress that some form of sexual oppression may be a necessary prerequisite for the creation of the subjective attitudes necessary to create and maintain any form of class-divided society. They emphasize that any form of class domination requires authoritarian personalities in nearly all people, and that sexual repression is one of the foundations of the authoritarian personality. Therefore, they argue that sexism can be seen in some ways prior to, and more fundamental than, the class oppression that Marx showed to be one of the defining features of any class-divided mode of production, including capitalism.

The majority of Marxist feminists would agree that sexism has existed in many class-divided societies before capitalism, and they would agree that the authoritarian and paternalistic psychology of sexism is a vital and important feature of all known class societies. Both groups of Marxist feminists would stress that the oppression of women helps to increase capitalist profits and to divide men and women workers—which ultimately weakens the working class both politically and economically. According to the majority of Marxist opinion, however, because sexism performs such a necessary function for capitalism, it will always be the prevailing ideology under capitalism, regardless of how many laws are passed against it. Therefore, these Marxist feminists contend that the struggle to abolish capitalism is the most important and fundamental way to fight sex oppression.

A minority of Marxist feminists insists that unless the fight to abolish both sexist institutions and attitudes is made coequal with the fight to abolish the class division of society, it is probable that the society that results from a socialist revolution will itself become a class-divided, exploitative society. In the majority view, all class oppression must be abolished and socialism established as the *necessary prerequisite* for the liberation of women and all human beings. The majority of Marxist feminists would agree with the minority (as against some vulgar Marxists) that a socialist revolution is not a sufficient guarantee of women's liberation, that a continuing movement for women's liberation is needed both *before* and *after* the socialist revolution.

CONTEMPORARY CRITICS OF AMERICAN CAPITALISM

The civil rights, antiwar, and women's liberation movements led to a burgeoning literature critical of the basic institutions of American capitalism. Like earlier critiques, this literature censured the grossly unequal distribution of income, wealth, and power in the United States. These critics, like the leftist Keynesians, deplored the extent to which post-World War II economic stability had been purchased at a cost of thoroughgoing militarism (discussed in Chapter 12).

On these points radical and liberal critics have been in agreement.

Liberal critics, however, believe that political reform and electoral politics are sufficient to correct these perversions of the American economy. Radical critics believe inequality and militarism are inherent in a capitalist economy and that it also necessarily involves (1) imperialistic exploitation of underdeveloped countries as a means of maintaining high output and large profits in the United States, (2) endemic discrimination against minority groups and women, (3) inability to control pollution and resource exhaustion, and (4) a degrading commercialism and social alienation. In the remainder of this chapter some of the literature in these four general areas is described. Much of this literature has appeared in the *Review of Radical Political Economics*, published by the Union for Radical Political Economics (URPE). (Its address is 41 Union Square West (Room 901), New York, New York, 10003.) URPE is the main organization of U.S. radical economists.

American Imperialism

One of the first and most influential of these critics was Paul A. Baran. His book *The Political Economy of Growth,* first published in 1957, has been translated into several languages; it has sold very well in the United States and even better in most less developed countries. Baran argued that, before a less developed country could industrialize, it would have to mobilize its *economic surplus,* or the difference between what is produced and what has to be consumed in order to maintain the economy's productivity. It is the source of investment capital with which the country can industrialize. Under present institutional arrangements, most less developed countries either waste their surpluses or lose them to imperialistic capitalist countries.

"Far from serving as an engine of economic expansion, of technological progress and of social change, the capitalist order in . . . [underdeveloped] countries has represented a framework for economic stagnation, for archaic technology, and for social backwardness." The peasant agriculture usually produces a sufficiently large surplus in these countries. In fact, Baran pointed out that the surplus is frequently as high as 50 percent of the total amount produced. "The subsistence peasant's obligations on account of rent, taxes, and interest in all underdeveloped countries are very high. They frequently absorb more than half of his meager net product" (Baran, pp. 164–165).

The problem is in the disposition of this surplus. Part goes to middlemen, speculators, moneylenders, and merchants—petty capitalists who have neither the interest nor the wherewithal to finance industrialization. A much larger part goes to the landowning ruling class, which uses its "share" to purchase luxury consumption goods, usually imported from capitalist countries, and to the extensive military establishments needed to maintain their internal power.

Importing luxuries and military hardware necessitates sending exports to the industrialized countries; exports usually consist of one or two primarily agricultural products or mineral resources. The capitalist countries with which they trade have a great deal of monopsonistic buying power (that is, there are many sellers and only a few collusive buyers), and thus can set the terms of trade in their own interest. The large multinational corporations that purchase the raw materials are not interested in the industrialization of these countries. Thus foreign capitalist investment is limited to that necessary for the profitable extraction of resources.

An alliance between the reactionary landowning class and foreign capitalists protects the interests of both by suppressing all opposition and keeping the masses at a subsistence standard of living. Thus landowners can maintain their position, and capitalists are guaranteed cheap labor and large profits.

> Small wonder that under such circumstances Western big business heavily engaged in raw materials exploitation leaves no stone unturned to obstruct the evolution of social and political conditions in underdeveloped countries that might be conducive to their economic development. It uses its tremendous power to prop up the backward areas' comprador administrations, to disrupt and corrupt the social and political movements that oppose them, and to overthrow whatever progressive governments may rise to power and refuse to do the bidding of their imperialistic overlords. (Ibid., p. 198)

Baran believes the American government works hand in hand with American big business. Most U.S. economic and military aid provided to less developed countries is given, in his opinion, in order to prop up client governments. Often such governments are not strong enough to survive on their own, even with this aid. Under these circumstances the United States intervenes, either clandestinely (through CIA sabotage and intrigue) or directly (through the use of military force).

Baran and like-minded critics see the interventions in Guatemala, Iran, Korea, Cuba, the Dominican Republic, Vietnam, Nicaragua, and El Salvador as examples of American endeavors to protect business interests, both current and potential, against threats from more progressive social and political movements. They point to 53 different "U.S. defense commitments and assurances" that commit the United States to the use of military force to maintain existing governments, very often against their own people (Magdoff, pp. 203–206).

The dependence of less developed countries on a small number of export commodities is documented in a study based on International Monetary Fund data. Each of the 37 countries considered earns 58 percent to 99 percent of its export receipts from one to six commodities. Furthermore, the United States depends on imports as the principal source for most of the 62 types of materials the Defense Department classifies as strategic and critical. For 38 of these, 80 to 100 percent of the new supplies are imported; for 14 others, 40 to 79 percent are imported.

A large and increasing percentage of U.S. corporate sales and profits result from exports and sales of foreign subsidiaries (many of which are, of course, in less developed countries). Moreover, detailed examination reveals that the foreign trade of the less developed countries is very lopsided. Raw materials and metals in their first state of smelting constitute 85 percent of exports and manufactured goods (mostly textiles) only 10 percent, but about 60 percent of imports are manufactured goods. Because most manufactured imports are consumer goods, such a pattern of trade cannot lead to development but only to continued economic dependence.

Critics of this point of view (that is, defenders of American economic foreign policy) argue that although foreign trade and foreign investments are important to American corporations, they also benefit the less developed countries. The orthodox argument is expressed in a widely used textbook:

> In general, a restrained optimism as to the future prospects for underdeveloped countries in their trading relations with the developed countries seems to be warranted. The most encouraging sign is the growing recognition on the part of developed countries that opening their markets to the export products of underdeveloped areas is an essential part of their accepted program to assist underdeveloped countries to grow. (Snider, p. 548)

Yet this position does not deal directly with radical critiques of American economic foreign policy. It simply assumes that all the less developed countries need is *more* trade and more private investment. Another orthodox scholar who has studied the problem more thoroughly admits that "increasing the flow of private capital to underdeveloped countries will probably require a *recasting of economic policies* in both underdeveloped and advanced countries" (Higgins, p. 593). He does not go on to analyze what obstacles prevent this "recasting of economic policies."

Conservative defenders of American policies grant that developed capitalist countries have had immense economic, political, and military power, which they have used to influence and control peoples around the world. They deny, however, that this "imperialism" is basically economic in nature. Thus the widely respected economic historian Professor David S. Landes writes:

> It seems to me that one has to look at imperialism as a multifarious response to a common opportunity that consists simply in disparity of power. Whenever and wherever such disparity has existed, people and groups have been ready to take advantage of it. It is, one notes with regret, in the nature of the human beast to push other people around—or to save their souls or "civilize" them as the case may be. (Landes, p. 510)

One radical critic has answered this assertion by noting that the modern capitalist drive to save people's souls from communism and to civilize them is perfectly compatible with economic motives. He cites the following quotation from an officer of the General Electric Company: "Thus, our search for profits places us squarely in line with the national policy of stepping up international trade as a means of strengthening the free world in the

Cold War confrontation with Communism." The critic Harry Magdoff summarizes his position: "Just as the fight against Communism helps the search for profits, so the search for profits helps the fight against Communism. What more perfect harmony of interests could be imagined?" (Magdoff, pp. 200–201).

Many books written since the 1960s have attempted to explain contemporary American foreign policy—and the cold war between the United States and the Soviet Union—in terms of American economic imperialism. One of the most persuasive and scholarly of these books was Edward S. Herman's *The Real Terror Network.* Herman showed that the United States' foreign policy consistently involves attempting to destabilize or overthrow governments not friendly to multinational corporations while doing everything possible to promote, train, arm, and protect governments that do the bidding of these multinational corporations. Under U.S. influence or domination, tyrannical governments that are dependent on American support have come to power in nearly every Central American and South American country, in Thailand, Indonesia, the Philippines, Zaire, and elsewhere. These regimes always represent jointly the interests of tiny indigenous elites and multinational corporations. Nearly every one of these governments maintains control over the people of its country by use of systematic terror, including virtually all known modern forms of torture. In his final chapter Herman concluded:

> State terrorism, the quantitatively important terrorism, has escalated in scope and violence in recent decades. This is evidenced in the rise of torture as a serious problem, death squad murders, and the use of direct state violence to intimidate millions . . . There is a *system* of terroristic states . . . that has spread throughout Latin America and elsewhere over the past several decades, and which is deeply rooted in the corporate interest and sustaining political-military-financial-propaganda mechanisms of the United States and its Allies in the Free World. (Herman, p. 213)

Racism and Sexism

Radical critics also point to the pervasive effects of discrimination based on race and sex that exist in capitalist countries, particularly in the United States. Virtually everyone agrees that racism and sexism create severe discrimination. Defenders of American capitalism explain this discrimination in one of two ways. The more reactionary argue that job discrimination merely reflects the innate inferiority of women and blacks. Few, if any, intellectuals embrace this position, but it apparently is accepted by a large minority in the United States. The other contention is that racism and sexism are products of a fairly universal human bigotry and are not related to capitalism or any other economic system.

Critics of capitalism point out that the wages of blacks and women make up a significant part of capitalists' wage costs. In 1984, for example,

American women earned only about 68 percent of the earnings of men. On that basis it would appear that as much as 10 percent of all manufacturing profits might be attributable to the lower wages paid to women. Profits made as a result of racial discrimination are smaller, but they are still significant.

In one of the most influential socialist critiques, Paul A. Baran and Paul M. Sweezy have argued that it is necessary to

> consider first the private interests which benefit from the existence of a Negro subproletariat. (a) Employers benefit from divisions in the labor force which enable them to play one group off against another, thus weakening all . . . (b) Owners of ghetto real estate are able to overcrowd and overcharge. (c) Middle and upper income groups benefit from having at their disposal a large supply of cheap domestic labor. (d) Many small marginal businesses, especially in the service trades, can operate profitably only if cheap labor is available to them. (e) White workers benefit by being protected from Negro competition for the more desirable and higher paying jobs. (Baran and Sweezy, pp. 263–264)

They also assert that, in addition to increasing profits, discrimination increases social stability in a capitalist economy. The class structure of capitalism, they hold, leads to a situation in which

> each status group has a deep-rooted psychological need to compensate for feelings of inferiority and envy toward those above by feelings of superiority and contempt for those below. It thus happens that a special pariah group at the bottom acts as a kind of lightning rod for the frustrations and hostilities of all the higher groups, the more so the nearer they are to the bottom. It may even be said that the very existence of the pariah group is a kind of harmonizer and stabilizer of the social structure. (Ibid., pp. 265–266)

Although Baran and Sweezy's assertions pertain to racism, many critics argue that sexism performs a similar function in a capitalist society. These critics generally do not believe that capitalism is the original creator of racism and sexism, but they do argue that capitalism perpetuates and intensifies racism and sexism because these serve valuable functions.

> Today, transferring the locus of whites' perceptions of the source of many of their problems from capitalism and toward blacks, racism continues to serve the needs of the capitalist system. Although an individual employer might gain by refusing to discriminate and agreeing to hire blacks at above the going rate, it is not true that the capitalist class as a whole would profit if racism were eliminated and labor were more efficiently allocated without regard to skin color. . . . The divisiveness of racism weakens workers' strength when bargaining with employers; the economic consequences of racism are not only lower incomes for blacks but also higher incomes for the capitalist class coupled with lower incomes for white workers. Although capitalists may not have conspired consciously to create racism, and although capitalists may not be its principal perpetuators, nevertheless racism does support the continued well-being of the American capitalist system. (Reich, pp. 109–110)

Similarly, the critics argue that sex prejudice helps divide the labor, civil rights, and radical movements to the benefit of American capitalists.

Alienation

Many contemporary radical critics have refined and elaborated on Marx's theory of the human alienation inherent in the capitalist economic system. Baran and Sweezy, for example, maintain that total alienation pervades and dominates contemporary American capitalism:

> Disorientation, apathy, and often despair, haunting Americans in all walks of life, have assumed in our time the dimensions of a prolonged crisis. This crisis affects every aspect of national life, and ravages both its social-political and its individual spheres—everyman's everyday existence. A heavy strangulating sense of the emptiness and futility of life permeates the country's moral and intellectual climate. High level committees are entrusted with the discovery and specification of "national goals" while gloom pervades the printed matter (fiction and nonfiction, alike) appearing daily in the literary market place. The malaise deprives work of meaning and purpose; turns leisure into joyless, debilitating laziness; fatally impairs the education system and the conditions of healthy growth in the young; transforms religion and church into commercialized vehicles of "togetherness"; and destroys the very foundation of bourgeois society, the family. (Baran and Sweezy, p. 281)

The fact of alienation, like the facts of racism and sexism, is explained by many defenders of capitalism as an unfortunate but inevitable by-product of industrial civilization. They point to all the boring and dangerous work that must be done, as well as to the narrow and fragmented personalities of the enormous number of bureaucrats. Any industrialized socialist economy would, they assert, create the same type of alienation. Few people, regardless of political and economic views, would be willing to forgo the advantages of industrialization in order to combat alienation. Moreover, even if people did want to return to preindustrial society, there is simply no practical way of turning back time to some imagined golden age.

Socialist critics reply that although some amount of alienation will surely exist in any industrialized society, capitalism significantly intensifies alienation and makes it more pervasive. Erich Fromm, the psychoanalyst, social philosopher, and author, argues that the most important single cause of alienation is the fact that the individual feels no sense of participation in the forces that determine social policy. Individuals see these forces as anonymous and totally beyond their sphere of influence. "The anonymity of the social forces," writes Fromm, "is inherent in the structure of the capitalist mode of production" (Fromm, p. 125).

Fromm identifies several types of alienation created by the capitalist mode of production. Conditions of employment alienate workers. Their livelihoods depend on whether capitalists and managers are able to make a profit by hiring them, and thus they are viewed as means only, never as ends. The individual worker is "an economic atom that dances to the tune of atomistic management." Managers "strip the worker of his right to think and move freely. Life is being denied; need to control, creativeness, curiosity, and independent thought are balked, and the result, the inevitable result, is flight or fight on the part of the worker, apathy or destructiveness, psychic regression." The worker feels that the capitalist controls his or her whole life; both workers and consumers (and voters) feel weak and insignificant compared to the colossal power of the corporations over working conditions, prices, and even government policy.

Yet Fromm argues that the "role of the manager is also one of alienation," for managers are coerced by the ineluctable forces of capitalism and have very little freedom. They must deal "with impersonal giants; with the giant competitive enterprise; with giant impersonal markets; with giant unions; and the giant government." Their position, status, and income— in short, their very social existence—all depend on the generation of ever-increasing levels of profits. Yet managers must do this in a world in which they have little personal influence on the giants surrounding them.

Fromm also maintains that the process of consumption in a capitalist society "is as alienated as the process of production." The truly human way of acquiring commodities, according to Fromm, would be through need and the desire to use: "The acquisition of bread and clothing [should] depend on no other premise than that of being alive; the acquisition of books and paintings on my effort to understand them and my ability to use them" (Fromm, pp. 115, 116, 120). In capitalist societies, however, the income with which to purchase these commodities can come only through sales in the impersonal market.

As a consequence, those who have money are subjected to a constant barrage of propaganda designed to create consuming automata. Capitalist socialization processes make consumption-hungry, irrational, compulsive, buying machines of us all. Acts of buying and consuming have become ends in themselves, with little or no relation to the uses or pleasures derived from the commodities.

> Man today is fascinated by the possibility of buying more, better, and especially, new things. He is consumption-hungry. The act of buying and consuming has become a compulsive, irrational aim, because it is an end in itself with little relation to the use or pleasure in the things bought and consumed. To buy the latest gadget, the latest model of anything that is on the market, is a dream of everybody in comparison to which the real pleasure in use is quite secondary. Modern man, if he dared to be articulate about his concept of heaven, would describe a vision which would look like the biggest department store in the world, showing new things and gadgets, and himself having plenty of money with which to buy them. He would wander around open-mouthed in his heaven of gadgets and commodities, provided only that there were ever more and newer things to buy, and perhaps that his neighbors were just a little less privileged than he. (Fromm, p. 123)

Finally, the most severe alienation is the alienation of a person from his or her "self." A person's "worth" in a capitalist market economy is determined in the same way as the "worth" of anything else: by sales in the marketplace. In this situation, man experiences himself as a thing to be employed successfully on the market. He does not experience himself as an active agent, as the bearer of human powers. He is alienated from these powers. His aim is to sell himself successfully on the market. His sense of self does not stem from his activity as a loving and thinking individual, but from his socio-economic role . . . If you ask a man "Who are you?," he answers "I am a manufacturer," "I am a clerk," "I am a doctor." That is the way he experiences himself, not as a man, with love, fear, convictions, doubts, but as that abstraction, alienated from his real nature, which fulfills a certain function in the social system. His sense of value depends on his success: on whether he can sell himself favorably, to make a profit of himself. Human qualities like friendliness, courtesy, kindness, are transformed into commodities, into assets of the "personality package," conducive to a higher price on the personality market. If the individual fails in a profitable investment of himself, he feels that he is a failure; if he succeeds, he is a success. Clearly, his sense of his own value always depends on factors extraneous to himself, on the fickle judgment of the market, which decides about his value as it decides about the value of commodities. He, like all commodities that cannot be sold profitably on the market, is worthless as far as his exchange value is concerned, even though his use value may be considerable. (Ibid., pp. 129–130)

Thus socialist critics argue that the impersonal nexus of the capitalist market mediates all human relationships. It makes profit and loss the ultimate and pervasive evaluative criteria of human worth. This means that human alienation must inevitably be extremely severe in a capitalist market economy.

Environmental Destruction

Capitalism must either experience economic growth or else suffer depression, unemployment, stagnation, and their attendant social problems. Yet economic growth can also create situations in which the pursuit of profits comes into direct conflict with the public welfare. Critics of capitalism have argued that corporate profit seeking is generally accompanied by very little concern for conservation or the maintenance of a clean, livable environment.

Pollution is of concern to defenders of capitalism as well as to its critics. Defenders argue that it is a problem common to all industrialized economies. Critics maintain, however, that the problem is worse in a capitalist economy. Furthermore, they point out that it is virtually impossible to control pollution effectively in a capitalist system because the basic economic cause of pollution in a capitalist economy is that business firms do not have to pay *all* the costs incurred in the production process. They pay for labor, raw materials, and capital used up in production. Generally, however, they pay little or nothing for the use of the land, air, and water for the disposal of waste products that are created in the process of production. Thus the environment is treated as a garbage disposal.

It has been estimated that each year businesses are responsible for over 25 billion tons of pollutants being spewed into the air and dumped into the water and on the land. This is about 125 tons of waste per year for every man, woman, and child in the United States. Included in this figure are about 150 million tons of smoke and fumes that blacken the skies and poison the air, 22 million tons of waste paper products, 3 million tons of mill tailings, and 50 trillion gallons of heated and polluted liquids that are dumped into streams, rivers, and lakes each year (D'Arge, et al.). Critics argue that it is extremely difficult if not impossible for a capitalist economy to deal with these problems because those who receive the profits from production do not pay these social costs, and those who do pay the social costs have little or no voice in the operation of the business.

In response to the widespread public demand for control of pollution and polluters, the government has given contracts to many corporations to devise new methods of combating pollution. In effect, the government is asking private corporations to act as the controllers of other private corporations. Critics are convinced that this corporate integration of polluters and controllers will never lead to any substantial improvement. Most of the important pollution-control companies have become subsidiaries of the giant corporations that do most of the polluting.

One radical critic has analyzed the effects of this corporate control as follows:

> It is the chemical industry . . . that best illustrates the consequences of the incest between the pollution control business and the industrial polluters. First, the chemical industry is in the enviable position of reaping sizable profits by attempting to clean up rivers and lakes (at public expense) which they have profitably polluted in the first place. To facilitate this practically every major chemical company in the U.S. has established a pollution abatement division or is in the process of doing so . . . A second consequence of placing the "control" of pollution in the hands of big business is that the official abatement levels will inevitably be set low enough to protect industry's power to pollute and therefore its ability to keep costs down and revenues high. According to a recent study by the FWPCA (Federal Water Pollution Control Administration) if the chemical industry were to reduce its pollution of water to zero, the costs involved would amount to almost $2.7 billion per year. This would cut profits almost by half (Gellen, pp. 469–470).

Under such circumstances the critics do not expect much progress in cleaning up the environment unless fundamental social, political, and economic changes occur first.

The Energy Crisis

In 1973 the American public suddenly found that there had developed a shortage of gasoline. They were told that it was because the Arab countries, where much of the world's crude oil is extracted, had formed a cartel called the Organization of Petroleum Exporting Countries (OPEC), and that the cartel was cutting back on production and charging higher prices.

Very shortly thereafter the shortage led to long lines at gas stations and much higher prices. Once the shortage forced prices up approximately 50 percent, however, it mysteriously disappeared. The giant oligopolistic oil companies realized a colossal increase in profits; for some of these massive corporations profits increased in excess of 200 percent. Higher profits having been achieved, there was suddenly plenty of oil (at the higher prices) for everyone.

So that Americans would not see themselves simply as victims of a hoax perpetrated by greedy, profit-hungry oil companies, however, they were told that there was a general "energy crisis." The speed limit on major highways was reduced from 70 to 55 miles per hour. People were exhorted to use lights, appliances, and air conditioners very sparingly. They were repeatedly told that it was patriotic to pay much more to the energy-supplying corporations for the use of less energy.

Again in 1979 there developed another gasoline shortage. The results were once again, long lines and soaring prices. Again Americans were told that the OPEC countries were to blame for not extracting and exporting enough crude oil and for charging higher prices. Yet this time Americans were not as gullible as the big oil companies and the government thought. They realized that the official explanation left facts unexplained. First, for a period of 15 years the oil companies had purposely refrained from expanding their productive capacity as fast as demand was expanding and thereby had purposely created a situation in which at some point a shortage would become inevitable (and very profitable for them). Second, during the winter months of 1979 the oil companies cut back on the percentage of their refining capacity they were utilizing, thereby purposely creating the immediate acute shortage. Third, the higher prices the oil companies paid to the OPEC countries came nowhere near accounting for all of the increases in the price of gasoline that Americans were paying, and once again the profits of the oil companies soared.

During the 1980s the oil companies have been less successful in colluding to curtail oil production and concern with the "energy crisis" faded. This is, however, a "crisis" that will recur any time the capitalists in any industry of vital importance to society succeed in colluding to restrict production and increase prices and profits.

Radical critics pointed out that there was absolutely nothing "unnatural" or even unusual about all of this. The energy crisis perfectly reflects how private enterprise capitalism works. Capitalists have always tried to create oligopolies and monopolies that can "corner a market." Once they have control of a market, then they increase the price at whatever level the "traffic will bear" in order to maximize profit. Maximizing profits is what private enterprise is all about.

The more the general public needs the product in question, the higher the price that can be charged and the profit that can be made. In the case of petroleum, our entire society is an automobile culture, in which driving a car is absolutely necessary for most working-class people to get to work and to shopping centers. Hence gasoline is an absolute necessity of life.

Therefore, both the wealthy Arab kings who own the crude oil and the giant oil companies who refine it and sell it have behaved exactly as one would have expected them to behave. Depending on values and intellectual perspective, one can call it gouging and robbing the public through monopoly power over a necessary commodity—or one can call it ingeniously successful free enterprise at work.

Radicals point out that it is a form of gross social stupidity to allow a few greedy individuals to engage in what is tantamount to blackmail simply because they have monopolized ownership of things that are daily necessities. They further point out that the oil companies dominate the ownership of such alternative energy sources as coal, shale oil, and tar sands oil, so we have no choice but to submit to their blackmail.

Radicals insist that only when the production of all necessities is owned and controlled by the general public—that is, only with socialism—can this grip of blackmailing giants be broken. Only then can a rational energy policy be built around a program of low-cost, efficient public transportation for everyone. In the meantime, we all wait for the next crisis with its long lines, soaring prices, and mushrooming profits for the oil companies.

Inflation

As a result of prolonged massive military expenditures, financed in part through deficit spending, together with the steadily increasing debt levels of individuals, business, and government, there has not been a depression of the magnitude of the Great Depression since World War II. This form of stimulating expenditures, however, creates difficulties of its own. Each year levels of debt must be increased to service past borrowing and to stimulate new expenditures. This means that the amount of debt as well as the money supply have increased much faster than any increases in productivity and output. The result has been prolonged chronic inflation. By early 1980 the rate of inflation was 18 percent per year. During the early 1980s the effort to decrease the rate of inflation severely increased the rate of unemployment. Because there were 7 million or more unemployed workers since the early 1970s, decreasing the rate of inflation by increasing unemployment risked precipitating a major depression.

Inflation, however, does not harm everyone. It merely *redistributes* wealth and income. The hardest hit by inflation are people on fixed incomes and pensions. Their buying power continuously shrinks. Next hardest hit are workers. According to the government index of labor productivity, productivity between 1967 and 1978 increased by 16.5 percent, whereas during those same years real wages (that is, wages after adjustment for inflation) increased by only 2.4 percent. Thus more than 80 percent of the workers' increased productivity was taken from them by higher prices. The beneficiaries of inflation are the capitalists. They own the commodities that are going up in price and realize windfall gains. Bankers are the most significant beneficiaries of the current inflation. They have managed to keep the interest rate above the rate of inflation and have continuously expanded their loans. Throughout the 1970s bank profits soared to all-time highs.

The general benefits of inflation for capitalists can be seen in the profits of the largest 500 industrial corporations for 1978 as reported in *Fortune* magazine. The editors of *Fortune* wrote that in 1978, when most people were reeling under the blows of inflation, "profits were absolutely sensational . . . and the median profit margins reached . . . the highest level in a decade. The median return on stockholders equity . . . was the highest on record."

Radicals point out that even the massive expansion of credit cannot eliminate the boom-bust cycle of capitalism. To the degree that this credit expansion has mitigated the severity of depressions it has involved two significant social costs. First, it has redistributed income and wealth from the old, the poor, and the working class to capitalists. Second, it has created a worldwide superstructure of credit in which A owes B, B owes C, C owes D, and so forth, so that solvency at any level depends on ever-increasing borrowing. Thus, the possibility now exists for a chain reaction of default that could precipitate a crisis potentially worse than the depression of the 1930s. The underlying problem of the inherent instability of capitalism always remains.

At the end of the 1980s the economy had been expanding continuously since the recession of 1981–1983. President Reagan's tax cuts had given the economy a very powerful stimulus. These tax cuts created, however, the largest government deficits in the history of any capitalist government. President Bush must find some way of dealing with these deficits. He pledged not to increase taxes. To do so would risk setting off a chain reaction that could lead to a socially disastrous depression. To allow the deficits to continue at record levels, however, threatens a worldwide financial collapse, the consequences of which would be much worse than a depression. Capitalism is inherently unstable and President Bush has an unenviable task.

LIBERAL VERSUS RADICAL CRITIQUES OF CAPITALISM

The glaringly unequal distribution of wealth, income, and political power and the facts of militarism, imperialism, vicious discrimination, social alienation, environmental destruction, irrational use of resources and energy sources, and severe inflation are all recognized and decried by both liberal and radical critics of capitalism. There is, however, an immensely important difference between the positions of liberals and radicals.

Liberals tend to see each of these social and economic problems as separate and distinct. The problems, they believe, are the results of past mistakes or random cases of individual perversity. Liberals also tend to regard the government as disinterested, as motivated by a desire to maximize the welfare of all its citizens; hence they generally favor government-sponsored reforms designed to mitigate the many evils of capitalism. These reforms never threaten the two most important features of capitalism—private ownership of the means of production and the free market.

Radicals, however, see each of the social and economic problems we have discussed as the direct consequence of private ownership of capital and the process of social decision making within the impersonal cash nexus of the market. The problems cannot be solved until their underlying causes are eliminated, but this means a fundamental, radical economic reorganization. If private ownership of capital is eliminated and if significant restrictions are placed on the area in which the market determines social decisions, the resulting system would no longer be a capitalist economic system. It would of necessity be some type of socialist society. This view implies that no government in the United States, whether Democratic or Republican, can solve the problems of capitalism.

Capitalism and Democracy in the United States

There is very little risk of any member of Congress in the Democratic or Republican parties trying to fundamentally change capitalism. In American capitalism voters vote much as they spend their money on consumer goods—in response to massive, expensive public relations and advertising campaigns. Capitalists contribute millions of dollars to the campaigns of candidates who take the capitalists' point of view. These politicians, in turn, pass laws that ensure and enlarge the economic power of capitalists. Poor people and working people have a choice of two parties reflecting competing capitalists' views, but no relevant choice of an anticapitalist candidate who can afford the hundreds of thousands of dollars necessary to make his or her views known.

In response to the upsurge of grassroots organizing in the 1960s and early 1970s, capitalists sought to cement their political control by increasing dramatically the amounts of money spent on congressional and senate races. Table 14.1 shows the average cost of a winning campaign for the U.S. House of Representatives and Senate for four elections between 1976 and 1986.

Table 14.1   AVERAGE COST OF A WINNING
CAMPAIGN FOR THE U.S.
HOUSE AND SENATE

Year	House	Senate
1976	$ 87,200	$ 609,100
1978	$126,900	$1,208,600
1982	$263,000	$2,066,308
1986	$355,000	$3,099,554

Source: Philip M. Stern, *The Best Congress Money Can Buy*
(New York: Pantheon Books, 1988), p. 25.

In 1986 the cost of winning a seat in the house was 407 percent of the 1976 cost while the cost of a senate seat was 509 percent of the 1976 figure.

Where did these millions of dollars necessary for Republicans and Democrats to get elected come from? The answer to this question is mainly from the "political action committees (PACs)"—a euphomism for special interest groups of mostly corporate executives and wealthy capitalists. Although unions, school teachers and other noncapitalists and noncorporate groups do have PACs, these PACs are smaller in number and much, much smaller in financial resources than the thousands of PACs representing corporate and capitalist interests. Table 14.2 shows the growth in the number of PACs and the size of their financial contributions to congressional candidates between 1974 and 1984. It is not an exaggeration to say that American politics of the 1980s is controlled by PACs representing the rich and the powerful.

In his carefully documented study, Philip M. Stern (1988) not only provides the statistics of Tables 14.1 and 14.2, he also describes case after case of clear-cut domination of politics by the wealthy. For example, in 1984 Senator Robert Dole initially opposed legislation that would give a tax break worth at least $300 million to 333 wealthy commodities traders. Each of these 333 multimillionaires stood to gain an average of $866,000 per individual. A special PAC was formed and run by and for Robert Dole. The commodities industry and various individual traders gave $10,500 to Dole's PAC. Then a group of individual commodities traders gave several thousand more dollars to a fundraiser hosted by Dole's PAC. Three weeks after the fundraiser, Senator Dole reversed himself and helped pass the huge tax break for these wealthy individuals. Stern's study is replete with similar examples of the political power of wealthy capitalists.

In an equally illuminating study, Frances Fox Piven and Richard A. Cloward (1988) describe in scholarly detail a series of electoral changes

Table 14.2   NUMBERS OF PACS AND AMOUNTS
OF THEIR CONTRIBUTIONS TO
CONGRESSIONAL CANDIDATES

Year	Number of PACs	PAC contributions to congressional candidates
1974	608	$ 12.5 million
1978	1,653	$ 34.1 million
1982	3,371	$ 83.6 million
1986	4,157	$132.2 million

Source: Philip M. Stern, The Best Congress Can Buy (New York: Pantheon Books, 1988), p. 24.

in the United States, from the late nineteenth century to the present, that have tended to disfranchise the poor and to make Republicans and Democrats unresponsive to the needs of the poor, racial minorities, and the industrial working class.

In this context it is obvious that electoral politics in the United States, at present, reinforces the power of capitalists and is not a vehicle for changing capitalism in any fundamental way. For electoral politics to become responsive to the needs of the poor, racial minorities, and workers would require a grassroots, mass movement to change the financial basis of American politics and then either the emergence of a new and powerful third party or a major, fundamental overhaul from top to bottom of the Democratic party. In the meantime electoral politics remains, in the main with a few notable exceptions, an institution for capitalist control of workers, for the rich controlling the poor.

RADICAL POLITICAL MOVEMENTS IN THE 1960s, 1970s, AND 1980s

In the 1930s and 1940s the "old left" political movements gained substantially in both numbers and influence. The old left was almost entirely socialist, and its growth had been a consequence of the Great Depression of the 1930s, which had convinced many people that capitalism was an irrational, dying system. The principal organizations of the left were the Communist party, the Socialist party, and the Socialist Workers party. Although their memberships constituted only a tiny percentage of the American population, they had an influence in labor organizations and in American social and political life that was far greater than their numbers would indicate.

The economic recovery of the late 1940s and 1950s, combined with the harsh influence and political repression of McCarthyism, had almost destroyed the leftist movement by the late 1950s and early 1960s. The civil rights and antiwar movements led to a widespread rebirth of the belief that many of the worst evils of American society were the inevitable outcomes of the structure and organization of capitalism. These movements thus led to a rebirth of the socialist movement.

Yet the radicals of the 1960s were generally very different from their counterparts in the 1930s. These differences—which resulted in their being called the "new left," in contrast to the "old left" of the 1930s and its surviving organizations—can be categorized under three headings. First, many believed that moral and emotional contempt were more important than the old left's intellectual dogmas as potential sources for transforming American society. American revolution was just around the corner. Second, many were so contemptuous of intellectual dogmatism and old left sloganeering that they refused for several years to accept very many of the theoretical and empirical insights of the Marxist tradition. Third, their dislike of authority, authoritarian structures, and the suppression of the individual was so great that they were unable to create any effective organizations through which to further their aims.

The organization most typical of, and influential among, the new left was the Students for a Democratic Society (SDS). Organized in the early 1960s, it was most instrumental in disseminating the facts about the Vietnam War and in mobilizing massive student resistance against the war. By 1968, however, two things had become obvious. First, its aversion to leftist dogma was so great as to degenerate at times into anti-intellectualism. As a result, there was amazing diversity in its members' opinions about the nature of American society and the best tactics to use in attempting to restructure that society. Second, the aversion to authority had resulted in an organization so loosely and ineffectively structured that it was hardly capable of any well-coordinated mass action at all (it was euphemistically extolled as "participatory democracy").

It is not surprising that in 1969, shortly after President Nixon was elected, relatively little effort was required on the part of government agents and provocateurs to precipitate the immediate and almost total disintegration of SDS. By this time, however, the antiwar movement had a momentum of its own and was able to survive the demise of SDS. Many moderate and liberal leaders had joined the bandwagon, and the Socialist Workers party and the Communist party had become active in the leadership of the radical wing of the antiwar movement.

By early 1973 several things became apparent. With the end of the Vietnam War, hundreds of thousands of Americans who had opposed the war and had sometimes been thought to be a part of the movement lapsed into a mood of relief and what appeared to be social and political indifference. People were weary of social conflict and hopeful that a peaceful, tranquil mood would come to prevail in the United States. The Watergate revelations and subsequent disclosures of widespread, illegal operations of the American CIA and FBI showed Americans how far their government would go to crush political criticism at home and to maintain the worldwide American empire.

The result of these revelations was not, as leftists hoped, a widespread indignation and determination for radical social change. The more usual response was apathy and a naive hope and faith that these abuses and excesses had simply been the result of a few corrupt and unscrupulous politicians. Both the Republican and Democratic parties chose presidential candidates for the 1976 election who could be portrayed as simple and honest—"just plain folks." Jimmy Carter was widely seen as uncorrupted by national office. He was elected president.

The 1970s saw several important changes in the radical movement. Many new left radicals of the 1960s came to see their hopes for radical social change in the near future were unrealistic. They saw that promoting such change would require a more adequate knowledge of the structure and functioning of capitalist society. It would also require a much more effectively organized movement.

The first of these requirements led to a widespread tendency to study Marx and the ideas of Marxist theoreticians of the last 100 years. Radical students of the 1960s became radical professors in the 1970s. Organizations, such as the Union for Radical Political Economics (URPE), devoted themselves to the promotion and propagation of radical understanding of American capitalism. The URPE currently has about 2000 members and publishes analyses of the current economic and political trends in the United States as well as studies aimed at increasing radicals' understanding of the nature and functioning of capitalism. These are published regularly in two journals—*The Review of Radical Political Economics* and *Dollars and Sense*—and a newsletter. Informal study groups have sprung up around the United States. Several universities have academic departments where radical professors now regularly teach Marxist views on history and the social sciences.

The widely felt need for better organization affected members of the new left in very diverse ways. A large part of them felt that no satisfactory nationwide socialist organization existed, so they concentrated their efforts solely on local organizing. Another major segment joined the various old left organizations. During the 1970s several Maoist organizations (political organizations that base many of their ideas on the writings of Mao Tse Tung and the Chinese Communists), the Communist party, the Socialist Workers party, the Progressive Labor party, the International Socialists, the Socialist party, and other old left organizations grew more rapidly than at any time since World War II.

A sizable number of former SDS members as well as many other members of the new left retained their dissatisfaction with the old left organizations, but they still hoped to reorganize on a nationwide basis. The most important organization to come out of this group was the New American Movement (NAM), which was formed in 1973 with approximately 50 chapters in various cities across the United States. The NAM aimed to create a democratic socialist society in the United States, in which racism, sexism, imperialism, and all other forms of human oppression were to be eradicated. It believed that the old left socialist organizations were too thoroughly affected by mistakes and outworn attitudes to be effective means for the economic, social, and political alterations that it believed were ultimately necessary to create a humane, moral society in the United States.

In the early 1970s, as a result of a number of internal conflicts, the Socialist party broke into three separate factions. One group remained the Socialist party. Another group, calling themselves the Democratic Socialist Organizing Committee, was the largest of the three. In 1982 the Democratic Socialist Organizing Committee and the New American Movement merged to form the Democratic Socialists of America (DSA). In 1989 the DSA is the largest American socialist organization since the 1930s. The

Socialist party, while small, continues to maintain the traditions of Eugene V. Debs, perhaps the greatest socialist in American history.

By 1980 very little of the civil rights, or black, movement remained as a separate movement. Most of their more moderate demands for economic reform have been taken up by the liberal wing of the Democratic party. Their more radical demands for fundamental change in the social, political, and economic institutions as a means of achieving human equality have been taken up by most of the socialist organizations (which have always fought for racial equality). The black separatist movement of the 1960s, which advocated a separate all-black nation, appears virtually to have disappeared.

The women's movement also changed in the 1970s and 1980s. The women's separatist movement appears to be following in the footsteps of the black separatist movement. Its members, like those of the SDS in the 1960s, have an aversion to nearly all organizational forms and, consequently, have never been able to create a nationwide organization. Generally, their dislike of authority renders their political organizations ineffective.

The National Organization of Women advocates few, if any, fundamental changes in social, political, or economic structures of capitalism. Consequently, although they do have a large and effective nationwide organization, they are definitely not socialist—though their rhetoric has recently become very radical on a number of important issues.

The Marxist feminist movement has had a considerable impact on several socialist organizations. This component of the women's movement has no effective national organization with an all-women membership, nor is it devoted solely to feminist issues. Marxist feminists, however, constitute a significant portion of the Democratic Socialists of America (whose leadership bodies have always had more than 50 percent women), and feminist issues are very prominent in the DSA's program and activities.

The socialist movement in the United States is much smaller and less effective than its counterparts in most advanced capitalist countries. In several western European countries, coalitions of communists and socialists regularly receive somewhere near a majority of votes in national elections. Socialist and communist parties in these countries have memberships in the millions. Because the United States is the most powerful of all capitalist countries, it is not surprising that its socialist movement is the weakest.

As we have seen in earlier chapters, socialist ideas and movements came into being with the Industrial Revolution, and socialists have always fought to eradicate the worst effects of capitalism. Socialists have also always fought and will continue to fight for the complete abolition of capitalism and its replacement by a democratic socialist society. As long as capitalism involves poverty, inequality, imperialism, unemployment and economic crises, environmental pollution, racism, sexism, and alienation, there will undoubtedly be socialists speaking, writing, organizing, and acting in their efforts to create a better society.

SUMMARY

From the late 1950s to the early 1970s, the civil rights movement, the women's liberation movement, and the antiwar movement generated a resurgence of radical criticism of American capitalism. The radicals argue that inequality, discrimination, alienation, environmental destruction, militarism, irrational use of resources, instability, inflation, and imperialism are integral parts of a capitalist economy. Unlike liberals, who believe that these evils are accidental and that the system can be reformed, radicals contend that these evils cannot be overcome until the basic structure of capitalism is fundamentally changed.

The principal obstacle to the achievement of such reforms is the fact that political power is derived from economic power. Radicals see capitalist governments as plutocracies hidden behind phony facades of democracy. Both political parties, they point out, spend millions of dollars on each election. As a consequence, both political parties, they point out, spend millions of dollars on each election. As a consequence, both political parties are almost completely controlled by the wealthiest 2 percent of the population, who own most of the income-producing capital (see Domhoff, 1967, 1970). In this situation one would not expect the wealthy elite to support any government that threatened to destroy the basis of their wealth, privileges, and power. Therefore, fundamental reform seems unlikely unless a reform movement can establish a base of power independent of wealth. In the 1960s at radical gatherings one often heard the slogan "Power to the People!" A strategic plan to peacefully and legally transfer power from this elite to the democratic control of common people remains the most difficult task of the left.

REFERENCES

Alperowitz, Gar. *Atomic Diplomacy: Hiroshima and Potsdam.* New York: Simon & Schuster, 1965.

Baran, Paul A. *The Political Economy of Growth.* New York: Monthly Review Press, 1962.

———, and Paul M. Sweezy. *Monopoly Capital.* New York: Monthly Review Press, 1966.

Belfrage, Cedric. *The American Inquisition, 1945–1960.* New York: Bobbs-Merrill, 1973.

Bidwell, Percy W. *Raw Materials.* New York: Harper & Row, 1958.

Cook, Fred J. *The Nightmare Decade: The Life and Times of Senator Joe McCarthy.* New York: Random House, 1971.

D'Arge, R. C., A. V. Kneese, and R. V. Ayres. *Economics of the Environment: A Materials Balance Approach.* Baltimore: John Hopkins Press, 1970.

Domhoff, G. William. *The Higher Circles: The Governing Class in America.* New York: Random House, 1970.

————. *Who Rules America?* Englewood Cliffs, N.J.: Prentice-Hall, 1967.

Fleming, D. F. *The Cold War and Its Origins.* Garden City, N.Y.: Doubleday, 1961.

Fortune. May 7, 1979.

Fromm, Erich. *The Sane Society.* New York: Fawcett World Library, Premier Books, 1965.

Gellen, Martin. "The Making of a Pollution-Industrial Complex." In *Problems in Political Economy: An Urban Perspective.* Edited by David M. Gordon. Lexington, Mass.: Raytheon/Heath, 1971.

Herman, Edward S. *The Real Terror Network, Terrorism in Fact and Propaganda.* Boston: South End Press, 1982.

Higgins, Benjamin. *Economic Development.* New York: Norton, 1959.

Hole, Judith, and Ellen Levine. *Rebirth of Feminism.* New York: Quadrangle, 1971.

Horwitz, David, ed. *Corporations and the Cold War.* New York: Monthly Review Press, 1969.

Horwitz, David. *Empire and Revolution.* New York: Random House, 1969.

Huberman, Leo, and Paul A. Sweezy. "The Road to Ruin." In *Monthly Review,* April, 1965.

Jalee, Pierre. *The Pillage of the Third World.* New York: Monthly Review Press, 1969.

Landes, David S. "The Nature of Economic Imperialism." *The Journal of Economic History,* December 1961.

Magdoff, Harry. *The Age of Imperialism, the Economics of U.S. Foreign Policy.* New York: Monthly Review Press, Modern Reader Paperbacks, 1969.

Piven, Frances Fox, and Richard A. Cloward. *Why Americans Don't Vote.* New York: Pantheon Books, 1988.

Reich, Michael. "The Economics of Racism." In *Problems in Political Economy: An Urban Perspective.* Lexington, Mass.: Raytheon/Heath, 1971.

Sheehan, Neil. "The Story Behind the Vietnam War, Based on a Pentagon Study." In *New York Times News Service,* June 13, 1971.

Snider, Delbert A. *Introduction to International Economics.* Homewood, Ill.: Irwin, 1963.

Stern, Philip M. *The Best Congress Money Can Buy.* New York: Pantheon Books, 1988.

Wise, David, and Thomas B. Ross. *The Invisible Government.* New York: Random House, 1964.

PRICES AND POVERTY

An Introduction to Microeconomics

Chapter
15

Market Allocation of Resources: Efficiency Versus Fairness

Part One of this book sketched some of the highlights in the history of economic thought and in the evolution of the private enterprise, or capitalist, system. In Parts Two and Three the actual working of the capitalist system is discussed. Part Two concentrates on *microeconomics*, the economics of individual enterprises and individual workers and consumers; Part Three deals with *macroeconomics*, the operation of the economy as a whole. Thus in Part Two we discuss, among other things, how enterprises set prices and make profits under competition and monopoly, how workers' wages are determined, how the government affects the distribution of income, and the economics of racial and sexual discrimination.

A private enterprise economy is one in which the factories, tools, and stocks of goods with which production is carried on are owned by private individuals. Individual ownership includes, of course, the corporate form of ownership. In the corporation individuals own the whole capital, but each person's ownership is specified in the form of the stock or shares that he or she holds.

Most modern private enterprise economies are distinguished by socially and technologically complex methods of production and distribution. It is possible to imagine an economy of small farmers and artisan-producers in which each individual owns his or her own means of production and is a fairly independent producer. In the reality of the modern private enterprise economy, however, this type of individual independence is completely impossible. The factory system, ushered in by the Industrial Revolution, has made individual producers completely dependent. A worker in an automobile factory, for example, owns no tools of production. Alone, one worker cannot produce anything. Individual workers depend for continued existence on being able to sell their labor time to a company that employs hundreds of thousands of other workers. Their work generally consists of one small, insignificant, and tedious operation (such as screwing a particular nut onto a particular bolt) repeated endlessly for 8 hours each day.

In the American economy about 1.8 percent of the population owns 80 percent of all corporate stock. Most of the remaining 98.2 percent own little or no capital and depend on the *market* for their labor services to earn a living. Workers who succeed in selling labor services are paid a wage that is then spent in the market for goods and services. By purchasing these goods and services, the individual worker plays a small (usually *very* small) role in creating the demand that provides jobs for the other workers who produce these goods and services. In fact, in the U.S. economy the continued employment of any individual may depend on the actions and behavior of hundreds of thousands or even millions of other people. All these people are related to this individual through only one social institution—the market. It is therefore vitally important to understand how the market functions.

In a private enterprise economy the market determines what is to be produced. Capitalists, or their hired managers, are motivated primarily by the drive to maximize profits. They use the market to hire labor and buy raw materials, which they combine with the factories, machinery, and tools they own in order to produce an output. Many capitalists are strictly intermediaries and financiers and are not directly connected with productive output, but we shall examine only those who do own a productive facility. They sell their output in the market.

Their objective is to maximize the difference between their sales proceeds and their money expenses incurred in buying raw materials, hiring labor, and replacing used-up capital. This difference is, of course, profits. They constantly search for commodities that can be produced and sold profitably.

The capitalists' costs of production represent income to laborers and the owners of raw materials. Profit is the income that accrues to the capitalist. The recipients of these incomes spend them in the market for the goods produced by the capitalists' business firms. Thus money circulates from the business firms to the general public in the form of incomes generated in the production process. The money then returns to the business firms when the public purchases the goods and services these firms sell in the market.

There is thus an amazingly complex circulation of money from hundreds of thousands of business firms to hundreds of millions of people and back into the hands of the business firms. At all points the guiding force is the capitalists' constant search for profits. The decisions concerning what goods to produce (or even whether to produce), what inputs to buy, what wages to pay, and so forth are all determined by the criterion of profitability. All economic relations between people are mediated by the institution of the market. The market is obviously one of the most important social institutions in a private enterprise economy. In this and the several following chapters, we attempt to achieve a clearer understanding of what markets are and how they function.

It is important to begin by distinguishing a particular market from the market system (or, as it is often referred to, *the* market). Historically, a market was an area, usually near the center of a village or town, where producers and traders would meet and exchange goods. Later, any place where a merchant regularly sold commodities was a market. Today the word *market* is sometimes used to refer to a grocery store, but it is more generally used as an abstract concept. It refers, in this usage, to the negotiation of exchange transactions that normally involve money, and the determination of the prices at which these exchanges are transacted.

We speak of the stock market, the labor market, or the automobile market when we are referring to the buying and selling of stock, labor services, or automobiles. We speak of the market or the *market system* when we wish to refer to monetary exchange and price determination in general. It is obvious that any market system that successfully facilitates price determination and exchange must contain complex systems of customs and traditions, laws and agencies of law enforcement, as well as the physical buildings in which business is transacted.

In this part of the book, physical settings of markets and many of the customs and laws that enable markets to function are ignored. We concentrate instead on exchange (buying and selling) and the determination of price.

A market is basically a two-sided phenomenon, with buyers facing sellers. Buyers have money they wish to exchange for goods, and sellers have goods they wish to exchange for money. The amount of a good that buyers would like to purchase at any given time is referred to as the *demand* for that good. Similarly, the amount of the good that sellers would like to sell is referred to as the *supply* of the good.

It should be stressed that demand is not necessarily related to need or desire. A penniless child longingly gazing through the window of a candy store adds nothing to the market demand for candy. Similarly, in the Great Depression of the 1930s millions of people went hungry while tons of wheat and thousands of cattle and sheep were destroyed and wasted because of the lack of any market demand for them. The problem, of course, was that, like the child at the candy store, the unemployed millions had no money to exchange for food.

DEMAND AND SUPPLY

Restated more formally, the definitions of demand and supply are as follows: *Demand for a good refers to the amount of that good buyers would like to purchase during a given period, at a given price.* Obviously demand must be expressed in terms of a given period if it is to have any meaning. The

Table 15.1   NUMBER OF FORD
            ESCORTS DEMANDED
            AT VARIOUS PRICES

Price	Quantity demanded per year (in 100,000s)
$7000	10
7500	8
8000	6
8500	4

number of automobiles people wish to purchase is certainly very different over the course of a week than over a year. Moreover, a given price must be specified. Clearly the number of Ford cars people would like to buy will be very different if the price is $500 than if it is $5000. The lower the price of Ford cars, the more of them people will want to buy.

The definition of supply is very similar to that of demand. *Supply of a good refers to the quantity of that good sellers would like to sell during a given period, at a given price.*

If the reactions of buyers and sellers at different prices are considered, it becomes possible to define a demand schedule and a supply schedule. A *demand schedule relates various prices* of that good with the *amounts* of that good people would like to buy at each of the various prices (given the incomes and preferences of the buyers). If the people of the United States were polled in order to determine the number of Ford Escorts they would like to buy at various prices, the results might be similar to those given in Table 15.1.

The information contained in this demand schedule can be shown on a graph as a demand curve (Figure 15.1). A *demand curve,* like a demand schedule, relates prices to quantities demanded. The DD curve makes it possible to select any price and ascertain the quantity buyers would like to purchase at that price.

Why does the demand curve usually have a downward slope? At higher prices, people have a small demand—both because other goods appear more attractive and because people simply do not have enough income to buy at those prices. As prices decline, people demand more—both because they can afford more and because these goods are now cheaper relative to other alternatives. We discuss these issues in more detail in later sections.

In a similar manner it is possible to find the number of Escorts the Ford Motor Company would desire to sell at various prices. Table 15.2 summarizes this hypothetical information. In Figure 15.2 the same information is expressed in the form of a supply curve, demonstrating the quantities sellers would like to sell at various prices.

Why does the supply curve usually slope upward? Ford is in business

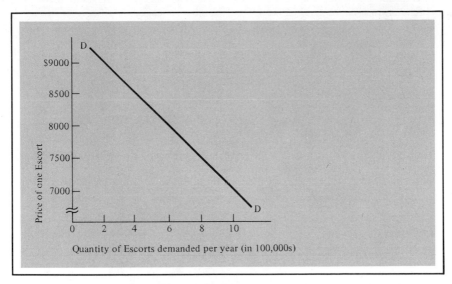

Figure 15.1 Demand for Ford Escorts.

for profit. At higher prices it can make more profit, so it is willing to supply more Escorts at higher prices. This issue is also discussed more fully in later sections.

Market prices are determined by the forces of supply and demand. Sellers wish to exchange products for money, and buyers wish to exchange money for products. When a particular price is established, a specific quantity will be offered for sale and a specific quantity will be demanded. If these two quantities are equal, both sellers and buyers will be able to conduct transactions in the desired quantities. For example, in Figure 15.3 the demand curve for Escorts (from Figure 15.1) is superimposed on the supply curve (from Figure 15.2). If a price of $8000 is established, the point at which the curves intersect indicates that buyers and sellers want to buy and sell 600,000 cars.

Table 15.2   NUMBER OF FORD
ESCORTS SUPPLIED
AT VARIOUS PRICES

Price	Quantity supplied per year (in 100,000s)
$7000	2
7500	4
8000	6
8500	8

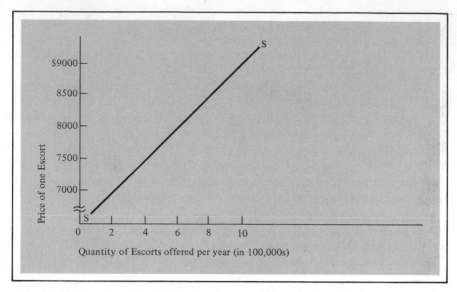

Figure 15.2 Supply of Ford Escorts.

EQUILIBRIUM

When the desires of buyers and sellers are consistent and both are able to conduct their desired exchanges, the market is said to be in *equilibrium*. The notion of equilibrium is central to most economic theories. It generally

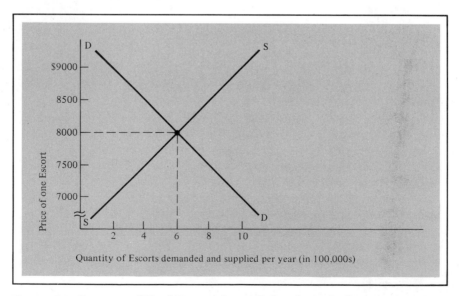

Figure 15.3 Quantity of Ford Escorts demanded and supplied.

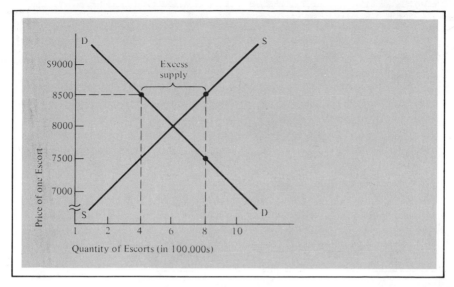

Figure 15.4 Excess supply of Ford Escorts.

means that supply and demand are equal and that the exchange desires of buyers and sellers are mutually consistent. At equilibrium prices everyone is able to buy or sell all that one chooses to buy or sell within one's budget

If a price that is higher than the equilibrium price is established, then supply will exceed demand. This is called a situation of excess *supply*. In Figure 15.4, if the price of Escorts is set at $8500, an excess supply exists. Ford would like to sell 800,000 Escorts at that price, but buyers would like to buy only 400,000. There is an excess supply of 400,000.

In many markets there is a tendency for the forces of supply and demand to cause price changes that will eliminate excess supply and equilibrate the market. In the situation illustrated in Figure 15.4, thousands of Escort dealers will find that at the established price of $8500 they are unable to sell the quantity of cars they had anticipated. As unwanted inventories of unsold cars accumulate, the dealers cut back or eliminate entirely their orders with the Ford Motor Company. With production geared for the 800,000 cars the manufacturer had hoped to sell, it is not long before unwanted inventories pile up at the factory.

In order to reduce these inventories and stimulate sales, the manufacturer *may* reduce the price, which definitely would improve the imbalance between supply and demand. As long as the price remains above $8000, however, the excess supply will persist, and the motive to cut the price further will continue to exist. Only at the equilibrium price of $8000 will excess supply disappear and the market be cleared.

At a price below $8000 demand would exceed supply (Figure 15.5). Dealers would find long lines of customers waiting to buy the few available cars. Orders sent to Ford would go largely unfilled because these orders

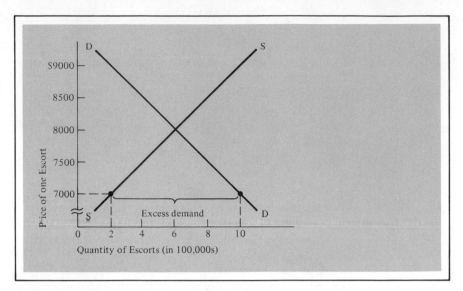

Figure 15.5 Excess demand for Ford Escorts.

would far exceed the number of Escorts being produced. Figure 15.5 shows that at the low price of $7000, Ford will offer to supply only 200,000 cars, but consumers wish to buy 1,000,000 cars. There is therefore an excess demand of 800,000 cars.

Under these conditions it would be obvious to the dealers and the manufacturer that more cars could be sold at higher prices. The search for higher profits would dictate that the price be raised. As the price is raised, the amount of excess demand declines. Yet at any price below $8000 there will continue to be some excess demand. There will therefore continue to be an upward pressure on the price until it reaches the equilibrium level of $8000.

The rate at which price changes bring the market into equilibrium varies greatly from market to market. In some markets, sellers are very sensitive to unwanted changes in inventories, so adjustments in price occur very quickly. The New York Stock Exchange is highly sensitive to hour-by-hour fluctuations in supply and demand. Frequent price changes serve to keep the market near equilibrium at all times.

At the other extreme, what is for most people the most important of all markets—the labor market—may remain for years in a situation of disequilibrium. With only a few exceptions (mostly in time of war) this market has had a persistent excess supply, which means, of course, involuntary unemployment for some people. This is a subject that receives considerable attention in Part Three.

There are also many cases in which control of supply or demand gives an individual or group of individuals the power to *fix* prices. In this case excess supply or demand may not lead to price changes if those changes

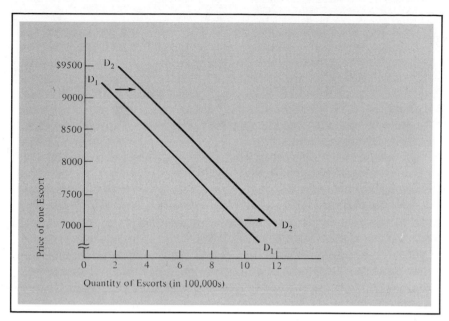

Figure 15.6 Change in demand for Ford Escorts.

are not in the best interest of the price fixer. We examine this fact and its implications in Chapters 20, 22, and 23, which examine imperfect competition, oligopoly (when a few firms control supply), and monopoly (when one firm controls supply), respectively.

CHANGES IN DEMAND

There are three main factors that can change the demand for a particular commodity: (1) changes in price, (2) changes in tastes or preferences, and (3) changes in consumers' available income. We have already discussed price changes. With a given demand schedule, a lower price means more demand, whereas a higher one means less demand.

Suppose there is change in preferences, with consumer preferences shifting from big, gaudy cars to small, economical ones like the Escort. What happens to the demand schedule? At any given price, more will be demanded. This upward shift in demand is illustrated in Figure 15.6. The old demand curve, D_1D_1 is replaced by a new and higher demand curve, D_2D_2.

Now consider another influence on demand. Suppose that there was a general increase in the incomes of all people consuming Escorts. With the new, higher incomes individuals would probably buy *more* Escorts at *every* possible price. The higher incomes cause a shift in the demand curve. This produces a new demand curve (line D_2D_2). At any price the new demand curve shows that people wish to buy more at that price than they formerly did (when line D_1D_1 was the demand curve).

This increased demand is the result of the increase in income. In general, whenever there is a change in any of the factors (other than price) that affect demand, this change will be shown as a shift in the demand curve.

A bit of terminology here will make you sound like a sophisticated economist and may save you some confusion later on. Whenever economists say flatly "demand has changed," they mean *the whole demand curve has shifted.* An increase in demand means a shift of the curve outward (to the right, from D_1D_1 to D_2D_2); it means *more* Escorts are demanded at any given price. A decrease in demand means a shift in the curve inward (to the left, from D_2D_2 to D_1D_1); it means fewer Escorts are demanded at any given price.

When everything else stays the same (i.e., the curve does not shift) and only the price changes, economists will *not* say "demand has changed." They will just say there has been *"movement* along the demand curve," or a change in quantity demanded. The economist will say, "at a higher price, less quantity was demanded" or "at a lower price, more quantity was demanded," but with no change or shift in the demand curve as a whole. In other words, with no shift in demand Ford could sell more Escorts only by lowering the price (and if Ford raises the prices it will sell fewer Escorts).

Of course, in reality both things often happen at once: (1) prices of Escorts change, and (2) income and other factors affecting demand change. As a result of both (1) and (2), the quantity of Escorts demanded has changed. Yet it is impossible to be sure how much of the demand change was a result of the price change (movement along the demand curve) and how much was a result of changes in income and other factors (shift in the demand curve). In other words, reality does not draw curves; only economists draw curves to try to analyze what is happening.

CHANGES IN SUPPLY

The explanation of shifts in demand and movements along demand curves may be repeated for changes in supply. The student should work this through in Figure 15.7. Consider, for example, the way higher or lower prices per car would cause Ford to move along the supply curve (S_1S_1), offering more or fewer Escorts to the consumer market at different prices. But also consider the way lower costs per car (such as a lower price of steel per ton) might motivate Ford to offer more Escorts at each given price (i.e., a shift from supply curve S_1S_1 to S_2S_2).

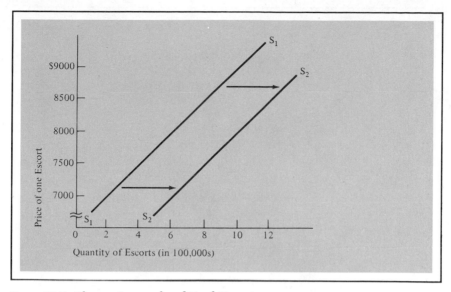

Figure 15.7 Change in supply of Ford Escorts.

CHANGES IN SUPPLY AND DEMAND

Finally, by putting the changes in supply and demand together, it is possible to explain how prices are forced to change. The effect on the price of Escorts of an increase or decrease in demand (with supply conditions remaining unchanged) is shown in Figure 15.8.

An increase in demand for Escorts can be explained as a shift up from curve D_1D_1 to D_2D_2, or as a movement along the supply curve SS up and to the right. Both descriptions are correct. Either way, the fact is that Ford can sell *more* Escorts at a *higher price*. The quantity sold went from 600,000 to 800,000; the price went from $8000 to $8500. Of course there is nothing mysterious about that delightful result for Ford. It happened because it was assumed that demand shifted to Escorts (from Chevrolets or Volkswagens, perhaps). In the example in which Ford could sell more Escorts only at a lower price, it was assumed that there was *no* shift in demand to Escorts.

Similarly, in Figure 15.8 a decrease in demand for Escorts means a shift down from curve D_2D_2 back to D_1D_1. Suppose consumers shift demand from Escorts to Honda Civics. Then Ford will sell *fewer* Escorts at a *lower* price per car, assuming that the supply curve remains as drawn.

Now, on the other side, consider the changes in the supply of Escorts while the demand remains the same (Figure 15.9). An increase in supply means a shift over from curve S_1S_1 to S_2S_2. For some reason, perhaps lower costs per car or competition from Volkswagen, Ford is offering to supply more Escorts at each price. There is an outward shift in the supply curve, or a *movement* out along the demand curve. With demand un-

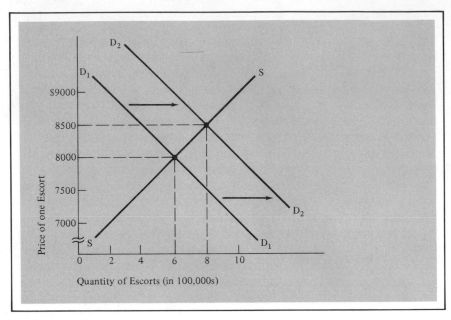

Figure 15.8 Changes in demand and price of Ford Escorts.

changed, Ford is selling more Escorts by lowering their price. Whereas it previously sold 600,000 Escorts at $8000 each, it now sells 800,000 at only $7500 each.

A decrease in supply means shifting back from S_2S_2 to S_1S_1. Suppose,

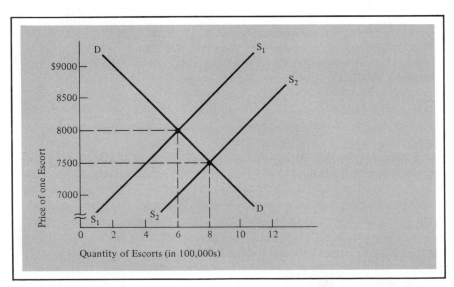

Figure 15.9 Changes in supply and price of Ford Escorts.

for example, that Ford's production costs rise for some reason. It may then charge higher prices *and* sell fewer cars. The supply curve has shifted, moving back along the demand curve, so that prices have gone up and fewer Escorts are being sold.

Of course, in reality *both* curves may shift in the same period. Because of this possibility, it is usually impossible to tell which curve has shifted and which has remained stationary (or by how much each has moved) in the real world.

THE MARKET AS AN ALLOCATIVE DEVICE

One of the central problems with which economics deals is the allocation of scarce resources. Perhaps the most universal of social and economic problems faced by all societies is the fact that no society's capacity to produce or secure goods has yet been sufficient to satisfy all the wants, needs, and desires people have for these goods. Any good is considered by economists to be a *scarce good* when demand would exceed supply *if the good were to be given away freely with no price charged for it.* In this sense, most objects people need and desire are scarce goods.

Any society must devise a method of dividing up or allocating scarce goods among its citizens. In a slave economy, the slaves, like productive domesticated animals, were given enough to keep them fairly healthy so that they could work and reproduce themselves; the rest of the economy's output went to their masters. In the feudal economy, the feudal serf, like the slave, was provided with a minimal subsistence income, whereas the feudal lord, like the slave's master, received a much larger share of the fruits of production.

In a private enterprise economy, the market allocates scarce resources and goods. If the needs and desires for a particular good far exceed the available supply (as is the case with most goods), then the good goes to those who are willing and able to pay the highest price for it in the market.

It may be the case that many people desperately need a car like the Escort but cannot afford its present price, although they could afford to pay a lower price. Now suppose the government fixed the price by law below the point at which supply and demand meet. Since there will be more demand than supply at the fixed price, people at the end of the line will not be able to purchase Escorts in spite of the fact that they would have been willing and able to pay even the higher price. This kind of shortage might have become a common situation in America if the wage-price controls begun in late 1971 had been continued for a long period. In some socialist countries, such as the Soviet Union, price fixing of this type is fairly common. This explains the frequent reports of "shortages" and long queues in these countries.

Obviously, to the extent that markets tend to be self-equilibrating in a private enterprise economy and that there is no government price fixing, there will be a tendency for these shortages to be eliminated. It must be emphasized, however, that economists use the term *shortage* in a way that has no necessary relation to the abundance or lack of abundance of a good relative to people's need for it. The shortage is only relative to the demand *in money terms* by paying customers.

For example, imagine two economies, one in which an efficiently self-equilibrating market exists and another in which goods are all given away free on a first-come, first-served basis. In the first economy, there may be an extreme paucity of provision with only a tiny elite minority receiving most of the meager supply of available goods. If the markets are all in equilibrium, there are no shortages in the economist's sense, despite the fact that many may be dying of starvation. In the second economy, there may be an abundance of goods that are given away at no charge. Even though virtually everyone might be very well off relative to even the richest citizens in the first economy, if some people want more than is available to them, there will be an economic shortage.

It is important to understand clearly the economist's meaning of the word *shortage* because the assertion that a market economy has fewer shortages than a nonmarket, or planned, economy is often misconstrued to imply that the material welfare of people in a market economy must be higher than that of people in a nonmarket economy. This welfare may or may not be higher, but it has nothing to do with the existence or nonexistence of economic shortages. In fact, in economies where the decision has been made *not* to use the market as the primary device to allocate scarce resources, the people have chosen to divide the produce of society by some nonmonetary means. They will no longer exclude those who cannot afford to pay the market price for a scarce good but they must use some other principle of distribution.

How can market versus nonmarket means of allocating scarce goods be evaluated? Such an evaluation would require the weighing of many diverse considerations. Neoclassical economists emphasize that the market tends to allocate scarce goods with a minimum of inconvenience and bureaucratic red tape and that the whole process is generally quite efficient and impersonal. By contrast, look at two widely used nonmarket allocative mechanisms. First, there are rationing coupons like those used by the United States during World War II, which limit the amount of a scarce good any individual can purchase, regardless of the amount of money he or she has. Second, there is the first-come, first-served technique, in which those at the end of the queue are automatically eliminated when the supply of the good in question is exhausted.

The first of these nonmarket allocative mechanisms involves the high cost of extensive record keeping and some inevitable bureaucratic inefficiencies in the control and distribution of the coupons. The second method causes much wasted time when people who can afford to buy the scarce commodity wait in line for a long time, only to find the supply exhausted when they finally reach the head of the line. Thus neoclassical economists contend that, in terms of convenience and efficiency, the market is superior to these two nonmarket allocative mechanisms as a means of allocating goods to customers.

The market is frequently criticized, however, on the grounds that the resultant allocation of scarce goods is inequitable, unfair, and unjust. It is argued that in a private enterprise economy like the United States, where a few people receive the overwhelming bulk of all profits generated by the economy, an unjustly lopsided concentration of income and purchasing power is created. Many economists feel that as a consequence of this concentration of purchasing power the private enterprise economy emphasizes production primarily for the wealthy. In allocating scarce medical care, for example, the private enterprise system places more importance on psychiatric care for the neurotic pets of the wealthy than it does on the provision of minimal health services for the children of the poor.

To illustrate this last point, imagine a hypothetical island economy that is periodically struck with an epidemic of a disease that affects only children. From past experiences the islanders have found that when the disease strikes it randomly affects 80 percent of the children. They have also discovered a preventive antidote that reduces the chances of death if it is taken before the disease strikes. A child who has taken no doses of the antidote has a 90 percent change of dying when he or she contracts the disease. With one dose of the antidote, the chance of death is reduced to 10 percent. Two doses reduce the chance to 8 percent; three doses reduce the chance to 6 percent; four doses reduce the chance to 5 percent. Beyond four doses the antidote has no further effect, and the chances of death remain at 5 percent.

Suppose that the island has 1000 children and that at the first sign of a new outbreak of the dreaded disease the people have produced and accumulated 1000 doses of the antidote. The antidote must be used immediately if the children's lives are to be saved. What system of allocation should the people use to distribute this extremely important scarce good? If the government on the island issues rationing coupons so that each child gets one dose of the antidote, then the following results could be expected: 800 children will get the disease, but since each has had one dose of the antidote, only 80 children will die; 920 children will survive the epidemic.

On the other hand, suppose there is the relative distribution of income and wealth that exists in the United States today. According to this income distribution, the islanders leave the allocation problem to the private enterprise, free-market system, with the following results: the 250 children who have the wealthiest parents will each take four doses of the antidote; of these 250, about 200 will get the disease and about 10 will die; of the remaining 750 children, 600 will get the disease and about 540 will die.

Using a nonmarket allocative mechanism, the islanders were able to save 920 children while 80 died. Given the unequal distribution of income and wealth that exists in the private enterprise market allocation, they were able to save only 450 children while 550 died. This is admittedly a farfetched example with hypothetical percentages chosen to illustrate our point dramatically. Nevertheless the point remains, and perhaps exaggeration is the most effective method of illustrating it. The student is urged to read Daniel Schorr's *Don't Get Sick in America,* a frightening but scholarly study that shows that this example is by no means as distorted as it might appear at first glance.

In ending this discussion on market allocation, it should be noted that one's view of the desirability of the market system depends on whether one is more impressed with the efficacy and impersonality of this allocation mechanism or with its lopsided results. Thus one defender of capitalism writes, "The case for capitalism is at its strongest on the simple thesis that the market knows best how to allocate and use the scarce resource of capital" (Webley, p. 41). A critic of capitalism sees it differently: "The main reason that freedom of contract has never been as free as advertised— and it is a painfully obvious reason—is that sellers and buyers are not equal in buying bargaining power. So the terms of sale will simply reflect the power, or lack of it, that each party brings to the market place. So a market is also a financial slaughterhouse, where the strong chop up the weak" (Bazelon, p. 52).

Even the "efficiency" of the capitalist market has been criticized as a very narrowly limited concept. As is seen in Chapters 20–23, such efficient allocation of resources operates only under pure competition; America, however, is characterized by a high degree of monopoly power. In Chapter 25 we explore the fact that if there is discrimination the market will reflect it and may reinforce it. In examining the aggregate economy in Part Three, we demonstrate that "efficient" use of resources applies only to employed resources but that the market system may leave many resources, both machines and human beings, unemployed. In Part Three we also note that private efficiency may ignore social costs such as pollution. This list of qualifications to market "efficiency" is lengthened still further in Part Three, particularly when we consider the international market mechanism that includes the less developed two-thirds of the world.

SUMMARY

In a competitive market economy, prices are determined by the conditions of supply and demand. Demand is based on consumers' desires and incomes—no cash, no sale. *If* there is pure competition, the market mechanism will allocate resources to each industry according to the cash demand for its product. Supply is based on the firm's costs of production. Thus, as costs go up, higher prices are required in order to induce the firm to supply more. As the price goes up, however, consumers demand less. The equilibrium price is the point at which supply and demand are in balance. Defenders claim that this system of production for private profit is efficient, even if it is not humane. Even its efficiency, however, is challenged by its critics.

REFERENCES

Bazelon, D. T. *The Paper Economy.* New York: Random House, Vintage Books, 1963.

Schorr, Daniel. *Don't Get Sick in America.* Nashville, Tenn.: Aurora Publishers, 1970.

Webley, Simon. "The Utilization of Capital." In *The Case for Capitalism.* Edited by M. Ivens and R. Dunstan. London: Michael Joseph, 1967.

Chapter
16

Prices and Income: The Neoclassical Theory

In Chapter 15 we examined the ways in which competition in the market allocates all resources under private enterprise capitalism. We explored the mechanics of price determination by supply and demand. All economists agree on the mechanics of supply and demand. Economists disagree, however, on the forces that determine supply and demand themselves, particularly the supply and demand for capital and labor. In this chapter we examine the neoclassical theory of how demand is determined by utility and how supply is determined by marginal cost and the cost of each "factor of production" is determined by its marginal product. In Chapter 17 we examine the Marxist or radical theory of these subjects.

UTILITY AND DEMAND

It has been demonstrated that the competitive market tends to allocate resources to produce things according to the pattern of consumer demand (with each customer's desires weighted according to how much money he or she has to spend). The heart of neoclassical economics, from early theorists like Stanley Jevons to most present-day textbook writers, is the notion that consumer demand, in turn, is determined by the utility of each commodity to the consumer. *Utility* is defined as *the pleasure or satisfaction one receives from consuming a good*. Most neoclassical textbooks state that utility alone determines how much people will be willing to pay for the good or how much of the good people will buy at various prices. However, several qualifications to this statement of the importance of utility must be made.

First, consumers often are persuaded by false and misleading advertising that they will receive a great deal more pleasure from a commodity than is in reality attainable. On this basis they purchase the commodity, only to be disappointed and receive little or no satisfaction from it. Second, many actions are guided not by a search for pleasure, satisfaction, or utility but only by habit, caprice, impulse, or any one of dozens of motives psychologists could list. Third, and most generally, a market society tends to inculcate a "buying mentality" in many consumers. The objective in making purchases sometimes becomes simply the spending of money per se rather than the satisfying of real needs or desires for the things purchased. This finding has been particularly emphasized in recent works in psychology concerning feelings of emptiness and alienation (see Chapter 14).

For these reasons we believe that the pattern of consumer demand is forced into a particular form by many things other than the actual pleasure or satisfaction derived directly from consumption of each commodity. But because the term *utility* is almost always used to explain demand, it will be retained but redefined for our purposes. We conceive of utility as synonymous with desire. If we say that a particular good possesses utility for a particular person, we simply mean that that person *desires to buy* the good in question. The desire may be the result of any number of motives. It may be a healthy desire that will, if satisfied, increase the person's well-being, or it may be a perverted or morbid desire that will, if satisfied, lead to pernicious or harmful results. In other words, the satisfaction of any particular desire cannot be said, a priori, to be either morally good or morally bad until there is sufficient information available to make an independent moral judgment.

DIMINISHING MARGINAL UTILITY

The neoclassical theory of demands begins with the principle of *diminishing marginal utility*. The marginal utility of a good is defined as the strength of the consumer's desire to purchase *one additional unit* of the good. The principle of diminishing marginal utility states that *as more and more of a good is acquired, the marginal utility of the good diminishes.*

On a hot summer day, for example, a person may desire a malted milk very intensely. If he has one malted milk, however, the intensity of his desire for another diminishes. If he has two malted milks, the intensity of his desire for a third will be very low. He may have no desire at all for a third. Another way of stating this is to say that the marginal utility of malted milks diminishes as one more is bought.

HOW CONSUMERS MAXIMIZE UTILITY

When consumers spend their income, they strive to maximize their utility. Suppose their income permits them to purchase a large number of different groups, or *bundles*, of commodities. They will try to choose the bundle that satisfies their strongest or most urgent desires; that is, they will attempt to maximize their utility.

The consumer comes to the market with (1) a set of preferences or desires and (2) a certain amount of money income. Because the consumer's desires are constrained by his or her income, the consumer must pay attention to prices. It turns out that the consumer will maximize satisfaction or utility when income is spent so that *the marginal or additional utility derived from the last unit of each good purchased is exactly in proportion to the price paid for each good.* Another way to state this rule is to say that the consumer's satisfaction is maximized when an additional dollar spent for any one good yields exactly the same marginal utility as an additional dollar spent for any other good. This rule is explained further in a simple example whose calculations are shown in Appendix A to this chapter.

ELASTICITY OF DEMAND

Economists have developed concepts to describe demand curves in terms of how much the amount demanded reacts to a price change. If a small price change up or down causes a very big change in quantity demanded, the demand is said to be very *elastic.* But if a significant price change causes almost no change in quantity demanded the demand is said to be very *inelastic.*

What kind of commodities have elastic demands (big reactions to price changes)? Mostly luxuries, such as movies or cake or Cadillacs. If the price is low enough, a consumer will be happy to buy a piece of cake or go to a movie or buy a new car. But if the price of one of these luxuries goes up while his or her income stays the same, the consumer will have to reduce the purchase of luxury items in order to buy more necessary goods. Demand for luxuries is very sensitive to prices; it is elastic.

The demand curve for cake might look like the one in Figure 16.1. The demand is elastic because when price declines, the rise in quantity is more than proportionate, so the total expenditure (or revenue to the seller) actually rises. Thus, at $3 only 100 cakes are sold and the total revenue is $300. But if the price goes down to $2, then 300 cakes are sold and the total revenue rises to $600.

What kind of commodities have inelastic demands (small reactions to price changes)? Mostly necessities, such as medicine or basic foods. If you are diabetic and need insulin to stay alive, then you will still buy almost the same amount if its price doubles. If you live in China and your main food is rice, then if the price rises considerably you will reluctantly look for a substitute; but you may still demand quite a bit. If the price of rice falls, you may demand more; but if it was already 80 percent of your diet, you will not demand much more.

The demand curve for rice in China might look like one in Figure 16.2. The demand is inelastic because when the price declines, the rise in quantity

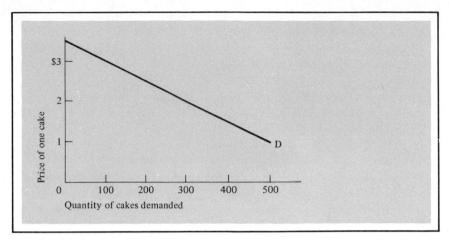

Figure 16.1 Demand for cakes.

is *less than proportionate,* so the total revenue declines. Thus, at $3 the quantity demanded and sold is 100 pounds and the total revenue is $300. But if the price goes down to $1, the quantity demanded only goes to 200 pounds and the total revenue *declines* to $200.

These, then, are the concepts of elastic and inelastic demand. They can be expressed in a general formula to measure elasticity. Defined more precisely,

$$\text{elasticity} = \frac{\text{percentage rise in quantity demanded}}{\text{percentage cut in price}}$$

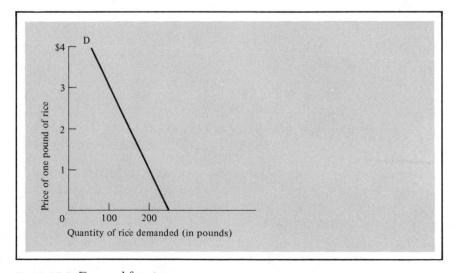

Figure 16.2 Demand for rice.

Of course it is just as easy to talk about a decline in quantity demanded due to a price rise or, in general, the percentage *change* in quantity demanded due to a percentage *change* in price. Exactly how to calculate elasticity is shown in Appendix B to this chapter.

SUPPLY AND MARGINAL COST

Consumer behavior and demand have been examined in great detail. In order to complete the picture it is necessary to examine the behavior of business enterprises in supplying goods, but only in enough detail to supply the information needed for an understanding of price determination in the competitive market. The details of business price and output behavior are very different for pure competition and for various degrees of monopoly power; these details are discussed in the chapters on competition and monopoly.

A firm's decision regarding the quantity of its product it wishes to supply at various prices depends on many things. The most important factor, though, is usually its costs of producing different quantities of its product. Just as neoclassical economics emphasizes marginal utility in determining consumer demand, it emphasizes marginal cost in determining business supply to the market.

Marginal cost is the additional cost of producing one more unit of output. Suppose a firm owns a single factory with 100 machines. It can increase its output only by adding more raw materials and more workers. Here, however, there is a law of increasing marginal cost for firms that is similar to the law of diminishing marginal utility for consumers.

Assume a given factory and machines (and no time to add more or improve technology). Then the lowest cost per unit is reached at some particular flow of raw materials and some *given number* of workers. To make it simple, assume that raw material flow is always adjusted to the number of workers. As the number of workers is increased, the cost changes. If there are too few workers, they will not be able to handle the whole factory efficiently. As the number of workers increases beyond some point, however, they add less and less to the product; or, the marginal cost of one more unit of output rises. For example, if there are only 100 machines and each machine needs only one worker, what can more than 100 workers contribute? Certainly some are needed to bring in raw materials and to take them away, clean up, and repair. At some point, however, whether it is 125 or 150 or even 200, an additional worker could only add less than the previously hired worker.

Within these rigid assumptions it is hard to quarrel with this law. On this basis it is possible to picture marginal costs rising with output (after some minimal cost point is passed). Entrepreneurs will obviously not supply additional goods to the market at a price below their additional cost.

Therefore, as the marginal cost of production rises for additional output, the prices at which additional supply will be offered must also rise.

In a perfectly competitive market the firm's supply curve is identical to its marginal-cost curve. The reason firms will supply goods at "cost" is that the traditional neoclassical definition of cost includes a "normal" profit. (The implications of this peculiar neoclassical definition are examined in Chapter 21.) With imperfect competition or monopoly, the amount a firm will supply is not determined solely by its costs. (This is also discussed in Chapters 22 and 23.) In the present context, however, it is sufficient to know that the firm's marginal cost is important in determining how much it will supply to the market.

THE PRICE AND OUTPUT OF AN INDUSTRY

Based on an understanding of the ways in which consumer desires (and income levels) determine demand and the ways in which enterprise costs determine supply to the market, it is possible to sum up the action of supply and demand for a whole industry. The mechanics of it were studied in Chapter 15. Here the main point is recapitulated in this new concept.

We can illustrate the general way in which supply and demand determine price by examining a mythical commodity called "Gadgets." It is assumed that the mythical industry of Gadget producers is composed of thousands and thousands of purely competitive firms. We are forced to use a fictitious commodity made by a fictitious industry because *few, if any, actual industries are purely competitive.* Later, in Chapters 22 and 23, we explain the importance of the degree of competition in a given industry.

Figure 16.3 shows the usual supply and demand curve for Gadgets, a competitive industry. Supply SS is based on marginal cost; demand DD is based on marginal utility.

The point at which supply and demand meet determines both the price of the Gadget and the number of Gadgets produced. At any lower price level, there is excess demand, and therefore the industry can produce more Gadgets *and* raise their price, hence making more profit. At any higher price level, there is excess supply, and therefore the industry is forced to produce fewer Gadgets and lower its prices.

The supply behavior is based on the marginal cost (always including a "normal" profit) of a Gadget to the Gadget Production Company.

This is a much oversimplified statement of the current view of price determination. Before it can be further refined and compared with earlier theories, one more tool is required—elasticity of supply.

ELASTICITY OF SUPPLY

It is not necessary to become involved in a detailed discussion of elasticity of supply because the concept is exactly analogous to that of elasticity of demand. Supply is elastic if it responds more than proportionately to a

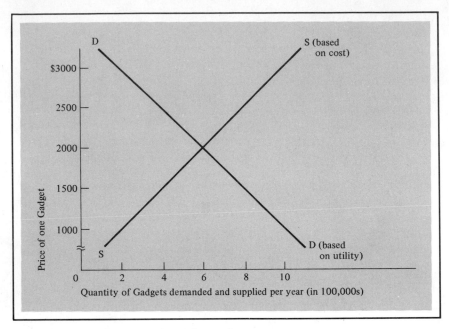

Figure 16.3 Supply and demand for Gadgets.

price change, and it is inelastic if it responds less than proportionately to a price change. More precisely,

$$\text{elasticity of supply} = \frac{\text{percentage rise in quantity supplied}}{\text{percentage rise in price}}$$

Unlike demand, the quantity supplied moves in the same direction as price because a higher price means a higher profit (costs remaining the same), which induces a business to produce and sell more.

Inelastic supply reaction is found most often with perishable goods. Ripe tomatoes *must* be sold quickly, regardless of the price that can be obtained in the market. Durable goods such as furniture, however, may show an elastic (sensitive) supply reaction to price changes. If the price of furniture falls, it can simply be stored and not offered for sale.

MOMENTARY SUPPLY AND PRICE EQUILIBRIUM

Even in the preceding examples, the length of time considered is clearly important. In addition to tomatoes already in the market, what about the longer-run reaction of tomato growers? If the price falls for a long enough time, the number of tomatoes grown *will* decline considerably.

In the 1890s Alfred Marshall used this notion to clarify the concept of price determination. He distinguished the supply reaction to a price or

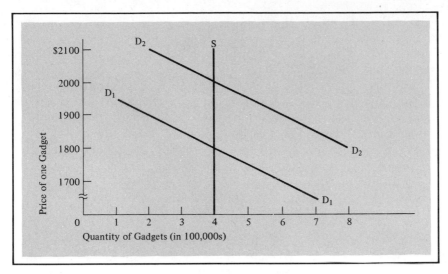

Figure 16.4 Momentary equilibrium of Gadgets.

demand change in three periods: momentary, short run, and long run. The momentary period is so short (an hour, a day, or a week, depending on the product) that the amount of supply in the market cannot be varied at all. The short-run period is long enough for a factory to produce more or less for the market within its capacity but too short for any new factories to be built or put into use. The long-run period is long enough for as many new factories to be built as are necessary to bring the supply up to the demand.

How does this time factor affect elasticity of supply (and thus, indirectly, prices)? Assume that at a given moment Gadget dealers have a certain supply of Gadgets on hand. No matter what sudden change there is in demand, they cannot sell more until they receive more: Momentary supply is perfectly inelastic.

Assume now that the one gadget dealer in a town usually sells ten Gadgets a week and that the factory delivers ten Gadgets each Monday. One week the dealer sells six Gadgets up through Thursday. So on Friday there are four Gadgets to sell. But that Friday eight customers want to buy Gadgets immediately (and are not willing to wait until Monday).

In this case the supply is fixed at four, so the price will be raised to take advantage of the higher demand. Suppose the dealer has been selling at a price of $1800. Because eight cannot be sold at $1800, the dealer may try to sell the four in stock at $2000 (see Figure 16.4).

The Gadget dealer was ready for the usual demand D_1D_1, but the demand shifted that day to D_2D_2. Still, the supply is perfectly inelastic for that day; the dealer simply cannot get more Gadgets to sell in that period. So the higher demand reaches equilibrium with the fixed supply at a higher price.

Most of the early utility theorists (from the crude J. B. Say to the very sophisticated Carl Menger) concentrated on market exchange and gave little consideration to changes in supply conditions. Consequently, it seems that this given momentary supply is the only case they considered. They stated (and it is true in this case) that marginal utility determines demand and that demand changes largely determine price changes. These theorists used this case to attack the older theory (of Marx and the classicals— Ricardo and Smith) that labor cost determines supply, which ultimately determines price. Certainly *in this case*, where supply is perfectly inelastic, supply cannot change and therefore cannot explain changes in price.

Short-Run Supply and Price Equilibrium

What price will bring an equilibrium of supply and demand in the short run? Or how do supply and demand changes affect price in the short run? These are the questions emphasized by Alfred Marshall and in every neo-classical beginning text to the present day.

Briefly, in the short run marginal cost tends to rise when a firm tries to produce additional units of output beyond some point because the short run is, by definition, a period in which the firm has a *given* factory and machinery and no time to expand it. Technology requires some particular number of workers to run the plant at capacity (or at the cheapest cost per unit). When the firm tries to produce more than the capacity for which the factory is designed by adding more workers, the product per additional worker declines, that is, the marginal cost rises.

Because supply will never be below marginal cost, the supply curve naturally rises (up and to the right, as in Figure 16.5) as output expands. In other words, with rising costs the firm will supply more goods only at higher prices, that is, the supply curve is more or less elastic, depending on the product, but is certainly no longer perfectly inelastic.

A shift upward in demand will raise prices, as in the previous case, but now the new equilibrium price is clearly also affected by the movement along the supply curve.

Figure 16.5 shows that an increase in demand for Gadgets raises *both* the price (from $2000 to $2500) and the quantity (from 600,000 to 800,000). The quantity rises because the supply curve is somewhat elastic. This reflects the fact that existing Gadget plants have the capacity to turn out more Gadgets, *though at rising costs per Gadget.* It is clear in this case that both the quantity supplied and the quantity demanded change and so together determine the new price equilibrium.

Alfred Marshall thus emphasized that supply and demand operate like the two blades of the scissors. Supply behavior is based on marginal costs. Demand behavior is based on marginal utility. It follows in the modern neoclassical view that both utility and cost together determine prices or values.

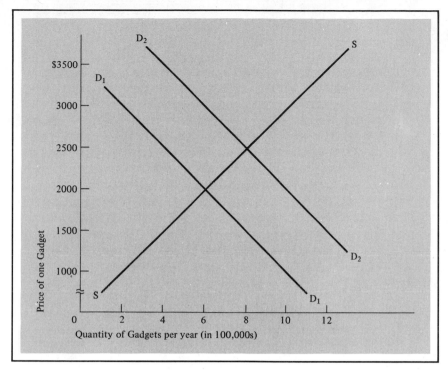

Figure 10.5 Short-run equilibrium of Gadgets.

Long-Run Supply and Price Equilibrium

In the long run new factories can be built. Capital and labor can shift to industries where demand has risen. Therefore in the long run the quantity supplied can always rise as much as demand does.

Moreover, if Gadget Producers Company builds a new factory to produce more Gadgets, the new factory need have no higher cost per Gadget than the older factories. Hence the average cost (and the marginal, too) remains the same in the long run. Of course this is a rough approximation. In some cases better technology may allow the new factory to produce Gadgets at a lower cost per Gadget. In other cases expanded production with more use of a scarce raw material may drive the price of the raw material up, thus raising the cost per Gadget. Here, for simplicity, the most common case—*constant cost per Gadget in the long run*—is assumed.

If, however, marginal costs are constant in the long run, then the supply curve will also be constant. It will be flat or a horizontal straight line on the graph. In short, supply will be perfectly elastic. Figure 16.6 illustrates this situation. In the long run what is the effect of an increased demand for Gadgets? More factories are built, and the supply adjusts completely to the demand. Moreover, the new factories have about the same cost per

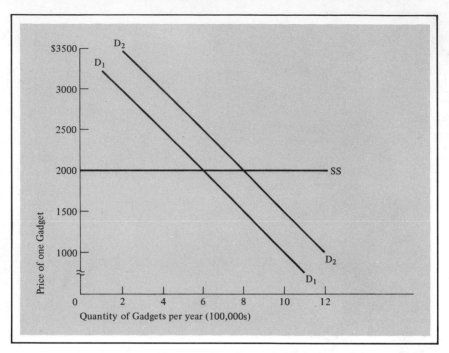

Figure 16.6 Long-run equilibrium of Gadgets. (The SS line also represents price level.)

Gadget as the previous ones—assuming additional cost from greater use of resources is about canceled out by better technology.

In the long-run case, therefore, it can be asserted that the sole effect of an increase in demand is an equal increase in quantity produced. The rise in demand has no effect on the price level, however. Of course at the initial moment of rise in demand, prices rose. That called forth more supply from existing factories in the short run, however, and therefore prices dropped a bit. In the long run the entire rise in demand was met by an equal increase in supply from new factories. Since the new factories have the same cost per Gadget as before, the price dropped back to its old level.

Therefore in the long run *demand determines the amount of production* (or the allocation of resources), *but supply alone determines the price level.* It can be said that the relative marginal utilities of different commodities determine the demand for them and the proportionate amounts of each produced. The long-run price level, however, is determined solely by the level of costs per unit—that is, the supply conditions.

This is the case emphasized by the classicals and Marx. They were not so much interested in momentary or short-run market exchange and demand as in the long-run price or value of commodities. This they found to be determined solely by the cost of human effort or, as Marx put it, the total amount of human labor embodied in the product. He includes the labor involved in mining the raw materials and building the factories and machines used up in that production. This case, in which the long-run labor cost determines price, is further explained in Chapter 18.

Marshall and the modern neoclassicals would agree that in this particular case of long-run supply, assuming constant costs, a change in marginal utility *does not* affect the price, but a change in the cost per unit *does* affect the price. The argument comes over the exact meaning of *cost.* The neoclassicals maintain that capitalists as well as workers put out an effort of some kind. The capitalist's "effort" may be purely subjective "sacrifice" of immediate higher consumption for a later return on capital invested. Marx, however, insisted that it is only the worker's objective expenditure of labor that determines long-run price or value.

This dispute arises, of course, because these economists are concerned not only with the mechanics of price determination but also with the equitability of income distribution. If the contributions to production by labor and capital are viewed differently, this obviously has much to do with how the distribution of income is viewed. Should Gadget workers or owners of Gadget stock receive the income from Gadget sales? This question of income distribution is discussed in Chapters 17–19.

SUMMARY

According to neoclassical theory, demand for a good is based on its marginal utility, or the desires of the consumer plus the consumer's income. Supply is based on the marginal cost of production. At any given moment when supply is fixed, the changing demand sets the price. In a short run just long enough so that a factory may produce more or less, both supply and demand change and effect the price. In a long run long enough to build new factories, the demand will still determine how much is to be produced—that is, the allocation of resources to different industries. In the long run, however, any quantity that is demanded can be produced, so the price level will simply be determined by the cost (including an average profit). In other words, in the long run twice as much demand will mean twice as much production of the commodity, but *if cost per unit stays constant*, then the price will also stay constant. (Most neoclassical economists would say that cost usually does not remain constant even in the long run.) This issue is discussed further in Chapter 18 on the labor theory of value.

APPENDIX A

Marginal Utility and Demand

Suppose that a consumer can spend income on only three commodities: apples, bread, and cake. It is then possible to determine the quantities of each to be bought in order to maximize utility. Utility will be maximized if the consumer buys the

Table 16.1

Quantity (in pounds)	Marginal utility of apples (in units of utility)	Marginal utility of apples per dollar (price: $1)
1	12	12
2	11	11
3	10	10
4	9	9
5	8	8
6	7	7

particular quantities of apples, bread, and cake that will leave the marginal utilities of each at a level at which the following condition holds:

$$\frac{\text{marginal utility of apples}}{\text{price of apples}} = \frac{\text{marginal utility of bread}}{\text{price of bread}}$$

$$= \frac{\text{marginal utility of cake}}{\text{price of cake}}$$

The equality of these three ratios means that utility is maximized when the last dollar spent on apples yields the same utility as the last dollars spent on bread and cake. A numerical example will help explain this principle.

Table 16.1 shows amounts of apples ranging from 1 pound to 6 pounds. The number of units of marginal utility for each pound of apples and the number of units of marginal utility per dollar for each pound of apples can be determined by reading across the table. The same kinds of assumptions are stated for bread and cake in Table 16.2. Of course, in reality it is not so clear that each consumer exactly measures or knows how many units of subjective utility is gotten from each additional commodity. (Could you measure *exactly* the relative desire or utility to you of one more apple versus one more loaf of bread?)

Table 16.2

Quantity (in pounds)	Marginal utility of bread (in units of utility)	Marginal utility of bread per dollar (price: $2)	Marginal utility of cake (in units of utility)	Marginal utility of cake per dollar (price: $3)
1	24	12	30	10
2	22	11	27	9
3	20	10	24	8
4	18	9	21	7
5	16	8	18	6
6	14	7	15	5

Still, the theory does help elucidate consumer behavior in a rough sort of way. Now imagine that a consumer with an income of $24 buys 6 pounds of cake for $18, 2 pounds of bread for $4, and 2 pounds of apples for $2. The consumer has spent the entire $24 income, but has not maximized utility. The ratios of marginal utility to price are not the same for three commodities. The ratios are as follows:

for apples: $\dfrac{11 \text{ units of utility}}{\$1}$ = 11 units of utility for last dollar

for bread: $\dfrac{22 \text{ units of utility}}{\$2}$ = 11 units of utility for last dollar

for cake: $\dfrac{15 \text{ units of utility}}{\$3}$ = 5 units of utility for last dollar

The utility received from the last dollar spent on cake (5 units of utility) was considerably smaller than that of the last dollars spent on apples and bread (11 units each). Obviously this individual's utility could be increased if some purchases were shifted from cake to apples and bread.

If the consumer gives up 3 pounds of cake, 54 units of utility will be lost, but $9 will be gained to be spent on apples and bread. With this $9, the consumer purchases 3 more pounds of apples (thereby gaining 27 units of utility) and 3 more pounds of bread (thereby gaining 54 units of utility). Thus by shifting $9 worth of purchases the consumer gives up 54 units of utility and gains 81 units.

Obviously the second bundle of goods has more utility than the first. If the units of utility in the first bundle are added, they total 204 (6 units from cake = 135; 2 units from bread = 46, and 2 units from apples = 23). The total number of units of utility in the second bundle is 231 (3 units from cake = 81; 5 units from bread = 100; and 5 units from apples = 50). The ratios of marginal utility to price for the three goods in the second bundle are as follows:

for apples: $\dfrac{8 \text{ units of utility}}{\$1}$ = 8 units of utility for last dollar

for bread: $\dfrac{16 \text{ units of utility}}{\$2}$ = 8 units of utility for last dollar

for cake: $\dfrac{24 \text{ units of utility}}{\$3}$ = 8 units of utility for last dollar

Thus maximizing the condition holds; that is,

$$\frac{8}{\$1} = \frac{16}{\$2} = \frac{24}{\$3}$$

Purchases cannot be shifted among the commodities any further without losing some utility. The reader should experiment with such shifts in order to be convinced that this is a maximum.

With this information it is now possible to demonstrate why demand curves slope downward and to the right—that is, why the quantity demanded *increases* as the price *decreases*. (See Chapter 15.) Imagine an initial position at which all consumers are maximizing their utility—that is, they have equated the ratios of their marginal utilities and prices for all the goods. It is then possible to trace the effects of a decrease in price.

If the price of one good, say apples, were to decrease, consumers would find that the utility received for the last dollar spent on apples would be higher than that received for the last dollar spent on other goods. Consumers would immediately shift some of their purchases from other goods to apples. Thus the initial result of a decline in the price of apples is an increased quantity of apples demanded.

But what determines exactly how much demand will shift to apples? Exactly how much will the demand for them increase when the price declines? That depends on their marginal utility (the desire for an additional apple) relative to the marginal utility of other goods (the desire for more bread and cake). As consumers buy more and more apples, their desire for an additional one declines. (This is just one illustration of the law of diminishing marginal utility.) At the same time consumers are buying less of all other goods (less bread and less cake). So the *marginal* utility of other goods rises; at the margin, their desire for an additional piece of bread or cake is now increased. The process of shifting demand from bread and cake to apples stops when an additional dollar spent for more apples (even at the new, lower price) yields just the same marginal utility as that spent for bread or cake (even at their old, unchanged prices).

APPENDIX B

Elasticity of Demand

Elasticity of demand was defined in words as

$$\text{elasticity} = \frac{\text{percentage change in quantity demanded}}{\text{percentage change in price}}$$

For those who prefer symbols to words, let us call elasticity E, quantity demanded Q, and price P, and let Δ mean "the change in." Then

$$E = \frac{\Delta Q/Q}{\Delta P/P}$$

The concept is important; the details of calculation are not. Nevertheless, the details may help you get the concept more firmly in mind.

Assume a move down the demand curve from some point 1 to point 2. The change in quantity demanded is $\Delta Q = Q_1 - Q_2$. The change in price is $\Delta P = P_2 - P_1$ because the price went down while quantity went up. The base for figuring the percentage could be either Q_1 or Q_2 with somewhat different results. As a convention economists always use the average, so $Q = (Q_1 + Q_2)/2$. Similarly, by convention $P = (P_1 + P_2)/2$.

The elasticity of demand for cake (shown in Figure 16.1) works out this way. Rise in quantity demanded is $300 - 100 = 200$. Average quantity, on which the percentage is based, is $(300 + 100)/2 = 200$. Fall in price is $\$3 - \$2 = \$1$. Average price is $(\$3 + \$2)/2 = \$2.5$. Therefore

$$E_{\text{cake}} = \frac{200/200}{1/2.5} = \frac{1}{0.4} = \frac{100\%}{40\%} = 2.5$$

The percentage change in demand (100 percent) is much greater than the percentage change in price (40 percent); therefore the demand is elastic. More precisely, demand is elastic if E is greater than 1, and here E is 2.5.

Similarly, the elasticity of demand for rice (shown in Figure 16.2) works out this way. Rise in quantity of demand is $200 - 100 = 100$. Average quantity is $(200 + 100)/2 = 150$. Fall in price is $\$3 - \$1 = \$2$. Average price is $(\$3 + \$1)/2 = \$2$. Therefore

$$E_{\text{rice}} = \frac{100/150}{2/2} = \frac{0.67}{1} = \frac{67\%}{100\%} = 0.67$$

Here the percentage change in demand (67 percent) is less than the percentage change in price (100 percent); therefore the demand is inelastic. Or, if you wish, it is inelastic because E is 0.67, which is less than 1.

To complete the concept, economists say that the demand curve is of *unitary elasticity* when E is 1. In this intermediate case the percentage change in demand is just the same as the percentage change in price.

At one extreme, a *perfectly inelastic* demand curve is shown by a vertical straight line. There is no change in demand when price changes. Thus E equals zero when demand is perfectly inelastic. However a *perfectly elastic* demand curve is shown by a horizontal straight line. When demand is perfectly elastic, E equals infinity. The firm can sell an infinite quantity of goods at the present price. Although these extreme cases are unrealistic, the concepts will be helpful later.

APPENDIX C

The Ethical Implications of Utility Analysis

In Appendix A we saw that when we assume (1) that individuals receive marginal utility from consumption of commodities determined solely by the quantities of commodities they consume, and (2) that they arrange their purchases of commodities in such a way as to maximize their utility, then they end up by equating the marginal utility per dollar spent on each and every commodity.

More advanced textbooks on orthodox microeconomic theory show, on the basis of similar assumptions in the theory of production, that competitive capitalists maximize their profits when the cost of producing an additional marginal unit of any two commodities is proportional to the prices of the two commodities. Furthermore, they show that competitive profit maximizing also leads to a situation in which the price of any factor of production, such as land, labor, or capital, is exactly equal to the value of the productive contribution of that factor in producing the last units of any commodities that require the use of that factor.

The entire analysis is based upon the assumptions of (1) diminishing marginal utility in the consumption of every commodity by each individual, (2) diminishing marginal productivity of any factor of production in the creation of all commodities, (3) utility and profit maximization, and (4) the uniform existence of competition in all markets. With these assumptions the conclusions of the previous paragraph follow from the logical principles of how constrained maxima are attained.

Traditional microeconomic theory does not stop there, however. It contains ethical or ideological elements as well. Neoclassical welfare economics accepts the above assumptions and conclusions and adds some important ethical assumptions. These assumptions are (1) an individual's utility is identical with his or her well-being or welfare, (2) the collective total of all individuals' utilities is identical with the social well-being or social welfare, and (3) the marginal utilities of different persons for all commodities in general (or the marginal utility of money) cannot be compared between any two persons.

On the basis of these ethical assumptions, neoclassical welfare economics concludes that a competitive capitalist economy results in the following:

1. Each individual orders his or her purchases such that no change could take place without diminishing his or her welfare.
2. No alterations in the free-market allocation of commodities among different individuals could take place without reducing at least one person's welfare.
3. No change in the allocation of productive factors, such as to change the proportions of the various commodities produced, could take place without reducing the total amount produced.
4. No change in the income payments to the owners of the various factors of production would be possible without either reducing the total amount produced or without some coercion that would leave some persons worse off than before.

The intricate arguments by which the conclusions are derived are too complex for this book. They are contained in intermediate and advanced microeconomic theory textbooks. All that we wish to do in this short appendix is to make two points. First, neoclassical welfare economics is the ultimate extension of the invisible hand argument of Adam Smith, which we discussed in Chapter 4. This theory attempts to show that a competitive capitalist economy maximizes social welfare and is therefore a perfect, ideal economy. Since it is not possible to compare individuals' utilities, and since each factor of production is paid the value of its marginal contribution to production, neoclassical welfare economics assumes that the social distribution of income is efficient and just.

The second point that we wish to make is that when microeconomic theory is used in this way (i.e., as an ideological justification for laissez-faire capitalism), it is subject to a large number of devastating criticisms. We mention only a few of them.

First, the notion that a person's welfare is identical to his or her utility or desire for commodities ignores several important facts. Most desires are socially learned. Is it not possible to argue that some of the desires that are socially learned are really harmful to the true welfare of an individual? The ultimate consequences of using some electronic gadget or taking some variety of medicine may be so complex that no ordinary individual could possibly know their long-range influence on his or her welfare, but still want to consume them because others have said they will be beneficial. Since it is usually from capitalists and their advertising campaigns that we learn that we "want" something, we would have to assume that capitalists advertise in order to promote the social welfare rather than in order to make more profits—a most unlikely assumption. The absurdity of equating utility and welfare is most clearly seen when we look at small children or drug addicts. Everyone knows that these persons frequently want and feel that they need things that are harmful to their welfare. In short, to assume that each of us always wants that which best promotes our own welfare would require that we believe all individuals to be omniscient, perfectly adjusted saints.

Second, the assumption that we cannot compare the increase in the welfare of two different individuals when each receives an extra increment of income violates the most basic common sense of everyday life. Most of us feel certain that an extra dollar means much more to the welfare of a starving man that it does to the welfare of a millionaire. The assumption that we cannot make such comparisons is tantamount to arguing that the present extreme inequalities of wealth and income cannot be shown to be any worse than any alternative. The millionaire may believe this, but neither the starving man nor most of the rest of us believe this.

Third, factors of production are not people. At least land and capital are not. Even if it could be shown that they received a reward equal to their marginal productivity (which the present writers believe to be impossible when sophisticated critiques of this theory are understood) it could never be concluded that the tremendously concentrated ownership of these factors in the hands of a tiny minority of the population is either fair or just.

There are many other ethical and theoretical arguments that show the weaknesses of neoclassical welfare economics, but we believe these three suffice to show the reader that economic theory never has been able to show, and cannot now show, that free-market capitalism is any sort of ethical ideal. Unfortunately, at the level of intermediate and advanced microeconomic theory (where these criticisms could and should be made with force and rigor) conservative economists dominate most universities. It is therefore important, even at the elementary level, to inform the reader about the tenuous nature of the welfare economics that are usually constructed upon the basis of orthodox utility theory.

REFERENCE

Fromm, Erich. *The Sane Society*. New York: Fawcett World Library, Premier Books, 1965.

Chapter
17

Income Distribution: The Neoclassical Theory

Of all the issues in economics, the distribution of income is one of the most controversial. The distribution of income is the chief factor determining the relative levels of material well-being that different individuals, groups, or classes attain. It reflects the structure of economic power but it also perpetuates the inequalities on which economic power is based.

The intensity of the controversy reflects the fact that different economic theories are not purely neutral, "detached" theories with no moral or ethical overtones. On the contrary, the two main theories—the conservative (neoclassical) theory and the radical (labor) theory—clearly rest on very different assumptions, which have very different ethical implications. The neoclassical theory tends to support the existing income distribution (or at most supports only minor alterations), whereas the labor theory tends to support critics' claims that substantial changes should be made.

In this chapter, we extend our discussion of neoclassical theory to the question of the distribution of income. In Chapter 18 we will examine the labor theory of value, including the views on income distribution inherent in that theory. Before beginning our discussion of income distribution theory, however, we must first examine poverty and inequality in the United States.

POVERTY AND INEQUALITY

In 1986 the United States government stated that an urban family of four lived in poverty if it received less than $11,203 per year. In that year more than 32.4 million persons received lower incomes than this officially

Table 17.1   INCOME INEQUALITY FROM 1947 TO 1981

Income group of family	Percentage of income received							
	1947	1950	1955	1960	1965	1970	1975	1986
Lowest fifth	5.1	4.5	4.8	4.8	5.2	5.4	5.5	4.6
Second fifth	11.8	11.9	12.2	12.2	12.2	12.2	12.0	10.8
Middle fifth	16.7	17.4	17.7	17.8	17.8	17.6	17.5	16.8
Fourth fifth	23.1	23.5	23.5	23.9	23.9	23.9	24.0	24.0
Highest fifth	43.3	42.7	41.8	41.3	40.9	40.9	41.0	43.7
Highest 5 percent	17.5	17.3	16.8	15.9	15.5	15.6	15.5	17.0

Source: U.S. Department of Commerce, Statistical Abstract of the United States, 1988 (Washington, D.C.: GPO, 1988), p. 428

defined poverty level. That income figure, however, was absurdly low. The government's figure would more aptly describe a family in a state of desperate destitution. Inflation so eroded the purchasing power of the dollar in the 1970s that an average American working family could just get by. In fact, the median household income (generally earned by more than one wage earner living in the same household) for 1986 was $24,897. Some have argued that this is a reasonable figure for the poverty level and that at least one-half of Americans live in poverty.

The government's definition of poverty is based on computations made by scientists working for the U.S. Department of Agriculture. They computed the poverty line on the assumption that a person who knew all about nutrition and was a skilled calculator of budgets could just get by if he or she carefully and skillfully used every penny of his or her food budget for food that would just suffice for "emergency or temporary use when funds are low." Even the government did not believe that anyone could subsist on that amount for very long! Most poor people, however, remain poor year after year.

Furthermore, the percentage of total income received by the poorest 20 percent and the second poorest 20 percent has not changed much since World War II. Table 17.1 shows the percent of total income received by each fifth of the population, from lowest to highest, since 1947. Also included is the percentage received by the highest 5 percent.

Two conclusions are obvious from Table 17.1. First, the distribution of income remains amazingly stable over the years. There is no observable trend toward a decrease in the degree of inequality. Indeed, the inequality seems to be increasing. Second, on the average for the entire period, the highest 5 percent of income recipients receive more income than the lowest 40 percent combined.

Moreover, these data do not really show the extent of inequality of incomes because they are taken from census reports that use biased data. The rich use legal loopholes to report less income, more frequently do not respond to surveys, and are counted as having only up to $100,000 (the Census does not count above the amount in the annual survey). If true incomes were reported, the higher incomes would be much larger than those shown.

INCOME BY SOURCE

The most important factor differentiating incomes is their source. Capitalists receive income from owning, whereas nearly all other individuals get their income from working. The very wealthy who receive extraordinarily high incomes are capitalists. Table 17.1 gave the figures for the highest 5 percent of income recipients; included among these are many doctors, lawyers, corporate executives, and so on. Yet the truly wealthy are capitalists, who constitute at most 2 percent of the population.

Of this 2 percent about one-half, or 1 percent of the population, are the elite, powerful capitalists. Three different scholarly studies have attempted to ascertain what percentage of the ownership of corporate stocks was in the hands of the wealthiest 1 percent of Americans. For 1958, Robert Lampman estimated that this wealthy 1 percent owned 75.4 percent of all corporate stock. A study for the year 1972, by James D. Smith and Stephen D. Franklin, produced the somewhat more conservative estimate that this 1 percent owned 56.6 percent of all corporate stocks. Andrew Winnick found (based on new government studies) that in 1983 the top $\frac{1}{2}$ of 1 percent of U.S. families owned 35 percent of all U.S. wealth, 89 percent of corporate stock, and 94 percent of business assets. Regardless of the exact estimates, it is obvious that this tiny percent of the population, which receives the bulk of the income from ownership, is truly a wealthy power elite. Incomes in this elite range up to highs of over $100 million per year (or more than $270,000 per day, 365 days per year).

Those who receive property income, such as profits from corporate stocks mentioned above, may be called the "capitalist" class. Property income includes corporate profits, the profits of unincorporated businesses, income from rents, and income from interest. Among the very wealthy, defined as those individuals with income over $1 million, more than 95 percent of their income (in 1971) came from such ownership of property, so these were truly capitalists (Bowles and Gintis, p. 90).

Every year Forbes magazine publishes a list of the wealthiest 400 people in the United States. In the fall 1987 issue of Forbes, the amount of the wealth of these individual capitalists ranged from a "low" of $225 million to a high of $8.5 billion. The exact return that each of these capitalists received on his or her investments varied widely. Over 116 of these 400 received a yearly return of over 50 percent on their wealth. Although Forbes did not compute an average return received by all of the 400 capitalists, we estimate that the average return was about 30 percent.

To give the reader an indication of what this means, we can calculate that an annual rate of return of 30 percent of $8.5 billion is $2,550 million. In other words, if you had $8.5 billion of income-yielding assets, you would receive $2.55 billion in income each year over and above the $8.5 billion. This amounts to a daily income of $7 million, or an hourly income of $291,000. This means $291,000 of income every hour, every hour of every day of the year. Measured against—and supporting—these capitalists are the millions who live in abject poverty in our society. These 400 capitalists are the richest of those who receive nearly all of their income from ownership. At the other end of the spectrum, for all those individuals with incomes under $25,000, wage and salary income from labor comprised more than 90 percent of their total income, so these were truly "working-class" people.

We can also make some estimate of the total shares of labor income and property income in the United States. Government data, however, do not exactly fit the categories of any economic theory, so conservative, liberal, and radical economists always fight over how to define these amounts, even when the same government data are being used. In 1986 the total amount of property income (in billions of dollars) was as follows:

Business proprietor's income	$290
Rental income	17
Corporate profits before tax	32
Net interest income	326
Total property income	$865

These data on property income (showing $865 billion) are still badly understated because they are based on what has been reported for tax purposes, so they do not include the property income that, through tax loopholes, goes unreported. Moreover, as can be seen in Table 17.2, Treasury Department, Internal Revenue Service audits show that only 2–3 percent of wage and salary income goes unreported, whereas up to 50 percent of various types of property income goes unreported.

The total amount of wages and salaries in national income in 1986 was $2,089 billion. This amount is drastically overstated relative to property income, whereas many loopholes exist for property income. Second, wages and salaries include vast amounts of "managers' and executives' salaries," which are often property income in disguise (so they can be claimed as deductions from corporate profits for tax purposes). The most interesting comparison is what Marx called the rate of exploitation or the rate of surplus value, which is roughly translatable into the ratio of property income to labor income:

$$\text{rate of exploitation} = \frac{\text{property income}}{\text{labor income}} = \frac{\$865}{\$2089} = 41.4\%$$

Table 17.2   UNREPORTED INDIVIDUAL INCOME AS A
PERCENT OF AMOUNT REPORTABLE,
BY TYPE OF INCOME, 1976

Type of income	Percent unreported
Wages and salaries	2–3
Dividends	8–16
Interest	10–16
Pensions, annuities, estates, and trusts	12–16
Capital gains	17–24
Self-employment	36–40
Rents and royalties	35–40

Source: Treasury Department, IRS, *Estimates of Income Unreported on Individual Income Tax Returns,* Publication 1104 (9–79) (Washington, D.C.: GPO).

Finally, how many people are in which class according to the source of their income? Again, the government does not use exactly the same categories as we do, but some of the main trends can be obtained from the government data. Table 17.3 shows the results.

From Table 17.3 we see that wage and salary workers are now the overwhelming majority (or 83 percent) of Americans. Yet their income share is far, far below 83 percent, especially since the labor income data reported by the treasury include managers' salaries as labor income. For example, in 1987, Jim P. Manzi, the 36-year-old chairman of Lotus Development Corporation, collected a total compensation (including salary, bonus, and a commitment for long-term income) of $26.3 million; in 1987 Chrysler paid Lee A. Iacocca $19.9 million and they paid Gerald Greenwald $6.6 million. Reebok paid its chairman, Paul Fereman, a salary alone of $15.4 million. Assuming Fereman worked as many as 60 hours a week, this amounts to $5,000 per hour pay as compared to Jim Manzi, to whom

Table 17.3   EVOLUTION OF THE U.S. LABOR FORCE

Year	Wage and salary workers (percent)	Self-employed (percent)	Managers and officials (percent)
1780[a]	20	80	0
1880	62	37	1
1974	83	8	9

[a] The data from 1780 excludes slaves.

Source: Michael Reich, "The Evolution of the U.S. Labor Force," in R. Edwards, M. Reich, and T. Weisskopf, eds. *The Capitalist System,* 2nd ed. (Englewood Cliffs, N.J.: Prentice-Hall, 1978), p. 180.

Lotus paid about $8,400 per hour—in about three hours, Manzi collected more than the average working class family (usually with two or three wage earners) earned in a full year. The top 25 executives received an average remuneration of $9.75 million per year for 1987 ("Who Made the Most and Why," in *Business Week*, May 2, 1988). According to *Business Week*, some 288 business executives received pay of over $1 million that year. Thus, by including managers' salaries as a part of labor income, government statistics significantly understate the differences between the incomes of capitalists and workers.

Managers and officials are now a not-insignificant 7 percent of the labor force. The 80 percent of the population self-employed in 1780 were mostly farmers. Today they number only 9 percent, including 2 percent farm owners, 4 percent independent professionals and artisans, and 3 percent self-employed businesspersons. So this 9 percent is what remains of the old middle class; even adding managers and officials we get only 16 percent "middle class."

But where is the capitalist class? The government data hide the capitalist class. The top corporate executives are hidden among the managers and officials. The biggest millionaire "coupon clippers" are hidden among the employed businesspersons. Nevertheless, from the estimates of wealth stated earlier, especially holdings of corporate stock, we find that the entire capitalist class is only 1 percent of the population.

The Mechanics of Income Distribution

Adam Smith talked about *rent* going to owners of land, *wages* going to labor, and *profits* going to the owners of capital. What determines the share of each of these types of income in the net national income? Economists' answers to this fundamental question differ greatly according to their basic world views. In fact, there are really two closely related questions: (1) What determines the share of each type of income? (2) Is the present distribution of income among different types good or bad?

To simplify the question, in this chapter we shall ignore the rent of land. In the modern United States and most industrialized economies, it is a very small category and thus not essential to the argument. That leaves two of Smith's categories—wages and profits. We define *wages* as all labor income, including time and piece wages, monthly salaries, commissions, bonuses, and managerial salaries. We define *profits* as all the return on capital. For the purposes of this argument profits are included both as the return on the entrepreneur's own capital (*dividends*) and as the return on borrowed capital (*interest*). For other purposes in later chapters, it will be necessary to distinguish between these two forms of profits. *Capital* is the factories, machinery, raw materials, and money with which production and commerce are conducted.

The modern corporation owns its capital goods—factory, machinery, and raw materials. It pays wages and salaries to workers (including managerial salaries and bonuses). The workers use the capital goods to produce a product. The product is owned and sold by the corporation. What is the difference between a corporation and an unincorporated business? The most important difference is that the individual capitalist owners are not liable for the debts of the corporation.

The owners of the corporation are its stockholders. They each own a number of shares of stock, which represent their portion of the value of the corporation. To get the stock, of course, they paid money to the corporation. It uses that money to buy capital goods and to pay for labor. It may also borrow money; usually it issues bonds, which show how much the lender is owed (and how much interest he or she gets). The stockholders receive dividends, which are all the revenue of the corporation from sales less all of the costs paid out (including wages, depreciation of capital, and interest to bondholders). If the corporation is unable to pay its debts, it is ruled bankrupt by the courts. Those who have lent money to it will divide all its remaining assets. If there are any assets left over, they go to the stockholders. If there are insufficient assets to cover the debts, that's just too bad; no one can sue the stockholders.

THEORIES OF INCOME DISTRIBUTION

In discussing how income is distributed between wages and profits, economists have advanced two distinct and opposing views. The conservative view has generally dominated and is taught as gospel in most American textbooks. It is a justification and apology for the status quo of U.S. capitalism. According to the conservative theory, (1) profits result from the sacrifices and productivity of capitalists (as wages result from the labor of workers), and (2) therefore the present distribution of income, in which many high incomes are made from profits, is just and equitable. The radical view has been advocated for at least 50 years, but it is now gaining prominence in the United States. According to it, (1) capitalists are unproductive and extract their profits from the product of labor, and (2) therefore we need a new economic system in which private profit is eliminated. The radical theory is discussed in Chapter 18.

The Conservative Theory

The concept of profit as the reward to a capitalist for abstaining from immediate consumption was developed in the early nineteenth century by the economists N. Senior and J. B. Say. Each argued that provision of capital for production is a subjective cost, or disutility. Capitalists practice abstinence from consumption in order to invest capital and therefore are morally justified in making a profit from their investments. Similarly, wages result from subjective unpleasantness, or disutility, in providing labor.

In the 1870s Alfred Marshall substituted *waiting* for abstinence. He

Table 17.4

Number of machines	Number of workers	Total product per week	Marginal product per week
5	10	$1000	—
5	11	1090	90
5	12	1170	80
5	13	1240	70

argued that when capitalists invest their capital in production they must wait to get the return from it until a future date. The fact that they must wait to use all their wealth for consumption justifies their making a profit. Indeed, because they will not invest otherwise, a normal profit is simply a necessary cost of production.

The modern conservative theory of marginal productivity first appeared in full detail in John Bates Clark's *The Distribution of Wealth*, published in 1899. It is dedicated to the propositions that workers and capitalists each receive in income exactly what they contribute as their marginal product and that this is an ethically just system. In other words, a worker's wage will just equal the additional (or marginal) product he or she adds to output. Likewise, the capitalist's profit will just equal the additional (or marginal) amount of product added by the piece of capital he adds to the productive process. This theory is gospel in all conservative textbooks, among them Paul Samuelson's famous *Economics*.

The theory of marginal productivity is basically a very simple argument. Assume that there is a fixed amount of capital—that is, a particular factory and machinery. How many workers should be added by the rational capitalist to maximize profits? Assume next that each additional worker adds something to the product, but that each additional worker adds less than the one before. This is the case because there is a fixed number of machines for them to use; therefore workers can add very little beyond the optimum capacity of the given factory. Suppose that there are five machines and ten workers and that the most efficient functioning requires two workers per machine. Table 17.4 demonstrates the contribution to the marginal product of additional workers in this hypothetical factory.

The capitalist should continue to add workers until the last worker's product just equals his or her cost, or wage. If the wage rate is $70 a week, the capitalist should hire only 13 workers (or 12). Because the thirteenth worker makes no additional profit for the capitalists, no more workers should be hired. The wage will just equal the additional (or marginal) product of the last worker.

Notice that what this theory has arrived at is a rule for capitalists to follow if they wish to maximize profits. If they do act this way (and they usually do), then the assertion that the wage is the same as the marginal product is at best a platitude. Workers are not hired if they produce a marginal product that is lower than the wage. This is simply because the addition of workers would reduce the capitalist's profits. Yet some conservatives believe that they have thereby proved that this is a just and ethical distribution of income.

The conservative theory does exactly the same things for profits. Assume that the capitalist employs a fixed number of workers. How much new machinery should he or she add? Suppose each machine adds less than the one before it. This is the case because the number of workers is fixed; therefore additional machines cannot be used efficiently. Even if the capitalist could enforce a speedup, 100 workers could not handle 1000 machines. Stated with these rigid assumptions, the theory of diminishing marginal productivity is likewise a truism. Yet in the real world the capitalist adds both workers and machines, and new technology to boot, so there may be no diminishing productivity.

In this simple example, however, each additional machine adds less to the product than the previous one (because workers and perhaps factory space are limited). Thus the capitalist should add machines until the additional marginal product of one more machine will just equal its cost. Beyond that point more machines give no more profit, so no more machines should be bought. Therefore, the cost of providing an additional machine (whether out of the capitalist's own capital or from borrowed capital) will just equal the value of its additional (or marginal) product. Conservatives conclude that what is paid to capital is *its own* marginal product and that profits are a necessary cost of production and may be ethically justified.

Of course, this argument applies only under pure competition; it does not apply in our present situation of pervasive monopoly power. Even Samuelson's conservative textbook agrees that *extra profits* (beyond the marginal product of capital) *are made under monopoly* to the degree that monopoly power controls the market. We shall see in Chapters 20–23 that monopoly power exists in nearly all American industry.

Radical Critique of Marginal Productivity Theory

It is important to note the grain of truth in Samuelson's conservative argument. It does show that marginal productivity theory provides a general notion of how to make profits. It tells the capitalist to keep hiring workers (or adding machines) as long as they produce extra profit. When the additional profit approaches zero (because the additional product drops to the cost level), then the capitalist should stop adding workers (or machines).

Samuelson also shows that these are useful rules even for socialist planners to follow in allocating resources among investment projects. They must "introduce first those investment projects with the higher net productivity," and use every additional worker and every additional machine in each project up to the point at which an additional unit would cost more than it adds to the product (Samuelson, p. 580). In relation to the allocation of capital (factories and machines), this means that socialist planners must use something like a profit or interest rate to calculate which projects will bring in the most return to society and which have returns too low to make investment worthwhile. This argument, however, assumes that prices are useful measures of social benefits and social costs. Most radicals believe that prices, which are determined solely by the free play of supply and demand, are not useful indicators of social benefits and social costs.

Finally, Samuelson quietly adds a point about interest, or profits, under socialist planning that should be loudly and repeatedly stressed: "But, of course, no one necessarily receives interest income from them" (ibid.). In other words, a planned socialist economy would have to calculate rates of return on different uses of capital to decide where to allocate it, *but it would not have to distribute any of these returns as income to any individual.*

We are concerned here, however, with the issue of how a capitalist system distributes income to individuals and groups. In relation to income distribution, radicals have attacked the marginal productivity theory on several levels. They claim (1) that it is a tautology, (2) that the marginal product of capital cannot really be measured, and (3) that it confuses the productivity of capital and the productivity of the capitalist.

On the first level, it was indicated earlier that, given its assumptions, the analytic conclusions of marginal productivity follow practically by definition (but not its political-ethical conclusions). If it is assumed that the capitalist always acts to maximize profit, then he or she will never hire an additional worker who would cost more than the worker produces. The capitalist will only keep on hiring workers who produce a surplus above their wages. If the product of the last worker hired is defined to be the marginal product, then it follows that his or her wage must be equal to that, neither more nor less. Similarly, a unit of capital will be utilized only if the additional product from its use equals the additional cost of its use. Given the assumption of profit maximization, these are tautologies in the sense that the conclusions are hidden in the definitions. It does tell the capitalist how to manipulate labor and other inputs to maximize profits, but it does not say whether this is good or bad for society.

It is possible that in some society it may be correct to allocate machines so that the return, or profit, from adding one more machine to production equals its cost. This allocation rule certainly does not prove, however, that it is necessary to have a society in which private capitalists provide the money to buy the machines. Nor does it prove that the capitalist's profit is justified even if it equals the marginal product of capital. This theory provides a particular description of the process of allocation of capital, but it represents no advance beyond older ethical justifications of profit income in terms of the capitalist's abstinence or waiting. (Incidentally, these older theories have long been ridiculed by radicals on the ground that capitalists make very little sacrifice in abstaining from consuming their whole income or waiting for their profit return. Should we sympathize with the sacrifice of people who sit on their yachts and decide to invest 50 percent of their $1 million income rather than consuming it all?)

The second radical criticism is that the marginal productivity theory is unrealistic because it does not refer to anything measurable. What is meant by a *unit of capital?* If it means a particular machine, of what relevance is theorizing about transferring it to a more productive use? Particular machines are designed to do particular jobs. If we find that its marginal product generates less than its cost in an industry, how can the machine be moved to another industry? It is not designed for other work. Furthermore, the theory assumes that small units of capital can be added or subtracted at the margin. Yet most machines represent very considerable investments; they are not infinitely divisible.

Third, even admitting that the theory offers insights about how capitalists should invest and that it has some roughly definable meaning, still it pertains only to the production contributions of labor and physical capital. It says nothing about the capitalists' contributions. This is probably the most important point of criticism. Radicals admit that a machine may increase production, that workers need them, and that they increase the workers' productivity. In that sense Samuelson is right to say that "capital" has a "net productivity." Yet it is only the physical capital (jointly with the worker) that is productive: capitalists are not. They may own the machine, but they themselves perform no work. It is the machine (operated by workers) that performs work. Capitalists reap the profits of this work.

Radicals agree that machines are a necessary, or "productive," part of the physical productive process; they would even agree to the importance of managerial labor. Radicals argue, however, that this productivity of physical capital goods (created by another labor process in the past) is significantly different from the capitalist owners' ability to capture a certain portion of the product as interest or profit. "It is, of course, true that materials and machinery can be said to be physically productive in the sense that labor working without them, but physical productivity in this sense must under no circumstances be confused with value productivity" (Sweezy, p. 61). In other words: "Under capitalism 'the productiveness of labor is made to ripen, as if in a hothouse.' Whether we choose to say that capital is productive, or that capital is necessary to make labor productive, is not a matter of much importance . . . What is important is to say that owning capital is not a productive activity" (Robinson, p. 18). This is clear in the case of a mere coupon clipper (as most stockholders are today). The fact that a few capitalists may otherwise perform productive labor through their own managerial work does not contradict the fact that they also receive huge incomes from the mere ownership of capital.

SUMMARY

Income is very unequally distributed in the United States. Depending on the definition of poverty used, anywhere from 34 to 44 million Americans live in abject poverty while wealthy capitalists receive income ranging up to $600 million a year. Conservative neoclassical theory justifies this inequality by arguing that capitalists' painful abstinence entitles them to receive the productivity resulting from their capital. Radical critics argue that there is no such thing as a measurable productivity of capital and that mere ownership involves no socially useful function. In the radical view, capitalists are extremely wealthy parasites.

SUGGESTED READINGS

The best data on income and wealth are given by Andrew Winnick, "The Changing Distribution of Income and Wealth in the United States, 1960–1985," in *Families and Economic Distress,* edited by Patricia Vaydanoff and Linda Majka (Beverly Hills, Calif.: Sage Publishers, 1988), pp. 232–260.

REFERENCES

Bowles, Sam, and Herb Gintis. *Schooling in Capitalist America.* New York: Basic Books, 1975.

Clark, John Bates. *The Distribution of Wealth.* New York: Augustus M. Kelley, 1966. First published 1890.

Marshall, Alfred. *Principles of Economics.* New York, Macmillan, 1953. First edition 1890.

Robinson, Joan. *An Essay on Marxian Economics.* New York: St. Martin, 1960.

Samuelson, Paul. *Economics.* 10th ed. New York: McGraw-Hill, 1977. First published 1948.

Sweezy, Paul A. *The Theory of Capitalist Development.* New York: Monthly Review Press, 1958.

Business Week. "Who Made The Most and Why." May 9, 1983.

Statistical Abstract for the United States, 1975. U.S. Department of Commerce, Bureau of the Census. Washington, D.C.: GPO, 1976.

Statistical Abstract for the United States, 1982. U.S. Department of Commerce, Bureau of the Census. Washington, D.C.: GPO, 1983.

Chapter
18

The Labor Theory
of Value

The radical alternative to the utility theory discussed in the preceding chapter is the labor theory of value. The labor theory, however, has not always been used exclusively by radicals. Many of the rudiments of this theory were developed in Adam Smith's *The Wealth of Nations*, written in 1776, even though Smith is best known for his "invisible hand" argument for unregulated laissez-faire capitalism (see Chapter 5). The theory was refined and given a much more elaborate and logically consistent presentation in David Ricardo's *Principles of Political Economy and Taxation*, first published in 1817. Ricardo was a capitalist who made his fortune on the London Stock Exchange and was a consistent spokesman for the capitalists' point of view in nearly all practical, economic, and political issues of his era.

After Ricardo, however, most of the proponents of the labor theory were radical critics of capitalism. Karl Marx formulated the definitive version of the theory. He made substantial improvements in Ricardo's version. Most of the developments in the labor theory made over the last 100 years have been refinements, elaborations, and extensions of Marx's version. One outstanding and important exception to the last statement was a book entitled *Production of Commodities by Means of Commodities* by Piero Sraffa, published in 1960. Although Sraffa for several decades had been a sympathizer of the Marxist tradition, in his book he developed Ricardo's version of the theory rather than Marx's version. Sraffa's contribution contained insights and theoretical tools that could be reformulated in such a way as to refine and give added precision to the Marxist version. Our account is not an attempt to reproduce the ideas of Marx, but to give a simplified version of the theory in its current state.

THE NATURE OF PRICES

The differences between the utility theory and the labor theory of value begin with the very question of the essential nature of prices. In the utility theory, prices are a reflection of the peculiar properties of commodities by virtue of which they satisfy desires. Since any commodity—for example, a loaf of bread—has the same physical qualities (assuming it to be made using the same recipe) in all societies, in all times, and in all places, it follows that the utility analysis is unaffected by the particular historical situation or social setting being analyzed. Thus, the utility theorists deem their theory to be applicable everywhere at all times. Even when a society does not use money and does not price, buy, or sell the products of its labor, the utility theorists claim that people in that society behave *as if* they are pricing, buying, and selling and that they can impute *implicit* prices. Thus, in their analysis, prices are a characteristic of all products of human labor in all societies. The major difference between capitalist societies and traditional societies that do not buy and sell is that in the former the prices are explicit and in the latter they are implicit.

The labor theory of value starts with a very different conception of prices. In all societies there is some division of labor. Without such a division each individual would be economically independent and autonomous and there would be no need for a society. This can be restated by simply noting that production is always social; it always involves human productive interdependence and economic coordination. In most traditional, premarket societies, the fact that labor is social is obvious. People coordinate their productive endeavors in accordance with their customs and mores. They generally work in proximity to one another and it is clearly visible that each individual is working for all of the others, that is, for the group as a whole. Moreover, in such societies the product of labor generally belongs to them *all* as a group, and it is used or divided according to their customs and mores. This, of course, does not imply that these premarket societies are egalitarian and that each individual receives a share equal to that of every other. Like capitalism, these societies are generally exploitative societies with a minority of individuals enjoying a disproportionate share of the products of social labor. Our point is that the social nature of labor is obvious in these societies; it is equally obvious that only labor transforms the resources of nature into useful products.

In capitalism the situation is different. Each producer works in relative isolation from others. Each producer uses the products of other individuals, and they use his or her product. Their productive interdependence, however, is not simple and direct. Producers neither know nor care who will use their products, nor do the producers care whose products they use. Therefore, while capitalist production, like the production in every society, is social, it is only *indirectly social*. In capitalism, a given producer's labor, say, a baker's labor, is not immediately *social*. A baker, together with the employees if he or she is a capitalist, produces bread. The baker does not produce it for any particular individual or group of individuals, however; the baker produces it merely as a commodity for sale in the market. Only as a commodity, with a price attached to it, can others acquire the bread through buying it. Thus the baker's labor becomes social when it takes the form of (or is embodied in) a commodity with a price tag.

But when we buy our bread, clothing, cars, and other commodities, we are unaware of, and have no concern for, who the particular human producer was or what particular kind of endeavor was necessary to produce the commodity being purchased. The labor is, for us, undifferentiated, *abstract* labor, and we care about it only as it is represented by, or embodied in, the commodity.

Therefore, in capitalism labor is social only in the form of abstract labor embodied in a commodity that is symbolized by and manifested in the price of that commodity. When I buy my bread and eat it, the baker is shown to have been laboring for me (among others). But my connection to the baker is solely the impersonal institution of the market. The baker's labor became social for me purely in the form of the price of bread.

The market and the price system is the method, in capitalism, of allocating and coordinating social labor. In this economic system, labor becomes social only in an abstract form, embodied in a commodity, that has meaning for you or me only as the price of that commodity. Therefore, in the view of the labor theory of value, prices are the *forms* in which we realize our productive interdependence or the social nature of labor. But the relation between the quantity of labor embodied in a commodity and the price of that commodity is rarely simple and obvious. It is not easy to see the quantitative relation between labor and prices even though prices are merely the social form of labor in a capitalist society. Because of this we shall approach the labor theory of value with a series of approximations, each taking us successively closer to an understanding of the quantitative relation between labor and prices.

THE LABOR THEORY OF VALUE: FIRST APPROXIMATION

Capitalist society is a very complex mechanism in which we must explain the market value of products, the wage rate of workers, and the profits taken by capitalists. To make the learning process easier, we shall begin with the explanation of prices in a much simpler society, then slowly add complexities until we achieve a fully realistic picture of modern capitalism. At the beginning we assume pure competition, perfect knowledge by all economic actors, very little government, full employment, and no international relations. Then, one by one, each of these unrealistic assumptions will be dropped, some in this chapter and some in later chapters.

As a first approximation, let us imagine a simple society in which each individual producer performs all of the labor necessary to bring a particular commodity to market. This might be a society of independent farmers,

Table 18.1   EQUILIBRIUM LEVEL OF EXCHANGE

	Labor time	Exchange for	An equilibrium pair of prices
1 pair of shoes	4 days	2 loaves of bread	$2.80
1 loaf of bread	2 days	½ pair of shoes	$1.40

hunters, and handicraft people. Producers have free access to the natural environment. With their own labor, they fashion all of the tools and gather all of the raw materials necessary to produce their commodity. They then perform the necessary labor to produce their commodity, using their own tools and raw materials, and sell their commodity on the market. With the proceeds of their sales they purchase, from other independent producers, those commodities that they need and desire.

In such a society, prices will perfectly reflect the amount of labor embodied in commodities. That is, prices will reflect the relationship between any given individual's productive effort and the productive efforts of all other individuals upon whom he or she is dependent. Let us suppose, for example, that the average amount of labor embodied in a pair of shoes is 4 days and that embodied in a loaf of bread is 2 days. In this society the forces of supply and demand will tend to adjust the prices of shoes and bread to that level at which two loaves of bread will exchange for, or cost as much as, one pair of shoes.

If money is used in the society, the same 2:1 ratio will tend to exist in the prices of the two commodities. Suppose a loaf of bread is $1.40 (an arbitrary sum of money). Then a pair of shoes will tend to be $2.80 as long as it requires twice as much labor. The resulting equilibrium level— *equilibrium* being defined as the point at which no further change is expected—is shown in Table 18.1.

If prices do not start at these equilibrium ratios, they will tend to move there by a series of adjustments based on the competition and self-interest of the individual producers. To illustrate this process of adjustment, let us assume that the price of bread is $1.00 per loaf and shoes are $3.00 per pair. At these prices one pair of shoes exchanges for three loaves of bread. Now in order for bread producers to obtain a pair of shoes they must work 6 days (needed to produce three loaves of bread). On the other hand, shoe producers need only spend 4 days to obtain a pair of shoes. Similarly, for the shoe producers 4 days of labor (needed to produce one pair of shoes) will exchange for three loaves of bread. Yet it takes the bread producers 6 days of labor to obtain three loaves of bread. In this circumstance, some bread producers will begin producing shoes. This situation of disequilibrium is portrayed in Table 18.2.

As the shift of producers from the bread industry to the shoe industry takes place, two things will happen. First, there will be a decline in the

Table 18.2   DISEQUILIBRIUM IN EXCHANGE

	Labor time	Exchange for	Prices
1 pair of shoes	4 days	3 loaves of bread	$3.00
1 loaf of bread	2 days	$\frac{1}{3}$ pair of shoes	$1.00

supply of bread available. With less bread available, the market mechanism will allocate the smaller supply by a competitive bidding-up of the price by those most able to afford bread at a higher price. Those with less money, or a lesser desire to buy bread, will reduce their purchases at the new, higher price. Secondly, there will be an increase in the supply of shoes available. In order to sell this increased supply, producers will bid down the price to induce consumers to buy more shoes.

These two price changes will continue until two loaves of bread exchange for one pair of shoes. For example, the price of shoes might decline to $2.80 a pair and the price of bread might increase to $1.40 a loaf. Only when the prices have adjusted to that point, at which they are proportional to the labor embodied, will there be no incentive for producers to leave one industry and enter another. Thus the market forces of supply and demand create equilibrium prices, the ratios of which are equal to the ratios of the labor embodied in the various commodities.

Effects of Changing Demand

One criticism of the labor theory often made is that it seems to rely only on the supply cost in labor units, but it ignores changes on the demand side. This is a misunderstanding of the labor theory. The labor theory says that equilibrium exchange ratios and prices will be set by proportionate amounts of labor, but it does not say that demand has no role to play. The demand will not set the price, but it will determine the *amount* produced.

Suppose an equilibrium price is achieved at $2.80 for a pair of shoes and $1.40 for a loaf of bread. Now suppose, by some quirk of consumer tastes, that the demand for bread doubles, while the demand for shoes declines. At first, the price of bread would increase. But then producers of shoes would shift to producing bread. Eventually, the amount of bread would reach the new, higher ratio of demand to the amount of shoes produced.

The demand will have determined the *amounts* of each produced. The price of bread, however, will drop back to its old ratio to shoes. If not, we would again have a disequilibrium situation. So changes in demand cause temporary or short-run price changes, but their lasting effect is only on the amount produced. With a given long-run demand for goods equal to the amount produced, the equilibrium *price* or exchange *value* is determined solely by the amounts of human labor embodied in each commodity.

The Value of Tools

Another, often heard objection to the labor theory is that prices must be determined by value of the tools (and raw materials) used in addition to the human labor used. This is another misunderstanding of the labor theory. It was assumed in the above example that individual producers made their own tools and obtained their own raw materials. The farmer makes plows and scythes, grows wheat, and bakes the bread. The shoemaker (of, say, wooden shoes) makes axes and chisels, cuts down trees, and finally makes shoes.

All tools are produced by human labor. Any work in procuring raw materials is human labor. Therefore the labor theory includes *all* labor—for tools, processing raw materials, and production of the final product—in the exchange value or equilibrium price. Thus the $2.80 for a pair of shoes includes the labor that went into the tools and the processing of raw materials as well as the labor that went into the final manufacturing; the same is true of the $1.40 price of the loaf of bread.

Socially Necessary Labor

One naive objection to the labor theory stresses the fact that some labor produces nothing useful and, therefore, its product has a market value of zero. Marx always qualified the labor theory by referring only to "socially necessary" labor. For example, if a silly person labors for a year to produce a "What's-That," a commodity of no use to anyone, the commodity has zero exchange value even though it embodies a year's labor.

Slightly more complicated is the point that production is assumed to be at the present average level of technology. If a commodity is produced with less than the average level of technology, it requires more than the average labor necessary in the society but its exchange value will be only the amount of socially necessary labor. For example, if a person were silly enough to produce a Ford auto in the backyard by hand, if it required 20 years of labor from 1971 to 1991, and if it were exactly identical to a 1991 Ford, then its price would also be identical.

Different Types of Labor

Another persistent objection to the labor theory of value is that various types of labor involve differing levels of skills, and that a commodity in which highly skilled labor is embodied would ordinarily seem to command a higher price than one in which unskilled labor is embodied. It is certainly true that commodities produced by an hour of skilled labor cost more than those produced by an hour of unskilled labor. Yet—apart from minor differences at birth—most work skills reflect the labor that went into producing that higher skill. For practical purposes, it is a sufficiently accurate representation of reality to assume that all differences in actual skills are a result of differences in training. When all of the labor time spent in teaching and acquiring skills is considered, all labor time can be reduced to a comparable equivalent of simple unskilled labor.

For example, in the above account of the production of shoes and bread, we can suppose that producing shoes requires much more skill than producing bread. Shoe producers must undergo a period of training to achieve their skills. We can then compute the additional time spent by the teachers and the trainees and then apportion this extra time over the average period during which shoe producers use these acquired skills. Perhaps it takes only 3 days of actual labor to produce a pair of shoes. But after apportioning the training time for the acquisition of skills, we find that the equivalent of 4 days of unskilled labor time is spent producing each pair of shoes. Although this computation, which reduces skilled labor to an unskilled labor equivalent, becomes more complex when we introduce profits into the pricing scheme, it is always consistently solvable as long as skill differentials can be reduced to differences in the labor embodied in the acquisition of skills.

In the simple economy described in this first approximation, there are no wages or profits. All income results from the sale of commodities embodying the labor of the producers and all income accrues to the immediate producers. Individual producers specialize in and then exchange the material embodiment of their labor for the material embodiment of the labor of the other producers upon whom their continued existence depends. In this simple case it was easy to prove that the amounts produced were determined by consumer demands, but that the long-run exchange values or equilibrium prices were determined by the amount of labor expended by each producer (including the labor expended on tools and training).

THE LABOR THEORY OF VALUE: SECOND APPROXIMATION

The second stage of our discussion of the labor theory of value provides a closer approximation to modern reality by introducing the central social relationship of capitalism, the class relationship between workers and capitalists. We now assume that different sets of workers extract raw materials, produce tools and machinery, and produce final commodities for consumption. The essence of capitalism is that capitalists own the raw materials, the tools and machinery, and all commodities up to that time at which the final consumer purchases a commodity. Capitalists also, at any given time, own most of the money in the economy. Laborers, in general, own nothing but their capacity to work—their labor power.

Production and the "Factors" of Production

In traditional economic theory, production is viewed as a process in which three separate and distinct factors of production—land, labor, and capital—are combined to produce a variety of outputs. Each factor is said to make a definite, measurable contribution to production. The rewards to the three factors are believed to be determined by the contributions that each factor makes to the production process. Thus landlords receive rent for the use of their land, workers receive wages for the use of their labor power, and capitalists receive profits according to the productiveness of their capital (for more details of the traditional theory, see Chapter 17).

The labor theory of value begins with a completely different view of the production process. Production is seen as a purely human activity in which humans expand labor on material objects given in nature. The labor theory starts with the fact that, unlike many species of animals, human beings rarely find a natural environment that is immediately adaptable for the satisfaction of their material needs. Subsistence requires the material necessities of food, shelter, and clothing. The enjoyment of pleasures beyond mere subsistence requires other material objects. Nature almost never provides the material prerequisites for human subsistence and pleasure in a directly usable form.

To sustain life, people must transform the natural environment from its unusable state to a state that is serviceable for human needs. This transformation is solely and purely a human activity. The outer crust of the earth existed for untold thousands of years before the appearance of the first human beings. No person is responsible for its existence, nor is anyone responsible for the particular properties of the natural environment, by virtue of which it can be adapted to fulfill people's needs.

People cannot live in a vacuum, nor can they live in the void of outer space. This seemingly obvious statement must be stressed, because distortions and misrepresentations of the labor theory have asserted that the theory ignores the "contributions" of the natural environment. The labor theory begins by taking the earth or natural environment as given independent of any human being or human endeavor.

In traditional theory, production is viewed as a process in which people and resources are coequal contributors, and in which some people ought to be paid for "nature's contribution." In the labor theory of value, production consists *solely* of human exertion applied to raw materials in order to transform them into products of human labor that are capable of sustaining life.

The earliest and most primitive forms of production were probably very simple and direct. Shelters were made from caves or with trees and branches; fruits and nuts were picked and gathered; small animals were killed for food and clothing. From this simple state of affairs, in which life must have been very difficult and precarious, all human progress was based on finding new, more complex methods of producing that would increase human productivity. This usually meant developing tools with which people could more effectively transform their environment. All human beings of which we have any direct or indirect knowledge have used tools. Increases in human productivity have been the result of increased knowledge of ways in which the natural environment could be transformed and of increasingly sophisticated and complex tools with which to effect the transformation. Traditional economic theory defines *capital* to include tools, machines, factories and partially processed raw materials. In this view, not only human labor, but also capital, is and always will be a factor of production. Therefore, the owners of capital are said to receive profits because capital is "productive." This assertion confuses material things with human relations.

In the labor theory, on the contrary, factories, tools, machinery, and partly finished raw materials are defined as *means of production.* (In previous societies land was the most important means of production, but now it plays a relatively minor role.) The means of production are the physical aspect of capital. But capital in our economy also has a monetary aspect. When a banker loans a billion dollars to a corporation, and the corporation uses it to buy means of production (or physical capital), that billion dollars is not just money, it is financial capital.

Both the physical and monetary aspects of capital are important, but they do not sufficiently define capital. For example, if a worker has $10 in money, and if that is not enough to go into business, the money is not "capital." Or if a worker has a tool, such as a lawn mower, that the worker uses for his or her own private purposes, the tool is not "capital." So what determines when a tool is "capital"?

In a capitalist society there are a particular set of human relationships. One class, called capitalists, "owns" the physical and monetary capital. Another class, called workers, uses the physical capital to produce things. Workers produce both consumer goods and more physical capital. The *human relations*—codified into laws—between workers and capitalists *determine what we call capital.* For example, if a capitalist hires many workers to cut lawns as a paid service to consumers, then the lawn mowers he owns are capital—and if he spends $10 to repair one of those lawn mowers, that $10 is capital.

Of course, the reason that economists study such human relations—and argue about definitions of capital or theories of value—is ultimately to justify or attack the system of private profit. This is why conservatives insist that private ownership of capital and production based on profit motives is the only way to organize an economic system; radicals offer the alternative of capital being owned by a collective group or all of society, with profit being collective or social rather than private.

The argument about profits becomes confused because human relations of production under capitalism have a superficial appearance that deceives us into thinking they are relations between things rather than people. Personal and social relationships appear, in a capitalist society, as the ratio of prices among commodities, for example the price of shoes compared to the price of hammers. Yet we have seen that prices do not reflect intrinsic values of shoes or hammers, but are determined by human relationships in production, and human expenditure of labor.

This identification of human relationships as commodity relationships is not, however, simply an illusion based on an erroneous perception or imagination. One of the defining features of capitalism is that, in this social system, and this system alone, the human element of the production process is reduced to a commodity—labor power—to be bought and sold on the market in the same manner as any other commodity. Labor power can never be made into a commodity unless and until the people who produce are effectively denied any means of living independently of employers. Workers can remain alive only by selling their power to produce—their labor power—to those who have the control over whether or not production can take place. Workers must sell their labor power or starve—so labor power becomes a commodity. Thus, human relations (between workers and employers) are seen as commodity relations (for example, between hammers and shoes).

Origins of the Worker-Capitalist Relationship

In Chapters 2–4 of this book we described in some detail the evolution of capitalism from the earlier, feudal economy. The feudal economy was centered about isolated agricultural estates, with some independent handicraftsmen in the guilds in the few urban areas. Rather than review that complex evolution here, we have chosen to highlight one feature—the origins of the worker-capitalist relation—by means of an unrealistic, but dramatically clear, parable.

Imagine a tropical island on which neither clothing nor shelter need be produced. The only necessary production on this island is the catching of fish. In order to catch enough fish to feed everyone, each of the 100 inhabitants of the island must spend 6 hours a day fishing. When the fish are caught, they are divided equally among the 100 citizens of the island. The fish are caught by hand.

One day, after the fishing is completed, several people are discussing the process of fishing, and it occurs to them that hemp, which grows wild on the island, could be dried and woven into ropes; the ropes could be tied together in a fashion such as to produce a fishing net; the net would enable them to catch substantially more fish per hour spent fishing. So they decide that for a period of time 50 people will work full-time producing nets, while the other 50 will fish 12 hours a day to produce enough fish to feed everyone.

The people who are producing nets are laboring only in order that more fish can be caught, so the net producers are, in reality, working to catch fish in the future. When the nets are completed, they represent partially caught fish; they are the material embodiment of a part of the labor that will go into the catching of fish. The islanders discover that, using the nets, each fisherman can catch twice the average number of fish in each hour of fishing than before the nets were used. It appears as though the 100 islanders can spend only 3 hours per day fishing and 3 hours per day producing various luxury goods to enhance their enjoyment of life.

But the most cunning and unscrupulous of the islanders has an idea. He gathers nine of the strongest and most brutal islanders, and in a secret conference explains his plan. The next day they announce to the other islanders that a new principle called private property ownership is being instituted. The ten of them are the owners of all of the hemp, all of the rope, and all of the nets, and have ownership of the waters surrounding the island. "We will have," they proclaim, "a private enterprise economy." They explain that this means that each of the other 90 people will be perfectly free to choose to work for them or not. Those who work for them will be paid a wage equal to one-half of the nets they make or one-half the fish they catch. Those who do not work for them will get nothing. Anyone using the hemp, the rope, the nets, or the water without their permission will be punished for violating the laws of private property.

Two or three of the most daring of the islanders refuse and begin fishing for themselves. They are immediately beaten up and tied to trees and forced to go without food or water for 2 days. The other islanders are told that this is the punishment for violating the laws of private property. In fear of receiving the same punishment and not wanting to starve, the other islanders "freely" apply for jobs. Fifty of them are put to work catching the same number of fish as were previously caught by all 100 of the islanders. Ten are put to work repairing nets and producing new nets as replacement for nets that wear out, and 30 are put to work producing luxuries for, or being servants of, the 10 capitalists.

Only this new relationship between the 10 capitalists and the 90 workers transforms the water, the hemp, the rope, and the nets into privately owned capital. If all of the islanders had continued using the nets and dividing the produce among themselves, there would be no capital and no profit. Profit now consists of the fish eaten by the capitalists and the luxuries or personal services provided for the capitalists. Considered another way, only the labor of the net producers and fishermen is actually necessary as a minimum if the islanders are to continue to produce and survive. The 30 luxury producers and servants provide *surplus labor*. This surplus labor is equal to the capitalists' profit, which is extracted from the net producers and fishermen.

Thus private ownership of the means of production is essentially a *social relationship* between the owners and the nonowners. In the parable, as in reality, it is a coercively established and coercively maintained system of privileges for the owners and sanctions for the nonowners. (Of course, capitalism was not the result of a conscious conspiracy by a few people; moreover, workers today are persuaded more by propaganda than by force.) Only when such a social relationship exists do the nets, tools, and other means of producing things become privately owned and used as a means to get workers to produce private profit.

To complete our parable, we find the capitalists announcing that there are inheritance laws, so that when they die their children will own the means of production. When the second generation of capitalists takes over, productivity has increased sufficiently to reduce the amount of labor necessary to provide food at the given level of technology in the society. The new capitalists, accustomed to a life of ease and luxury, now appoint some of the islanders as policemen to enforce the laws of private property. The capitalists now have no function but to enjoy their leisure, their luxuries, and the services provided for them.

They fear, however, that since the workers greatly outnumber the policemen, there may be a revolt that would put an end to their privileges. They decree that each worker needs to be schooled in "social science." They hire "social scientists" who devise a theory that the production of fish requires both labor and capital. The workers, these social scientists proclaim, receive a wage, determined by the productivity of their labor, and the capitalists receive profits, determined by the productivity of their capital. Each worker is free to work or starve, and each person, whether capitalist or worker, receives a reward determined by the productivity of the factor of production (either labor or capital) he or she owns. Therefore the system is fair and just. (This theory was examined at some length in the previous chapter.)

To the extent that the workers believe the social scientists, all is peaceful and tranquil. If they do not accept this "theory" and attempt to withhold some or all of their surplus produce from the capitalists, the police punish them for violating the laws of private property. Such is the parable that illustrates the essential social feature that transforms a society of free and independent producers into a society of a few capitalists (who receive all profit) and many, many workers (who receive only wages).

Commodity Exchange Under Capitalism

A *commodity* is defined as any product sold in the market. Some societies do not produce commodities for the market. In the parable above, when the 100 fishermen fished collectively and then divided the product equally, there was no market exchange. They produced products only for their use value. *Use value* is defined as all of the concrete, particular characteristics of a product, by virtue of which individual consumers can derive utility from the product.

Capitalists, on the contrary, do not invest money in a business to produce use values, but to obtain exchange value. *Exchange value* is defined as the quantity of other commodities—or the quantity of money—for which a commodity will exchange in the market. For example, General Motors does not produce autos as use value for its workers. GM produces autos strictly for sale in the market, to obtain exchange values.

Capitalists have no personal interest in the use values they produce; that is, they have no concern about the nature of their commodity— whether it be guns or medicine—or what use is made of it, as long as they receive their exchange value. They have only the indirect concern that if no person buys their commodity, then its exchange value will not be realized in money. Money is the medium of exchange, and, as such, it is the universal expression of exchange value. The exchange value of a commodity is only realized when it is exchanged for money. Persons having money can, through exchange, give up possession of generalized exchange value (money) for possession of the use value of a commodity. Capitalists' only concern therefore is that someone will have both the money and the desire to possess the use value of their commodity so that they may realize its exchange value.

The society of independent producers in our first approximation was, like capitalism, a society that produced commodities for exchange in the market. The *form* of the process of exchange, however, is strikingly different in a simple economy of independent producers (our first approximation) and in a capitalist economy. In the simple economy of independent producers, each producer expended his or her own labor to produce a commodity. This commodity was then exchanged for money. The money, in turn, was exchanged for other commodities that the producer wished to consume. The circulation of commodities and money could thus be depicted as follows:

commodities → money → commodities

In this simple economy, exchange is an exchange of use values, with money merely mediating the exchange. Thus in our earlier example the shoemaker exchanged a pair of shoes for $2.80 in money, then used the money to buy two loaves of bread. The shoemaker bought the bread for direct consumption as a use value.

The situation looks quite different to a capitalist in a capitalist economy. Eventually, of course, the capitalist—like the independent producer— exchanges his or her commodities in the market for money and uses the money to buy other commodities, both for personal consumption and for expanding production. Unlike the independent producer, however, the capitalist does not begin by expending his or her own labor to produce a commodity.

On the contrary, the capitalist begins by investing money, with which raw materials, plant, and equipment (which are commodities), and labor power (which is now also a commodity) are bought. The commodities that the laborers, using the capitalist's tools and materials, produce are then sold, with the capitalist receiving the exchange value. Thus the new circulation of commodities and money can be depicted as follows:

money → commodities → money

In this process the capitalist begins with money and ends up with money.

The acquisition of commodities now merely mediates in the exchange of money for money.

But why should anyone wish to exchange money for money? The answer is obvious: The capitalist expects to end up with more money than that which he or she started with, and in the usual operation of a capitalist economy, this is exactly what happens. Thus a more accurate description of circulation in capitalism would be

money → commodities → more money

Profits and Prices

We must now explain how a capitalist can begin with a fund of exchange value (money), make a series of exchanges, and then end up with another fund of exchange value (more money), which is greater than the original amount. This "more" or "extra" exchange value is called *surplus value*, and at the present stage of the argument, surplus value is the equivalent of profits. The question to be answered, then, is: How do all capitalists, as a class, make profits by buying and selling?

To begin, we must reject the notion that profits are made because a capitalist buys commodities from other capitalists at prices below their equilibrium exchange values, or sells commodities to other capitalists at prices above their equilibrium exchange values. This may be the source of profits for some particular capitalists, but it can never be the source of profits for all capitalists as a class. This is so because any time a profit is made by buying below the exchange value, the seller incurs an identical loss. Similarly, when a profit is made by selling above the exchange value, the buyer incurs an identical loss. It is obvious that, in the aggregate, such gains and losses exactly cancel out. But capitalists, as a class, make profits. We must therefore seek the source of aggregate profits elsewhere.

Another possible source of profits might be the monopoly power of certain capitalists. By securing a monopoly, they can charge as high a price as the "traffic will bear" and secure high profits. Although monopoly power is certainly a source of extremely high profits for certain capitalists, it is not the source of profits for all capitalists. Capitalists operating in industries that are highly competitive also receive profits. Therefore to get at the basic and ultimate source of profits, we shall, at this stage in the argument, assume that there is pure competition and *there are no monopolies.*

Does this system of competitive capitalism have the same results for prices as the system of independent competitive producers described in our first approximation? Remember, there we found that the equilibrium price or exchange value was solely determined by the labor embodied in each commodity. When capitalists employ workers for a private profit, does this result change? In our example bakers sold bread for $1.40 a loaf, while shoemakers sold shoes for $2.80 a pair. Now suppose there is the same technology under capitalism. A loaf of bread still requires 2 days' labor, while a pair of shoes still takes 4 days' labor. What will be the exchange rates and prices under capitalism?

Suppose we begin with some other, arbitrary prices, such as only $1.00 for bread but $3.00 for shoes. In this case, the shoe-producing capitalists make a higher than average rate of profit (an extra 20¢ a pair), since they are selling above the value of the product, measured in labor days. The bread-making capitalists, however, are making below the average rate of profit because they are selling below the value (40¢ a loaf below) of the product, measured in labor days.

With competition among capitalists prevailing in every industry, however, the principal result would be that an equal rate of profit would tend to be established in each and every industry. The *rate of profit* measures the ratio of the increase of money (profit) to the money invested. With pure competition capitalists can enter or leave any industry with relative ease. This means that if different profit rates exist in different industries, then capitalists (seeking to maximize their profits) will leave those industries having low profit rates and enter those industries having high profit rates.

In our example this would reduce the supply of bread, and hence raise the price of bread in this low-profit industry. Simultaneously it would increase the supply of, and hence lower the price of, shoes. These price changes would then increase profit margins in bread (the low-profit industry) and reduce those in shoes (the high-profit industry). As long as any difference in profit rates remains, the process will continue. It is obvious that where competition prevails, the forces of supply and demand will tend to equalize all rates of profit. Therefore, eventually the prices of shoes and bread will reach an *equilibrium* 2:1 ratio of $2 to $1, or at $2.80 to $1.40, or some other combination, that matches the ratio of labor expended on their production. Therefore we can conclude that, in the long-run equilibrium under capitalism, competitive profit-making ensures that prices will be in the same ratios as exchange values determined by the labor expended.

How Capitalists Make Profit

We seem, however, to be further than ever from explaining profit. If capitalists must sell at equilibrium prices equal to the labor value of the product, how do they ever make a profit? The answer to the mystery lies not in selling prices and exchange but in the human relations of the capitalist process of production.

The capitalist begins with money, with which material commodities, such as plant, equipment, and raw materials can be purchased. The capitalist also purchases some units of the commodity *labor power*—that is, the right to direct workers' expenditure of labor power for some hours or days. We assume that both the material commodities and the labor power have been bought at their equilibrium prices. The labor power works with the material commodities. The use value of the labor power—the actual exertion of muscular and intellectual energy in producing—is used up. New commodities are produced. They are sold at their equilibrium value. Somehow, the process ends with the capitalist having more money than the amount with which he or she started. The whole process may be depicted this way:

money → commodities → production →

more commodities → more money

Since the capitalist both bought commodities and sold commodities at equilibrium prices, the extra money must have been made in the production process. In other words, the commodities bought to be used as productive inputs must have created more value in production than their own value. The answer to the origin of surplus value (or profit) is just this: *The capitalist buys the worker's labor power as a commodity in the market at its market value, then sells the product of the worker at a higher value.*

To show how this happens, let us consider the process for a single individual. A capitalist begins by using his or her money to buy two kinds of commodities, which Marx called constant capital and variable capital. *Constant capital* is defined as all the money spent for raw materials, machinery, factory construction, and any other products of previous labor purchased by the capitalist. The term is generally used to refer both to the money spent and the commodities bought, since they are two forms of the same thing.

Since these products are all the result of previous labor, they may also be considered simply as so many units of labor. A *unit of labor* is defined as the product of the work of one laborer for one production period. In our example we assume that the capitalist buys constant capital embodying four units of labor. Why did Marx call these commodities (such as machinery) constant capital? Because he wished to stress that this type of commodity enters the production process with a certain value (such as four units of labor) that remains constant during the production process.

Variable capital, on the other hand, is defined by Marx to be the amount of money expended on the wages of labor during the production period. The term variable capital may be used to refer both to the money expended on wages and the commodity that is bought for that money, namely labor power, the worker's ability to expend muscle and energy. This type of "capital" is variable in that it does *not* transfer its original value to the product. The value of the product of one unit of actual labor performed differs from the value of one unit of labor power. In our example we assume the capitalist buys the labor time of ten workers, that is, ten units of labor power.

In order to purchase this labor time, the capitalist pays the laborers the market value of the only commodity they sell, namely ten units of labor power. What is the value of a unit of labor power? We do *not* mean the ethical value of an honest day's work, nor do we mean the product of a day's work, since that is called a unit of labor. We mean: How much must the capitalist pay in the marketplace to hire one worker's labor power for a day?

In Marx's terms, what is the labor value of the commodity labor power? The reader will recall that one of the distinguishing features of capitalism is that human productive endeavor becomes a commodity—labor power. The exchange value of labor power is determined in the same way as that of any other commodity. A certain amount of labor must be expended in order to create and maintain an adequate supply of labor power. In order that laborers be able to continue offering their labor power for sale to capitalists, they must consume a certain amount of those commodities necessary to sustain life. In order that the labor force be maintained over a longer period it is necessary for laborers to receive a sufficient amount of these necessities for them to rear a family and, in effect, generate their own replacements.

Those commodities that a laborer must have to sustain himself or herself are socially necessary costs of production, just as the food and shelter for farm animals are a necessary cost of producing agricultural products. Thus *the labor embodied in the production of the commodities that a worker and that worker's family must consume to sustain themselves is the labor value of the commodity labor power.* As in the case of any other commodity, this is an average long-run result, which is the effect of all the factors affecting competition for jobs and wages in the labor market. These include the size of the unemployed army of workers kept in reserve, the strength of individual capitalists and their associations, the opposing strength of the trade unions, and the role of the capitalist state in labor struggles. Of course, in some short-run situations, such as a depression, a worker may be paid less than the value of his or her labor power.

How many hours a day must workers work in order to produce the (long-run) value of their labor power? The answer is many hours less than they actually do work in a day, since the extra labor (beyond the value of their labor power) is the source of surplus value for the capitalist.

For simplicity, in our example we assume it takes exactly one-half of the worker's day to produce the market value of his or her labor power, say, 4 hours out of an 8-hour day. This means that one-half of labor exerted creates the market value of labor power, and one-half of the labor exerted creates surplus value. Looked at in another way, each worker labors one-half of the day for his or her own subsistence (wages) and one-half a day for the capitalists' surplus value (profit). We can call the first half of the worker's day *necessary labor,* because it is a socially necessary cost of production. The second half of the day can be called *surplus labor* because it is not a socially necessary cost of production. Surplus labor creates commodities; these constitute the surplus value or profits. Because surplus labor represents labor expended beyond that period during which a worker produces the value equivalent of his or her wages, it can be called unpaid labor. Unpaid labor is the ultimate, real and only source of profits.

Our example of capitalist production is illustrated in Figure 18.1. The picture shows that the capitalist buys 4 labor days' worth of constant capital that is, raw materials, plant, and equipment. The capitalist also buys 10 days of labor power—that is, he or she hires ten workers for a day. In the production process, the 4 days of labor embodied in the raw materials, machinery, and other material inputs are used up to produce 4 days of labor embodied in new commodities (say, a commodity called "widgets"). The 10 days of labor power are used up in the production process to produce commodities (widgets) embodying 10 days of labor. By our assumption of the wage level, however, the workers are paid an amount of money sufficient only to buy 5 days of labor embodied in commodities (widgets). This leaves the capitalist with commodities embodying 5 days of labor; this is the surplus value, or profit.

If we add together the value of the constant capital used up (4 labor days' worth of commodities), plus the value of the variable capital used up (wages in the form of commodities embodying 5 days of labor), plus surplus value (profit in the form of commodities embodying 5 days of labor), then the total value of the commodities produced is 14 days of labor. Thus:

total value = constant capital + variable capital + surplus value

or

14 days of labor = 4 days + 5 days + 5 days

In modern accounting terms, which blur and disguise some important concepts, the same equation may be expressed as

price = material costs (including depreciation) + wages + profit

What is disguised here is that the commodities represented by each of these terms actually embody a certain number of units of labor. Money often disguises labor values. With this warning—and given certain unrealistic assumptions to be modified in stage three of our argument—the terms in the equation may be transformed from days of labor into money terms. If we arbitrarily assume that the value produced by 1 day of labor is valued at $10 in the market, then the equation becomes

price of $140 = $40 material costs + $50 wages + $50 profit

Exploitation, or surplus value, is defined here as the difference between the value produced by the worker and the worker's wage (value of labor power). It is a strictly scientific concept, although the word also has ethical

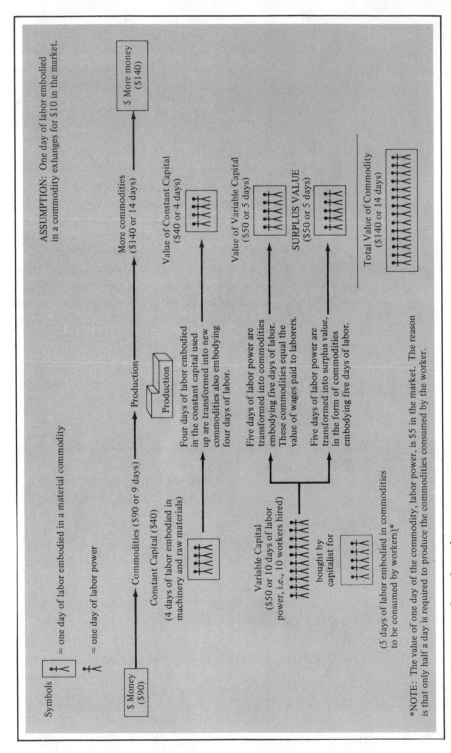

Figure 18.1 The origin of surplus value.

connotations (like every concept in economics). The *rate of exploitation* is defined as

$$\text{rate of exploitation} = \frac{\text{surplus value}}{\text{variable capital}} = \frac{\text{profit}}{\text{wages}}$$

or, in this example,

$$\frac{5 \text{ units of labor}}{5 \text{ units of labor}} = \frac{\$50}{\$50} = 100\%$$

The rate of exploitation is defined from the worker's point of view.

On the other hand, the *rate of profit* is a capitalist concept, designed to measure the profitability of various capital investments. It is defined as

$$\text{rate of profit} = \frac{\text{surplus value}}{\text{variable capital} + \text{constant capital}}$$

$$= \frac{\text{profit}}{\text{wages} + \text{material costs}}$$

In this example,

$$\text{rate of profit} = \frac{5 \text{ days of labor}}{9 \text{ days of labor}} = \frac{\$50}{\$90} = 56\%$$

Obviously, the rate of profit depends not only on the ratio of profits to wages but also the ratio of material costs (constant capital) to wages (variable capital). This latter ratio is defined as

$$\text{organic composition of capital} = \frac{\text{constant capital}}{\text{variable capital}} = \frac{\text{material costs}}{\text{wages}}$$

In other words, the *organic composition of capital* is the ratio of material costs (past labor) to present labor costs in production. In our example, it is

$$\text{organic composition} = \frac{4 \text{ days of labor}}{5 \text{ days of labor}} = \frac{\$40}{\$50} = 80\%$$

Our second stage, or second approximation to reality, could also be extended to the circulation of *all* capital. This task is accomplished mainly in Part Three of this book. Here, we may briefly note that capitalists as a whole will produce the constant capital directly in the form of new machinery and raw materials to replace those used up. For example, 4 million labor-days' worth of constant capital might be used by workers to produce 4 million labor-days' worth of new constant capital. Capitalists as a whole will produce the value of variable capital in the form of consumption goods for workers. To pay wages to 10 million workers (days of labor power), they will order the workers to produce 5 million days of labor power in the form of consumable commodities. This leaves 5 million days of labor power for production of surplus value or profits. The capitalists will take their profits in two forms. Some, perhaps 2 million days of labor power, will go to produce commodities for luxury consumption. The rest, perhaps 3 million days of labor power, will be used to produce new capital goods for expansion of business, thus leading to larger production and larger profits in the next period.

THE LABOR THEORY OF VALUE: THIRD APPROXIMATION

So far we have swept under the rug one complication in the labor theory. We showed how competition among capitalists forces an equal rate of profit in all industries. Yet competition of workers for jobs   and the strug gle between workers and capitalists in each industry—also tends to produce an equal rate of exploitation in all industries (assuming, for the moment, that there are *no* unions or business monopolies). If there are equal rates of profit and equal rates of exploitation in all industries, that does not seem to pose any problem.

It sounds logical, and is logical, that equally exploited workers should produce equal rates of profit. The problem is, however, that the rate of profit is measured against not only living labor but also the previous labor embodied in constant capital (costs of raw materials and depreciation of machinery). Remember that the rate of profit is equal to profit divided by wages *and* the constant capital. *This implies that the rate of profit is determined not only by the rate of exploitation of labor but also by the ratio of labor costs to material costs (the organic composition).* Thus, where labor is equally exploited, lower material costs will mean higher rates of profit. That is, rates of profit are different in different industries depending upon the ratio of labor to material costs.

Yet we know that competition leads to equal rates of profit. In earlier sections we solved this problem by just assuming (implicitly) that technology or the organic composition was the same in all industries. Realistically, that is not true. So how can there be the same rate of profit in all industries if there are differing ratios of labor to machinery and material costs?

The answer is that in this more realistic approximation, when the organic composition differs from industry to industry, money prices will diverge from labor values in such a way as to redistribute the surplus value systematically from one industry to another. In this stage of our presentation, money prices will no longer be identical to labor values, and profits will no longer be identical to surplus value when surplus value is stated in terms of labor values. Two points must emphatically be made, however. Both underline the fact that the modifications introduced in this section do not in any way alter the conclusions arrived at in the first two stages of the argument. First, prices still reflect the social division of labor and the production by separate capitalist firms, in which all coordination of production is affected by the market. Second, living labor power remains the sole source of surplus value, and surplus value is the sole source of profit. In particular, the source of profit remains the difference between the price of labor power and the prices of commodities, where the commodities embody the labor into which that labor power was transformed in the production process.

A significant part of the reasoning at the third stage of our presentation is analytically more difficult than the main body of this chapter. We must therefore refer the interested reader to some literature that is somewhat more technical (see, e.g., Hunt; Meek). The reader who works through this literature will see that even though prices may deviate from labor values, and the profit of any capitalist may deviate from the surplus value generated by the labor power he or she purchases, the ratio of the money value of all commodities produced to the money value of all labor power is equal to the ratio of the labor value of all commodities produced to the labor value of all labor power. Thus the nature and source of profits remain the same as in the second stage of our analysis, even though they are redistributed among capitalists.

If competition equates the rates of profit in all industries, and if differing organic compositions of capital exist, then the *surplus value must be redistributed through price changes* that equate the rates of profit. Some surplus value must be taken from those industries with a low organic composition and given to those industries with a high organic composition. The latter industries have more constant capital and therefore require more surplus value to achieve the socially average rate of profit. The former industries have less constant capital and therefore require less surplus value to achieve the socially average rate of profit. To effect this redistribution of surplus value it is necessary for competition to raise the prices in industries with a high organic composition and lower the prices in industries with a low organic composition. A commodity produced with the socially average organic composition will have a ratio of money price to labor value that is equal to the ratio of the total monetary value of all goods to the total of all labor embodied in those goods. That is, a commodity with an average organic composition will have a price that is proportional to the labor embodied in it.

Thus, in its third approximation to reality the labor theory of value does not assert that all money prices will be proportional to labor values. It does assert that *deviations from this proportionality will be systematically predictable.* In any science it is not expected that a valid theory is one that permits no exceptions or deviations. The most that is ever expected of a scientific theory is that in its most complex and complete form it be capable of systematic prediction of when and how observed phenomena will deviate from the general outcome that the theory predicts in its most simplified and qualified form. The labor theory of value, when judged by this standard, is seen to be scientifically sound.

THE LABOR THEORY OF VALUE: FURTHER APPROXIMATIONS

Our exposition of value, wages, and prices is still at a very high level of abstraction. Several further approximations are needed to be more realistic, and many chapters of this book will deal with those more realistic situations. First, there is *not* pure competition but a high level of industrial concentration, as described in fact and theory in Chapters 20–23. Second, all workers are not treated equally; there is discrimination, by race and sex and other prejudices, as discussed in Chapter 25. Third, there is not equilibrium at all times but rather frequent periods of unemployment and price inflation, as explained in Chapters 26–32 and 34–37. Fourth, there is not a purely private economy but extensive government intervention through regulations, laws and police, military spending, business subsidies, taxation, and other means, all of which are discussed in Chapters 24 and 33. Fifth, goods and services are not all measured only in the market but have non-economic benefits and losses, such as polluting products, discussed in Chapters 38 and 39. Finally, the U.S. economy does not form its prices in isolation from all other economies but has vital international relationships, as discussed in Chapters 40 and 41.

SUMMARY

The labor theory of value is based on an intellectual perspective that views production as a transformation of unusable resources into usable products of human labor. The only ingredient in this transformation is human labor. The natural resources represent the material that is transformed (production could certainly not take place in a vacuum with nothing to transform), but the natural resources contribute nothing toward their own transformation. They simply exist—and their existence and potential for being transformed are prerequisites for human life and human production. Although tools and machines are used in production, they are merely natural resources that have been previously transformed by human labor.

Means of production that have themselves been produced—that is, tools—have been used in every human society of which we have any knowledge. By themselves, however, these means of production are not capital. They become capital only in a market-oriented, commodity-producing society in which they are owned and controlled exclusively by a small social class—the capitalists. The existence of a capitalist class that owns and controls the means of production necessarily involves the co-existence of a working class with no means of sustaining itself except through the sale of the commodity labor power. The widespread sale of labor power as a commodity is one of the most important distinguishing features of capitalism.

In the first stage of our presentation of the labor theory of value we showed that in a commodity-producing society in which each producer owned his or her own means of production, commodity prices would be proportional to the labor embodied in the production of the commodities. Prices would reflect the social division of labor and the mutual interdependence of all producers—an interdependence that is expressed in millions of market exchanges.

In the second stage, or second approximation, of our argument we showed that the basis of profits is the fact that only a portion of a laborer's productive effort is needed to produce the value equivalent of his or her means of subsistence (that is, the value of his or her own labor power). The remainder is surplus (or "unpaid") labor, that is, profits.

The third approximation, increasing the realism of the argument, showed that differing organic compositions of capital cause prices to deviate from strict proportionality to quantities of labor embodied in commodities. These deviations, however, follow a predictable pattern and do not alter any of the important conclusions arrived at in the first two approximations of the argument.

Further approximations to reality show how production, prices, and wages are affected by monopoly power, trade union struggles, discrimination, unemployment, government activity, and international relationships.

REFERENCES

Hunt, E. K. *History of Economic Thought, A Critical Perspective.* New York: Harper & Row, forthcoming.

Meek, Ronald L. "Some Notes on the 'Transformation Problem.' " In *Economics and Ideology and Other Essays.* London: Chapman and Hall, 1967.

Chapter
19

The Labor Movement

It is obvious from our discussions of the neoclassical theory of income distribution (Chapter 17) and the labor theory of value (Chapter 18) that conservative and radical economists have very different views of labor unions and the labor movement generally. Conservative neoclassical economists see unions as monopolistic sellers of labor power who are constantly trying to raise wages above the value of labor's marginal product. There are, however, liberal neoclassical economists who recognize the enormous monopoly power of the giant corporations and therefore support labor unions as the appropriate means for workers to avoid being exploited by the corporate giants. The radical economists view labor unions as workers' only means, in a capitalist system, of decreasing the degree of their exploitation. In the radical view, labor unions are very important in establishing the value of labor power and thereby determining the degree of exploitation. Whichever view one takes, the labor movement is one of the most important institutional influences on the distribution of income. In this chapter we very briefly trace the history of the labor movement.

THE LABOR MOVEMENT BEFORE THE CIVIL WAR

The labor movement was very weak in the United States before the Civil War. There had been a few strikes and a few unions, but most unions were very temporary and soon disappeared. One reason was that the industrial working class was such a small part of the population. In the North most of the population in the early nineteenth century was composed of small farmers, whose whole families ran the farm. In the South slaves did the majority of the labor, though there were also many poor white farmers. In 1860 there were still only 1.3 million factory workers. The Civil War greatly stimulated industry, however, so by 1870 there were 2 million factory workers and 3.6 million other wage workers (see Boyer and Morais; also Foner).

Another factor that made the organization and maintenance of unions so difficult was the fact that workers were split by all kinds of prejudices, in part stimulated by the employers. Throughout American history there have been large numbers of new foreign-born workers who could be pitted against the native-born. There was also a slow influx of women into industry; they were paid very low wages and were prohibited by men from entering most unions until after the Civil War (and are still underrepresented in leadership positions in most unions).

The most important prejudice weakening American labor, however, was the racial prejudice of whites against blacks, as well as the objective fact of slavery in a large section of the nation. The South made no apologies for its slave-based economic system. The *Charleston Mercury* newspaper, for example, stated, "Slavery is the natural and normal condition of the laboring man . . . and the Northern states will yet have to introduce it. The theory of a free society is a delusion" (Boyer and Morais, p. 13). Moreover, before the Civil War slave owners often elected the president, dominated the Supreme Court, managed Congress, had a strong control over both political parties, and pushed racism as God's will through organized religion in the South and to some extent even in the North. They used their power to buy up much of the press, to control some of the few existing universities (and all of the southern schools), to dominate the officers' corps in the U.S. Army, and to push the nation into a war with Mexico in order to expand into the West. In 1857, in the Dred Scott case, the U.S. Supreme Court held that slavery was legal *everywhere* in the United States regardless of state laws. In pure economic terms, this meant that white workers in the North could not get high wages or maintain strong unions because the South was always willing to produce the same product more cheaply with slave labor.

After the Civil War, the northern industrialists took over control of the country, pushed capitalism into the West and the South, and made enormous fortunes (some begun by selling poor-quality goods to the Union armies). This was the era of the robber barons, who made fortunes by ripping oil, timber, gold, and coal from the earth, often leaving ruined land and dust bowls behind them. At the same time millions of people lived in abject poverty in unsanitary slum conditions.

THE NATIONAL LABOR UNION

The Civil War provided the basis for trade unions by the resultant abolition of slavery and by the stimulation of industry, which resulted in a growing class of poorly paid factory workers. William H. Silvis helped organize and lead the first nationwide labor federation. He was born in 1828, in Penn-sylvania, into a family of ten children (which was typical in those days) with little money in the family and little food to eat. He worked as an iron molder, and in 1863 helped to organize a national union of iron molders. He was appalled by the poverty of the working class—for example, the fact that in New York City little girls worked from six in the morning till midnight for $3 a week! As a union organizer he set out on a national organizing tour with only $100 in his pocket.

Not only did he see the poverty of the workers, but he also noted that employers were beginning to organize on a national scale (for example, the Iron Founders Association was organized in 1866). Silvis pointed out these facts not only to thousands of individual workers but also to many other trade union leaders. As a result, in August 1866, in Baltimore, the National Labor Union was formed and Silvis became its president. But labor was still divided. Many delegates were opposed to admitting women, but Silvis fought for and won the inclusion of women in the National Labor Union (NLU), though many of its constituent unions would not admit women for many years.

Silvis also fought for the inclusion of blacks, 4 million of whom were now free workers, in the NLU. On this point, however, he was defeated. Not only were many of the delegates prejudiced against blacks, but they were single-mindedly interested in a campaign for the 8-hour workday and did not want to hear about any other issue. The only major resolution passed declared: The first and great necessity of the present to free the labor of this country from capitalistic slavery is the passing of the law by which eight hours shall be the normal working day in all the states of the American Union (quoted in Boyer and Morais, p. 32).

The campaign for the 8-hour workday spread like wildfire, and Eight-hour Leagues were formed all over the United States—50 in California alone. By 1868 the U.S. government was forced to pass an 8-hour workday for all of its own employees. Yet private industry resisted, state laws were declared unconstitutional by the Supreme Court, and a federal law was passed only in 1938 by the New Deal. Before that time, many congressional investigations found incredibly long working hours even for women and children in most parts of the United States. Still, the agitation of the NLU did result in the average workday being reduced from 11 hours in 1865 to 10.5 hours in 1870.

Silvis worked so hard as an organizer that he died in 1869 at the age of 41. As a memorial, the NLU finally admitted blacks to membership at its 1869 convention. But it was too late for this gesture to succeed. The NLU was already becoming a largely middle-class reformers' organization, with almost no white or black workers in it. By 1868 two-thirds of its membership were doctors, lawyers, farmers, preachers, and other non–working-class people. As a result, after the 1869 convention the NLU lead-ership declared that trade unions were not the best road to reform. Their union affiliates began to fall away, and by the 1871 convention only two union delegates showed up. The NLU, like many other organizations of this period, turned to the crank ideas of a currency reform that would make easy money available to everyone. In 1872 the NLU supported a National Labor Reform party, running on the single plank of currency reform, which left workers so uninterested that it received only 30,000 votes. Thus, the NLU killed itself by acting, not like a labor federation, but like a middle-class reform group with crankish ideas. This pattern repeated itself in many "labor" organizations in the last half of the nineteenth century.

THE KNIGHTS OF LABOR

After some years of rapid industrial expansion following the Civil War, a major depression began in 1873 and lasted for six lean and hungry years. By 1877 there were about 3 million unemployed, a huge percentage of the labor force. In 1873 there had been 30 national trade unions, but unemployment, lockouts, and blacklists destroyed most of them, so only eight or nine national unions remained by 1877. Yet workers and the unemployed were becoming more militant under the intolerable conditions. There was a large demonstration in New York City, where signs proclaimed, "The Unemployed Demand Work, Not Charity." The police, bought and paid for by big business, attacked the demonstrators with clubs and sent many women and children to hospitals. The *New York Times* said that all of the demonstrators were foreigners and communists, a theme that has been repeated ever since.

In Pennsylvania in the 1870s the police fought pitched battles with the miners' union. Because many of them were Irish immigrants who belonged to the Ancient Order of Hibernians, most of the union leadership was charged with being Irish revolutionary terrorists. The police and the newspapers invented the name "Molly McGuires" for them, though this organization never existed in the United States. Ten of the miners were charged with killing a policeman, rapidly convicted in a witch-hunting atmosphere, and hanged on June 21, 1877.

In another action, in July of 1877, a strike against the Baltimore and Ohio Railroad erupted in violence when strikebreakers tried to move the trains. The Philadelphia militia came to Pittsburgh, was met by a large hostile crowd, and fired into it, killing 20 men, women, and children. That night militiamen were surrounded in their barracks by thousands of miners and steel workers. They ran away at midnight to escape the wrath of these many thousands of people. The newspapers again reported that the strikers and all their supporters were communists and anarchists, so the newspapers praised the police and militia for their violence. The *New York Tribune* said, "These brutal creatures can understand no other reasoning than that of force and enough of it to be remembered among them for generations" (quoted in ibid., p. 69).

At the same time, a new national union federation was growing from a small and strange beginning. In 1869 a small union called the Garment Cutters Association was disbanded and immediately reconstituted itself as the Knights of Labor. Its national officers were called the Master Workman, the Veritable Sage, the Worthy Foreman, the Unknown Knight, and the Treasurer. People wishing to become members paid $1, went through a large number of ritual initiation ceremonies, and were sworn to secrecy. There had been so much violence against the labor movement that the Knights felt that only secrecy would allow them to survive. No women were admitted until 1882. For a long time the Knights of Labor was a very small organization; it was known only for its secrecy, so the newspapers charged that it was a subsidiary of the Irish Molly McGuires, trying to overthrow the government of the United States.

By 1877, however, the National Labor Union had disappeared, and the great strikes, as well as the violence with which they were met, convinced many workers that some new national organization was needed. By the end of 1877, the Knights had expanded to 14 district assemblies from Massachusetts and New York to Indiana and Illinois, with much strength in Pennsylvania. The Knights had a program opposed to monopoly corporations, which they thought should be publicly owned; specifically, they argued for public ownership of the railroads, telephones, and telegraph companies. In 1881 the Knights finally decided to abandon their secrecy and go public, though they retained secret initiation rites. In 1878 the Knights had only 9,287 members, but membership rose to 52,000 by 1883 and to more than 600,000 by 1886.

Part of the secret of their swift growth was that local assemblies would accept anyone from any trade or occupation, male or female, black or white. Their slogan was "An injury to one is the concern of all." Yet their admission of anyone, without limitation by trade, was also a weakness. Many of their assemblies had a middle-class composition and were more interested in grand reforms than immediate issues of labor versus capital.

The Grand Master of the Knights of Labor in the years 1880 to 1886 was Terrence V. Powderly. A rather conventional believer in reform policies, he stressed the popular panacea of currency reform. On the other hand, he absolutely opposed strikes and actually acted as a strikebreaker in some circumstances. He felt that strikes could never give rise to reforms, change unjust laws, or solve labor's problems. He even attempted in 1886 to stop the tide of workers organizing in favor of the 8-hour workday, which he also felt to be a side issue. When millions of workers organized to strike for the 8-hour workday on May 1, 1886, Powderly did all he could to oppose this movement. That was the last straw for many members of the Knights, and membership in the Knights declined as fast as it had previously risen.

THE AMERICAN FEDERATION OF LABOR

A third national federation of labor unions also grew out of the depression of 1873 and the violent strikes of the late 1870s. In 1881 a number of unions met together to form the Federation of Organized Trades and Labor Unions of the United States and Canada, which changed its name in 1886 to the American Federation of Labor (AFL). The AFL was formed by a number of labor leaders who considered themselves socialists, its leader Samuel Gompers among them. In 1886 the AFL adopted a preface to its constitution that said:

> A struggle is going on in the nations of the world between the oppressors and oppressed of all countries, a struggle between capital and labor which must grow in intensity from year to year and work disastrous results to the toiling millions of all nations if not combined for mutual protection and benefit. (Quoted in Boyer and Morais, p. 90)

Moreover, the first main action of the AFL was a very militant one. The AFL became the main force behind the 8-hour workday movement. The AFL called on all labor to strike for the 8-hour workday on May 1, 1886. It is ironic that many years later the AFL declared it was subversive and communistic to demonstrate on the first of May. These demonstrations, supported by many hundreds of thousands of workers, were peaceful and very successful for their publicity. The day after, however, at a protest meeting against police brutality in Haymarket Square in Chicago some unknown person tossed a bomb that killed one policeman. Using this as an excuse, the police rounded up several trade union leaders and some anarchists, a long frame-up trial took place, and four of the men—who had been nowhere near Haymarket—were executed.

The AFL gradually took an entirely different, very peaceful, and less and less militant path as time went by. Its leaders declared that they had no ultimate ends for social change, that they were interested only in immediate monetary gains for the workers. Moreover, the AFL came to rely more and more heavily on organization of the highly skilled workers in very narrowly defined craft unions. At no time until the 1930s did the main leaders of the AFL willingly organize masses of unskilled workers in industrial unions. On the contrary, they often had a large number of small craft unions all competing for members among the skilled workers and totally neglecting the unskilled, especially black and women, workers. They practiced what came to be known as "business unionism," meaning a dollars-and-cents orientation toward higher wages as their first and last priority, the amassing of huge treasuries to support their power, the use of large staffs of highly paid professional organizers, and the payment of large salaries for their top executives.

There were many attempts to reform the AFL, to bring it closer to the needs of the millions of unorganized workers. This was particularly true in the period of 1900 to 1920, when the Socialist party flourished in the

United States. By 1912 the Socialists had elected over a thousand local and state officials and two congressmen, published newspapers that were sold to millions of people, and had hundreds of thousands of dues-paying members. In 1912 Eugene Debs, who was born and raised in Terre Haute, Indiana, ran for president of the United States as a Socialist and received over a million votes. Even later, in 1920, when he was in prison for opposing World War I, Debs still received almost a million votes again, despite the fact that he could do no personal campaigning from his prison cell. Throughout this whole period, the Socialists opposed the business unionism and narrow craft organization of Samuel Gompers and other AFL leaders. The Socialist candidate for president of the AFL frequently took about one-third of the votes.

Although the Socialist party produced many leaders, Eugene Debs was by far the most remarkable. He grew up in the Midwest, was very tall and a powerful speaker, and reminded people of Abe Lincoln. Debs worked on the railroads for many years. He wrote,

> As a locomotive fireman, I learned of the hardships of the rail in snow, sleet and hail, of the ceaseless danger that lurks along the iron highway, the uncertainty of employment, scant wages and altogether trying lot of the workingman, so that from my very boyhood I was made to feel the wrongs of labor . . . (Quoted in Boyer and Morais, p. 115)

In 1893 Eugene Debs organized a single railway union to replace the 22 squabbling craft unions of the AFL on the railways. At that time Debs was still quite conservative in much of his thinking, was not a Socialist, and supported the Democratic party. In 1894, however, Debs's fledgling union was manipulated into a strike when it was still growing and not yet mature. Even then the union (the American Railway Union) would have won against the bosses, but U.S. Army troops were called into the center of the strike, in Chicago, and broke the strike with violence. At the same time Debs and all the union leadership were put in jail for 6 months for violating the Sherman Anti-Trust Act on the theory that they had restricted trade and competition! (Yet up to that time, no monopoly corporation executive had ever been tried under the act, much less been sent to prison.) During his time in prison, Debs studied Marxist political economy and became a socialist.

In the 1920s Debs died, the Socialist party split into many warring sects of socialists and communists, and government repression was very severe. The president of the National Association of Manufacturers said, numerous times, that the American trade union movement was an un-American, illegal, and infamous conspiracy of communists and anarchists. After the Bolshevik revolution in Russia, "Innumerable . . . gentlemen now discovered they could defeat whatever they wanted to defeat by tarring it conspicuously with the Bolshevist brush" (Boyer and Morais, p. 204). On January 2, 1920, a *New York Times* banner headline screamed: "200 Reds Taken in Chicago. Wholesale Plot Hatched to Overthrow U.S. Government." That night Attorney General Palmer, who was very probusiness and antilabor, had indeed arrested 10,000 American workers, mostly union members and union leaders, who were taken out of their beds and thrown into prison. They were all charged with being illegal or undesirable aliens and indicted for deportation. As it turned out, about 6,500 were released with no charges at all—they were not aliens but American citizens. The other 3,500 were held for deportation, but the great majority of these also won their cases and were acquitted.

In all of this period, the AFL continued placidly to organize small numbers of skilled, almost all white, mostly male workers. The more militant unions were independent of the AFL—such as the Western Federation of Miners, which in the period 1896–1914 fought to organize the miners of the West. Particularly in Colorado, where the government was "owned" lock, stock, and barrel by the mining and banking interests of the Rockefellers, the miners fought pitched battles against scabs supported by local, state, and even federal troops. There were a number of massacres in which wives and even children of the miners were killed. For a time the Western Federation of Miners was the most important founder and supporter of the International Workers of the World (IWW). The IWW, organized as a rival federation to the AFL, was highly militant, explicitly socialist, and did win some important strikes, such as the strike by (mostly women and children) textile workers in Lawrence, Massachusetts, in 1912. Yet the IWW did not pay enough heed to the immediate needs of the workers, nor to the necessity for routine organizing in an efficient manner at times other than the most red-hot strike situations. So the IWW faded away after a short, but glorious, history.

THE GRAPES OF WRATH AND THE RISE OF THE CIO

The 1920s were a time of little trade union activity and very little radical political activity, partly because of government repression, partly because of splits in the socialist movement, and partly because of a long business upswing with only mild recessions. In 1929, however, the Great Depression began, and it continued through 1930 and 1931 and 1932 and 1933, with only a slight recovery after that, with production reaching the 1929 level only in 1937. World capitalist production fell by 42 percent and U.S. capitalist production by 50 percent between 1929 and 1932. At least 50 million people were unemployed throughout the world, with over one-fourth of the U.S. labor force unemployed, according to official statistics. The capitalist system planted the grapes of wrath in workers and reaped a major expansion of the trade union movement in the United States.

The AFL did very little in the first years of the Great Depression, even coming out against unemployment compensation. For a while the most important organized activity of workers was that of the National Unemployed Council, which had branches all over the United States. Its main activity was the prevention of evictions. Where families could not pay the rent and the police were sent to evict them, members of the local National Unemployed Council would show up to prevent them, as thousands of people determined not to allow such evictions. For example, in the eight months ending June 30, 1932, in New York City, 185,794 families got eviction notices, but about 77,000 of these were moved back into their homes by people from the National Unemployed Council.

Although there were big increases in the votes for the Socialist and Communist parties, the main political event of the 1930s was the election of Franklin Roosevelt and the advent of the New Deal. The New Deal, supported by the labor unions, promoted the Civilian Conservation Corps to give employment to the unemployed. In 1935, it passed the Wagner Act, or National Labor Relations Act, which guaranteed the right to strike and collective bargaining and made illegal some antiunion activities of corporations. In 1938 the New Deal passed the Fair Labor Standards Act, which legislated maximum hours of work and minimum wages.

With some support from the New Deal legislation, workers at first tried to organize in the AFL. But the AFL unions were not interested in or designed to accommodate millions of unskilled workers. Moreover, the employers counterattacked with huge expenditures on propaganda claiming that the trade unions as well as Roosevelt and the New Deal were all part of a communist plot. In addition to propaganda, General Motors, alone, from January 1934 to July 1936 spent $994,855.68 to hire private spies and private police to sabotage and attack the labor unions.

One memorable strike that did occur was that of the longshoremen on the West Coast in 1934. When they first tried to bargain with the employers, the employers simply fired all the union leaders. When the leaders were reinstated by order of the regional labor board, the employers still refused to recognize or bargain with the union. Eventually, about 35,000 maritime workers were out on strike, the center of the strike being the Embarcadero at the port of San Francisco. The strikers wanted pay of $1 an hour and a union hiring hall to replace the usual "shape-up" system whereby employers hired on whim from those who showed up at the docks. On July 3, 1934, the police decided to break the mass picket lines to allow scabs to work. One reporter wrote,

> The police opened fire with revolvers and riot guns. Clouds of tear gas swept the picket lines and sent the men choking in defeat. . . . Squads of police who looked like Martian monsters in their special helmets and gas masks led the way, flinging gas bombs ahead of them. (Quoted in Boyer and Morais, p. 285)

But this was only the preliminary. The pickets returned on July 5 (known as Bloody Thursday), and they were joined by many young people from the high schools and colleges as well as hundreds of other union members. The police charged, using vomiting gas, revolvers with live ammunition, and riot guns. Hundreds were badly wounded and two workers were killed.

The pickets finally were driven away and the employers thought they had won. But many union locals as well as the Alameda Labor Council called for a general strike. In spite of a telegram from the president of the AFL forbidding any strike, the workers of San Francisco launched a general strike to support the longshoremen and in protest against the killings by the police. The general strike was amazingly successful:

> The paralysis was effective beyond all expectation. To all intents and purposes industry was at a complete standstill. The great factories were empty and deserted. No streetcars were running. Virtually all stores were closed. The giant apparatus of commerce was a lifeless, helpless hulk. (Ibid., p. 287)

During the general strike, labor efficiently allowed into the city emergency food and medical supplies, but nothing else. Thousands of troops moved into the city, but there was no violence; labor simply refused to go to work. The general strike lasted until July 19, when the local AFL officials, refusing to hold a roll-call vote of the central labor council, announced that a majority of the council had called off the strike.

After that, however, the longshoremen's pickets were not disturbed, lest the general strike should break out again. The longshoremen had their wages raised to 95 cents an hour and won the union hiring hall. Later, the U.S. Immigration Department tried five times to deport the union leader, Harry Bridges, who had come from Australia, on charges that he lied when he said he was not a communist—but after five long cases, the U.S. Supreme Court finally ruled that all the cases were frame-ups and there was not sufficient evidence that he was a communist.

By 1935 the U.S. government had recognized the right of collective bargaining for most workers, wages were still very low, unemployment was still very high, and millions of workers were in a very militant mood. Many unorganized workers tried to organize new locals of the AFL, but the AFL was not much interested in them, and the very narrow jurisdictional rules of the AFL craft unions made organizing very difficult in the mass industries. Thus, when John L. Lewis pulled out of the AFL and organized a new federation, it was welcomed with open arms. In addition to Lewis and the United Mine Workers, the AFL was left behind by the Typographical Union; the Amalgamated Clothing Workers; the Textile Workers; the Mine, Mill and Smelter Workers; the International Ladies' Garment Workers' and a few other unions. Altogether, some 1 million workers left the AFL to form the Congress of Industrial Organizations (CIO).

There were immediately a number of mass organizing campaigns and strikes, many of them in the new form of the "sit-down." In this form, workers simply sat down in a plant and took it over till their demands were met. The advantage was that scabs could not be brought in unless the workers were forcefully pushed out, but that was difficult without damaging the company's equipment, which most companies were loath to do. On January 29, 1936, at 2 A.M., the rubber workers in Firestone Tire Plant No. 1 in Akron, Ohio, simply pulled the switch to stop the assembly line, and sat down. In three days they won their strike, including union recognition. The wave of sit-down strikes spread rapidly across the nation, partly as a fad, but mostly as a serious new offensive by workers for their rights. Most of the new unions—the Rubber Workers, the Electrical Workers, the Steel Workers, and the United Automobile Workers, each of which became massive unions—went into the CIO. Within a year of its formation, the CIO grew from 1 million to 2 million members. The AFL—and numerous newspapers—denounced the CIO as a communist conspiracy, but nobody paid much attention.

One of the hardest-fought strikes was against the automobile companies in Michigan, where working conditions pushed the men to desperate organization in the summer of 1936:

> During July, a torrid heat wave sent the thermometer boiling to over 100 degrees for a week straight. But the assembly lines pounded away mercilessly while many workers fell at their stations like flies. Death in the state's auto center ran in the hundreds within three or four days . . . (Ibid., p. 299)

The auto companies would not even recognize the unions. The new United Auto Workers struck the main plant of General Motors in Flint, Michigan. On December 30, 1936, the Flint workers staged a sit-down in the plant—as did GM workers in many other plants around the country. But GM had always completely owned the town of Flint, being the only major employer in town. Some GM officials organized vigilante squads, the police cooperated closely with GM, and the courts willingly issued injunctions against the strikers. But the workers held firm in the plant for day after day, their beards growing longer and longer. The hardest fight was by the wives of the strikers, who had to bring in food to them in a running battle against the local and state police. One woman wrote later:

> Motorists had been warned to drive elsewhere. The police stationed themselves around the plant with tear gas and guns. They had gas masks on when the women came with the evening meal. . . . The women began passing the food through the windows. . . . Then came the tear gas. (Quoted in ibid.)

On the worst day, 14 women fell from gunshot wounds, but the food continued to come into the plant.

All of the nation's newspapers said this was a prelude to revolution; they quoted Alfred Sloan, head of GM, who said it was all a communist attempt to Sovietize the auto industry and then the whole country. Enormous pressure was brought to bear on the young liberal governor of Michigan to bring in the National Guard to clear the plant of strikers. At last, he capitulated and went to tell John L. Lewis of his decision, but Lewis reminded him of the governor's own grandfather, who had been an Irish revolutionary. Lewis promised that he himself would go to the plant and be the first to fall from the National Guard's bullets. The governor retreated and finally decided not to use the National Guard. Then, on the forty-fourth day, General Motors surrendered to the strikers' demands (because

Table 19.1   UNION MEMBERSHIP, 1930–1984 (UNION MEMBERS
AS PERCENT OF ALL EMPLOYEES)

Year	Percent unionized	Year	Percent unionized	Year	Percent unionized
1930	11.3	1955	33.2	1970	27.3
1945	35.5	1960	31.4	1980	23.0
1950	31.5	1965	28.4	1984	18.8

Source: U.S. Department of Labor, Bureau of Labor Statistics (Washington, D.C.: GPO), 1988.

their competitors were taking the market away from them). The union was recognized, the speedup was reduced, and wages started to rise from their level of 30 cents an hour.

Soon after, there was an enormous effort to organize the steel industry. After seeing the GM strike, United States Steel gave in and recognized the United Steel Workers union. But Republic Steel held out, using their own police to massacre ten peaceful picketers on Memorial Day 1937. Nevertheless, before long all the steel companies had recognized the union. By 1938 the CIO grew to nearly 4 million members, and even the AFL had awakened enough to begin to seek new members.

Then came World War II, during which the corporations made record profits while thousands of soldiers were dying. Nevertheless, the war did bring full employment and another vast growth in union membership. Women, particularly, flooded into the war industries, and female union membership grew from 800,000 in 1938 to 3,500,000 by the end of 1944.

The overall data on the growth of unions from 1930 to 1984 are shown in Table 19.1. The data show that, excluding agriculture, in which unions have had few members, the percentage of unionized workers was only about 11 percent in 1930. The militant organizing drive of the CIO brought in many millions of unorganized and unskilled workers, raising union membership to about 30 percent of the working population in the late 1930s. The full employment of World War II brought union membership to a high of 35.5 percent in 1945 (after that it declined for the reasons discussed in the following section).

THE COLD WAR AND THE DECLINE AND FALL OF THE CIO

At the end of World War II the prospects for American labor looked very bright. Allied with the Soviet Union, we had won a war against fascism. Our country was filled with democratic, prounion propaganda, and the government was run by a Democratic party, supposedly allied with labor. There had been a great deal of discussion of civil rights in the U.S. government, and black soldiers came home expecting to find equal opportunities. Women had been widely recognized as equal workers, and both parties accepted the Equal Rights Amendment into their platforms. Then a counterattack was launched by all the most antiblack, antiwomen, antilabor, and probusiness forces in the United States.

The main weapon of this attack was the cold war, in which it was said that the one and only threat to Americans came from the Soviet Union and the communist "conspiracy." The first success of this attack was the election of an overwhelmingly conservative Republican Congress in 1946, which immediately passed the very antilabor Taft-Hartley Act, cancelled all rent and price controls, attacked child-care centers as a communist device, and totally ignored the need for civil rights for minorities. One of the main instruments of the antilabor attack was the House Un-American Activities Committee, which helped the Republican party as early as its 1944 anti-Roosevelt presidential campaign by stating, "The political views of the Communist Party and the CIO Political Action Committee coincide in every detail."

Although the Un-American Activities Committee and its supporters had been attacking labor unions as a communist conspiracy ever since 1938, they stepped up the level of their slanders in the period 1946–1948 (and to some extent throughout the 1950s). Every union that showed the slightest militancy immediately had its leaders subpoenaed before the House Un-American Activities Committee—and later before Senator Joe McCarthy's committee.

The Taft-Hartley Act of 1946 must be seen in the context of this cold war against Russians and communists. It restored to courts the power to issue antiunion injunctions. It gave the National Labor Relations Board the right to order a 60-day cooling-off period during which a strike would be illegal. It outlawed mass picketing, the closed shop, and the right of labor to contribute to political campaigns—but gave employers the right to sue unions for "unfair labor practices." And it forced all union leaders to take an anticommunist oath, which meant that they could be sentenced to prison if a jury could be convinced that they were communists. In those days of hysteria, it was easy to get juries to convict alleged communists. For example, Clinton Jencks of the Mine, Mill, and Smelter Union was accused by a stool pigeon of being a communist, tried in a farcical trial, and sentenced to five years in prison. It required many years of legal fighting, during which Jencks suffered both personally and as a union organizer who could no longer help the union, before the U.S. Supreme Court held many aspects of the trial and "evidence" to be insufficient and unconstitutional. This was the experience of many thousands of Americans who lost their jobs or careers because they were too strongly prolabor and had been labeled "communist" by some committee or prosecutor (the FBI even went around asking employers, "Did you know that Mr. X is a communist?").

Under this kind of red-baiting pressure, the CIO finally caved in and split. In 1948 the CIO leadership issued an order that all of their unions must vote for Harry Truman and the Democratic party or risk expulsion, though many of the CIO unions had already declared for the new Progressive party. As a result, by 1949 the CIO expelled all unions suspected of leaning to the left: the United Electrical Workers; the International Longshoremen's Union; the Mine, Mill, and Smelter Workers; and seven other unions. Union activists realized that they had better be silent or be expelled by the CIO or smeared by Senator McCarthy or by the House Un-American Activities Committee.

In this situation not only the independent unions, but also the AFL and the CIO, all lost members. Most union leaders became very timid and/or corrupt and/or collaborated with the management. The AFL and CIO merged in 1955, but even this merger did not restore their strength or vigor; it merely marked the end of the militant CIO. Thereafter, total union membership fell from 35.5 percent of the nonagricultural labor force in 1945 to only 18.8 percent in 1984. The loss of bargaining strength— with a lower percentage of the labor force enrolled in unions—helps explain the weakening position of labor versus capital.

SUMMARY

Income distribution in the United States is very unequal. It is not just a matter of the impersonal forces of supply and demand but of the very direct personal confrontation of workers and employers as part of those forces. The history of labor unions in the United States has been very violent. There were few unions till the Civil War and the industrialization following it. The most important labor organization for many decades was the American Federation of Labor, which mainly organized highly skilled, white, male workers and left most of the labor force unorganized. During the New Deal of the 1930s, the situation changed enough that the Congress of Industrial Organizations (CIO) was able to organize millions of new workers. All unions grew during World War II. Then in the following period of repression against so-called "communists," the labor movement split and declined, and the percentage of union members has been declining ever since, although some signs of renewed militancy have appeared in the unions in the 1980s.

SUGGESTED READINGS

A very thorough, but always exciting, history is Philip S. Foner, *History of the Labor Movement in the United States* (New York: International Publishers, several volumes, 1947–1980). The nature of the labor process and labor markets is revealed in Richard Edwards, Michael Reich, and David Gordon (eds.), *Labor Market Segmentation* (Lexington, Mass.: Heath, 1978).

REFERENCES

Boyer, Richard O., and Herbert M. Morais. *Labor's Untold Story.* 1st ed., 1955; 3d ed., 1970. New York: United Electrical, Radio, and Machine Workers of America.

Foner, Philip S. *History of the Labor Movement in the United States.* New York, International Publishers, several volumes; first volume, 1947.

Chapter
20

Monopoly Power

The world of numerous, small competitive capitalist enterprises, which Adam Smith thought would produce the best possible economic system, is gone forever (if it ever existed). Since the period of the 1890s and early 1900s, western Europe and the United States have been characterized by the domination of a relatively few giant firms. This new stage of concentration and centralization of corporate power has not ended capitalism, but it has intensified many old qualities and added some entirely new and unpleasant features. In this new stage of capitalism the setting of prices and outputs may be quite different from what occurs under competition. The amount of waste, manipulation of the consumer, limitation of the worker's wages, and conflict between the search for profits and the furthering of social needs (such as the need for a decent environment) exist on entirely new scales.

THE TREND OF CONCENTRATION

In a purely competitive economy each competing business unit would be so small that its actions taken alone could not appreciably influence the quality of goods or the price in the market. Such, more or less, was the U.S. economy during the early nineteenth century. Small farms and small businesses produced most of the output, and there were no giant corporations dominating an entire industry (though there were many local monopolies). As late as 1860 there were still no incorporated business firms in many of the major urban industrial centers. Since that time the picture has changed drastically.

The size of corporations rose rapidly in the post-Civil War period. By 1900 the share of manufacturing output produced by corporations had grown to two-thirds. Some of the big corporations developed by virtue of rapid internal growth; others arose through mergers of formerly independent firms.

Mergers have come in waves. The first massive movement, which lasted from the early 1890s to the outbreak of World War I, was characterized by *horizontal* mergers, in which a big corporation absorbed other corporations that were its direct competitors. The result of such mergers was of course industries dominated by fewer and much larger corporations. The second wave came in the 1920s. It was characterized by *vertical* mergers, occurring between firms producing goods in sequence, as when a giant corporation absorbs its suppliers or absorbs the firms to which it sells its output. The 1960s witnessed a third and unique wave. Most of these mergers were of the *conglomerate* variety, in which a giant corporation absorbs other corporations that have no relation to its primary product line. The aim is simply to establish a colossal corporate empire that will give its controllers immense economic and political power.

From 1950 through 1959 there was an average of 540 corporate mergers a year. From 1960 through 1967 the average was 1100 a year. In 1968 there were 2655 mergers. More and more of these were conglomerate mergers between giants in different industries. From 1948 through 1953 conglomerate mergers accounted for 59 percent of the total. From 1960 through 1965 they comprised 72 percent of the total. In 1968 conglomerate mergers accounted for 84 percent of all mergers. Throughout the Reagan administration, the strongly probusiness, *laissez-faire* attitude led to a vertical mushrooming of mergers and corporate buyouts of other corporations. All evidence points to the 1980s as being, perhaps, the most dramatically rapid increase in industrial concentration in American history. As yet we know of no reliable studies that accurately quantify the extent of that increase.

The enormous size and power of the 100 largest conglomerates may be seen in the data on how many large firms in each separate industry are under their control. "In more than half of the 1014 product classes in manufacturing as a whole, at least one of the 100 largest was among the 4 largest producers, and in 31 percent at least 2 came from the 100 largest. It is thus obvious that the 100 largest companies are not limited in their operations to only a few large-scale industries but rather are broadly represented among the largest producers of manufacturing products throughout most of the wide spectrum of U.S. industry" (Blair, pp. 53–54).

Today there are millions of very small industrial enterprises, but a few hundred corporate giants hold most of the wealth and do most of the producing. Table 20.1 reveals the extremely high concentration of corporate assets in comparatively few firms. At the bottom, a large number of small corporations held a minuscule portion of total corporate assets. At the top, a few giant corporations hold 75 percent of all assets. The fact that some

Table 20.1   DISTRIBUTION OF CORPORATE ASSETS (ALL U.S. CORPORATIONS, 1984)

Size (in assets)	Corporations (number in group)	Corporations (percent in size group)	Assets (percent owned by group)	Assets (billions owned by group)
$0–100,000	1,773,719	56%	0.5	$ 56
100,000–500,000	811,649	29	1.9	209
500,000–5,000,000	420,417	13	5.1	571
5,000,000–250,000,000	68,591	2	17.3	1,916
250,000,000 and over	3,663	0.12	75.2	8,355
Total	3,078,039	100.12%[a]	100%	11,107 billion

Source: U.S. Internal Revenue Service, Statistics of Income. Corporation Income Tax Returns July 1983–June 1984 (Washington, D.C.: GPO, 1987).

[a] Data add to more than 100 percent because of rounding.

3663 U.S. corporations hold well over $8 trillion in assets is incredible; such an amount is more than the total value of all western European assets. Among those 3663 corporations there is even a greater concentration within just the top 200 or 300 corporations.

The figures for all corporations average out differences in various sectors. In the important sector of banking alone, for example, there are approximately 13,775 commercial banks, but a mere 14 of them hold 25 percent of all deposits, and the 100 largest banks hold 46 percent of all deposits (House Committee on Banking and Currency, p. 15).

Another function of banks is to hold assets in trust for individuals and corporations. Banks exercise the voting power for these stocks, which gives them immense power without having legal ownership. Forty-nine of the largest banks hold over 5 percent of the common stock in 147 of the 500 largest industrial corporations in the United States. They also hold at least 5 percent of the common stock in 17 of the largest companies in the fields of merchandising and transportation. These banks are represented in the boards of directors of the majority of the largest corporations in the fields of manufacturing, merchandising, utilities, transportation, and insurance.

Finally, let us turn to the decisive sector of manufacturing taken alone. In the general category of manufacturing enterprises, there were 180,000 corporations and 240,000 unincorporated businesses in 1962 (Mueller, pp. 111–129). Ninety-eight percent of all manufacturing assets were owned by the corporations. Of the 420,000 manufacturing firms, the 20 largest (not 20,000, but 20!) owned 25 percent of total assets of manufacturing firms. The largest 50 firms owned 36 percent, and the largest 200 owned 56 percent. If adjustment is made for giant firms that are owned by even larger giants (i.e., if their ownership is added together), we arrive at a much higher percentage of control. The fact is that, after adjustment for ownership of subsidiaries, a mere 100 firms owned 58 percent of the net capital assets of all the hundreds of thousands of manufacturing corporations. Another index of the imbalance of economic power is the fact that the largest 20 manufacturing firms owned a larger share of the assets than the smallest 419,000 firms combined.

When profits earned are examined, the contrast is even more striking. The net profits of the five largest corporations were about twice as large as those of the 178,000 smallest corporations combined. In order to appreciate the size of these giants, consider just one of them, General Motors. "General Motors' yearly operating revenues exceed those of all but a dozen or so countries. Its sales receipts are greater than the combined general revenues of New York, New Jersey, Pennsylvania, Ohio, Delaware, and the six New England states. . . . G.M. employees number well over 700,000 and work in 127 plants in the United States and 45 countries spanning Europe, South Africa, North America, and Australia. The total cash wages are more than twice the personal income of Ireland" (Barber, p. 20).

If the individual industries that are the arenas of most direct competition are examined, the picture of economic concentration may be even more sharply drawn than in the aggregate data. Let an *industry* be defined so that there is easy substitution among the products of all firms within it, and very little possible substitution with products of outside firms. In most industries, three or four giant monopolistic firms control most of the production, and most of these top firms, as shown above, are part of the 100 largest conglomerates. Many small firms also exist in most industries, but altogether they produce a small percentage of the total output. U.S. government data for 1963, adjusted slightly for more precise market definition, showed that 39.6 percent of all industries were moderately concentrated— that is, had 50 percent or more of their product sold by four companies (Blair, p. 14).

Moreover, among the top companies are many interlocking directorates. In 1965, the 250 largest corporations had a total of 4007 directorships, but these were held by just 3165 directors (ibid., p. 76). Among these directors, 562 men each held two or more directorships, and 5 men held six each! Other studies have traced control to eight main groups: three that each held large blocs of stock in several corporations were Rockefeller, Mellon, and Du Pont; two that held financial control over several corporations were Morgan-First National and Kuhn-Loeb; three were groups known for their local control in the cities of Boston, Chicago, and Cleveland. In addition, as seen earlier, there is now formal control by large conglomerates (themselves usually part of one of the major interest groups) of top corporations in each of several industries.

Since 1950, one out of every five of the 1000 largest manufacturing companies has been swallowed by an even larger giant. Since 1959 big business has been absorbing other business firms with $410 million or more in assets at a rate exceeding 60 a year. In 1966, 101 companies, each with assets of more than $10 million, were absorbed by other companies; in 1967 the number was 169; in 1968 it was 192. Obviously oligopolistic business giants are far from satisfied with the immense size and power they already have. Nothing leads us to believe that these mushrooming industrial empires are about to discontinue merging.

The economy of the United States has thus changed from a predominantly competitive to a highly concentrated system of production. The corporations are still growing through conglomerate mergers of giants in different industries. The apparent degree of concentration may not change in each industry, but the same conglomerate may now control a large firm in each of many industries. Thus the data on particular industries, which indicate that the shares of the three or four largest have not increased much for several years, severely understate the trend toward concentration of power in the 100 largest manufacturing firms.

THE REASONS FOR MONOPOLY

One fundamental cause of the emergence of the giant corporation is the economies of scale that can be derived from large production units that turn out cheaper goods by using more specialized machinery, more specialized workers, and mass-production assembly lines. Small firms are driven out of business by the cheap goods produced through large-scale applications of technology. The large firm gains a monopoly by selling at a lower price while making more profit.

In addition to improved technology based on the economies of scale, there is another reason for the greater profitability of some huge firms such as General Motors. These firms grow internally or via merger far beyond the technologically necessary minimum because they wish to exercise monopoly power over the market. With small competitors eliminated or dominated, the few remaining giant firms can restrict output and set higher prices or make higher rates of profit.

The giant firms attempt to eliminate risk and uncertainty, not only by controlling their own industry's output, but also by (1) buying out raw material suppliers, (2) buying out dealers and outlets for the finished product, (3) using vast nationwide advertising, and (4) linking up with banks and other financial sources. With these motivations there is no clear upper limit to desirable size. The motto seems to be "the bigger the better."

PRICES AND PROFIT MAXIMIZATION

What is the effect of monopoly on the price structure? The essence of the monopolist's position is the ability to keep competitors out of the market by means of greater efficiency, control of natural or financial resources, control of patents, or any other legal or illegal methods. Thus prices can be as high as the market will bear, and there is no competitive mechanism to bring the higher profit back down to the average rate of profit in industry as a whole. We shall see in Chapters 21 and 22 that monopolies receive a much higher profit for a lower output than do competitive firms. The number of pure monopolies in the U.S. economy is rather small, however. We shall see in Chapter 23 that most U.S. business firms operate in monopolistic competitive industries and that most highly concentrated industries are oligopolies.

The quest for greater size, for control over dealers and outlets, for nationwide markets and for more political influence are all motivated by the general desire for more profits and more economic, social, and political power. But as one or two firms in a given industry gain more power there is a tendency for others to follow suit. In this way, the firms in an industry must constantly expand in order to remain competitive. Moreover, when a few firms succeed in destroying most of their rivals, as they did in the U.S. automobile industry between 1910 and 1960, and thereby succeed in getting oligopolistic and monopolistic super-profits, the markets are most generally attacked by their foreign competitors. Thus, just as General Motors, Ford, and Chrysler were succeeding in gaining control of the American automobile market in the 1960s, the German, Japanese, and other foreign competitors began to make important inroads in the market. Thus, most giant corporations operate in either monopolistically competitive or oligopolistic industries. We will discuss output and pricing in these industries in Chapter 23.

One of the great advantages of size is the diversification of risk and the ability to sustain temporary losses in some plants or take other actions that are not necessarily dictated by the short-run quest for maximum profits. This flexibility makes possible the calculated pursuit of maximum long-run profits. Contrary to our view, many economists claim that modern businessmen do not always attempt to maximize profits. The capitalist today, however, is not the individual businessperson but the corporation. Whether the businessperson is rational and calculating in private life is essentially irrelevant to the functioning of the system. In corporate decisions there can be no doubt that the generation and accumulation of profit hold as dominant a position today as they ever did. Like the individual enterprise of an earlier period, the giant corporation is an engine for maximizing profits, but it is not merely an enlarged version of the personal capitalist. There are two differences: (1) The corporation has a much longer time horizon, and (2) it is a much more rational calculator (see Earley, pp. 333–335).

Having said that much, it is important to avoid a dogmatic notion that every corporate decision is made in terms of immediate dollars-and-cents returns. As we have stated, very large corporations can afford to sacrifice short-run profits to ensure the security of their market control, to spur company growth, and to follow any other short-run policy that seems advantageous in the long run. Thus prices are not always set as high as the market will bear. It could be said that management maximizes a multiple set of objectives. Equally well (because the difference is only semantic), it could be emphasized that each of the other objectives is merely a rational way to achieve maximum long-run profits, which are the real sole objective.

WHO CONTROLS THE CORPORATION?

Liberals agree that monopoly is an evil aspect of capitalism, but they believe in a remedy short of eliminating capitalism. Some rely on stricter enforcement of antitrust laws. Others admit that these laws have clearly proved inadequate and advocate stricter laws. Still others claim that a process of internal change in giant corporations is automatically eliminating most of capitalism's negative qualities. John Kenneth Galbraith is the leading spokeman of the latter view.

Galbraith maintains that there is a great contradiction between the notion that the modern corporation is controlled by the management and the fact that it nevertheless ruthlessly tries to maximize profits for its stockholders. Furthermore, he argues that the most important factor of production is no longer capital but the specialized talents of scientists and technologists, and that real power passes from stockholders and top management to the members of the *technostructure*—that is, the technical personnel, including scientists and technicians. According to Galbraith, the members of the technostructure do not receive the profits they are supposed to maximize. Because the technostructure supplies talent, rather than capital, of what concern to them is the return to capital? He says that the modern corporation has the capacity to shape society, but its resources are used to serve the deeper interests or goals of the technostructure, which possesses the real power (Galbraith, 1967, chaps. 5–8).

Galbraith agrees that a few hundred giant corporations control the market, regulate output and prices, and exercise enormous political control. Yet, with a wave of the hand he eliminates the corporate executive and puts the control of the corporation in the hands of scientists and technically skilled workers. He then finds that the technostructure really manages the corporation and that, for their own reasons, they manage it in the best interests of all of society. In other words, Galbraith is very critical of capitalism, especially of the tremendous centralization of the means of production, but nevertheless is apologetic in the sense that he concludes that the industrial system has actually solved (or is in the process of solving) its problem.

The radical view is that Galbraith ignores the real position of modern corporate management. In the first place, the fact that so many top executives hold stock means their motivations cannot possibly be inconsistent with profit seeking. For example, in early 1957, 25 managers of General Motors owned an average of 11,500 shares each (Kolko, p. 13). They might not be able to affect policy even with that amount of stock in General Motors, yet each owned roughly $500,000 in the company, so it is improbable that any of them were indifferent to profits. Further, among stockholders there are more managers than representatives of any other group, and a larger proportion of managers own stock than any other group.

Galbraith, of course, argues that it is not the motivation of the managers but the motivation of the technostructure that is decisive. Radicals counter that the goals of the technostructure are the same as those of the managers—survival of the firm, growth, and independence from outside control. All these demand profit-making activity. More important, it flies in the face of reality to believe that the technicians control the corporations. The managers hire and fire the technicians, not vice versa. In the end it is the boss rather than the hired hand who makes the decisions (and uses expert advice only to make more profitable decisions).

INDUSTRIAL CONCENTRATION AND WASTE

To some extent, large firms are more efficient because of economies of scale. Production cannot reach optimum efficiency below a certain quantity of output. The fact that large firms account for most U.S. output means that most of the economy is able to produce at lower costs than ever before. Studies of cost data reveal the possibility of high efficiency at a fairly constant level beyond the necessary minimum scale of production. Of course, because the very large firms also have disproportionately larger research facilities and control a very large percentage of all unexpired patents, they have the greatest potential for increasing efficiency. Moreover, many investment projects require resources beyond the means of small firms.

But the large, entrenched firm stands to lose most from the obsolescence of present machinery and from product improvements that reduce the number of units the customer needs to buy—for example, a longer-lasting light bulb. Therefore if the large firm has an oligopolistic position and faces no serious competitive pressure for improvement, it may develop and patent but not use important inventions. Thus monopoly power has a paradoxical effect on innovation. Giant firms have a rapid rate of technological progress, but they retain a large amount of technologically obsolete equipment.

Monopoly power may also be used to restrict supply in order to raise prices. Thus, as is seen in Chapter 36, monopoly power is one of the principal causes of inflation. Monopolies will expand production as rapidly as possible only in extraordinary periods of unlimited demand. This usually occurs only when government demand skyrockets, as in World War II. In wartime, monopolies can cease restricting output but still charge prices as high as the government will allow.

Moreover, as is also shown in Chapter 36, the existence of economic concentration may have increased the severity and possibly the number of depressions because of (1) its destabilizing effects on remaining small businesses and (2) its lowering of workers' ability to consume. This is another reason why the net effect of monopoly seems to be a reduction in the rate of economic growth.

On the other hand, breaking up large firms into smaller units would probably not increase economic growth. Reducing the American economy to small firms would certainly cause a major decrease in economic efficiency because of the loss of economies of scale—and most likely would have a negative effect on investment. It is impossible to go backward to a competitive small business economy; the only answer seems to be to go forward to public and workers' control of the giant corporations.

The rate of growth (and waste) under monopoly is also affected by the fact that the sales effort has greatly expanded. Once a relatively unimportant feature of the system, sales effort has become one of its most important nerve centers. In fact, the impact of advertising and related expenditures on the economy is surpassed only by that of militarism. In all other aspects of social existence, the influence of advertising is second to none. In an economic system in which competition is fierce and relentless, but in which the small number of rivals rules out price cutting, advertising becomes to an ever-increasing extent the principal weapon of the competitive struggle. Under atomistic competition there is little room for advertising; in monopoly it is perhaps the most important factor in the firm's survival.

Relatively large firms are in a position to exercise a powerful influence on the market for their output by establishing and maintaining a pronounced difference between their products and those of their competitors. This differentiation is sought chiefly by means of advertising, trademarks, brand names, distinctive packaging, and product variation. If successful, it leads to a condition in which consumers believe that slightly different products can no longer serve as substitutes for each other.

Advertising involves a massive waste of resources, a continual drain on the consumer's income, and a systematic destruction of the consumer's freedom of choice between genuine alternatives. Furthermore, advertising in all its aspects cannot be meaningfully dealt with as some undesirable excrescence on the economic system that could be removed if we would only make up our minds to get rid of it. Advertising is the very offspring of the monopoly form of capitalism, the inevitable by-product of the decline of price competition: It constitutes as integral a part of the system as the giant corporation itself. The economic importance of advertising lies partly in its causing a reallocation of consumers' expenditures among different commodities. Even more important, however, is its effect on the magnitude of aggregate effective demand and thus on the level of income and employment. In other words, it generates useless expenditures by consumers, who relieve the monopoly of part of its overproduction by spending money beyond their direct needs.

Advertising affects profits in two ways. First, part of advertising and other selling expenses are underwritten through an increase in the prices of consumer goods bought by productive workers. Total profit is maintained by the higher prices, but workers' real wages are reduced by this amount.

The other, more complicated effect is that the profits and wages some capitalists and workers make from the business of advertising constitute an expense for other capitalists. This component of the outlays on advertising and sales effort does not constitute an increase in total profit but does cause its redistribution. Some individuals living off profit are deprived of a fraction of their incomes in order to support other individuals living off profit—namely, those who derive their incomes from advertising itself.

Furthermore, in making it possible to create the demand for a product, advertising encourages investment in plant and equipment that otherwise would not take place. The effect of advertising on the division of total income between consumption and saving is not measurable but is clear in direction and probably very large. The function of advertising, perhaps its dominant function today, is to wage a relentless war on behalf of the producers and sellers of consumer goods against saving and in favor of consumption.

Actually much of the "newness" with which the consumer is systematically bombarded is either fraudulent or related trivially, and in many cases even negatively, to the function and serviceability of the product. Moreover, other products are introduced that are indeed new in design and appearance but serve essentially the same purposes as old products they are intended to replace. The extent of the difference can vary across an entire spectrum from a simple modification in packaging to the far-reaching and enormously expensive annual changes in automobile models.

In addition, most research and development programs, which constitute a multibillion-dollar effort in the United States, are more closely related to the production of salable goods than to their much-touted mission of advancing science and technology. For example, if monopoly profit and dealers' markups were excluded, then the real cost of production of the 1945 automobile, built with the technology of 1975, would have been far less than it was in 1945. The big three automakers have always spent enormous sums on changes in automobile styles each year that are of no use to consumers but help sell more cars. The total waste from all the time and effort devoted directly and indirectly to selling products under monopoly must considerably lower the rate of economic growth.

Not only does monopoly greatly increase the waste of capitalism, but it also raises pollution and environmental destruction to a new level. In the competitive model, apologists could claim that consumer preference dictated what was produced and therefore that pollution was merely an unfortunate by-product of the demands of the public. The apologists argued that these unfortunate by-products of public preference could be handled by some minor public action to beautify the environment. Under monopoly, such apologies are no longer possible; it is clear that consumer preference is manipulated toward whatever products are most profitable to produce; therefore, "environmental damage becomes a normal consequence of the conflict between the goals of the producing firm and those of the public" (Galbraith, 1967, p. 477).

So far, only the civilian wastes and peacetime pollution caused by monopoly have been considered. The full effect of monopoly power, however, depends on its political influence (see Chapter 24), its close relationship with the military (see Chapter 33), and its vast international spread (see Chapters 40 and 41).

SUMMARY

In several waves of mergers since the late 1890s, the American economy has been converted from one of numerous small competitive industrial enterprises to one dominated by giant corporations. In each industry three or four corporations together make the decisive output, investment, and pricing decisions. All small businesses together produce a small percentage of total output and receive an even smaller percentage of profits. The high degree of concentration increases instability and unemployment in at least two ways. First, driven to the wall, small businesses reduce employment and sometimes set off depressions; they may also go bankrupt, thus worsening the depression. Second, the giant corporations keep their own prices and profits high by restricting the supply of output and further reducing employment.

Giant firms increase their prices rapidly during prosperity, causing inflation by pushing profits up through the use of monopoly power over the market. Since the 1950s, they have even had the power to continue to raise prices during recessions (though more slowly than during expansions). The giant firms also mount enormous advertising campaigns, wasting vast resources in an attempt to prove that their products are better than others. Finally, the giant firms contribute pollution to the air, land, and sea; it is simply not profitable to spend their money on purifying devices for their industrial processes or for their consumer products, such as cars.

SUGGESTED READINGS

The fullest data on monopoly power are in John Blair, *Economic Concentration* (New York: Harcourt Brace Jovanovich, 1977). The relation of monopoly to private waste and government waste is explored in Paul Sweezy and Paul Baran, *Monopoly Capital* (New York: Monthly Review Press, 1967).

REFERENCES

Bain, J. S. "Price and Production Policies." In *A Survey of Contemporary Economics.* Edited by Howard S. Ellis. New York: McGraw-Hill, 1948.

Barber, Richard. *The American Corporation.* New York: Dutton, 1970.

Blair, John. *Economic Concentration.* New York: Harcourt Brace Jovanovich, 1972.

Earley, James. "The Impact of Some New Developments in Economic Theory Discussion." In *American Economic Review*, May 1957.

Federal Reserve Bank of Cleveland. *Economic Commentary*. May 12, 1969.

Galbraith, John K. *The New Industrial State*. Boston: Houghton Mifflin, 1967.

————. "Economics as a System of Relief." In *American Economic Review*, May 1970.

Kolko, Gabriel. *Wealth and Power in America*. New York: Praeger, 1962.

Mueller, Willard F. "Economic Concentration." In *Hearings Before the Subcommittee on Antitrust and Monopoly of the Committee on the Judiciary, United States Senate, 88th Congress, 2nd Session, Part I: Overall and Conglomerate Aspects*. Washington, D.C.: GPO, July 1964.

U.S. Bureau of the Census. *1963 Census of Manufactures*. In: Blair, John. *Economic Concentration*.

U.S. Department of Commerce. "Concentration Ratios in Manufacturing." In *1972 Census of Manufacturing*. Washington, D.C.: GPO, 1975.

U.S. House of Representatives, Committee on Banking and Currency. *Commercial Banks and Their Trust Activities*. Washington, D. C.: GPO, July 1968.

Chapter
21

Prices and Profits in Pure Competition

In the preceding chapter we said that monopolies are able to charge higher prices and to reap higher profits than competitive business firms. This implies, of course, that the processes of price formation are different among different enterprises depending on the number and strength of their competitors.

For many years traditional economic thinkers assumed that the majority of business firms operated within what they called *purely competitive* industries (which we shall define below). Monopolies were generally treated as isolated, exceptional cases. This method of analyzing the process of price formation had particularly great ideological advantages for conservative thinkers, because it is only when one assumes that the majority of businesses are purely competitive that one can derive the conservative implications of the utility theory—implications that were summarized in Appendix C to Chapter 16.

Because of this ideological advantage many conservative economists continue to this day to use the analysis of pure competition as the theory of prices applicable to the majority of businesses. Yet this analysis, as we shall see, is based on excessively restrictive or empirically unrealistic assumptions. Consequently, many economists now differentiate between pure competition and "imperfect competition." Imperfect competition is generally broken down into three categories, or three types of market structures: monopolistic competition, oligopoly, and monopoly. Adding pure competition to these three market structures we arrive at four theories of price determination based on four types of market structures. We shall see that the market structures are defined according to the nature and extent of the competition a firm faces in each structure.

In this chapter we discuss pricing and profit maximization in a purely competitive market structure. In Chapter 22 we discuss the same aspects for a monopolistic market structure, and in Chapter 23 for monopolistically competitive and oligopolistic market structures. At the outset we should state that very few firms operate in a situation of pure competition or of monopoly, so analysis of these situations is not realistic for understanding most pricing procedures. Nearly all businesses in the United States today are in either monopolistically competitive or oligopolistic industries. Yet it remains important to understand pure competition and monopoly. The importance of understanding the analysis of pure competition is largely ideological. Among conservatives, this analysis is (depending on the forthrightness of the conservative) either depicted as the actual state of affairs or as the desired or ideal state of affairs. The analysis of monopoly is important because, as we shall see in Chapter 23, even though there are very few actual firms that fit the usual definition of a monopoly, nevertheless, most oligopolistic firms operate to some degree as though they are monopolies.

MARKET STRUCTURES AND THE DEGREE OF COMPETITION

A *purely competitive industry* is one in which four essential conditions are present: (1) The industry is made up of a very large number of firms, and there is also a large number of buyers of the produce they sell. (2) Each seller supplies so small a percentage of the market that its actions have virtually no effect on the price at which the industry sells the product. Each buyer demands so small a percentage of output that the buyer's purchases alone also have virtually no effect on the price at which the industry sells the product. (3) It is very easy for new firms to enter the industry or for old firms to leave it. (4) Each firm produces a product that is so nearly identical to the product of the other firms that consumers are largely indifferent about which firm within the industry produced the product they buy.

A *monopoly* exists when there is only one seller of a product that has no close substitutes. In a monopolistic industry one firm *is* the industry. If the monopolist's position is to be maintained, it must erect barriers that prevent competitors from entering the industry. If it is successful in doing this, the payoff is generally very large. Because it has complete control over the price of its product (within the limits set by the demand schedule), it can set the price at the level that will maximize profits. We shall discuss monopoly pricing in Chapter 22.

Between the extremes of pure competition and monopoly, economists make two further classifications. Closer to pure competition is *monopolistic competition*. A monopolistically competitive industry has a large number of small sellers who engage in some slight amount of *product differentiation*.

A product may be differentiated in various ways; for example, one seller packages the product more attractively or gives friendlier service. In any event, some consumers prefer one or another particular seller's product. For this reason, firms have a small degree of control over price, and a firm cannot enter the industry as easily as it can enter a purely competitive industry.

Closer to a monopoly (and often tantamount to it) is an *oligopoly*. An oligopolistic industry has a few giant sellers, each of which controls a significant share of the market. Entry into an oligopolistic industry is very difficult, often as difficult as entry into a monopolistic industry. There is generally, but not always, some product differentiation. The most significant feature of an oligopoly is the fact that, because of the interdependence of its members, no firm can make significant changes in price without taking into account the reactions of its competitors.

The analyses of monopolistic competition and oligopoly include, within their definition, nearly all of the business firms in the United States today. We will discuss these market structures in Chapter 23. For the remainder of this chapter, we turn our attention to the discussion of pure competition.

DEMAND AND PRICE FOR A PURELY COMPETITIVE FIRM

For a whole industry, a larger amount can be sold only at a lower price (or lower average revenue). This is not the case for a single competitive firm. In a purely competitive industry, each firm is so small that whatever quantity it chooses to sell will have a negligible effect on the supply for the entire industry. Therefore, it can sell all that it wishes at the going price.

The situation for a purely competitive industry and one firm within that industry is demonstrated graphically in Figure 21.1. Figure 21.1(A) shows the supply and demand for coats, which is assumed to be a purely competitive industry. Figure 21.1(B) shows the price curve (or demand curve, since they are the same in this case) for the individual coat-making firm.

The price of a coat ($100) is determined in the industrywide market for coats by the intersection of the industry supply and demand curves. The graph shows that *at this price the individual firm can sell any quantity it wishes.* It has been assumed that the individual firm cannot affect supply for the entire industry, and that the market demand is equal to the supply at the prevailing price ($100). Therefore, the firm never experiences any problem in selling all it wishes to sell at this price.

As a result, the demand curve for the individual firm's output is a horizontal line at the industry-determined price. The firm sells any quantity it chooses at this price. Let us assume that it decides to raise its price in order to increase its revenue. Because all the firms in a purely competitive industry produce an identical product, no consumer will pay more than $100 for one firm's product when he or she can buy an identical product from a competitor for $100. Similarly, the firm will never sell any quantity

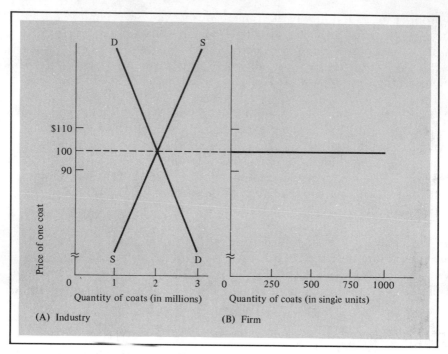

Figure 21.1 Supply and demand for coats.

at a price below $100. Because it can sell any quantity it chooses at $100, there would be no incentive for it to lower the price. Thus the firm in a purely competitive industry faces a given price; it cannot vary it upward and it does not wish to vary it downward. (The situation is very different for a monopoly.)

SUPPLY AND THE COSTS OF PRODUCTION

A firm's decision regarding the quantity of its product that it wishes to supply at various prices will depend, to a large extent, on the costs of producing different quantities. In this section we shall analyze the firm's cost during the short run, when its output is limited to the productive capacity of its current plant and equipment. Over a longer period the firm could construct a larger plant and install new equipment, thus expanding its scale of operations; but for the shorter period considered here, these capital goods are fixed in size and number.

Because the amount of a firm's plant and equipment is fixed in the short run, some of its costs must be considered fixed whether it produces nothing or operates at capacity. *Fixed costs* include the maintenance of plant and equipment, rent, and salaries of watchmen, caretakers, and others. Obviously, if the firm produces more goods, then the *average* fixed cost will decline because the same cost is spread over, or divided by, more units.

Even during the short run, however, some costs—notably those of labor and material—are variable. The firm can produce more or less of its product by hiring more or fewer workers and using more or less raw materials.

The *average* variable cost for a unit of output is obtained by taking the total cost of labor and raw materials and dividing it by the quantity produced. If one laborer combined with a given amount of raw materials produced ten coats, and if each additional laborer combined with the same amount of raw materials continued to produce ten coats, then the average variable cost per unit produced would remain the same regardless of the amount the firm produced. The average-variable-cost curve would be a straight horizontal line, showing that the quantity of coats produced had no effect on its magnitude.

This situation does not obtain in most types of productive processes. Generally the firm's plant and equipment have been designed and constructed to operate most effectively at a particular level of output. The production of a single commodity usually involves numerous production processes, which occur at different rates and are difficult to coordinate. For maximum efficiency no single process should be halted or stopped because it is moving faster than the other processes, nor should other processes be stopped because this process cannot keep pace.

After engineers have calculated the various rates at which the different productive processes will take place, the plant is constructed and equipped in such a way that there is some *optimal* level of production at which all production processes can be effectively coordinated. Average variable costs are lowest at the optimum level of production, but higher both below and above that level.

Because average fixed costs fall continuously, the total result is that average cost per unit may fall rapidly at first and continue to fall until the optimal point is achieved; then average cost may slowly rise. This usual short-run behavior of average costs (a U-shaped curve) is illustrated in Figure 21.2.

According to Figure 21.2, the quantity of 1000 coats is the production level at which all production processes are most effectively coordinated and plant and equipment are most efficiently utilized (the cost is only $75 per coat). At smaller quantities, bottlenecks occur and some equipment is *underutilized;* consequently, average costs are higher. At larger quantities, plant and equipment are being *overutilized* and various other bottlenecks and inefficiencies are encountered; consequently, average costs are higher. The further a firm moves from the optimally efficient quantity (1000 coats in this case), the higher its average costs are. This is true whether the firm produces smaller or larger quantities than the optimal amount.

Because it is the basis of the supply curve, marginal cost is even more important than average cost. *Marginal cost* is defined as follows:

$$\text{Marginal cost} = \frac{\text{increase in total cost}}{\text{increase in quantity}}$$

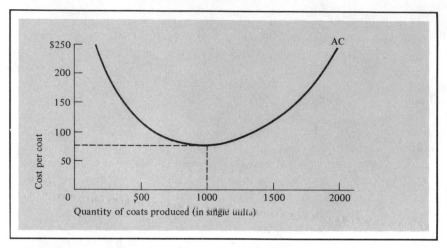

Figure 21.2 Average cost (AC) of coats.

Because we may speak of decrease as well as increase, we may substitute the word *change* for *increase* in the definition to make it more general.

In Figure 21.3, marginal cost represents the increase in total costs of production attributable to an increase in output of one additional coat. If the change in cost attributable to producing one more coat is lower than the average cost of producing the product, then it may be said that the lower marginal cost is pulling the average cost downward. This is similar to the case of a person taking several tests. The last test score pulls the average score up or down, depending on whether it is higher or lower than the average. Thus it is possible to conclude that as long as the average cost is declining, the marginal cost must be below it. When the average cost is rising, the marginal cost must be above it, pulling it upward. These relations between the average and marginal are illustrated in Figure 21.3.

Notice that at low production levels, those at which each additional coat is produced at less cost, marginal cost is very low (only $25 at 500 coats) and is well below the average. But at production beyond the optimal capacity, when the average cost of producing coats is rising, marginal cost rises rapidly to a high level ($150 at 1500 coats) and goes higher and higher above the average as more coats are produced.

These mechanical relations may be summarized as follows: (1) average cost is at its minimum when it is equal to marginal cost; (2) when marginal cost is below average cost, it is pulling average cost downward; (3) when marginal cost is above average cost, it is pulling average cost up.

CLARIFYING THE MEANING OF COSTS

Two more points relating to the traditional (neoclassical) economist's treatment of costs must be clarified. The economist's concept of costs differs from the accountant's definition of the term. For the accountant a cost

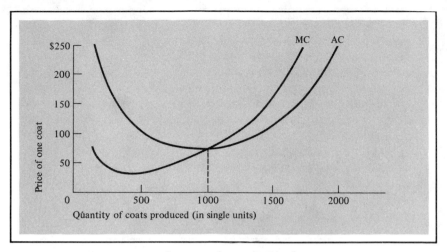

Figure 21.3 Average cost and marginal cost (MC) of coats.

must involve a monetary outlay. In other words, costs are recorded only when money changes hands. Economists include two types of costs in their analyses: explicit costs and implicit, or imputed, costs. *Explicit costs* are the costs considered by the accountant—that is, those involving the transfer of money. *Implicit costs* include those that the company's owner would have to pay if, for example, he or she did none of the managerial work; thus a normal wage for the managerial and other labor he or she performs is counted among implicit costs.

Assume, for example, that someone saves $20,000 and opens a service station. During the first year an accountant calculates the total revenue from the station was $32,000 and the total costs of operating that station was $22,000. The accountant informs the owner that the profit from the station was $10,000. A traditional economist would assess these costs differently. Suppose that the owner worked 60 hours every week and that it would have cost him $3 per hour to hire somebody to do this work. The economist subtracts the imputed wage of $9,360; the profit now becomes $640 rather than $10,000. All economists agree that everyone deserves pay for his or her own labor, including managerial labor.

The traditional economist, however, would consider another, more dubious implicit, or imputed, "cost." The owner invested $20,000 in the station, thus forgoing the opportunity to invest it elsewhere—say, in 6 percent government bonds. Therefore the neoclassical economist factors in an implicit cost of $1,200 in interest forgone, so that the gas station owner has "really" lost money.

For neoclassical economists *profits* means only *excess* profits—that is, they are excess over all explicit and implicit costs, including a "normal" or average profit (or interest). Although this definition is useful in one way, it has a very conservative bias in another sense. It is useful in that

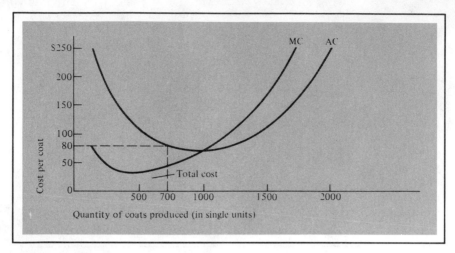

Figure 21.4 Average, marginal, and total costs of coats.

the capitalists *do* require the bribe of an average rate of profit to get them to use their capital in production. They usually consider normal and necessary the rate that has been the average for the previous few years. Thus only if an average profit is included with costs can it be said that supply behavior is determined completely by costs. This definition is employed here because it is convenient to be able to say, in agreement with all current economics books, that in pure competition the supply curve is identical with the marginal-cost curve. This point is examined later.

The neoclassical definition of costs is conservative in the sense that it introduces the concept that capitalists *deserve* to receive an average profit as a cost of providing capital for production. It is true that physical capital goods are necessary for production, that in any society limited capital goods must be allocated to maximize returns, and that allocation is a social cost because it means other areas cannot use those capital goods. It is also true, given a private enterprise system, capitalist entrepreneurs must be bribed with the average profit to get them to furnish their capital. It was shown in Chapter 16, however, that the productivity of capital goods implies neither that the capitalists are productive nor that they deserve their profit. In other words, a socialist society would provide capital to itself out of public funds; it would consider provision of capital a cost of production; and it might even calculate rates of profit in each industry to decide where to allocate capital (see Chapter 44). But a socialist society would not pay the profits to any private individual.

There is only one other essential point to be made in this discussion of costs. Total costs can be shown quite easily on a graph of per-unit costs. Because the average cost is the total cost divided by the quantity produced, it follows that total cost is given by multiplying the average cost by the quantity produced. In Figure 21.4 total cost is shown as a shaded rectangle.

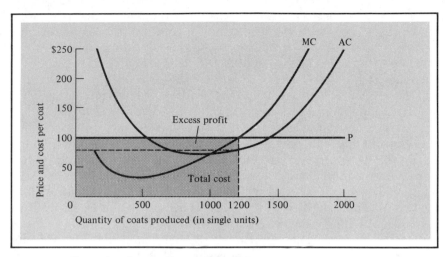

Figure 21.5 Price (or demand) and cost of coats.

Taking any quantity (for example, 700 coats in Figure 21.4), we go up the average-cost curve and then over to the cost axis of the graph. Here the average cost per unit required to produce 700 coats is found: $80. We know that the total cost will equal 700 × $80. But because line 0–700 and line $0–$80 are adjacent sides of a rectangle, their product is equal to the area of the rectangle. Therefore, the shaded rectangle in Figure 21.4 represents the total cost of producing 700 coats: 700 × $80 = $56,000.

MAXIMUM PROFIT UNDER COMPETITION

In an earlier section it was shown that once the price of the industry's product is determined, the individual competitive firm faces a demand curve (or a given price) that is a straight, horizontal line. It is further assumed that each firm has the U-shaped short-run average-cost curve described earlier. In Figure 21.5 the demand curve has been superimposed on the cost curves in order to present the whole picture for the competitive firm.

In order to understand the firm's reaction to the market price ($100), it is necessary to ascertain what motivates the firm's owners (or managers). The answer provided by the vast majority of economists, from Adam Smith to the present, is that the one overriding objective of all capitalists, or their managers, is to maximize their profits. We accept this answer provisionally and treat each firm as a profit maximizer.

The manager whose cost and revenue curves are pictured in Figure 21.5 will maximize his profits by producing and selling 1200 coats. At this quantity the firm's marginal cost is equal to its price. The rule for maximizing profit under competition is to produce the quantity *that equates marginal cost and price.* The combined area of the two shaded rectangles in Figure 21.5 is equal to the firm's total income from sales or revenue (because it represents the price times the quantity the firm sells). The area of the lower rectangle is equal to the firm's total cost (because it is the product of the firm's average cost and the quantity produced). The area of the upper rectangle is equal to the firm's profit (because it represents the total revenue minus total costs, which is, by definition, profit).

In order to understand why 1200 coats is the quantity that maximizes the firm's profit, imagine that the firm produces and sells a smaller quantity of the product. For any quantity below 1200, the firm's price per unit is higher than its marginal cost. Consequently, if the firm produces and sells an additional coat, this last coat will add more to the firm's profit. As long as the firm is producing fewer than 1200 coats, it can add to its profit by producing and selling more coats.

However, imagine that the firm is producing more than 1200 coats. For any quantity above 1200 the firm's marginal cost exceeds its price per unit. If the firm were to produce and sell one less coat, the reduction in its costs would exceed the reduction in its revenue. Its profit would therefore increase. As long as the firm continues to sell more than 1200 coats, it can add to its profit by producing and selling less. It is now easy to see why the competitive firm maximizes its profit by equating its marginal cost and its price.

For any price that prevails in the market, the marginal-cost curve will indicate what quantity the firm would like to sell. But a line showing the quantities a firm would like to sell at various prices is exactly what we defined a supply curve to be; therefore *in pure competition a firm's marginal-cost curve is its supply curve.* Because the industry is simply the total of the firms within it, the industry's supply curve is the summation of the marginal-cost curves of all these firms.

EQUILIBRIUM FOR THE FIRM AND THE INDUSTRY IN PURE COMPETITION

In the purely competitive industry, price is determined by the intersection of the industry supply and demand curves. The individual firm adjusts its quantity in order to maximize profit. Figure 21.6(A) shows an individual firm's cost and revenue curves.

In Figure 21.6 the firm and industry are in short-run, but not long-run, equilibrium. The firm is in short-run equilibrium because it is producing at the point where its price and marginal cost are equal. But the firm is receiving excess profits. In long-run equilibrium, neither the industry nor the firm is making excess profits.

Two points should be made about the firm's excess profits: (1) It is assumed that all firms in an industry have access both to the same technology that this firm is using and to inputs of comparable quality. Therefore

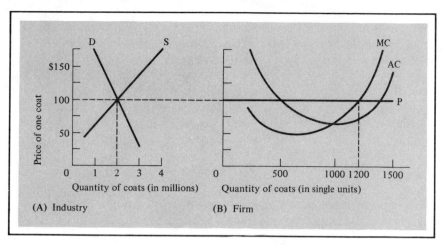

Figure 21.6 Competitive equilibrium in the coat market.

it can be concluded that the cost curves of virtually all firms in the industry are nearly identical to those of the firm pictured in Figure 21.6(B). (2) It must be remembered that the firm's cost curves include an imputed cost covering an average return on the owner's capital; thus normal, or average, profit is included in the cost.

Therefore, it must be concluded that the firms in this industry are making excess profits above an average return on capital. Because it is easy to enter a purely competitive industry, capitalists who are making only an average profit in other industries will be attracted to this industry by the lure of excess profits.

An industry is said to be in long-run equilibrium when there is no tendency for firms either to enter or to leave it. The industry pictured in Figure 21.6 is not in long-run equilibrium because it is earning excess profits, and hence new firms will be entering it.

As new firms enter, their additional outputs must be added in order to derive the industry's new supply curve. This means that the supply curve will shift to the right. Figure 21.7 illustrates the original situation depicted in Figure 21.6, and also shows what happens as the supply curve shifts to the right (from the original position, S_1). When the supply curve shifts, it must ultimately shift to S_2. If it stops short of S_2, excess profits will continue and more firms will be attracted, shifting the curve farther to the right until it reaches S_2.

With the greater supply provided by the new firms entering the industry, all excess profits have been eliminated. At the new, lower price of $75, the firm reduces its output from 1200 to 1000 coats in order to equate its marginal cost with the new price. This lower output maximizes the firm's profits in the new conditions. At that point, however, it is also true that the firm's average cost is just equal to its price per unit. The decline

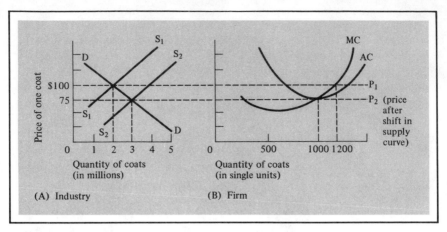

Figure 21.7 Change in equilibrium in the coat market.

in price from $100 to $75 has eliminated the firm's excess profits (because its average cost is also $75).

With no excess profits there is no longer any incentive for new firms to enter the industry. The firms within the industry are receiving a normal, or average, rate of return on their capital and labor; therefore there is no tendency for firms to leave the industry. It can now be said that when the new supply curve results in the establishment of a new price equal to the long-run average cost of each firm, then the industry is in long-run equilibrium because the number of firms within the industry has been stabilized.

Thus, when both the individual firms and the purely competitive industry are in long-run equilibrium, the following equality holds for each firm:

Price = marginal cost = average cost

The fact that price equals marginal cost indicates that the firm is satisfied that its profits are maximized by its current level of output. The fact that price equals average cost indicates that there will be no tendency for firms either to enter or to leave the industry (because the average cost includes just an average rate of profit).

Our account of long-run equilibrium in a purely competitive market differs somewhat from the accounts that are found in many conservative textbooks. When the firm was making excess profits by producing and selling that quantity of output at which the industry price equaled its marginal cost, the conservative economists depict two different series of changes that lead to long-run equilibrium for both the firm and the industry. First, they say that new firms will enter the industry for the same reasons that we have already given. Second, they say that the existing firms may expand their productive capacity and generate entirely new and different *long-run cost curves*. The expansion of each individual firm's productive capacity was ignored in our account, and we must explain why we omitted this consideration.

In the standard conservative textbook it is argued that in the long run the firm has no fixed costs because all factors of production, including the size or productive capacity of the factory, can be varied. Therefore all costs become variable costs in the long run. If all costs are variable, then there is no immediate or obvious reason why the U-shaped cost curve is derived from the fact that a particular factory was designed to operate most efficiently when a certain number of workers are employed in the factory. If either fewer or more workers than this optimum number of workers are employed, the production process will be less efficient. A short-run, U-shaped average-cost curve reflects the fact that a given factory operates most efficiently when producing that level of output for which it was technically designed, and that if either more or less than that amount of output is produced, then production will be less efficient and costs will be higher.

In the long run the firm can expand its factory size or the number of factories it owns. It is our belief that if a firm multiplies the number of factories it owns while each factory incorporates the same technology as all of the other factories, then the firm's long-run average costs will be relatively constant—that is, the average cost per unit of output for a second factory, utilizing exactly the same technology as the first factory, ought to be identical, at a given level of output, to the average cost per unit of output in the first factory. If this is true, and we believe that in general it is, then in the long run the firm could produce larger quantities without increasing its average costs per unit of output simply by constructing more factories. Therefore, the long-run average-cost curve would be a horizontal line showing constant returns to scale as the firm multiplies the number of factories that it owns.

If we drop the assumption of a fixed technology and allow for technological change, then the effects of such changes in technology as have generally occurred in the history of capitalism are to make production more efficient and hence to make average costs decline in the long run. Therefore, we conclude that in the long run a firm's average-cost curve will probably be constant (or horizontal) or else declining—depending on whether technology remains constant or changes.

This poses a problem for conservative economists. They like to argue that in the long run something approximating pure competition can reasonably be expected to obtain in a capitalist economy. But if a single firm can, in the long run, produce ever-larger quantities of output at a constant or a declining average cost, then what is there to prevent a single firm from growing so large as to take over the entire industry and create a monopoly? Or what prevents a few firms from growing so large as to create an oligopolistic industry? In our opinion, this is exactly what has happened in many of the more economically significant industries in most capitalist economies. But this is precisely what most conservative economists would like to deny.

One way in which they can deny this tendency to oligopoly or monopoly in capitalism is to argue that long-run average-cost curves are U-shaped and that the point of optimum efficiency or the point of minimum average cost per unit of output occurs when the firm is producing only a small, insignificant part of the total output of the entire industry. If the firm then attempted to expand its output, it would incur higher costs and would therefore be unable to compete profitably at that higher level of output. Therefore the U-shaped average-cost curve "saves" the "realism" of the theory of pure competition.

But the reasons that the conservative economists put forward to support the idea of a long-run U-shaped average-cost curve seem to us to be quite unconvincing when applied to actual conditions in most industries. Therefore, we generally reject the notion that such cost curves characterize most actual industries. Because we reject this notion, in our demonstration of long-run equilibrium we had to show the change in the industry supply curve as being entirely the result of new firms entering the industry.

In our view, it is only when the increase in the industry's supply curve is the consequence solely of new firms entering the industry that the notion of a purely competitive industrial equilibrium for a long-run period can be defended. Therefore, without asking why existing firms do not expand their capacity, we simply showed that if they do not do so, then it is theoretically possible for a long-run purely competitive equilibrium to exist. The important question, of course, is why we should ever expect this type of solution to occur in reality. This raises the issue of the relevance of the competitive model.

RELEVANCE OF THE COMPETITIVE MODEL

The reader has probably wondered which industries in the contemporary American economy are purely competitive. Only one or two industries (out of many thousands) in the entire American economy present a factual resemblance to the model just worked through.

The most obvious choice of a purely competitive market might be from agriculture. Traditionally, in the wheat industry, for example, each farmer produced a homogeneous product, and no farmer produced enough to affect the price significantly. Each would take as given the price determined in the market. Whether all or none of the individual farmer's crop was sold at this price was virtually irrelevant to the determination of price.

Over the past several decades, however, two important changes have occurred in agricultural markets: (1) The government has intervened extensively in the market through various schemes of subsidies and production controls; (2) the agricultural industry has increasingly come under the control of giant corporations that in no way resemble the small, relatively powerless firms pictured in the theory. These two developments have so fundamentally altered the agricultural market that the model of pure competition definitely does not explain or describe it.

If only one or two industries even resemble the model, then a question must be asked: What is the relevance of this analysis to the American economy of the 1980s? The answer is that such analysis reveals more about the thinking of many economists that it does about the functioning of the economy.

The model of pure competition is the basis of the neoclassical economists' claim that the unencumbered private enterprise market system results in a situation of optimum production and distributional efficiency. In Chapter 8 we saw that neoclassical economics arose as an apology for the status quo in capitalism. From the analysis just presented it can be seen that in pure competition each firm, in equilibrium, produces the quantity at which its costs are minimized and its production is most efficient. The firm receives only the socially defined normal rate of profit. No excess profits exist. The consumer is able to purchase the product at the lowest possible price. The theory also claims that every factor of production receives in return the value of what it contributes to production (although the theory says nothing about the inequitable ownership of factors of production that prevails).

Thus the neoclassical analysis is generally used to show that the free enterprise market economy is the best and most just of all possible worlds. Therefore, the theory of pure competition is studied here primarily to understand the basis of a very important conservative ideology supporting capitalism. (The model of pure competition, in its simplest form, also provides analytic tools that can be used to study more realistic cases.)

SUMMARY

Orthodox price theory usually distinguishes four different types of market structures within which firms operate—pure competition, monopolistic competition, oligopoly, and monopoly. In this chapter, after defining the four market structures, we focused our attention on pure competition. We found that in pure competition the firm has no control over the price it charges for its product. When a purely competitive industry is in a long-run equilibrium, firms receive only the socially average (or "normal") rate of profit, costs (which include that normal profit) are minimized, and consumers pay a price for the product that equals the minimum cost of production for the profit. This analysis depicts the ideal state of affairs for conservative economists, and despite the fact that almost no industries meet the criteria defining this market structure, some conservative economists hold that this analysis describes the actual state of affairs in American capitalism.

Chapter
22

Prices and Profits
of a Monopoly

From the very beginning of the capitalist system, capitalists have understood that very large profits could generally result if they could "corner the market" for a particular commodity—that is, if they could achieve a monopoly. After a firm has achieved a pure monopoly, or complete control over an entire industry, its most important task is to erect barriers that can prevent competitiors from entering the industry and taking some of the excessively high profits.

Also from the beginnings of capitalism, firms with monopoly power have sought to use the government to help exclude competitors. In the term *monopoly power* we include any firm with significant power over the market, including firms in imperfect competition, oligopolies, and pure monopolies. We saw in Part One that in the mercantilist era the great trading companies were granted monopolies by their governments. We also saw how the monopoly power of these companies inhibited the growth of industrialization, calling forth the classical liberal cry for a reduction of government interference in the market.

With industrialization, however, there came a new and inexorable drive for monopoly power. We saw in previous chapters that the enforcement of antitrust laws and the actions of the numerous government regulatory commissions have consistently aided and abetted the creation and maintenance of monopolies.

Although it is intuitively obvious that a monopolist can charge higher prices, it is not true that the monopoly firm can simply fix its price at any level it chooses. If that were true, then any given monopolist could make such high profits that after a few years the firm might own all the wealth. In fact, monopolists face both cost constraints and revenue constraints. In

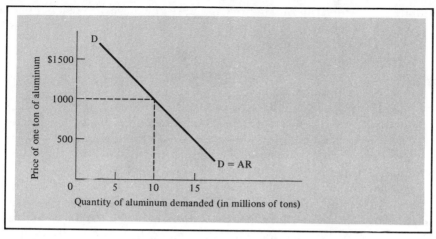

Figure 22.1 Demand and average revenue (AR) from aluminum.

this chapter we examine the nature of these constraints and the manner in which they affect the monopolist's profits and its decisions regarding levels of output and pricing.

DEMAND AND REVENUE FOR A MONOPOLY

A monopoly exists when a single firm constitutes the entire industry. The firm sells a product for which there are no close substitutes, and potential competitors are prevented in one way or another from entering the industry.

Under competition, the demand curve for a whole industry slopes down and to the right (because the quantity sold increases only when the price falls). The demand curve for a competitive firm, however, is a horizontal straight line (because the firm's output is so small, it can sell as much as it wishes at the same price). A monopoly firm, by definition, is the only seller of a commodity; it is the industry. Therefore the *demand curve for a monopoly firm is exactly like the demand curve for a whole competitive industry:* It slopes down and to the right. Unlike the owner of a competitive firm, who must sell at a given price, the monopolist can therefore *choose* to sell more goods at a lower price or fewer goods at a higher price (he or she is not a price taker but a price fixer).

Thus a market demand curve shows the maximum revenue per unit of the commodity that a monopolist will receive at any particular level of sales chosen. When they view it from this seller's standpoint, economists call the demand curve an *average-revenue curve.* It shows the average revenue per unit of the commodity sold for any level of sales.

Figure 22.1 shows a demand curve for a monopolized commodity, aluminum, over which the Aluminum Company of America (ALCOA) had a pure monopoly for many years. It can be labeled a demand curve or an average-revenue curve. The curve in Figure 22.1 is labeled D = AR to underscore this equivalence. At $1000 per ton, consumers wish to purchase 10 million tons. Alternatively, if the monopolist wishes to sell 10 million tons, the $1000 is the maximum price he can charge.

When ALCOA (assumed here to be a pure monopoly) decreases the price of aluminum and hence increases its sales of aluminum, two separate effects result in a change in its total revenue: (1) the *quantity effect* and (2) the *price effect.* More aluminum can be sold only by lowering the price of aluminum. The decline in the price of aluminum multiplied by the quantity of aluminum sold at the old price is the amount of revenue that the firm loses in order to expand sales. This is the price effect. The increase in the quantity sold multiplied by the new and lower price is the quantity effect. Thus when the quantity sold is increased by a lower price, the quantity effect always increases total revenue, whereas the price effect decreases total revenue. The net change in total revenue may be positive or negative, depending on whether the quantity effect or the price effect is larger.

Assume that ALCOA (or any monopoly) wishes to know how much total revenue will be increased if sales are increased by 1 ton. The information ALCOA is looking for is what economists call the *marginal revenue,* which may be defined as the change in the total revenue the firm will receive as a result of sale of one additional unit, in this case one more ton of aluminum. Marginal revenue is defined as follows:

$$\text{Marginal revenue} = \frac{\text{change in total revenue}}{\text{change in quantity sold}}$$

The average and marginal revenue curves of a monopoly are illustrated in Figure 22.2.

Notice that at any quantity of aluminum the marginal revenue is lower than the average revenue. Whenever the average revenue is decreasing, the marginal revenue must be lower than the average revenue. Again, this is similar to the case of a person taking a series of tests. If the average score declines as more tests are taken, it must mean the marginal score (or the score on the last test taken) is below the average. In fact, it is the lower marginal score that pulls the average score down. Similarly, if the average revenue is decreasing, the marginal revenue must be below it and pulling it down.

When 10 million tons of aluminum are sold, marginal revenue is zero, or total revenue can be increased no further with the given demand—the quantity effect just offsets the price effect.

At quantities below (to the left of) 10 million, the quantity effect is more significant than the price effect; as the quantity effect minus the price effect is, in fact, the numerator of the above equation, under these circumstances it—and thus the marginal revenue—is positive. As the quantity of

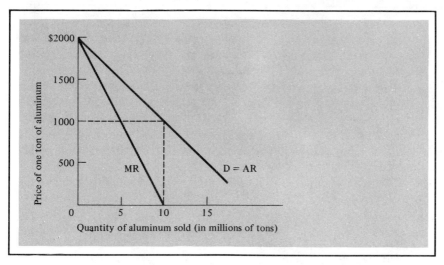

Figure 22.2 Average revenue and marginal revenue (MR) from aluminum.

aluminum sold increases, the price effect becomes more important and the quantity effect less important, until at 10 million they are equal. At higher quantities of aluminum (to the right of 10 million), the price effect is greater, so that the numerator—and therefore the marginal revenue—becomes negative. It is possible to conclude from this that a monopolist would always sell a smaller quantity than 10 million tons because at sales of 10 million, the increase in revenue as a result of the last unit sold is zero. Sales of greater quantities would result in a loss of revenue because marginal revenue is negative at quantities above 10 million.

EQUILIBRIUM FOR A MONOPOLY

In order to see the equilibrium price a monopolist will charge and the quantity the firm will sell, the revenue curves must be superimposed on the cost curves. From the discussion in the previous section, it is known the average-revenue curve will slope downward and to the right and that the marginal-revenue curve will be below it and have a steeper slope. These curves are drawn in Figure 22.3. The profit-maximizing position is reached when the monopolist produces and sells the quantity (6 million tons) at which *marginal revenue equals marginal cost.* The reason for this is easy to comprehend. Below this level, one additional ton of aluminum brings in more revenue than its additional (or marginal) cost. Above this point, one additional ton of aluminum costs more than the average it brings in to ALCOA. Notice how the monopoly rule differs from the competitive rule that price should equal marginal cost. Because the monopolist has the entire market, his demand curve slopes downward, and therefore his mar-

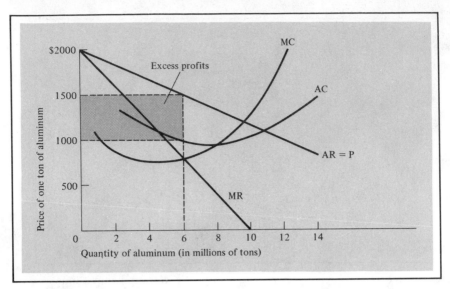

Figure 22.3 Equilibrium for a monopolist selling aluminum.

ginal revenue is below his average revenue. In the competitive case, the firm is so small that the demand curve appears purely elastic in relation to it. Therefore, the competitive price or average revenue *equals* its marginal revenue. Because the monopolist's marginal revenue is lower (and the more general rule is that marginal cost equals marginal revenue), the monopolist chooses to supply less output to the market than would be the case in a competitive industry with similar cost and demand curves.

The average-revenue curve in Figure 22.3 indicates that $1500 is the maximum price at which 6 million tons can be sold. The shaded area shows the excess profits received at that price. For a monopoly, unlike a purely competitive firm, the making of excess profits is the usual and expected case. Nothing in the short or the long run tends to reduce these excess profits (except for changes in general business conditions as the economy undergoes cyclical fluctuations, a topic that will be examined in Part Three).

In addition to the high price monopolists charge and the excess profits they make, they almost never produce at the most efficient level of production. As shown in Figure 22.3 monopolists stop producing before reaching the point at which their average costs are minimized. They do this, of course, because they are interested in maximum profits, not maximum efficiency. Had they produced the quantity that minimized their costs, they would have been forced to sell their product at a much lower price, thus reducing their excess profits. The reader can now easily see what is meant by the age-old charge that monopolies restrict output and sales in order to increase their excess profits. The reader can also see why, from the very beginning of the capitalist, private enterprise economic system, most businessmen have tenaciously fought to acquire monopoly power.

MODIFICATION OF MONOPOLY ANALYSES

In the discussion of the market equilibrium for a monopolist, it was assumed both that monopolists took their revenue and cost curves as given and that they maximized profits by equating marginal cost and marginal revenue within the fixed constraints of externally determined revenue and cost curves. These assumptions enabled us to examine only one aspect of the monopolist's ceaseless drive for more excess profits. Monopolists can also increase excess profits by shifting their cost curves downward and their revenue curves upward.

Shifts in revenue curves can be effected in several ways. The first and most obvious method is through advertising. If monopolists can persuade more consumers that they want or need their product, then they will be able to sell more of it at all prices along the demand curve—that is, the demand curve will shift upward and to the right. Thus we are literally bombarded with advertising, as business endlessly attempts to convince us to consume ever-increasing amounts of their products.

Another way monopolists can increase the demand for their products is by convincing the government that it should erect and maintain protective tariffs to eliminate foreign competition. Although a firm or a group of firms often manages to achieve a monopoly within national boundaries, only very infrequently can a worldwide monopoly be achieved (however, many American-based multinational firms are working feverishly in that direction). To the extent that consumers are able to buy a close foreign-made substitute for a monopolist's product, the demand for that product is reduced. Protective tariffs can eliminate foreign competition and thereby increase demand for the monopolist's product. Over the past several centuries business leaders have—generally with considerable success—sought the aid of governments in creating and protecting their firms' domestic monopolies by enacting protective tariffs. Such tariffs increase monopoly revenues at the expense of the consumer, who is forced to pay a higher price for "protected products." They are much like a tax levied by the government against all consumers, part of the proceeds of which is turned over to the monopolists to augment their excess profits.

Many large business firms are also able to increase the demand for their products through massive sales to the government. The bulk of these sales is connected with military procurement. For many of the largest U.S. corporations, these sales represent from 5 to 100 percent of their total sales. This topic is examined in greater depth in Part Three.

There also are many ways business firms can shift their cost curves downward. They can press for government legislation that weakens labor unions; the Taft-Hartley Act of 1947 is an example of very restrictive legislation. They can also work to elevate "cooperative" and "reasonable" people to positions of leadership in unions—people who will not press very hard for wage increases that would disturb the status quo in the wage and profit distribution. They can also get the president to appoint business-leaning "public" people to positions in regulatory agencies. These measures enable large firms to keep their wage costs to a minimum.

Monopolies, in many instances, seek to achieve a monopsonistic position. A *monopsony* exists when a firm is the *only buyer* of a particular resource or intermediate product. Monopsonists can offer a very low price for the resource they are purchasing; sellers must accept the offer or not sell their resource. Thus resource costs can be decreased if the firm can achieve monopsonistic buying power, which is no less actively sought than monopolistic selling power.

The immense political power that stems from their economic power permits giant corporations to reduce costs in other ways. The government is often persuaded to allow them to use government-owned facilities for production connected with the armaments they are selling to the government. These facilities are generally used *free of charge.* And when the government has charged rent, it has reimbursed the corporations and given them extra profits on this rent: this is the so-called cost-plus contract. In other words, the government has actually paid the giant corporations to use government-owned facilities free of charge. Such a case was described by a U.S. Senate Committee report on pyramiding missile profits:

> Much of Western Electric's Nike production was done at two government surplus plants, which under the ordinary method of doing business with the government would have been supplied to Western Electric without cost. However, Western Electric instead of having the plants supplied free, rented them from the Government. Western Electric included the rentals as part of its overall costs and then charged the government a profit on these costs. The total rentals paid to the government by Western Electric for these plants amounted to over $3,000,000. When added to Western Electric's costs, the rentals generated additional profits to the company of $209,000. In such a situation, there could be little resistance on the part of Western Electric to having the government raise the rent, because as the rent went up, so did Western Electric's profit, since the complete amount of the rent was repaid by the landlord back to the tenant together with a profit. (U.S. Congress, 1964)

These are only a few of the ways large monopolistic corporations are constantly striving to use their economic and political power to maximize profits.

WHO ARE THE MONOPOLISTS?

Most introductory economics textbooks identify pure competition and monopoly as the extreme cases along the spectrum of industrial organization. They argue (and we agree) that there are almost no purely competitive industries. Most pure monopolies, they assert, are either local or regional in scope, ranging from the single grocery store in a small village to the single giant real-estate developer in a large city. They maintain that national monopolies are as rare as purely competitive industries. According to these textbooks, monopoly theory is of intellectual interest primarily as an extreme case with little actual or practical applicability at a national level in the American economy.

This view, we believe, is erroneous because it adheres strictly to the definition of monopoly as existing when there is only one seller. It interprets one seller to mean one firm. Admittedly, there are very few national markets where a single business firm is the only seller. Most important nationwide markets are dominated by a few giant corporations, which are oligopolies. In the next chapter, however, we shall see that despite some distinct differences between oligopolies (a few firms) and monopolies (a single firm), most oligopolies act as if they were monopolies. We shall argue that our analysis of monopolies applies generally to oligopolies on questions of pricing, output, and the shifting of both revenue and cost curves. If our analysis is correct, so that we can redefine monopolies to include industries that behave *as if* they were a single seller, then monopolies dominate almost all of the important national markets in the United States.

NATURAL MONOPOLIES AND GOVERNMENT REGULATION

There are some industries that economists call *natural monopolies*. The technology used in these industries creates a cost curve on which the minimum average cost is not reached until a firm is producing a very large quantity. Generally, before the minimum average cost is reached a single firm can supply the entire market with the commodity in question. If two firms divided the sales between them, each would produce such a small quantity that its average cost would be much higher than that of a single firm supplying the entire market. In this circumstance a free market will always lead to one firm's acquiring a monopoly position.

The most common examples of natural monopolies are public utilities such as electric and telephone companies. Because these companies supply a commodity that is a vital necessity for most individuals and most other business firms, they are almost always regulated by the government. This regulation generally takes the form of an imposed price ceiling (although the regulating agencies are often controlled by the monopolies, so the price ceiling is usually high enough to allow considerable excess profits).

The governing agency can reduce the monopolist's excess profits by lowering the price they will charge the public and/or increasing the quantity of the product they will sell. If the government wishes to increase the public welfare and still allow monopolists to choose a profit-maximizing quantity to sell, it will generally attempt to set the price at the level at which monopolists' marginal costs are equal to their average revenue. This type of price ceiling is illustrated in Figure 22.4.

For quantities at which the price ceiling is below the firm's average-

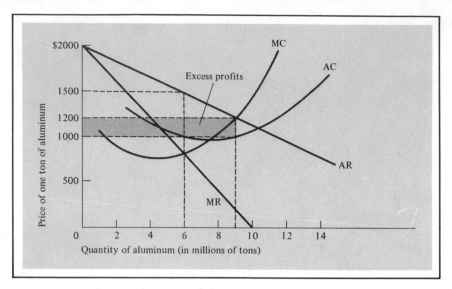

Figure 22.4 Ceiling on the price of aluminum.

revenue curve, that ceiling becomes, in effect, an average revenue and a
marginal revenue for the firm. The reasoning is analogous to that for a firm
in pure competition, whose price is determined independently of its actions.
The monopolist, unlike the purely competitive firm, however, cannot sell
any quantity it wishes at that price. For quantities at which its original
average-revenue curve falls below the price ceiling, the maximum price
it can charge is determined by its average-revenue curve. In Figure 22.4,
for quantities up to 9 million tons, the price ceiling serves as an average-
revenue and marginal-revenue curve. At quantities larger than 9 million
tons, the firm reverts back to its original revenue curves. If the firm is not
regulated, it will charge $1500 and sell 6 million tons. The price ceiling
is imposed at the price ($1200) that will equate the firm's average revenue
and its marginal cost (as under competition). The firm then treats the price
ceiling as a marginal-revenue curve for quantities up to 9 million tons
(where the price ceiling equals the average revenue and the marginal cost).
It is then selling more at a lower price and receiving less profit.

　　Although the welfare of the general public and other business firms is
improved by the imposition of the price ceiling, it is obvious that the monopolist firm is still making large excess profits (that is, its average-cost
curve is still below its average-revenue curve). But as long as monopolists
are allowed to choose the quantity they wish to sell, there is no price that
will both clear the market (that is, equate supply and demand) and in any
way result in better service for the public. For example, if the price ceiling
were set at a lower level, the quantity the firm wished to sell would fall
short of the quantity the public wished to buy, resulting in a market disequilibrium. If the price ceiling were set at a higher level, the government

would merely be returning the monopolist firm closer to its original profit-maximizing position at the expense of the general public's and other business firm's welfare. This happens frequently because of the monopolists' control of the regulatory agencies. Moreover, government-regulated monopolies frequently own the firms that supply them with materials and component parts. Most generally these subsidiary firms are not regulated. This permits the monopolist to direct its subsidiary firm to charge the monopoly firm very high prices. In that way, the excessive profits do not appear on the books of the regulated monopoly firm but appear on the books of its unregulated subsidiary.

SUMMARY

A monopolist is a single seller controlling an entire industry. Because monopolists face no direct competitors, the industry demand curve becomes the average-revenue curve for the monopolist. By producing and selling that level of output at which the monopolist firm's marginal cost is equal to its marginal revenue, it is nearly always the case that its average revenue will exceed its average costs (which already contain a calculation for "normal" profits), and so its profits will exceed the social average or normal rate of profit. The monopolist does not produce efficiently and charges a higher price than would a competitive firm. There are ways in which the government can regulate monopolies, but these regulations do not eliminate excess profits. Moreover, such regulation frequently either has very little impact or even aids the monopolist in securing higher profits.

REFERENCE

U.S. Congress. Senate Report No. 970. Washington, D.C.: GPO, 1964.

Chapter 23

Prices and Profits in Monopolistically Competitive and Oligopolistic Industries

In the United States today there are about 12 million business firms (of which nearly 14 percent are corporations). If agriculture is excluded as a special case not clearly fitting into any market structure, well over 99 percent of the remaining firms fit into the category we call monopolistic competition. Judged in terms of number of firms, it is by far the most important category of industrial organization.

The overwhelming majority of business firms are, however, minute firms in the fields of retailing, wholesaling, and the service industries (for example, small drugstores, hot dog stands, barber shops, and so forth). In a very important sense the more basic industries (for example, mining, agriculture, banking, transportation, manufacturing, and communications) are the foundation on which the prosperity of the nation depends. The people who control these industries dominate the entire economy. Almost all the basic or fundamental industries are completely controlled by giant oligopolistic corporations. Therefore, judged in terms of economic power, oligopoly is by far the most important category of industrial organization. Of the approximately 180,000 U.S. manufacturing corporations, for example, a mere 100 (or 0.004 percent) own 58 percent of total net capital assets.

If we were to describe America's industrial landscape, we would begin with a vast plain of millions of tiny pebbles, representing all the economically powerless, monopolistically competitive business firms. At the center of this enormous plain would rise a few hundred colossal towers, representing the important oligopolistic corporations. These few hundred towers would be so large as to make insignificant the entire plain below them.

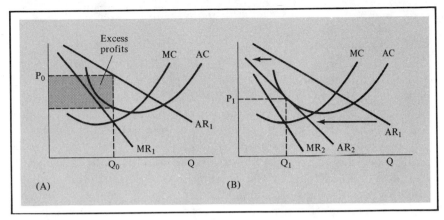

Figure 23.1 Average revenue before (A) and after (B) new firms enter.

EQUILIBRIUM FOR A MONOPOLISTICALLY COMPETITIVE FIRM

Monopolistic competition exists in an industry composed of many small firms, each producing a slightly differentiated product. An example of a monopolistic competitor is the neighborhood gas station, which differs slightly, but only slightly, from its competitors. The differentiation may be merely in the packaging, the location of a retail store, or the service offered, but in any case it creates a certain amount of consumer loyalty, which creates demand curves that slope downward and to the right. If a firm raises its price, it will lose only a portion of its customers to competitors. Many will continue to buy the product at higher prices. If a firm lowers its price, however, it will attract some of its competitors' customers.

The monopolistically competitive firm maximizes its profits when it equates marginal cost and marginal revenue. In many cases, if the firm has recently substantially differentiated its product it may make large, monopolistic excess profits. Such a situation is shown in Figure 23.1.

A monopolistically competitive market, however, has no significant barriers capable of preventing the entry of new firms. New firms, seeing the excess profits, will begin producing and selling highly similar products and will drain the demand away from the firm pictured in Figure 23.1(A). As a consequence, the original firm's average-revenue curve will shift downward and to the left. As long as excess profits remain, new firms will continue to enter and the average-revenue curve will continue to shift downward and to the left. Therefore, as shown in Figure 23.1(B), the downward shift will come to a halt only after the average-revenue curve just touches but does not cross the average-cost curve. At that quantity the firm's marginal cost is equal to its marginal revenue and the firm maximizes its profits by producing at this point. It is also the quantity at which the firm's average revenue is equal to its average cost. All of the excess profits have been squeezed out by the entry of new competitors.

Notice, however, that the new equilibrium is always above the minimum point of the firm's average-cost curve. In Figure 23.1 (B) the new demand curve, because it is still not flat as in pure competition, meets the average-cost curve above the minimum point. The price is above the minimum cost level, but there are no excess profits because at the actual production level costs are also higher than the minimum. In other words, the firm in monopolistic competition produces less output at a higher price and higher cost than the purely competitive firm in long-run equilibrium. We can therefore say that, in equilibrium, monopolistically competitive firms incur waste by never producing at their most efficient level. (In fact, only a purely competitive firm can be shown to produce efficiently in a private enterprise economy.)

The only way in which the firm can hope to regain some of its lost excess profits is to convince the public, usually through advertising, that its product is substantially different (i.e., better) than those of its competitors. But when one firm advertises and attracts new customers, its competitors generally retaliate by competitively advertising their own products. The net result is often that relative distribution of sales returns to the point at which it was before the first firm began to advertise. Now, however, no firm is willing to curtail its advertising for fear of losing its customers to competitors who continue to advertise.

Advertising becomes almost a pure waste that is locked into the system. We say "almost" a pure waste because we grant that advertising may occasionally impart useful information. Most advertising, however, is so notorious for its use of half-truths, emotional appeals, brainwashing, and psychological appeals to people's most basic frustrations that few people can tell when any genuinely useful information is being offered. Most of us consciously dismiss advertising as a totally unreliable source of information, even though we may unconsciously be affected by the constant barrage of advertising aggressively directed at each of our senses.

Another waste of monopolistic competition is needless duplication of the same service. For example, how many times have you seen four gas stations on all four corners of the same street crossing? From a social point of view this is totally inefficient.

Thus, we have sketched the picture of monopolistic competition, a picture that fairly adequately describes the overwhelming majority of small businesses in a private enterprise economy. Millions of tiny, nearly powerless businesses work feverishly to create or protect some amount of monopolistic excess profits. Millions of competitors try equally hard to take away those excess profits. No competitor is able to sustain the acquisition of excess profits for very long, but each perpetually struggles, worries, competes, connives, and battles in a never-ending war in which there are no victors. Millions of firms almost never produce at the most efficient, lowest-cost level of production; billions of dollars are wasted on the aggressive propagation of inane, mind-dulling, and obnoxious advertising.

OLIGOPOLY

An oligopoly exists when a few business firms dominate an industry. Unlike any of the industrial categories discussed up to this point, an oligopolistic firm does not face a definite, unambiguous demand curve for its product. The amount oligopolists can sell at any price can be substantially affected by their rivals' actions. Furthermore, because the actions of an oligopolistic firm similarly affect its rivals, any time it changes its price it must assume that other competitors will react in some way to this change. Its rivals' reactions will, in turn, affect the customers' response to its initial price change. All firms must be prepared to respond to any unexpected moves by their competitors. Thus the fact of *interconnectedness* and *mutual interdependence* of oligopolistic firms is the outstanding feature of an oligopolistic industry.

How can the effects of competitors' reactions be analyzed? First, their reactions to a price increase and to a price decrease can be differentiated. If a firm raises its price, it will automatically lose many of its customers to its rivals, who sell a highly similar product. Consequently, its action is not likely to provoke a reaction from its rivals. They are happy to acquire new customers.

However, if the firm lowers its price it will attract its rivals' customers unless the rival firms retaliate. Rather than lose their customers, they are likely to lower their prices by the same amount. It might seem that these price changes would cancel each other out, leaving each firm selling the same quantity at a lower price. This is not the case, however. When all the firms lower their prices, they attract new customers. Furthermore, old customers may buy more of the product sold by the industry.

Figure 23.2 provides two demand curves for an oligopolistic firm in an oligopolistic industry: Ford Motor Company (and our old friend the Escort). Demand curve D_1D_1 is constructed on the assumption that rivals ignore price changes made by Ford. Demand curve D_2D_2 is constructed on the assumption that rivals follow suit and change their prices by the same amount. For demand curve D_1D_1, marginal-revenue curve MR_1 is constructed. For demand curve D_2D_2, marginal-revenue curve MR_2 is constructed. Demand curves D_1D_1 and D_2D_2 intersect at the price and quantity that prevailed before the price change.

From the discussion of oligopolistic behavior it is assumed here that, beginning at $5000, Ford's rivals will not react if it raises its price. Therefore, for all prices above $5000 (and quantities below 600,000 Escorts), the curves D_1D_1 and MR_1 are Ford's actual demand and marginal-revenue curves. If Ford lowers its price below $5000, its rivals will lower their prices accordingly. Thus for prices below $5000 (and quantities greater

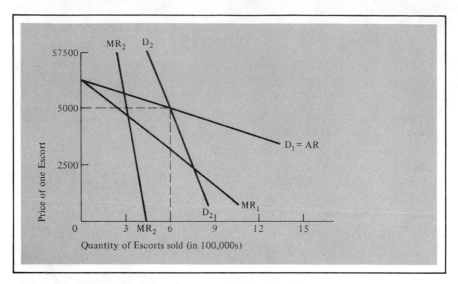

Figure 23.2 Oligopoly demand curves for Ford Escorts.

than 600,000 Escorts), the curves D_2D_2 and MR_2 are the firm's actual demand and marginal-revenue curves.

By eliminating the irrelevant sections of the two demand curves, it is possible to construct the firm's actual demand and marginal-revenue curves. In Figure 23.3 these curves are constructed and the firm's cost curves superimposed upon them. Two things should be carefully noted: The av-

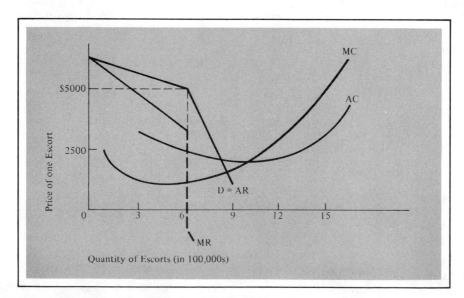

Figure 23.3 Kinked demand curve for Ford Escorts.

erage-revenue or demand curve is kinked (where the demand curve abruptly turns down), and the marginal revenue (at 600,000 cars) suddenly falls off into the negative quadrant of the graph.

It is clear from the graph that Ford will lose profits if it changes its price either upward or downward from the initial price of $5000. It is also clear that it would be highly unlikely that the revenue curves could ever shift so far downward and to the left that Ford would lower the price it charged. An increase in costs or an increase in the revenue curves would have to be fairly substantial for the firm to raise its price, unless business conditions have already led rival firms to raise their prices.

This analysis helps explain the historically observed fact that prices in oligopolistic industries are very stable in the face of small short-run variations in demand. It also helps explain why, over the longer run, oligopolistic prices almost never fall; rather, they show a persistent tendency to rise during periods of inflation and remain stable during periods of recession or deflation.

OLIGOPOLISTIC PRICES

The analysis does not show, however, how the price charged by oligopolists is determined. Whatever price is established, a kink will develop at that price. But how is the price established in the first place?

Most textbooks develop elaborate models of oligopolistic behavior based on the assumption that regardless of how many times the actions of rivals upset their expectations, the rivals never learn that they are mutually dependent (Bilas, pp. 213–219). The German economist H. von Stackelberg developed a sophisticated analytical model of oligopolistic behavior to prove that under oligopolistic rivalry a stable price cannot be established unless all the firms accept a single firm as a price leader and all other firms accept positions as price followers (von Stackelberg, pp. 194–204). In other words, stability requires that a single firm (or any other single decision-making body) make the decision in the oligopoly and that the remaining firms accept this decision.

What type of decisions will be made by the oligopolistic leader in a private enterprise economy? The answer to this question is simple once the absurd assumption that oligopolistic firms do not recognize their mutual dependence is rejected. "If we assume that they recognize it [their mutual dependence], then they will set industry price at the monopoly price. The number of firms in the industry does not matter so long as they realize their interdependence" (Bilas, p. 219).

In other words, the large corporations prevent price competition, although they do compete through alleged quality differences and advertising. In the absence of price competition the sellers of a given commodity have a collective interest in seeing that the price or prices established are such as to maximize the profits of the group as a whole, so each product is priced *as if it were sold by a single monopoly corporation.* This is the decisive fact in determining the price policies and strategies of the typical large corporation. It means, moreover, that the appropriate price theory of an economy dominated by such corporations is not competitive price theory but, rather, monopoly price theory. What nineteenth-century economists treated as a special case is now the general situation.

It is true that there is little open collusion in the United States because of the antitrust laws. Yet some kind of tacit collusion probably exists to a large degree in most industries, reaching its most developed form in what is known as *price leadership.* It is a mutual security pact in which no formal communication is necessary.

In this situation, when one firm raises or lowers the price, all the others will follow. When collusion is forbidden, the price leader calculates the share of the total market demand that his rivals will supply at various prices. It then chooses the price at which the remaining demand (after the rivals have chosen their appropriate supply quantities) will maximize its profits. For the industry as a whole, this solution approximates the pure monopoly solution. So long as all firms accept this solution, which is really nothing else but a corollary of the ban on price competition, it becomes easy for the group as a whole to feel its way toward the price that maximizes the industry's profit. In the appendix to this chapter we examine the exact mechanism of price leadership and other mechanisms by which oligopolies set a monopoly-like price.

In equating monopoly with oligopoly there is the qualification that oligopoly prices do not in fact move upward or downward with equal ease, as they would in a pure monopoly. If one seller raises its price, this cannot possibly be interpreted as an aggressive move. The worst thing that can happen to this firm is that the others will stand pat, and it will have to rescind (or accept a smaller share of the market). In the case of a price cut, however, there is always the possibility that aggression is intended—that the cutter is trying to increase its share of the market by violating the taboo on price competition. If rivals interpret the initial move in this way, the result may be a price war with losses to all. Hence firms are likely to be more careful about lowering prices than about raising them. Under the present situation of oligopoly, in other words, prices tend to be stickier on the downward side than on the upward side, and this fact introduces a significant upward bias into the general price level in a capitalistic economy dominated by oligopolies.

OLIGOPOLY OR MONOPOLY?

In Chapter 21, four general classifications of market structures—pure competition, monopolistic competition, oligopoly, and monopoly—were described. We found that there were almost no purely competitive industries. In the preceding section it was argued that, in their decisions regarding pricing, output, and sales, there is very little difference between oligopolies and monopolies.

Are there other differences of sufficient importance to make the oligopoly category a useful analytical tool? Or would it be better to drop oligopoly and simply refer to all industries that are dominated by a few giant corporations as monopolies?

The principal difference between oligopolistic and monopolistic firms is the rivalry that exists among the former. Although they have found by experience that this rivalry is mutually disastrous when it is extended to competitive pricing, they remain rivals. Their competition is generally confined to advertising, sales promotion, and cost-reduction campaigns, and their actions do not differ substantially from the monopolist's behavior, particularly in attempts to shift revenue curves upward and cost curves downward.

It seems, therefore, that only when the passage of time results in a substantial shift of relative power within an oligopolistic industry are there important differences between a monopoly and oligopoly. During such a situation a struggle for the industry's price leadership might develop. Such a struggle might result, temporarily, in destructive price competition (or worse). Once a new leader emerges, however, the industry will generally return to the types of policies that make it hardly distinguishable from a monopoly.

Thus, the oligopoly category is useful for analyzing temporary situations during which destructive competition takes place. It might also be useful to differentiate between monopolies and oligopolies in analyzing differences between advertising and sales promotion techniques for firms that sell commodities for which there are close substitutes (oligopolistic firms) and for those that sell products for which there are no close substitutes (monopolistic firms).

In almost any other situation or context, the differences between monopolistic and oligopolistic firms are insignificant. In most discussions it is quite appropriate to refer to all giant corporations as monopolistic firms, as is generally done in ordinary conversation. The economist's narrower definition of monopoly, although sometimes helpful, is so restrictive that it eliminates almost all existing business firms. Yet the formal analysis of a monopolist's pricing and output decisions forms the basis for understanding the behavior of most giant corporations.

A perfect example of oligopolists acting as a monopolist was the gasoline shortage of 1978. Although spokespersons for the government and the oil industry continually told the public that the shortage was the result of difficulties in importing sufficient quantities of crude oil, independent investigators soon discovered that the oil companies had curtailed both domestic production of crude oil and the refining of oil. So, while motorists canceled vacation plans, ran out of gas on the streets and freeways, and endured hours of waiting in long lines at gas stations, the price of gasoline soared from around 70 cents a gallon (to which it had risen in the previously planned "crisis" of 1973) to over $1.00 a gallon, and the oil companies raked in ever higher excess profits. All of this would have been impossible had the oil companies not been able to act as a monopoly.

SUMMARY

Most American business firms fit into the market structure of monopolistic competition. Our analyses have shown that although these firms generally do not receive excess profits, they incur waste by never producing at their most efficient level and by spending enormous sums of money on competitive advertising.

A comparatively few powerful oligopolistic giants dominate the industrial landscape of American business. Oligopolies generally set prices as if they were monopolies (this point is developed further in the Appendix that follows). Large excess profits and inefficiency characterize their operations. Thus, the general public's faith that the competitive market of American capitalism automatically results in efficient production is not theoretically or empirically warranted. That faith is a part of the general folklore of our culture by which the status quo of capitalism is ideologically maintained.

APPENDIX

Price Determination in an Oligopoly

The simplest and most direct method of oligopolistic pricing occurs when the oligopolistic firms form a formal cartel. A *cartel* is an association that acts as a monopoly. Within a cartel each firm is treated as if it were merely a separate plant owned by the monopoly.

Figure 23.4 shows that a cartel's price determination is identical to that of a monopoly. The monopolist has a single marginal-cost curve; the cartel's marginal-cost curve is determined by adding together the marginal-cost curves of the various individual oligopolists. The industry price is set at $5000, and 3 million compact cars is the quantity sold by the industry. Each firm produces the quantity at which its own marginal cost is equal to the industry's marginal cost (and marginal revenue).

Cartels, as such, are illegal in the United States. Yet many oligopolistic industries have found several ways of engaging in covert collusion that enables them to cooperate in such a manner that their pricing and output decisions are tantamount to a formal cartel.

When this type of collusion is not possible, many oligopolistic industries rely on the price leadership of the dominant firm within the industry. The dominant firm may be either the largest or the most efficient; sometimes it is both. In this situation the dominant firm sets the price. The other firms take that price as given in the same way a purely competitive firm accepts the industry price as given.

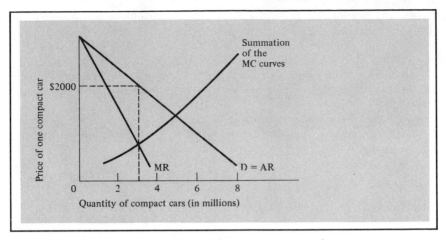

Figure 23.4 Oligopoly equilibrium in the compact car industry.

They produce up to the point at which their marginal cost is equal to that price (which they take as their marginal revenue).

In order for the dominant firm to maximize its profits, it must know approximately the marginal costs for the other firms. For some time U.S. Steel was the price leader in its industry. Figure 23.5 illustrates how price is determined in such an industry: DD is the industry demand curve; the demand curve for U.S. Steel is labeled $D_{USS}D_{USS}$. The summation of the marginal-cost curves for all firms other than the price leader is also shown.

The demand curve for the price leader (D_{USS}) is computed in the following manner: Whatever price the leader (U.S. Steel) selects, it knows the other firms will produce up to the point at which their marginal cost equals that price. U.S.

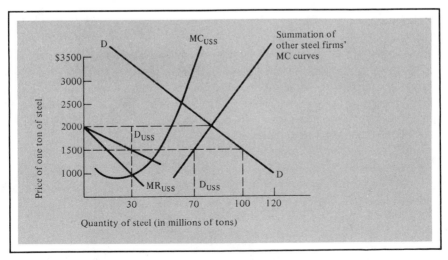

Figure 23.5 Price leadership by U.S. Steel (USS) in an oligopolistic industry.

Steel knows, therefore, that the other firms, taken collectively, will produce the quantity (in Figure 23.5, 70 million tons) at which the summation of their marginal-cost curves equals the price it has established. The demand for the leader's output will be the total market demand at that price minus the quantity the other firms sell. In other words, the leader's demand curve at any price will be equal to the difference between the market demand curve and the summation of the other firms' marginal-cost curves.

For example, if the leader establishes a price of $2000, the other firms will produce all that can be sold at that price (because at that point market demand equals the summation of the marginal-cost curves). At prices below $2000 the summation of the marginal-cost curves falls successively farther to the left of the demand curve. Therefore, as price declines, the demand remaining for the leader increases.

The marginal revenue (MR_{USS}) is derived from U.S. Steel's demand curve. The leader will maximize its profit by producing the quantity (30 million tons) and establishing the price ($1500) for the industry. The remainder of the firms will produce, among them, 70 million tons, and the entire industry will produce 100 million tons (equal to U.S. Steel's 30 million plus the others' 70 million).

It should be stressed that the follower firms only very superficially resemble firms in a purely competitive market. Although they take the price that has been established and adjust their output so that their marginal cost is equal to that price, their long-run normal position is one in which they also make monopolistic, excess profits. Because the oligopoly, like the monopoly, manages to prevent new firms from entering the industry, there are no market forces that would tend to erode profits.

A third method of establishing a monopoly price is through the creation of a government regulatory agency to supervise the industry. Although these agencies ostensibly exist to protect the general public's interests, very often they function as means of coordinating the industry and establishing a monopoly price (as was discussed in Chapter 9).

REFERENCES

Bilas, Richard A. *Microeconomic Theory.* New York: McGraw-Hill, 1967.

von Stackelberg, H. *The Theory of the Market Economy.* Translated by A. T. Peacock. New York: Oxford University Press, 1952.

Chapter
24

Government and Inequality

In Chapter 17, we examined the distribution of income in the United States and found that there exist a small number of very rich people, who are mostly recipients of profit income from capital, and a very large number of poor and low-income people, who are mostly wage workers or unemployed workers. In Chapter 20, we found that even in the corporate world there are a few very big fish and millions of small ones. Clearly, economic power lies in the hands of the few thousand owners and executives of the major corporations.

In this chapter the relationship of economic power to political power is examined. First, we explore the degree to which their vast economic power gives disproportionate political power to that same relatively small number of top corporate owners and executives. Then we examine how the resulting government affects economic inequality via taxation, welfare, farm subsidies, antitrust laws, and education. In Chapter 33, government policies, particularly military spending, are considered in relation to unemployment and inflation.

HOW ECONOMIC INEQUALITY PRODUCES POLITICAL INEQUALITY

In spite of our formal political democracy, money has the same power in politics that it has elsewhere. Thus it is no surprise that many writers, not all of whom are radical, have alleged that those with economic power dominate in U.S. politics. While he was president of the United States, Woodrow Wilson wrote: "Suppose you go to Washington and try to get at your Government. You will always find that while you are politely listened to, the men really consulted are the men who have the biggest stake—the big bankers, the big manufacturers, the big masters of commerce, the heads of railroad corporations and of steamship corporations. . . . The masters of the Government of the United States are the combined capitalists and manufacturers of the United States" (Wilson, pp. 57–58).

How far can Wilson's hypothesis be substantiated by the facts? Who dominates U.S. politics—the large number of low-income workers or the few high-income, upper-class capitalists? The economics of class structure has been examined; now we must ask about consciousness of class background because this will affect political behavior. A careful study conducted in 1964 found, contrary to the myth of an all middle-class America, that 56 percent of all Americans said they thought of themselves as "working class." Some 39 percent considered themselves "middle class." (It is true, however, that 35 percent of all those questioned said they had never thought of their class identification before that moment.) One percent said they were "upper class," and only 2 percent rejected the whole idea of class (Irish and Prothro, p. 38).

An individual's political behavior is strongly influenced by class background. But that leads to a puzzle. If a majority identifies with the working class, and everyone has one vote, why do parties favorable to the working class not win every election? Why do government policies usually support not working-class interests but (as Woodrow Wilson asserted) those of the wealthy capitalist class? More precisely, given formal democracy and capitalism, exactly how does our extreme economic inequality tend to be translated into political power?

In the first place, there is the simple fact that the degree of political participation tends to vary with class background. "The average citizen has little interest in public affairs, and he expends his energy on the daily round of life—eating, working, family talk, looking at the comics [today, television], sex, sleeping" (ibid, p. 165). More exactly, 86 percent of those identified as middle class voted, but only 72 percent of the working class voted. Similarly, 40 percent of the middle class had talked to others about voting for a party or candidate, but only 24 percent in the working class had talked about it. Among the middle-class people interviewed, 16 percent gave money to a political cause, 14 percent attended political meetings, and 8 percent worked for a party or candidate; in the working class, figures on the same activities were 4, 5, and 3 percent, respectively (ibid., pp. 165, 38).

Thus, political participation of every kind increases with income. Some of the reasons are obvious. Lower-income workers have less leisure, less money, above minimum needs, and more exhausting jobs. Furthermore, detailed studies show that because workers have less education and less access to information, they have less knowledge of the importance of various issues, which accounts, in part, for their lower participation. The same studies show more cross-pressures on workers—for example, the racial antagonisms that conveniently divide and weaken their working-class outlook.

One result of the low political interest and participation of the average American is the continuing trend to lower voting turnout. In 1960, of the eligible voters, 58.5 percent voted for president, but in 1976 only 49.5 percent voted. In the congressional elections of 1978, only 35 percent voted. Hence a minority elects the president and a smaller minority elects Congress.

Unequal political power is also achieved through control of the news media. Even if the average worker "had an interest in politics, he would have great difficulty getting accurate information; since the events of politics unfold at a great distance, he cannot observe them directly, and the press offers a partial and distorted picture" (ibid., p. 42). Even the quantity of news is limited. Although 80 percent of Americans read newspapers and 88 percent have television sets, only 2.8 percent of total newspaper space and even less television time is devoted to political news.

If the quantity of political news is deplorable, its quality is abysmal or worse. The first problem is that only one view is available to most because of increasing concentration of newspaper ownership. In 1910 some 57 percent of American cities had competing daily papers, whereas in 1960 only 4 percent had competing dailies. Furthermore, news media tend to have a conservative bias because (1) they do not want to offend any powerful interests, (2) they especially do not want to offend major advertisers, all of which are big businesses, and (3) most important, "Since the media of communication are big businesses, too, the men who control them quite naturally share the convictions of other businessmen" (ibid., p. 184).

Economic power also worsens the substantial inequality of political power available to different pressure groups. Thus, a standard political science textbook points to *status* as the most important factor in determining the influence of a pressure group. After listing other sources of status, it concludes: "Finally, since status is so closely tied to money in the United States, the group with greater status will almost automatically be able to command greater financial resources. And it costs money to engage in pressure politics" (ibid., p. 245).

Economic power weighs all the more heavily because advertising is now a vital component of politics. "Pressure groups . . . are now spending millions of dollars every year on *mass propaganda.* Not only broad groups like the National Association of Manufacturers, but even individual companies maintain elaborate bureaucracies to sell 'correct' ideas on general policy questions along with favorable attitudes to the company" (ibid., p. 249). Several large corporations have given millions of dollars to promote capitalist propaganda in the universities, such as the $20 million subsidies for the Institute of Constructive Capitalism at the University of Texas.

The vast amount of business advertising reinforces the general ethos of capitalism. Its message is that we live in a lovely country, material luxuries represent the ultimate goal, and everyone can have these material luxuries.

A certain percentage of business advertising is devoted to specifically political issues. Yet the government permits *all* business advertising to be
counted as a cost, which can be deducted from income when taxes are
computed. Of course, labor unions are not allowed this tax deduction for
political advertising.

ECONOMIC POWER AND THE PRESIDENT

There is no great mystery about how economic power gains dominance
over the president. Enormous sums of money are required for presidential
campaigns. For example, in just the few months of primary campaigns in
1972, Edmund Muskie spent about $2 million. It is estimated that President
Nixon spent $29 million in the 1968 campaign and about $55 million in
the 1972 campaign. With the inflation of the late 1970s and early 1980s
the cost of electing a president went up dramatically. The 1988 political
campaigns cost several hundred million dollars. Two traditional political scientists admit that "because campaigns are exceedingly costly, the
wealthier a person is, the more strategic his position for bringing pressure
to bear on politicians" (Dahl and Lindblom, p. 249).

In return for the money showered on the Republican party, President
Bush appointed mostly millionaire businesspersons or their functionaries
to his cabinet and appointed friends of business to head most government
agencies. Obviously these powerful positions are desired and used in furthering the interests of these individual businesspersons and of all business.
This process, by which the president is elected by economic power and
then appoints economically powerful people to positions from which they
can further extend and defend economic power, may be called a feedback
mechanism. In later sections, we look at how the political feedback mechanism causes presidential bias in favor of big business through tax cuts for
business and the rich, military spending, and cuts in spending for social
services for the middle class and the poor. More direct feedback mechanisms to influence the political process itself include the use of police to
stop demonstrations, the CIA and FBI to attack "radicals" (meaning anyone
opposed to the administration), and the president's prestige in TV and
press announcements to promote big-business politics.

When conservatives talk about "law and order," they mean primarily
the protection of private property here and abroad—by any means available. Thus letting the police shoot California farm workers because they
are striking is "law and order." The attempts to overthrow the government
of Nicaragua by mining its harbors and other acts of subversion—even
though unconstitutional because Congress did not authorize them—are
"law and order" because they protect the friends of capitalism abroad.
Thus the conservative view of "law and order" is always to protect property
(or "national security," which is the same thing) but not people. *This*

function of "law and order" (or protection of private property) is the primary function of the U.S. government.

The connections between business and politics can be seen in the careers of most of our prominent politicians. In 1966, just after Ronald Reagan became governor of California, he sold some land to Twentieth Century Fox. The corporation paid him 30 times what he had paid for the land in 1952 and triple its assessed market value at the time of the purchase. Reagan thus received a capital gain of nearly $2 million, but it was not considered a political donation, so he could spend it any way he chose. Twentieth Century Fox never used the land and later sold it. These kind of transactions permit persons like Ronald Reagan to devote all their time to politics. With the new federal laws that give government money to finance the campaigns of the major party candidates, these types of "gifts" become all the more important.

CONGRESS AND ECONOMIC POWER

Nor is Congress immune to the lure of economic power. Members of Congress need money to get elected and reelected; they need it for advertising, to pay for television, to pay air fares, and for many other basic necessities of political life. Lincoln is said to have spent only 26 cents on his campaign, but in the 1950s members of Congress spent about $15,000 to $25,000, and in the 1970s many members of Congress were spending over $100,000 on each campaign. In the 1976 race for governor of West Virginia, Jay Rockefeller spent $1.6 million in the primary contest alone, or $8.85 per vote. By the 1988 election, the average campaign expenditure for each Senate seat exceeded $6 million. Senator Pete Wilson, Republican from California, spent $13 million for his 1988 Senate seat. In the House of Representatives, an average of more than one-half million dollars was spent in each race. Representative Robert Dornan, Republican from California, spent $1.8 million to win his seat in the House of Representatives. A total of $458 million was spent in 1988 electing representatives and senators.

One investigation found that the Democratic party's money comes about 55 percent from large corporations, 20 percent from big labor, 15 percent from racketeers and gangsters, and 10 percent from middle-class Americans in small contributions. The Republicans usually collect about twice as much money in total, mostly from big business. Conservative Senator Russell Long guesses that "about 95 percent of congressional funds are derived from businessmen." During the 1970s several legal reforms ostensibly designed to reduce the political power of the rich by restricting the size of the political contributions of wealthy individuals were enacted. These reforms have greatly increased the political power of large corporations. Whereas in the past a relatively small number of capitalists would each give hundreds of thousands of dollars to the candidates they believed would best promote their interests, now they organize Political Action

Committees (PACs). In a corporate PAC, all of the corporation's executives, managerial personnel, and major stockholders are asked to give up to $5000 a year. A large corporate PAC can raise hundreds of thousands of dollars each year.

In 1974 there were 608 PACs; by 1986 there were 4157. Thus by 1986 the emphasis in financing political campaigns had shifted from a relatively few extremely wealthy individuals to a few thousand corporate PACs. The *New York Times* reported, however, that in the 1980 congressional elections there were 1585 corporate and commercial or trade PACs that contributed $36 million to their candidates, whereas 240 labor organizations contributed $13 million to theirs. Clearly, the corporate PACs are enormously more powerful than the labor PACs, and this is reflected in the very conservative, antilabor Congresses that were elected in the 1980s. The imbalance between the influence of business and labor is understated by those figures, however. In politically conservative regions such as the South or the Intermountain West, labor is weak, and business need spend relatively little to maintain its dominance. In states where the populace is less conservative and labor is stronger, business spends proportionately more. In 1982, for example, in the elections in California, business outspent labor by more than a 7:1 ratio.

Members of Congress are also indirectly affected by economic power through the strong influence of the president. Furthermore, big business can threaten to open or close plants in a particular congressional district. Business can give a member of Congress free time on radio or television or a free plane ride. In addition, there are about 5000 full-time lobbyists in Washington, about 10 for each representative (and many are ex-members of Congress or good personal or business friends of members of Congress). Except in emergencies, lobbyists do not directly buy votes. They merely serve as the main channel for the largest campaign contributions; buy lunches and dinners; and supply petty cash, credit cards, profitable investment opportunities, legal retainers to members of Congress (most of whom are lawyers), lecture fees, poker winnings (members of Congress always win), vacations, and fringe benefits ranging from theater tickets to French perfume. The two largest lobbies are the oil interests (with corporate income of billions of dollars because of tax loopholes) and the military armaments industry.

All of these interests are so strong—and so necessary for election— that even liberals will be found voting consistently for the direct needs of business concerns in their districts, no matter how they may vote on broader issues. For example, in 1980, liberal Democrats from Michigan all voted for government charity (in the form of guarantees for loans) to be given to the ailing Chrysler corporation. Thus one friendly senator, Boies Penrose, said to a meeting of businessmen (back in 1900, when such things were said more frankly): "I believe in a division of labor. You send us to Congress; we pass laws under . . . which you make money . . . and out of your profits you further contribute to our campaign funds to send us back again to pass more laws to enable you to make more money" (Green, Fallows, and Zwick, pp. 7–8).

An example of the influence of corporate PACs is their political effort to destroy the "lemon law." In the late 1970s, the Federal Trade Commission formulated an administrative ruling that required used-car dealers to make their customers aware of any known defects in the cars they were buying. The ruling was called the "lemon law." The "law" benefited tens of millions of used car buyers and reduced the profits of a few thousand car dealers. The car dealers formed a PAC called the National Automobile Dealers Association (NADA). During 1981 and 1982 the PAC raised and contributed over a million dollars. In 1982 Congress passed a law permitting them to veto FTC rules such as the "lemon law." Of the senators and congressmen who received more than $4000 in NADA PAC money, 90 percent voted against the lemon law. Of the senators and congressmen who received no money from the dealers' PAC, only 34 percent voted against the lemon law. The car dealers' contributions were sufficient, however, that their will prevailed in both houses of congress by a margin of more than two to one.

ECONOMIC BACKGROUNDS OF POLITICAL LEADERS

Upper-income members of the capitalist class (mostly white, male, Anglo-Saxon Protestants) hold a disproportionate percentage of the top political positions. Between 1789 and 1932, the fathers of U.S. presidents and vice-presidents were 38 percent farm owners and only 4 percent wage earners or salaried workers. Similarly, from 1947 to 1951, the fathers of U.S. senators were 22 percent professionals, 33 percent proprietors and officials, 40 percent owners, and only 4 percent wage earners or salaried workers. Between 1941 and 1943, the fathers of U.S. representatives were 31 percent professionals, 31 percent proprietors and officials, 29 percent farm owners, and only 9 percent wage earners or salaried workers.

Data for 1978 show that 153 of the 435 members of the House of Representatives had financial ownership of wealth of over $100,000, not including houses, automobiles, jewelry, insurance policies, or retirement funds. With regard to special interests (in conflict with their impartial lawmaking), 150 representatives have speculative real estate investments, 107 own shares in banks, large numbers own stock in top defense contractors, oil and gas industries, radio and television industries, and airlines and railroads. Thus very wealthy men, with fortunes ranging from many tens of thousands of dollars up to the slightly under $3 million listed for Representative Pierre Du Pont, sit in Congress.

What are the sources of their wealth? A total of 102 members of Congress held stock or well-paying positions in banks or other financial institutions; 81 received regular income from law firms that generally represented big businesses; 63 got their income from stock in the top defense

Table 24.1   WEALTH AND IDEOLOGY IN THE U.S. SENATE, 1975

Wealth group	Senators in group	Average liberal rating by ADA, 1975
Under $50,000	5	92%
$50,000–$250,000	30	59
$250,000–$500,000	18	53
$500,000–$1 million	4	53
$1 million or more	21	29

Source: Ralph Nader study, reported in Jim Chapin, "The Rich Are Different . . . ," Newsletter of the Democratic Left, November 1976, p. 3. The results are for 78 senators for whom questionnaires or other data were available; no data on 22.

contractors; 45 from the giant (federally regulated) oil and gas industries; 22 from radio and television companies; 11 from commercial airlines; and 9 from railroads. Ninety-eight members of Congress were involved in numerous capital gains transactions; each of them netted a profit of more than $5000 (and some as high as $35,000).

In the executive branch, upper-income, business-oriented individuals have held a majority of all the important positions throughout U.S. history. This includes the members of the cabinet, their assistants and department heads, and heads of most regulatory agencies. They quite naturally, with no conspiracy in mind, tend to consult big business leaders and business groups as experts (such as for the Committee for Economic Development or the Council on Foreign Relations). Wealthy families have also contributed a majority of federal judges, top military men, and top leaders of intelligence agencies. Finally, it should be noted that there is much crossing over at the top: Ex-generals often become corporate executives, and corporate executives often get to be cabinet members.

The results of the importance of wealth in getting elected, as well as the effects of wealth on ideological outlook, can be seen clearly in Table 24.1. There are at least 21 millionaires in the Senate but only 5 whose total wealth is below $50,000 (though this lowest category includes the vast majority of all Americans). Table 24.1 also shows an inverse relation between wealth and a liberal political outlook. The poorest senators (though not very poor) were given a liberal voting rate of 92 percent by the Americans for Democratic Action (ADA), but the ADA gave only a 29 percent liberal voting record to the 21 millionaires. These results fit almost too well with a vulgar Marxist economic determinism. There are certainly many exceptions—for example, Senator Edward Kennedy is both a millionaire and very liberal.

Of course, no serious critic would state the thesis of big-business control of government as if it were total. There are many qualifications. For example, although most members of Congress are rich, white males, the influence of wealth in Congress is much less than it is in the cabinet and in other executive offices. Similarly, in state and local governments, the influence of the wealthy is strong, but certainly they do not have exclusive control. Moreover, even among the members of the capitalist class in high positions there are many differences of opinion, mistakes in perceiving their own interests, and conflicts of interest between different business groups. Thus, the rule of the capitalist class is by no means monolithic; it rules through the forms of shifting coalitions and liberal or conservative styles, as reflected in the Democratic and Republican parties. Finally, the working class (including farmers, industrial workers, intellectual and professional workers, the poor and unemployed, and workers from minority groups) can sometimes organize sufficiently to overcome the power of money by pure weight of numbers, may exert pressure, elect a few representatives, and sometimes even prevail on particular issues.

EFFECTS OF GOVERNMENT ON ECONOMIC INEQUALITY

Although there is no question that extreme inequality exists in the United States, liberals argue that the inequality is much reduced by higher tax rates on the rich, welfare payments to the poor worker, subsidies to the poor farmer, public education for the poor, and antitrust laws, which decrease the concentration of income and power. Thus, Paul Samuelson asserts the U.S. government has reduced income inequality, though he admits that it has not been much of a change: "The welfare state, through redistributive taxation and through educational opportunity . . . has moved the system a bit toward greater equality" (Samuelson, p. 804). Radicals object to this conclusion on several grounds.

First, radicals present the facts on the history of income distribution, which were given in Chapter 17. These facts show that (1) there was very, very little overall change in income distribution between 1910 and 1977; (2) the share of the poorest 20 percent of the population has actually declined; and (3) the share of the richest 20 percent has fluctuated, going down very, very slightly by 1970, but rising throughout the 1970s. Therefore, in spite of many promises by liberal U.S. government administrations, there has been no reduction of inequality since 1910. In fact, after 1980 the Reagan administration actually increased inequality.

Second, the main function of the system is the preservation of "law and order," which means that police and armies and courts and prisons all protect the private ownership of the vast fortunes of the rich. Government thus preserves capitalist control of land and factories. With the help of government in breaking strikes, the rich can continue to pay low enough wages to farm and industrial workers to continue to make the high profits by which they grow richer.

Third, radicals have shown that the administration of every program from taxation to welfare has been such that the rich have benefited more

Table 24.2   MARGINAL TAX RATES
                    FOR 1989

Gross income	Marginal tax rate
$ 10,000	14%
20,000	15
50,000	28
100,000	33
200,000	28
1,000,000	28
10,000,000	28

Source: U.S. Internal Revenue Service.

and the poor less than the law would seem to indicate at first glance. We look in detail at each program in the following sections.

Taxation

Taxes are controlled by governments at the local, state, or national (federal) levels. The most important kinds of taxes are income taxes (at the federal, state, and sometimes local levels), property taxes (at the state and local levels), sales taxes (at the state and local levels), and excise taxes (at all levels). There are a number of other taxes as well.

Taxes are said to be progressive if as income increases by a certain percentage, the tax increases by an even larger percentage. Taxes are said to be proportional if they increase by the same percentage that income increases. Taxes are said to be regressive if, as income increases by a certain percentage, taxes increase by a lesser percentage. Traditionally the federal income tax has been given as the prime example of a progressive tax. At one time, the nominal, or apparent percentage taxation for extra income was as high as 90 percent for the very rich (although as we shall see, the rich never pay as high a rate as the Internal Revenue Service tax schedule would suggest).

In 1986, a major reform of the federal income tax return took place. The major features of this reform included reduction of the marginal tax rates at the high end of the income distribution. The maximum rate (which had once been as high as 90 percent) was lowered from 50 percent to 28 percent for wealthy individuals and from 46 percent to 34 percent for corporations. Table 24.2 shows the marginal tax rates (the tax on each additional dollar of income for a person with that level of income) for income levels ranging from $10,000 to $10,000,000, i.e., from a poverty level to the level of a rich capitalist.

From Table 24.2, one can see that Federal income taxes are progressive for workers and professionals. For incomes between $10,000 and

$50,000—the income range that includes nearly all workers—the tax rate doubles. Thus, the workers with the highest salaries pay twice as high a marginal rate as the lowest paid workers. But a capitalist with an income of $10 million per year pays the same rate as the better paid worker—indeed, a capitalist with an income of $1 billion a year would pay the same rate.

These official IRS tables grossly understate the inequity of the Federal income tax system. It would certainly seem unfair that the well-paid worker earning $50,000 per year pays the same tax rate as the multibillionaire whose income exceeds $1 billion. The real situation is much worse than that, however. In practice, rich taxpayers find many loopholes that allow them to pay much lower tax rates. Thus in 1957 the highest tax rate had risen to an apparently confiscatory 91 percent, and yet that category of taxpayers paid only 52 percent to the government (Kolko, chap. 2). In 1969, the tax rate paid by all taxpayers with incomes reported over $1 million was only 34 percent, and because they are not required to report all of it, the rate was actually only 20 percent (Gurley, p. 11). While we do not have similar studies showing just how much billionaire capitalists actually pay under the 1986 tax law, we do know that these types of tax loopholes will suffice to make working people pay much higher taxes as a percent of their incomes than are paid by wealthy capitalists.

One very large loophole is the tax-free bond. The interest on federal bonds cannot be taxed by states, and the interest on municipal bonds cannot be taxed by states or by the federal government. Of course, to make a significant amount of money from bonds, a very large investment is necessary, and bonds are typically sold in large lots that only the rich can afford. Other loopholes include homeowners' preferences, dividend exclusion, depreciation allowances, and depletion allowances (especially gas and oil).

As a result of these loopholes, some startling statistics have appeared. In 1965 a certain taxpayer had an income of $20 million but paid no taxes. In 1974 some 3302 people earning more than $50,000 paid no federal taxes—and that included 5 people with incomes over $1 million in that single year. *It has been estimated that the total loss of government revenue from all loopholes in the income tax laws is about $77 billion a year* (Lechman and Okner, pp. 13–40).

Whereas the rich, with income from property, can find many tax loopholes, none exists for the average worker with wage income. Consequently, there is in fact only the slightest redistribution of income as a result of the federal income tax. The data for 1962 indicate that the richest fifth (or top 20 percent) of the population had 45.5 percent of all income before taxes. After taxes, their percentage of national income had decreased by only 1.8 percent. The poorest 20 percent had increased their share by only 0.3 percent; the second fifth, by only 0.6 percent, and the third fifth, by only 0.5 percent. *After* taxes the richest 20 percent still had far more income than the poorest 60 percent. With the Reagan tax law of 1986, the inequities of the Federal income tax are sure to become worse.

Even more important to the perpetuation of income inequality in the United States is the fact that the federal income tax amounts to only 40 percent of all taxes and is the only tax that is progressive to even a slight extent. The other 60 percent of taxes are mainly *regressive*, according to most observers, in that they fall more heavily on the lower income groups. "We might tentatively conclude that taxes other than individual income taxes do not reduce, and probably increase, income inequality (Ackerman, p. 24).

Most of the regressive taxes are state and local, such as the sales tax and the property tax. In terms of percentages these fall much more heavily on lower- and middle-income groups than on the rich. For example, a tax on gasoline or telephone service is spread quite equally among the population; therefore these taxes take a much higher percentage of a poor person's income. A number of studies have shown that the burden of state and local taxes is definitely regressive. The lower one's income, the higher the rate at which one pays these state and local taxes (Cantor, 1976).

In addition, a large amount of taxes are paid in the form of compulsory contributions by workers to the social security system. These taxes are highly regressive because there is a minimum tax. After the rich person receives income above the point at which the maximum tax is incurred, the remainder of his or her income becomes tax free.

When all kinds of taxes—federal, state, and local—are added together, the proportionate burden on the poor seems to be actually larger than on the rich. Although the rich pay a larger total amount of taxes, the percentage of their incomes going to taxes is actually less than the percentage of poor families' income going to taxes. In 1967 the poorest families, those with less than $3000 income, paid 34 percent of their income in taxes. In the same year, the richest families, those with incomes over $25,000, paid only 28 percent of their income in taxes. In fact, in 1967 the richest 5 percent of taxpayers had 15 percent of all income before taxes; but they had 17 percent of all income after all federal, state and local taxes were paid (Pechman, pp. 113–137). From all evidence, it would appear that taxes in the mid-1980s are even more inequitable.

In the last 40 years, the tax burden has actually been moving from rich capitalists to all workers and the poor. In 1944 corporate income taxes were 34 percent of all federal revenue, but by 1984 corporate taxes had fallen to only 6 percent of federal revenue. At the same time, social security taxes (paid mostly by workers) rose from 4 percent of federal revenue in 1944 to 29 percent in 1974. In the 1970s and 1980s, the social security taxes were rising faster than any other form of taxes.

The real windfall for corporations, however, came with the Reagan tax cuts of 1981. These cuts contained two provisions by which large corporations could escape federal taxes. First, they were given an accelerated depreciation schedule; second, they were given "tax leasing" provisions.

The notorious "tax leasing" law allows corporations whose tax breaks exceed their profits to sell those tax breaks to other firms. This has resulted in a situation in which hundreds of firms make profits ranging into the millions of dollars and pay absolutely no federal taxes. Even worse, many of them not only pay no taxes, but receive tax refunds after paying no taxes. For example, in 1981 General Electric Co. bought so many tax breaks that it paid absolutely no taxes on its profit of $2.55 billion and received an approximately $100 million tax refund for its previous year's taxes. By 1986 the average tax rate actually paid by corporations was estimated to be less than 10 percent and the economy was rapidly moving toward a state in which corporations do not pay taxes. At current rates, and assuming the Reagan tax changes are not repealed, by 1990 every single American tax payer will have paid, on average, an extra $7330 in taxes to finance $500 billion in tax cuts for corporations. It is not hard to see why the corporate PACs have had such enthusiasm for Reagan, Bush, and their political supporters.

A newspaper report in the *Los Angeles Times* of February 3, 1985, entitled "Well-to-do benefit from lower taxes, don't feel cutbacks," examined some professional and business families in detail, showing that their taxes were way down while none of the spending cuts hurt them. A second article right next to it, entitled "The working poor losing ground in fight for survival," examined some working-class families earning lower-income wages. It showed that these working poor actually have higher taxes (including social security tax) than before Reagan, while the spending cuts lowered their incomes as well as ended some government services (a mother in one family said, "Sometimes, I've just went to bed and cried"). The Congressional Budget Office finds that for the country as a whole, Reagan's policies made the rich richer and the poor poorer. For families with less than $10,000 income in 1984, Reagan's policies lowered their taxes by $20, while cutting government payments to them by $410, a net loss of $390. For families in the $40,000 to $80,000 income bracket, Reagan's policies lowered their taxes by $3,080, while cutting government payments to them by $170, a net gain of $2,910 (*Los Angeles Times*, February 3, 1985). Thus the Reagan policies effected a massive redistribution of income in favor of the rich.

In conclusion, the whole tax system redistributed very little, if any, income from the rich to the poor. In recent years it has redistributed income in the opposite direction—that is, from the poor and the working class to the wealthy. Over longer time periods it has never systematically done anything to mitigate poverty or reduce inequality.

Welfare

Liberals assert that absolute poverty is the only income problem left, ignoring the fact that extreme inequality of income creates a relative, or social, poverty as well. They argue that because a growing number of people are receiving large welfare payments, the poverty problem will be solved. But poverty is not defined simply as an absolute income level of less than $3000; it is *relative* to the society in which a person lives. The people in India live on a median income of $100. There a person earning $3000 per year might be considered wealthy. But there can be no doubt that an American family living on that income can afford neither the cultural nor the physical necessities of life. Even if a person earns $3000, in a society as affluent as the United States that person is living in relative poverty. Therefore, "brutalizing and degrading poverty will exist as long as extreme income inequality exists" (Edwards, p. 244).

Because taxation does not redistribute income, the question is whether welfare programs have a significant effect in that direction. In the first place, expenditures for welfare have been fairly small. In 1968 welfare spending under all federal, state, and local programs was only $26.9 billion. This included public aid, unemployment payments, workers' compensation, health and medical programs, public housing, and educational aid to low-income students. These payments do help the poor somewhat, but the effect is small; they do virtually nothing to alter the relative positions of the poorest or the richest segments of society. Moreover, this $26.9 billion for welfare represents only 3.82 percent of all personal income in 1968. Therefore, although it could improve the lot of a few people, it could not change things very much.

What has been the historical trend of welfare payments? In 1938, welfare payments were 6.7 percent of personal income; in 1950, welfare was down to 3.9 percent; in 1960, it was down a little more, to 3.3 percent. In 1968 it was 3.8 percent whereas in the 1980s, the figure fluctuated between 4 and 5 percent. These figures generally reflect the general state of economy. In 1938 unemployment was very high and poverty was widespread. By 1968, the rate of unemployment as well as the poverty rate had improved. Between 1968 and the decade of the 1980s, however, the economic situation deteriorated. Thus, the 5 percent in 1988 does not reflect liberalized welfare payments—on the contrary, the Reagan administration discontinued or reduced the funding for many programs—but an increase in the number of unemployed and poor people.

Moreover, the poor help pay for welfare, so the net amount received is even less. It is estimated that the poorest 40 percent of the population paid taxes that financed about 25 percent of all welfare payments. Thus, nearly one-quarter of all welfare payments represents money taken from some poor people and then given to others who are poorer. It is no wonder, then, that our tax and welfare systems have not resulted in any significant redistribution of income.

Interestingly, this pattern of small effects and no significant reductions in income inequality over many decades also holds true for the capitalist countries of western Europe. Even in Denmark and Sweden, where taxation and welfare programs are supposed to be extremely progressive, recent studies have shown little change in income distribution (after taxes and welfare) for several decades. A U.N. report reveals that for all western Europe "the general pattern of income distribution, by size of income, for the great majority of households, is only slightly affected by government action" (U.N. Economic Commission of Europe, pp. 1–15).

The problem is that the social and economic conditions of a private enterprise economy lead to a psychology in which one works only if one has to work. Thus, only by offering extremely unequal incomes for differing amounts of work performed can work incentives be maintained under this system. It would take very different institutions with very different education and propaganda to change this psychology. Therefore, U.S. welfare programs are very carefully designed to assist those who do not work—children, the old, the blind. Very little welfare income goes to those who work hard but are paid low wages (who constitute about half of the poverty group) because that might lower their "incentive." A few programs give the low-paid worker minimum health and education so that he or she is able to work but are very careful to avoid providing any food, clothing, or shelter. This philosophy of welfare leads to extreme degradation of welfare recipients. In order to "motivate" the working poor to ever-greater effort, welfare recipients are kept in such a pitiful, dehumanized condition that anyone would rather work, even at the most disagreeable jobs and at the lowest pay.

The "dole" a welfare recipient receives is grossly insufficient for even the barest subsistence livelihood. Moreover, in return for this insignificant sum the individual loses many basic civil rights supposedly guaranteed to everyone. The single woman supporting a family on welfare, for example, must permit welfare workers to search her house and subject her to a demeaning interrogation to ascertain whether her personal sexual conduct is proper and fitting. This is only one of many ways welfare recipients are degraded and dehumanized. It is patently absurd to argue that programs like these will ever eliminate poverty.

Farm Subsidies

The rural poor have suffered the most pathetic poverty. For most of the twentieth century the incomes of small-farm owners and farm workers have lagged far behind other U.S. incomes. For that reason, liberals have persuaded Congress to pass various bills aiding farmers with subsidies. What has been the practical effect of these subsidies?

First, the high economic concentration among the business firms engaged in farming should be noted. At present the richest 7 percent of all farms produce 56 percent of total agricultural output. The poorest 66 percent of all farms produce only 9 percent of farm output. The data showing the concentration of power in agriculture appear in Table 24.3. Concentration in agriculture has greatly increased in the period since subsidies were initiated.

Second, the farm support programs benefit mainly the richest farmers

Table 24.3   BREAKDOWN BY FARM SIZE OF 2.37 MILLION FARMERS FOR 1985

Size class	Number of farms in class	Farm size (acres)	Percent of national farm sales	Percent of profit from farming
Smallest	1,645,000	0–180	10	2
Middle	700,000	180–1000	60	48
Largest	25,000	1000+	30	50

Source: New York Times, Sunday, Feb. 17, 1985, Section 4, p. 15.

and provide very little support for the poorest farmers. A study done a few years ago showed that the poorest 20 percent of all farms received only 1 percent of the farm subsidies given in sugar cane, rice and feed grains, 2 percent of those in cotton, 3 percent of those in wheat, 4 percent of those in peanuts and tobacco, and 5 percent of those in sugar beets. At the same time, the richest 20 percent of all farms (with the highest incomes before subsidies) received 83 percent of the farm subsidies given in sugar cane, 69 percent of those in cotton, 65 percent of those in rice, 62 percent of those in wheat, 56 percent of those in feed grains, 57 percent of those in peanuts, 53 percent of those in tobacco, and 51 percent of those in sugar beets. There is no evidence to suggest that the subsidies are any less unequally distributed now than they were during the period covered by that study.

Third, it appears in fact that the net result of the farm program has been to increase the percentage of total farm income going to the richest farmers and to decrease that going to the poorest farmers. The data from this study show that subsidies are more equally distributed than is income from farming. Thus not only do most of the benefits go to the richest farmers, but their share of the subsidies is higher than their share of the pre-subsidy income, so the disproportionate subsidies increase even further the extreme inequality in farm income. Although these subsidies are certainly regressive, we cannot say just how regressive: "the net effect of these programs may be less regressive than the data suggest—or possibly more regressive—but the pattern is clear" (Bonnen, pp. 235–243).

The discussion up to this point has shown the effects of the farm programs on farmers who own their farms. There is a fourth factor: What are the effects on farm workers, who own nothing but their labor power? The answer is very simple. The main farm programs provide farm owners—mainly on the largest, richest farms—price supports to maintain prices at a certain level above costs, and payments to keep some land out of production in order to reduce the supply of farm goods. No money from these programs goes to farm workers. In fact the programs may hurt farm workers to the extent that the programs pay to keep land out of production, thereby increasing unemployment. "The State pays the *owners* of farm property not to produce, but pays virtually nothing to farm *workers* who become

unemployed as a result of this dole to property owners" (Wachtel, p. 12).
Moreover, less available employment for farm workers will naturally exert
a downward pressure on the wage levels paid for work on the land under
production.

The net result of this program—to help farm workers not at all, to
help poor farmers slightly, and to help rich farmers very much—is not at
all surprising. Indeed it represents the continuation of a consistent pattern
in U.S. history. Large corporations have always been the ones helped
by government subsidies. In the nineteenth century, for example, three-
fourths of all railroad construction was paid for by the government, and
huge amounts of land were given to the railroads. Merchant shipping today
receives large subsidies. Largest of all is the amount the government gives
business for "research and development" ($17 billion in 1969 alone) both
directly and indirectly through academic institutions. President Reagan
recommended giving military contractors over $25 billion for "research
and development" just for the "Star Wars" project—that is, for military
weapons in space.

Education and Inequality

Government-subsidized education is often thought to decrease the inequality of incomes. "The government gives free education to all," goes
the argument, "so anyone can improve his or her station in life by going
to school for a longer period."

Clearly there is a significant positive correlation between amount of
education and level of income. Over the years a number of studies have
shown that on average the more education a person has, the higher will
be his or her income. In large part, however, more and better schooling
is the *effect* of having a higher income (and to some extent individuals from
high-income families may get high-income jobs merely because their parents own the business in which they work).

Children of richer parents receive more schooling largely because their
parents can afford to help them in school longer than poor parents can.
They can pay high tuitions in private schools that admit students even with
low grade averages. Even in the public universities, where the tuition may
be much lower or nonexistent, there are still living expenses. Many students
must drop out of college or are unable to enroll simply because they have
no money on which to live while in school.

Furthermore, children of richer families have a better chance to do
well in school and learn more. Opportunities and encouragement provided
in the home and community are much more likely to produce highly motivated children who know how to study. Cultural background is very important in the performances on IQ tests and college entrance examinations.
These examinations, which purport to test general ability, in reality are
designed to conform to the middle class, white, urban experience. A student
from a poor or rural background will lack the necessary cultural references

to understand the questions or have any intuition of the answers. This has been proved again and again, but the tests are still used. They determine which "track" (discussed below) an elementary student is put into, and they determine who enters college. Thus it is no surprise that only 7 percent of all college students come from the poorest 25 percent of all families.

Another condition that hurts students from poor families and helps those from richer families is the fact that schools in different areas receive very different amounts of money. Central-city slum schools often are given less money per student and almost always attract less competent teachers. Suburban township schools are apt to receive more money per student and attract better teachers.

Students in elementary and high schools are put into different tracks. One track is vocational training, which prepares the poor for manual labor. Another track, college preparation, prepares students from upper-middle-class and richer families for college, so that they can move into high-income jobs (so that their children can go to college and so forth). In elementary schools it is often called *ability grouping* of the bright and the stupid. But the degree of ability is determined by IQ tests that are not objective measures of innate intelligence but, as noted previously, discriminate on the basis of class background.

The tracking system exists both within and between high schools. Within some high schools, counselors push the poor and the minority groups into vocational training and the rich into college preparation. Within others, such pushing is hardly necessary because of the vast differences among schools. Schools in the black slums provide only basic, or vocational, training. Schools in the richest areas give only college preparation. These different tracks are enforced both formally by the tests given and informally by counselors and teachers. One investigation in New York showed that middle-class white children were usually offered voluntary classes in how to pass college examinations, but that in Harlem even seeing the old tests was "against the rules" (Howe and Pautner, p. 234).

We may conclude with certainty that our educational system does not reduce inequality from generation to generation. On the contrary, the richer students have more opportunities to obtain a good elementary and high school education, to be accepted into college, to remain in college, and therefore to be hired for a higher-income job after college—and then to send their own children to college. Thus the educational system seems to transmit inequality from one generation to the next.

GOVERNMENT AND BUSINESS

In the United States the Industrial Revolution commenced after the Civil War. During more than a century of American industrial capitalism, the relationship between government and big business is seen by some observers as having been desultory and often contradictory. This is because many government programs and legislative acts have been designed to promote big business, whereas some laws, particularly antitrust legislation, have ostensibly been designed to curb the size and power of big business.

Thurman Arnold, former "trust-busting" head of the federal government's antitrust division, believes that these contradictory policies and laws have stemmed from "a continuous conflict between opposing ideals in American economic thinking" (Arnold, p. 151). The power of "economic thinking," taken alone, explains very little, however. A more realistic explanation of these seeming contradictions would be based on the two broadest objectives of government in its dealings with big business.

First, the government has been committed to the maintenance of the capitalist system and the promotion of the interests of big business. This commitment has generally dominated the relationship between government and business. The interests of various capitalists and business firms, however, are not always mutually compatible. Many conflicts are so intense that, if left unresolved, they could eventually threaten the very existence of the capitalist system. Government's second objective, therefore, is to act as the arbiter in these rivalries and to resolve the difficulties before they become so extremely serious.

The antitrust laws have given the federal government a measure of power to enforce its function as arbiter. Interpreted in this way, the government's policy toward business has not been contradictory. Nor has this policy been designed, as many liberals believe, to curb the immense power of giant corporations. Rather, it has always attempted to promote the general interests of all capitalists and all businesses. Sometimes the individual interests of capitalists have coincided—as, for example, in the late-nineteenth-century attempt to crush labor unions. But in instances of industrial or commercial rivalry between two giant corporate empires, the interests have been in conflict. In such cases the general interests of all capitalists would depend on at least partial restriction of one or both of the rivals.

American industrialization was aided significantly by the intimate association of government and business. Big business was supported by protective tariffs, which began with the Morrill Tariff of 1861 and were expanded significantly in 1890, 1894, and 1897. The protection from foreign competition thus afforded large corporations removed all restraints on their use of domestic monopoly powers to charge high prices.

The due process clause of the Fourteenth Amendment had been intended to give equal rights to blacks. In the late nineteenth century, however, it was not used to help blacks at all; rather, it was interpreted to prohibit state regulation of corporations (who were considered legal "persons"). The courts denied state governments the right to interfere in any way with even the most abusive, malicious, and socially deleterious corporate behavior.

The railroad magnates were among the most important entrepreneurs in the American Industrial Revolution. Through bribery, chicanery, and fraud, they amassed great personal fortunes. Building railroads was never more than the vehicle from which they launched their financial schemes. The federal government responded by generously giving federal lands to the railroads. Between 1850 and 1871 the railroads were handed 130 million acres of land, an area as large as all the New England states plus Pennsylvania and New York. During the same period, state governments gave the railroads another 49 million acres. All this, and yet some economic historians still refer to the second half of the nineteenth century as an age in which government stayed out of business affairs! (This is, of course, true only if one is speaking of regulatory activity rather than the dispensing of largesse.)

Toward the end of the nineteenth century, the relationship between the federal government and big business became a symbiosis in which the government governed in ways big business wanted it to govern and big business furnished the money, organization, and power structure through which politicians could come to power in the federal government. When progressive elements of the Democratic party saw that Democratic President Cleveland's relationship with big business was hardly distinguishable from the Republican big-business relationship, they captured control of the party and nominated William Jennings Bryan, a champion of the workers and farmers. William McKinley, the big-business Republican candidate, raised campaign funds estimated to total as much as $15 million, 50 times Bryan's $300,000. From that time on, the Democratic party has been more careful to pick candidates who are in favor of at least a segment of big business.

Regulatory Agencies

Since the late nineteenth century the U.S. government has established many regulatory agencies, such as the Interstate Commerce Commission, supposedly designed to protect consumer and environmental interests. Thus telephone and electric companies are given monopolies, but public agencies are placed above them to regulate their profits. These commissions are commonly thought to be the watchdogs of the public interests, but they often turn out to be merely a legal way of giving monopoly powers to an oligopoly. The commissions are generally dominated by those interests they are supposed to regulate and usually neglect the public interest. For example, when the public does not give them careful attention, the public utilities commissions normally grant most price increases desired by the regulated companies. Similarly, when California passed a new law by voters' initiative (against strong pressure from the construction industry) to regulate building on the California shoreline in the interest of environmental protection, Governor Reagan appointed to the agencies responsible for enforcement mostly representatives *opposed* to the protection of the shoreline.

President Reagan's appointments also were blatantly probusiness. He appointed James Watt to the Department of the Interior, where he gave away much of the wilderness area to businesses. And he appointed Ann Gorsuch Burford to the Environmental Protection Agency, where she protected business while it destroyed the environment. President Bush's appointments appear to be continuing this tradition.

Antitrust Laws

There have been four major laws designed ostensibly to decrease the monopoly power of big business. The first was the Sherman Anti-Trust Act of 1890 which forbade any contract, combination, or conspiracy to restrain trade. In fact, it forbade any agreement not to compete, regardless of how the agreement was achieved. It also forbade monopolies or attempts to monopolize.

The Clayton Act of 1914 forbade corporations to engage in price discrimination—that is, to force some customers to pay more than others. It also prohibited *interlocking directorates* where this would lead to a substantial reduction of competition.

The Federal Trade Commission Act of 1914 outlawed *unfair* methods of competition and established the FTC to investigate the methods of competition used by business firms. Finally, the Celler-Kefauver Act of 1950 forbade the purchase of either the stock of a competing corporation (which had already been illegal) or the assets of competing corporations (hitherto a big loophole in the laws).

The antitrust laws were supposed to limit the concentration of economic power among corporations. Yet, as one observer has written, "the fact that after the passage of the Sherman Act the country witnessed a spectacular merger movement, another wave after the passage of the Clayton Act (1914), and again after the Celler-Kefauver Act, indicates that the laws have been ineffective in 'limiting the concentration of control' " (Dowd, p. 49).

For the first two decades after the passage of the Sherman Act, the antitrust laws were used almost exclusively to break the power of labor unions to strike against employers. Although there have been periodic convictions of business firms throughout the twentieth century, most observers agree that virtually all the important oligopolistic corporations are constantly violating most of the antitrust sanctions. There is almost no price competition among the giants. There are numerous instances of interlocking directorates and almost no one doubts the pervasive existence of illegal collusion among giant corporations.

Why, then, are a few corporations occasionally convicted for violations of which virtually all corporations are guilty? We believe that in these cases the government uses the antitrust laws to act as arbiter in the irreconcilable conflicts among various corporations. Antitrust convictions are generally mild punitive actions, taken when the government decides which group of corporations should be supported in a particular conflict of interest. This was most apparent recently when the U.S. government acted against certain conglomerate mergers in which "young newcomers" tried to take over old, established corporations.

The antitrust laws were never strongly enforced. Under President Reagan, however, the Justice Department nearly ignored the antitrust laws. New indictments declined drastically. A very strong case against AT&T was dropped in favor of a settlement that gave AT&T tens of millions of dollars of extra profits from telephone users.

The government does not really attempt to eliminate the pervasive illegal policies of corporations. Throughout American history the government has done everything it could to create and promote the interests of monopolistic businesses. For the good of all, a few must occasionally be slapped on the wrists. Antitrust laws make this possible. They therefore operate to blunt some of the traditional antimonopoly sentiment and to resolve come conflicts among different corporate interests.

Government Purchasing Policy

Federal, state, and local governments buy one-quarter to one-third of our national product. Corporations selling to government earn much higher than average profit rates. The largest single government purchase is of military supplies, where the most spectacular profits are made. Through this mechanism, government purchasing policies tend to shift income to the corporations and to their rich stockholders. Government spending is analyzed in detail in Chapter 33.

SUMMARY

The economic power of a comparatively few corporations and individuals, examined in previous chapters, was shown here to result in a disproportionate degree of political power for this group. This is not an accident but a perfectly natural result of their control over the press, television and radio, advertising, financing for political campaigns and for lobbying, foundations, and the many other avenues of control open to those with wealth.

Because of this natural influence (not a conspiracy), government policies do not decrease inequality in the American economy. In fact, after considering only the policies that are supposed to reduce inequality (such as taxation, farm subsidies, and education), we can conclude that many of them actually increase the degree of inequality. If we had considered all government policies, the net effect would undoubtedly have been a substantial increase in inequality. Given the present sources of political power, it appears very doubtful whether the government will ever take actions that will substantially reduce poverty and inequality.

SUGGESTED READINGS

The best single survey of radical political analysis is Albert Szymanski, *The Capitalist State and the Politics of Class* (Cambridge, Mass.: Winthrop Publishers, 1979). The socioeconomic role of education is explained in a potent fashion in Samuel Bowles and Herbert Gintis, *Schooling in Capitalist America* (New York: Basic Books, 1978). An excellent book on the economic bases of Congress is Philip M. Stern, *The Best Congress Money Can Buy* (New York: Pantheon Books, 1988). An outstanding book on our low voting turnout is Frances Fox Piven and Richard A. Cloward, *Why Americans Don't Vote* (New York: Pantheon Books, 1988).

REFERENCES

Ackerman, F., et al. "Income Distribution in the United States." In *Review of Radical Political Economy.* Summer 1971.

Arnold, Thurman. "Economic Reform and the Sherman Anti-Trust Act." In *Historical Viewpoints: Volume Two, Since 1865.* Edited by J. A. Garraty. New York: Harper & Row, 1969.

Bonnen, James. "The Effect of Taxes and Government Spending on Inequality." In *The Capitalist System.* Edited by R. Edwards, M. Reich, and T. Weisskopf. Englewood Cliffs, N.J.: Prentice-Hall, 1972.

"Business Outspends Labor 7 to 1 in State Elections." *Riverside Press-Enterprise,* October 7, 1982.

Cantor, Arnold. "State Local Taxes: A Study of Inequity." In AFL–CIO *American Federationist,* February 1974.

Congressional Budget Office data. In "The Poor Get Poorer; the Rich Get Richer." *Los Angeles Times,* February 3, 1985.

Cummings, Milton, and F. Wise. *Democracy Under Pressure.* New York: Harcourt Brace Jovanovich, 1971.

Dahl, Robert, and Charles Lindblom. *Politics, Economics and Welfare.* New York: Harper & Row, 1953.

Dowd, Douglas F. *Modern Economic Problems in Historical Perspective.* Lexington, Mass.: Raytheon/Heath, 1965.

Edwards, Richard. "Who Fares Well in the Welfare State." In *The Capitalist System.* Edited by R. Edwards, M. Reich, and T. Weisskopf. Englewood Cliffs, N.J.: Prentice-Hall, 1972.

"Financial Disclosure." *Congressional Quarterly* 36. September 2, 1978.

Green, Mark, James Fallows, and David, Zwick. *Who Runs Congress?* New York: Bantam, 1972.

Gurley, John. "Federal Tax Policy." In *National Tax Journal.* September 1967.

Howe, Florence, and Paul Pautner. "How the School System Is Rigged." In *The Capitalist System.* Edited by R. Edwards, M. Reich, and T. Weisskopf. Englewood Cliffs, N.J.: Prentice-Hall, 1972.

Irish, Marian, and James Protho. *The Politics of American Democracy.* Englewood Cliffs, N.J.: Prentice-Hall, 1965.

Kolko, Gabriel. *Wealth and Power in America.* New York: Praeger, 1962.

Lechman, J., and B. Okner. "Individual Income Tax Erosion by Income Classes." In *Economics of Federal Subsidy Programs.* U.S. Congress, Joint Economic Committee. Washington, D.C.: GPO, 1972.

The Nation. Editorial column. November 6, 1976.

The New York Times, August 4, 1981.

Pechman, Joseph. "The Rich, the Poor, and the Taxes They Pay." *The Public Interest,* Fall 1969.

Samuelson, Paul. *Economics.* 9th ed. New York, McGraw-Hill, 1973.

United Nations Economic Commission of Europe. *Incomes in Postwar Europe: A Survey of Policies, Growth, and Distribution.* Geneva: United Nations, 1957.

"Vote Would Close Loopholes for Rich." *Riverside Press-Enterprise,* May 13, 1976.

Wachtel, Howard. "Looking at Poverty from a Radical Perspective." In *Review of Radical Political Economics.* Summer 1971.

Wilson, Woodrow. *The New Freedom.* Garden City, N.Y.: Doubleday, 1914.

Chapter
25

Economics of Discrimination

Many elementary economics books ignore racial and sexual discrimination as social phenomena outside the purview of economics. These phenomena, however, have political-economic roots and, in turn, affect the economy in important ways.

TYPES OF DISCRIMINATION

Racism in the United States involves prejudice and discrimination against a number of minorities. In its most common form, racism uses an ideology claiming that another race is inferior in order to justify profit-making activity and discrimination against the members of that other race. For example, the white colonists in America declared that the Indians were inferior and then stole their land and almost eliminated them. Today, American Indians have a median income only one-third of the national average, over one-half of the Indian population lives below the official poverty line, and unemployment on Indian reservations ranges between 20 and 90 percent.

Ironically, each succeeding wave of white settlers was met by a form of discrimination called *nationalist* prejudice, which was directed at them by those who were already here. Thus all eastern Europeans were held to be backward in culture; Italians were all lazy; and Irish were all loud and uncouth. Chinese and Japanese immigrants faced a combination of nationalist and racist prejudice. During World War II all Americans of Japanese ancestry on the West Coast were confined to concentration camps. (German Americans were never imprisoned.) Finally, nationalist and racist prejudice also combine to support discrimination against Americans of Mexican and Puerto Rican origin. (Both groups were incorporated into the United States through imperialist expansion, one group in the war against Mexico and the other in the war against Spain.)

Religious bigotry is another form of discrimination closely related to national chauvinism and racial prejudice; indeed, all three forms of discrimination are similar both in cause and in effect. In Europe, Protestants and Catholics killed each other for centuries; in America, the Catholic minority is still subjected to a certain amount of prejudice and discrimination. Much worse, of course, is the centuries-old oppression of the Jews, who were forcibly converted, limited to certain occupations, often taxed to bankruptcy, and periodically massacred. In the late nineteenth and early twentieth centuries, it appeared that anti-Jewish sentiment was finally dying away, and it has never been as severe in America as in some other countries, although it is certainly present. But just as the Jews began to feel secure, Hitler's fascism unleashed the worst racist atrocity in the history of humankind. More than 6 million Jewish men, women, and children were tortured, gassed, and burned to death.

Another racist atrocity was the enslavement of black Africans throughout three centuries and their shipment under horrifying conditions to various places of prison and work, especially the American South. This enslavement was not done in the name of Aryan domination, as was Hitler's killing of the Jews and other "inferior" people, but in the gentle name of Christianity, it being the white man's burden to bring civilization and the true faith to the black man. One result of this enslavement is that blacks today constitute the largest single minority in the United States, and one of the most oppressed.

When blacks were slaves doing simple agricultural work in the South, racism played its usual function of explaining that blacks were inferior to whites, that slavery was their natural condition, that such simple labor was all they could do, and that they were very happy in this condition. Now that blacks are a majority in some American cities and do all the complex tasks required to run American industry and urban life, the prejudices have changed somewhat, but the discrimination is still fierce.

Last but not least, there is sexist discrimination against women in America. It will be shown that both the attitudes and the actual discrimination against the female 51 percent of Americans are very similar in nature to the discrimination against racial, national, and religious minorities.

THE IDEOLOGY OF RACISM

Racism is the conviction that minority groups are biologically inferior. Racism is an "ideology" that contains a systematic set of beliefs claiming the superiority of one group to others. Racism is a "prejudice" in that no amount of evidence can shake these beliefs—and even inconsistent beliefs do not bother the true believers.

Adolf Hitler carried racism to its ultimate point in the 1930s, when he proclaimed that white, male, non-Jewish Germans (called "Aryans") were a "master race," superior to all other groups. He created a stereotype, or ideal picture, of all Aryans as big, strong, blond, and of superior intelligence—even though Hitler himself was none of these. His stereotypic Jew was small, dark, greedy, and cowardly. His stereotype of all other peoples was likewise physically weak and mentally inferior. In his stereotype, all women were stupid and good for nothing but sex and childbearing; Aryan women were no different but were beautiful as well. Such stereotypes were far more than harmless nonsense; on this basis Hitler killed millions of Jews and Russians, and enslaved hundreds of millions of people, particularly women.

Similarly, slave owners in the American South before the Civil War claimed that blacks were biologically inferior. Stereotypic blacks were stupid and lazy, shuffled their feet when they walked, and liked to sing and dance (to celebrate their happy life as slaves). The stereotype also said that blacks were oversexed. This has long provided an excuse for white men to rape black women, while lynching black men for imaginary rapes of white women.

There are still racists who claim that all blacks are mentally inferior. For example, Dr. William Shockley, a white male physicist, claimed in 1973 that in data "from Negro populations with average IQ's of 80 in Georgia and 90 in California that each 1 percent of Caucasian ancestry raises average IQ by one point for these low IQ populations" (quoted in United Press, 1973, p. A2). So the blood of the "master race" raises intelligence! Yet over and over again anthropologists and psychologists have demonstrated that IQ scores are dependent on socioeconomic status and cultural background (because of the way the tests are designed) and are thus not true measures of intelligence.

Such unscientific stereotypes are common in everyday thinking and strongly affect and harm blacks in occupational and professional roles. The following incident illustrates the awful power of prejudiced stereotypes:

> A young Negro lawyer recently recalled his first case, in which he was called upon to defend a burglar. The thief, white, appeared before the judge dressed as he had been when apprehended by the police, in dirty work clothes, his hair mussed, an unshaven face. The lawyer . . . was neatly dressed in a business suit, was well-shaven, and was carrying a briefcase. The judge looked at both men and asked, unjokingly, "Which man is the lawyer?" (Quoted in Epstein, 1971, p. 180n)

How much attention do you imagine the judge paid to the black lawyer's arguments?

FACTS OF RACIST DISCRIMINATION

Black families have much lower income than white families. Because of the victories of the militant civil rights movement of the 1960s, the median family income of blacks rose from 54 percent of white income in 1964 to 61 percent in 1969. Because of white backlash in the 1970s and 1980s, black income fell back to 56 percent in 1987. In fact, black family income in 1987 in terms of real purchasing power was considerably below the 1973 level. (All data in this section are from U.S. government sources, particularly the U.S. Census Bureau.) An amazing 33 percent of all black families in 1987 were below the poverty level. In 1985 the median wealth of black families was only $13,397, while the median wealth of white families was $39,135.

One of the reasons for the number of blacks living in poverty is the job discrimination that results in much higher unemployment rates among blacks than among whites. Decade after decade black unemployment rates have been more than double those for whites. In 1985, for example, black unemployment was 15 percent, compared to 6 percent for whites. Black teenage workers face particularly severe discrimination; their unemployment rate in 1983 was 45 percent. All of these unemployment figures are official U.S. Labor Department data, but we shall show in Chapter 26 that these official data are drastically understated. Black females are even worse off than black males because they suffer from both racist and sexist discrimination. Black female adult unemployment in 1983, during a period of economic recovery, was still 17.1 percent, although white female adult unemployment had fallen to 7.9 percent. Most of their poverty, however, was due to the fact that, although most black female family heads were hardworking, full-time workers, they were being paid below-poverty wages.

In the political sphere, although blacks comprise 11 percent of the U.S. population, blacks in 1987 comprised only 5 percent of the U.S. House of Representatives (there were no black members of the U.S. Senate). In the same year, blacks made up only 4 percent of state legislators and less than 1 percent of elected city and county officials.

Another basic area of continuing discrimination is education. By 1984, only 14 percent of blacks in the 25–34 age group had completed four years or more of college, while 25 percent of whites had finished four years or more of college. Most blacks who dropped out of school did so because of economic pressures. Even with a college education, blacks face discrimination. The unemployment rate in 1984 for whites with one to three years of college was 6 percent, but it was 13 percent for blacks with the same education. Black college graduates have about the same unemployment rate as white high school graduates! In 1985, black male college graduates earned only 78 percent as much as white college graduates (see Winnick).

Finally there is continued job segregation against blacks. Black men and women are overrepresented among poorly paid factory workers and domestic servants. Blacks represent only a very small percentage of highly paid managers, professionals, and administrators.

WHAT CAUSES RACISM?

The most conservative view now, as always, is that inherited biological differences make blacks (and Mexicans, Indians, Jews, Catholics, and other minorities) intellectually and physically inferior. This inferiority is the cause of lower income, less educational achievement, and so forth. Moreover, they are lazy and like to live in squalor. Because these arguments cannot be validated by any scientific evidence, and because refutations do not diminish the prejudice one bit, we may leave this view without further comment. Races are, of course, defined by their superficial physical differences, but there are no important biological differences among the races of humankind, much less any inherited intellectual differences.

Most sociologists are liberal enough to admit that blacks are not inherently inferior. They still insist that the problem lies in the minds of blacks and whites. Many assume that all whites have racist attitudes. Many assume that all blacks have attitudes making it more difficult for them to get good jobs, such as "low aspiration patterns that set limited achievement goals" (Ferman, Kornbluh, and Miller, p. 32). The traditional sociologists' solution would seem to be that an unprejudiced psychoanalyst (from Mars?) must be employed to change the attitudes of all whites and blacks through therapy.

Radicals agree that most whites have racist prejudices. It is also a fact that some blacks still have attitudes of inferiority that impede their progress, though most of the reports on black attitudes are myths used to excuse discrimination. It must be emphasized that the discrimination caused by white racism is a thousand times more of a barrier to blacks at present than any remaining black attitudes of inferiority.

But the most important question is, "Why do these white racist attitudes persist?" Hundreds of comparative studies of other societies show that whites are not born with attitudes of racial superiority and blacks are not born with attitudes of racial inferiority. These attitudes are inculcated by society. They are given to children by the older generation in the family, by the educational system (e.g., in stereotypes in textbooks), by the media (e.g., in stereotypes on television, in newspapers, books, and magazines), and by political leaders.

This leads to the next question: "Why does the establishment permit and encourage racist stereotypes?" Of course, the degree of open stereotyping has been reduced in recent years but only under the pressure of the civil rights movement. It is the contention of radicals that racism plays an important function in supporting the status quo and that the capitalist establishment benefits from it both directly and indirectly.

WHO BENEFITS FROM RACISM?

Conservative economists agree with the conservative sociologists that no one benefits from discrimination, that it is merely a matter of irrational and inexplicable tastes or preferences. Conservatives emphasize that discrimination by business is irrational because (so they claim) profits are lost as a result. They argue that if there is discrimination in other areas of the economy, then each capitalist is presented with a supply of qualified blacks willing to work for wages below the going wages. Since the capitalist can purchase these workers at lower wages, profits can be increased by doing so. Therefore, capitalists who are willing to hire blacks (below the going wage) will make more profits, whereas those who refuse to hire blacks at any wage will lose profits. Thus the conservative Milton Friedman claims,

> a businessman or an entrepreneur who expresses preferences in his business activities that are not related to productive efficiency is in effect imposing higher costs on himself than are other individuals who do not have such preferences. Hence, in a free market they will tend to drive him out. (Friedman, p. 108)

The conservative economists conclude that the capitalists who discriminate do so for irrational reasons and lose money because of the discrimination. They further argue that under pure competition capitalists who discriminate will eventually be put out of business because of their higher costs per unit. Thus competition will tend to end discrimination and push black wages ever closer to white wage levels.

Most liberal economists seem to agree with most of these premises, which flow from good neoclassical economics. They argue, however, that the U.S. economy is characterized by a high degree of monopoly rather than by pure competition. By the exercise of their monopoly power in the labor market and in the commodity market, firms can hold down all wages and pass on to consumers some of the cost of discrimination. In other words, although the liberals agree with the conservatives that racism is an inexplicable attitude, they contend that it costs the capitalist only a little to indulge his strange preference. Therefore, they believe it might be a long time, if ever, before capitalism ends discrimination, and so they support the passage of legislation to end discrimination.

Radicals, on the other hand, do not believe that capitalists lose money from discrimination or that their attitudes are inexplicable. How could discrimination continue for such a long time if capitalists lose from it? Capitalists gain in many ways from racist discrimination and hence have an interest in continuing it. They gain because (1) racist prejudice divides workers, making unions weaker and resulting in lower wages for all workers; (2) the same division makes capitalist politicians safer from attacks by labor; (3) racist discrimination makes it easy to keep blacks as an unemployed reservoir of cheap labor for boom times; (4) racism provides white politicians with a scapegoat for many social problems; and (5) racism helps inspire soldiers when they are supposed to kill people in third world countries. As a result white capitalists as a whole benefit from racism, although white workers as a whole lose from racism (Reich, 1988).

Radicals maintain that in the pre-Civil War South racism was a useful apologia for slavery, alleviating guilty consciences on the part of slave owners, promoting an easier acceptance of their lot among slaves, and preventing Northerners from interfering. Racism declared that slavery was divinely ordained by God as a benefit to the inferior black. Its first function was to justify economic exploitation.

The function of racism continues today, when apologists contend that black and Chicano workers are poorly paid only because they are inferior workers. More important, to the extent that white workers believe the racist ideology, unions are weakened by excluding black workers—or by accepting them reluctantly and preventing them from having equal power. White and black workers have frequently broken each others' strikes in the past, though they are now learning to work together. In the areas of strongest racism and weakest unions, such as the South, black workers' wages are very low, but white workers' wages are almost as low. For this reason, one liberal economist has concluded, "Far from being indifferent to the existence of discriminatory attitudes on the part of workers, the capitalist gains from them and may find it profitable to invest in their creation" (Morris Silver, quoted in Franklin and Resnick, p. 23).

Another reason that racism is profitable to capitalists is its provision of a handy, but disposable, labor force. If an employer has ten black and ten white workers, and must fire half for a couple of months, which will he fire? If "he is rational and seeks to minimize his labor turnover costs, he will lay off his ten black workers on the assumption that they will be unlikely to get permanent or better jobs elsewhere because of the discriminatory practices of other employers" (ibid., p. 20). Thus the capitalist can (and does) fire black workers in each recession, easily hiring them back in times of expansion. He also gains by not having to pay the fringe benefits due workers who stay on the job for a longer time.

Radicals assert that blacks are exploited within the United States, both as an internal colony and as workers. Blacks today constitute about one-third of the entire industrial labor force and an even larger percentage of unskilled manual laborers. Racial discrimination keeps them "in their place" as a large pool of unskilled and often unemployed workers to be used to hold down wages in times of high demand for labor; racial prejudice justifies this discrimination. Thus racism is in this respect only an additional apologia for considerable extra profits extracted at the expense of the lowest-paid part of the American working class.

Because that exploitation is at the heart of the system, legal reforms cannot give much help to most blacks. Radicals claim that

> the system has two poles: wealth, privilege, power at one; poverty, deprivation, powerlessness at the other. It has always been that way, but in earlier times

whole groups could rise because expansion made room above, and there were others ready to take their place at the bottom. Today, Negroes are at the bottom, and there is neither room above nor anyone ready to take their place. Thus only individuals can move up, not the group as such: reforms help the few, not the many. For the many, nothing short of a complete change in the system—the abolition of both poles and the substitution of a society in which wealth and power are shared by all—can transform their condition (Baran and Sweezy, p. 27).

Radicals maintain that the primary political function of racism is to find a scapegoat for all problems. For example, the white is told that the dirt and violence of the modern city are all due to the blacks. Similarly, Hitler told German workers that unemployment was all due to Jewish bankers, while the middle class was told that all the agitation was due to Jewish communists.

The second political function of racism, according to radicals, is to divide the oppressed so the elite can rule. For example, few Americans are more oppressed or poverty-stricken than white southern sharecroppers. But they have always fought against their natural allies, the blacks. Instead, the poor white has given political support to the wealthy white southerners who not only monopolize southern state and local politics but also wield disproportionate influence in Congress because they succeed to and hold key committee chairmanships and leadership positions by virtue of seniority. The same kind of divide-and-rule tactic is used in northern cities.

Radicals also claim that racism is a particularly handy tool of imperialism. England especially has long used the strategy of divide and rule: Hindu against Moslem, Jew against Arab, Protestant against Catholic, Biafran against Nigerian, black against Hindu in Guyana. And America is quite willing to use the same tactic: Vietnamese against Cambodian, Thai against Laotian. Moreover, "inferiority" (inherited or acquired) is still being given as a reason for lack of development—where imperialism is the real reason. Finally, national chauvinism, or patriotism, always asserts that aggression comes from the other, evil people and that "our" pure motives should not be questioned.

SEXIST IDEOLOGY: STEREOTYPES OF WOMEN

Just as the ideology of racism relies on stereotypes of blacks, the ideology of sexism relies on stereotypes of women. One stereotype of women is that they are all sentimental and impulsive, emotional and foolish—not hard-headed, stable, and logical, as in the stereotype of men. For example, Vice-President Spiro Agnew, who was forced to resign because of his criminal activity, has said: "Three things have been difficult to tame—the ocean, fools, and women. We may soon be able to tame the ocean; fools and women will take a little longer" (quoted in Amundsen, p. 114).

Yet the opposite stereotype of women also exists. Women are narrow in vision, interested in little material things, and grasping and evil. For example, the men who wrote the Bible claim: "And the Lord God said unto the woman, What is this that thou has done? And the woman said, The serpent beguiled me, and I did eat." On this basis medieval men stereotyped all women as sly, sharp, aggressive witches.

Of course, these two stereotypes are contradictory. How can all women be greedy, sharp, and aggressive at the same time they are being sentimental and foolish? Such inconsistencies, however, never seem to bother prejudiced people. Nor are racists and sexists bothered by conflicting evidence; they see things the way they wish to see them: "Thus, an anti-Semite watching a Jew may see devious or sneaky behavior. But in a Christian he would regard such behavior only as quiet, reserved, or perhaps even shy" (Goldberg, 1971, p. 168). Since prejudice distorts "evidence," no amount of objective evidence can change prejudice.

As an example of how prejudiced stereotyping is much too stubborn for evidence, imagine an employer interviewing a series of people for an executive job. Suppose he possesses the usual stereotype of women. Suppose the first woman is sophisticated and careful before speaking. He thinks she is too passive and "feminine" for the job. Suppose the second woman objects to something he says. He thinks she is too aggressive. Suppose the third person is a man: he gets the job. In many real cases like this imaginary one, prejudiced stereotypes are not harmless; they lead directly to discrimination.

Above all, sexist stereotypes are intended to justify the domination of women by men. This is very apparent in a statement by Napoleon Bonaparte:

> Nature intended women to be our slaves . . . they are our property, we are not theirs. They belong to us, just as a tree that bears fruit belongs to a gardener. What a mad idea to demand equality for women! . . . Women are nothing but machines for producing children. (Quoted in Morgan, p. 7)

Sexism, or the theory of male supremacy, is an ideology that serves to justify discrimination against the majority of Americans. Although sexism is similar to the pattern of discrimination and in ideology to racism, it is more pervasive, more deeply ingrained, and harder to combat. Clearly the black woman is held to be doubly "inferior" and suffers the most discrimination.

SEXIST DISCRIMINATION

In 1890, women constituted only 17 percent of the labor force, although many more were unpaid workers on farms owned by their husbands. (All data in this section, unless otherwise stated, comes from the U.S. Department of Labor, Womens Bureau.) From this period comes the myth that all women are housewives and play no role in the paid labor force. This myth no longer has even a semblance of truth. By 1940 women made up 25 percent of the labor force. In World War II women suddenly became 36 percent of the labor force, then dropped to 28 percent in 1947 as they were pushed out of jobs by returning veterans. Since then, there has been a steady rise, until in 1986 women represented 44 percent of the labor force.

A majority of all women (64 percent) in the working ages (20–64) were in the labor force in 1986. Moreover, 58 percent of all working women were married at that time. So most women work at a paid job. Most women workers really have two jobs, a paid job plus the unpaid job of housewife. Even women with small children now work outside the home; in 1986, 64 percent of women with children under 17 were in the labor force.

Working women generally work for the same reason as men—economic necessity. About 42 percent of women workers are single, divorced, separated, or widowed, so have no choice but to work. Women head 12 percent of U.S. families, with about half of those families living in poverty.

But why are more and more married women working in paid jobs? Because of inflation, their wages are more and more necessary to attain a minimum decent standard of living. Women work more if they have more years of education and fewer small children. If we look at women with the same education (e.g., 4 years of high school) and the same age level of children (e.g., ages 6 to 17), then we find that the percentage of women working declines as the husband's income level is higher. In fact, 71 percent of all working women are single, divorced, separated, widowed, or have husbands earning less than $10,000 per year and so are working because of dire need.

Because of discrimination most women forced to work outside the home are paid less than male workers receive for the same jobs. The wage gap is large and has been improving only very slowly. The median full-time, year-round woman worker earned only 65 percent of men's median wages in 1955, but this percentage rose to 70 percent in 1987. Wage discrimination is true even in specific professions where everyone has high educational qualifications; in 1985 female social scientists earned only $25,000 a year, while male social scientists earned $34,700 a year.

Some of the wage gap is thus caused by direct discrimination within an occupation. Another factor causing the wage gap is discrimination in promotion. For example, on all college and university faculties women account for 51 percent of the low-paid category of instructors but only 33 percent of the higher category of assistant professors, only 19 percent of the still higher category of associate professors, and only 10 percent of the highest paid category of professor. The same pattern is true of all occupations. For example, 90 percent of all bank tellers are women, but only 19 percent of bank officers.

The largest single cause of the wage gap, however, is the segregation that keeps women out of many high-paying occupations and pushes them into a few low-paying occupations. These low-paying occupations are then relatively overcrowded with the large supply of women workers forced into them, so the employers can continue to pay low wages. Thus in 1984 some 26 percent of all women workers were crowded into just 20 narrowly defined occupational groups: for example, women were 97 percent of nurses and 84 percent of elementary schoolteachers. Men, on the other hand, were spread out over a wide range of occupations.

At the other end of the spectrum, women are present in very small numbers in the high-paying occupations and professions. The percentage of women in high-paying jobs did increase in the late 1960s, the 1970s, and the 1980s as a result of the women's movement. Pressure from the women's movement achieved the passage of antidiscrimination laws. Propaganda from the women's movement changed the consciousness of men and women and opened up new vistas on possible careers for women. Even with this movement, which caused large increases in the percentages, in 1980 only 4 percent of all engineers were women.

In the political arena, even though women represent 51 percent of the U.S. population, in 1989 they made up only 2 percent of the U.S. Senate, 4 percent of the U.S. House of Representatives, 1 percent of federal judges, 4 percent of governors, 5 percent of state senators, and 10 percent of state representatives.

Because of the women's movement—and out of economic necessity— women began to overcome prejudice in the professions. In 1960, women were only 2 percent of all lawyers, 7 percent of doctors, and 2 percent of dentists. By 1980 women were 13 percent of lawyers, 13 percent of doctors, and 4 percent of dentists. In 1986, there were still only 32,000 women economists but 132,000 male economists.

Yet there are small numbers of women in the higher-paying professions. The earnings gap between men and women has continued to increase because (1) most new women workers have gone into the poorest-paying occupations, (2) some discrimination in wages for the same jobs continues, and (3) women are still not promoted as often as men.

WHAT CAUSES SEXISM?

The ideologies of racism and sexism are similar in many ways. Both are based on the supported inferiority of some groups of human beings to others: "All discrimination is eventually the same—Anti-Humanism" (Chisholm, p. 45). Even in the present "enlightened" age, the ideology of sexism continues unabated. Thus the conservative view still justifies lower pay for women: "If a woman were more like a man, she'd be treated as such" (Black, p. 37). This view ignores the main point: that millions of women receive less pay for doing the same work as men.

Tests show that men and women are equal in intelligence, although they usually progress at different rates of learning in childhood, with women leading in the early years.

Certainly there are physical differences between men and women. With respect to working ability, however, the evidence indicates that on the average male and female workers are equal. In fact, in some primitive societies women normally carry heavier loads than men. The question is one of training and expectations. Listen to the lot of a slave woman of the American South as expressed by the great black abolitionist Sojourner Truth: "Look at my arm! I have ploughed and planted and gathered into barns, and no man could head me—and ain't I a woman? I have borne thirteen children, and seen most of 'em sold into slavery, and when I cried out with my mother's grief, none but Jesus heard me—and ain't I a woman?" (Quoted in Bird, p. 25)

Even in social and sexual matters, in the radical view, it is not a given, eternal fact that man must always dominate. In some primitive societies men and women appear to have about equal social and sexual roles. This is especially true in societies in which the economic roles of the two are roughly equal in importance, as when women gather wild food and men hunt. In other primitive societies, in which women conduct agriculture and hunting is unimportant, women appear to play the dominant role. If nothing else can be said without controversy, at least modern anthropology makes clear that there are many types of family organization (including various kinds of group marriages), not just one eternal type in which man dominates.

Only with the coming of civilization—meaning economic stratification and the possession of property in land, cattle, slaves, or serfs—did the women also become articles of property. In fact, for purposes of clear inheritance of property the upper class woman in ancient civilizations was very well guarded; only the male could freely violate the theoretical monogamy system. This was the beginning of the double standard.

The particular attitudes of American men and women are carefully inculcated, not inherited. "Women are taught from the time they are children to play a serving role, to be docile and submissive . . ." (Goldberg, 1970, p. 35) by the family, the schools, the media, the church, corporations, and the government—areas in which white males are usually dominant.

It has often been said that the position of women in a society mirrors the general condition of human rights in a society. Even in the nineteenth century, the connection was pointed out to those radicals who wished to ignore it: "Every socialist recognized the dependence of the workmen on the capitalist . . . but the same socialist often does not recognize the dependence of women on men because the question touches his own dear self more or less clearly" (Bebel, 1892). In the twentieth century, the ideology of women's inferiority reached its high point in Nazi Germany. The Nazi directive to women was to be with "children, kitchen, and church."

WHO BENEFITS FROM SEXISM?

As in the case of racism, conservative economists argue that capitalists actually lose by discriminating against qualified women. Such discrimination, they say, means paying men for a job that women could do equally well for less pay. In the words of establishment economist Barbara Bergmann,

> We come . . . to the allegation, usually made by radicals out to discredit capitalism, that women's subjection is all a capitalist plot. Who benefits financially from maintenance of the *status quo?* The most obvious beneficiaries of prejudice against women are male workers in those occupations in which women are not allowed to compete . . . It is not the male workers or their wives who do the discriminating, however. The employers of the male workers (almost entirely males themselves) are the ones who do the actual discriminating, although of course they are cheered on in their discriminatory ways by their male employees. The employers actually tend to lose financially since profits are lowered when cheap female help is spurned in favor of high-priced male help. (Bergmann, 1973, p. 14)

So in her view it is not the capitalists but only the male workers who gain from discrimination. The poor capitalists, who are actually responsible for the discriminating, lose by it. But why do capitalists in business for profits systematically choose to lose money? She says they lose financially but gain psychologically: "It feels so good to have women in their place." Neither she nor any one else with this view answers the obvious question: If it causes financial losses (even small ones), why hasn't such discrimination tended to decline and disappear under capitalism?

The truth is, according to radicals, that capitalists do not merely gain psychologically while incurring losses from sex discrimination. On the contrary, capitalists gain from sexism both in power and in *profits.* Moreover, all workers, male as well as female, lose from sexist attitudes.

How do capitalists make profit from sexism? Obviously they use it as an excuse to pay women lower wages. More important, sexist prejudice divides male and female workers, making it more difficult to organize strong unions. In the United States one of every four men workers are unionized, as compared to only one of every seven women workers. The prejudice of union men is apparent in the fact that women constitute 20 percent of all union members but less than 1 percent of all union executive board members. Even in unions like the International Ladies' Garment Workers' Union, which is over 75 percent female, only a few token women are on the executive board. Furthermore, in the past unions have done little, if anything, for women's specific grievances and have even joined employers in agreements for lower wages and worse job categories for women.

Union men often pay for their prejudices in broken unions and lower wages. For example: "Standard Oil workers in San Francisco recently paid the price of male supremacy. Women at Standard Oil have the least chance

Table 25.1   EDUCATION AND INCOME OF WORKERS, 1970 (ALL DATA FOR
             FULL-TIME, YEAR-ROUND WORKERS; ALL OCCUPATIONS LISTED
             CONTAIN AT LEAST 51 PERCENT WOMEN)

Occupation	Percent whose median education in occupation is above median education of all U.S. male workers		Percent whose median wage in occupation is below (or above) median of all U.S. male workers	
	Men	Women	Men	Women
Librarian	+38%	+35%	+1%	−19%
Dietician	+3	+5	−21	−41
Registered Nurse	+10	+8	−8	−26
Therapist	+30	+33	+3	−29
Clinical lab technician	+20	+19	−5	−27
Therapy assistant	+5	+2	−9	−50
Religious worker	+34	+20	−21	−68
Social and recreational worker	+34	+33	+4	−19
Elementary teacher	+37	+35	+7	−14
Kindergarten teacher	+31	+29	−31	−60

Source: Department of Commerce, *1970 Census of Population,* Subject Report PC(2)-7A. Occupational Characteristics, Table 1 (Washington, D.C.: GPO).

for advancement and decent pay, and the union has done little to fight this.
Not surprisingly, women formed the core of the back to work move that
eventually broke the strike" (McAfee and Wood, p. 156). Because it reduces union bargaining strength, sexism causes lower wages for *both* men
and women.

The evidence shows that in areas where most of the labor force is
female the pay for both men and women is lower than average, even though
the workers in many of those areas have higher qualifications (shown
in more education) than the average worker. Government data reveal
that this is true for all occupations in which women predominate. (See
Table 25.1.)

The table shows that in these occupations women's education is far
above the median of U.S. workers, but their wages are far below. Moreover,
the same is true of the men in these predominantly female occupations;
their education is much above, while their wages are much below the U.S.
median. Therefore, *sexist discrimination not only hurts female workers but
also hurts male workers*—and the lower wages produce higher profits.

In addition to weak unions, another reason for low wages in the predominantly female occupations is that women have few other economic
options—they are systematically excluded from other occupations and
pushed into these. Such segregation causes overcrowding or oversupply
in the areas where women are allowed to work, thereby lowering wages
in these jobs. Some economists admit that males in these occupations will

be hurt, but they argue that males in other occupations will have higher wages because the exclusion of women lowers labor supply. Thus they claim that some male workers may gain from sexism. This is partially true, but it ignores the weakening of unions in all areas and the other unfavorable sociopolitical effects for all workers to be mentioned below. It might also be noted that the sectors employing mostly white males are sectors with strong monopoly power, where higher wages are passed along in higher prices to all consumers.

Again, like blacks, women have a much higher unemployment rate. This is partly because the employer knows that they will not easily find other jobs because of discrimination and is thus able to keep a core of skilled white males, (cheaply) hiring blacks and women from the army of unemployed during peak seasons when they are needed most. Thus the capitalist also avoids paying women fringe benefits, which accrue only to workers employed for a long time.

The glorification of housework can also be profitable. In the words of one male advertiser, "properly manipulated . . . American housewives can be given the sense of identity, purpose, creativity, the self-realization, even the sexual joy they lack—by the buying of things" (quoted in Friedan, p. 199). Thus advertisers use the sexist ideology to instill "consumerism" in women. The sexist image of the good woman shows her in the kitchen surrounded by the very latest gadgets, using the best cake mix, and made up with miracle cosmetics. Commercials imply that she is a failure if her floors are not the shiniest and her laundry is not the whitest in the neighborhood. This image helps business sell billions of dollars of useless (or even harmful) goods.

Sexism is also profitable because women's unpaid work in the home is crucial to provision of the needed supply of labor. Housework is equivalent to about one-fourth of the GNP, though it is not counted in the GNP. If business had to pay women in full to raise and clean and cook for the labor force, profits would be seriously reduced. The labor of women as housewives is vital to industry; there would be no labor force without it, and yet it goes unpaid. Furthermore, women in the family are not only profitable to capitalism through their unpaid material labor but perhaps even more in the psychological jobs that women (under sexist conditioning) do in the family. The woman in the sexist family helps provide "good" workers: "A woman is judged as a wife and mother—the only role she is allowed— according to her ability to maintain stability in her family and to help her family 'adjust' to harsh realities. She therefore transmits the values of hard work and conformity to each generation of workers. It is she who forces her children to stay in school and 'behave' or who urges her husband not to risk his job by standing up to the boss or going on strike" (McAfee and Wood, p. 156). Moreover, as a result of their dependent role in the sexist family, women themselves are socialized to be passive, submissive, and docile as workers.

The last, but not the least, important profit to capitalism from sexism comes in its increased support for political stability. The woman's psychological role in the sexist family tends to create submissive political behavior: (1) it tends to make her more fearful and conservative, (2) she tends to influence her husband in this direction, and (3) she tends to pass it on to her son and, especially, to her daughter. Much like racism, sexism is also used as a political divide-and-rule tactic. White politicians blame all urban problems on blacks. During the Nixon administration, Secretary of the Treasury George Schultz blamed unemployment (and accompanying pressure for low wages) on the competition of women workers. Thus conservative politicians try to make women a scapegoat for men's problems so that men do not see in women their natural ally against a system that oppresses them both.

LIBERATION MOVEMENTS

Discrimination causes terrible socioeconomic conditions for many minority groups. These poor conditions have led to strong protest and liberation movements by many minority groups, including blacks, Chicanos, and Indians. There are reform groups, such as the National Association for the Advancement of Colored People, who believe laws against discrimination can achieve equality under capitalism. There are also radical groups that do not believe full equality is possible under capitalism but want to see an entirely new, restructured system to achieve full equality in a democratic socialist society.

The same reformer-versus-radical split exists among groups favoring women's liberation. There are many reforms on which all of those fighting against sexism can agree. For example, women need free child-care centers, equal pay for equal work, equal access to all education, equal access to equal kinds of jobs, free birth control information and devices so that they can determine if and when they wish to have children, and as a last resort, free and legal abortions when necessary.

The problem is that it is unlikely that these reforms will change basic attitudes, nor is it at all clear that these reforms can actually be achieved under capitalism. It is a fact that the lower wages of women are a source of additional profit. Perhaps even more important, it is a fact that the submissive attitude of women, encouraged by both religion and the media, serves as an important prop to the status quo. There are thus strong and vested interests in favor of maintaining the ideology of male supremacy and the practice of sexual discrimination so long as capitalism exists.

SUMMARY

National, religious, and racial discrimination exist in America against blacks, Mexican and Puerto Rican Americans, and other ethnic groups, such as Native Americans, Japanese and Chinese Americans, Catholics, and Jews.

The well-documented oppression against blacks is very severe in housing, education, jobs, health, and every other area of life—and even in death (there are segregated cemeteries). The racist ideology against blacks originated as an apology for slavery, but it continues as an apology for low wages, high ghetto rents, exclusion of blacks from the political process in the South and elsewhere, and many other profitable reasons for maintaining racist myths.

Prejudice and discrimination against women are much older, having been present in many previous societies. American women continue to suffer from fewer educational opportunities, fewer job opportunities, lower pay for the same jobs, and a sexist ideology that says they are inferior. The ideology and discriminatory patterns continue to be supported, in part, because some important interests find them very profitable.

Women as well as blacks, Chicanos, and other minorities have organized liberation movements. They are achieving some limited reforms under capitalism. Their more radical groups are also playing a major role in the fight for a better—egalitarian and socialist—society.

SUGGESTED READINGS

An excellent and comprehensive book on sex discrimination is Barbara Sinclair Deckard, *The Women's Movement: Political, Socioeconomic, and Psychological Issues* (New York: Harper & Row, 1983). The most thorough study of racism against blacks is Michael Reich, *Racial Inequality, Economic Theory, and Class Conflict* (Princeton, N.J.: Princeton University Press, 1980). The best history of Chicanos and analysis of discrimination against them is by Mario Barera, *Race and Class in the Southwest* (Notre Dame, Ind.: Notre Dame University Press, 1980).

REFERENCES

Amundsen, Kirsten. *The Silenced Majority.* Englewood Cliffs, N.J.: Prentice-Hall, 1971.

Baran, Paul A., and Paul A. Sweezy. *Monopoly Capital.* New York: Monthly Review Press, 1966.

Bebel, August. *Women and Socialism.* New York: Schocken, 1971.

Bergmann, Barbara. "Economics of Women's Liberation." In *Challenge.* May–June, 1973.

Bird, Carolyn. *Born Female.* New York: Pocket Books, 1971.

Black, Angus. *A Radical Guide to Economic Reality.* New York: Holt, Rinehart and Winston, 1970.

"Black America in the Seventies." *Dollars and Sense,* July–August 1979.

"Black Elected Officials." *Economic Notes,* May 1978.

"Black Labor Since Reconstruction." *Dollars and Sense,* Summer 1976.

Chisholm, Shirley. "Racism and Anti-Feminism." In *The Black Scholar*, January–February 1970.

Epstein, Cynthia. *Woman's Place*. Berkeley: University of California Press, 1971.

Ferman, Louis, Joyce Kornbluh, and J. Miller, eds. *Negroes and Jobs*. Ann Arbor: University of Michigan Press, 1968.

Franklin, Ray, and Solomon Resnick. *The Political Economy of Racism*. New York: Holt, Rinehart and Winston, 1973.

Friedan, Betty. *The Feminine Mystique*. New York: Dell, 1963.

Friedman, Milton. *Capitalism and Freedom*. Chicago: University of Chicago Press, 1962.

Goldberg, Marilyn. "The Economic Exploitation of Women." In *The Review of Radical Political Economics*, Spring 1970.

Goldberg, Philip. In *The Professional Woman*. Edited by Athena Theodore. New York: Schenkman Publishers, 1971.

"Know Your Enemy." In *Sisterhood Is Powerful*. Edited by Robin Morgan. New York: Vintage, 1970.

McAfee, Kathy, and Myrna Wood. "Bread and Roses." In *Female Liberation*. Edited by Roberta Salper. New York: Knopf, 1972.

Morgan, Robin. *Sisterhood is Powerful*. New York: Vintage, 1970.

Riverside Press-Enterprise, October 23, 1973

Reich, Michael. "The Economics of Racism." In *Problems in Political Economy*. Edited by David M. Gordon. Lexington, Mass.: Raytheon/Heath, 1971.

San Francisco Chronicle, July 17, 1970.

Winnick, Andrew. "The Changing Distribution of Income and Wealth in the United States, 1960–1985." In *Families in Distress*. Edited by Patricia Woydanoff and Linda Majka. Beverly Hills, Calif.: Sage Publishing, 1988.

PART Three

UNEMPLOYMENT AND INFLATION

An Introduction to Macroeconomics

Chapter
26

Unemployment
A Macroeconomic Problem

What is macroeconomics? Macroeconomics deals with the behavior of the economy as a whole, by contrast with microeconomics, which deals with the behavior of individual consumers, workers, and enterprises. Thus, macroeconomics is concerned with such problems as the following:

1. Why is the whole economy sometimes depressed? What causes the decline of output in the aggregate? What causes unemployment of workers? Why are millions of workers suddenly left without jobs and feeling miserable?
2. What causes inflation, that is, the increase of prices? Why does inflation sometimes proceed slowly, but other times at a gallop? Why do all prices sometimes decline together, as they did in the Great Depression of the 1930s?
3. What causes economic growth? What are the relative contributions of labor, machinery, and technology to the growth of advanced capitalist countries? Is growth good or bad? What about pollution? What causes underdevelopment and lack of growth in the Third World countries?

We begin with the problem of unemployment.

HISTORY OF UNEMPLOYMENT IN THE U.S. ECONOMY

Unemployment means willing and able workers with no jobs. The most unemployment takes place during recessions or depressions. A depression is a large downturn in output and employment. A recession is a small downturn in output and employment. Since no one agrees on what is "small" or "large" in this context, the terms are best defined by means of an ancient, but accurate, old joke: A recession is when the other guy is out of work; a depression is when you are out of work. Whatever the term, it means a lot of human misery.

Alternating periods of expansion and decline of output and employment—called business cycles—have occurred regularly in the United States for more than 150 years. The very earliest cycles were clearly tied to events abroad. In its infancy, from 1776 to 1840, the American economy depended heavily on the export trade to Europe. The country prospered with every quickening in the flow of ships and goods from Atlantic ports. When this flow was interrupted, distress in the coastal towns persisted until some new stimulus brought a return of strong demand for American shipping. Most profits came from commerce, and large foreign commerce at that. It was in commerce and shipping that the most important capital investment was occurring. Therefore, between 1800 and 1815, a remarkably close correlation existed between the demand for American exports and the health of the American economy as a whole (see Smith and Cole). In 1836, when European economic activity declined and American expansion faltered, Europeans sold many of their holdings and withdrew their funds, intensifying the major depression that followed.

After 1840 foreign influence persisted, but the course of the economy was increasingly shaped by the domestic environment. By midcentury, American business cycles were more clearly generated internally; a pattern of fluctuation characteristic of modern capitalist economies had set in. In the nineteenth century, depressions or recessions began in 1857, 1860, 1865, 1869, 1873, 1882, 1887, 1893, and 1899. The twentieth century witnessed depressions or recessions beginning in 1902, 1907, 1910, 1913, 1918, 1920, 1923, 1926, 1929, 1937, 1948, 1953, 1957, 1960, 1969, 1973, 1980, and 1981. There has been a somewhat regular pattern of expansion and contraction in business activity. The average business cycle of peacetime expansion and contraction lasts about 45 months. The economy always expands in wartime, so cycles including a war are much longer.

During the period of American industrialization (1870s through 1920s) "millions lived in abject poverty in densely packed slums. . . . They struggled merely to maintain their families above the level of brutal hunger and want for such little pay that their status was a tragic anomaly in light of the prosperity enjoyed by business and industry" (Foster R. Dulles, quoted in Boyer and Morais, p. 34). Prosperity was enjoyed by business and industry in most years. Output, productivity, and profits all climbed impressively. Yet the last decades of the nineteenth century saw frequent periods of distress and depression. From 1873 to 1879, thousands of small businesses failed, farms were lost to foreclosure, and the accumulated savings of thousands of families disappeared in bank failures. Estimates of unemployment during the long depression that began in 1873 range from 1 to 3 million. When recovery came in the 1880s, output expanded more rapidly than at any other time in U.S. history, and yet the decade was interrupted by three years of depression. Vigorous expansion did not return to the economy until late in the 1890s; the depression of the early 1890s is generally regarded as the most severe on record prior to the Great Depression of the 1930s. More than 4.5 million workers, or almost 20 percent of the labor force, were unemployed in 1894 and unemployment remained high until 1899 (see Lebergott).

In the early nineteenth century, most of the people in the U.S. economy were self-employed farmers or craft producers. A cyclical downturn meant they sold less, but they were not unemployed. By the end of the nineteenth century most people in the U.S. economy were employed by capitalists and were paid wages or salaries. A cyclical downturn then became more painful because it was reflected in large-scale unemployment.

The inadequacies and deficiencies of the banking community and of the monetary system operated to aggravate the mild as well as the severe cyclic disturbances, not only in nineteenth century, but also well into the twentieth century. As the economy matured, the frequency of banking crises accelerated. Precipitous monetary failures occurred in 1873, 1874, 1890, 1893, and 1907.

World War I brought economic expansion. It was followed, however, by the severe depression of 1920–1921, when production fell 20 percent and employment dropped 11 percent within a year (Figure 26.1).

The rebound out of the 1921 depression was strong, and notwithstanding the downturns of 1923–1924 and 1926–1927, the 1920s were growth years. Major advances in productivity took place, employment was high, and prices were steady or gently falling. Major new industries led the expansion. Automobile production tripled during the decade, making up one-eighth of the value of manufacturing by 1929. The automobile's stimulus to the construction, steel, glass, rubber, oil, retail trade, and service industries led to widespread increases in production. These were boom years for new housing and business construction, as well. Radio was a new growth industry, and production of other consumer durables reached record levels.

In October 1929 the stock market collapsed. It would be difficult to support a view that the stock market breakdown was the basic cause of the depression of the 1930s. Manufacturing had begun to falter at least three months earlier, and the construction industry had been depressed for almost two years. But the collapse of the stock market was spectacular. Buyers for securities vanished as everyone rushed to sell. Debts that could not be paid encompassed the lenders in the downward spiral of asset values. Moreover, the loss of wealth was being matched by the loss of income as prices, sales, and production continued to fall. There were signs that the debacle had ended in early 1931, but instead of beginning to recover, the downward momentum suddenly quickened. By 1933 at least 25 percent of the labor force was unemployed. The homeless, the hungry, and the desperate were never fully counted. The economy improved slightly until

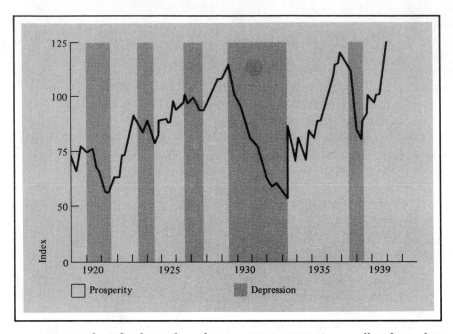

Figure 26.1 Index of industrial production, 1919–1939. Seasonally adjusted. Base: 1935–1939 = 100. *Source:* Federal Reserve Board, reprinted in U.S. Department of Commerce, Bureau of the Census, *Historical Statistics of the United States, 1789–1945* (Washington, D.C.: GPO, 1949), p. 330. Depression dates from the National Bureau of Economic Research.

1938, when it took another downward plunge. Full employment was restored only by the all-out war spending of World War II.

Since World War II the American economy has been plagued by instability, although depressions approaching the seriousness of the Great Depression have been avoided. Several small recessions in the 1950s were followed by prolonged prosperity in the 1960s, but in 1969 another recession hit the economy. In the period 1974–1975 the economy suffered from a deep and long depression, with unemployment officially recorded at over 9 percent. An even worse depression occurred in 1981–1982, when the official unemployment rate rose to 11 percent, the highest since the 1930s.

Table 26.1 records the dates of business cycle peaks and troughs since World War II. A trough is the low point of business activity and employment. A peak is the highest point of business activity and employment. A business cycle is defined as the expansion of business activity from initial trough to peak plus the following contraction of business activity from peak to final trough.

Table 26.1   TIMING OF BUSINESS CYCLES IN THE
UNITED STATES SINCE 1949

Standard reference dates (monthly)

Trough	Peak	Trough	Peak
Oct. 1949	July 1953	Mar. 1975	Jan. 1980
Aug. 1954	July 1957	July 1980	July 1981
Apr. 1958	May 1960	Dec. 1982	
Feb. 1961	Nov. 1969		
Nov. 1970	Nov. 1973		

Sources: U.S. Department of Commerce, *Business Conditions Digest* (monthly).
Methods of dating first proposed by Wesley Mitchell and Arthur Burns, *Measuring Business Cycles* (New York: National Bureau of Economic Research, 1946).

THE MISERY OF UNEMPLOYMENT

Even in minor depressions, millions of people are unemployed and suffer extreme deprivation; for example, cases of malnutrition were found in 1975 and again in 1982 among families of those long unemployed. For the society as a whole, recessions and depressions mean periods of unused resources, lower output and employment, and a much slower long-run rate of growth. Many attempts have been made to calculate the amount of loss to society from unemployment. One careful estimate put the total loss for the years 1953 to 1972 at 45 million labor-years, valued at $1.8 trillion in 1970 dollars (see Keyserling). A *labor-year* is the amount of work one person can produce in one year. If these calculations were extended back to cover all the depressions in U.S. economic history, the total loss would be astronomical.

Depressions and economic instability have other effects, however, that cannot be calculated in economic terms. There are sociological effects, as reflected in population growth, higher divorce rates, crime, physical and mental ill health, and even suicide rates. (For data from even before the Great Depression, see Thomas.) If few resort to suicide, the total effect is nonetheless incalculably great on all who lose jobs, small businesses, or farms, or who wander about on an enforced "vacation" with meager subsistence provided by private or public charities, or who find all of their previous plans destroyed.

Even in the Great Depression, most unemployed workers tortured themselves with the idea that each of them, individually, was at fault:

> The suddenly-idle hands blamed themselves, rather than society. True, there were hunger marches and protestations to City Hall and Washington, but the millions experienced a private kind of shame when the pink slip came. No matter that others suffered the same fate, the inner voice whispered, "I'm a failure." (Terkel, p. 5)

Unemployment thus caused millions of individual tragedies as well as vast social wastefulness.

Conservatives do a lot of shouting about "law and order," yet they ignore the causes of crime. As Tom Wicker noted, unemployment is one of the most prominent causes of crime:

> In 1974, as a declining economy progressively forced people out of work, the rate of crime rose by 17 percent nationally, compared to a rise of only 0.75 percent in 1973. The rate of violent crime doubled, the rate of property crime tripled, and . . . [a] link to rising unemployment was suggested. (Wicker, p. 33)

What suggested the link between crime and unemployment to Wicker were three facts. Those cities that had the largest increases in unemployment also had the largest increases in crime. Those months that had the largest increases in unemployment also showed the largest increases in crime. Finally, the type of crime that increased most was the type most likely to be committed by a poor, unemployed person, that is, street crimes of muggings and robberies for small sums of money. Nor is the relation between unemployment and crime purely economic; the unemployed are angry and frustrated and live in a society where affluence is flaunted at them every day.

When a newspaper casually mentions that 11 million Americans want to work but cannot find jobs, these are not just 11 million statistics but 11 million afflicted individuals. If a large firm closes down or moves to a new location, it leaves behind engineers and executives suddenly reduced from a useful job at high pay to enforced idleness on unemployment compensation, as well as a large number of unskilled workers with no future prospects. At times, whole mining towns seem to lose animation, and hundreds of miners' wives line up at soup kitchens and welfare departments for food allotments. In the "prosperous" year of 1959, a 38-year-old unemployed auto worker was representative of millions of others when he said: "I've been looking for work all over but I can't get a job. I hate being on welfare. It's enough to make a man jump into the river" (Raskin, p. 1). When the majority of the people are working for good wages, very few really want to subsist on a few dollars a week.

One careful study finds that each one percent increase in the unemployment rate causes statistically significant increases in suicide, mental illness, homicide, and deaths from heart strokes and kidney disease (Brenner, p. 2).

> In 1975 even experienced, skilled workers lost jobs: Robert Cleland, age 26, was a draftsman at Chrysler in Detroit. He has a wife, two children, a new house, a car, and many payments to make. In February 1975 he was unemployed and said "Once upon a time, I believed in the American Dream. Everything I have, I earned by long hard work, and now it seems a total hassle to hang onto it. The good things of the dream are slipping away. You're damn right there's a depression." (Graham, p. C2)

The depression of 1974–1975 put many white middle-class suburban families on food stamps for the first time. Many, many small businesses went bankrupt. Many small farmers were forced off the land.

The 1981–1982 depression was worse. A volunteer worker who was spending her time trying to get jobs for other people wrote in August of 1982, "Anyone who thinks that people on welfare ought to go out and get a job ought to try to get one from where I sit, at a desk shared with three other volunteers at the Inner City Law Center down on Skid Row" (Holub, p. 5). She says she knew job hunting might be tough, but learned that it is impossible for many people. For example, there was one job opening with 1800 applicants in three hours. In another case, she says: "An exemplary client, a highly skilled industrial technician, sends out 150 applications. . . . After 10 months of daily searching, he gets a job. We celebrate with roses. Two weeks later, the plant closes down" (ibid., p. 5).

There is a perception that many unemployed don't really want to work. But in one town in Ohio, 15,000 people lined up in the early morning to apply for 90 to 100 jobs (Associated Press, March 4, 1981); that is not unusual. A poll found that 75 percent of unemployed Americans would be glad to go to work in menial jobs at the minimum wage (Associated Press, April 6, 1981a).

THE TRUE EXTENT OF UNEMPLOYMENT

According to official data (U.S. Labor Department, 1983), there was a 25 percent rate of unemployment in the worst of the 1929–1933 depression and a 20 percent unemployment rate in the worst of the 1938 depression. Unemployment rates were only 6–8 percent in the worst months of the recessions of the 1950s and 1960s. The rate rose to 9 percent in 1975. In December 1982 there were 12,036,000 Americans out of work, or an officially recorded rate of 10.8 percent of the labor force. The official data are bad enough, but they drastically understate the true extent of unemployment.

In December 1982, for example, the civilian labor force was calculated at 113 million people, so 12 million unemployed was 10.8 percent. But another 62 million people were defined—by the U.S. Labor Department—to be "not in the labor force." Most of these 62 million were sick or retired or voluntarily housewives or househusbands. There were, however, 7 million people not counted in the labor force who stated that they did want jobs. These 7 million were not counted as unemployed workers in the labor force because they had given up actively looking for work. They are the "discouraged" workers, some going back to school, some doing housework, some just doing nothing after months or years of looking.

Because the government does not count the discouraged workers as unemployed, some strange things happen to the unemployment rate. For example, in the midst of a recession or depression, suppose there is a month in which 100,000 workers are newly unemployed; but 300,000 workers are so discouraged that they give up looking for jobs. There are then 200,000 fewer unemployed by the official definition—that is, the 300,000 leaving the labor force are no longer counted as unemployed, while only 100,000 are newly unemployed. In fact, in every recession or depression, the number of discouraged workers rises rapidly, so the number in the labor force falls. Therefore, the unemployment rate does not rise as rapidly as it would have if we counted the discouraged workers—hence the picture looks rosier by the official definition.

If, using the data for December 1982, we add 7 million discouraged to the 12 million unemployed (and add the same 7 million to the 113 million in the labor force), then the unemployment rate becomes 19/120, or 15.8 percent.

The second largest cause for the official understatement is the peculiar handling of part-time workers. The department states: "persons on part-time schedules for economic reasons are included in the full-time employed." What does the term "economic reasons" mean? By economic reasons the department means that people wanting full-time jobs could only get part-time jobs because the economy was in such a bad condition. So the department's statement really says "persons on part-time schedules who wanted, but were unable to get, full-time jobs are included in the full-time employed." Peculiar indeed!

According to the Labor Department's own data, in December 1982 there were over 6 million persons (6,472,000) who could find only part-time work "for economic reasons," though they desired full-time work. The average hours worked by these people were only 21 a week, or about half the full-time work week. Therefore, they should be counted as half-employed and half-unemployed, the equivalent of an average of 3 million additional unemployed. If we add 3 million involuntary part-time workers to 7 million discouraged and 12 million officially unemployed, then total unemployment was 22 million. Out of a labor force of 120 million, this means the adjusted unemployment rate was 22/120, or 18.3 percent.

Unfortunately, even that correction does not necessarily correct all downward biases in the Labor Department unemployment data. The department treats as fully employed many unpaid family workers, including at least 700,000 in agriculture. This phenomenon of work without pay in the family unit—because no other job is available—is called disguised unemployment. The person may add little or nothing to the family income (as on a very small farm) but shares in that small income. During a depression, disguised unemployment always increases as more people are forced to share the limited family resources.

The averages at a given time also hide the extent of the spread of insecurity among workers. For example, in 1981 there were only 7.6 percent unemployed on the average, according to U.S. Labor Department data, but the same data showed that 20 percent of the labor force—23.4

million Americans, or 1 out of 5 in the labor force—was unemployed at some time during the year (see Combined News Services).

UNDEREMPLOYMENT

There is also what some economists call *subemployment* or *underemployment*. Because of general widespread unemployment, a skilled person may accept an unskilled job at low pay if nothing else is available. The threat of unemployment holds millions of workers at very low pay in jobs below their qualifications. In 1972, for example, a year of expansion and relatively low unemployment, there were 6 million full-time employed workers who earned less than the government's own official poverty standard. In the 1980s, with continued underemployment and a high rate of inflation, the condition of the working poor has considerably deteriorated.

Underemployment means that millions of unskilled workers work full-time but are paid below the poverty level. Underemployment means that millions of skilled workers must work in unskilled jobs far below their capacity. Finally, underemployment means that hundreds of thousands of college graduates work at jobs requiring almost no education. For example:

> In one case in 1975 Jim Stephens (a fictitious name, but a real case) earned his bachelor's degree in biology. He was unable to gain immediate acceptance to the limited number of spots in medical schools, so he tried to get work as a lab technician. Since it was the middle of the depression, he was unable to get even a lab technician job. Therefore, he became a cab driver. (LaBelle, p. 11)

A survey of placement services found that among the college graduates of 1975, many architecture B.A.s became construction assistants, many English B.A.s were reduced to clerical work, some people with education degrees were forced to work in factories (because cities and states are too cheap to employ more teachers), and a few Ph.D.s were discovered working as bartenders. A year after the 1974 graduation, 27 percent of graduates "said they had more education than their jobs required and 24 percent said their work didn't make use of their skills" (LaBelle). This high rate of underemployment of college graduates continued for years after the 1974–1975 depression and rose again in the 1982 depression.

UNEMPLOYMENT OF WOMEN AND MINORITIES

All women and both sexes in many minority groups—including blacks, Chicanos, Puerto Ricans, Jews, Italians, Irish, and many others—suffer discrimination in the United States. The discrimination is justified by various kinds of prejudices, which falsely claim the groups are "inferior." There is discrimination in housing, education, loans, types of jobs, and employment. Here we consider only that facet of discrimination that results in

Table 26.2 WHITE UNEMPLOYMENT AND BLACK
UNEMPLOYMENT (PERCENT)

Year	White rate	Black rate
1950	4.9	9.0
1960	4.9	10.2
1970	4.5	8.2
1980	6.3	13.1
Dec. 1982	9.4	18.2

Source: Council of Economic Advisors, *Economic Report of the President* (GPO, 1982), p. 271, and U.S. Bureau of Labor Statistics, *Employment and Earnings* (Jan. 1983).

higher unemployment rates. In the case of young people, some unemployment results from prejudice against youth, but some also results from lack of qualifications, to the extent that training and experience are qualifications. In the case of women and minorities, since anthropologists find that all groups are created with equal qualifications, all higher rates of unemployment must be due to discrimination, including some present employment discrimination and some previous discrimination in education, training, or previous jobs.

Because of racial discrimination, the data show that blacks (including "others") have always had higher unemployment rates than whites. Table 26.2 shows the gap. The rate for "blacks and others" is consistently twice the "white" rate.

The official unemployment rate for women sometimes appears higher and sometimes lower than that of men. In December 1982, according to official data, only 9.6 percent of women were unemployed, but 11.3 percent of men were unemployed. Unfortunately, the unemployment rate for women is drastically understated relative to men.

The main reason is the greater number of "discouraged" workers among women than men. In the fourth quarter of 1982, among men who were actually unemployed, but counted as "not in the labor force," there were 2,390,000 who wanted a job but had given up looking for some reason.

Among women actually unemployed, but counted as "not in the labor force," there were 4,605,000 who wanted a job, but had given up looking for some reason. Suppose we correct the unemployment rates for men and women by adding these "discouraged" workers to both the unemployed and all those in the labor force. Then the corrected unemployment rate for men would be 14.59 percent, while the corrected unemployment rate for women would be 17.5 percent.

Furthermore, the category "white" includes Chicanos and Puerto Ricans, whose unemployment rates are far higher than average. On the other hand, the category "black and others" includes several other small racial minorities, particularly Chinese and Japanese, whose unemployment rates are much lower than the rates for blacks. Thus the unemployment gap between whites and blacks is somewhat larger than it appears in the official data.

Finally, subemployment or underemployment is far more prevalent among young workers, women, and minorities than it is among white male adults. For example, the average wage of full-time employed black women is less than the official poverty line, so it is easy to see how most families headed by black women were in poverty even though most of them worked full time.

In addition to underemployment as a cause of their low wages, underemployment is also reflected in the poor jobs given some highly qualified groups. For example, in 1972 women with college degrees had only a slightly higher median wage than men with an eighth-grade education. Among women with four years of college, 17 percent take jobs as unskilled or semiskilled workers. Even among women with five years or more of college, 6 percent take unskilled or semiskilled jobs. (See Deckard, chap. 5.)

Why is unemployment so high among minorities? The reason lies both in prejudice and in the fact that this unemployment pattern is also profitable to employers. If an employer has ten black and ten white workers, and must fire half for a couple of months, which will be fired? If "he is rational and seeks to minimize his labor turnover costs, he will lay off his ten black workers on the assumption that they will be unlikely to get permanent or better jobs elsewhere because of the discriminatory practices of other employers" (Franklin and Resnick, p. 20). Thus the capitalist fires black workers in each recession and hires them back in times of expansion. The employer also gains by not paying the fringe benefits due workers who stay on the job for a longer time.

TWO VIEWS OF UNEMPLOYMENT: TRADITIONAL AND CRITICAL

There are two differing views of unemployment, reflecting two differing approaches to macroeconomics. One view may be called traditional or conservative and is represented by the classical and neoclassical schools of economics. The other may be called the critical view and is represented by the post-Keynesian followers of John M. Keynes, the liberal institutionalist followers of Thorstein Veblen, and the radical Marxist followers of Karl Marx. Both of these views will be spelled out in detail in later chapters, but a brief statement of them in relation to unemployment is necessary here.

The traditional, conservative view contends that the economy always tends toward equilibrium at full employment. So most recorded unemployment is really voluntary, consisting of workers looking for a better job or resting between jobs. A temporary dislocation may cause temporary unemployment, but the economy always adjusts toward full-employment equilibrium. Dislocation is caused by outside forces, such as government mistakes or international shortages, not by the system itself. The economy always returns to equilibrium if left alone. It follows that the best government policy to cure unemployment is to leave the economy alone.

The critical view says that the present institutions of capitalism cause instability. When the economy grows under these institutions, unemployment grows. But when these institutions of capitalism cause a recession or depression, massive involuntary unemployment results. Critical economists who are liberal believe that particular economic institutions can and should be reformed by government policy to achieve full employment. Critical economists who are left-wing radicals believe that capitalism must be replaced by democratic socialism to achieve full employment.

FRICTIONAL UNEMPLOYMENT

Frictional unemployment is supposed to apply to those workers who are temporarily unemployed only because they are moving from one job to another, usually in the wake of technological progress. For example, workers building stagecoaches may be unemployed for a short time until they move into the automotive industry. This concept contains a small grain of truth, but it has been used in deceptive ways.

Many traditional, conservative economists say that frictional unemployment is natural because it results from technological progress in all economic systems, so nothing can be done about it. Liberals argue that all such workers could be retrained by the government. Moreover, liberals argue that conservative economists tend to overestimate frictional unemployment in order to deny that there is much (or any) general unemployment caused by capitalist business cycles.

In World War II, when there was unlimited government demand, unemployment fell to 1 percent. Since frictional unemployment results from technological progress, and since such progress was very rapid in World War II, frictional unemployment should never be higher than the 1 percent recorded in World War II. Yet, in the Truman era, government economists started saying frictional unemployment was 1.5–2 percent, Eisenhower's economists said frictional unemployment was 2.5–3 percent, Johnson's economists spoke of 3.5–4 percent. Then, Nixon's economists talked about 4.5–5 percent, and Carter's economists talked about 6–8 percent, while Reagan's economists set frictional unemployment at 8–9 percent. What will "frictional" or "natural" unemployment be under President Bush?

UNEMPLOYMENT AND THE BUSINESS CYCLE OF CAPITALISM

The main tools for careful measurement of the business cycle and its effects on unemployment were developed by the great American economist Wesley Mitchell (1874–1948). As a critical, institutionalist economist, he felt it was urgent to understand in detail how the business cycle of capitalism produces unemployment. In the first place, Mitchell studied all the available evidence in every form, from newspapers to statistics, to find out exactly when recessions and depressions occurred. The dates given earlier in this chapter were all obtained by him or by his methods. These dates are now published officially by the U.S. Department of Commerce.

Second, in order to study unemployment over the business cycle, Mitchell created a method of describing and measuring the business cycle in a systematic fashion. He wanted to see what all cycles held in common as well as what was unique about each. He divided each business cycle into nine stages. Stage 1 is the initial trough or low point at the beginning of the cycle. Stages 2, 3, and 4 divide the expansion period into three equal stages. Stage 5 is the peak of business activity. Stages 6, 7, and 8 divide the contraction period into three stages. Stage 9 is the final trough or low point of the depression. Mitchell explained how each stage of the cycle led to the next stage.

Figure 26.2 shows how Mitchell measured the value of a variable— gross national product (GNP) in this case—at each stage of the cycle. He presented it as a percentage of its average value over the entire cycle. The data on the GNP in Figure 26.2 is presented in real terms—that is, after allowing for price inflation. The GNP rises in the entire expansion and falls in the entire contraction of the business cycle.

Mitchell's methods allow us to describe the systematic behavior of unemployment over the business cycle, illuminating its involuntary nature. In every expansion period, all the indicators show that jobs are plentiful, but the same indicators show few available jobs in the contraction periods. Based on U.S. Department of Commerce data, in the average of the last seven expansion periods, factory employment rose 11 percent, the number of hours worked per week rose 3 percent, average number of overtime hours rose 32 percent, and—most revealing of all—the ratio of help-wanted ads to the number of unemployed rose 74 percent! Of course, all the indicators of unemployment fell in expansion. Thus, in the average of the last seven expansions, the unemployment rate fell 43 percent (as shown in Figure 26.3), claims for unemployment insurance fell 44 percent, the average number of weeks of unemployment fell 29 percent, and the long-run unemployment rate (persons unemployed more than 14 weeks) fell 71 percent.

Conversely, in the average of the last seven recessions or depressions, factory employment fell 8 percent, hours worked per week fell 3 percent, overtime work fell 28 percent, and the ratio of help-wanted ads to the

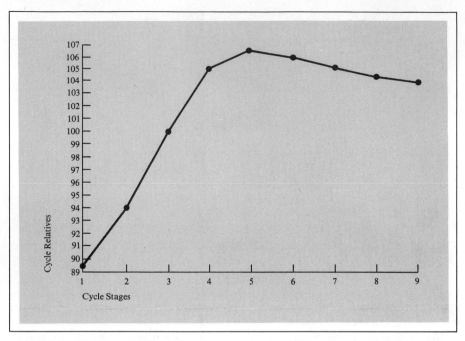

Figure 26.2 Gross national product, average, 7 Cycles, 1949–1982. *Source:* Series no. 50 from U.S. Department of Commerce, *Handbook of Cyclical Indicators* (Washington, D.C.: GPO, 1984).

number of unemployed fell 78 percent! In other words, no matter how hard they looked, the unemployed could not all find jobs because few new jobs existed while millions of more workers became involuntarily unemployed. Finally, in the average of the last seven depressions or recessions, the unemployment rate rose 49 percent (as shown in Figure 26.3), claims for unemployment insurance rose 54 percent, and the long-run unemployment rate rose 83 percent.

SUMMARY

The U.S. economy is subject to alternating periods of expansion and contraction. In each contraction period, the amount of unemployment rises to extremely high levels, causing many kinds of individual and social misery. Traditional, conservative economists believe that most unemployment is temporary or voluntary, when workers voluntarily leave their jobs to look for higher pay or because they prefer leisure. Critical economists, however, point out that the capitalist system suffers from business cycle contractions, in which workers are fired because demand for goods and services is insufficient.

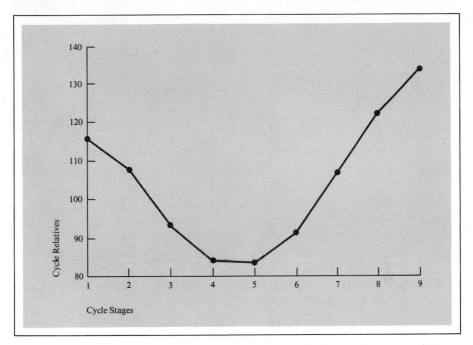

Figure 26.3 Unemployment rate, 7 cycles, 1949–1982. *Source:* Series no. 43 from U.S. Department of Commerce, Handbook of Cyclical Indicators (Washington, D.C.: GPO, 1984).

SUGGESTED READINGS

The best understanding of people's feelings in the Great Depression is to be found in Studs Terkel, *Hard Times: An Oral History of the Great Depression* (New York: Pantheon, 1970).

REFERENCES

Associated Press. *Los Angeles Times,* March 4, 1981, pt. 4, p. 1.

Associated Press. *Los Angeles Times,* p. 1. April 6, 1981.

Boyer, Richard O., and Herbert Morais. *Labor's Untold Story.* New York: Marzani & Munsell, 1955.

Brenner, Harvey. *Estimating the Social Costs of National Economic Policy.* Prepared for the Joint Economic Committee, U.S. Congress. Washington, D.C.: GPO, 1976.

Combined News Services. "One Out of Five Jobless at One Time." *The Honolulu Advertiser,* p. 1. July 21, 1982.

Deckard, Barbara Sinclair. *The Women's Movement.* New York: Harper & Row, 1982.

Franklin, Ray, and Soloman Resnick. *The Political Economy of Racism*. New York: Holt, Rinehart and Winston, 1973.

Graham, Victoria. "The Unemployed." *Riverside Press-Enterprise*, February 9, 1975.

Holub, Margaret. "There Are No Jobs for Some People," *Los Angeles Times*, August 30, 1982.

Keyserling, Leon. "What's Wrong with American Economics." *Challenge* 16 (May–June, 1973).

LaBelle, G. G. Associated Press release. *Riverside Press-Enterprise*, August 27, 1975, p. 11.

Lebergott, Stanley. *Manpower in Economic Growth. The American Record Since 1800*. New York: McGraw-Hill, 1964.

Mitchell, William, John Hand, and Ingo Walter, eds. *Readings in Macroeconomics*. New York: McGraw-Hill, 1975.

Raskin, A. H. "People Behind Statistics: A Study of the Unemployed." *New York Times*, March 16, 1959.

Smith, W. B., and A. H. Cole. *Fluctuations in American Business, 1790–1860*. Cambridge, Mass.: Harvard University Press, 1925.

Terkel, Studs. *Hard Times: An Oral History of the Great Depression*. New York: Pantheon Books, 1970.

Thomas, D. C. *Social Aspects of the Business Cycle*. New York: Knopf, 1927.

U.S. Department of Labor. *Employment and Earnings*. January 1983.

Wicker, Tom. "Unemployment and Crime." *New York Times*, April 25, 1975.

Chapter

27

Unemployment and the Institutions of Capitalism

Why are millions and millions of people unemployed in the U.S. economy? It seems strange—like a scene from *Alice in Wonderland*—that millions of people lack jobs when there is so much to do. After all, by official government count, millions of people live in poverty, lacking the necessary food, clothing, and shelter for a decent life. Couldn't the millions of unemployed be put to work producing those urgently needed amounts of food, clothing, and shelter? It seems barbaric and inexplicable to have even one person languishing in unemployment while so much needs to be done.

Our economy experiences periods of prosperity and depression, or boom and bust. These are caused by the imbalance of aggregate supply and aggregate demand. Aggregate supply is defined as the total output that business produces and plans to sell. Aggregate demand is defined as the total dollar amount of goods that consumers, investors, and governments plan to buy. Sometimes the aggregate supply of produced goods is either too small or too great in terms of the aggregate demand for goods. Certainly, if aggregate supply and demand were always equal, there would be no depressions. Depressions occur when the aggregate demand is insufficient (in money terms) to purchase the aggregate supply.

J. B. SAY VERSUS WESLEY MITCHELL

J. B. Say (1767–1832) was a classical economist, who stated what has come to be known as Say's law, that aggregate demand will always automatically adjust to aggregate supply. This law meant that there could never be a depression caused by lack of demand and there could be no general unemployment for any long period of time (only brief unemployment caused by outside shocks to the system). We shall discuss Say's Law in depth in Chapters 29 and 30. Here it is only necessary to note that Say's argument was based on analysis of a precapitalist type of economy. He (and other classical economists) analyzed a simple economy, such as that of Robinson Crusoe, in which the economic unit produced for its own collective use (rather than for a private profit by selling for exchange in the market) and there was barter of goods (rather than use of money).

In Chapters 29 and 30, we shall examine the theoretical critiques of Say's Law by Marx and by Keynes. Here we begin with the institutionalist critique by Wesley Mitchell. Institutionalists believe that economics should be a science of the evolution of economic institutions (rather than static and supposedly eternal laws of psychology (the founder of institutionalism was Thorstein Veblen, 1857–1929).

Mitchell argued that the business cycle causes unemployment when the economy is depressed. Depressions are caused by the basic institutions of capitalism, which are very different in important respects from feudal economic institutions. Say's law is true under precapitalist, feudal institutions, but is not true under capitalist institutions.

In all precapitalist systems, there was never a problem of lack of demand, though many other problems existed. Under capitalism, however, effective demand is only demand backed by money. The poor may desire more food, but that is not an effective demand unless they have the money to buy the food. Only demand backed by money is effective in inducing a capitalist to produce and to hire more workers.

THE CAPITALIST SYSTEM

What exactly is meant by capitalism? Capitalism may be defined as a system in which one class of individuals, the capitalists, owns the means of production. These means of production, such as factories and equipment, are called capital goods. The capitalists hire another class of individuals, called workers, who own nothing productive but their power to labor. The product of the workers' labor is owned by the capitalists. The capitalists sell the product in the marketplace for a certain amount of money. The capitalists will produce only so long as they expect to make a profit in the market above and beyond all their expenses.

It is this system that creates the possibility of an alternative cycle of boom and bust, with episodes of massive unemployment, sometimes accompanied by high rates of inflation. Previous economic systems, such as slavery or feudalism, did have unemployment at times, but only rarely and usually as a result of some natural catastrophe such as a flood or an epidemic. Only modern capitalism shows a systematic business cycle with periodic mass unemployment caused by a lack of effective demand. It is worth noting these differences from previous systems in some detail to understand the nature of the business cycle.

PRODUCTION FOR THE MARKET

It is characteristic of the private enterprise economy, which was fully developed in England by the end of the eighteenth century, that most production was directed solely toward sale on the market. This was hardly ever true of earlier societies. In the most primitive societies, almost all productive activity was directed at the collection of food by gathering or hunting. These activities were necessarily carried out by the collective unit of all the males and/or females of the tribe. Generally, almost all of the produce was distributed according to some fixed scheme among the tribe's membership. Even at a somewhat higher economic state, production was still for use, not for sale. None of the Indian tribes of the Americas, not even the Aztecs, bought or sold land or produced crops to sell for a profit to others. In fact, "for the red man soil existed only in order to meet the necessities of life, and production, not profit, was the basis of his economy. . . . Unemployment was certainly never a problem in the Indian communities of early America" (Crow, p. 54). Because there was little division of labor within the tribe, there was little if any trade among its members. Furthermore, very little commerce was transacted between the most primitive tribes, and that "was virtually restricted to materials small in bulk and precious for their decorative or magical qualities" (Clark, p. 96). We find that all over the world for thousands of years almost all economic systems, whether tribal or feudal, were based on relatively self-sufficient agricultural units.

In the Roman Empire, there was a great deal of trade, but most of it was in luxury goods (Walbank, pp. 11–13). This trade therefore did not affect the self-sufficiency of the basic agricultural unit, the slave-run plantation, although a lack of surplus food could bring starvation to large numbers of city dwellers. As one author says: "Notwithstanding the phenomenal expansion of trade and industry, the vast masses inside the Empire still continued to win their livelihood from the soil. Agriculture remained throughout the antiquity the most usual and most typical economic activity, and land the most important form of wealth" (ibid.).

The same was true of feudal England, where the primitive level of technology made impossible the supply of large urban populations and even greatly restricted trade between the villages. As a result, in the England of that day "towns developed slowly; each group of burgesses solved their local problems on their own initiative and in their own time. Even in 1377 not much more than eight percent of the population were townsmen, and only a minority of these had independent dealings with continental markets" (Gibbs, pp. 7–8).

If there happened to be a surplus from the slave or feudal estate, then it might be marketed in return for foreign luxury items to be used by the lord of the estate. Finding a market, however, was not a matter of life and death for the economic unit. If the surplus found no market, the manor was still supplied with its necessities for that year, and it could and would continue the process of production for the next year's needs. Such economically self-sufficient societies could be disturbed only by the catastrophes that were more or less external to the economy—natural disasters such as droughts, plagues, or floods, or political troubles such as government interference, war, or revolution. These phenomena could and did depress production at various randomly spaced intervals as well as seasonally because of the special seasonal sensitivity of agriculture.

This type of economy could not, however, conceivably face the problem of lack of effective demand for all commodities because the economic unit directly consumed most of the products of its own land and could do without trade altogether. Thus in discussing the business cycle of depression and prosperity, Mitchell observes that "business cycles are phenomena peculiar to a certain form of economic organization which has been dominant even in Western Europe for less than two centuries, and for briefer periods in other regions" (Mitchell, 1926, p. 47).

During the period of transition from feudalism to capitalism in England of the sixteenth, seventeenth, and eighteenth centuries, the majority of the people still lived on the land and consumed their own products. As time went on, however, more and more products, both agricultural and industrial, were delivered to the marketplace. By the end of the eighteenth century, the private enterprise system of production for the market embraced most economic activity. By the nineteenth century, one business entrepreneur might own a factory producing millions of shoes, though his whole family was capable of consuming only a few pairs. The shoes had to be sold in order to buy other consumer goods for his family, pay wages to his employees, and replace and expand the plant and equipment of his business.

In the United States, the transformation to a market economy took place in the nineteenth century. In 1800 two-thirds of the U.S. population labored in agriculture, and most of the remainder were employed in commerce and shipping. Except for the foreign trade sector, markets were small and local. Many families and communities were almost self-sufficient. Native industry, which had a foothold in 1800, spurted during the War of 1812, when imports from England were cut off. By 1815 New England mills and factories were capable of supplying textiles and simple manufactures to the nation. Transportation networks were built to link communities and regions. This permitted farmers to specialize in commercial crops for cash income with which they purchased in the market the necessities of life. By 1840 a large national market for manufacturers had been created. Families turned away from self-sufficiency and purchased cloth, flour, farm implements, and household items. Rapid industrialization followed. In 1860 the United States was producing more than one-fifth of world manufacturing output, and by 1913 American production had risen to one-third of the world total.

The process of industrialization, starting first in England and spreading to the rest of western Europe and the United States, had changed the character of production and employment. Production required a greater number of stages, or steps, as materials and products became less simple. Labor grew more specialized, and labor's employment came to be linked with the expanded use of capital.

In the modern market economy, every person's productive effort is related to sales in the market and every person's income depends on the income of others. A man or woman working in an automobile factory, for example, depends for his or her continued employment on millions of people buying cars each year. In turn, most of these car buyers depend on millions buying the products they produce. If consumers are unable to buy their cars, the automobile worker immediately loses his or her job. The car manufacturer needs less steel, less rubber, less paint, and so on. Each of these industries, in turn, lays off workers. The process goes on and on because of the interconnectedness of the market economy. Each time more workers lose their jobs, their income ceases. They can no longer buy the hundreds of goods and services they normally purchase, and the crisis widens and becomes more severe.

The sale in the market of privately produced goods and services generates all income. Decisions to purchase are made by thousands of small- and large-income receivers, and the total of these purchasing decisions comprises the total, or aggregate, demand. In previous economic systems, the self-sufficient economic unit—the craftsman producing a trickle of handmade items for known customers—could not possibly be troubled by lack of demand for his or her product. When almost all that was produced by the economic unit was consumed by it, supply had to equal demand. In the industrialized private enterprise system, however, the businessperson produces for the market and cannot continue production if there is no market demand for his or her products. This, then, is the first major institutional feature of the private enterprise economy. Appearing in the eighteenth century and continuing to the present day, it is one of the factors that make business cycles possible.

REGULAR USE OF MONEY

Another institutional condition that opens up the possibility of a lack of aggregate demand is the regular use of money in exchange. The monetary system takes the place of the barter system of exchanging good for good. It was seen that production for the market makes cyclical unemployment possible. Use of money in the market exchange will be shown to be a second necessary condition for the emergence of business cycles.

The Uses of Money

Money replaced the barter system because it is much more convenient to use. What precisely are its functions in the modern economy? Traditionally, money is said to have four functions:

1. Money is the unit of accounting, or the standard of value—that is, a measuring stick for everything else. All contracts are drawn up in money terms, with so much money to be paid for a certain product at a certain time. We think of a coat or a table as being worth so many dollars.

2. Money is the medium of exchange, or actual intermediary between commodities (including services). Under barter, one commodity is exchanged for another commodity. In the monetary economy, a commodity is exchanged for money; then the money may be exchanged for another commodity.

3. Money is a store of value, or a device for hoarding. When money is received as an income, it need not be spent immediately. Instead, if it is in a nonperishable form such as gold, it may be buried or stored away and hoarded until the possessor chooses to use it. In the modern world money is deposited in a bank account, which is completely nonperishable; the money may even grow by earning interest while it is on deposit.

4. Money is a standard of deferred payment, or a unit of accounting for future payments on debts. In other words, I may buy something from you now and promise to pay for it later. My promise is always in terms of so many units of money, not, for example, in so many pairs of shoes. In the United States paper money is a legal tender (or legally acceptable unit) for the payment of any debt.

Our "money" today is (1) coin and paper currency in circulation, plus (2) all demand deposits (checking accounts) in commercial banks. We shall see that money has evolved from commodities such as gold to its present complex forms in the U.S. economy, including paper money and credit.

The four traditional concepts of the use of money listed above are grossly oversimplified and misleading. For one thing, a piece of paper cannot produce an automobile; only human beings can produce things. The piece of paper has power to command labor only because it faithfully reflects the human relationships on which our society is built. It is not really money but people who command and manipulate other people.

Moreover, the monetary system is often inadequate to fulfill these functions, which traditional views assume it will smoothly achieve. We shall see that it fails in all its functions during an inflation. We shall also see that the monetary system helps make depressions possible and tends to intensify them.

The Abuses of Money

Money does not serve its four functions equally well under all conditions. Imagine that there is a catastrophic inflation, with prices doubling every hour, which means that the value of money falls by half each hour. Money then functions badly as a unit of accounting because the same product sells at such rapidly changing prices that neither consumers nor sellers can keep track of them. With rapid inflation, money is also a poor medium of exchange. People may refuse to accept it at all because its buying power is so uncertain and may diminish further before it can be spent.

With rapid inflation, money is also a very bad store of value because money hoarded away now will buy so very much less in the future. Instead of keeping money, everyone rushes to buy goods or real property that will be worth more and more units of money as the inflation continues. Anyone with cash savings in paper money, bank accounts, or government bonds is badly hurt, so it may happen that no one will put money in banks or buy government bonds at almost any interest rate. Finally, with rapid inflation, money cannot function as a standard of deferred payment because the standard itself keeps changing. If someone lends $100 today and it is worth only $1 when it is paid back tomorrow, then the lender is very badly hurt. When people refuse to accept the medium of exchange because they have lost confidence in it, economic activity falls to the level that can be maintained only by barter.

The use of money, even in ancient times, brought many new complications onto the economic scene. In the Roman Empire, for example, vast amounts of money were needed by the government to support wars of expansion, large standing armies, police and bureaucracy, and an unfavorable balance of trade (due to the importation of luxuries from the East). The emperors were eventually forced to the expedient of debasing their coins by "clipping" (decreasing the metallic content of coins) or mixture with less valuable metals. As the government debased the coins and as production of goods declined in the later days of the empire, the amount of goods that could be bought with the coins declined rapidly; in other words, a catastrophic inflation occurred (Walbank, pp. 42–43, 51–52).

Despite their difficulties with it, the regular use of money did not lead to the modern type of depression because most of the Roman economy was still contained in self-sufficient agricultural units (ibid., p. 18). The luxury trade did suffer from the extreme inflation, but only as one more affliction in addition to colonial wars and slave revolts, the extreme inefficiency of employing slave labor, and the Roman citizens' attitude that any participation in the work process was degrading (because only slaves should work).

With the breakup of the Roman Empire, trade suffered a considerable decline. In early feudalism the pattern was overwhelmingly that of the isolated, self-sufficient manor. Barter therefore grew in importance, and the use of money declined. On each manor, in return for the lord's protection, the serf provided all the services and consumer goods needed and required by the lord, his family, and his retinue. However, when technology began to improve, industry and commerce slowly began to revive in western Europe. The widespread trade of the later medieval period eventually led to the replacement of barter by a money economy; at the same time, following the pattern discussed in the previous section, production was increasingly designed for sale in the market rather than use at home.

The modern private enterprise economy demands continuous use of money as the go-between in market exchange by the entire population. In a barter economy it is possible for one commodity to be brought to market in larger supply than there is demand. There may be a mismatch of particular supplies and demands, but there can be no lack of aggregate demand; in other words, total supply cannot exceed total demand. For example, those who bring cows to market may find more shoes and fewer coats produced than they desire—that is, they would rather "spend" their cows for fewer shoes and more coats than are available. The excess supply of shoes is balanced by the excess demand for coats. The result is only a temporary, or frictional, unemployment of shoe producers, which could be cured by a shift to coat production. It is true that in the actual medieval economy rigid feudal restrictions did not allow many such shifts in production or occupation, but it is just these restrictions that the classical economists wish to abolish from consideration.

The mistake made by the classical economists, who argued that total demand automatically equals supply, was to apply rules of a barter economy to a money economy. They extended the argument by means of the general observation that money is merely the means of exchanging two commodities, so that the operation of the money economy is "essentially" the same as that of the barter economy. Thus we find Ricardo contending that "productions are always bought by productions, or by services; money is only the medium by which the exchange is effected" (Ricardo, p. 275). One function of money is to facilitate the exchange of commodities, but it has other uses as well. In the modern economy, the seller obtains only money for commodities, money that may or may not be used immediately or later to buy other commodities. Thus money functions as the means of storing value for future use. The wants of humankind may be infinite, but it is not always the case that all buyers have money to buy what they want. There is therefore no inherent necessity in a money economy that sellers should find buyers for all commodities brought to market.

The problem is not an aggregate lack of money in the economy. Those who wish to buy may have no money, whereas those who have money may be taking it out of circulation and not using it in any way—that is, hoarding it. The chain of circulation may then be broken at any point at which the flow of money is stopped or withdrawn from the system. In that case the reduction of the flow of circulation, like the reduction of the volume of water flowing in a stream, causes a slowdown in the movement of products being circulated by this means. Although it is basically true that products exchange for products even after the introduction of money, the mere necessity of the money bridge makes all the difference in the world. If the bridge is absent, finished commodities may pile up in warehouses while potential consumers are unable to buy them. Only money can make a possible consumer into an actual buyer in the private enterprise system.

An excess of supply in this economic system does not mean that everyone is fully satisfied. People's wants are elastic; we may have as much of a particular commodity as we want at one time, but there is always an infinite amount of other things that we desire, things that will have use value or utility for us. Therefore, the problem is not overproduction of the total commodities relative to what people want or desire. The problem is rather that there may be too many commodities on the market relative to the effective demand, which is limited by definition to desires that are backed by money in the marketplace.

Credit Money

In the United States at present, the largest part of the money supply— about four-fifths of the whole—is pure credit money. Credit money consists of demand, or checking, deposits at banks, which are dollar amounts owed by the banks to the holders of the accounts. Credit money is created whenever a bank makes a loan to a customer and "credits" his or her checking account with the amount of the loan. Except for the legal constraints on the lending of money, banks could go on creating money without limit as long as people had confidence in the acceptability of the money. Only the smallest portion of the money supply consists of coins and paper money issued by the U.S. Treasury. A somewhat larger portion is paper money issued by the Federal Reserve System (Fed). Technically, even these portions of the money supply are credits to the private sector because they are debts of government agencies that are payable on demand. Dollar bills, however, are no longer payable in gold, so a $10 bill presented to the Treasury or the Fed could be paid by any legal tender—say, two $5 bills. Thus the Treasury or the Fed may create money simply by using the printing press. Although Congress does impose a legal limit, it often raises that limit.

The use of credit intensifies all money problems; not only may a person sell something and not immediately purchase something else, but also it is possible to sell something and not receive the proceeds of the sale for some time. If Brown owes Smith, and Smith owes Johnson, and Johnson owes Martin, a break anywhere along this chain of credit circulation will be disastrous for all of the later parties in the chain. Moreover, the credit chain in the modern private enterprise economy is usually circular in nature, so the reverberations reach the starting point and may begin to go around again. This does not, of course, explain why the chain should ever break in the first place.

It has been amply demonstrated that when money and credit institutions become the usual way of doing business, the business cycle of boom and bust becomes a possibility. Does this mean that these institutions are sufficient to explain the business cycle? We know that money and credit existed in ancient Rome and in the sixteenth to eighteenth centuries in western Europe, and yet the financial disturbances of those times do not seem to have been the same phenomena as the modern type of business cycle. It is true that after the development of money and credit every catastrophic natural happening or violent political event might be reflected in a financial panic. For example, when the English fleet was burned by the Dutch in 1667, and when Charles II stopped payments from the Exchequer in 1672, there were sudden runs on the London banks. In the eighteenth century, financial crises resulted from the Jacobean conspiracy in 1708, the bursting of the South Sea stock speculation "bubble" in 1720, the fighting with the Pretender to the throne of England in 1745, the aftermath of the Seven Years' War in 1763, and the disturbances caused by the American Revolution (Mitchell, pp. 583–584). These panics were unlike the modern business cycle, in both cause and effect, because they originated in external causes and resulted in only limited depressions in a few trades for brief and random periods. The first truly general industrial depression of the modern type appeared as late as 1793 in England (Ibid.).

In summary, there is evidence of a long period of extensive use of money and credit with only temporary and externally caused financial panics. Conversely, in the nineteenth and twentieth centuries there have been depressions, as well as many minor recessions, that did not produce financial panics. There is no reason, all other things being equal, why money and credit should not flow steadily through the process of circulation, so long as business expectations remain optimistic. It may be tentatively concluded that the regular use of money and credit is a necessary prerequisite, but not a sufficient explanation, of business cycles.

PRODUCTION FOR PRIVATE PROFIT

We have examined two conditions—production for the market and regular use of money—that must be present if business cycles are to occur. These are cycles in which demand fluctuates below the full-employment level of supply. But at least one more institutional condition is necessary before we can contend that total demand may not equal total supply in this economy. It is the existence of private ownership of production facilities and production for private profit. Even in an economy characterized by exchange in the market through the medium of money, supply and demand can be kept in balance, or quickly brought back into balance, if both supply and demand are consciously planned by the same national agency.

A centrally planned economy is one in which the government owns and plans the use of all means of production. Most business cycle economists admit that industrialized planned economies do not experience the business cycle phenomena that are characteristic of industrialized private enterprise economies. This is the case because a centrally planned economy can make one unified plan for growth without concern for private profit. Thus all of the data on Soviet economic development indicate continuous full employment (except for retraining time or movement between jobs).

In a private enterprise economy, each individual enterprise makes it own plans on the basis of its own estimate of whether it will obtain a private profit by undertaking production. In the national plan of a planned economy, the same agency decides both the aggregate supply and the aggregate demand. It sets the aggregate consumer demand by setting wages, and it controls the aggregate investment demand directly through the government budget.

Of course, planners may make mistakes in allocation of resources and new investment, especially because there are changes in technology and other new conditions each year. They may allocate resources to uses that are not as productive as others, or even order the production of one commodity (say, automobiles), but not order enough production of other commodities going into it (say, rubber tires). In such cases there may be supply bottlenecks holding back production in some industries and temporary oversupply and unused capacity in others. Such mistakes may lower the rate of growth or even cause output to fall (as in Czechoslovakia in 1963 and in Poland early in the 1980s).

In an economy based on private ownership of individual competing units, the sum of decisions to produce may not equal the sum of decisions by other individuals and businesses to spend—that is, to consume and invest. If the sum of the outputs produced at present prices is greater than the sum of the monetary demand, then there is not enough revenue to cover the costs of production and also yield a profit for the private entrepreneur. This criterion is decisive because if the private entrepreneur can make no profit, he or she will not continue production, machinery will stand idle, and all of the workers in that business will be unemployed.

SUMMARY

Some classical economists believed aggregate demand always automatically adjusts to aggregate supply. This was true of earlier societies in which production was for self-sufficient isolated units, and the little exchange that existed was by barter. It is also roughly true in socialist economies, where production and investment are planned for social use. Automatic full employment is not true of modern private enterprise, capitalist economies, in which (1) production is for the market, (2) exchange operates by means of money and credit, and (3) the aim of production is private profit. Thus, despite its impressive long-run growth, the American economy has been plagued by instability. The growth of large-scale, oligopolistic, corporate capitalism in the late nineteenth century only increased this instability. As a result, ever since the Industrial Revolution and the establishment of full-blown capitalist systems, western Europe and the United States have been subject to periodic depressions from "overproduction," in which output falls, factories are idle, and millions of workers are unemployed and on relief. This unemployment means that every worker and small-business owner lives with uncertainty and great tension every day. While society loses much product, millions of individuals lose jobs, are plunged into poverty, have a feeling of total helplessness and uselessness, and suffer greatly increased physical disease (including malnutrition) and mental disease (including rises in every indicator of ill health from insomnia to suicide).

Chapter 28 will develop a precise accounting framework for examining instability in the modern economy. Chapters 29 and 30 will then use that accounting framework to discuss in detail the neoclassical arguments for Say's Law versus the arguments by Keynesians and Marxists against Say's Law.

SELECTED READINGS

The importance of the capitalist economic system to the coming of the business cycle is traced in Philip Mirowski, *The Birth of the Business Cycle* (New York: Garland Publishing Company, 1985).

REFERENCES

Clark, Grahame. *From Savagery to Civilization.* London: Cobbett Press, 1946.

Crow, John A. *The Epic of Latin America.* Garden City, N.Y.: Doubleday, 1948.

Gibbs, Marion. *Feudal Order.* London: Cobbett Press, 1949.

Mitchell, W. C. *Business Annals.* New York: National Bureau of Economic Research, 1926.

———. *Business Cycles.* Berkeley: University of California Press, 1913.

Ricardo, David. *The Principles of Political Economy and Taxation.* London: Gonner, Bell and Sons, 1891.

Walbank, F. W. *The Decline of the Roman Empire in the West.* London: Cobbett Press, 1956.

Chapter
28

National Income Accounting

How to Map the Circulation of Money and Goods

The U.S. Department of Commerce publishes detailed national income accounts. These accounts report the total flow of money and goods in the nation for a given period the same way that private accounting reports the flow of money and goods in a single private enterprise. Many economists have labored to map this circulation of money and goods in the nation—just as biologists trace the circulation of blood through the body. Some famous economists who have labored at this task are Quesnay, Marx, and Keynes.

The extensive contribution of Karl Marx to national income concepts was long ignored, not only because of his radical views, but also because classical and neoclassical economists did not admit any problems of aggregate supply and demand, so no detailed accounts were necessary. The Great Depression so shook up economic theory that government agencies and some economists were receptive when J. M. Keynes proposed certain aggregate concepts as the basis for a whole new area of economics now called *macroeconomics.*

John Maynard Keynes (1883–1946) made his major contributions in the midst of the Great Depression of the 1930s. He wanted to trace the total flow of money and goods in order to learn how it was possible for a nation to have a lack of demand for goods while millions of people were hungry, poorly clothed, and ill-housed. He found the answers by tracing how money may leak out of the system, how those who have money may hoard it and not spend it, while those who badly need goods have no money. He concentrated on the total or aggregate demand for goods coming from consumer spending on consumer goods and the demand from investors' spending on goods necessary for production.

The aggregate concepts of Keynes constituted a radical new way of thinking for orthodox, mainstream economists. Before Keynes, most orthodox academic economists denied the possibility of aggregate disequilibrium (depression or inflation); they had thus seen no need for aggregate concepts. Keynes changed all that and made the aggregate concepts the basis for a whole new aggregate or macroeconomic analysis. The concepts are now used by the U.S. Department of Commerce, so the following discussion is based on their data.

THE CIRCULAR FLOW OF GROSS NATIONAL PRODUCT

Gross national product (GNP) is defined as the total value of all the finished goods and services produced by a nation during a year. Each good or service is valued at its market selling price. The market pricing system thus provides a yardstick by means of which totally different and otherwise unrelated items can be compared and aggregated.

The national flow of production and income in the private domestic sector may be thought of as a circular flow of supply and demand between households and businesses. Understanding the circular flow in this uncomplicated economy is essential to understanding the concepts of aggregate supply and aggregate demand. The same concepts underlie the construction of the national income and product accounts.

In a capitalist economy some households own property while others own only their power to work. The workers' households supply certain amounts of labor. The capitalist owners of property buy this labor and add to it the appropriate amounts of factories, machinery, and raw materials. At each given level of technology this will enable business to supply households with a certain amount of consumer goods and to supply other businesses with new capital goods. Capital goods are defined as new factories and new machinery as well as raw materials supplied to business.

Consumer goods keep the households alive and ready for labor, and the new capital goods are available for further business expansion. Of course, the services supplied by households to business as well as the products supplied by businesses to households are furnished for payment, not free of charge. In a primitive economy, services can be bartered directly for products, but a complex economy cannot be based on such a system of exchange. Payment must be made by means of money, which is the only type of effective demand in the U.S. economy. This concept of effective demand, based on spending, was Keynes's main analytic tool.

The payment for the supply of services from households may be similarly divided into various income streams; wages, rent, interest, and profits. Wage income includes hourly wages, piecework wages, salaries, and commissions. Profit income includes profits of both corporate and unincorporated business. Rental income includes the rent from land as well as from buildings. Interest income includes all returns on borrowed money. It is

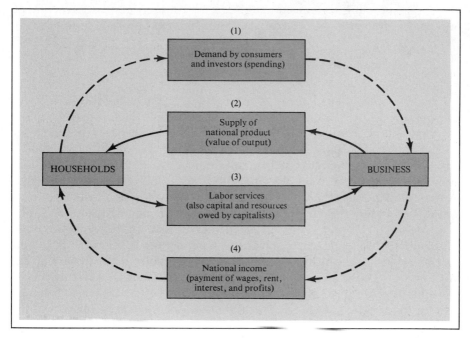

Figure 28.1 The circular flow of supply and demand.

assumed at this point that all of these business incomes are actually paid out to households.

The circular flow of supply and demand is depicted in Figure 28.1, which indicates how (1) money spending flows from households to business to buy consumer and investment goods. This spending pays for flow (2), the transfer of products from business to households. At the same time, flow (3) shows the movement of services from households to business. These services are paid by flow (4), the flow of money income from business to households. Notice that money moves in one direction around the circuit, with goods and services mirroring it in their equal and opposite movement. If there is no hitch, the supply and demand will flow smoothly and just balance each other in both sets of transactions. All four flows are supposed to be equal and are different ways of looking at our aggregate economic activity.

HOW TO CALCULATE THE GROSS NATIONAL PRODUCT

Gross national product (GNP) may be calculated in terms of money in two different ways, corresponding to the money flow from households to business or the equal money flow from business to households. In the first, we examine the aggregate money demand for all products—that is, the flow of money spending on consumer goods, investment goods, government purchases, and net exports (exports minus imports).

$$\$ \text{ GNP} = \$ \text{ spending} = \$ \text{ consumption} + \$ \text{ investment} \tag{1}$$
$$+ \$ \text{ government} + \$ \text{ net exports.}$$

This flow of money spent for products must correspond to the equal and opposite flow of products to their final buyers. In the market place the money flow from purchasers is precisely the measure of the value of the GNP sold by business. Thus in Figure 28.1 the two upper loops, labeled (1) and (2), show the movement of money in one direction and the equal movement of goods and services in the other direction. The two are equal by definition because the exchange price has been agreed to by both buyers and sellers. In the next chapter we will see how Keynes analyzed the problems that result when buyers intend to spend less than the value of goods supplied at present prices. The second way of calculating GNP is to add up the money paid out by businesses for all of their costs of production. Most of these costs of production constitute flows of money income to households. These incomes include wages paid for the services of labor, rent for the use of land, interest for the use of borrowed capital, and profit for capital ownership. Thus the two lower loops of Figure 28.1, labeled (3) and (4), depict the movement of goods and services to business in one direction and the equal movement of money as income to households in the other.

Actually businesses have another major cost that has not yet been discussed. This cost makes the second way of calculating GNP a little more complicated than is suggested by the simple diagram in Figure 28.1. This cost is depreciation, or the funds set aside to replace the machinery and factory buildings that are used up or eventually worn out in the process of production. These funds are paid out not to any individual but to other businesses when it is time to replace the worn-out instruments of production. So when depreciation is added to the flows of money incomes, we get

$$\$ \text{ GNP} = \$ \text{ wages} + \$ \text{ rent} + \$ \text{ interest} \tag{2}$$
$$+ \$ \text{ profits} + \$ \text{ depreciation}$$

Marx emphasized this second way of looking at the flow of GNP. He agreed that the business pays out wages to workers. He also noted that business pays other businesses to replace the depreciated machinery. He emphasized the property incomes—rent, interest, and profit—that capitalists exploit from workers by grouping them together. Thus, he calculated GNP as

$$\$ \text{ GNP} = \$ \text{ wages} + \$ \text{ property incomes} + \$ \text{ depreciation} \tag{3}$$

We can calculate GNP, as Keynes did, in terms of all spending to purchase output; or we can calculate GNP, as Marx did, in terms of all the money flow through business to workers and capitalists (and for depreciation to other businesses). By definition, the GNP calculated by either method must be equal to the same money value. Indeed, the U.S. Department of Commerce, which makes these calculations, does always arrive at the same amount by either method (after allowing for statistical mistakes).

GROSS NATIONAL PRODUCT IN REAL TERMS

To know whether a change in GNP reflects a change in national welfare, we must determine whether the change was due to a change in the economic measuring rod (prices) or a change in the real quantity of goods and services produced. If the national product doubles in money value but the price level has also doubled, then the real product—the goods and services available to the nation—has remained the same. Or, if GNP in current prices has risen 5 percent but the overall price level has risen 3 percent, physical output has increased by only 2 percent.

In calculating GNP the government must use current prices. But to make comparisons between years when price changes have occurred, the money value of GNP can be deflated by dividing the current value by an index showing how much prices have changed:

$$\$ \text{ GNP/Price Index} = \text{real (or deflated) } \$ \text{ GNP} \tag{4}$$

The Department of Commerce compiles price indexes for the many components of GNP. It also deflates each component by its index. Each index is constructed from the price changes that have occurred in the items that make up that component. By choosing a base year, such as 1929 (i.e., 1929 = 100), against which all price changes are measured, deflated GNP data can be made comparable over the years.

POTENTIAL GROSS NATIONAL PRODUCT

Many times, part of the nation's productive capacity goes unused. Factories may stand idle or only partially used while millions of unemployed workers search for jobs. During such periods economists can calculate the approximate potential GNP that would exist if the unemployed laborers could be put to work and if the factories not being utilized could be used to full capacity. The difference between potential and actual GNP is a widely used measure of the economic costs of recessions and depressions.

PER CAPITA GNP

We have noted that the actual GNP in real terms is used as a reflection of national welfare. Suppose, however, that we want to measure the welfare, not for the nation, but for each individual. If China has the same national product as England, then the average Chinese is much worse off than the average Englishman because of the tremendous difference in population. Therefore, to measure the individual welfare, the GNP of a nation must be divided by the number of its population. This result is the per capita GNP. Notice, however, that per capita GNP is only an average; it does not say anything about how the GNP is distributed among individuals.

NET ECONOMIC WELFARE

Finally, suppose we have deflated GNP by price rises and by population increases. Is the resulting real per capita GNP a good measure of individual human welfare? More and more economists are coming to the conclusion that it is not a good welfare measure.

On the one side, there are some goods and services not included in the GNP because they are not given a value in the market. For example, the work of housewives is not counted in the GNP. Yet women work long, hard hours in the home, and their labor equals about one-fourth of the official GNP value. This exclusion is very inconsistent. Suppose a woman works as a maid for a man who owns a house. That woman's labor is counted in the GNP to the amount of her salary, yet if she marries the house owner, her labor is no longer counted and GNP is reduced. The reason for this exclusion is the sexist idea that women do not really work very hard, plus the capitalist notion that services have value only if they are sold in the market.

On the other side, many costs to the public are not subtracted from GNP, even though they are caused by the private capitalist production of GNP. For example, the production and use of cars and trucks cause air pollution. This pollution costs the public in terms of health, such as eye and respiratory diseases, and even property damage, such as harm to trees and plants. Thus GNP should be reduced by the amount of this damage.

Moreover, some large portion of GNP is composed of wasteful or harmful goods that reduce or do not increase human welfare; this portion should not be included in GNP. For example, cigarettes are part of GNP, but they are harmful. Advertising "service" is part of GNP, but over 90 percent of it is pure propaganda or misinformation. The largest single waste is military spending, yet the billions of dollars spent to build and then stockpile bombs and tanks are included in GNP.

It might also be noted that some projects benefit the public beyond the cost shown in GNP. For example, a dam built by the government to provide water and power (and counted in GNP at cost) may also produce recreation and beauty. Therefore a new measure is needed, and some economists have argued for net economic welfare (NEW) to replace the official GNP. The NEW would equal the GNP, but would in addition (1) add housewives' labor, (2) add unpriced benefits (e.g., recreation from dams), (3) subtract unpriced costs (e.g., pollution from industry and cars), and (4) subtract all harmful and wasteful products.

THE NATIONAL INCOME ACCOUNTS IN DETAIL

In Figure 28.1, we noted that if government and foreign trade are omitted, then GNP may be calculated as spending for consumption plus spending for investment.

We are now ready to bring government in more detail into the calculation of GNP and to admit that goods are bought and sold abroad. Government can be viewed as a giant household or business, but because government output of services is not sold in the marketplace, there is no obvious way to value the services it provides. The U.S. government is not to any appreciable extent an owner of any instruments of production; it receives its income by taxing the incomes of labor and of privately owned instruments of production. Yet government spending in the private sector is a very significant part of overall demand, and government employs about 18 percent of the labor force.

For our purposes the role of government in the economy will be simplified by assuming that it merely siphons money from the circular flow by imposing taxes and returns money to the spending stream by buying goods and services from businesses. The types of goods and services government buys and the uses to which it puts them are considered in later chapters. The GNP, with government spending in the economy and with foreign trade, when calculated from the expenditure side, becomes

$$\$ \text{ GNP} = \$ \text{ spending} = \$ \text{ consumption} + \$ \text{ investment} \qquad (5)$$
$$+ \$ \text{ government} + \$ \text{ net exports}$$

In 1987, the GNP was $4486 billion, which equaled $2966 billion personal consumption spending plus $716 billion gross investment spending plus $924 billion government purchases minus $120 billion net exports (because U.S. exports were less than U.S. imports).

Net exports are the difference between what is sold and what is bought abroad. Exports bring a flow of dollars into the country in exchange for goods produced at home but sold abroad. Imports result in a flow of dollars out of the country for the purchase of goods produced abroad. If more is exported than imported, the net figure is an addition to the total amount of spending for domestically produced goods and services. But if imports are greater than exports, money flows out of this country.

With governments in the picture another cost of doing business must enter the calculation of production costs: sales or excise taxes. These taxes include general sales taxes on all or most commodities, such as a 5 percent state tax on all sales. They also include special taxes, such as the tax on cigarettes, that affect only the purchasers of one commodity. In either case, the governments extract the money at the point of purchase before it can be considered as income by business. These are sometimes called *indirect taxes* because they are not a direct tax on the income of any individual or business. From the income or cost side the GNP includes the sales taxes as a cost of doing business. Thus

$$\$ \text{ GNP} = \$ \text{ cost of production} = \$ \text{ wages} + \text{interest} + \text{profit}$$
$$+ \$ \text{ rent} + \$ \text{ sales taxes} + \$ \text{ depreciation} \tag{6}$$

NET NATIONAL PRODUCT

Net national product (NNP) differs from GNP in only one respect: NNP does not include the amount of depreciation that has occurred during the year. Depreciation is defined as the amount of capital used up in the production process. The NNP is very useful as a measure of what part of the economy's total production is actually available for use. Certainly, production that merely replaces machinery that has worn out and is no longer usable should not be considered as adding to the amount of capital available to the economy.

Thus, to compare useful production in two countries, we would compare NNP, not GNP, because when we compare product actually available for use, we are not interested in the amount of depreciation or capital used up in producing the available product. To arrive at the figure for NNP, we simply subtract depreciation from GNP,

$$\$ \text{ NNP} = \$ \text{ GNP} - \$ \text{ depreciation} \tag{7}$$

In the national accounts, depreciation is called *capital consumption allowance.* Unfortunately, the capital consumption allowance does not always reflect physical depreciation accurately because it involves many problems of estimation that are affected by the practices of accountants. These accountants must view not only the expected life of capital equipment but also the implications for tax liability. From the cost or income side NNP can be calculated by eliminating depreciation (or the capital consumption allowance).

$$\$ \text{ NNP} = \$ \text{ wages} + \$ \text{ rent} + \$ \text{ interest}$$
$$+ \$ \text{ profits} + \$ \text{ sales taxes} \tag{8}$$

If we were still excluding government, NNP and national income would be identical. National income is defined as the income of the nation in a year's time that is wholly derived from the production of final, usable goods and services. It is the income going to all the economic classes: wages to workers, rent to landlords, interest to lenders, and profit to capitalists. Sales taxes and all other indirect business taxes go to the government and do not become income to any class of citizens. When they are subtracted from NNP, the national income is simply

$$\$ \text{ national income} = \$ \text{ wages} + \$ \text{ rent} + \$ \text{ interest} + \$ \text{ profits} \tag{9}$$

In 1987, U.S. national income was $3636 billion, which was composed of $2647 billion of wages and salaries plus $19 billion of net rental income plus $337 billion of net interest income plus $305 billion corporate profits plus $328 billion of noncorporate profits (called proprietors' income).

PERSONAL AND DISPOSABLE INCOME

The government imposes various taxes on the national income but also adds to the income stream many kinds of welfare payments. The total of payments to all classes in production (i.e., the national income) is therefore not the amount of income that households actually have at their disposal. Households' income comes from production plus various welfare payments minus various taxes.

In order to proceed from national income to the income that actually goes to people (i.e., personal income), various additions and subtractions must be made. First, corporate profits do not go directly to any individual; corporate profits must be subtracted from national income in the process of determining the personal income actually going to individuals. Second, individuals pay out of their wage income certain compulsory contributions for social insurance to the government (these are usually payments for Social Security); these also must be subtracted from the national income. Third, individuals make various payments of interest on loans to financial institutions and to government; these also must be subtracted to find personal income.

On the positive side, the government makes many transfer payments that shift income to individuals, thus adding to personal income. These transfers include unemployment compensation, farm subsidies, business subsidies, and Social Security benefits. Second, corporations pay dividends out of profits. Third, business makes a few transfer payments, such as retirement benefits. Fourth, a great many wealthy individuals receive interest payments from the government or from corporations. All such payments must be added to national income if we wish to calculate personal income. Totaling all the additions and subtractions from national income, the result is total personal income. The procedure is indicated by the following unwieldly equation:

$ personal income

$$
\begin{aligned}
= \; & \$ \text{ national income} - \$ \text{ corporate profits} \\
& - \$ \text{ interest paid by individuals} \\
& - \$ \text{ social security taxes} \\
& + \$ \text{ government transfer payments} + \$ \text{ dividends} \\
& + \$ \text{ business transfer payments} \\
& + \$ \text{ personal interest income}
\end{aligned}
\tag{10}
$$

DISPOSABLE PERSONAL INCOME

Finally, there is disposable personal income, which is the amount of money actually at the disposal of individuals and households for spending on consumption or for personal saving. In order to find this quantity, personal income taxes, which are the taxes an individual or a household must pay in proportion to its yearly income, must be deducted. The result is expressed as

$ disposable personal income

(11)

 − ⓢ personal income − $ personal income taxes

Consumers may now spend and save out of disposable personal income. If consumption expenditures are subtracted, we arrive at personal saving. A simplified listing of the accounts discussed here (with actual figures for 1987) is shown in Table 28.1.

SAVING AND INVESTMENT

It is necessary to distinguish between the concepts of wealth, capital, and investment. Wealth, the broader concept, is the total holding by everyone of all durable consumer goods plus the ownership of natural resources plus

Table 28.1   NATIONAL INCOME ACCOUNTS FOR 1987
                     (BILLIONS OF DOLLARS)

Gross National Product	$4486	
− Depreciation (or capital consumption)		−8479
= **Net National Product**	= 4007	
− Indirect business taxes (mostly sales taxes)		−397
= **National Income**	= 3636	
− Corporate profits		−305
− Interest paid by individuals		−337
− Social security taxes		−394
+ Government transfer payments		+520
+ Dividends		+88
+ Business transfer payments		+23
+ Personal interest income		+516
= **Personal Income**	= 3746	
− Personal income tax		−565
= **Disposable Personal Income**	= 3181	
− Consumption expenditures		−2966
− Interest paid by consumers to business		−95
= Personal saving	= 120	

Source: Council of Economic Advisors, *Economic Report of the President* (Washington, D.C.: GPO, 1988), pp. 272–275.

the total holding of the entire stock of capital. Wealth is not measured in the national income and product accounts. A high level of production certainly means that a large stock of wealth exists in the form of productive capital.

The national accounts, however, measure only the value of the flow of production, and hence income. They are not designed to measure the holding of wealth either as capital or, for that matter, in the form of claims measured in money—that is, financial wealth. *Capital* is defined as the total value of all existing buildings and factories, machines and equipment for production, and inventories. Inventories are defined as the existing stocks of raw materials, goods in process, and finished goods stockpiled.

Investment may then be defined simply as the change in capital, its increase or decrease within one year or some other period. This means that any individual investment that does not increase the amount of capital, such as the purchase of old shares of stock by one individual from another, does not count as new investment for the nation. Even if a corporation sells new stock, the proceeds do not become net investment in the economy until the corporation actually uses the money to purchase new factories, equipment, or inventories. In other words, the investment discussed here is not mere financial dealing or individual investment of money, but the real, or physical, expansion of the nation's economic capacity. More specifically, this year's investment consists of new construction, new producers' durable equipment, and the change in business inventories.

Only one more distinction in this area of analysis need be made. The total investment in the economy is called *gross investment*. It includes both net investment, or investment to expand productive capacity, and replacement investment, or investment needed to replace the depreciation of present productive capacities.

There is, of course, a close connection between net and gross investment and net and gross national product. The connection can be easily stated through the spending approach to national product. Leaving aside government spending and net export spending, we find that

$$\text{\$ gross national product} = \text{\$ consumption} + \text{gross investment} \qquad (12)$$

In this equation gross investment includes replacement investment, which is equal to depreciation. Similarly, without government or new export, we find that

$$\text{\$ net national product} = \text{\$ consumption} + \text{net investment} \qquad (13)$$

Having defined investment, we must now define saving. Most of our national product goes for consumption—that is, the aggregate purchase of consumer goods and services by all U.S. households. Whatever part of national income or product is not used for consumption is defined as saving.

Thus the following definition may be written (aside from government and foreign trade):

$$\text{\$ net national product} = \text{\$ consumption} + \text{\$ saving} \tag{14}$$

Aside from the government, there are only two sources of saving in the economy. These are (1) the personal saving of individuals and households and (2) the retained profits of businesses. Notice that the depreciation funds put aside by business, a form of gross savings, come out of the gross national product. Therefore net saving is what remains from net national product after consumer spending, whereas gross saving is what remains from gross national product after consumer spending.

Notice that both saving and investment are each by definition equal to national product (net or gross) less consumption. Therefore they must by definition equal each other. Leaving out government and foreign trade, we may write

$$\begin{aligned} \text{\$ consumption} + \text{\$ net investment} \\ = \text{\$ consumption} + \text{\$ savings} \end{aligned} \tag{15}$$

The equality between saving and investment is an accounting identity. Both are equal to national income minus consumption, by definition. Had we started from GNP, depreciation funds would have been included on both sides, making gross investment equal to gross saving of business and individuals. (The following equations will hold for net or gross amounts, so we do not distinguish between them.)

With government included, the identity becomes

$$\begin{aligned} \text{\$ consumption} + \text{\$ investment} + \text{\$ government} \\ = \text{consumption} + \text{\$ saving} + \text{\$ taxes} \end{aligned} \tag{16}$$

This is so because national product is now the sum both of the three spending flows and of the three allocations between consumption, saving, and tax payments. The sum of investment spending and government spending is identical to the sum of private saving and taxation. If government spending and taxation are equal, the government budget in the national accounting framework is in balance. In practice, the difference between government spending and government taxation is called *government saving*, which may be positive if taxes exceed government spending or negative if there is a budget deficit.

When foreign trade is added, the identity becomes:

$$\begin{aligned} \text{\$ consumption} + \text{\$ investment} + \text{\$ government} + \text{\$ exports} \\ = \text{\$ consumption} + \text{\$ saving} + \text{\$ taxes} + \text{\$ imports} \end{aligned} \tag{17}$$

This identity can be understood as representing, on the left side, the expenditures for goods and services by the four spending sectors and, on the right side, the uses of national income. The difference between exports and imports is often called *net exports*.

If it is positive, it indicates that foreigners cannot pay for all U.S. exports with the money spent on imports from them. Hence they are increasing the total demand for U.S. goods. Since they are putting money into the U.S. economy, net exports is also called *net foreign investment.*

By rearranging accounting terms and subtracting consumption from both sides, the overall identity between saving and investment can be written as follows:

$ investment + ($ exports − $ imports)

$$= \$ \text{ savings} + (\$ \text{ taxes} - \$ \text{ government}) \qquad \textbf{(18)}$$

The sum of net domestic private investment and net foreign investment is identical to the sum of net private saving and governmental saving; or, in brief, saving equals investment in the national accounts.

THE VALUE-ADDED CONCEPT

The GNP of the United States includes only final products. It avoids counting the value of the same product more than once when this product appears at various intermediate stages of the production process. Suppose both the value of all the steel produced and the value of all the automobiles produced were counted in the GNP. Since a great deal of steel is used in automobile production, we would be counting the value of that steel twice, once by itself and once as a principal ingredient in automobiles.

The correct procedure is to include only the value added by capital and labor (and land) in each industry—that is, the increase in the worths of the product in the production process of that industry beyond the worth of the raw materials bought from other industries. Therefore the value added by capital and labor (and land) to the raw material in the steel industry would be counted. Then the value added by capital and labor (and land) in making automobiles out of the steel would also be counted. But the value of the steel, or any other product from another industry, used by the auto industry would not be counted again. The whole calculation of gross product (using the cost of production, or income, approach) may be illustrated as follows:

gross product in steel and auto industry

$$= \text{steel (wages + profits + rent + interest + depreciation)} \qquad \textbf{(19)}$$

$$+ \text{auto (wages + profits + rent + interest + depreciation)}$$

Notice that neither the cost of the iron or coal used in the steel industry or that of the steel or rubber tires used in the auto industry is included; both are values produced by other industries and not values added by this industry. The value added is thus less than the price in each industry by exactly the amount of goods and materials bought from other industries.

SUMMARY

Goods flow from business to households, and labor services flow from households to business. Money travels in the opposite direction around the circle; that is, money flows from households to business in order to buy goods, and money flows from business to households to buy labor services. For the purposes of analysis, economists try to keep accounts that measure all of national output. Everything put together is called the gross national product (GNP), the demand for which comes from consumers, investors, government, and foreign buyers. The GNP is the money value of all the goods produced in a year. Although it is an important measure, we should not be mesmerized by the size of GNP because it includes many wasteful or even harmful goods and services (advertising, cigarettes, military). It should be corrected for inflation of prices or increase of population if it is to begin to measure welfare. It should also be corrected to add housewives' labor and other benefits not priced in the market, and to subtract all harmful and wasteful products (including the military) as well as all the costs of pollution and other environmental destruction. Only with these major corrections would a new measure of GNP reflect human welfare.

A second concept is the net national product (NNP), which equals GNP minus depreciation. Third, national income equals NNP minus sales taxes (and a few similar taxes). Fourth, personal income is what actually winds up in the hands of individuals; it thus equals national income earned in the usual ways plus welfare and subsidies and interest payments from the government minus profits kept by corporations and corporate taxes and employees' Social Security taxes paid to the government. Fifth, disposable income is equal to personal income minus personal income taxes. Finally, savings equals disposable income minus consumption. Because investment is also defined as all income or output minus consumption, saving and investment are equal by definition in the national income accounts (but, as is seen in Chapters 29 and 30, what some people plan to save and others plan to invest may not be equal).

SUGGESTED READINGS

The classic, detailed statement of the national income accounts is R. and N. Ruggles, *National Income Accounts and Income Analysis* (New York: McGraw-Hill, 1956).

Chapter
29

Say's Law and Its Critics
Three Views of Macroeconomics

In this chapter we discuss three very different analyses of how the macro economy is structured, why unemployment and inflation occur, and what are the correct political policies to cure these problems. The first is the conservative position, presented by J. B. Say and almost all the classical and neoclassical economists. The second is the liberal position, presented by J. M. Keynes and his followers (which is similar to the liberal view of Thorstein Veblen, Wesley Mitchell, and other institutionalists, discussed in Chapters 26 and 27). The third is the radical position, presented by Karl Marx and many other radicals.

THE CONSERVATIVE VIEW OF J. B. SAY

The conservative view, first presented by J. B. Say (1767–1832), is that unemployment and inflation are accidents caused by factors external to the economy. They are always minor and temporary; the capitalist economy, if left to itself, will always automatically come back to full employment and stable prices in a short time. *Say's law states that any supply of goods calls forth its own demand*, so there can never be overproduction relative to demand for any length of time. Every supply of output leads to income, which leads to an equal amount of demand.

In its most rigid form, Say's law states that aggregate demand must always equal aggregate supply at any level of supply, including the full-employment level. This denies the possibility of either a deficiency or an excess of aggregate demand and therefore denies the possibility of depressions or general unemployment. Say's law does not state that aggregate supply and aggregate demand are "identical" or are equal by definition: ". . . Though Say's law is not an identity, his blundering exposition has led a long series of writers to believe that it is one . . ." (Schumpeter, p. 618). Rather, Say's law says that an increase of supply, through various automatic processes, calls forth an equal amount of demand. The economy always behaves so as to bring back an equilibrium of supply and demand at full employment.

Aside from a few dissenters, whole generations of economists refused to accept the possibility that there could be involuntary unemployment or an excessive supply of goods. Furthermore, they never challenged the assumption that all commodities could always be sold at prices equal to their full, long-run costs. They admitted only the possibility of temporary, accidental maladjustments in one or a few industries. Such maladjustments were sure to be corrected as soon as competition could force capital to switch from one industry to another. In a typical statement Ricardo argued, "Too much of a particular commodity may be produced, of which there may be said to be such a glut in the market as not to repay the capital expended on it; but this cannot be the case with all commodities" (Ricardo, p. 276).

The kernel of truth in Say's law is the platitude that every purchase constitutes a sale, and every sale means some money income to someone, which again may, and ordinarily will, be used for more purchases. Ricardo phrased the case for Say's law in this way: "No man produces but with a view to consume or sell, and he never sells but with an intention to purchase some other commodity which may be useful to him or which may contribute to future production. By purchasing them, he necessarily becomes either the consumer of his own goods, or the purchaser and consumer of the goods of some other person" (Ricardo, p. 273). Because Say's law predicts that the economy will always return to full employment equilibrium, the argument implies that there can be no depressions in modern private enterprise economies.

Yet observation reveals that such economies have never been without periodic depressions within the last century or more. Say's law is, indeed, true for certain earlier types of economies. These economies could not have had less aggregate demand than supply because production was for the use of self-contained communities with little external trade and little use of money. Under capitalism, however, the economy has changed. As we shall see in the next chapter, under capitalism (1) production is for private profit and ceases if there is no expectation of profit; (2) output is not bought by those who produce it and must be sold in the market for a profit; and (3) money is used as a medium of exchange and may be hoarded rather than respent.

By ignoring these historical changes, the classical economists, such as Say or Ricardo, built an analytic model that fit a primitive economy or a Robinson Crusoe island but is inadequate for modern capitalism. Leaving aside government and foreign trade for the moment, the essentials of J. B.

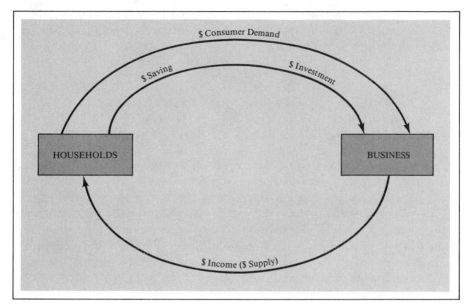

Figure 29.1 The macroeconomy according to J. B. Say.

Say's view of the economy can be portrayed in a very simple diagram (Figure 29.1).

This figure shows one important truth in what Say claimed. It is true that output, which is supplied to the market and sold there, generates income. The capitalist pays out wage income, rental income, and interest income, while the residual from sales is profits income. These incomes all go to households (if we assume that corporations pay out all profits to stockholders). The households normally use all the money for consumption and investment. Thus, saving—or the money that is not consumed—is automatically equal to investment in this case. Unfortunately, this is not always the case. It is not true that households always spend all of their money, so we shall see that—according to the critics—Say's law does not hold.

The classical economists, however, concluded that the capitalist system will automatically restore full employment with stable prices after any temporary dislocation. So the government should do nothing if there is unemployment, because it will always be temporary.

Say's law and the policies that follow from it are not merely a historical curiosity. Modern conservatives, such as the monetarist school led by Milton Friedman, still believe in Say's law and therefore advocate no government action to cure unemployment, no matter how severe it is. In fact, all neo-classical economists begin their analysis with the preferences of individuals and ordinarily assume all economic activities are voluntary. Because he begins with the analysis of individual preferences, the leading neoclassical analyst of unemployment says: "To explain why people allocate time to

. . . unemployment we need to know why they prefer it to all other activities" (Lucas, p. 38). Moreover, Michael Boskin, who is the head of President Bush's Council of Economic Advisors, advocates the same policy; he is in favor of reduction of the government role in the economy largely on this basis.

BLAMING THE VICTIM

Conservative economists have always tended to blame the unemployed for unemployment. Some conservative politicians still claim that anyone who really wants a job can get one. Using the strange proposition called Say's law, conservative economists for many decades proved to their satisfaction that a general depression is impossible, so involuntary unemployment on a large scale is impossible. They admitted only frictional unemployment—that is, a temporary depression in a few industries until workers can move to other industries that are booming.

On the basis of these arguments, conservative economists concluded that all unemployed (beyond the frictional unemployed) must be lazy loafers unwilling to work at the prevailing wage. The unemployed must, according to these economists, all be people who voluntarily leave their jobs to look for easier or better-paying jobs elsewhere. Imagine arguing this notion during the 1930s when official unemployment was over 25 percent. Do all workers periodically get fits of laziness or greed? Are millions only pretending to be unhappy when out of a job and living on a thin handout from the government?

As we shall see in a later chapter, this argument always leads conservative economists to the conclusion that all workers would be fully employed if only they would accept lower wages. These views have been revived in more sophisticated technical form by modern conservatives. For example, Armen Alchian argues that when demand declines, workers are faced with a choice (see Alchian). They can agree to continue working at a lower wage or voluntarily quit their present jobs and go hunting around for a better one. Since many workers are ignorant of the true facts of the job market, they spend many months hopping around looking for nonexistent jobs at their old wages. Meanwhile, these millions of ill-informed workers may be considered voluntarily unemployed or frictionally unemployed or "employed" in acquiring information. But most workers are just fired, not offered such a choice. We shall see, moreover, in Chapter 30 that accepting lower wages would not lower the unemployment rate.

Alchian's argument about voluntary, frictional unemployment while looking for better jobs has been particularly applied to women workers and young workers. Three authors of a recent textbook say

> The size of frictional unemployment is rising. Voluntary quits and job hopping represent a large and growing phenomenon in the United States labor market.

Unusually large numbers of younger (and inexperienced) workers and middle-aged women have been entering the labor force recently. These workers are typically more selective about the types of jobs they will accept. . . . Unemployment during job search to improve wages or working conditions is considered to be voluntary and not a proper concern of government policy. (Mitchell, Hand, and Walker, p. 152)

So women and young workers "voluntarily quit" and "job hop" and "are typically more selective about the type of jobs they will accept." The mildest comment one can make about this argument is that it is both illogical and a travesty of the facts. Logically, one would expect that women and young workers would be far more anxious to hold on to any job, no matter how bad and lowly paid, than an older male because they know that they will face discrimination in getting a better job. They are certainly not more selective because they cannot afford to be. The fact is—according to numerous U.S. Labor Department surveys—that fewer women voluntarily quit any given job than men at that job. The argument, therefore, seems compounded less of evidence and more of prejudiced notions about women and unemployed young workers (of whom a high proportion are black, though this is not always mentioned).

The conservative economists extend the argument to blame the victims not only for unemployment but also for inflation. Alchian's view is that voluntary unemployment lowers the supply of willing workers, so raises wages and thus raises prices. In Alchian's view workers must suffer several months of futile job hunting before they learn to accept lower real wages—and only these lower real wages will stabilize the price level. Conservatives now view some level of unemployment as natural. The natural level of unemployment is that level necessary to stop inflation; and they argue that any steps to lower that natural level will only result in more inflation. Thus, conservatives have the view—satisfying to the wealthy—that workers are themselves responsible for unemployment and inflation.

THE LIBERAL VIEW OF J. M. KEYNES

John Maynard Keynes (1883–1946) is perhaps the most important economist of the first half of the twentieth century. His background does not appear to be that of a radical or an earthshaker. Born into a respected English family and educated in the best British schools, Keynes worked for His Majesty's Civil Service, headed the Bank of England, edited the *Economic Journal,* and wrote careful treatises on Indian finances and formal logic as well as on the general problems of money. Keynes was always considered one of the establishment in cultural, governmental, and financial circles, yet he rocked the establishment both in England and the United States by demolishing the myth of Say's law and automatic full employment.

Say's law had been attacked by such unorthodox economists as Malthus and Marx. Keynes, however, was the first establishment economist to attack it in detail, using the respectable academic tools of the classical and neo-classical economists. In his most famous book, *The General Theory of Employment, Interest and Money*, written at the depths of the Great Depression, he destroyed Say's law and proved that the equilibrium level of the economy might be either at a point of heavy unemployment or at a point of overly full employment and inflation.

EQUILIBRIUM OF AGGREGATE SUPPLY AND DEMAND

Keynesian economists use the idea of an equilibrium of the forces of aggregate supply and demand as their important analytical tool for understanding the level of output and employment. Aggregate supply is defined by Keynes as the total output that is produced and offered for sale by all U.S. economic units. Aggregate demand is defined as the total dollar amount of final goods and services that consumers, investors, government, and foreigners (net of U.S. spending abroad) plan to buy from all U.S. economic units. Equilibrium exists when planned aggregate demand equals planned aggregate supply at present prices.

Planned spending is defined as all spending—except the spending on unwanted and unplanned increases in inventories. Planned supply and planned demand will be equal only when the economy is at equilibrium. Equilibrium means that buyers' and sellers' desires exactly agree at present prices. If, however, 1000 bushels of ripe tomatoes go unsold, then the supply at present prices is greater than the planned demand.

The problem may be explained another way by saying there is equilibrium only if consumption plus planned investment are equal to consumption plus planned saving. Saving is defined as the difference between income and planned consumption spending. Keynes argued that equilibrium is maintained only if saving out of income is just equal to planned investment spending.

The problem of economic equilibrium, as seen by Keynes, is illustrated in its simplest form in Figure 29.2. Business pays the national income to households. Then, if there is equilibrium, all of that income is spent by households to buy goods from business. This implies that all income that is not spent for consumption is saved in the form of investment spending. If some savings are not invested but are diverted into hoards of money, then there will not be equilibrium of supply and demand.

The Keynesian picture in Figure 29.2 assumes that

$$\text{\$ Saving} = \text{\$ investment demand} \atop + \text{\$ hoarding or \$ dishoarding} \tag{1}$$

On the contrary, the picture painted by J. B. Say (Figure 29.1) assumes that there is no hoarding in the economy.

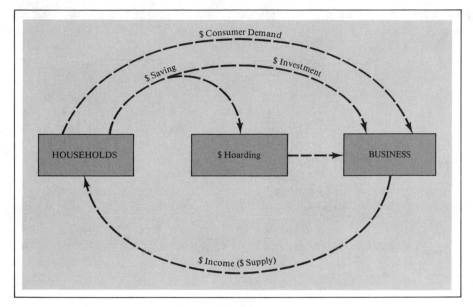

Figure 29.2 The macroeconomy according to J. M. Keynes.

DISEQUILIBRIUM, UNEMPLOYMENT, AND INFLATION

Say assumed that all output supplied to the market meant income and that all income is invariably spent, either for consumption or investment. Keynes, on the contrary, points out that some income may not be spent for either consumption or investment in a given period. "Hoarding" means not spending income. If all income is not spent, then some income drops out of the circular flow of money into inactive hoards. For example, money deposited in banks, if the banks do not lend it to anybody, is not spent.

Keynes pointed out that if some of the money income—wages, profit, interest, and rent—from supplying goods to the market is not spent, then there may be disequilibrium. Disequilibrium here means simply that the total money demand for all goods is less than the value of all goods at present prices. When demand is less than supply, inventories accumulate and capitalists lose money, so they cut back production and fire workers. According to Keynes, the economy may reach equilibrium again only at a much lower level of supply, where a vast number of workers are unemployed.

On the other hand, a situation of excess of demand over supply may result in inflation. Remember that inflation means rising prices (whereas deflation means falling prices). Suppose that planned demand is greater than supply, or that planned investment is greater than saving. As a result, at present prices, excess demand drives prices and outputs upward. When the barrier of full employment is reached, output can rise no higher, so a still higher demand can result only in higher prices or inflation. In the case of inflation, according to Keynes, spending may be greater than national income because additional money moves out of hoards into investment, as shown in Figure 27.2. This movement of money out of hoards is called *dishoarding.* Spending can also exceed income if the spenders are borrowing from banks and the banking system as a whole is creating new money.

Keynes's solutions to unemployment and inflation are those of the liberal reformer. He proves that unregulated capitalism may produce long periods of unemployment or inflation. Nevertheless, he believes that capitalism can be saved by government intervention. If there is unemployment, aggregate demand can be raised by more government spending or lower taxes. If there is inflation, aggregate demand can be lowered by less government spending or by higher taxes. This Keynesian argument about government action to affect demand will be explored in detail in Chapter 34.

THE RADICAL VIEW OF KARL MARX

Long before Keynes was born, Karl Marx (1818–1883) made the same critical attack on Say's law; he also proved that capitalism is subject to periodic attacks of mass unemployment. Unlike Keynes, however, he argued that the capitalist diseases of unemployment and inflation could be cured not by reforms but only by completely replacing capitalism with the new economic system of socialism. These policy differences are discussed in later chapters.

Marx's distinctive contribution to macroeconomic analysis is to point out the very different demand behavior resulting from workers' wage income and from capitalists' property income. This distinction is shown in Figure 29.3.

Marx divides income into two flows:

$$\$ \text{ Wage income} + \$ \text{ property income} = \$ \text{ national income} \qquad (2)$$

Wage income here includes all income earned from labor, such as piecework wages, hourly wages, and salaries. Property income includes all unearned income deriving from ownership of property, such as profits from ownership of capital, rent from ownership of land, and interest from ownership of money. Marx argued that all property income is derived directly or indirectly from the labor done by workers.

The important point here is that workers' wages and capitalists' property income reveal very different spending patterns. On the one hand, most workers' income is in the lower income categories. Thus most of workers' income is spent for consumption, and very little, if any, is saved. For simplicity, Marx considers that the low wages of debt-ridden poor workers are balanced by the higher wages of better-paid workers. Therefore, Marx assumes that aggregate wages just equal the consumer spending of workers:

$$\$ \text{ Wage income} = \$ \text{ workers' consumption} \qquad (3)$$

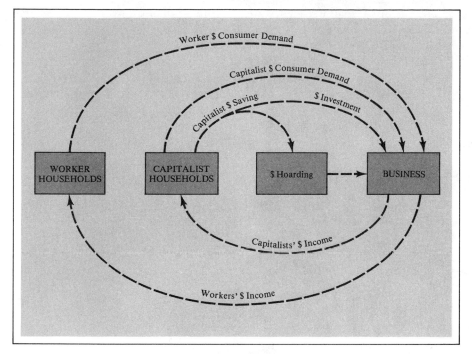

Figure 29.3 The macroeconomy according to Karl Marx.

The data in later chapters will indeed indicate that the average worker—the average of the poorly paid and the better paid, in good times and bad times—saves almost nothing.

Capitalists, on the other hand, receive very high incomes from profits, rent, and interest. Therefore, as will be shown in later chapters, capitalists do save large parts of their income. As a result, the pattern of spending from capitalist income shows two flows. Capitalists not only spend on consumer goods, including luxuries, but also save some of their income:

$$\$ \text{ Capitalist consumption} + \$ \text{ capitalist saving} = \$ \text{ property income} \qquad (4)$$

What happens to capitalists' savings? In what forms do they save? A large part of it will be invested for profit. The capitalist buys stocks and bonds in corporations, and the corporations invest the money in factories, equipment, and inventories of goods on hand. Some of the money is invested indirectly through deposits in banks and insurance companies, who lend it to corporations, who use it to buy capital goods. It often happens, however, that there are no more profitable ways to invest the remaining amounts of capitalist saving. In that case, some of capitalist savings are not profitably invested but are held idle in banks or other hoards. As a general proposition,

$$\$ \text{ Capitalist investment} + \$ \text{ capitalist hoarding} = \$ \text{ capitalist saving} \qquad (5)$$

Of course, in a year with very high profit expectations, capitalists may invest beyond their current income by lowering their saving hoards or dishoarding.

Marx thus agrees with Keynes that saving may be greater than planned investment (causing unemployment) or saving may be less than planned investment (causing inflation). Marx, however, stresses that these problems arise because of (1) the unequal distribution of income under capitalism and (2) the behavior of capitalists seeking profits.

SUMMARY

This chapter shows three views of income determination. The conservative, J. B. Say, sees an automatic adjustment mechanism keeping the circular flow of the economy uninterrupted at full employment. The liberal, J. M. Keynes, sees the flow interrupted by hoarding, with no automatic return to full employment, but believes the capitalist government can correct the imbalance. The radical, Karl Marx, agrees that capitalism often operates with unemployment, but finds the problem to be caused by the basic relations of capitalism and to be unsolvable within capitalism.

SUGGESTED READINGS

An excellent article, discussing in a critical manner those theories that claim that all unemployment is voluntary, is Lars Osberg, "The 'Disappearance' of Involuntary Unemployment," *Journal of Economic Issues* 22 (September 1988), pp. 707–728.

REFERENCES

Alchian, Armen. "Information Costs, Pricing, and Resource Unemployment," *Western Economic Journal* 7 (June 1969), pp. 107–129.

Lucas, Robert. "Models of Business Cycles." Mimeographed paper given for the Yrjo Jansson Lectures. Helsinki, Finland (March 1986).

Keynes, John Maynard. *The General Theory of Employment, Interest and Money.* New York: Harcourt Brace Jovanovich, 1936.

Mitchell, William, John Hand, and Ingo Walter. *Readings in Macroeconomics.* New York: McGraw-Hill, 1975.

Ricardo, David. *The Principles of Political Economy and Taxation.* (London: Gonner, Bell, & Sons, 1821 [reprinted in 1891]).

Schumpeter, Joseph A. *History of Economic Analysis.* New York: Oxford University Press, 1954.

Chapter
30

Aggregate Supply and Aggregate Demand

Most neoclassical economists follow Say's law, stating several arguments in its favor. These arguments reply on a particular view of aggregate supply and aggregate demand. When looking at an individual product, neoclassical economists think of a demand that declines as the price rises, because consumers find it relatively less attractive as its price goes up. This view of demand is combined with a view of supply that thinks of supply as rising when prices rise, because capitalists are willing to supply more at higher prices, since they then expect a higher profit. Suppose we begin at a very high price, where there is a big supply but not enough demand. They argue that competition will force prices down in that case. Then the supply will fall and the demand will rise until an equilibrum is reached. Neoclassical economists use this same type of analysis to look at aggregate supply and aggregate demand, which they picture as simply the sum of individual demand and supply. As we shall see below, Keynes disputed this view.

AGGREGATE SUPPLY, DEMAND, AND PRICES IN THE NEOCLASSICAL VIEW

Suppose that the economy is operating at the full-employment level of supply, but that for some reason there is a temporary lack of demand for all goods and services. In the neoclassical view, this lack of demand will cause a fall in the price level. At the lower price level, consumers will have a greater demand for goods and services. Thus demand will rise to meet

449

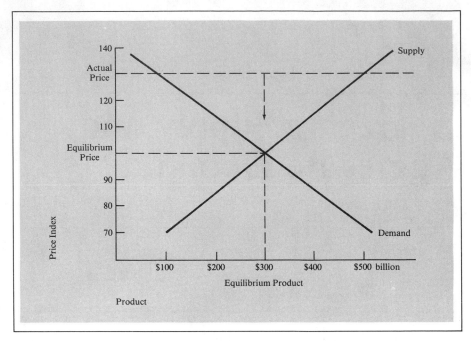

Figure 30.1 Neoclassical view of aggregate supply, demand, and prices.

the supply, so that equilibrium of supply and demand will be restored at the full employment level of supply.

This viewpoint is illustrated in Figure 30.1. This graph illustrates the assumption that the existing price is above the equilibrium level. In that case we see that there is a gap between the supply and the demand. The aggregate demand is too small to purchase the aggregate supply at the existing price. But the graph also shows an arrow pointing down from the existing price level toward the equilibrium. The reason for the falling price is that capitalists are unable to sell all of their goods at the existing price, so they lower their prices to attract more customers. As the price declines, the demand increases, while the supply decreases. Finally, an equilibrium of supply and demand is reached at the lower price level. Capitalists can then sell all of the goods that they are producing at the going price, so there can be no overproduction.

Thus, the first neoclassical argument for Say's law argues that if there is insufficient demand, prices will decline until equilibrium is reached at a point where all supply is bought.

SAVINGS, INVESTMENT, AND INTEREST RATES IN THE NEOCLASSICAL VIEW

A second neoclassical argument claims that all income that is not consumed will always be invested, so there can be no hoarding. What households do not consume is called savings and these savings are the source of loans.

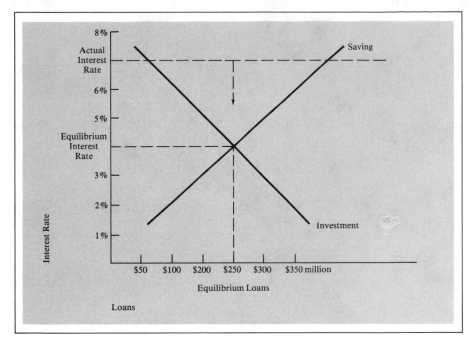

Figure 30.2 Neoclassical view of savings, investment, and interest rates.

Assume that all capital to invest in business is borrowed. The price of loans is the interest rate. They argue that if there is a deficient amount of investment to soak up all savings available for loans at the present interest rate, competition among lenders will cause the interest rate to decline until a new equilibrium is reached—at which point all savings will be invested, thus preventing hoarding.

The argument is illustrated in Figure 30.2. This picture shows that the existing interest rate is too high for all savings to be lent to investors. The arrow shows the downward pressure on interest rates caused by competition. As the interest rate goes down, we see that investment goes up because it costs less to borrow. At the same time, the falling interest rate means that people have less incentive to save, so they will consume more of their income. Eventually, the interest rate falls to an equilbrium where the supply of loans (saving) is equal to the demand for loans (investment). At the equilibrium point, saving (which is all of the nonconsumed income) is therefore all invested. Thus, all income is spent on either consumption or investment, so there is no hoarding, and aggregate supply is all purchased by the aggregate demand.

LABOR SUPPLY, LABOR DEMAND, AND WAGES IN THE NEOCLASSICAL VIEW

Suppose that for some reason there are too many workers seeking work at the present wage, so that there is more of a supply of labor than employers are demanding. There is then temporary unemployment. But neoclassical

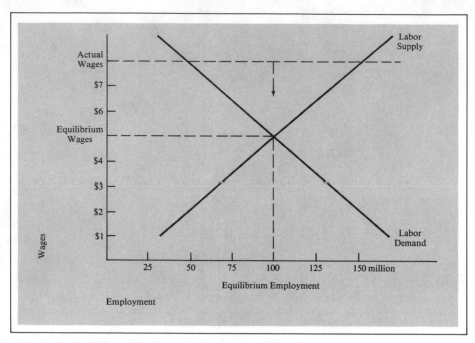

Figure 30.3 Neoclassical view of labor supply, demand, and wages.

economists believe that this oversupply of workers will be automatically cured as competition among workers forces the wage to drop. At some lower wage, an equilibrium will be reached where all workers seeking jobs will find jobs.

Figure 30.3 illustrates the neoclassical view of employment and wages. At a too high wage level, more workers will be attracted to the labor market to find jobs. But at that too high wage level, employers will reduce the number of jobs that they are willing to offer. Therefore, Figure 30.3 shows a temporary unemployment gap at the existing wage. Wages are pushed down, however, by the competition among workers for the small number of jobs. As the wage level declines, fewer workers go into the job market, while employers are offering more jobs. There will therefore be an equilibrium of supply and demand for labor at full employment—that is, all workers who want jobs at the equilibrium wage will find jobs offered at that wage.

THE KEYNESIAN VIEW OF AGGREGATE SUPPLY AND DEMAND

Keynes contended that this neoclassical view of aggregate supply and aggregate demand was completely incorrect for many reasons. For one thing, he pointed out that the same rules do not apply in the aggregate as in

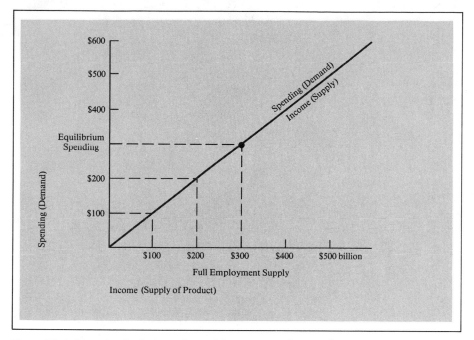

Figure 30.4 Neoclassical view of equilibrium spending and income.

individual markets. In an individual market for workers, a lower wage means that employers will hire more workers if nothing else changes. But in the aggregate, if all workers' wages are lowered, then they have less income. If all workers have lower income, there will be less demand for consumer goods, which means less demand for workers. So in the aggregate, we cannot keep separate the costs of production from the demand for production. One person's costs are another person's income—and demand in the aggregate is composed of everyone's income.

So Keynesians have constructed a very different picture of aggregate demand and supply that does not allow one to forget their interconnections. In Figure 30.4 the relations of aggregate demand and aggregate supply are shown in what is usually called the Keynesian cross.

On one axis is the income of all people in the nation, which we may call the national income, defined in Chapter 29. On the other axis is the spending that is done by everyone. Total spending is, of course, the aggregate demand for goods and services in the United States. The spending is composed of consumer spending, investor spending, government spending, and net exports. In the graph, we see a dashed line rising at a 45-degree angle, which merely traces the path that would be followed if the economy were always at equilibrium, in which supply and demand (or income and spending) were always equal. If income is $100 billion and spending is $100 billion, then a line from each axis at the $100 billion level will cross the other line at a point on the 45-degree line. Similarly,

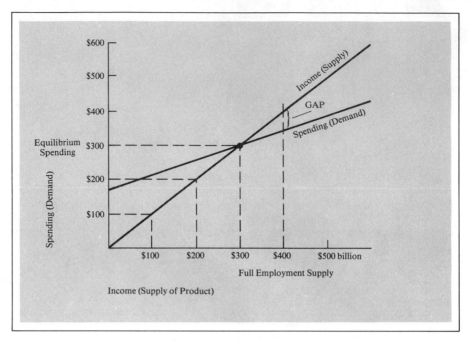

Figure 30.5 Keynesian view of the aggregate employment gap.

they will cross each other on the 45-degree line if income is $200 billion and spending is $200 billion—or if both are $300 billion, and so forth. Thus Figure 30.4 shows each equilibrium level of spending and income or of aggregate supply and aggregate demand. It so happens that if there is full employment, the labor force will produce $300 billion dollars, so that is a full-employment equilibrium if the economy happens to land at that point.

In reality, however, Keynes found that aggregate income is not always spent. As shown in Chapter 27, he described the process whereby money income sometimes leaks out of circulation into inactive status (hoarding). At a very low level of income, however, people may borrow a great deal of money and spend more than their present income. There is simply no magical reason to guarantee that the economy is always at equilibrium at the level of full employment. Figure 30.5 shows a Keynesian picture in which demand is less than supply at the full employment level, causing a recession and unemployment.

In this figure, the level of spending is actually above the level of income at a very low level of income. Then the spending level rises more slowly than the income level, for reasons to be investigated in the next chapter. Eventually, at the full-employment level of output and income, there is a big gap between the total national income and the total national spending. Income in real terms—that is, after allowing for inflation—is the same as the value of all the goods supplied. Spending is the expression of aggregate

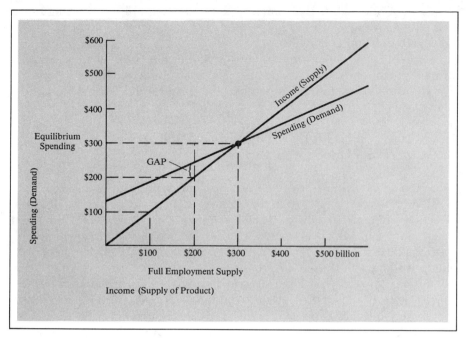

Figure 30.6 Keynesian view of the aggregate inflation gap.

demand. So when Keynes says there is a gap between spending and income, he is also saying that there is a gap between aggregate demand and aggregate supply. When the effective or money demand for goods and services is less than the supply of goods and services, there is overproduction at the full-employment level of output and income.

This overproduction (relative to spending) causes capitalist employers to cut back production and fire workers. This creates unemployment. Keynes argues that as the supply of output is reduced and employment declines, there is less income than at full employment, so the amount of spending declines. But he does expect spending to decline less than income (as we shall see in the next chapter), so eventually a new equilibrium is reached. For Keynes, however, it is important to stress that *this new equilibrium will be below the point of full employment*. The gap between the equilibrium point and the full-employment point is a measure of unemployment—and it is not automatically cured by the usual operation of supply and demand. Supply and demand for goods are equal at a low equilibrium point, but millions of people are unemployed.

Finally, the Keynesian cross can also be used to illustrate the opposite problem: inflation. Figure 30.6 shows a situation in which spending is much higher than income and output, so there is inflation.

In this figure, the level of full employment is below the equilibrium point of income and spending. Suppose, for example, that the country is at war and the government is spending hundreds of billions of dollars for military supplies—but that much of a supply is simply not available. In that case, as shown in the figure, spending is above income and output, aggregate demand is above supply, and inflation results. Why can't capitalists simply produce more to meet the higher demand? If the country is already at full employment and full use of all capacity, then there is no way to produce any more. The excess of demand simply drives up prices.

KEYNESIAN REFUTATION OF NEOCLASSICAL ARGUMENTS FOR SAY'S LAW

Since the 1960s, there has been not just one set of economists who are considered Keynesian, but two sets of Keynesian economists who disagree in many ways. These two warring Keynesian camps were created when fiscal policy ran into problems not predicted by the theory, so that the previous consensus in which everyone was Keynesian vanished. For simplicity we may call these two groups conservative Keynesians and liberal Keynesians, though the differences are far more complex than that. The conservative brand of Keynesian economics has been dominant in U.S. economics and has slowly diluted Keynes' analyses till it resembles the neoclassical view in many ways, though still mildly disagreeing on Say's law. The liberal brand of Keynesian economics, which has been more significant in England, particularly at Cambridge University, disagrees strongly with neoclassical economics and is most often called Post-Keynesian.

Critique of Neoclassical View on Prices and Demand

The first neoclassical argument for Say's law alleges that if there is too much supply and not enough demand, competition will force prices to decline, so that demand will increase until a new full-employment equilibrium is reached. The conservative Keynesians admit that this mechanism would restore full employment if it worked as it is supposed to work. But they argue that many things prevent prices from falling and that price levels are quite rigid, at least downward. For example, the monopolistic power of giant corporations may be used to maintain higher prices in many areas where competition does not operate. Since prices remain high, there is no adjustment and demand may remain insufficient. Some conservative Keynesians argue the policy position that what is needed is better enforcement of antitrust laws to restore competition and allow price flexibility. So long as there is price rigidity, however, Say's law will not work.

The liberal Keynesians present a much stronger refutation of the first neoclassical argument. Suppose, they say, prices are flexible downward, so that an excess of supply leads to falling prices. Falling prices mean less revenue to firms and less income for employers and employees. When people have less income, they spend less. Therefore the fall in prices may result in a rapid further decline in spending, so that there is a cumulative downward spiral of demand and supply, which certainly does not lead to full employment. It is worth stressing that their argument is based on the fact that in the aggregate a decline in prices has a different effect than for an individual product, because a decline in all prices means a decline in aggregate income, which leads to a decline in aggregate spending and demand.

Critique of the Neoclassical Argument on Interest and Investment

The second neoclassical argument for Say's law contends that if there is insufficient investment in the economy, competition among lenders will force the interest rate to drop—which will make borrowing to invest easier and more attractive, so that it will restore investment in new plant and equipment to a level sufficient for full employment of all workers seeking jobs. The conservative Keynesians answer that there are many reasons (some given by Keynes) that the interest rate may not drop as expected. One reason given by Keynes for thinking that the interest rate may not drop below a certain point is the fact that potential lenders often speculate that a particularly low interest rate may soon turn upward again, so that they hold cash and refuse to lend while speculating on the future. If there is an inflexible or rigid interest rate for any reason, then investment will not rise, it will be less than saving, and there will be some hoarding of income. Thus income and output (at full employment) will be greater than spending, so output will decline to some lower equilibrium point and unemployment will result. Many conservative Keynesians reach the policy conclusion that the government need only force lower interest rates to solve unemployment in such a case.

The liberal Keynesians criticize the neoclassical argument in a more fundamental way. They point out that there will be investment in new plant and equipment only if there is an expectation of future profits. But if there is a deficient aggregate demand, capitalist entrepreneurs may fear future losses from new investment. No matter how cheaply a firm can borrow money, it will not do so if it does not expect future profits. Again, they stress the aggregate demand problem that may not be solved by lower costs in particular industries.

Critique of the Neoclassical View on Wages and Employment

The third neoclassical argument is considered to be their ultimate and unanswerable proposition. They argue that if there are too many workers offering to work compared to the demand from employers, then the wage level must fall so that employers will hire more workers. The conservative Keynesians agree that lower wages would automatically bring back full employment. They argue, however, that wage rates are rigid and unflexible because of the actions of unions, government, and tradition. Unions use their monopoly power over the sale of labor to raise wages. Governments unwisely enforce minimum wage standards. The conservative Keynesians agree with the neoclassicals that if the barriers to competitive demand and supply were removed, then the competitive market system would automatically restore full employment. Thus they conclude that Say's law would work only if there were a pure private competitive system that allowed wages to be flexible downward.

The liberal Keynesians point out that it is true that lower wages may increase employment in an individual firm if its demand holds steady. But they argue that, in the aggregate, if all wage incomes fall by 15 percent, then all consumer spending will fall by 15 percent. So, in the aggregate, lower wages just mean lower demand. The lower demand causes further reduction in output and employment, so that there may be a downward spiral of demand and supply—and certainly no restoration of full employment.

Another way to state the liberal Keynesian argument is to point to a paradox. Any individual capitalist would like lower wages in his or her own enterprise; if workers were paid less (all other things being equal), then more profit would be made. But each capitalist would like all other capitalists to pay high wages; high wages throughout the economy would translate into higher demand for the product of this individual capitalist. Higher wages in the aggregate mean not only higher demand but also higher costs. Lower wages in the aggregate mean not only lower demand but also lower costs. It appears that neither lower nor higher wages will, by themselves, cure unemployment.

SUMMARY

This chapter has considered three neoclassical arguments for Say's law, which depend on lower prices raising demand, lower interest rates raising investment, and lower wages raising employment. Conservative Keynesians refute these arguments by alleging that prices, interest rates, and wages are rigid in a downward direction, so they will not fall. They usually consider that relatively minor reforms could make prices, wages, and interest rates more flexible and make Say's law work in the economy. The liberal Keynesians, however, argue that even if prices, wages, and interest rates were flexible downward, this would not restore full employment. Lower prices and lower wages lead to lower aggregate demand, so that the lower costs are counteracted. If there is a lack of aggregate demand, then no positive level of interest rate would get investors to invest. They recommend more drastic government intervention to prevent unemployment.

Chapter
31

Consumption

The largest single element of spending for U.S. products comes from the consumer demand for goods and services. What determines consumer demand?

KEYNES AND CONSUMER BEHAVIOR

Keynes gives particular attention to understanding the psychological bases for the decision of households to save or consume at different economic levels. For Keynes, consumer demand is determined for the most part by the level of national income. His reasoning as to consumer behavior is based on certain broad psychological presumptions: (1) At a very low income level, the average individual still needs some minimum consumption and therefore will spend all his or her income on consumption and may even dip into savings or go into debt to spend more than his or her whole current income on consumption. (2) As the individual's income rises, a smaller percentage of it is needed to cover minimum needs, so at some break-even point he or she reaches an equality of income received and consumption spending. (3) As income rises to a very high level, consumption needs and desires may be filled through the use of a smaller portion of income, so an increasing percentage may be saved.

This usual behavior of consumers is illustrated in Figure 31.1. The line labeled *income* shows the total income at each point; it is equal by definition to the income spent for consumption plus the income saved. If there were no saving, so that income exactly equaled consumption at every income level, then the *income* line would also show consumer spending. In reality

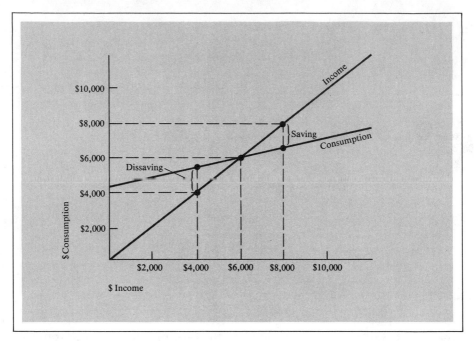

Figure 31.1 Consumption and income.

they are different. The line labeled *consumption* shows how much consumer spending there actually is at each level of income. The space between these two lines obviously reflects the amount by which consumption differs from income. At low levels of income, consumer spending by the poor is greater than their income, so there is dissaving (using up of reserves or going into debt) by these consumers. At high levels of income, consumer spending by the rich is much less than their income, so there is saving by this group.

This Keynesian schedule of aggregate consumer spending at different income levels is called the consumption function. It tells us that in the short run consumption is not some constant proportion of income; rather, as income rises, consumption rises, but consumption rises more slowly than income. Therefore, as income rises, the proportion of income spent on consumption declines.

CONSUMPTION AND INCOME

For a concrete example of the relation of consumption to income, we examine consumption and swing patterns for one year in one city in Table 31.1. This table reveals that in 1970 the people of Washington D.C. followed exactly the predicted consumption pattern according to income level.

Table 31.1   INCOME AND CONSUMPTION IN WASHINGTON, D.C., 1970

Income	Disposable personal income	Consumption	Saving	Percentage of consumption to income
$ 1,000–$ 2,999	$ 1,873	$ 2,013	–$ 140	107.5
3,000– 3,999	3,302	3,345	– 43	101.5
4,000– 4,999	3,900	3,697	203	94.8
5,000– 5,999	4,668	4,355	313	93.3
6,000– 7,499	5,780	5,266	514	91.1
7,500– 9,999	6,828	6,002	826	87.9
10,000– 14,999	9,507	8,062	1,445	84.8
Over $15,000	19,719	14,020	5,699	71.1

Source: Conway Lachmann, "Value-Added Tax vs. the Property Tax: A Case Study," Real Estate Law Journal 8 (Summer 1979), pp. 34–46.

People in the lowest income groups in Washington, D.C., spent more on consumption than their total income. As income rises for each group above that level, more was spent on consumption. But the increase in consumption did not equal the increase in income; there was a slightly higher percentage of saving at each income level. Roughly, people with a $4,000 disposable income consumed 95 percent and saved only 5 percent, whereas people with a $20,000 disposable income consumed only 70 percent and saved 30 percent. In addition, of course, successful corporations saved a high proportion of income in retained earnings.

CONSUMER PSYCHOLOGY AND SOCIAL STRUCTURE

Keynesian economists use certain shorthand terms to describe the relationship between consumption and income. The *average propensity to consume* is the percentage of income spent for consumption—that is, consumption/income at any particular level of income. In Table 31.1, for example, in the $6,000–$7,499 income group the average person had a disposable income of $5,780 and spent $5,266 for consumption; therefore the average propensity to consume of this group was 91.1 percent. Similarly, the *average propensity to save* is the ratio of saving to income at this particular level of income. (Remember that saving is defined as all income not consumed.) In Table 31.1, for example, the average person in the $6,000–$7,499 income group had an income of $5,780 and saved $514 a year; therefore the average propensity to save of this group was 8.9 percent.

Keynesian economists also speak of the *marginal propensity to consume*, which can be thought of as the portion that will be spent out of any additional increment to income. It is defined as the ratio of the change in consumption to the change in income. For example, in Table 31.1 the average increase in income from the $6,000–$7,499 group to the $7,500–$9,999 group was $1,048, while the average increase in consumer spending was $736; therefore, the marginal propensity to consume was 70 percent (736 as a percentage of 1048). Similarly, the *marginal propensity to save* is the percentage of the increase in saving to the change in income. For example, in Table 31.1 the average increase in income from the $6,000–$7,499 group to the $7,500–$9,999 group was $1,024, while the average increase in saving was only $312; therefore the marginal propensity to save was 30 percent (or 312 as a percentage of 1024).

The Keynesian use of the term *propensity* to describe consumer behavior seems to imply that consumers follow some purely innate psychological laws. On the contrary, according to other economists, consumer behavior is determined not by any natural drives but by social conditioning. We are not born with a desire for television sets. Nor is there any innate compulsion to consume exactly 90 percent of our income and save 10 percent. Our desires for television sets, as well as our decisions on the ratio of consumption and saving to income, are determined by society's attitudes, ideologies, and institutions. Certainly family background has a significant influence on consumption habits, as do secular and religious educational systems. And, last but not least, the vast volume of advertising in the U.S. economy affects the pattern and even the aggregate amount of consumption.

Thus consumer psychology is largely socially determined. Even more important than consumer psychology or desires, however, are the objective social facts of how income is distributed. Even if they have the very same psychological attitudes, an unemployed worker with a tiny income will not be able to save anything (and may dissave, or go into debt), whereas a businessperson with a million-dollar income may consume only 10 percent of his or her income (and still have a very high consumption standard). Thus the data show that groups with very low incomes spend all (or more than all) their incomes on consumption. In the terminology of Keynesian economics, low-income groups have a high propensity to consume. On the other hand, the data show that groups with very high incomes spend only a small proportion on consumption. The high-income groups spend a large number of dollars on consumption, but this leaves them with a high proportion of unused income, which they save in various forms. In the terminology of Keynesian economics, the high-income groups have a low propensity to consume and a high propensity to save.

Obviously, a change in the distribution of income will affect the proportion of income spent on consumption. Hence, if society taxes the rich and gives to the poor, the proportion of income spent on consumption (the propensity to consume) will usually rise. But if society taxes the poor and gives to the rich, the proportion of income spent on consumption will usually fall.

Propensity to consume for the whole nation therefore depends mainly on just two factors (although it is influenced by many others): (1) consumer psychology as determined by social conditioning and (2) how society distributes income. In this context the term propensity to consume is perhaps misleading. A more neutral term, perhaps consumption ratio, might more easily include behavior based on both psychological desires and income distribution. Because most economic literature does use propensity to consume, it is used here; but the reader must remember that it refers, not to innate drives, but to socially conditioned psychology and the objective facts of income distribution.

Using the usual terminology, we can say that an income shift from the rich to the poor will tend to raise the national propensity to consume because the poor have to consume all their income. An income shift from the poor to the rich will tend to lower the national propensity to consume because the rich consume a much lower proportion of their income.

Further, most of the income of the rich comes from ownership of property (profits, rent, interest, and dividends). But most of those whose income comes almost solely from wages and salaries fall into the lower-income groups. Thus we expect to find workers forced to spend almost all of their low incomes, whereas capitalists are able to save a good-sized proportion of their high incomes. This theoretical expectation is confirmed by the data, as shown in the next section.

The effects of shifts between property income and wage income are therefore similar to those of shifts between rich and poor. If less goes to capitalist property owners and more to wage workers, the result is a higher propensity to consume because wage workers consume almost all their income. If less goes to wage workers and more to property owners, the result is a lower propensity to consume because property owners consume a small percentage and save a very large percentage of their income.

INEQUALITY OF INCOME DISTRIBUTION

Consumer demand is affected by total income and by distribution of income. Obviously, as Keynes argues, the total amount of income available is an important factor. Rich and poor, however, have very different spending patterns. Therefore, another factor determining consumer demand is the degree of inequality in the distribution of income between rich and poor.

The facts of inequality in U.S. income distribution have been presented in many other places, so we need only summarize the data here. First, a large percentage of U.S. families live below the officially defined poverty level. Second, distribution of income is very unequal, with the richest 10 percent of families getting more income than the poorest 50 percent of families put together. Third, there has been little, if any, change in inequality in this century (though inequality did worsen during the Reagan administration). Fourth, the richest one-tenth of 1 percent of families control most property, particularly corporate stock, so that 90 percent of their income is from profit, rent, or interest. Fifth, the poorest 70 percent of the population own almost no capital and obtain no interest, rent, or profit income, so that almost 100 percent of their income is wage or salary income in return for their labor.

CONSUMER BEHAVIOR OVER THE BUSINESS CYCLE

The changes in consumption to income ratios over time may also be illustrated by actual data. In 1929, at the peak of prosperity, the level of consumer expenditure reached its highest point of the decade, as did national income. Personal saving was also at a record level of over $4 billion. By 1933, in the depth of the Great Depression, aggregate income had fallen by half. Consumption had also fallen, but not as swiftly, because people were spending on consumption more than their aggregate income by dipping into their savings accumulated in previous years and by going into debt. As a result, personal saving was actually negative in 1933, at −$648 million (dissaving).

From these data, the conclusion is: Total consumer spending rises when national income rises and falls when national income falls. Consumption, however, rises more slowly than income and also falls more slowly than income. In a recession, when income suddenly falls, all or more than all income is often spent on consumption. In other words, when national income rises in prosperity, the average propensity to consume (the percentage of consumption to income) generally falls. When national income declines in a depression, however, the average propensity to consume generally rises.

There is, in fact, a great deal of evidence from U.S. history to indicate "that as income falls in the business cycle, consumption will fall proportionately less than income; and again when income rises cyclically, consumption will rise proportionately less than income." (Hansen, p. 76). This historical behavior still is true for the present. Thus, over the three business cycles from 1970 to 1982, the average propensity to consume was 78 percent. At the peak of the business cycle, however, the average propensity to consume fell to 76 percent. But at the trough of the average recession or depression, the average propensity to consume rose to 80.5 percent.

We may illustrate the patterns of consumer behavior in Figure 31.2, using Wesley Mitchell's method of measurement, described in Chapter 26. Remember that Stage 1 is the low point or trough at the beginning of the cycle, Stage 5 is the cycle peak, and Stage 9 is the final low point or trough. The standing of consumption at each of the nine stages is shown as a percentage of its average value over the cycle, called the *cycle base*.

Figure 31.2 reveals that total real consumption rose throughout the expansion. In the contraction phase of the cycle, real consumer spending fell for a while, then rose a little heralding the recovery. National income

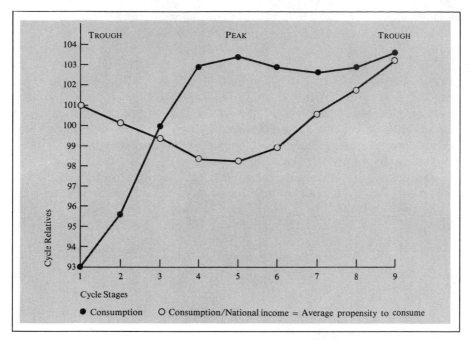

Figure 31.2 Consumption, 1970–1982, average, 3 cycles. *Source:* U.S. Department of Commerce, *Handbook of Cyclical Indicators* (Washington, D.C.: GPO, 1984).

rose more rapidly than consumption in expansion, then fell more rapidly throughout the contraction.

Figure 31.2 also shows the pattern followed by the average propensity to consume (consumption/income) over the cycle. Since consumption rises and falls less than income, the average propensity to consume falls in expansions and rises in contractions. The average propensity to consume out of income fell in every stage of the average expansion and rose in every stage of the average contraction period.

CONSUMER BEHAVIOR OF CAPITALISTS AND WORKERS

Many economists have considered the differing consumer behaviors of affluent capitalists and lower-income workers. As capitalist income rises in an expansion, capitalists do consume a smaller and smaller proportion of it. Partly this is because they still consider their earlier consumption level normal and satisfactory. Partly it is because the profit outlook has become more optimistic, so they wish to save a larger part of their income in order to invest it in profitable enterprises.

Workers, on the other hand, continue to spend in the expansion almost their whole income on consumption. Since their standard of living was below normal at the bottom of the depression, they use most of their increased income to pay off debts and buy necessities. At any rate, their propensity to consume remains very high even at the peak of the cycle.

Interestingly, the conservative economist Milton Friedman confirmed this difference in class behavior in some data for the period 1948–1950 (Friedman, pp. 69–79). Friedman found that the average business owner spent 77 percent of his or her additional income for consumption, but the average (nonfarm) wage worker spent 96 percent of his or her income for consumption. Although a few better-paid workers save some money, most workers are forced to spend all their income for consumption, while poorer-paid workers go into debt.

If we include not only the personal profit income of individual capitalists, but also corporate profits, interest income, and rental income, then in the period 1949–1982, capitalists consumed only 13 percent of all property income and saved 87 percent. Different definitions of profits and wages will give somewhat different estimates of the consumption out of profits and out of wages. In all the estimates, however, the percentage of profit income spent for consumption is much lower than the percentage of wage income spent for consumption.

SHIFTS IN CONSUMPTION AND INCOME DISTRIBUTION

Why does the average propensity to consume tend to fall in each business cycle expansion (and rise in each business cycle contraction)? Many mainstream Keynesian economists simply argue in terms of psychological behavior. They claim that the average psychological propensity of consumers is fixed at the norm of their previous spending levels. It is a psychological law, they say, that consumers are slow to change their habits when their income changes. So their percentage spent on consumption falls in the upswing and rises in the downswing of the economy.

Other economists, of several different viewpoints, have stressed that the cause could be shifts in income distribution. Since the capitalists have a much lower propensity to consume than the workers, the distribution of income between worker and capitalist is very important in determining the national average propensity to consume. Even if there were no changes in psychological propensities to consume in either class, a shift in income distribution could explain a change in the average propensity to consume. The declining average propensity in an expansion may be explained by a shift of income from workers (with high propensities to consume) to capitalists (with low—and falling—propensities to consume). The rising propensity to consume in a depression could be explained by an income shift back from capitalists to workers.

Wages do rise and fall proportionately less than aggregate income, while profits fluctuate more than the total national income. The aggregate data demonstrate that the ratio of wages to national income falls in economic expansion (while profits are a rising percentage of national income). Thus there is an income shift toward high-income capitalist profits in the ex-

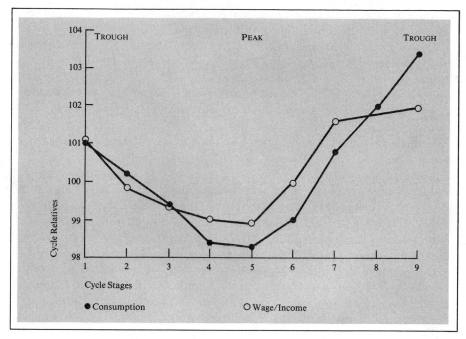

Figure 31.3 Average propensity to consume and labor share. *Source:* U.S. Department of Commerce, *Handbook of Cyclical Indicators* (Washington, D.C.: GPO, 1984).

pansion and back toward lower-income workers' wages in the contraction. This was a major reason for the declining propensity to consume in the expansion and the rising propensity to consume in the contraction.

To avoid confusion, it must be stressed that real wages, profits, consumption, and income all rose in the expansion and all fell in the contraction. But the ratio of consumption to income and the ratio of wages to profits both declined in the expansion and both rose in the contraction. In the expansion, workers have more real income but a smaller proportion of all income—and vice versa in the contraction.

The wage share (wages/national income) falls in expansions and rises in economic recessions or depressions. For the average cycle from 1949 to 1982, this pattern of a falling wage share in expansion but a rising wage share in contraction is portrayed in Figure 31.3.

Why do wages rise so slowly in expansions, particularly in the early half of expansion? In the recovery phase of the cycle, there are still large numbers of unemployed willing to take new jobs at low pay. The bargaining power of unions in the early phases of business expansion is also relatively weak, partly because of the existence of a reserve of unemployed workers and also because of the general attitudes toward wage changes. The public is sympathetic to workers resisting wage cuts but less sympathetic to fights for wage increases. Even workers are more easily aroused by anger and militancy to resistance to wage cuts than they are enthusiastic to strike for wage increases. Another factor that prevents unions from raising wages—

or from raising them more rapidly than productivity and prices are rising—is the existence of fixed labor contracts for two or three years.

In early expansion, however, the big profit increases come primarily from increased productivity. Partly, this is due to investment in new machinery, which increases productivity of workers and lessens the need to hire more workers. Partly it is due to the fact that factories were running at a low percentage of capacity—and are now starting to increase their use of capacity. The organization and use of labor and machines become more efficient when that level of production is reached for which the factory was designed.

Most important is that at low levels of production capitalists may fire production-line workers. They are forced, however, to keep employed large numbers of administrative workers, maintenance workers, security people, and sales and distribution workers. The need for these types of workers does not decline much with lower production. Neither does it rise much with higher production. For example, a bookkeeper or a security guard is needed whether production is high or low. Therefore, as production rises toward full use of capacity, there is also a decline in the number of these nonproduction workers relative to the amount of production—or per unit of production. This decline in the unit cost of production means higher profits for capitalists, but these profits are not automatically passed on to workers in higher wages. Therefore, the share of production going to labor drops in every period of industrial recovery.

Why do wages usually keep rising to the peak of expansion? At the peak of expansion, there is much less unemployment. This gives unions greater bargaining power. Worker militancy also increases as workers become fully aware that productivity increases and higher prices are raising profits. For these reasons, real wages as well as money wages usually continue to rise to the peak of expansion.

Why do real wages fall relatively slowly in contraction? During the recession, workers strongly resist wage cuts, while prices usually rise much more slowly than in expansion (because of declining demand). Fixed labor contracts prevent wages from declining immediately. Productivity falls, mainly because there is a higher and higher proportion of nonproduction workers; thus the recession usually witnesses a shift to a lower ratio of profit to wages as profits fall faster than wages. In the next chapter we shall examine why profits usually rise so rapidly in early expansion, level off in late expansion, decline rapidly in early contraction, and usually bottom out in late contraction.

INTERACTION OF INCOME DISTRIBUTION AND CONSUMPTION

Earlier sections have implied that cyclical changes in income distribution affect the behavior of consumer demand, but it will be useful to make this explicit. Early in cyclical expansions the wage share (the ratio of wage

Table 31.2   CONSUMPTION AND INCOME DISTRIBUTION
Imaginary Data for Illustration Only

Before income distribution shift (with total income of $200 billion)

Wages $100 billion	Profits $100 billion
Workers consume 100%	Capitalists consume 5%
Workers consume $100 billion	Capitalists consume $5 billion

Total consumer demand = $105 billion

Therefore, average propensity to consume is 53%
($105 consumption/$200 income)

After income distribution shift (with income grown to $300 billion)

Wages $100 billion	Profits $200 billion
Workers consume 100%	Capitalists consume 5%
Workers consume $100 billion	Capitalists consume $10 billion

Total consumer demand = $110 billion

Therefore, average propensity to consume is 37%
($110 consumption/$300 income)

income to national income) falls drastically, while the profit share rises. This income shift (from the poor to the rich) lowers the ratio of consumer demand to income and output. In the later stages of expansions the wage share stops declining, but it is still below the cycle average until the business peak is reached. This relatively low wage share keeps the average propensity to consume quite low, so consumer demand rises only very slowly.

In the early part of most contractions wages fall, but profits fall even more rapidly. The higher wage share and improved equality of income distribution raises the ratio of consumption to income. Therefore consumption does not fall as rapidly as income, so consumer demand sets some floor to the contraction.

A numerical example may clarify how a shift in income distribution affects consumer demand. In Table 31.2, consumer demand is shown before and after a shift in income distribution. In this table we assume that workers have a much higher propensity to consume than capitalists—which is true. We also assume that all of the increase in income in an industrial recovery goes to capitalists, increasing the ratio of profit to wages. This simple assumption is made for simplicity, but it is true that in the early stage of every expansion on record the profits of capitalists have risen faster than the wages of workers, so there has been a shift in income distribution.

The shift of income to capitalists, who have a lower propensity to consume, causes a lower average propensity to consume in the nation. This decline means a widening gap between consumer demand and output as the expansion continues. The reverse happens in contraction, when profits fall faster than wages, so that the propensity to consume rises.

CONSUMPTION IN AN INFLATIONARY ERA

The existence of inflation in consumer prices in the United States has distorted and changed the usual patterns of consumer behavior. When there is inflation, people expect that the price of each good or service, among those they desire, will increase in the future. This expectation makes people more prone to buy things now, rather than to postpone buying, because the item is believed to be cheaper now than it will be in the future. So consumers spend more rapidly, which makes inflation still worse.

The principle of buying now as much as possible begins to pervade our social consciousness. One result is that consumers become less rational in their buying habits. Everything looks cheaper than it will in the future, so there is more impulse buying.

During inflation, there is a huge increase in consumer buying on credit. Even if it costs 10 percent to borrow money, this is very cheap if the rate of inflation is 13 percent. If I borrow $100 at 10 percent for a year, then I must pay back $110 at the end of the year. But if the inflation rate is 13 percent, the $110 will only buy $97 worth of goods. Some consumers consider this actually making money by buying now and paying later.

It is not so clear that one actually makes money if one consumes these goods. It is true, however, that it is cheaper to spend $100 now for a coat than to spend $113 next year—even if you also pay $10 in interest. The problem is only that some consumers buy coats that they do not need or want. Of course, some people do make money this way if they buy things to resell rather than to consume. If I buy a house for $100,000 and pay $10,000 in interest, but then sell it for $113,000, I make $3,000 profit. On the other hand, a creditor that lends money at a nominal rate of 10 percent interest will be losing money if the rate of inflation is 13 percent. The creditor lends $100 and gets back $110 a year later, but the $110 will only buy what $97 would have bought the year before. Thus, if the nominal rate of interest is 10 percent, but inflation is 13 percent, then the real rate of interest is minus 3 percent. This means that all commercial and credit transactions become much more uncertain depending on predictions of the inflation rate. So both borrowers and lenders may make various unwise decisions.

What effect has this huge increase of credit had on the business cycle? The buy-now pay-later syndrome has caused a rising propensity to consume (on credit) during the whole inflationary period. This has been a major factor bolstering consumer demand in the expansion phases of the cycle, so it tends to postpone the collapse.

Once a collapse occurs, however, this increase in credit tends to intensify the situation in several ways. Consumers who have been deeply in debt may now lose their jobs or be afraid of losing their jobs. Therefore, consumers suddenly restrict their buying, so sales may fluctuate rapidly downward. For this reason, the decline in sales in the early months of the 1980 recession was the most rapid since the Great Depression of the 1930s.

Even more important, if millions of consumers are deeply in debt and lose their jobs in a recession, then they cannot continue payments on the things they have bought. Their cars and refrigerators and TV sets may then be lost to the loan companies. This is obviously very painful to consumers.

But it is also painful and often disastrous to the lender, whether a bank or other finance company. The flow of principal and interest to the bank has stopped. They own some secondhand goods, but in a recession these are very hard to resell for anything like the original price. As a result, many lending companies and banks may go bankrupt. This hurts their depositors and stockholders and sends negative reverberations throughout the economy.

INCOME DISTRIBUTION IN AN INFLATIONARY ERA

In a period of inflation there tends to be a shift in income distribution from the poor to the rich and from workers to capitalists. The reason is that anyone with a relatively fixed income, such as aged workers on pensions or any worker on a fixed wage or salary will be hurt more by rising prices than will those whose income may go up with prices. When prices rise, the rich are able to buy property on speculation—and often have access to the right information on what property to buy—and thus may make a lot of extra money. A rich person who owns real estate in an inflationary era automatically gains a rising value for the property. When it is sold, the rich person then has a capital gain. But, as we saw in an earlier chapter, capital gains have been taxed much lower than other income, so the rich not only gained in income but paid less taxes by this device.

Similarly, when prices are rising rapidly, a giant corporation can invest in all kinds of property, including stocks of raw materials or finished goods, which continually rise in price. A small business, on the contrary, cannot afford to hold the goods long enough for the price to rise significantly in value.

Another reason that wages fall behind profits in inflation is the increased difficulty of getting higher real wages. With constant prices, a rise of 1 percent in money wages means a rise of 1 percent in real wages. It may be possible in a labor struggle to win that 1 percent. If, however, there is an inflation rate of 13 percent, then it requires a money wage increase of 14 percent to get a real wage increase of 1 percent. This may be much more difficult for workers to obtain, since it sounds much different, not only to the workers themselves, but especially to the general public when the media report it in glaring headlines. Thus it is not only difficult to win public support for a labor action to obtain a 14 percent increase (even if it is only 1 percent in buying power), but it is even harder to convince a state legislature to give such an increase to employees in the public sector.

The result of all these obstacles to real wage gains during an inflation can be seen in many types of evidence now available. First, the real average weekly earnings of all workers declined from $198.35 in 1973 to $169.28 in 1987 (this was in constant 1977 dollars for all private, nonagricultural, nonsupervisory workers). Such a decline over a long period in peacetime is unprecedented. Second, income distribution has worsened. The poorest 20 percent of families received only 4.6 percent of all income in 1985 (the lowest on record since this series started in 1947). The richest 20 percent of families received 43.5 percent of all income (the highest on record). Third, wealth distribution has worsened. By 1983, the super rich—or top $\frac{1}{2}$ percent of all families—held 43 percent of all U.S. wealth (excluding homes), a large increase from the 1960s when the last study was made. Also in 1983, the richest 10 percent of families had 83 percent of all the wealth (excluding homes), another large increase. (The data here comes from Winnick.)

This worsening inequality between low-income workers and rich capitalists has been the main effect of deep recessions and continued inflation in the 1970s and 1980s. All this is quite contrary to the usual picture given in the media. Workers are shown on strike, disrupting the normal flow of commerce and economic activity. If the strike is won, the headlines proclaim the higher pay in current dollars, but ignore the fact that it often represents lower pay in real purchasing power.

The fact that income distribution becomes more unequal in an inflation has a considerable effect on consumption spending. Since the rich spend a much lower percentage of their income than the poor on consumer goods, the average propensity to consume tends to decline. This means that it is harder and harder to sell the output produced.

On the other hand, as we saw in the previous section, workers and the poor turn more and more to the use of credit to keep up with inflation. For a time the use of credit may postpone the decline in the propensity to consume, thereby postponing the downturn in sales. When the recession does hit, however, we also saw in the previous section that this will make the recession much harder on workers who are deep in debt—and may lead to the bankruptcy of the banks and finance agencies who have lent them money.

It is worth emphasizing that not all capitalists gain from inflation. Those capitalists who are producing goods and selling them generally gain from mild inflation. But those capitalists who make interest from lending money generally lose from inflation because the value of the money that is repaid has declined. Thus all capitalists who have lent money are opposed to inflation. Furthermore, very rapid inflation hurts all capitalists by weakening the economic system and making it unmanageable. Therefore, the U.S. government—and all governments in which capitalists have great influence—worry far more about inflation than about unemployment.

SUMMARY

Consumer behavior is determined by both social conditioning and income distribution. Income is distributed very unequally—a few rich families having very high incomes, a large number of poor having a very low income. The poor (mostly wage earners) consume a very high percentage of their income. The rich (mostly profit and interest receivers) consume a small percentage of their income.

In expansion periods the average propensity to consume falls, partly because of the psychological behavior of capitalist profit makers, but also partly because of a shift of income from low-income wage earners to high-income profit makers. In depression periods the average propensity to consume rises, partly because of the psychological behavior of capitalist profit makers, but also partly because there is a shift in the percentage of income going to low-income wage workers (though their absolute income levels are falling).

In periods of inflation the use of credit tends to expand at a rapid rate. This gets consumers to spend more money, often unwisely. There also tends to be a shift in income distribution from the poor to the rich. When the recession comes, the poor consumer cannot repay debts, causing bankruptcy, not only for the consumer, but also for the bank that made the loans.

REFERENCES

Friedman, Milton. *A Theory of the Consumption Function.* Princeton, N.J.: Princeton University Press, 1957.

Hansen, Alvin. *Guide to Keynes.* New York: McGraw-Hill, 1953.

Winnick, Andrew. "The Changing Distribution of Income and Wealth in the United States, 1960–1985." In Patricia Voydanoff and Linda Majka, *Families and Economic Distress.* Beverly Hills, Calif.: Sage, 1989.

Chapter
32

Investment

Attempts to explain investment behavior constitute the heart of many theories of cyclical unemployment. Economists have long realized that, from the standpoint of understanding unemployment, investment spending is the most crucial component of aggregate demand. It also fluctuates the most and is thus the most difficult to explain and to predict accurately.

GROSS AND NET INVESTMENT

Gross investment is defined as the total value of all capital goods produced in a year. Net investment is simply the change in the stock of capital within a given period. The stock of capital grows as new capital goods are produced and purchased. On the other hand, the stock of capital is steadily diminished through use, wear and tear, and obsolescence. To determine net investment, the amount by which the old capital stock has diminished in the period is subtracted from the amount of gross investment.

For example, in the crucial year 1929, $8.7 billion was invested in new construction and $5.8 billion in new producers' durable equipment, and there was a $1.7 billion increase in business inventories, or a total of $16.2 billion gross investment. Because allowances for depreciation (or decline of the old capital stock) amounted to $8.6 billion in that year, it can be assumed that $8.6 billion of the gross investment was for replacement. By definition the net investment must have been at the level of $7.6 billion (because $16.2 billion gross minus $8.6 billion depreciation equals $7.6 billion).

Although it is assumed that the amount of replacement investment can

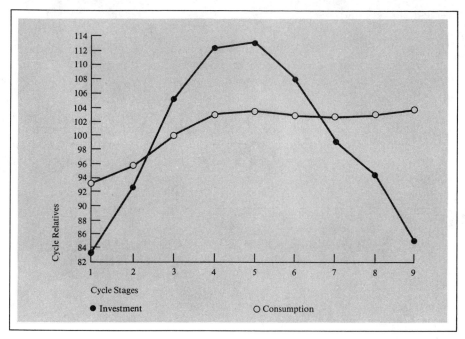

Figure 32.1 Investment and consumption, 3 cycles, 1970–1982. *Source:* U.S. Department of Commerce, *Handbook of Cyclical Indicators* (Washington, D.C.: GPO, 1984).

be measured by the estimated depreciation, the decision to replace depreciated capital goods is not automatic. In 1933, gross investment was only $1.4 billion, but depreciation was still $7.2 billion. Therefore net investment was actually at the negative level of minus $5.8 billion, meaning that capital declined by that amount. The capital stock, and hence the economy's productive capacity, was rapidly diminishing. (Note that gross investment could never be negative, for at worst no new capital goods would be produced. In that event, net investment would be negative and equal to depreciation.)

INVESTMENT FLUCTUATES VIOLENTLY

In Chapter 31 it was shown that consumption fluctuates much less than national income. Entrepreneurs raise investment rapidly in expansions, and let it decline rapidly in contractions. It is therefore no surprise that investment fluctuates far more violently than consumption.

Figure 32.1 shows dramatically that consumer spending rises much slower than investment in expansions. But consumption falls much slower than investment in contractions.

DECISION TO INVEST

The businessperson who contemplates the purchase of new plant or equipment will not decide to make the purchase unless the profit he or she expects to receive from this investment is greater than the purchase price of capital goods. Obviously, profits (revenue minus cost) are exceedingly important in determining the level of investment—and hence output, income, and employment—in the U.S. economy. Indeed, the prime motivation for investment in a private enterprise economy is the expectation of future profit on the new investment. Yet, because future profits cannot be known with certainty, it is mainly on the basis of the present level of profits and changes in profits that businesspeople base their expectations. Accordingly, high or rising profits will lead to optimistic expectations and a decline in new investment.

The other, and quite distinct, reason for the importance of profits is the fact that increased profits provide funds for increased investment. Without profits, the firm may lack funds to increase investments even if it wishes to do so. Although the capital funds can sometimes be borrowed, increased profits make it easier for the firm or its stockholders to obtain credit (and lower interest rates). Moreover, most firms are quicker to invest from internal sources, and in practice most expansion is financed with retained profits.

There is a close relationship between investment decisions and profit rates and also between total profits and investment in every business cycle. The long-run investment decision between different industries is probably most influenced by the rate of profit on investment in each industry. On the other hand, in making a decision on whether to invest in a particular phase of the business cycle, businesspeople seem most heavily influenced by the movements of profits in the previous few quarters. At any rate, there is no reason to doubt that investment behavior is most influenced by the recent profit performance of corporations.

THE ACCELERATOR

We have seen that the basis for investment decision making is the expected profit from the investment. Yet it is difficult to estimate expected profits, so economists and businesspeople use crude substitutes to make rough guesses. The most widely used index on which to base guesses of the profitability of investments is that of changes in demand for output.

This approach examines the ratio between increased demand for output and increased capital investments. If this ratio is known and stable, we could predict the change in capital (that is, investment) from a change in output demanded. The accelerator is defined as the ratio of investment decisions to changes in output demanded. In other words, the accelerator is the coefficient by which we multiply a change in output demanded to predict the level of investment.

Notice that the businessperson invests in (net) new machinery only to increase his or her output. So the accelerator coefficient relates investment decisions, not to the level of demand for output, but to the change (increase or decrease) in demand for output. The fact that the rate of change of demand fluctuates more than the level of demand helps explain why investment fluctuates more violently than the level of output. In an appendix to this chapter the accelerator concept is discussed in detail, with its weaknesses examined as well.

PSYCHOLOGICAL ATTITUDES

Because investment decisions are based on projections of future sales, revenues, and profits, it would be easy to say that fluctuations in aggregate investment are caused by changes in investor confidence about economic conditions. Although it points to a vital aspect of economic behavior, such a formula actually explains nothing. There can be no denying the sensational effects of changes in expectations on real economic conditions in the private enterprise system. Between 1929 and 1932, children did not have enough to eat, men jumped from tall buildings, and rich women pawned their fur coats. What caused the trouble? Pessimism? Certainly there was pessimism in the Great Depression of the 1930s. But what caused the pessimism? In 1929 most indexes of production, new investment, and profits turned down in the summer, but the stock market crash and the collapse of expectations did not occur until autumn. For example, the industrial peak was reached in June 1929, but stock prices did not peak until October 1929. In a competitive, private enterprise economy, especially one that is increasing in complexity and interrelatedness, a single enterprise cannot accurately predict its future costs and receipts; therefore it tends to keep an optimistic outlook until it encounters obstacles. In fact, the usual order of events in depressions appears to be that production and profit indices decline first, despite the most extreme optimism. Only then, because of the change in objective economic conditions, does the optimism change to pessimism, thus reinforcing the depression and possibly postponing the recovery. The reverse process seems to occur in economic expansions, when rises in production and profits are followed by a shift from pessimism to optimism.

Of course, after an expansion begins, it is true that the optimism of businesspeople goes beyond a rational response to profit increases, carrying the expansion far beyond the point that cold calculation would carry it. Such frenzied speculation helps make the peak conditions into a "bubble" that is easily burst. Similarly, after a depression begins, pessimistic businesspeople (usually overreacting in an irrational manner) cause a much greater decline in business activity than the objective condition warrants.

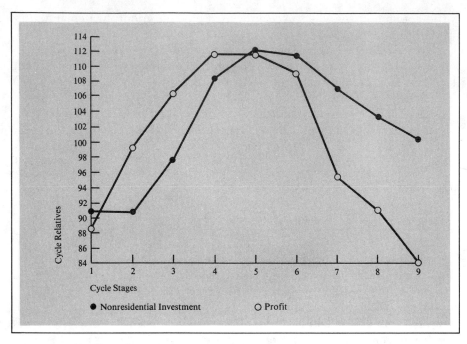

Figure 32.2 Profit and investment, 3 cycles, 1970–1982. *Source:* U.S. Department of Commerce, *Handbook of Cyclical Indicators* (Washington, D.C.: GPO, 1984).

But the ultimate cause of pessimism in businesspeople's attitudes is the previous objectively recorded decline in profits or profit rates.

INVESTMENT DETERMINED BY PROFITS

In the expansion phase of the cycle, particularly in the early expansion, profits and profit rates rise rapidly. This causes a powerful spurt of investment. At the peak of expansion, profits and profit rates are squeezed by various forces. This profit squeeze causes—via still more pessimistic expectations of future profits—a decline in investment.

The decline in investment continues throughout the contraction as profits continue to decline. Toward the end of the recession, profits and profit rates bottom out and expectations become more optimistic. This ending of the profit squeeze (and expected upturn of profits) leads to the beginning of a new investment boom.

Let us see the degree to which the messy facts of the real world bear out that scenario. Figure 32.1 shows the behavior of investment and profits, in the average of the three cycles from 1970 through 1982. Investment in this graph is defined to be gross private domestic nonresidential investment, while profit is defined as profits before taxes for all manufacturing corporations. In the average expansion, profits turn down first, followed by investment. In the average contraction, profits level off near the end, while investment is still declining. Investment closely follows the movements of profits, but with a time lag. Profits are important because they supply funds for investment and because they motivate investors to invest or to withhold their funds.

PRODUCTION AND REALIZATION OF PROFIT

Investment is a function of profits (and profit rates). What, then, determines how much profit is made in the U.S. economy? In making profits the capitalists perform three operations. First, they use their money to buy certain inputs. They buy physical capital goods, such as machinery and raw materials. They also buy living labor—that is, the contractual right to use workers' power to labor for so many hours a day. Second, they use the capital and labor in a production process that produces commodities with a higher revenue than the cost of the capital and labor that went into them. Third, they sell the new commodities for money. Profit shows up here because the capitalists sell the commodities for more money than they used originally in buying the capital and labor. In summary, the three operations are:

1. Money → commodities (labor and capital goods)
2. Commodities → production process → more commodities
3. More commodities → more money (including profit).

In this way capitalists make a profit if all goes smoothly.

Obstacles to profitability may arise in any of these three areas. The first two operations may produce problems in the production of profits. For example, there may be problems in the first capitalist operation, the purchase of capital and labor. If the price of labor (wages) or the price of physical capital goods (such as raw materials imported from abroad) begins to rise more rapidly than output prices, profits suffer. There may also be problems in the second capitalist operation, the production process itself. Less profit will be made if workers are less exploited, by working shorter hours or at a slower pace, or if the productivity of labor declines. Both of these sets of obstacles to making profit refer to higher costs per dollar of output, so both are considered as obstacles to the production of profit.

But there may also be problems in the third operation, selling the goods produced. Even if the costs per dollar of output have remained constant, profits may be threatened if the capitalist cannot sell the product at the present price. For this reason, the profit that is actually made depends on the effective demand for all commodities, including the demand for consumer goods and services and the demand for investment goods and services. In Chapter 31 we examined the limitations of consumer demand. If a capitalist has produced a consumer commodity embodying a profit above costs, but there is no consumer demand for it, the capitalist cannot realize a profit and sustains a loss. Thus lack of demand leads to problems in realizing profits, even when workers have produced a commodity with much potential profit in it.

WAGE COSTS OVER THE CYCLE

Since the problem of demand was examined in some detail in Chapter 31, we can concentrate here on the cost problems met by the capitalists in buying labor and capital or in exploiting labor most productively. Let us begin by examining one kind of cost—wage costs.

Several theories of the business cycle allege that high wages during a period of expansion reduce profits and thereby cause the downturn. In this view, labor is itself responsible for unemployment—again, blaming the victim. But for workers to be able to receive high wages there would have to be a shortage of labor during these booms. Actually, there is chronic long-run continuing unemployment in the United States. Even at the peak of the boom, considerable unemployment continues. Except in wartimes, the only authenticated nationwide shortages of labor occurred in one or two railway booms in the nineteenth century—although there are often shortages of particular types of skilled labor. Otherwise, there is enough unemployment even in peacetime expansion, so workers' wages cannot rise rapidly.

The net output is a single pie over which workers and capitalists fight, with the share of each determined by their bargaining power. If the share of workers (wages to income) goes up, then the profit share (profit to income) must go down. We define wages to include salaries and fringe benefits, with profits defined to include rent and interest, so that together they equal the total net national output. If the profit share declines, then—assuming all other things stay constant—the rate of profit on invested capital will decline.

In Chapter 31 we found that real wages rise in economic expansions, but real profits rise faster, so that the profit share rises. In most contractions, real wages fall, but profits fall faster, so that the profit share declines, helping to cause a large decline in the rate of profit on invested capital.

The share of wages in output may be broken up into two components: the hourly wage—that is, the real wage per hour of labor; and labor productivity—that is, the product per hour of labor. The wage share must, by definition, equal hourly wages divided by hourly product:

$$\text{Wage share} = \frac{\text{total wages}}{\text{total output}} = \frac{\text{wage per hour of labor}}{\text{output per hour of labor}} \tag{1}$$

In most expansions, real hourly wages do rise, though slowly. This normal pattern marks some increase in hourly labor costs to capitalists. In most contractions, real wages fall slowly. This fall in hourly wages is some relief to capitalists, again a normal part of every recession or depression.

We discussed in Chapter 31 why hourly rates rise slowly in expansion and fall slowly in contraction. In expansion, hourly wages rise slowly because (1) the recovery begins with a large pool of unemployed workers, (2) it is hard to mobilize workers for further wage increases when the (real) wage is slowly rising, (3) labor contracts are generally fixed for 1–3 years, (4) it is not necessary to hire administrative workers as production rises, and (5) it is not necessary to rehire as many production workers as before the recession because of advancing technology. Each of these factors works in reverse in a downturn, so real hourly wage rates also fall very slowly.

Capitalists, however, are not only concerned with the real hourly wage, but also with labor productivity. The real hourly output per worker—that is, labor productivity—usually rises rapidly in expansions and falls rapidly in contractions. Thus, profits are increased in expansions and decreased in contractions by the rise and fall of labor productivity.

BEHAVIOR OF COSTS

The entrepreneur faces various types and categories of costs. We may divide these into (1) labor costs, (2) costs of borrowing, and (3) physical capital costs (costs of plant, equipment, and raw materials). The first category, labor costs, was discussed above. Labor costs rise in expansion, but not usually as much as the product. Thus, labor costs do not usually reduce the profit margin. In depressions and recessions, labor costs decline, but usually not as much as the product—so the lower labor costs do not usually restore the profit margin.

Costs of Borrowing Capital

The cost of borrowing capital on credit also rises and falls with the business cycle, though with a time lag. Availability and cheapness of credit greatly affect profits and investment. The details will be explored in Chapter 33.

Cost of Physical Capital

In a careful study of costs of physical capital and consumer prices, Frederick Mills collected data for many cycles, from the 1890s to the 1930s (see References). He compared the prices of consumer goods with the costs of plant and equipment as well as the costs of raw materials. In the average business expansion period, he found that consumer goods prices rose very slowly. The costs of plant and equipment rose more rapidly. Fastest of all, however, was the very rapid rise in raw material prices. Similarly, in the average business contraction period, he found that consumer goods prices fell slowly, costs of plant and equipment fell faster, and costs of raw materials fell most rapidly.

The prices of raw materials rise and fall most rapidly because their supply is relatively fixed and hard to change, while demand for raw materials fluctuates very rapidly. Thus the higher costs of raw materials cut into profit margins in expansions, while lower costs of raw materials help restore profits in recessions.

In the 1970s and early 1980s, a similar pattern continued. In the average business expansion period from 1970 to 1982 (three cycles) the consumer price index rose 22 percent, but the price index of crude materials rose 34 percent. Thus, costs of raw materials reduced profit margins by rising much faster than revenue from sales of consumer goods.

In the average business contraction of 1970 to 1982, the consumer price index rose by 9 percent. It continued to rise in recessions because of the strong long-run inflationary trend. In spite of strong general inflation, however, the price index of crude materials rose only 1 percent in the average business contraction. Since consumer prices rose nine times faster than raw material prices, this helped profit margins to recover from the recession (data from U.S. Department of Commerce, 1984).

PROFITS DETERMINED BY DEMAND AND COSTS

Profits cannot be squeezed from one side alone. The profit squeeze at the peak of expansion must be explained by both the limited demand for goods and services (the problem of realizing profit) and the rising costs of wages, equipment, and raw materials (the problem of producing profit). In Chapter 31 we saw that consumer demand is limited in the expansion by a falling propensity to consume among capitalists and a shift in income from workers' wages to capitalist profits. In this chapter we have seen that prices of raw material, equipment, and other intermediate goods all tend to rise faster than the prices of finished goods, especially consumer goods.

The results of the squeeze by limited demand and rising costs are reflected in declines in total profits and profit rates during the late phases of the expansion. These changes in profits and profit rates explain why businesspeople change their levels of investment. In the early expansion period, rapidly rising profits lead to high levels of investment. The profit squeeze at the peak of expansion reduces investment. Falling profits during the depression cause rapid declines in investment. Finally, a slight recovery in profits leads to recovery in investment.

The capitalist system is thus once again temporarily "cured" of its illness by the drastic means of a depression. The rising profit margins lead to new investment and new prosperity for business.

SUMMARY

Investment shows violent fluctuations over the business cycle. In percentage terms, consumption fluctuates much less. Investment depends on profit expectations. Profit expectations depend on expected revenues from sales and expected costs of production. Actual profits rise rapidly in early expansions as costs are low and demand rises rapidly. Then profit is squeezed by limited demand and high costs.

In contractions, profit falls rapidly, reflecting falling demand. Finally, profit recovers as demand levels off and costs per unit fall. Business investments rise and fall even more than the objective increases and declines in profit rates would indicate because of irrational and exaggerated psychological reactions (confidence or lack of confidence).

APPENDIX

The Accelerator

What is the systematic reasoning that links investment to a change in output? With a given technology, a factory needs a certain amount of capital equipment to produce a certain output. Assume that there is an increase in demand for a factory owner's products, so that the owner wishes to increase the factory's output beyond the present capacity. If the technology stays the same, capital equipment must be increased in proportion to the increase in output demanded. Therefore the factory owner's demand for new capital (net investment) bears a precise relation to the increase in output.

This reasoning may be extended to the determination of net investment in the whole economy. At a given level of technology, aggregate output can be increased only with a certain aggregate increase in capital (net investment). Therefore the demand for an increase in capital is in some ratio to the decision to increase output. That ratio is by definition the accelerator. Thus, in general, we may say that

$$\text{change in capital} = \text{accelerator} \times \text{change in output} \qquad (1)$$

By definition capital means the value of productive facilities. But the expenditure to increase productive facilities is by definition net investment. Because net investment is precisely the change in capital, we may write

$$\text{investment} = \text{accelerator} \times \text{change in output} \qquad (2)$$

Isolating the accelerator in the above equation we obtain:

$$\text{accelerator} = \frac{\text{investment}}{\text{change in output}} \qquad (3)$$

It should be remembered that this theory claims that the accelerator ratio is some precise and roughly constant number.

In the United States yearly output runs at about one-third of the value of all capital. It may therefore be assumed that roughly three units of new capital are required to add one unit to national product. The accelerator coefficient thus may be thought of as relating about three units of net investment to each added unit of output.

For example, the output of shoes may be related to the investment in new

Table 32.1   THE ACCELERATOR IN SHOE PRODUCTION[a]

Time period	Shoe production output	Change in output	Shoe machinery (capital)	Change in capital (net investment)
1	$100	$10	$300	$30
2	110	20	330	60
3	130	5	390	15
4	135	0	405	0
5	135	−5	405	−15
6	130	−20	390	−60
7	110	−10	330	−30
8	100	0	300	0
9	100	10	300	30
10	110			

[a] We assume that $3 more of capital is required to produce $1 more of output. The figures for output of shoe machinery are chosen arbitrarily. The figures for shoe machinery (capital) must then be three times the output of shoes. The change in output is the difference between output one period and the next. The change in capital (net investment) is the difference between capital one period and the next but is also always three times the change in output.

show machinery. More demand for shoes means more investment in equipment. But if demand for shoes stays the same, there should be no further investment in shoe machinery. Finally, if demand for shoes declines, then the accelerator causes disinvestment. Disinvestment here means that some shoe machinery is allowed to wear out and is not replaced. If the value of the accelerator is known, then what will happen to net investment for any movements of output can be predicted exactly. Table 32.1 picks some arbitrary changes in the output of shoes to see what will happen to investment in shoe machinery (given an accelerator set at 3).

The movements of shoe production are given arbitrarily; the rest of Table 32.1 follows by assumption and definition. Thus, from period 1 to period 2, output rises by $10, but because $3 of capital is required to produce $1 of output, capital must rise by $30. In other words, under this assumption a change in output of $10 causes net investment of $30. Similarly, in the next interval, a $20 rise in output causes $60 of investment. A smaller ($5) rise in output from period 3 to period 4 causes a decline in investment to only $15, and in the next interval, output does not change. Thus net investment, or the change in capital, must be zero.

From period 5 to period 6, output declines slightly, but investment must decline by three times as much. Next, a larger decline in output means a much larger decline in investment, and then a smaller decline in output causes a rise in investment to a less negative level. When output stops declining for a period, investment rises to zero. Finally, a small ($10) rise in output again leads to $30 of investment. Throughout, the level of net investment, or the change in capital, is related to the change in output. The desired new investment will always be the excess of desired capital over actual capital.

To illustrate the most important features of this process, the movements of output (shoe production) and net investment (increase or decrease in shoe machinery) may be graphed. The data in Table 32.1 are used as the basis for the graph in Figure 32.2.

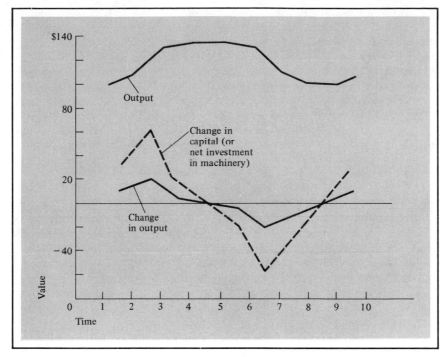

Figure 32.3 Output and investment in shoe production.

Notice that in Figure 32.3 the movements of net investment in shoe machinery do not resemble the movements in the output of shoes; investment moves earlier and more sharply. However, the movements of investment in shoe machinery are exactly similar to the movements of the change in the output of shoes (multiplied by 3).

Several studies have indicated that in the long run, when productive capacity must grow if output is to grow, there is a roughly stable relationship between net investment and the change in output. In any short-run period, however, concern is focused on investment as an immediate psychological reaction to prospective changes in the amount of output demanded. It is easy to see that in the short run the rigid relationship between investment and change in output posited by the accelerator theory must be qualified in many ways.

First, even if the accelerator holds true for a 10-year period, does investment react exactly in that ratio to a change in demand over a 2-month period or even over a whole year? In reality the time lag between changed demand and net investment varies from industry to industry and even from phase to phase of the business cycle. A long and complicated process takes place before investment spending actually results. If demand improves, the corporate directors must come to expect increased future demand. But entrepreneurial expectations may also be affected by noneconomic psychological or political factors. Then the directors must appropriate funds for investment purposes and perhaps arrange outside financing. Next engineers must design new factories or new machines. Even after the construction actually begins, it is some time before all the investment funds are fully spent.

Second, the accelerator assumes that each industry faced with higher demands is already running at full capacity. That is not true, however, in a depression or in the early stages of recovery from a depression. During a depression there is much idle machinery and many empty, unused factories, allowing any new demand to be met easily without net investment. Thus the accelerator is notably weaker whenever there is much unused capacity.

Third, the accelerator ignores the physical limitations on the amount of investment or disinvestment in any given period. No matter how much the demand increases at the peak of prosperity, the investment goods industries have just enough excess capacity to produce the called-for investment goods. Similarly, falling demand in a depression may indicate much disinvestment. But the whole economy can disinvest (or reduce its capital stock) in one year only to the extent of the depreciation of capital in that year. In other words, capital can be reduced in the economy as a whole only as fast as it wears out or becomes obsolete.

Fourth, the simple accelerator ignores the effects of changes in the relative levels of prices and costs. At the peak of prosperity, the great demand on the capacity of the capital goods industries may raise the cost of capital goods and thus weaken investment incentives. The level of wage costs also changes systematically over the cycle. Moreover, a firm needs financial capital for investment, which depends mostly on reinvestment of profits; if there is not enough profit, then the firm must borrow in the capital market and must face higher interest costs. On the other side, prices show long-run as well as cyclical fluctuations, which affect expected revenues.

These costs and price changes, which are summarized by profit changes, affect investment as much as or more than the simple amount of output demanded. Therefore, the profits—or the rate of profit—are a better predictor of investment than amount demanded. For both profits and output demanded, the change in the indicator may impress investors more than a continuing high or low level of that indicator (but the level of profits does control how much capital is actually available for investment).

Finally, the accelerator only tries to explain net investment. Since replacement is not automatic, it is gross investment that must be explained. Replacement investment—in addition to net investment—is sometimes accelerated and sometimes postponed. To explain these changes in replacement policy we must again turn to changes in expectations of profit and available funds from profits.

SUMMARY

The accelerator principle says net investment is related in a definite ratio to the change in output during the business cycle. Although this is roughly true, several factors indicate that there is no reliable single fixed figure for the accelerator ratio. First, there is a long and varying time lag from the first indication of increased demand for output to the actual investment expenditure. Second, in a recession, the accelerator is greatly weakened. Third, changes in investment cannot be as extreme as predicted because there is an upper limit, given by the capacity of the capital goods industries, and a lower limit, given by the amount of depreciation. Fourth, the simple accelerator is modified by changes in the relationship of prices and costs because these changes affect profits and, consequently, investments. There is no space here for a discussion of other modifications, such as the fact that the accelerator may work only in the aggregate and not at all in many individual industries. Nevertheless, the accelerator does contain a large grain of truth and emphasizes the basic fact that new capital goods are built to meet new demand. It also explains, in part, why investment fluctuates so much more violently than consumer demand; it is related not to the level but to the change in demand.

REFERENCES

Mills, Frederick. *Price-Quantity Interactions in Business Cycles.* New York: National Bureau of Economic Research, 1946, pp. 132–133.

U.S. Department of Commerce. *Handbook of Cyclical Indicators.* Washington, D.C.: GPO, 1984.

Chapter
33

Money and Credit

Before we can fully understand consumer and investor spending, we must consider the credit system on which it is based. This chapter begins by describing our monetary and credit system, as well as the evolution of money from primitive times to the present Federal Reserve System. Then we turn to the theories and policies advocated by Keynes, the conservative monetarists, and the liberal Post-Keynesians. Finally, we look at the actual behavior of money and credit in the U.S. economy to see how the facts compare with the theories.

THE MONEY SUPPLY

The present money supply consists of coins and paper currency outside of commercial banks, checking accounts (demand deposits) in commercial banks, and many new kinds of accounts on which a depositor may draw checks but also get interest in many cases. For theoretical purposes, these new, rapidly growing kinds of accounts may be considered to fulfill the same function as demand deposits. The growth of the component parts of the money supply is shown in Table 33.1.

Demand deposits are the debts of commercial banks owed to their depositors. These demand deposits have remained a fairly constant percentage of the U.S. money supply (around 75–78 percent). Banks create money in the sense that banks have the ability to create demand deposits. To understand the present situation more clearly, we present a brief history of the evolution of money and of the power to create money. This history is conjectural in that it is not of one specific place, but a logically consistent

Table 33.1   GROWTH OF THE MONEY SUPPLY (IN BILLIONS OF DOLLARS, AVERAGE FOR DECEMBER OF EACH YEAR)

Year	Currency	Demand deposits at commercial banks	Other check-drawing deposits
1960	29	112	0
1970	49	166	0
1980	116	267	27
1988	235	588	1470

Source: Federal Reserve data, reported in Council of Economic Advisors, *Economic Report of the President* (Washington, D.C.: GPO) 1988.

and approximately accurate description of the development of money in most places.

A HISTORY OF MONEY

Money is defined as any widely accepted medium of exchange. A commodity that is used as money does not necessarily have any intrinsic value; for example, the only value of paper money may be its general acceptability in exchange and for the settlement of debt. If the law requires that it be accepted in the settlement of debt, it is also legal tender.

Among the most primitive tribes exchange was conducted by the barter system. Barter means that one commodity is directly traded for another in the market without the use of money. For example, we may find trade in this form:

$$1 \text{ coat} = 2 \text{ hats} \tag{1}$$

If this exchange ratio persists for some time, people may come to think of one coat as worth two hats, or they may think of one hat as worth half a coat.

The second evolutionary step was to the crudest kind of money, a stage in which some particular commodity was used as money. Any convenient or often-used commodity might eventually attain the status of money if it were relatively scarce and therefore valuable. For example, in a community in which the number of cows owned was a status symbol, we might find that cows played the role of money. Thus

$$2 \text{ coats} = 1 \text{ cow} = 4 \text{ hats} \tag{2}$$

People in this society would calculate all their production and wealth in terms of cows. They might actually sell or trade coats for cows and then use the "cow money" to buy hats, or vice versa.

Cows, however, are not a very convenient money commodity. They are perishable and not easily divisible, problems that could be solved by using precious metals or stones. The need to have large numbers of pieces of money that are of equal value led to the third step of the evolution, the development of metallic money. Precious metals have several virtues as a medium of exchange: (1) They are valuable; one need carry only a small amount to buy other commodities. (2) They are easily divisible; uniform coins of various values can be made by melting, and thus the exact amount necessary for any purchase can be used. (3) They are nonperishable and hence can be stored indefinitely.

The durability and portability of metallic money mean it may be used not only for calculating value ratios but also in every exchange. Thus trade takes this form:

$$1 \text{ coat} = 1 \text{ oz. gold} = 2 \text{ hats} \tag{3}$$

Any commodity (such as a coat) may be sold for metallic money. Then the metallic money is put away until its holder wishes to buy another commodity (such as a hat).

The next step in the evolution came when paper claims were substituted for metallic money such as gold, but they were still payable in gold. These claims were originally issued by goldsmiths, private bankers, and merchants. Governments soon followed suit, issuing their own paper money, which consisted of IOUs, or promises by the government to pay in gold on demand. Of course it was possible to issue more paper money than gold because not everyone demanded gold at the same time.

The modern issue of inconvertible paper money is the fifth step in the evolution of money. Paper money looks the same as before, but a government declares that it will no longer convert or pay its paper IOUs in gold on demand. This method of money creation financed the American and French Revolutions and the U.S. Civil War. Almost all governments had recourse to this expedient in the monetary chaos following World War I and during the Great Depression. At the same time, governments usually prohibited private institutions from issuing paper money. One way governments made their paper money more acceptable to the populace was to accept it for tax payments and to declare it legal tender. Of course the value of inconvertible paper money today has no direct connection with gold reserves.

The most recently evolved form of money is the checking account. Sums of money in checking accounts are bookkeeping entries called *deposits.* They are actually promises to pay—that is, they are debts of the bank. Checks written against these accounts are orders to transfer deposit funds to others' accounts or to convert some of the deposit account into currency. The owner of such an account may have brought currency to the bank or may have deposited a check. He or she may have signed a note and borrowed the money. In such a case the bank and the individual merely exchange IOUs. But the bank's IOU, the demand deposit, serves all the functions of money. Checks drawn against the balance make payment without the use of currency or coin. Although a check is not legal tender, the deposit is convertible into legal tender, and the deposit account is money. It is apparent that the distinguishing characteristic of a bank is that, unlike any other private enterprise, the evidence of its debt to an individual is accepted as money.

THE EVOLUTION OF MODERN BANKING

Perhaps we can illustrate the role of the modern banker by returning to conjectural history. Centuries ago, when the market system was evolving, goldsmiths had large quantities of precious metals. To protect them, secure storage facilities had to be constructed. Other individuals sought the same security for their money but did not have enough money to justify the expense of constructing such facilities. The local goldsmith began to accept their coin (the sole form of money at the time) and precious metals. As evidence of these deposits the depositor was provided with a receipt. The goldsmith earned income by demanding payment from the individual depositor for the safekeeping function performed.

In time, goldsmiths who had developed reputations for honesty found that these deposit receipts began to circulate and could be used by the individuals holding them in payment of debt. For example, merchants, instead of carrying coin on business trips, would deposit it with a reputable and renowned goldsmith. The receipt could then be used to settle accounts in distant lands. Hence as long as the goldsmith was willing and able to redeem these deposit receipts, or paper claims, on demand for coin, they performed the function of money. Here we see the initial stages in the development of both the banking system and paper claims as money. The validity of the paper claims as money was a function of their general acceptability as money, which depended on the confidence that the public had in the goldsmith's ability to convert the paper claims into coin on demand.

Thus far, however, goldsmiths have not performed the primary distinguishing function of bankers, the money creation function. All they have done is to match their metallic assets with paper claims. Their balance sheets probably would resemble this:

Assets		Liabilities	
Coin in vault	$1000	Deposits	$1000
Total assets	$1000	Total liabilities	$1000

Sooner or later goldsmiths realize that they can create debt (demand deposits and notes payable on demand) in excess of the coin they hold in their vaults. Why can they do this? First, because the people have confidence in their ability to redeem their paper claims in coin on demand. Second, this confidence leads other people to accept the paper claims in settlement of their debts. Therefore, at any given time only a small portion of the paper claims need to be converted into coin.

As long as goldsmith-bankers can readily meet this small portion of claims for coin, they are in a position to increase their total liabilities beyond the actual amount of coin they have in their vaults. In other words, they are able to create money. And the total of coin, bank notes, and deposit receipts now in circulation exceeds the amount of coin that has been minted by government authority. The bank notes (issued by the goldsmith-bankers to those who borrow from them) and the deposit receipts are money, the same way coin is money, because people are willing to accept them in payment for any debt. It makes no difference to an individual whether payment is made in the form of coin, bank note, or deposit receipt, as long as he or she can use these interchangeably for making his or her own payments.

Goldsmiths—who are now bankers because they create money—will then keep in their vaults an amount of coin large enough to meet the demands for coin that will be made on them. Of course they can roughly estimate these demands from their experience. The banker-goldsmiths' balance sheets probably would resemble this:

Assets		Liabilities	
Coin in vault	$ 800	Notes payable	$ 600
Loans	800	Deposits	1000
Total assets	$1600	Total liabilities	$1600

The bankers' liabilities in this example clearly exceed the coin in their vaults. What they have done is lend money to individuals, of which $200 has had to be paid out in the form of coin (reducing their coin from $1,000 to $800). However, people are willing to hold the other $600 of loans in the form of bank notes. Thus the bankers have created new liabilities while holding only half of their total liabilities ($800) in the form of coin. They now have an additional form of income: the interest they earn from the loans they make. The banker has created money in excess of the coin in their vaults to the amount of $800.

The bankers' ability to create money is limited by the portion of notes and deposits they are forced to maintain in the form of coin because of institutional or other considerations. In this case, because they have to hold 50 percent of their deposits and note liabilities in the form of coin, they can expand the money supply by only twice the amount of coin in their vaults.

Here we see the development, in its initial stages, of the modern banking system. The bankers now create debts that circulate freely as money and that slowly come to form an increasing part of the total money supply. They have succeeded in converting their idle coins, which earn no interest, into loans for which they charge a rate of interest. The borrowing-lending function, formerly performed by moneylenders, is now performed by bankers. The uniqueness of bankers, however, lies in the fact that, unlike the moneylender, they can make loans in excess of the actual coin in their vaults.

OPERATION OF MODERN COMMERCIAL BANKS

The bankers' business consists of taking the money deposited with them, on some of which they pay interest, and lending it out at higher rates of interest. Money deposited in time or savings accounts pays interest to depositors, but it must stay frozen, or on deposit, for some definite time before the interest is paid (thus it is counted only as near money). Money deposited in checking accounts available on demand (and therefore counted as part of the money supply) generally pays no interest. In order to pay the interest on savings accounts, bankers must get higher interest rates on the money they lend to others.

Bankers are torn between two objectives. On the one hand, they want to make as much profit as possible by lending out as much as they can (and the riskiest loans pay the highest interest rates). On the other hand, they want safety; they want to be able to pay off easily any depositor who demands his or her money. Technically the banker is said to seek liquidity. The most liquid assets are those most easily available in cash to pay off depositors. Thus the most liquid asset is money in paper currency and coin (or even gold), which pay no interest to the banker. The next most liquid assets are government notes and bonds, sometimes called near money, which pay low interest but can be cashed immediately (although at variable prices if cashed before maturity). Least liquid are risky private loans, which may pay high interest but cannot be cashed for a long time and may never be paid back if the individual goes bankrupt. The precise way in which the entire American banking system holds its assets is indicated in Table 33.2.

Bank liabilities consist mainly of deposits, or the amount that is owed to depositors. The assets of the whole banking system include gold (held only by the government's Federal Reserve Bank), currency (a very small item), and U.S. government bonds. By far their largest assets, however, are the loans that banks will some day collect from individuals and businesses. For purposes of analysis we shall often classify all assets merely as reserves of money and near money or as loans to businesses, individuals, and governments. We shall soon discover that modern banks are required by the government to keep a certain ratio of their deposits in the form of reserves, which limits their power to make loans.

Table 33.2 shows the combined balance sheet of the whole U.S. banking

Table 33.2   CONSOLIDATED BALANCE SHEET FOR THE BANKING SYSTEM
OF THE UNITED STATES ON AUGUST 30, 1988

Assets (in billions)		Liabilities and capital (in billions)	
Loans and securities	$2523	Deposits	$2059
Cash	216	Borrowing	471
Other assets	192	Other liabilities	213
		Capital owned by stockholders	188
Total assets	$2931	Total liabilities and capital	$2931

Source: Federal Reserve Bulletin, September 1988, A17.

system. Most of the assets of the banks consist of money loaned to house-holds, corporations, and government—so Table 33.2 reveals loans and securities equal to $2.523 trillion. Most of the liabilities of the banks consist of money owed to those who have made deposits in the banks—so the table reveals $2.059 trillion in deposits.

THE FEDERAL RESERVE SYSTEM

On December 23, 1913, President Woodrow Wilson signed the Federal Reserve Act establishing the Federal Reserve System (Fed). It was the government's answer to the banking failures and monetary panics of the early 1900s. The Fed is the central bank of the United States, corresponding to the Bank of England or the Bank of France. Its original purposes were to give the country a currency flexible enough to meet its needs and to improve the supervision of banking. Today, however, these are only a part of broader and more important objectives, which include maintaining price stability, fostering a high rate of economic growth, and promoting a high level of employment.

Federal Reserve functions are carried out through 12 Federal Reserve banks and their 24 branches, but there is also central coordination by the Board of Governors in Washington. The Board of Governors consists of seven members appointed by the president and confirmed by the Senate. One of the board's duties is to supervise all Fed operations. The board participates in all of the principal monetary actions of the Fed. It has full authority over changes in the legal reserve requirements of banks (within the limits prescribed by Congress). The board "reviews and determines" the interest rates of the individual Federal Reserve banks, and it has the authority to establish the maximum rates of interest member banks may pay on savings and other time deposits. In addition, the board is responsible for the regulation of stock market credit.

The presidents of the 12 regional Federal Reserve banks are not publicly elected or appointed; they are usually conservative bankers (see *Reuss*, pp. 370–372). The president of each Federal Reserve bank is appointed by the board of directors of that bank. Each board of directors has nine members, six of whom are elected directly by the member banks, usually on the advice of the state bankers' association, their lobbying group. The other three directors (called Class C directors) "are supposed to be representative of a broader public. In fact, they represent the same narrow interests as the others: twenty-nine of the thirty-six current Class C directors are executives or directors of corporations, mostly large" (ibid., p. 371).

The House Banking Committee of the U.S. Congress surveyed all of the 108 directors (12 Federal Reserve banks times 9 directors) and concluded that the directors are "representative of a small elite group which dominates much of the economic life of this nation" (quoted in ibid., p. 371). These directors of the regional Federal Reserve banks include no women, no labor union members or worker representatives, no consumer organization members, no small farmers, and only two blacks. What is more incredible is that the Federal Reserve has existed 63 years and has had 1088 persons on its regional boards of directors, but none have been women, none have been workers or consumer representatives, and only four have been blacks.

There is also a Federal Open Market Committee (FOMC), which has the important function of buying and selling government bonds on the open market. The FOMC is composed of the seven members of the Board of Governors of the Federal Reserve (mostly conservative economists and big business representatives) plus five presidents of the regional Federal Reserve banks (the 12 presidents take turns on the FOMC, but they are all bankers). These are the people who determine the major part of U.S. monetary policy.

The Federal Reserve System controls the money supply in order to achieve its purposes. The real bases of the value of the nation's money supply are the goods produced and confidence in the government. Until recently, however, the money supply of the United States had as its legal base the country's gold stock, which stood at $11.8 billion on August 26, 1970. Congress had required the Federal Reserve to hold an amount equal to 25 percent of its liabilities in the form of gold, but this requirement was removed in 1968 with no significant effect on the efficiency with which money has performed its functions.

Although the Federal Reserve banks still hold gold certificates, this is merely one of several types of assets. Gold certificates need bear no necessary relationship to Federal Reserve liabilities (i.e., they bear no necessary connection to the U.S. money supply). The other principal types of assets are government securities and loans to the member banks. The principal liabilities are Federal Reserve note currency, which constitutes most of the paper currency held by the public, and member bank reserves, which, as will be seen, form the basis for the creation of credit money by the banking system.

The Fed specifies exactly how much reserve each member bank must hold in relation to its deposits. Congress has set the following limits on reserve ratios that the Fed may require: for the demand deposits of big city banks, a minimum of 10 percent to a maximum of 22 percent; for demand deposits of country banks, a minimum of 7 percent to a maximum of 14 percent; and for saving deposits in all banks, a minimum of 3 percent to a maximum of 10 percent. Actual reserve requirements set by the Fed are at 18.5 percent for city bank demand deposits, between 8 and 13 percent for country bank demand deposits (increasing with the size of the bank), and 3 percent on all saving deposits.

Banking reserves of money or "checking accounts at the Fed" may be kept either in the bank vault or in the nearest Federal Reserve bank. If it is kept as a deposit in a Federal Reserve bank, the member bank may even earn a small interest on its money reserves. Country banks are given a lower required reserve ratio, apparently on the theory that they may also use loans from the larger city banks as part of their emergency reserves.

The first purpose of the reserve system is, of course, to ensure that the bank has sufficient funds to meet its depositors' withdrawals. Yet in the Great Depression thousands of banks failed because runs on the banks by depositors exhausted their reserves. This purpose is now more fully met by the Federal Deposit Insurance Corporation (FDIC), which guarantees all deposits up to $100,000. The more important purpose that the Fed now serves is to control the money supply as a tool of general economic control.

THREE TOOLS OF MONETARY POLICY

Monetary policy is government policy designed to increase or decrease the flow of money and credit. Increases or decreases in money and credit will stimulate or depress demand. What are the tools with which the Fed influences money and credit?

In an inflationary situation exactly how should monetary policy be applied and how effective is it? The supply of money and credit may be restricted by monetary policy through three major controls: (1) raising the required Federal Reserve ratio, (2) raising the interest rate the Federal Reserve charges banks, and (3) sale of government bonds by the Federal Reserve. Let us see how each of these controls is supposed to work.

First, in order to restrict credit the Federal Reserve may raise the ratio of reserves banks are required to hold against their deposits. Furthermore, as soon as one bank decreases its loans, the effect on all banks may be several times as great by virtue of the money multiplier (see Appendix to this chapter). Thus, in theory, raising the Federal Reserve ratio from 10 to 20 percent would lower the multiplication of money by banks from tenfold to only fivefold. If all banks were fully loaned out, this would cause a great decrease of loans. A reduction in the volume of loans may then mean less money available for consumer and investor spending, thus reducing inflationary pressures.

Second, the Federal Reserve may also raise the interest rate that banks must pay if they wish to borrow from the Federal Reserve banks. Then a bank will either have to charge higher interest rates on loans to its customers or reduce the amount it lends in order to avoid borrowing reserves from the Fed. Either way, less money will be available for further consumption and investment spending, thus reducing demand and leading to a lower rate of price inflation.

Finally, the Federal Reserve may sell more government bonds to banks or rich individuals. The money to pay for the bonds must come from bank reserves or from individual bank deposits. In either case the ability of banks to make loans is reduced (manyfold, according to the money multiplier—see Appendix to this chapter). Thus again consumer and investment spending may be decreased and inflationary pressures reduced. These methods of reducing money spending in an inflation may encounter certain obstacles. First, each assumes banks had already made loans up to the maximum ratio of deposits to reserves. But banks often keep extra reserves above even the highest possible required reserve ratio and thus can keep lending until these reserves are exhausted. Second, these monetary controls assume that corporations must borrow from banks all the money they need for new investments. But corporations often keep their own internal savings, which they may decide to use regardless of bank policies. Third, in cases in which the government succeeds only in getting banks to raise their interest rates (by lowering money supply), there may be little effect on demand. If expected profit rates are rising even faster than interest rates, corporations may still be willing to borrow and invest more rapidly. In all of these cases the government may be able to restrict the money supply, but the velocity, or speed, of spending the present money supply may increase even more rapidly.

Despite these weaknesses, monetary policy, if applied strongly enough (and rapidly enough, because time is required for it to take effect), can choke off a general inflation. Of course, too severe a remedy may cause instability in the bond and stock markets, loss of confidence by domestic and foreign investors, and eventually a business downturn. There is, indeed, considerable evidence that Federal Reserve attempts to reduce inflation were part of the causes of the downturns of 1969–1970, 1973–1975, 1980, and 1981–1982.

In a depression exactly the opposite monetary policy may be applied. The supply of money and credit may be expanded by (1) lowering the required Federal Reserve ratio, (2) lowering the interest rate the Federal Reserve charges banks, or (3) having the Federal Reserve purchase government bonds in the open market to put more cash into the hands of individuals and banks. These measures are designed to increase the volume of borrowing and thus the volume of spending by increasing the supply of money for loans and lowering interest rates.

Obstacles to monetary policies intended to combat depression include most of those met by counterinflationary policies and a few that are different and more difficult to surmount. First, the interest rate cannot go below zero, and in actual practice lenders will not go below a floor that is somewhat above a zero rate. Yet during a depression it may require a zero or even negative interest rate to stimulate borrowing. Second, neither consumers nor most investors seem much stimulated to borrow by slightly lower interest rates. Businesspeople apparently consider their pessimistic expectations of smaller profits or even losses to be quantitatively much more important than low interest rates in investment decisions. Moreover, businesses prefer to invest from internal funds; when their profits fall drastically in a depression, they are not much attracted by any kind of loan.

The government may increase the banks' supply of money in order to combat a depression, but consumers and businesses may reduce the amount of borrowing and spending even more rapidly. In short, monetary policies may have some effect in minor recessions, but in a major depression monetary policy may be able to do little or nothing to expand the volume of spending.

KEYNES AND MARX ON MONEY AND CREDIT

This is an area of economics where J. M. Keynes followed Marx in some basic points. Keynes agreed with Marx that the money and credit system allows instability in capitalism and tends to intensify that instability (see Crotty, 1986, 1987). Marx said that in earlier economies commodities are exchanged with other commodities, with money merely acting as an intermediary. Let C stand for commodity and M stand for money. Then the form of exchange in most primitive and feudal economies is

$$C \rightarrow M \rightarrow C$$

A person exchanges commodities (including goods and services) for money, only to use the money to buy other commodities.

But in capitalism, the main preoccupation of capitalists is to turn money (M) into more money (M^+). So the most important form of exchange for businesspeople is

$$M \rightarrow C \rightarrow M^+$$

Money is used to buy commodities (capital and labor), which produce more commodities and are sold for more money.

Keynes complimented Marx on this astute analysis (Keynes, p. 81). Keynes used this analysis of the importance of money to destroy Say's law (that demand will equal supply at full employment). If commodities only exchange for other commodities (with money only a go-between), then demand must equal supply. But if money is used to buy commodities in order to produce more commodities for sale (in order to make more money), then it is possible that there will be insufficient demand to sell all the commodities at a high enough price to make more money; the result will be a depression with unemployment.

Keynes went further to note the vital importance of credit in the modern economy. Credit allows consumers to buy beyond their income. Credit allows business to buy capital goods beyond its net income. Thus credit is the usual source for an exaggerated boom. But what happens when the bubble bursts? In a depression or recession, consumers cannot pay their debts, businesses cannot pay their debts, and creditors (such as banks) go bankrupt.

Obviously, Keynes thought that money and credit were very important in making depressions intensify. But, as shown in the previous section, there are definite limits to the effectiveness of monetary policy in ending unemployment. So Keynesians in the 1950s and 1960s downplayed the importance of monetary theory and monetary policy, while putting their faith in government spending and tax cuts.

At the University of Chicago, however, economist Milton Friedman was publishing a series of articles in an effort to revitalize the more traditional monetary theories. From this effort an entire school of thought called monetarism eventually emerged.

MONETARIST TENETS

Generally, a strict monetarist would agree with the following propositions:

1. Unfettered free markets are efficient, will produce an equitable distribution of goods, will promote growth, and will generally solve their own problems without assistance. Serious economic disturbances are the consequence of random shocks (such as a bad harvest or the formation of a foreign oil cartel), which no one can control, or are due to misguided economic policy from a government that should not be interfering.

2. The expansion and contraction of the money stock will directly and unambiguously affect the level of nominal spending in the economy. The money stock is more closely correlated with that spending than such money-related variables as interest rates or bank credit. A change in the money stock, moreover, will affect only nominal variables in the long run (after the passage of a few months). In the short run, real variables are affected, but countervailing forces—after any monetary disturbance—return real variables such as output and employment to their old values. Hence, an excessive monetary expansion will generate inflation, but no change in output and employment. So, in the long run, expanding the money supply does

not fight unemployment. Most monetarists would probably also agree that most inflations have excessive monetary expansions as their ultimate cause.

3. There is a lag between changes in the money stock and their impact upon nominal spending, and that lag is variable and unknown. Policymakers trying to use discretionary monetary policy (using monetary policy to attempt to correct short-run problems) will tend to either overreact or underreact and will ultimately end up trying to chase down and stamp out the results of their own misguided policy. Additionally, their behavior will generate destabilizing expectations in the private sector. When all of this is combined with the argument that monetary policy cannot influence real income or employment anyway, monetarists have, in their judgment, sufficient reason to rule out the use of discretionary monetary policy. They therefore believe that monetary authorities should do no more than allow the money supply to expand at a fixed rate, perhaps 3 percent or 4 percent per year. This is the so-called monetary rule.

4. Discretionary fiscal policy cannot be used to solve problems of inflation, unemployment, or sluggish growth. Such policy will merely reallocate the distribution of goods and services, usually in favor of the government at the expense of the private sector (because private investment is "crowded out").

BASIC CRITICISMS OF MONETARISM

Critics have attacked each of the main propositions of monetarism:

1. It is asserted that the market system is distorted by monopoly, so that it is not efficient even in the narrowest sense. Workers are exploited by employers who make huge profits from the products created by workers, so the distribution of income is not equitable. Moreover, the capitalist market system results in periodic recessions and depressions, so growth is uneven and much slower than it need be. These periodic crises are internal to the system as evidenced by the fact that they keep recurring in the same patterns time and again. Particularly in those places where monetarist policy has been tried—such as by the junta in Chile, the Begin government in Israel, the Thatcher government in England, and the Federal Reserve System policies in the United States—the result has been millions of workers unemployed.

2. The critics point out that the money supply does not have any clear effect on spending for two reasons. First, the monetarists use a very narrow definition of money, such as cash and demand deposits. But the critics note that the economy today really operates mainly on credit, so it is the expansion and contraction of the broader credit aggregates that is really important.

Second, whether one speaks of money narrowly defined or of credit, the direction of causation is probably more from economic activity to money and credit than vice versa. When the economy is expanding rapidly, the corporations and the consumers wish to borrow, the banks are happy to comply and the Federal Reserve System is under pressure to allow it. In the contraction, everyone is afraid to borrow or to lend; this causes the supply and velocity of money and credit to decline.

3. Some critics argue that enough is known so that discretionary monetary policy, combined with fiscal policy, can achieve some short-run success. Others might agree that it is difficult to know what time lags will affect the money supply with a given policy, but they argue that this also undermines the monetarist idea that the money stock directly and unambiguously affects spending. How can it be unambiguous when the time lag is variable and unpredictable? There is obviously no way to test a relation with a variable time lag, so the connection must remain an unscientific assertion.

4. The monetarist argument that fiscal expansionary policies, which lead to deficits, must crowd out private investment has also been vigorously challenged. It is argued that public spending, through the multiplier mechanism, has a very strong positive effect on the economy and that this positive effect is much stronger than any negative effect on borrowing for private investment. The evidence on this point has been strongly disputed ever since Keynes wrote about it in the 1930s.

MONEY AND CREDIT IN BUSINESS CYCLES

Business cycles are intensified by the use of money and credit in a capitalist economy. Monetary panics have often closed and bankrupted hundreds of banks, as in 1907 and 1932. In every contraction the flow of credit is disrupted to some extent, further restricting both consumer and investor demand. The stock market crash of 1929 also drastically contracted the funds available for investment.

One good measure of the heavy use of credit in the late expansion period is the ratio of consumer installment credit to personal income. The cyclical behavior of this ratio for the last five cycles, 1958 to 1982, is depicted in Figure 33.1.

This picture reveals a rapid rise in the ratio of credit to income during most of the expansion period. The consumer credit ratio rises rapidly in the expansion because consumers have good jobs and are optimistic about the future. Obviously, this higher flow of credit increases the flow of spending in the expansion, so it supports more effective demand and postpones a depression.

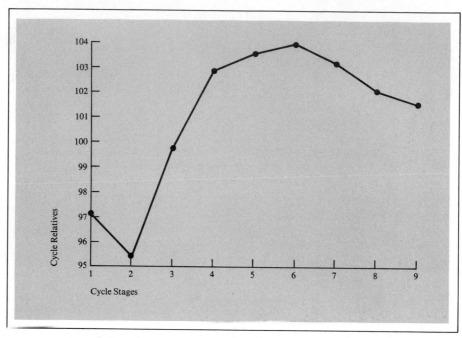

Figure 33.1 Credit/income. *Source:* U.S. Department of Commerce, *Handbook of Cyclical Indicators* (Washington, D.C.: GPO, 1984).

But the rising ratio of debt to income also makes consumer finances increasingly more fragile and vulnerable to a downturn. Thus Figure 33.1 shows that debt continues to rise or remain high (because consumers need credit badly to pay old debts) even after income starts declining in the first stage of depression—so the debt to income ratio rises further. After a while, however, lost jobs make it impossible to get more credit, so the ratio declines throughout the rest of the depression period. The ratio keeps declining even in early recovery as people use new income to pay off old debts. (Similarly, businesses pile up debts in the expansion, then are forced to borrow less in recession or depression as their credit rating falls. They also cannot pay back their debts.)

A closely related factor is the credit policy of financial institutions. During the middle of expansion they are free and easy with credit at relatively low interest rates. This encourages unrealistic speculative purchases by both consumers and businesses. Then, as the speculative frenzy increases, banks begin to worry about repayment and the higher demand allows them to raise interest rates. The best-known interest rate, the prime rate to the best credit risks, is shown in Figure 33.2.

This picture shows the very steep rise in interest rates in the last half of the expansion. The rise in interest rates comes at the worst time for consumers and small businesses, when they are using more and more credit.

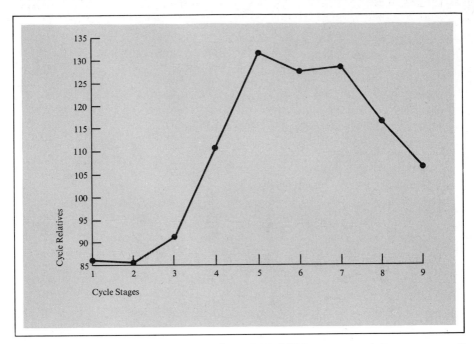

Figure 33.2 Prime interest rate, 7 cycles, 1949–1982. *Source:* U.S. Department of Commerce, Handbook of Cyclical Indicators (Washington, D.C.: GPO, 1984).

The inability to get credit at reasonable rates when it is most needed may be called a "credit crunch."

Figure 33.2 shows that the prime rate remains high in the first part of business contraction because so many businesses are demanding credit. The interest rates available to consumers and small businesses even increase in the early stages of business contraction. (Thus economists speak of the interest rate as well as the ratio of credit to income as lagging cyclical indicators—that is, effects of the business cycle rather than initiating causes.) Eventually, as the recession or depression becomes evident to everyone, there is great pessimism, and no one is willing to borrow more on speculation. Demand for credit collapses and the interest rate falls.

Easy availability of money and credit fuels the boom in the business expansion, but the collapse of money and credit during crises worsens the business contraction. So money and credit do not cause downturns by themselves, but their reactions can turn mild recessions into severe depressions.

TRENDS IN CREDIT

There is a trend toward more and more corporate borrowing from banks. This results from the constant drive of corporations to increase their profits by borrowing capital (say, a profit rate of 15 percent). This long-run trend

Table 33.3   BORROWING BY BUSINESSES FROM LARGE COMMERCIAL
             BANKS (BILLIONS OF DOLLARS)

	Loans (net credit borrowing by nonfinancial sectors)	U.S. gross national product (GNP)	Percent of loans to GNP
1960	36.2	506.5	7.1
1970	95.3	992.7	9.6
1980	343.2	2633.7	13.0

Source: U.S. Federal Reserve System, Flow of Funds Accounts (Washington, D.C.: GPO), 1983.

is quite clear in Table 33.3. For the last 20 years or more, business has not only borrowed more and more total dollars, but the amount borrowed has also risen as a percentage of gross national product.

Nonfinancial corporations owe banks debts amounting to a large percentage of their own sales. This means an enormous burden of interest payments. It is easy to meet these payments during a profitable business expansion. In a depression, however, these interest payments (and return of principal, since loans will not be extended) may lead to disaster.

On the other side, banks make the most profits by expanding loans as much as possible; if the bank pays depositors 5 percent but lends the money for 10 percent, the profit is considerable. The trick is not to let deposits sit idle but to lend as much as possible. In an expansion, when corporations look like very safe bets to return both principal and interest on time, banks rush to lend them money.

The long-run trend in large commercial U.S. banks has been to lend out a larger and larger percentage of deposits. (Thus, from 1950 to 1974, bank loans increased from 36 percent of their deposits to 82 percent of their deposits.) At the same time, their liquid reserves of cash and U.S. Treasury bonds and notes are becoming a smaller and smaller percentage of their deposits (falling from 54 percent to 14 percent from 1950 to 1974). This risky position makes big profits for banks in a boom when most loans are repaid with interest. In a depression, however, many corporations and many consumers cannot repay their loans, let alone pay interest. Banks are faced with falling profits and are caught in a bind for cash. They may not be able to meet withdrawal demands of depositors (which usually increase in a depression), causing some banks to fail and go bankrupt, thereby intensifying the depression.

SUMMARY

In this chapter we examined the money supply and its probable evolution from barter to paper money to credit. Today the most important component of the money supply is the demand, or checking, deposits owed to customers by the banks. The Federal Reserve System was established to regulate banks and stabilize the money supply. The Fed is controlled by big businesses and bankers, so it may sometimes act to control inflation, but its policies often increase unemployment. When corporations borrow too much, the risky credit structure may collapse for some corporations and some banks; the collapse may be too quick for the Federal Reserve to help them. Credit supports the expansion beyond reasonable expectations, but the collapse of credit is one cause of deep depressions.

APPENDIX

How Banks Multiply Money

Exactly how much new money can banks create with a given amount of new deposits? Obviously, this depends in large part on what reserve ratio the Federal Reserve requires them to hold. Part of each new deposit must be held in reserve, and part may be lent out. For convenience assume that the Federal Reserve ratio is set at 20 percent for all kinds of deposits in all kinds of banks. Then, if a bank receives a $1000 deposit, it deposits the $1000 at the Federal Reserve bank, thus increasing its reserves by $1000. It would seem that, with only 20 percent required in reserve, the new reserve of $1000 would permit the bank to make new loans totaling $4000 and thereby create $4000 in new money. Its new reserves of $1000 would be 20 percent of the original $1000 deposit and the $4000 in new deposits created by the loans. It might thus appear that a single bank could expand the money supply by a multiple of each new deposit it receives.

This is not the case, however. Something called adverse clearing balances prevents this. Assume that recipients of the $4000 in new loans write checks, totaling $4000, drawn on their newly created demand deposits. Now, assume (for simplicity of analysis) that these checks are all deposited with another bank. This second bank will immediately deposit these checks in the account it maintains at the Federal Reserve bank, which increases the reserves of the second bank by $4000 but simultaneously charges these checks against the reserve account of the original bank. This reduces the original bank's reserves by $4000.

The Federal Reserve bank then sends the checks back to the original bank on which they are drawn. The bank reduced by $4000 the demand deposits of the writers of the checks. Thus the bank finds its reserves reduced by $4000 and its demand deposits reduced by $4000. Because it had reserves equal to 20 percent of its demand deposits and because it is required to maintain this ratio of reserves to demand deposits, it can afford to lose only 20 percent as much in reserves as it loses in demand deposits.

When the bank lost $4000 in demand deposits, this permitted it to lose only $800 (20 percent of $4000) in reserves. Thus it had lost $3200 in reserves that it could not afford to lose. Obviously it overextended its loans by $3200. If the bank had lent only $800 instead of $4000, it would not have experienced this difficulty.

To avoid these adverse clearing balances with the Federal Reserve bank, a bank must restrict its loans to its excess reserves. When the bank received its new

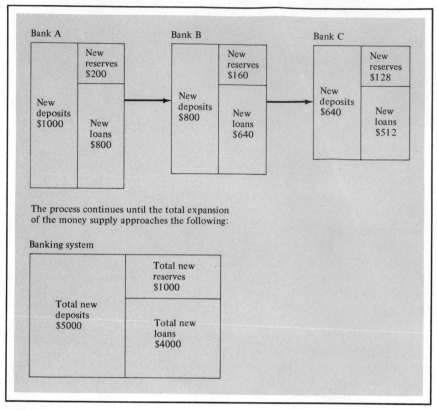

Figure 33.3 How the money multiplier works (with Federal Reserve ratio of 20 percent).

deposit of $1000, it was required to hold only $200 of it in reserves. This means it had excess reserves of $800 (the original $1000 it received minus the $200 it must hold as reserves). Thus it can be conclude that if a single bank received a new $1000 deposit, it must keep $200 in reserve but can lend out $800. It lends money by giving its customers a new demand deposit of $800, thus creating money. Yet a single bank may reasonably claim it adds nothing to the money supply. When the customer actually uses the loan, he or she draws his or her deposit down to zero, while the bank merely pays out the $800 in cash. It is when the whole banking system is considered that a new deposit will generally lead to a multiple expansion of the money supply. How this expansion works can be seen in Figure 33.3 and in Table 33.4.

When the $800 loan from Bank A (Figure 33.3) is spent, it becomes new deposits in Bank B, which are the basis for new reserves of $160 and new loans of $640. In the case of the whole banking system, the process will continue until all of the original new deposit ($1000) becomes required reserves in various banks. Because the new required reserves are then $1000 (or 20 percent of all new deposits), the new loans are $4000 (or 80 percent of all new deposits). Based on an initial new deposit of $1000 in money, the banking system has thus created a total

Table 33.4   HOW THE MONEY MULTIPLIER WORKS

1. Assume an initial increase in deposits of $1000.
2. Assume a required federal Reserve ratio of 20 percent.
3. Assume that banks are always fully loaned out.

Bank	Increase in loans	Increase in deposits (or money supply)	Increase in reserves (required)
Bank A	$800	$1000	$200
Bank B	640	800	160
Bank C	512	640	128
Bank D	410	512	102
Bank E	328	410	82
Bank F	262	328	66
...	...	262	...
...	...	...	...
...	...	...	...
...	...	...	...
...	...	...	...
All banks	$4000	$5000	$1000

increase in deposits of $5000 (assumed to be demand deposits and therefore counted as money).

For our analysis we use the concept of the money multiplier, which is analogous to, but not to be confused with, the investment multiplier of income determination. The money multiplier may be defined as follows:

$$\text{money multiplier} = \frac{\text{total increase in deposits}}{\text{initial new deposit}} \qquad (1)$$

A simple formula for deriving the money multiplier is

$$\text{multiplier} = \frac{1}{\text{required Federal Reserve ratio}} \qquad (2)$$

Assuming that each banker has to keep 20 percent of his or her deposit liabilities in the form of cash, the money supply can be expanded to five times the amount of cash that the banking system holds:

$$\text{multiplier} = \frac{1}{0.20} = 5 \qquad (3)$$

Thus the initial new deposit of $1000 is multiplied by 5 to get a $5000 total increase in deposits (or in the money supply).

The analysis does not yet take into account several kinds of leakage that may occur in varying degrees over time. The assumption that banks are always fully loaned up is not consistent with the facts. There are often some excess reserves— that is, reserves above the legal requirement. The volume of expansion of deposits therefore depends on the degree to which bankers decide to make the maximum loans on their reserves. It also depends on the degree to which businesspeople wish to accept these loans. Finally, the whole process takes time, and only a certain amount of the predicted expansion will occur in any given period. It is nevertheless generally true that banks lend in some multiple of their reserves and that total expansion of the money supply will be greater, the smaller the required Federal Reserve ratio.

REFERENCES

Crotty, James. "Marx, Keynes and Minsky on the Instability of the Capitalist Growth Process." In *Marx, Schumpeter and Keynes.* Edited by Suzanne Heldurn and David Bramhall. Armonk, N.Y.: M. E. Sharpe, 1986, pp. 297–327.

———. "The Role of Money and Finance in Marx's Crisis Theory." In *The Imperiled Economy.* Book 1. Edited by Robert Cherry, et al. New York: Monthly Review Press, 1987.

Reuss, Henry. "A Private Club for Public Policy," *The Nation* (Oct. 16, 1976), pp. 370–372.

Chapter
34

Government: Welfare or Warfare?

In American society the government exerts an enormous influence on the economy, although the government is itself dominated to a large extent by economic power. The U.S. government has always affected the economy in many ways, from the inflationary spending of the Revolutionary War period through the deficit financing of the 1930s. In recent years, however, an essentially new relationship has emerged. Since 1941 the government has become, by far, the largest single source of demand. The newly emerged economic structure is dominated not only by large private firms but also by pervasive governmental activity, mostly centered around military production. It follows that the actions of the U.S. government now form an integral part of the American economy.

GOVERNMENT AND THE EARLY ECONOMY

The history of U.S. governmental activity is a record of the conflicts between the interests of sectors, regions, and groups, and most often these interests have been economic. As James Madison said:

> But the most common and the most durable source of faction has been the various and unequal distribution of property. Those who hold and those who are without property have ever formed distinct interests in society. Those who are creditors, and those who are debtors, fall under a like discrimination. A landed interest, a manufacturing interest, a mercantile interest, a moneyed interest, with many lesser interests, grow up of necessity in civilized nations, and divide them into different classes, actuated by different sentiments and

views. The regulation of these various and interfering interests forms the task of modern legislation. (Madison, p. 3)

From the Revolutionary War through the nineteenth century, the government was concerned primarily with the protection of property, the promotion of business, and the establishment of the necessary institutional framework for a commercial, industrial economy.

An important function of the government in the eighteenth and nineteenth centuries was the creation of efficient transportation networks, a primary prerequisite for the growth of a commercial, private enterprise system. For example, in 1838 state governments borrowed $60 million to spend on canals, $43 million to spend on railroads, and $7 million to spend on roads. Although the market was potentially national in size, a huge investment in transportation was necessary before regional markets could be united. Between 1815 and 1860, federal and state governments made 73 percent of the total investment in canal development, and governments were large suppliers of capital funds for railway construction before the Civil War.

After the Civil War, the railroad boom became even more important to the American economy. Between 1865 and 1914, railroad mileage increased from about 37,000 to almost 253,000 miles. During this period, the federal government became a major source of railroad financing. Earlier, between 1850 and 1871, the U.S. Congress had given away 175,350,000 acres of choice public lands to the railroads—a gift to private enterprise of taxpayers' property worth about $489 million (Fite and Reese, p. 330). In addition, in the same period, the government had granted the railroads $65 million in special low-cost credit.

Thus, throughout the period when American capitalism was developing into an industrial giant, the government was instrumental in providing the institutional and economic framework in which profitable business could be conducted. Private enterprise profited handsomely as taxpayers subsidized many of the business and industrial ventures that helped provide these necessities.

FISCAL POLICY

The economic role of government that most directly influences the level of output, income, and employment is its taxing and spending of money, or fiscal policy. The effects of fiscal policy on output, income, and employment were ignored until the depression of the 1930s. The prevailing economic philosophy was that taxes should be used only to finance necessary government expenditures. It was thought to be an unsound financial practice for governments to borrow money. If a balanced budget, in which expenditures equaled taxes, could not be achieved, it was thought to be preferable to have taxes exceed expenditures so that any debts incurred in the past could be retired. Only the Great Depression and the World War II experiences forced a change in this policy. Since that time the view has spread that government spending and taxation should help stabilize the economy.

Federal government spending in the United States in 1929 was only 1 percent of GNP. In the period 1930–1940, as the New Deal responded to the Depression, federal government spending increased to 4 percent of GNP. With World War II government spending rose to the incredible height of 42 percent of GNP in 1944. After the war it fell somewhat, but it bounced up again to 18 percent of GNP in the Korean War, went up to 20 percent in the Vietnam War, and has averaged 24 percent in the 1980s.

Under President Reagan, two-thirds of government spending on goods and services was for military purposes. In addition to federal spending for goods and services (now only 8 percent of GNP), the federal government also made transfer payments amounting to 16 percent of GNP. These transfer payments among citizens included huge subsidies to big business and large farms, small welfare payments, unemployment compensation to individuals, payments of interest on government bonds to rich bondholders, and pension payments to people who had paid Social Security taxes.

There is also state and local spending, which rose from 7 percent of GNP in the 1950s to 13 percent of GNP in the 1980s.

GOVERNMENT AND AGGREGATE DEMAND

Figure 34.1 depicts the flows of money to and from government to households and businesses. The personal income tax takes money away from households, reducing demand. The corporate profit tax takes money away from business, reducing demand. Contributions to Social Security are taken from workers before any income goes to households, reducing demand. The sales tax also reduces the flow of money and demand going to business.

On the other hand, there is an enormous flow of demand from government to business for the purchase of goods and services. Finally, there is a large flow of transfer payments, both to households and businesses; these include subsidies, Social Security payments, and—very important quantitatively—interest payments on the national debt.

When spending is greater than taxes, there is a government deficit, which means a net flow from government to households and business, increasing demand. When taxes are greater than spending, there is a government surplus, which means a net flow from households and business to government, reducing demand.

THREE VIEWS OF DISCRETIONARY FISCAL POLICIES

Discretionary fiscal policy means current, conscious decisions by government to change spending or taxation levels (we shall later examine so-called automatic, or built-in, spending and tax policies). There are three

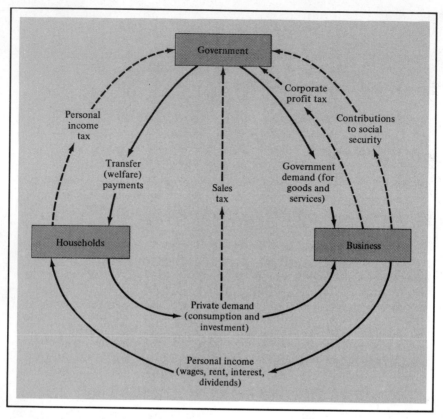

Figure 34.1 Circular flow of income, excluding exports and imports (net exports would appear as an additional demand for products).

different policy views of what government discretionary fiscal policy ought to be.

The most conservative economists, such as Adam Smith or the contemporary American economist Milton Friedman, argue that no discretionary fiscal measures are needed. The government should stay out of the economy. Friedman agrees with Adam Smith that the less government the better. He attributes many of our economic problems to too much interference with private enterprise, which would otherwise automatically adjust to all situations in a near-perfect manner. To the extent that conservatives admit any need for government policy, they say that only monetary measures are necessary. Conservatives favor measures affecting the money supply (via interest rates, for example) rather than any fiscal measures of spending or taxation because they feel that monetary measures do not directly interfere with business. They view an adequate money supply merely as one of the prerequisites for a private enterprise economy. Other prerequisites that they believe government should provide include police and armies to maintain "law and order," primarily to protect private property from its domestic and foreign enemies.

Contrary to the liberal view that government spending can employ workers and increase demand, Milton Friedman contends:

> Government spending does not increase employment. First, government spending has increased for the last 25 years, but so has unemployment. Two, government spending just takes money from private people who would have spent it, so there is no net increase in demand for labor. (Speech on CBS-TV)

As to his first point, the 1930s witnessed vast unemployment with relatively little government spending. Today, government spending is many times higher, but unemployment is much lower. As to the second point, it is shown below that money for spending may be borrowed from the rich (who might not spend it) or it may simply be printed.

The second, the liberal view is that of such economists as John M. Keynes or the contemporary American economist Paul Samuelson. Liberals admit that capitalism has real problems, such as general unemployment and inflation. Liberal Keynesians argue that adequate government measures of increased or decreased taxation are necessary to correct these problems. Franklin Delano Roosevelt argued that every American has the "right to a useful and remunerative job in the industries or shops or farms or mines of the Nation" (State of Union address, 1944). Since Roosevelt, all liberals have favored full employment policies.

Liberal Keynesian economists have always suggested that unemployment can be cured by stimulating demand. Demand may be increased directly by government spending or, indirectly, by reduction of taxes. Lower taxes will increase consumer and investor income and spending. Keynesian economists have also argued that inflation may be cured by lowering demand. Demand may be lowered directly by less government spending or indirectly by higher taxes, which will reduce consumer and investor spending.

Liberals used to maintain that spending and taxation measures can always successfully bring about full employment with stable prices; however, some of them now define full employment as "only" 4 or 5 percent unemployment and stable prices as "only" 2 or 3 percent inflation per year. Others, including Samuelson, frankly admit that establishment economists have not developed a method for ending inflation and maintaining full employment at the same time: "Experts do not yet know . . . an incomes policy that will permit us to have simultaneously . . . full employment and price stability" (Samuelson, p. 823).

The radical view is expressed by Karl Marx or the contemporary American economist Paul Sweezy. Radicals argue that problems like periodic unemployment are deeply rooted in the capitalist system and cannot be cured by an amount of monetary or fiscal measures. They contend that the U.S. economy has reached full employment only during major wars. In normal peacetime years, they believe unemployment and/or inflation is the usual state of capitalism. They argue that the necessary drastic fiscal measures cannot be taken by capitalist governments because powerful vested interests oppose each such step aside from military spending.

PROBLEMS WITH KEYNESIAN FISCAL POLICY

Let us consider the liberal Keynesian argument that government intervention can prevent large-scale unemployment or runaway inflation. The basic fiscal formula, to which may be added certain monetary measures, is to raise taxes and lower spending during inflations, while lowering taxes and raising spending during depressions. There are, however, administrative, political, and economic problems with this formula.

Administrative Problems

Before an intelligent fiscal policy can be carried out, one must know the economic situation, decide what to do, and get it done—but all that takes time. First, information must be gathered and someone—usually economists—must decide if a change is temporary or permanent. Second, before spending, say, for a new bridge, engineers must design the bridge. Third, Congress must decide exactly what spending will be done or taxes cut. Fourth, the president must agree. Fifth, the actual spending must be done; but if the government builds a dam, it may take five years for all the spending to occur. Thus there are many time lags between an economic change and implementation of a new fiscal policy. Often, by the time the new policy takes effect, the economic situation is totally different, so that the policy has an opposite and detrimental effect.

Political Problems

The problem remains: Which spending? Whose taxes? Suppose we agree to spend the large amounts of money necessary to maintain full employment. Many outlets that would be socially beneficial conflict with the vested interests of large corporations or wealthy individuals. Larger welfare payments tend to raise the wage level; government investment in industrial ventures or in public utilities tends to erode monopolistic privileges. The issue is the political constraints to economic policies.

In the years immediately after World War II, the problem was to spend $15–20 billion annually. This might have been a very agonizing social and political issue except for the advent of the Cold War.

Dollars for Cold War armaments did not violate any vested interests. Military spending is considered an ideal antidepression policy by big business for three reasons. First, such expenditures have the same short-run effect on employment and profits as would expenditures on more socially useful projects. Second, military spending means big and stable profits, whereas welfare spending may shift income from rich taxpayers to poor recipients. Third, the long-run effect is even more favorable because no new productive equipment is created to compete with existing facilities. During the past 25 years, the main change has been that the necessary addition to the income stream has risen to at least $100–200 billion a year. If it were politically possible, the whole amount could be spent on useful public commodities, such as housing or health or education, rather than on military waste. These useful types of public spending are not politically feasible in such large amounts, however, as long as the U.S. government is dominated by big business.

One popular cure for depression is reduction of taxes to allow more money to flow into private spending. Given the interests dominating the U.S. government, however, tax cuts always end up benefiting mainly the rich and the corporations. Even during the liberal Kennedy administration, the taxes of the poor were reduced very little and those of the rich very much, resulting in a redistribution of income to the members of the wealthy class. In fact, on the excuse of stimulating investment, corporate income taxes have declined from 40 percent of net federal revenues in 1945 to only 11 percent in 1982. Especially during a depression, however, the wealthy will not spend their increased income. The consumption of the wealthy remains at adequate levels even during a depression, and they have no desire to invest in the face of probable losses. Hence the political restriction as to who gets the tax cuts makes this policy economically ineffective.

Similarly, many economists (and even many businesspeople) may see a need for more and more vast government spending under capitalism. The primary political question, however, is where this spending is to be directed, for it is here that vested interests come into play. Even small vital expenditures on medical care have sometimes been defeated by the American Medical Association. Powerful vested interests oppose almost every item in the civilian budget as soon as expansion proceeds beyond the necessary minimum. What interests must be defeated to have the necessary spending to fill a $200–300 billion deficiency in demand? Constructive projects such as a Missouri Valley Authority could develop dams, irrigation, and cheap power, but these have been fought tooth and nail by the private power interests (and, indeed, might lower private investment by direct competition). Government dollars could be usefully devoted to the construction of large-scale public housing, but private contractors have long kept such programs to a minimum.

Other kinds of welfare spending—for example, on hospitals and schools—would be sound investments; however, the rich see these as subsidies to the poor for things that the rich can buy for themselves out of their own pockets. Proposals to increase unemployment compensation or to lower taxes paid by the poor encounter even greater resistance because they would transfer income from the rich to the poor. Likewise, billions could usefully be spent in aid and loans to the less-developed world, where poverty and human suffering are so widespread. That, however, could be instituted only over the bodies of hundreds of members of Congress, who well represent the wishes of their self-interested constituents and have no concept of the long-run gain to world trade and world peace. If any of these measures are to some extent allowed, it is only after a long political fight and certainly not promptly enough to head off a developing depression.

We could list, one by one, all the areas in which powerful vested interests stand in opposition to the satisfaction of some of the nation's most basic social needs. These interests will not tolerate government competition with private enterprise, measures that undermine the privileges of the wealthy, or policies that significantly alter the relative distribution of income. They therefore tend to oppose all government nonmilitary spending—except direct business subsidies. The only major exception to this generalization is government spending on highways, which is actively promoted by the largest and most lucrative single industry after defense—the automobile producers.

MILITARY SPENDING VERSUS WELFARE SPENDING

From all of the facts just given, we conclude that welfare or constructive spending on a large scale is opposed by too many special interests to be politically feasible. Our hypothesis is that only large-scale military spending brought the United States out of the Great Depression of the 1930s, and only large-scale military spending has kept the United States out of another major depression. This view is contrary to those writers who believe it would be easy to change production from guns to plows. Certainly, it is technically possible to divert money from bombs to cleaning up rivers, from tanks to education, or from military to civilian aircraft.

The political reality is that vested interests oppose each of these programs with violent rhetoric and successful political pressure. Thus Congress does not even talk about building government factories for peaceful use—in fact, the Eisenhower administration sold profitable atomic energy plants to private capitalists for tiny sums of money. Presidents Nixon and Ford, both of whom were supported primarily by big business, vetoed a large number of liberal Keynesian bills to stimulate employment by more public jobs or by more spending for health, education, or welfare. President Carter promised in his 1976 campaign some Keynesian-type spending to bring the economy to full employment. Yet he also had many ties to business and had many conservative economic advisors. Therefore, Carter did not launch constructive projects of the magnitude needed to approach full employment but continued to allow a relatively high level of unemployment. Carter kept nonmilitary spending to a constant or declining amount in terms of purchasing power, restricting some existing programs, and prohibiting new programs in national health care, public housing, or public energy production (instead of these he used subsidies to business to promote energy production). On the other hand, Carter, in spite of his explicit promise to cut military spending, raised military spending by a large amount.

We have seen that political constraints make military spending the only allowable solution to unemployment. The political nature of the problem has become even more apparent in the inflationary situation of the 1970s and 1980s. The Korean and Vietnam wars caused so much government demand for military supplies that inflation resulted, with prices rising especially in 1950–1953 and 1967–1981. To cure inflation the simple Keynesian prescription is to increase taxes and reduce spending.

But whose taxes and which spending? Major increases in taxes on the wealthy are not easily passed by our government. And there is not that much room for further taxes on the poor and the middle class without provoking rising discontent. So it is easier to reduce government spending. But not military spending; politicians and spokespersons for industry and the military continue to convince the nation that these are absolutely necessary. Thus welfare spending is cut. Already a tiny percentage of the American government budget, welfare has nevertheless been cut further as a tool to fight inflation. Hence the burden of inflation has fallen on the common man and woman in the forms of rising prices, rising taxes, and falling welfare spending all at the same time. The question of social and political priorities often boils down to a conflict between the genuine needs of the majority versus the desires of the tiny minority that possesses immense economic and political power. The majority of Americans need more education, health, and welfare, but a powerful minority favors military spending.

ECONOMIC CONSTRAINTS ON FISCAL POLICY

In the next chapter we shall see that conservative presidents and liberal presidents end up with remarkably similar fiscal performances in most periods. Why does this happen? Not only are there administrative and political constraints on fiscal policy, but there are also objective economic constraints—not just on Keynesian fiscal policy, but on any fiscal policy. These economic constraints are given by the structure of capitalism. The three major constraints are limits on the redistribution of income, competition with private enterprise, and the incompatibility of anti-unemployment and anti-inflation policies.

First, if drastic redistribution of income toward equality were to be seriously legislated by a strongly liberal or mildly radical government, then capitalists might refuse to invest. This sabotage of the economy has not occurred in the past with minor tax reforms or increased welfare spending (as in the 1930s or 1960s). But a really drastic redistribution policy might "lower business confidence" and make capitalists hoard or flee the country with their capital. This did occur, for example, with the socialist Allende government in Chile. Of course, capital needs places to go that are safer and/or give higher returns. Such places might be difficult to find for large amounts of capital fleeing redistribution policies in the United States (it can't all go to South Africa).

Second, if the U.S. government sponsored a successful public energy corporation, the lower prices would compete with present private energy corporations. These private energy corporations might then go on strike by not investing or fleeing overseas. As conservatives frequently and correctly point out, any peaceful constructive direct investment by government does compete with private capital. Therefore, enough government investment might cause an investment strike or capital flight. Of course, one remedy would be still more government investment—that, however, is the road to socialism.

The same constraint may apply to regulations on elite professionals or competition with elite professionals. If free national health care were instituted, doctors might get reasonable payments instead of outrageous monopoly revenues. Doctors might also flee, but where would they go? Every other industrialized country (except South Africa) already has free national health care—and how many doctors could fit into South Africa?

Finally, fiscal policies for higher employment may conflict with anti-inflation policies, since one requires higher demand and the other requires lower demand. A drastic enough rise in demand to cause full employment would also probably lead to much greater inflation. A drastic enough fall in demand to cause stable prices (zero inflation) would also probably cause much more unemployment. There is thus no simple fiscal cure to a situation of simultaneous unemployment and inflation.

We now turn from the fiscal policies and fiscal constraints to what has actually happened in U.S. government activity. We begin with the military sector and wartime fiscal policies. Peacetime performance is considered in the next chapter.

THE MILITARY ECONOMY

The U.S. Department of Defense runs the largest planned economy outside of the USSR. It spends more than the net income of all U.S. corporations. It has over 8,000 major and minor installations, owns 39 million acres of land, spends over $300 billion a year, uses 22,000 primary contractors and 100,000 subcontractors, and employs about 10 percent of the U.S. labor force in the armed forces and military production (see Melman).

How big is U.S. military spending? It certainly includes all Department of Defense spending, but it goes considerably beyond that. How far is controversial, but the most careful study to date (see Cypher) includes half of all "international affairs" spending, veterans benefits, atomic energy and space appropriations (all military related), and 75 percent of the interest on the public debt (since at least 75 percent of the debt was used to pay for wars). Other military activities, on which it is too difficult to obtain exact expense data, are major parts of the research and development budget, the CIA, and other intelligence agencies; also part of military costs are the deaths, wounds, and alienation of young Americans. For the five quantifiable items in military spending, Cypher adds up the grand total of $1.7 trillion from 1947 through 1971—enough to buy our entire gross national product for 1969 and 1970. Similarly, Department of Defense spending was listed at "only" $127 billion in 1980, but if we include the military items cited by Cypher, then it comes to $223 billion.

Yet this amount of direct military spending (even if it included the things that cannot be quantified) still underestimates the impact of military spending on the U.S. economy. There is a very large indirect or secondary effect on (1) additional consumer goods from the spending of those who receive military dollars and (2) additional investment in plant, equipment, and business inventories by military industries. Economists measure the secondary effects of military spending by the government multiplier (discussed in detail in the Appendix to this chapter), which measures the ratio of the total increase in all spending to every dollar of increase in government spending. Estimates of the multiplier from military spending range from about $1.85 to $3.50 of total spending for every dollar of military spending.

Over the whole 1947–1971 period, direct military spending averaged 13.2 percent of GNP (according to Cypher). Now if we are quite conservative and assume a multiplier of only 2, it is apparent that direct and indirect military spending accounted for the demand for 26.4 percent of GNP. This means that if military spending and its indirect effects had not been present in this whole period (and all other things had been the same) we would have had a depression greater than that of the 1930s—when unemployment was 24.3 percent. Of course, if the military multiplier is actually 3, then total demand for GNP would fall by 39.6 percent if we ended all military spending—always assuming we did nothing else. Actually, we have seen that the U.S. government might increase welfare spending a little, but it is not politically feasible on the scale required.

HOW MUCH PROFIT IN MILITARY CONTRACTS?

Why is big business normally happy with such a high level of military spending? On the aggregate level, we saw that it is used to protect U.S. investments abroad, to pull the economy out of recessions, and to prevent a major depression. There is yet an additional incentive for the individual defense contractor—the rate of profit is very high in military production and most of these profits go to a few very large firms. Almost all military contracts go to some 205 of the top 500 corporations, and just 100 of them get 85 percent of all military contracts.

There are some studies of military profits, but all of them understate the profit rates. In reporting to the government, the military firms overstate their costs—and since they operate in a cozy relation with the Pentagon, not under competition, they probably overstate costs more than most firms. Thus they allocate costs of other parts of their business to military contracts and add in all sorts of other unrelated costs—some have even tossed in the costs of call girls to influence government inspectors (called "entertainment" in their accounts). In addition, much of the profits can be hidden through the use of complex subcontracting procedures to subsidiaries, unauthorized use of government-owned property, and obtaining patents on research done for the government.

Still, a study by the General Accounting Office (GAO) of the U.S. government has definitely spelled out their high profit rates (discussed in Cypher, Chapter 5). First the GAO asked 81 large military contractors by questionnaire what their profit rates were for 1966 through 1969. The replies, which were limited by self-interest, still admitted an average profit rate of 24.8 percent—much higher than nonmilitary profits in the same industries. But spot checks showed that these profit rates were very much underreported, so the GAO did its own audit of the books of 146 main military contractors. The study found that the profit rate of these merchants of death was a fantastic 56.1 percent return on invested capital!

FISCAL POLICY IN WARS

The largest discretionary fiscal changes take place in wars. In the World War II, the U.S. government under Franklin Roosevelt spent 40 percent of the GNP to support the war. Yet it would have been very unpopular and harmful to the war effort to raise taxes by that much. Therefore, there was an enormous amount of borrowing, very high deficit spending, and a rapidly growing national debt. Naturally, there was full employment so long as the government spent so much money.

In the Korean War business cycle (1949–1954) military spending again was the dominant economic factor. In the expansion of 1949–1953 under Truman during the war, total federal spending grew at 4 percent per quarter. Yet taxes (or total receipts) grew by only 0.6 percent per quarter, since Truman did not want to be made unpopular by raising taxes. Therefore, in the wartime expansion, the deficit grew by over 3 percent per quarter and the national debt rose. Production and employment continued to rise as long as the war continued.

Similarly, under President Johnson, spending on the Vietnam war rose rapidly from about 1965 to 1968. There are no neat dates for the Vietnam War and it did not take up the entire 1961–1969 expansion, but it certainly prolonged that expansion. In the actual war years, total government spending rose very rapidly. To remain popular, however, Johnson did not raise taxes. Therefore there was more borrowing, the deficit rose, and the national debt increased rapidly.

To sum up, in all wartime expansions military spending rises enormously. Taxes go up much less rapidly. Therefore, deficit spending balloons and the national debt increases rapidly. The large government demand ensures that production and employment continue to rise until the war ends.

SUMMARY

In the nineteenth century, federal and state governments subsidized canals and railroads. Since the 1930s the U.S. government has tried to modify the business cycle by increased government spending and lower taxes in depressions. The government reduces spending and increases taxes at the peak of each expansion to prevent full employment (supposedly to fight inflation). Government spending in depressions has never been directed toward constructive projects—schools, hospitals, housing—on the massive scale required because of the political power of the capitalist class, which opposes these projects and desires military spending for greater profits.

Military spending took the United States out of the Great Depression and has prevented a major depression ever since. Constructive government spending tends to compete with private enterprise and to redistribute income from the rich to the poor. Military spending alone does not compete with private enterprise; it indirectly stimulates private consumption and investment and redistributes income from the poor to the rich (because of the very high profit rates paid to military producers). Very powerful economic interests are therefore against constructive or welfare spending but favor military spending. Although enough military spending can produce full employment, it seems a highly irrational economic system that can guarantee full employment only in this way—since it also implies high taxes, inflation, and death.

In addition to the administrative and political problems, the most important economic constraint on fiscal policy has been the simultaneous existence of high unemployment and high inflation.

APPENDIX

The Government Multiplier

The obvious objectives of government fiscal policy are to increase that net flow of demand during depressions by increasing spending and lowering taxes and to reduce the net flow of demand during inflation by reducing spending and raising taxes. Both the direct and the secondary effects of these policies are important. For example, in a depression it is hoped that increases in government spending will mean more income to businesses or individuals and that this, in turn, will lead to further increases in private consumption and investment.

The secondary effects of a government expenditure may be quantified in terms of the *government multiplier*, which is the ratio of increase in national income to an increase in government spending. The reader will recall that the investment multiplier was defined as the ratio of an increase in national income to an increase in private investment.

Let us make the very simple assumption that consumption reacts in a given ratio to an increase in income (while investment remains constant). Then every increase in income automatically leads to a certain increase in consumption spending. This spending means a further, though smaller, increase in income, some of which will be spent for a second round of consumption, and so forth.

The formal apparatus for studying the government multiplier is exactly the same as that for the investment multiplier (as discussed in Chapter 32). It may help to review a numerical example in which we assume (1) a certain increase in government spending with a given marginal propensity to consume and (2) that the increase in government spending takes place without any change in tax receipts. Under these simple assumptions, the formula for the government multiplier is

$$\frac{1}{MPS}$$

or

$$\frac{1}{1 - MPC}$$

Remember that MPS stands for marginal propensity to save and MPC stands for marginal propensity to consume. Since income is divided into savings and consumption, MPS equals $1 - MPC$. And MPC is defined as the ratio of an increase in consumption to an increase in income. Thus in Table 34.1, where MPC is assumed to be 80 percent, the government multiplier is $1/(1 - 0.8) = 1/0.2 = 5$, so that the national income increases by $5000.

Suppose, in different economic conditions, that only half of additional income is consumed and fully half is saved. Then only half of new government spending will be respent for consumption. The multiplier in this case is $1/(1 - 0.5) = 1/0.5 = 2$. That is, the total additional consumption will just equal the additional government spending, so the total increase in income is just twice the initial increase in income received from the government. Thus if the government spends an extra $1 billion, a multiplier of 2 says that a total increase of $2 billion in national income will be generated, of which $1 billion will be the secondary consumer spending.

For similar reasons, if MPC rises to two-thirds, the government multiplier rises to 3. If, however, the marginal propensity to consume is zero, then the multiplier is 1. In this case there are no secondary effects because all of the first round of spending is saved. In the other extreme case, if MPC moves toward 1, the multiplier moves toward infinity—that is, the secondary effects are infinite because all income is immediately respent for consumption.

Of course, the government multiplier ratio is an artificial concept because it does not take into account all the changing factors and complications involved. The

Table 34.1   HOW THE GOVERNMENT MULTIPLIER WORKS

Increase in government spending[a]	Increase in consumption[b]	Increase in national income	Increase in saving
$1000		$1000	
0	$800	800	$200
0	640	640	160
0	512	512	128
0	410	410	102
0	328	328	82
___	___	___	___
___	___	___	___
___	___	___	___
___	___	___	___
$1000	$4000	$5000	$1000

[a] Private investment remains constant. [b] MPC = 80%.

first qualification is the fact that the second, third, and fourth rounds of spending do not occur instantaneously; it takes time before income is respent for consumption. Long or varying lags make it much more difficult to speak of an exact multiplier. Second, the multiplier explained here assumes that investment is a given constant and is not affected by changes in income. As has been seen in earlier chapters, however, there is probably a close connection between investment and the change in income. If this is so, changes in government spending, as well as the secondary changes in consumer spending, may directly affect investment. However, government spending may have negative psychological effects on investment if it is thought to take away funds by taxation or to compete by means of cheaper products. At any rate, government spending is likely to have some direct or indirect effect on investment, and as a result investment may not legitimately be considered a constant in this regard.

The third major set of qualifications to the government multiplier arises from the fact that MPC does not remain constant, yet it is the very rock on which the multiplier theory is founded. It does not remain constant because, for one thing, consumption is actually influenced by many factors other than income. The marginal consumption ratio also varies because there are different leakages from the process at different times. For example, the effect of an increase in government spending on national income may be partly siphoned off by the levy of higher taxes or merely by automatic movements into higher tax brackets. Furthermore, it may happen that increased spending for imports removes some portion of income from the domestic multiplier process. For all of these reasons, MPC may change too often for any accurate prediction of the multiplier beyond a short period of only one or two rounds of the process.

The fourth and last qualification has to do with how the government spending is financed. If the government takes back through taxation the same amount that it spends, then there is no net addition to consumer spending; only the initial government spending is added to the economy, and the multiplier will be only 1. The national income will increase by the amount of the increase in government spending.

If increased government spending is financed by sale of government bonds, or deficit spending, the effect on the private economy depends on how the bondholders would have used the money had they not lent it to the government. If they had spent it all for consumption or investment anyway, then there would have been no net stimulation to the private economy. If they had spent only a small percentage of it (which is often the case), then the government spending would have a very powerful net effect on the private economy.

Finally, the most inflationary method of financing government spending is to print new money because this withdraws nothing from the private sector either by taxation or borrowing. In a deep depression, a government may finance expenditures by printing money; at full employment, it will attempt to use only taxation; and with a small degree of unemployment, it may use borrowing.

SUMMARY

Government spending has both direct and indirect effects. The indirect effects occur through the additional consumer and investment spending the government stimulates. These indirect effects are called multiplier effects. The multiplier measures the total change in demand resulting from a change in direct government spending. Economists estimate it with the formula, multiplier = 1/MPS, but this formula is very rough and inaccurate because it leaves out many factors.

REFERENCES

Madison, James. *The Federalist*, Number 10, 1787.

Fite, G. C., and J. E. Reese. *An Economic History of the United States*, 2d ed. Boston: Houghton-Mifflin, 1965.

Friedman, Milton. Speech on CBS-TV on January 8, 1982.

Roosevelt, Franklin. State of the Union Address to U.S. Congress, January 11, 1944.

Samuelson, Paul. *Economics*, 9th ed. New York: McGraw-Hill, 1973.

Melman, Seymour. *Pentagon Capitalism.* New York: McGraw Hill, 1970.

Cypher, James. *Military Expenditures and the Performance of the Post-War Economy, 1947–1971.* Ph.D. dissertation. University of California, Riverside, 1972.

Chapter
35

Government Performance and Current Problems

The last chapter investigated discretionary fiscal policy and its constraints, as well as the resulting military expansion and discretionary fiscal policy in wars. This chapter turns to so-called automatic fiscal policy, the fiscal performance of the government in peacetime, and the theories and actions of the Reagan and Bush years.

AUTOMATIC FISCAL POLICY

Excessive or deficient demand can be combated in two ways—with *automatic* fiscal devices and with *discretionary* fiscal policies. Automatic fiscal policy is built into the present structure of governmental taxing and spending to react automatically to inflation or depression. Discretionary fiscal policies are changes in the fiscal structure made by current and conscious government decisions. Except for war periods, the government has placed considerable reliance on automatic fiscal measures. The fiscal structure is supposed automatically to expand net government demand in depressions and to decrease it in inflations. An automatic stabilizer is a government device built into the fiscal system that automatically increases or decreases government flows to or from the rest of the economy in response to changes in economic conditions.

In a depression, when the GNP tends to drop, the stabilizers should automatically increase money flows to businesses and households and/or decrease money flows from businesses and households to the government. This will prevent disposable personal income from dropping as rapidly as otherwise, and thus investment and consumption expenditures can be maintained at a higher level. Similarly, in an inflation, the automatic stabilizers are supposed to decrease the amount given and increase the amount taken away from business and households, thus decreasing the total amount of consumer and investor spending. In either case the net changes in government flows should have a multiple effect through the indirect respending of funds by consumers.

Now what are the magic devices by which the government is supposed to keep the economy automatically stable? On the spending side of the ledger, the government makes many types of welfare payments that automatically increase in depressions and automatically decrease in expansions. For example, as full employment is approached, there will be very little unemployment compensation; in a depression, however, with growing unemployment, this may become a significant source of buying power. Similarly, many subsidies for business and farming automatically decline in prosperity and rise in depression.

On the taxation side, the total amounts of federal income tax collected usually decline in most recessions faster than personal income declines. So, after income taxes, people are left with a higher percentage of their income to spend in recessions than in expansions. In recessions, individuals enter a lower tax bracket, so they automatically pay a lower rate. Thus, taxes decline not only absolutely, but as a percentage of income in each recession.

PEACETIME FISCAL PERFORMANCE

Table 35.1 shows the fiscal performance of the U.S. government in the five peacetime cycles from 1954 to 1982 (excluding the Vietnam War cycle of 1962–1969). Of course, military spending played a major role, but it was not dominant as it was in the war periods.

This table reveals that in business expansions government spending grows quite slowly, at an average of only 0.5 percent per quarter. Spending grows slowly partly because of the effect of the automatic stabilizers— that is, less need for unemployment compensation and so forth. Taxes (including all federal receipts of fees and so forth) grow much faster, at a rate of 1.6 percent per quarter on the average for these five cycle expansions. Taxes grow rapidly because income taxes automatically grow with income. In fact, since the tax system is progressive, people go into higher brackets, so the percentage of taxes out of income rises.

In the expansion, as taxes grow faster than spending, the deficit will decline. In fact, the deficit declined at an average 1.1 percent per quarter in these five peacetime expansions. The decline of the deficit does not seem to be effected very much, if at all, by the fiscal opinions of the political party in power. The effect of the decline in deficit spending—which means less net outflow of cash from government to business and households—is less and less stimulation of the demand for goods and services.

Table 35.1   FEDERAL SPENDING, TAXES, AND DEFICITS[a]
(5 Cycles, 1954–1982, Excluding Vietnam Cycle of 1962–1969)

A. Expansions

Expansion dates	President	Spending growth rate	Tax growth rate	Deficit growth rate
1954–57	Eisenhower	0.3	1.3	−1.0
1958–60	Eisenhower	0.1	2.4	−2.3
1970–73	Nixon	0.4	1.4	−1.0
1975–79	Carter	0.9	1.2	−0.3
1980–81	Reagan	0.8	1.7	−0.9
Average		0.5	1.6	−1.1

B. Contractions

Contraction dates	President	Spending growth rate	Tax growth rate	Deficit growth rate
1957–58	Eisenhower	3.2	−3.2	6.3
1960–61	Kennedy	1.9	−0.8	2.7
1973–75	Ford	2.9	−1.0	3.9
1979–80	Carter	3.0	−0.9	4.2
1981–82	Reagan	2.1	−2.0	4.0
Average		2.6	−1.6	4.2

Source: U.S. Department of Commerce, Handbook of Cyclical Indicators (Washington, D.C.: GPO, 1984).

[a] All data are in real terms, deflated for inflation. "Taxes" include all receipts, such as fees.

The contrary scenario is usually found in business contractions. In every recession or depression, the U.S. government is forced to spend more money for unemployment compensation, farm and business subsidies, and welfare. Thus, in the average contraction from 1954 to 1982 (excluding the Vietnam cycle), U.S. government spending rose rapidly by 2.6 percent a quarter. At the same time, falling personal and corporate income meant lower tax collections. Thus government revenue fell in the average contraction at 1.6 percent per quarter. Since spending was rising while taxes were falling, the deficit grew very rapidly (at 4.2 percent per quarter).

Notice that the deficit grew in every business contraction, with no regard for which party was in power—under the Republicans Eisenhower, Ford, and Reagan, as well as under the Democrats Carter and Kennedy. The growth of deficit spending meant more money flowing out of government than into government, so demand was stimulated by each of these administrations.

We can see this process pictorially for the average of the last three cycles (since the Vietnam War ended) in Figures 35.1 and 35.2. Figure 35.1 shows that spending rose in expansions, but rose somewhat faster in contractions. Taxes, on the other hand, rose rapidly in expansions but fell in contractions.

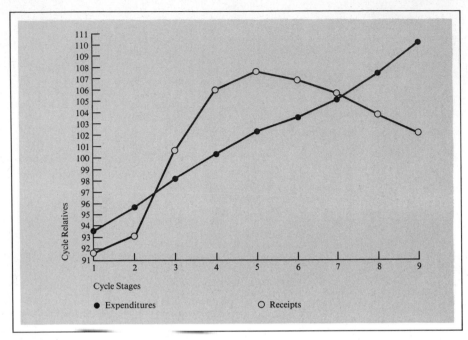

Figure 35.1 Federal spending and taxes, 3 cycles, 1970–1982. *Source:* U.S. Department of Commerce, Handbook of Cyclical Indicators (Washington, D.C.: GPO, 1984).

In Figure 35.2 we see that the federal deficit fell considerably in expansions, but rose very rapidly in business contractions. It is worth remembering that this behavior, which occurs in all peacetime business cycles (but not in wartime cycles), means that the economy is more and more stimulated by deficit spending in each contraction, but less and less in each expansion.

THE DECLINE AND FALL OF KEYNESIAN FISCAL POLICY

From 1945 to the late 1960s, Keynesian policies—in a very mild form— were dominant in the United States. Even the conservative President Nixon once said, "We are all Keynesians now." Keynesian policy meant stimulating demand to combat unemployment while reducing demand when inflation occurred.

By the early 1970s, however, the economy was subjected to rampant inflation as the result of a process that began with heavy government military spending in the Vietnam War. Yet the recessions of 1970 and 1974–1975 did not cure inflation. In spite of alarmingly high unemployment, prices continued to rise rapidly. There is no simple Keynesian answer to simultaneous unemployment and inflation because the government cannot

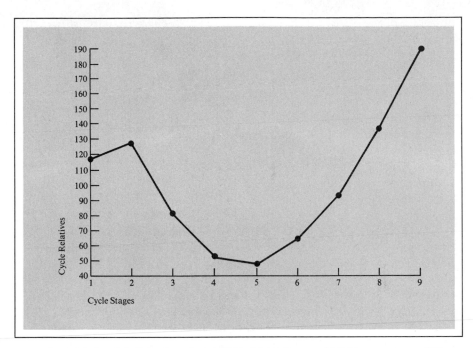

Figure 35.2 Federal deficit, 3 cycles, 1970–1982. *Source:* U.S. Department of Com merce, *Handbook of Cyclical Indicators* (Washington, D.C.: GPO, 1984).

both stimulate demand and reduce demand at the same time. Eventually, many economists and politicians declared that Keynesian economics had failed.

SUPPLY-SIDE FISCAL POLICY

The decline and fall of middle-of-the-road Keynesian economics opened the door to new doctrines on the right and left. In the late 1970s, radical economists, who advocated democratic socialism, grew in numbers. At the same time, supply-side economists found enormous support from big busi-ness and right-wing politicians. In fiscal policy, supply-side economics dominated government decisions in the early 1980s under President Rea-gan and Vice-President Bush.

Supply-side economics is based on reducing the costs of supply; tax cuts are seen as a magical weapon. Supply-siders agree with Keynesians that cutting taxes would reduce unemployment, but for different reasons. It is not necessary, they say, to stimulate consumer demand by cutting the taxes of the poor and middle class. It is only necessary to cut the taxes of the wealthy so that they will save more money. It is necessary to reduce the taxes paid by business so that business will have more incentive to invest. Thus, the agreement on tax cuts to solve unemployment is accompanied by disagreement over which class is to receive the largest tax cuts. Keynesians would weight their tax cuts toward the poor to increase demand. Supply-siders would weight their tax cuts toward the rich and the corporations to increase supply.

There is also profound disagreement between Keynesians and supply-siders over the impact of tax cuts on inflation. The Keynesians argue that tax cuts will increase demand and therefore increase inflation. The supply-siders argue, first, that tax cuts lead to harder work and more savings. Second, the savings are invested in new factories, which will reduce unemployment. Third, the new factories have higher productivity. Fourth, higher productivity means lower costs, which will reduce inflation. This is the supply-side argument by which tax cuts will reduce both unemployment and inflation, but there are problems with each step.

The first problem with the supply-side argument is that an increase in after-tax income does not necessarily result in an increase in saving. Some of the increased income will simply go for more luxury consumption for the rich. Second, Keynes's main insight was that greater income and greater saving do not automatically lead to more investment. If the profit outlook is pessimistic (for example, if there is insufficient demand), then the increased income may be saved but *not* invested. As Keynesians have emphasized, the excess of intended saving over intended investment may be used in many other ways. It may be hoarded in a Swiss bank account or it may be invested in some other country where the rate of return is higher. In 1981 and 1982 the large corporations and the wealthy received billions of dollars from the Reagan tax cuts. They did not use the money for new investment, however, because there was huge unused capacity and no demand for more goods.

Third, even if there is an investment in new plant and equipment, the new plant and equipment are not necessarily more productive than the old. Higher productivity depends on technological advance. Yet, increased tax breaks for the rich do not produce new inventions.

Fourth, even if there is more productivity and lower costs, corporations with monopoly power do not have to pass on the lower costs to the consumer. This would be true only under conditions of pure and perfect competition. All of the big corporations, however, have some degree of monopoly power. Therefore, there is very little price competition in the United States, and most lower costs are not passed on to consumers.

VOODOO ECONOMICS AND ITS RESULTS

When Ronald Reagan ran for president in 1980, he claimed that (1) he would greatly increase military spending for U.S. defense, (2) he would greatly decrease taxes to reduce the cost of supply, and (3) he would balance the budget. This was very crude supply-side economics and reflected an amazing faith in its promises. George Bush, running against

Reagan in the primaries, called this "voodoo economics." He explained that if the government made an enormous increase in military spending, while making an enormous cut in taxes, the result had to be an enormous deficit. Bush said that one could cut taxes, raise spending, and balance the budget only by the use of voodoo, or magical, economics.

The events of the eight years of the Reagan-Bush administration proved that candidate Bush was correct in calling Reagan's economic program voodoo economics. As we shall see, Reagan succeeded in pursuing a great increase in military spending. He also succeeded in enacting a tremendous decrease in taxes. According to supply-side economics, this tax cut was supposed to provide so much stimulation to the economy that total government revenue would actually increase. The higher revenue would be sufficient to fund the military spending. But the voodoo magic did not work. The combination of $100 billion more military spending and $100 billion less taxes naturally led to $200 billion of deficit spending.

Yet as vice-president, Bush switched his opinion and claimed that the supply-side incentive was enough, so that no new taxes would be necessary to reduce the deficit. As a candidate for president in 1988, Bush said, "Read my lips: no new taxes." If as president, Bush does not switch his view once more, the deficit will obviously persist.

The magnitude of the deficits and increase of debt in the Reagan-Bush administration must be stressed. There was a record increase of military spending, a record decrease of taxes, and, consequently, an historically unprecedented record level of deficit and debt in dollar amounts. The national debt was around $800 billion when Reagan took office. In his first speech on the economy as president he said: "Before we reach the day when we can reduce the debt ceiling, we may in spite of our best efforts see a national debt in excess of a trillion dollars. Now this is a figure that's literally beyond our comprehension" (quoted by Berry, p. 7). Yet by the end of fiscal 1988 (September 30) the national debt had gone beyond one trillion to reach $2.6 trillion—Reagan-Bush had tripled the debt.

HOW BUSH AND REAGAN PROVED KEYNES CORRECT AND FRIEDMAN WRONG

What has been the effect of the unprecedented deficit spending under Reagan and Bush? The most important effect is quite clear. The record deficits have been accompanied by a record long peacetime expansion of the economy. No other factor is large enough quantitatively to account for the unprecedented length of the economic expansion.

Just as Keynes argued, large enough deficit spending can pump enough money and effective demand into the economy to make up for the deficient private sector demand—so as to create a lengthy prosperity. Keynes talked about increasing effective demand by reducing taxes and increasing government demand. But Keynes never dreamed of increasing government spending by the amount that Reagan and Bush did. Nor did Keynes ever dream of a tax cut of the magnitude made by the Reagan-Bush adminis- tration. The Reagan-Bush experiment thus proved beyond a doubt the Keynesian proposition that larger government spending, a cut in taxes, and continuing deficits can give a continuing stimulation to the economy, sufficient to postpone a business contraction.

This deficit-created expansion also disproved the monetarist view of Milton Friedman that government deficit spending is self-defeating and cannot cause economic expansion. Friedman argues that massive deficits mean massive government borrowing. This government borrowing would result in higher interest rates and so crowd out private investment, which would decline by as much as deficit spending increased. Thus, expansion would not occur.

The Reagan-Bush experiment proved that monetarism was wrong. It may be that real interest rates (adjusted for inflation) have remained higher than otherwise would have been the case. But rising interest rates are normal in an expansion, so one cannot prove how much extra occurred. Moreover, regardless of interest rates, it is a fact that the high deficits were accompanied by expansion. So, if anything, Reagan and Bush proved that high interest rates could not prevent an expansion if there was sufficient effective demand. It is not the strongest peacetime expansion on record, but it is the longest.

A second conservative criticism of Keynes was that any deficit spending would lead to rapid inflation. Yet in the Reagan-Bush expansion, despite heavy deficit spending, inflation did not increase; rather, inflation declined. The Keynesian view is that, with heavy unemployment, deficit spending will increase output and employment but not cause inflation. Only when full employment is approached will deficits begin to cause inflation. The Reagan-Bush experiment, begun with very high unemployment, did not increase inflation so long as unemployment remained high. Thus, again the Keynesian view seems vindicated and the conservative view rejected.

A third conservative view was the supply-side argument that large tax rate cuts would so rejuvenate American enterprise that total government revenue would actually increase, so no deficit would result. On the contrary, massive tax cuts were followed by massive deficits. Supply-side assumptions were wrong and candidate Bush was right in calling it voodoo economics.

BUSH, REAGAN, AND INCOME INEQUALITY

The fact that deficit spending led to a lengthy expansion does not necessarily mean that high deficits and a rising debt are a good thing. One problem is that inequality in income distribution has increased in the Bush and Reagan period. In popular terms, the rich have gotten richer and the poor have gotten poorer. This effect has resulted from the type of government spend- ing, the type of tax cuts, and the rising national debt.

In the first place, the high national debt (tripled in the Reagan-Bush administration) has resulted in a crushing burden of interest payments. Ownership of Treasury bonds is highly concentrated among the rich; most treasury bonds are owned by less than 1 percent of all Americans (plus rich foreigners). The total interest, which must be paid by all tax payers, rose from $50 billion in 1980 to $151 billion in 1988—or 14 percent of the whole U.S. budget! Thus the Reagan-Bush national debt (which tripled in their administration) causes a huge giveaway from the poor and middle income groups to the super-rich.

In the second place, the very large tax cuts in the 1981 bill went primarily to the rich. An equal percentage was cut at all income levels—but a 20 percent cut across the board means a saving of $20,000 for someone with a $100,000 taxable income, yet only $2,000 if your taxable income was $10,000. Some of the poor pay no income tax, so they can have no savings. When all was finished, the personal income tax system had more loopholes and was less progressive than before. While on national television just before the tax cuts were voted, Representative Robert Michel, Republican leader in the House, told a conference of House Republicans to be sure to remind their wealthy constituents that the new tax law would be less progressive than the old.

At the same time, many kinds of corporate taxes were reduced to an enormous extent—even though 59 percent of Americans favor raising taxes on business and corporations (reported by Stacks, p. 23). Business deductions for depreciation were greatly increased. A very large additional tax cut was given to the oil companies. Finally, to help the very wealthy, huge reductions were made in all inheritance taxes. Even United Press International, the leading U.S. wire service, said in its summary, "Although the bill contains massive tax cuts for business and a host of tax breaks for special interests, there are only a handful of changes to help the average worker" (United Press International, August 5, 1981).

In 1986, a tax reform bill was passed. It did eliminate some loopholes; however, it also lowered the tax rate on wealthy taxpayers from 70 percent to 38 percent. This was the greatest decrease in progressivity in any one bill. In the same period, under Reagan and Bush, there was a considerable increase in the Social Security tax, which falls most heavily on the poor.

Finally, Reagan and Bush changed the whole composition of spending. Military spending to increase our power to kill rose from the range of $100 billion to $300 billion a year. This means even greater profits to a sector with extraordinary profit rates, as explored in the previous chapter. While wealthy owners of military corporations got richer, Reagan and Bush cut large amounts of spending to the middle class and the poor.

Under Reagan and Bush, large cuts were made in public service job programs for the unemployed, while the job-producing Young Adult Conservation Corps was eliminated. Other spending cuts tending to reduce employment were made in education programs, in aid to disadvantaged children, in many health programs, with less Medicaid payments to states, less Medicare for the elderly, lower Social Security benefits, less public housing (with increases in rents), fewer food stamps, less mothers' and infants' nutrition, cuts in school lunches, less day care, less aid to families with dependent children, cuts in the Economic Development Administration, cuts in the Appalachian Regional Administration, fewer urban development action grants, cuts in the Consumer Product Safety Commission, less mass-transit aid, less funds for water cleanup projects, less funds for more parks, less funds for arts and the humanities, less funds for legal services for the poor, less funds for the Postal Service, less funds for public broadcasting, and less funds for community action programs. There were no cuts in subsidies to big business.

It is worth noting that Reagan's specific proposals for 1981 and 1982 alone would—if all had been enacted—have cut *one-third* of all spending on children (reported by McDowell). These cuts included reductions in school funds for disadvantaged children, in supplementary funds for mothers and infants, in day care, in school breakfasts, in education for the handicapped, in youth employment funds, in Medicaid funds for children in poverty, in food stamps (50 percent of which go to children), and in aid to dependent children (800,000 children were dropped from the rolls in 1981). There are 11 million children living in poverty. Some 41 percent of black children are on welfare—which President Reagan said are "too many." President Reagan said he favors help to the "really needy." It would seem, however, that children on welfare were not really needy in his view.

In a poll in 1981, 60 percent of Americans answered that "Reagan represents the interests of business rather than the average American" (Stacks, p. 22). It is important to remember that the 1981 budget, which was hostile to the working class and supportive of capitalist interest, was written by the conservative Republican party. Nevertheless, the budget proposal of the liberal Democratic leadership had the same class bias, though to a little lesser degree. The Democrat's spending proposal made large cuts in all nonmilitary pro-working-class programs, though the cuts were smaller than those proposed by the Republicans. Even Tip O'Neill, Speaker of the House, admitted that the Democratic proposal "cut off the working class at the knees," but argued that the Republican proposal cut off the working class at the waist. The Democrat's tax proposal gave somewhat larger cuts to the middle class than the Republicans (indicating their somewhat different class support). Yet the Democrats' tax proposal also gave big business just as incredible a cut as did that of the Republicans. These giveaways to big business are clearly the only widely agreed upon program for stimulating the economy, which is completely understandable given the structural basis of capitalism. The liberal Democratic leadership not only went along with most of the Republican program, but had no alternative program.

In the second term, the Reagan-Bush budget proposals attacked women, children, and the poor as always, but also attacked the middle class. They proposed to eliminate altogether many programs for the poor and needy, including: the Legal Services Administration, community-development action grants, the Job Corps, and job training for welfare mothers. They would have cut money to many programs for the poor, including: Medicaid, Medicare, food stamps, and Aid to Families with Dependent Children. Yet they would also completely eliminate some middle-class programs, such as subsidies for farm-ownership loans, for Amtrak, and mass transit in several cities (e.g., Houston and Los Angeles), for air carriers, and for the Small Business Administration. Finally, Reagan-Bush wanted to cut funds to some important middle-class programs, such as financial aid to students in higher education, farm price supports, federal employee pensions, and veterans' medical care and pensions. In a poll in 1988, at the end of the second term of Reagan and Bush, 72 percent of Americans said the wealthy were better off under the Reagan-Bush administration, 54 percent said the poor were worse off, and 33 percent said the middle class were worse off (Associated Press, December 27, 1988).

As a result of the devastating cuts in spending for the middle-class, workers, and the poor, the increase in military profits to the rich, the very serious reduction in tax progressivity, and the huge payments of interest to the wealthy, Reagan and Bush significantly changed the distribution of income in favor of the wealthy. At the same time, the real hourly wage of all employees fell in the early 1980s and never got back to its peak level (it fell again in 1987). The lowest 40 percent of income recipients had less family income, even though more women took jobs. Poverty in 1988 still included 30 million people.

There were more homeless on the streets after Reagan and Bush ended many poverty and public housing programs. Yet on December 22, 1988, President Reagan alleged in an interview with David Brinkley on ABC-TV that "those people still prefer being out there on the grates or the lawn to going to one of those shelters." He added that there were plenty of jobs in Washington. Many neoclassical economists interpret all activity as the result of individual choice and preference, but this was too much even for many of them. (Note also that unemployment, a cause of homelessness, remained at 5 to 6 percent by official statistics, still quite high by historical comparison.)

SUMMARY

Automatic fiscal stabilizers are built in policies that increase demand in contractions by (1) lowering taxes or (2) raising government spending. The effect of these, plus discretionary policies, has been that in contractions (1) taxes fall, (2) spending rises, and (3) the deficit rises. In expansions, the opposite process occurs.

Keynesian policy could not cope with inflation-plus-unemployment in the 1970s. One substitute was supply-side economics, which promised that one could drastically lower taxes (while maintaining spending) and still balance the budget. But when Reagan and Bush used this approach, it resulted in enormous deficits.

The record deficit spending staved off a business contraction and resulted in a lengthy expansion. Another result, however, was a huge national debt, which meant very large interest payments to the wealthy. Coupled with extraordinary military profits, cuts in almost every important program for the middle-income groups and the poor, and tax breaks for the rich, the Reagan and Bush policies resulted in a large increase in income inequality.

SUGGESTED READINGS

A good book discussing some of the tendencies of this period is Bennett Harrison and Barry Bluestone, *The Great U-Turn* (New York: Basic Books, 1988).

REFERENCES

Berry, John M. "The Legacy of Reaganomics." *Washington Post National Weekly*, December 19–25, 1988.

Stacks, John. "America's Fretful Mood." *Time*, December 28, 1981.

United Press International. "Tax Cut Seen Having Small Initial Impact." *The Honolulu Advertiser*, August 5, 1981, p. 1.

McDowell, Charles. On "Washington Week in Review," a program of the Public Broadcasting System, February 20, 1982.

Associated Press International. "Majority Rates Reagan's Job Overall as Good, but Poor on Social Issues." *The Houston Post*, December 27, 1988.

Chapter
36

Unemployment and
Business Cycles

This chapter begins by discussing the conservative, liberal, and radical theories of cyclical unemployment, followed by a factual analysis of exactly what does happen in the business cycle.

CONSERVATIVE NEOCLASSICAL THEORIES

Until the 1930s, the main body of neoclassical economic theory did not try to explain, but rather tried to explain away, the business cycle. It was argued that the amount of general unemployment was exaggerated and that there were only partial and frictional fluctuations of production. Moreover, each depression was said to be the last. Indeed, in the 1920s they were said to be gone forever after more than 100 years of business cycle phenomena. In the 1960s, conservatives repeated that "the business cycle has disappeared." In the 1980s, conservative economists argued that all unemployment is voluntary.

These attitudes can be traced, in the main, to the general social outlook of economists, who supported the status quo. In part, however, they may have resulted from the lack of much theoretical interest in the movements of aggregate demand. Neoclassical economists dealt mainly with demand for particular products based on subjective utility to individual consumers. Individual desire, however, must obviously be limited and must begin to decline after some given quantity is consumed. Thus a typical neoclassical economist asserts, "It is natural . . . that after the brisk demand of the . . . American public for motor cars in 1922–1923, the intensity of the desire for these articles should fall away" (Robertson, p. 10). This neoclassical approach leads naturally to the view that unemployment is a problem of absolute overproduction, of too much production. When, however, the entire economy is examined, rather than each individual product, it becomes clear that the problem in a major depression is not that more is produced than people subjectively desire to consume. On the contrary, there is not nearly enough produced to fulfill the desires or even the minimum health needs of the population; there is too much output only relative to effective purchasing power.

As long as most economists accepted Say's law, maintaining that there cannot be a general deficiency of effective demand relative to supply, there were only a few logically possible explanations for the fluctuations of aggregate output. One such explanation was that external or noneconomic shocks to the economy may limit supply or bring sudden demands. For example, sunspots may cause bad weather, and bad weather leads to bad harvests; unions may go on strike; governments may foolishly interfere with production activities; wars may stop the flow of raw materials or bring sudden demands for military production; and so forth. Thus, one famous economist declares, "Major depressions have been produced by a variety of different types of 'shocks,' not by a regular cycle-producing mechanism" (Duesenberry, p. 11).

Certainly such shocks as wars and bad weather do affect the economy; but such occurrences do not always coincide with the major swings in the economy, some of which occur in the absence of any apparent outside shock. Furthermore, noncapitalist economies have reacted quite differently to outside shocks. Therefore we may at least ask what mechanisms in the American economy give rise to cyclical movements as a result of these random shocks. We shall also try to understand how the internal operation of the capitalist economy might produce a business cycle even in the absence of external shocks.

Since conservatives refuse to believe that the private capitalist economy could possibly generate its own depressions, they examine every other accidental or shock explanation with greater care. The modern conservative school known as monetarists believes the whole problem is due to government mistakes in handling the monetary system. They argue that fluctuations are not caused by the capitalist system but by the government issuing too much or too little money (see Mitchell, Hand, and Walter, pp. 271–272). Granted that the U.S. capitalist government makes mistakes in its monetary policies, is it conceivable that the government has made the same mistake every few years for the last 150 years? Such theories of "mistakes" do not explain the systematic behavior of the capitalist economy, in its expansions and contractions, which follow regularly one after the other.

Another conservative notion is that depressions are due to inexplicable waves of psychological pessimism. Such pessimism may cause temporary panics during which money is hoarded and credit is withheld. Typical of these explanations is the statement that "the chief cause of the evil is a want of confidence" (Marshall, 1881). The defect of such theories lies in the fact that no one has ever demonstrated cycles of optimism and pessimism in businesspeople independent of the economic cycle. In fact, the height of optimism is always reached, as in 1929, at the peak of the business cycle. Only *after* economic conditions have objectively worsened are there irrationally large reactions by businesspersons, which intensify the economic downturn. Similarly, irrational optimism may intensify an economic expansion after conditions have objectively improved.

LIBERAL KEYNESIAN THEORIES

The economist whose name is connected with the theoretical revolution of the 1930s is Keynes. As has been seen, Keynes's contribution was the demolition of Say's law. He recognized the possibility that the economy as a whole may be in equilibrium at other than full employment, that is, that more or less may be demanded than is supplied at full employment at the present price level. Yet, one of his most prominent followers comments, "Keynesian economics, in spite of all that it has done for our understanding of business fluctuations, has beyond doubt left at least one major thing unexplained; and that thing is nothing less than the business cycle itself" (Hicks, p. 1) Keynes's popularity perhaps is attributable to his having said, in a striking manner, the right thing at the right time, for he not only explained the possibility of depressions and inflations but also laid down possible solutions for these problems within the bounds of the private enterprise economic system.

The simplest Keynesian theory of the business cycle was stated by Alvin Hansen and Paul Samuelson (see Samuelson, pp. 75–78). It provides only a bare sketch of reality. The theory consists of just three relationships. First, aggregate demand is composed of planned consumption spending plus planned investment spending. Of course this demand may be greater or less than the full-employment supply of output.

How much income is spent for consumption depends on the second relationship: Consumption is determined by some given propensity to spend out of last year's income. Moreover, the average propensity to consume declines as income rises.

How much income is spent for investment depends on the third relationship: Investment is determined by the change in income or demand during the previous period (the so-called accelerator coefficient). If these three statements are accepted as reasonable approximations of reality, what kind of cyclical behavior results?

Assume that national income is expanding in the early expansion phase of the business cycle. The increase in income causes an even greater demand for new capital goods, or net investment. But an initial increase in investment spending causes a further increase in consumer spending and in national income. Then the process continues because the increase in income leads to more investment, which leads to more consumption and income, causing still more investment, and so forth. The consumption and investment relations together thus spell out a cumulative process: An initial expansion in the economy leads to continuing expansion.

Assume now that national income is contracting in the depression phase of the business cycle. The decrease in income causes a large disinvestment of capital. The vast decrease in investment spending means much less income and less consumption. The further decrease in income leads to further disinvestment, which causes a further lowering of consumption, and so forth. Thus the combination of consumption and investment relationships also explains the cumulative process of contraction in the depression. An initial decline leads to continuing decline.

What is more difficult to understand is why the economy ever passes from the process of continuous expansion to the continuous contraction of depression or, for that matter, how we move from depression back to expansion. The same theory can also explain these turning points, though not as persuasively as it explains cumulative expansion or contraction.

At the peak of expansion it is true that income, consumption, and investment are all increasing. Yet the careful observer can begin to discern strains and even cracks in the impressive facade of prosperity. Consumption increases, but the propensity to consume begins to decline as the proportion of income saved increases. As a result, the aggregate demand out of national income starts to rise more and more slowly. But a smaller increase in national income means, according to the investment relationship, an absolute decline in net investment. A decline in net investment, however, causes a decline in national income, which causes a fall in consumer spending. Thus begins the process of contraction into depression.

Similarly, at the lowest point in a depression (the trough) it is true that income, consumption, and investment are all contracting. Yet as total consumption declines, the propensity to consume rises. As a result, the aggregate demand out of national income starts to fall more and more slowly. But a *smaller* decline in national income means, according to the accelerator, an absolute rise in the level of investment (or at least less disinvestment). This causes a rise, no matter how small, in aggregate spending. Then the rise in spending means more income and a rise in consumption. Thus begins the process of recovery and expansion.

Some readers may gain understanding from an arithmetic example of the whole process of expansion, downturn, depression, upturn, and again prosperity. Such an example can be constructed from the simple assumptions about consumption and investment behavior. Assume that net investment always equals the preceding change in income (that is, the accelerator is exactly 1). Also assume that the marginal propensity to consume is 0.90, or 90 percent of the previous period's income, to which we must always add some arbitrary minimum consumption (say $96 billion). The resulting cyclical process of expansion and contraction is shown in Table 36.1.

Table 36.1   ARITHMETIC EXAMPLE OF SIMPLEST BUSINESS CYCLE THEORY[a,b,c]

Time period	Consumption	National income	Net investment
1		$996 ⎱	
2		1000 ⎰	
3	$996	1000	$4
4	996	996	0
5	992	988	−4
6	985	977	−8
7	975	965	−11
8	964	952	−12
9	953	940	−13
10	942	930	−12
11	933	923	−10
12	927	920	−7
13	928	925	−3
14	928	933	5
15	936	944	8
16	945	956	11
17	957	969	12
18	969	982	13
19	978	991	13
20	987	990	9
21	995	1000	5

[a] It is assumed that the consumption is always $96 billion plus 90 percent of the previous period's income, and that net investment is always equal to the change in income to one period ago from two periods ago. It is also assumed that national income is expanding from $996 billion in first period to $1000 billion in second period. All figures are in billions of dollars.

[b] Some of the numbers are not exact because of rounding.

[c] The arrows show lines of influence. Only the first two arrows are shown. The student should fill in the rest of the arrows. The result will show that the pattern is repeated in every period.

The time periods here may be taken as two or three months. Notice that after the initial rise the national income falls for ten periods (from $1 trillion to $920 billion), then rises for ten periods (from $920 billion to $1 trillion), and then begins to fall again. The same fluctuation will continue forever, or as long as we keep the same assumptions. Consumption is always determined by the preceding national income, and net investment is always determined by the difference between the two preceding national incomes. National income itself is always the sum of the consumption plus the net investment of the same period. Thus does the simplest (or multiplier-accelerator) theory give a consistent picture of how the economy produces depression out of expansion and expansion out of depression in a continuing business cycle.

THE UNDERCONSUMPTIONIST VERSION
OF LIBERAL THEORY

All economists agree that the simplest liberal Keynesian multiplier-accelerator theory is too simple to explain many of the facts. The liberal economist John Hobson argued that consumer demand is too restricted because wages are too low. (Hobson and other underconsumptionists are discussed in Haberler, chap. 5, and in Hunt, chap. 14.) Hobson believed unemployment cycles could be cured under capitalism if workers were given higher wages—a theory that appeals to many trade unionists.

Hobson did *not* say that workers' wages—or even their share of income—are always declining. That could explain how capitalism gets into a depression but not how it gets out of it. What Hobson argued is that while total wages rise in the expansion period, the *share* of wages in national income falls, as has happened in every expansion on record.

Hobson asked, "What is the effect on consumer demand of this shift from wages to profits?" He argued that profit makers have much higher incomes than wage workers and therefore save more and have a lower propensity to consume. Since they now have a larger share of national income, the national propensity to consume will decline, as has also happened in every expansion.

Hobson concluded that in every expansion period the propensity to consume tends to fall, mainly because of the shift from wages to profits. Hobson thought that this was sufficient to explain how inadequate consumer demand at the cycle peak causes a depression, while the opposite process would initiate a recovery.

Critics noted that this argument is not sufficient. Although there may not be enough consumer demand to buy all new production, investor demand may fill the gap. As one conservative economist says, "It will not do to explain insufficiency of investment by the insufficiency of effective demand because effective demand would be sufficient if aggregate investment were" (Fellner, p. 121). Of course, if consumption were not rising at all, more investment could only mean the production of factories to produce more factories to produce more factories, and so on.

The underconsumptionist argument may be buttressed in a modern Keynesian framework by explaining investment with the help of the accelerator principle. The accelerator says that investment is determined by the increase in aggregate demand. But consumer demand is the largest component of aggregate demand. When consumer demand rises more slowly at the peak, it means aggregate demand also increases more slowly. When the increase in aggregate demand is less and less, the accelerator principle says investment will actually fall. This sets off a depression. This process is depicted in Figure 36.1.

The opposite process at the bottom of the depression initiates a recovery and expansion. Wages do not fall as rapidly as profits in the contraction. For this reason (and others) consumer demand falls more slowly

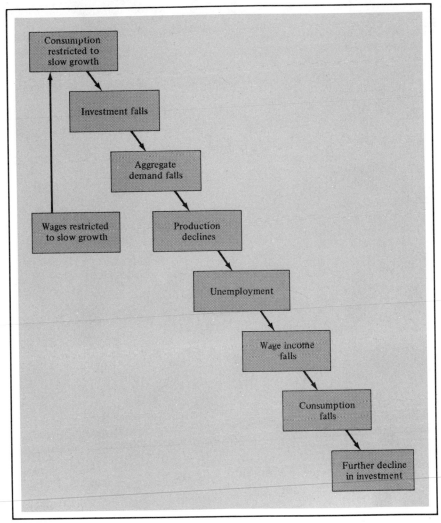

Figure 36.1 Underconsumption view of the crisis at a cycle peak.

than income or production. Therefore, aggregate demand reaches a floor and stops falling (or falls very slowly) at the trough of the contraction. When aggregate demand is constant, the accelerator principle says that net investment will stop falling and will actually rise from its negative level to become at least zero. Continued production at this stabilized level sets the stage for a renewed expansion.

Since the problem of a depression, as they see it, is lack of demand, the underconsumptionists argue for higher wages as a solution. Presumably, higher wages would increase consumer demand, allow capitalists to realize more profits, and keep the expansion going forever. They ignore the fact that wages are not only the largest component of consumer demand but also the largest component of costs. If costs rise, the capitalist makes less profit; the solution of higher wages thus leads to other problems.

THE CONSERVATIVE OVERINVESTMENT THEORY

Overinvestment theorists, such as Frederick von Hayek, argue that a crisis arises from high costs (see Haberler, chapter 4). The high level of investment and production leads to a demand for more labor and materials than are available, causing the price of labor and raw materials to rise. Some of Hayek's work also stresses the cost of rising interest rates at the cycle peak. Excessive investment may thus cause a problem of high costs in three different areas: (1) wage costs, (2) raw material costs, and (3) interest costs.

Some overinvestment theorists emphasize the threat to profits from rising wage costs as the economy nears full employment. In wage negotiations employers use this argument to prove that higher wages will lead to less investment and production, and thus eventually to unemployment. Therefore they tell unions to hold down wage requests.

In reality, the argument that high wages in expansion lead to low profits, which lead to a crisis, ignores some crucial facts. For one thing, labor costs per unit usually fall during most of the expansion because of rising productivity. Moreover, when labor costs rise somewhat near the end of expansion, they rise less than other more rapidly expanding costs.

Some overinvestment theorists also emphasize that the expansion leads to rising costs of new capital equipment, rising costs of raw materials, and rising interest rates, making borrowing more expensive. Assuming that these costs increase faster than the prices of the commodities produced, capitalist profits per unit must decline. When profit rates decline, there is a decline in investment and production, causing depression to begin. Paradoxically, in this view too high a level of investment leads to high costs, which eventually lead to a crisis characterized by declining investment. This view of the crisis is pictured in Figure 36.2.

To summarize the overinvestment theory: In expansion, rapidly rising demand for labor and investment goods (overinvestment) causes a sharp increase in the cost of these goods to investors. The prices of consumer goods rise more slowly, squeezing profit margins in that sector; as a result, the increase of total profits proceeds more slowly. Because investment is determined by the increase in profits, less increase in profits causes less investment. Less investment causes less income, which causes less consumption, and so forth until the depression is well under way.

The opposite process takes place in the contraction period and eventually leads to recovery. In the contraction there is a rapidly falling demand for labor and investment goods, so there is a fall in the cost of these goods to investors. Since the prices of finished goods fall more slowly (or rise more rapidly if there is an inflation in the midst of recession), the profit

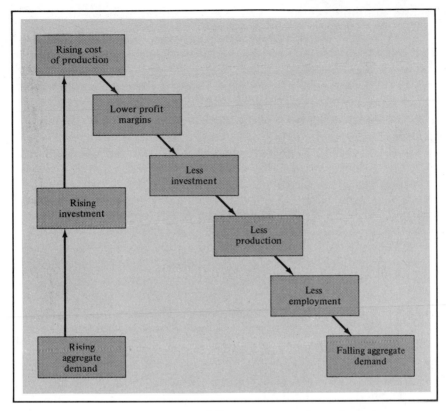

Figure 36.2 Overinvestment view of the crisis at a cycle peak.

margin eventually improves. This improvement of the profit margin then leads to more investment and a new expansion.

Since the problem causing the depression is a profit reduction owing to higher costs, these theorists argue the position that the government could cure the problem by taking appropriate steps. The steps they urge, however, are exactly the opposite of those suggested by the underconsumptionists. Their solution—which is pleasing to business—is to hold down costs, particularly wage costs. Those who emphasize the rising costs of labor claim that more employment can only come by cutting wages. One textbook says, "The general solution to involuntary unemployment is a reduction in real wages until the amount of labor demanded equals the amount supplied" (Leftwich and Sharp, p. 249).

The notion of solving unemployment by cutting wages ignores the fact that lower wages mean less demand for consumer goods. If there is less demand, it is harder for capitalists to sell their goods. Both Marx and Keynes emphasized this fact and the consequent lower profits from unsold goods.

The theme that higher costs, particularly wage costs, cause lower production and lower investment, is repeated again and again by conservative economists and the business press. In October 1974 an economist wrote in the *Wall Street Journal:*

> The cost of labor is soaring. . . . One reason many analysts view the trend as "ominous" is that it could soon begin to erode company profits sharply and trigger increasing layoffs. So far, corporations generally have managed to boost their prices even more rapidly than labor costs have risen. (Malabre, p. 1)

This article admitted that prices had actually risen faster than labor costs in the year from September 1973 to September 1974. In fact, real wages were falling while corporate profit rates were still rising in that period. This article merely worried that corporate profits might soon begin to fall, not that they are actually falling.

CRITICAL THEORIES

All critical economists agree that capitalism inevitably leads to economic crises and depressions. They also agree that the only way to end unemployment completely is to replace capitalism with a socialist system of democratic planning. But they disagree on the exact mechanisms that cause cyclical unemployment just as much as the various conservative and liberal views disagree.

One group of critical economists (see Sweezy) agrees with the liberal underconsumptionists that lack of effective demand is the most important problem. The underconsumptionists emphasize, however, that the problem begins in the capitalist production process. In that production process, workers are exploited—that is, their wages are less than the product they produce, so workers cannot buy all that is produced. In a capitalist expansion, the share of labor always declines further, so the gap between workers' income and the value of consumer goods widens. That gap leads to a cyclical downturn and unemployment.

A second group of critical economists (see Boddy and Crotty), however, has a version of the overinvestment theory. They argue that rapidly rising investment leads to a greater demand for labor. This condition of rising employment gives workers more bargaining power. They use their bargaining power to get higher wages and a slower pace of work. "Knowledgeable observers of the labor scene have pointed directly to an increasingly obstreperous labor force as an influence on the decline in productivity during expansion" (Ibid., p. 8). Again, the analysis begins with workers being exploited, but now the problem is seen as a rising wage share (or falling exploitation). The higher costs—and falling productivity—must lead to lower profits and a recession.

A third group of critical economists (see Kalecki) contends that in each expansion capitalist profits are squeezed from both the demand side and the cost side. As the expansion continues, the wage share declines, so the average propensity to consume declines. As consumption grows more slowly, aggregate demand is limited. At the same time, costs are rising. The price of raw materials and the interest rate rise rapidly. Therefore, entrepreneur's profit is squeezed between limited revenue and rising costs. This squeeze leads to a recession or depression.

This completes the survey of theories. Next, we present a narrative description of what actually happens in a typical U.S. business cycle.

EARLY EXPANSION

Demand

In the early stages of expansion, output is expanding very fast, so employment also expands. Since workers are earning more wages, consumer demand rises rapidly. In fact, the rising consumer demand soon outruns supply because the expansion begins at such a low level of production.

Costs

At the beginning of the expansion, wages are very low because of the high unemployment remaining from the last recession or depression. Wage rates rise very slowly for several reasons, including fixed labor contracts, continued fear of unemployment, and workers' contentment that wage rates have at least begun to rise. There are large excess supplies of raw materials and of machinery, so the prices of these inputs are also very low. Labor productivity per unit is rising, mainly because there is increasing use of capacity, but little or no increase in nonproduction overhead workers, such as bookkeepers or guards.

Profits and Investment

Because of the rising demand, low costs, and rapidly rising productivity, profits rise very rapidly. Profits rise faster than wages, and the rate of profit on capital rises very rapidly. Therefore there are plenty of funds for new investment and ample levels of optimism for higher profit rates in the future. As a result, capitalists both increase the use of their present capacity and invest in expansion of capacity. This in turn means more employment, more total demand, and further rising expectations.

LATE EXPANSION

For a period during the middle of the expansion, the outlook is very rosy, so there is a cumulative expansion of investment, employment, and consumer demand.

Demand

Under the surface, however, problems are arising. Since profits are rising more rapidly than wages in the first half of expansion, the average propensity to consume is falling (because capitalists have a lower propensity to consume). The falling propensity to consume eventually causes consumer demand to rise more and more slowly in the last half of expansion. If investment does not fill the gap, then total demand will also rise more and more slowly.

Costs

In the last half of expansion, wages continue to rise at about the same rate as before. There is a downward pressure on wages because the growth of output is slowing down, but there is an upward pressure on wages because workers and trade unions have more bargaining power as employment increases to higher levels. Raw material prices usually rise even faster than all prices in the last half of expansion because there is a rapid growth of demand by industry, but supply takes a while to catch up. Interest rates rise because there is a high demand for money to borrow. Productivity of labor is constant or even falling as the peak of expansion is reached. The reason seems to be that the use of capacity is not growing any more, both because it is close to optimum in some industries and because of weakening demand in other industries.

Profits and Investment

With most costs rising rapidly, while growth of consumer demand is reduced, profits are squeezed and there is a lower rate of profit. This profit squeeze at the peak of expansion is depicted in Figure 36.3. The lower present rate of profit reduces investors' expectations for the future. The slower increase of total profits means less funds available for investment. So investment finally declines, causing a decline in total output and employment. This begins the recession.

EARLY CONTRACTION

Demand

In the early stages of contraction, consumer demand begins to fall because employment is falling and because people begin to expect even less employment in the future.

Costs

Since employment is still high, though falling, wage rates (even in real terms) fall extremely slowly. Raw material prices also continue at high levels for a while, until current orders are all satisfied. Interest rates remain

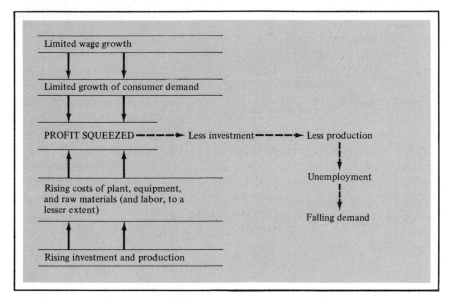

Figure 36.3 Profit squeeze at cycle peak.

high because small businesses rush to borrow more funds simply to keep afloat. Productivity of labor falls very rapidly. The main reason is that capitalists can fire some production-line workers but are hesitant to fire highly skilled workers and cannot fire many kinds of nonproduction workers whose labor is just as vital as ever. Therefore measured productivity per worker falls because there is a much smaller decline in employment than in output.

Profits and Investment

Since consumer demand is falling, although costs per unit of production are still quite high, there is a rapid decline in both total profits and the rate of profit. This causes a catastrophic decline in investment, since there is both a lack of funds and a very pessimistic expectation of future profitability.

LATE CONTRACTION

Demand

As the recession or depression continues, income declines, but more and more slowly. Workers are unemployed, but they pay lower taxes and receive unemployment compensation. Moreover, profits have fallen much more than wages. The shift to wage income as a ratio of total income means a rising propensity to consume (since workers have a higher propensity to consume than capitalists). Thus wages are declining and consumption is declining, but they are a rising percentage of output, and their decline is slower and slower.

Costs

At the bottom of the recession or depression, real wages are falling rapidly. Raw material prices fall very rapidly. Interest rates fall. And productivity per worker stops falling and sometimes begins to rise inasmuch as capitalists have now fired large numbers of workers, so the ratio of workers to output has begun to fall.

Profits and Investment

Since consumer demand has almost stopped falling, whereas costs per unit are rapidly declining, total profit and the rate of profit both stop declining. Sometimes they will even rise slightly at this point. Thus capitalists begin to have more funds available for investment (both their own and easy-to-borrow savings). More important, capitalists begin to have more optimistic expectations for the future since the present is less bleak. Then investment stops its rapid decline and eventually begins to rise again. Capitalists also begin to produce more with their present unused capacity, abundant raw materials, and plentiful cheap labor. In this way, the recovery begins.

OTHER IMPORTANT FACTORS

To make the description as simple as possible, a number of important factors were ignored.

Government

As has been shown in Chapter 34, the deficit falls throughout expansion. This is no problem in early expansion because aggregate demand is rising rapidly. At the business cycle peak, however, when consumer and investment demand has slowed down to almost zero growth, the further decline of deficit spending is a quite negative factor. The Federal Reserve also usually pursues a restrictive monetary and credit policy at the peak because the Fed worries most about inflation.

At the bottom of the recession or depression, however, deficit spending is rising, helping set the stage for recovery. The Federal Reserve also usually adopts an expansionary monetary and credit policy at the cycle trough, which also helps recovery.

International Relations

A later chapter will show that U.S. net exports tend to fall during U.S. expansions and usually rise during U.S. contractions. Net exports are an important demand factor. So falling net exports at the cycle peak will have a negative effect, but rising net exports at the cycle trough have a positive effect on the economy.

Credit

Chapter 33 explained why credit rises rapidly in business expansions, intensifying the expansion. On the other hand, in business contractions credit declines. If the credit decline is mild, the recession will be mild. If the credit system collapses (as it did in the early 1930s), then a deep depression is likely.

Monopoly

The existence of monopoly was ignored in our narrative description of the business cycle. In the next chapter, however, we shall see that monopoly power probably intensifies depressions—by keeping prices high, but lowering output and employment.

Technological Innovation

In a later chapter we explore the leading role of technological innovation in economic growth. Here we may merely note that in a depression new technology is seldom introduced and is usually postponed for better times. When recovery begins, however, many new inventions are taken from the shelves, dusted off, and put into production—so these innovations help fuel the expansion.

Types of Investment

Economic theories often speak just of net investment, but about half of all investment is the replacement of depreciated plant and equipment. Replacement is often postponed in a recession or depression, then done all at once in the beginning of recovery, so that it adds to demand at that time.

Economic theories also frequently concentrate only on the dramatic rise of investment in plant and equipment—or its dramatic fall in a major depression. But it actually takes quite a while to order, produce, and install plant and equipment. Short-run business cycles are usually dominated by fluctuations in inventory investment. In a recession, for example, retailers will quickly cut back their purchases of finished products to keep on hand, while manufacturers will try to reduce stocks of raw materials.

SUMMARY

Conservative neoclassical economists argue that there are no internal mechanisms inevitably producing business contractions, only external shocks. Liberal Keynesians contend that a lack of effective demand causes downturns through the multiplier and accelerator mechanisms. Underconsumptionists usually blame the lack of effective demand on the limitations of wages. Overinvestment theorists, on the contrary, claim that too much investment demand leads to rising prices of raw materials, rising interest costs, and other costs—all cutting into profits and causing economic downturns.

What actually happens in the cycle? In early expansion, rapid rise of demand and low costs result in rapidly rising profits. In later expansion, demand rises very slowly while costs rise much faster; this results in profits rising sluggishly, then often falling before the peak. When actual profits fall, business expectations fall, and there is recession or depression.

In early contraction, demand falls rapidly while costs fall slowly, so profits plummet downward. At the end of a business contraction, however, demand levels off while costs are still falling, so profits pick up again and a recovery begins.

SUGGESTED READINGS

All of these subjects are covered in much more detail in Howard Sherman and Gary Evans, *Macroeconomics* (New York: Harper & Row, 1984). The classic history of economic thought on business cycles is Gottfried Haberler, *Prosperity and Depression* (Cambridge, Mass.: Harvard University Press, 1960).

REFERENCES

Boddy, Raford, and James Crotty. "Class Conflict and Macro-Policy." *Review of Radical Political Economics* 7 (Spring 1975), pp. 1–15.

Duesenberry, James. *Business Cycles and Economic Growth.* New York: McGraw-Hill, 1958.

Fellner, William. *Money, Trade, and Economic Growth.* New York: Macmillan, 1951.

Haberler, Gottfried. *Prosperity and Depression.* Cambridge, Mass.: Harvard University Press, 1960.

Hunt, E. K. *History of Economic Thought: A Critical Perspective.* Belmont, Ca.: Wadsworth, 1975.

Hicks, J. R. *The Trade Cycle.* New York: Oxford University Press, 1950.

Kalecki, Michal. *Theory of Economic Dynamics.* New York: Monthly Review Press, 1988.

Leftwich, Richard, and Ansel Sharp. *Economics of Social Issues.* Homewood, Ill.: Irwin.

Malabre, Alfred. "Real Cost of Labor Outpaces Pay Gains as Productivity Lags," *Wall Street Journal*, October 31, 1974.

Marshall, Alfred, and A. P. Marshall. *The Economics of Industry.* New York: Macmillan, 1881.

Mitchell, William, John Hand, and Ingo Walter. *Readings in Macroeconomics.* New York: McGraw-Hill, 1975.

Robertson, D. H. *Banking Policy and the Price Level.* New York: Augustus M. Kelley, 1949.

Samuelson, Paul. "Interaction Between the Multiplier Analysis and the Principle of Acceleration." *Review of Economic Statistics*, 21 (May 1939), pp. 75–78.

Sweezy, Paul. *Theory of Capitalist Development.* New York: Monthly Review Press, 1958.

Chapter
37
Inflation

The Keynesian explanation of inflation boils down to the idea that inflation results when aggregate demand is greater than the aggregate supply provided by a fully employed labor force. It must also be understood that the aggregate monetary or effective demand includes not just coins and paper money and demand deposits, but all the forms of credit in the economy. Effective demand includes anything that allows an individual or business or government to purchase goods and services now, whether they pay now or later. The important effect of this is that demand may be expanded to some extent by banks and financial institutions and/or by government manipulation of the financial system.

We shall find that this Keynesian explanation of inflation by excess aggregate demand, including credit, is adequate to explain most of the inflation of past U.S. capitalist history up through the 1940s. In the 1950s and 1960s, however, traces of a new kind of inflation emerged that were confusing in Keynesian terms. The inflation of the 1970s and 1980s is definitely a new variety that the usual Keynesian model cannot explain; it is inflation at a time of deficient aggregate demand. We begin this chapter with a look at those types of inflation that a simple Keynesian model can explain; then we turn to the present type, which it cannot explain. The possibilities and the inadequacies of present government policy are also examined.

NORMAL INFLATION IN BUSINESS EXPANSIONS

In most business expansions in the United States prices have risen. In most U.S. business contractions prices have fallen. For example, in the Great Depression of the 1930s prices fell about 50 percent. The best index of

U.S. wholesale prices reveals that in 23 of the 26 cyclical expansions and contractions between 1890 and 1938, prices moved in the same direction as business activity and production (see Mills).

As Keynes argued, prices usually moved up in expansions because effective demand for all products was moving upward faster than the physical supply of products. In contractions, prices usually moved down (e.g., by about 50 percent in the Great Depression) because effective demand for all products was moving downward faster than the physical supply of products was decreasing. Higher prices took up part of the increased demand in expansion, while lower prices were part of the reaction to decreased demand in contraction.

Why does the flow of aggregate demand in money terms rise so rapidly during a period of expansion? On the one hand, the money supply expands because banks give credit (in the form of demand deposits). Businesses want to borrow in order to take advantage of profitable opportunities, and banks want to lend because it appears that businesses can easily repay the loans with interest. Therefore, the money supply in circulation will increase rapidly.

Not only is there more money in circulation, but it turns over faster because consumers and businesses both spend more rapidly. In Keynesian terms the level of consumption and investment both rise. Consumers wish to get bargains before prices rise further and also because they feel assured of future income. Businesses likewise dig into their hoarded savings—and borrow more on credit—to make the investments that appear attractive. In times of expansion everyone wishes to spend in order to buy goods rather than to hoard money.

In a depression, on the other hand, the flow of money demand usually decreases even faster than the transactions with the national product. Banks call in their loans, while businesses do not want to make new loans; therefore, the money supply rapidly declines. Furthermore, individuals and businesses hoard their savings for the rainy days ahead, especially because there are no attractive opportunities for investment. As a result, money circulates more slowly and hoarding increases considerably in a depression. For these reasons, during most of U.S. history, depression was normally a time of price deflation.

INFLATION IN WARTIME

The usual inflation experienced during peacetime prosperity has been very slow and very slight compared with the rapid and spectacular inflation stimulated by wartime spending. Just how closely price inflation is correlated with war may be seen in Figure 37.1. Very rapid price inflation accompanied the Revolutionary War, the War of 1812, the Civil War, and World War I. We shall see later that there was also rapid price inflation in World War II, the Korean War, and the Vietnam War.

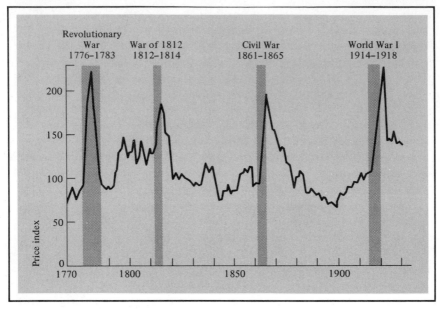

Figure 37.1 War and inflation in U.S. history. *Source:* Wholesale price index, 1770–1929, from U.S. Department of Commerce, *Historical Statistics of the United States, 1789–1945* (Washington, D.C.: GPO, 1949).

During wartime there is little production of consumer goods or private producer goods. At the same time there is full employment, with high wages and profits. All of the increased goods and services are in the military sphere and all are bought by the government—which finances most of its purchases by printing money or by borrowing, with only limited tax increases. Therefore, civilians have relatively high incomes and high monetary demand, but the amount of available civilian goods and services is very limited. Furthermore, as prices begin to rise rapidly, people rush to buy goods before prices rise further, thus increasing the spending flow even faster than income rises because their propensities to consume and invest are rising.

INFLATION IN THE MIDST OF UNEMPLOYMENT

In the Great Depression of the 1930s, there was vast unemployment and prices declined by over one-third between 1929 and 1933. Then prices recovered a little until a new recession in 1938 caused another sharp decline. In World War II, large military demand created intense inflationary pressure, but prices were held down by direct price controls. Following World War II, price controls were ended, so that prices rose rapidly in 1946 to 1948. Then, in 1949, a recession caused prices to fall. The Korean War in 1950 caused more inflation.

Up to this point, prices behaved as Keynesian theory predicts, rising in expansions and in wars, then declining in recessions. In the 1950s, however, a new phenomenon became evident. In the recession of 1954, overall prices remained constant. In the recession of 1958, prices actually rose, the first time this had ever happened in U.S. history—rising prices in a period of rising unemployment. In the 1961 recession, prices were again steady. In the recessions (or depressions) of 1970, 1974, 1980, and 1981, price inflation continued throughout the contraction period! This phenomenon of rising prices in contractions may be seen in Figure 37.2.

It is such evidence that forces us to distinguish the inflations during recent recessions from the ordinary *demand-pull* inflation, which is caused by the upward pull of aggregate demand. Here, instead, prices apparently are pushed upward by individual firms and industries. It is called *cost-push* inflation to indicate the belief that prices are pushed upward by either higher profit margins or higher wage costs. Many conservative economists argue that monopoly or oligopoly power of firms is not responsible for spiraling prices. On the contrary, conservatives argue that the bargaining power of labor unions pushes wages upward and that prices only follow wages. The opposite view, held by many liberals and radicals, is that prices are pushed up by monopolies to make higher profits. These economists maintain that wages mostly lag behind prices, and that wage increases are merely bemoaned as an excuse for higher prices

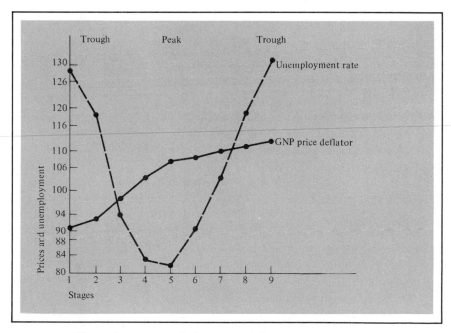

Figure 37.2 Unemployment and the price deflator, 1949–1980, as an average of six cycles. *Source:* U.S. Department of Commerce, *Business Conditions Digest*, April 1981.

STAGFLATION

Stagflation is defined as the condition of price inflation in the midst of stagnant or falling production and heavy unemployment. This is a new phenomenon in the United States. As mentioned earlier, in most cycles till the 1950s prices rose in the expansion and fell in the contraction. In all of these cycles, of course, unemployment declined in the expansion phases and rose during the contractions.

On the basis of such data, traditional economists found a relation between prices and unemployment. These economists argued that wages and prices always rise in periods of falling unemployment and economic expansion, while wages and prices always fall when unemployment rises in economic contraction. This assumed relationship of unemployment to inflation was first graphed by a Professor Phillips and is therefore called the Phillips curve. His curve portrays an inverse relation between unemployment and inflation. We present the annual data on unemployment and inflation in Figure 37.3.

For the 1960s we found the relationship pretty much as Professor Phillips described it. When the unemployment rate went higher, the rate of price inflation went lower. When the unemployment rate went lower, the rate of price inflation went higher. Thus, from 1960 through 1969,

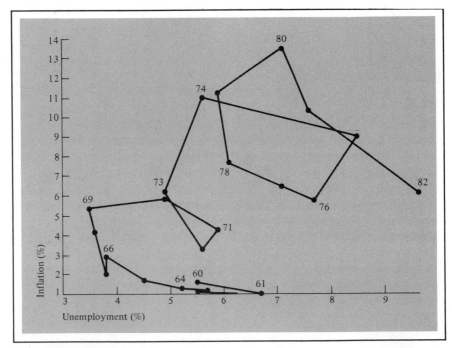

Figure 37.3 Phillips curve: annual data, 1960–1962. *Source:* Council of Economic Advisors, *Economic Report of the President.*

the monthly changes in the unemployment rate moved in the opposite direction from the consumer price index 73 percent of the time. The explanation given by most economists was that high unemployment goes with low demand for goods and for labor, which reduces inflation. On the other hand, a lower unemployment rate reflects higher demand, which leads to a higher rate of inflation.

Figure 37.3 also reveals the data for the 1970s. When we fit a curve to this data, the result is strikingly different. The Phillips curve for the 1970s reveals a higher rate of unemployment going along with a higher rate of inflation! In fact, in the 1970s monthly changes in these two rates moved in opposite directions only 54 percent of the time.

The long-run trend was for both unemployment and inflation to rise. The official unemployment rate moved from 4.8 percent in 1960–1969 to 6.2 percent in 1970–1979 and to 8.1 percent in 1980–1982. Yet the inflation rate (change in the consumer price index) also moved up from 2.3 percent in 1960–1969 to 9.2 percent in 1970–1979 and to 10 percent in 1980–1982.

In 1982, however, by pushing unemployment to the highest rate since the 1930s, the Reagan administration did finally lower the inflation rate. Vast unemployment will lead to lower inflation or even a decline in prices. On the other end, full employment (as in wartime) clearly leads to inflation. In between, there is a wide range in which unemployment and inflation may move together.

How can we explain the fact that in the 1970s high unemployment and high inflation occurred together, while lower unemployment and lower inflation also occurred together? Many economists, perhaps most, agree that this type of inflation could not be caused by a high demand pulling up prices. We know that demand was insufficient because there was much unemployment. These economists would all argue that there is a *supply-push* or *cost-push* inflation. But there is no agreement on the type of supply-side costs that pushed up prices. Some argue that the cost of foreign raw materials, such as oil, is the main villain. Most argue that the main villain is higher wages caused by powerful unions. Many others argue that there is *profit-push* inflation caused by monopoly power.

LABOR UNIONS AND INFLATION

There is no evidence that labor unions obtain such high wages as to cause inflation. The most important fact is that real wages decline in each depression or recession. In other words, although money wages have risen somewhat in recent contractions, they have risen much less than prices. This means that inflation during the contraction periods cannot be blamed on wages because they lag behind prices. In human terms, the worker's standard of living declines in each depression-plus-inflation period.

Nor can price inflation in expansions be blamed on high wages. Because productivity is rising, real labor cost per unit declines in most of the expansion. Therefore, the cost of paying wages cannot possibly be the cause—though it may be the excuse—for higher prices in most of the expansion period. The slight rise in labor costs in the later expansion period is not enough for wages to catch up with the earlier productivity rises. Again, these wage increases are only an excuse for price increases, not the determining factor.

Finally, union strength in most industries has been declining. The percentage of workers unionized reached a peak in 1956 of 36 percent of all workers in private, nonagricultural, business. Since then, the percentage of unionization has declined drastically to 18 percent in 1986. Declining labor unions can hardly be used to explain more rapid inflation (especially in contractions with high unemployment). The weakness of unions has helped business monopolies in their economic and political domination.

MONOPOLY POWER AND ADMINISTERED PRICES

In the Great Depression of the 1930s (and in the smaller depression of 1938), Gardiner Means found what he called administered prices in the monopoly sector (see Means; also Blair, 1972, pt. 4). In these more concentrated industries, Means found that prices were not set in a competitive market but were carefully administered or set in the best interests of the monopolies. He found that the competitive prices changed frequently, but the administered or monopoly prices changed very seldom.

More specifically, Means found that the prices in the competitive sector registered large declines in the depression, whereas the administered prices in the monopoly sector declined very little. Means defines the competitive sector as the 20 percent least concentrated industries; the monopoly sector is defined as the 20 percent most concentrated industries. From 1929 to 1932, prices in the more competitive sector fell 60 percent, whereas prices in the monopoly sector fell only 10 percent. A few prices in the monopoly sector even rose a little in the face of the Great Depression.

As shown in Table 37.1, the industries with great monopoly power lowered their prices very little, but they kept prices from going down more only by reducing their production by very large percentages. The more competitive sectors had no choice but to let their prices be forced down by lack of demand, while their production declined less because of greater demand at the lower prices. The monopoly sector thus held up its prices and profit per unit at the expense of great decreases in production and large-scale unemployment. The competitive sector lowered production less, fired fewer workers, but suffered much greater declines in prices and profits per unit. A highly monopolized economy is thus more apt to produce high rates of unemployment in every decline.

Since the 1930s, monopoly power has increased dramatically. In most industries only four or five firms sell most of the product—and most of

Table 37.1   PRICE AND PRODUCTION BEHAVIOR IN DEPRESSION, 1929–1932

| | Decline as percent of 1929 | | |
	Prices	Production	
Motor vehicles	12	74	⎫
Agricultural implements	14	84	⎬ High monopoly power
Iron and steel	16	76	⎭
Cement	16	55	⎫
Automobile tires	25	42	⎬ Intermediate levels of
Leather and leather products	33	18	⎬ monopoly power
Petroleum products	36	17	⎭
Textile products	39	28	⎫
Food products	39	10	⎬ Mostly competitive
Agricultural commodities	54	1	⎭

Source: U.S. National Resources Committee (under the direction of Gardiner Means), *The Structure of the American Economy* (Washington, D.C.: GPO, 1939), p. 386.

these top four or five firms are now owned by conglomerates with power in a number of industries. In 1978, the top 500 corporations made 80 percent of all profits. And the top 130 corporations had 530 directors sitting on more than one board so as to make interlocking decisions (see Roberts). If small business is defined as those firms with less than $1 million sales and fewer than 100 employees (a generous definition of "small"), then in 1982 small businesses were over 99 percent of all firms, but they produced only 38 percent of GNP! (See U.S. Small Business Administration, 1982.) Firms with fewer than ten employees accounted for 78 percent of all firms, but had only 11 percent of all sales.

Data for more recent contractions show patterns similar to the 1930s, becoming only more dramatic in the latest contractions. The competitive sector is defined in Table 37.2 as all those industries where concentration of sales by eight firms is under 50 percent. The monopoly sector is defined as all those industries where concentration of sales by eight firms is over 50 percent. Table 37.2 on the behavior of prices in the monopoly sector and of prices in the competitive sector is perhaps the most important in this book.

Table 37.2 reveals that the pattern for the 1948 recession was the same as in the 1929 and 1937 depressions. In all three cases, monopoly prices declined a little, whereas competitive prices declined by an enormous amount. In the 1954 and 1958 recessions, we see the first indications of the new stagflation behavior. Competitive prices decline as usual, though by a small amount. But monopoly prices actually rose in the recessions, though again by a small amount. The new situation is very clear in the 1970 recession, in which competitive prices decline by a significant amount, but monopoly prices reveal a considerable rise.

Table 37.2   COMPETITIVE AND MONOPOLY PRICES
Changes in Price Indexes from Cyclical Peak to Trough

Dates of cycle peaks and troughs	Changes in competitive prices	Changes in monopoly prices
Nov. 1948–Oct. 1949	−7.8%	−1.9%
July 1953–Aug. 1954	−1.5	+1.9
July 1957–Apr. 1958	−0.3	+0.5
May 1960–Feb. 1961	−1.2	+0.9
Nov. 1969–Nov. 1970	−3.0	+5.9
Nov. 1973–Mar. 1975	+11.7	+32.8

Sources: Price changes for 1948–1949, 1953–1954, and 1957–1958 from Robert Lanzillotti, *Hearings before the Joint Economic Committee of the U.S. Congress, Employment, Growth and Price Levels* (Washington, D.C.: GPO, 1959), p. 2238. Price changes for 1969–1970 from John Blair, "Market Power and Inflation," *Journal of Economic Issues* 8:2 (June 1974). Price changes for 1960–1961 and 1973–1975 from Kathleen Pulling, Market Structure and the Cyclical Behavior of Prices and Profits, 1949 to 1975 (Ph.D. dissertation, University of California, Riverside, 1978).

Price data on the 1973–1975 depression indicate that monopoly prices rose in the depression by an astounding percentage. This very large price increase throughout the now-dominant monopoly sector caused even competitive prices to show a considerable rise in the depression for the first time on record. This undoubtedly caused great disruption in the competitive sector, decreased production, increased bankruptcies, and increased unemployment.

PRICES OF AUTOS, OIL, AND FOOD

Before giving a systematic analysis of such price behavior, it is worth looking at three case studies of monopoly pricing and restriction of production. The most obvious is the auto industry, in which the big three control more than 90 percent of U.S. domestic production. The largest, General Motors (GM), is usually the price leader. In the early part of the 1973–1975 depression, from the third quarter of 1973 to the third quarter of 1974, demand for autos fell rapidly and GM sales were down 22 percent. Yet GM did not lower its prices as traditional economics would predict. Rather, GM raised its prices by $900 to $1000; the lower sales were met by further restriction of production and the firing of thousands of GM workers (see Edwards, pp. 217–218).

Oil prices rose dramatically during the 1973–1975 depression. The companies blamed the price rises on the Arab oil producers. But the fact is that the U.S. companies artificially restricted oil production for many years before that time. Internationally, most oil in the Arab countries was extracted by Anglo–U.S. companies, who carefully controlled the flow.

The Anglo–U.S. companies made profit rates in excess of 100 percent every year from 1950 to 1970 on the oil from that region (see Akhdar, pp. 89–95). In the United States, with immense oil deposits of its own, the oil companies have not built a new refinery since 1965, and they have cut back exploratory drilling by 60 percent since 1956. Even during the so-called shortage, the U.S. oil companies held immense amounts of oil off the market in reserve holding areas. So it is the U.S. oil companies that caused the shortage, raised U.S. prices, and made enormous profits from it (see Harrison).

Finally, U.S. consumers have been badly hurt by rising food prices and restricted food production. Yet, myth has it that food production is purely competitive, so the high prices could not possibly be the result of monopoly; thus the argument that high food prices must be due to Russian wheat deals (a very small percentage of the crop) or to a bad anchovy harvest off Peru or some other random factor, but not to monopoly because there is none. The fact is that, especially since the 1930s, the number of small farmers has been rapidly shrinking while the number of giant agribusiness corporations is rising. On the supply side, farmers must buy most of their implements and fertilizers from monopolies, such as International Harvester. On the selling side, Campbell sells 90 percent of soups, four firms sell 90 percent of breakfast cereals, Gerber sells most baby food, Del Monte sells most canned fruits and vegetables, and just 20 supermarket chains sell 40 percent of all food (see Robbins, p. 326).

The power of the monopolies in food sales was accurately summed up by one investigator of the high prices of our Thanksgiving meals: "The Smithfield ham comes from ITT, the turkey is a product of Greyhound Corporation, the lettuce comes from Dow Chemical Company, the potatoes are provided by the Boeing Company, and Tenneco brought the fresh fruits and vegetables. The applesauce is made available by American Brands, while both Coca Cola and Royal Crown Cola have provided the fruit juices" (Robbins, p. 325). In the 1973–1975 depression, prices received by farmers dropped, but these middlemen (canners, packers, and distributors controlled by conglomerates) increased their share of the food dollar to 60 cents, so that retail prices actually rose!

EXPLANATION OF PRICE BEHAVIOR

In all recessions before the 1950s, prices fell. That behavior was predictable and easily explained by traditional economic theory. Neoclassical theory leads us to expect that falling demand will cause both output and prices to decline. By reducing supply and also reducing prices to sell more of the supply, the amount of output supplied is brought back into equilibrium with the demand in each industry.

Similarly, Keynesian theory predicts that, in the aggregate, an excess supply will lead to falling production, unemployment, and falling prices. If there are institutional rigidities or monopoly power, then there will be stable prices. Keynesian theory predicts price inflation only when there is an excess demand above supply at full employment.

Neither neoclassical nor Keynesian theory predicts price inflation in the face of falling demand and unemployment. Yet that has been the fact in the monopoly sector in the recessions of 1954, 1958, 1970, 1975, and 1982. Of course, traditional theory would admit that firms with monopoly power can always set prices higher if they wish to restrict their supply enough to do so. But why, in the face of falling demand, should monopolies find it profitable to reduce their production so drastically as to actually increase prices?

Only a few unorthodox economists have provided some answers to this question. In most of the monopoly sector a single large firm in each industry sets prices; other firms just follow this price leader. These large firms mostly follow a policy of setting the price as a certain margin of profit added on to their cost level. This procedure of cost-plus pricing by the large corporations has been confirmed by a large number of empirical investigations (see Eichner).

The giant corporations do not maximize their short-run profit by setting prices as high as possible at any given moment. Rather, they set prices with a profit margin that will ensure their maximum long-run growth—and maximum long-run profits. This profit margin must therefore be enough to meet fully their expected needs for growth and expansion. Each corporation sets a target profit level based on its previous earning record and the record of the leaders in its industry.

What happens if a giant corporation finds its sales revenue falling in a recession or depression? The firm will try to regain enough revenue to reach its target profit by higher price markups on the remaining sales. This process has been illustrated very well in a numerical example in an excellent article by Wachtel and Adelsheim, who write,

> For example, say a firm operating in a concentrated industry has direct costs (raw material and labor) of $200 per unit of output and sets its profit markup above direct costs at 20 percent, therefore selling the product for $240 per unit and making a profit of $40 per unit. Let us say the firm has a target level of profits of $40,000; to realize this profit level it will have to sell 1,000 units at $240 per unit. Now we have unemployment and a recession which causes the volume of sales to fall, say, to 950 units. But if the firm still has a target profit level of $40,000, which it wants to attain, it will have to raise its prices to slightly over $242 per unit from the previous level of $240 per unit. It does this by raising its percentage markup over costs to 21 percent compared to the previous 20 percent. Having increased their profit per unit, the firm now achieves its target profit level, but the resultant manifestation in the economy

is the simultaneous occurrence of inflation and unemployment. (Wachtel and Adelsheim, p. 5)

This illustration assumes little or no further decrease in demand when the price is marked up. But Wachtel and Adelsheim point out that their conclusion—that monopolies will raise prices in a recession by implementing these policies—holds true even if the price increases cause some further decline in demand. Of course, even the tightest monopoly, in reality, will lose a few customers from any price rise, but most of them have strong enough market control—and a strong enough image from advertising—that they won't lose many customers. Just how high a price they can set is a function of their degree of monopoly power—a power that is roughly reflected in their high degrees of industrial concentration.

More specifically, their degree of monopoly power over price has three main constraints. First, if the industry raises its price (led by the price leader), how many customers are willing or able to switch to a substitute product? Second, if the price is raised and if this leads to a higher profit margin, how many new firms will be able to enter the industry, or how high are the barriers to such new entrants? Third, what is the realistic likelihood of any government intervention if the price gouging becomes too obvious to be overlooked?

It follows from this *cost-plus* behavior that such oligopolistic firms do not change their prices as frequently as competitive firms. Even if there is rapid inflation of prices and costs, these firms usually keep one price for quite a while, then raise it to the new level dictated by their usual profit margin above costs. Thus there is considerable evidence that in periods of business expansion and rapid inflation, it is the prices of the more competitive firms that rise more rapidly and change from day to day.

In a recession, however, the small, competitive firms are immediately forced to drop their prices as demand falls (since no one of them can restrict the industry supply), regardless of the effect on their profit rates. This is not so for the large, oligopolistic firms. In the recession, if their costs per unit remain the same (as they do in physical terms over a wide range of output), then they can and will adjust their prices so as to maintain total profits as near constant as possible. Of course, that entails extra reduction of production and unemployment of many more workers than in a similar competitive industry, but that is not their worry.

If, as in recent recessions, costs per unit actually rose in the early part of recessions (with declining productivity), they will actually raise prices as far as they believe necessary to maintain profit rates. Productivity per unit declines at first because the corporations hesitate to fire excess workers (at the lower production levels) since the decline may be only temporary. When the recession deepens and they realize it may be lengthy, the large corporations make very drastic employment cuts to be efficient at a much lower output.

MONOPOLY AND STABILITY OF PROFIT RATES

According to this cost-plus explanation of monopoly price and output behavior, the monopoly sector should show much more stable profit rates
than the competitive sector. And indeed it does. Profit rates rise almost
twice as fast in the competitive sector as profit rates in the monopoly sector
in the average expansion. But profit rates in the competitive sector also
fall almost twice as fast as profit rates in the monopoly sector in the average
contraction. Specifically, in the eleven most concentrated industry groups
in the cycles of the 1950s and early 1960s, the profit rate (on sales for all
U.S. manufacturing corporations) rose an average of 27 points in expansions
and fell an average of 30 points in contractions. In the same period in the
nine most competitive industry groups, the profit rate rose an average of
52 percent in expansions and fell by 58 percent in contractions (see Sherman, p. 171). The conclusion is that monopoly profit rates are far more
stable than competitive profit rates.

Table 37.3 presents similar data on cyclical fluctuations in corporate
profit rates on capital according to the size of the corporation from 1970
through 1982. These data on profit rate fluctuations by size are interesting
because most large corporations have monopoly power, and most monopolized industries contain very large corporations. Table 37.3 shows that
the profit rates of the larger corporations rise less in expansions and fall
less in contractions than the profit rates of the smaller corporations. Therefore, it may be concluded that the profit rates of large monopoly corporations are far more stable than those of small competitive corporations.

Why do the large monopoly corporations have more stable profit rates
in boom and bust? First, they attempt to set their prices so as to maintain

Table 37.3 CORPORATE SIZE AND PROFIT RATES ON CAPITAL[a]
Average, 3 Cycles, 1970 to 1982

Asset size	Change in expansion	Change in contraction
0–$5 million	+49	−58
5–10 million	+39	−43
10–50 million	+35	−41
50–100 million	+36	−42
100–250 million	+25	−37
250–1000 million	+21	−38
Over $1 billion	+22	−33

Source: U.S. Census Bureau, Quarterly Financial Reports of Manufacturing Corporations
(Washington, D.C.: GPO, 1970–1982).

[a] Quarterly data, all U.S. manufacturing corporations. Profit before tax to stockholders'
equity. Expansion change measures change in standing from initial trough to cycle peak.
Contraction change measures change in standing from cycle peak to final trough.

a stable profit rate. Second, their monopoly power allows them to set their prices at those levels. They maintain those prices in contractions by restricting their production and employment. In expansion they raise prices only slowly while rapidly increasing their production and employment to obtain or keep a high share of the expanding market. Third, the costs of the largest corporations may rise a little at lower output levels but nowhere near the cost increase per unit of the small corporations in each contraction. The unit costs of small corporations rise rapidly when they go below optimum capacity. Fourth, the effective interest burden in small corporations is greater than in large corporations both because they pay higher interest rates and because they borrow a higher percentage of their capital. Fifth, and very important, the small corporations have all their eggs in one basket (with no reserves), while the large conglomerates are very diversified with some investments in industries that may happen to grow in spite of a contraction. The conglomerates can shift reserve capital from strong to weak areas.

There is also some evidence that crises hit the small competitive firms long before they hit the large monopoly firms. In the business expansions in the period from 1947 to 1963, the profit margins of the nine most competitive industry groups turned down 6.7 months, on the average, before the expansion peak. Yet the profit margins of the monopoly industries (the 11 most concentrated groups) did not feel the squeeze for another 4 months, turning down on the average only 2.2 months before the expansion peak. It appears that the increased monopolization of the economy produces a more stable sector of high monopoly power but further destabilizes the competitive sector. And the instability of the competitive sector is the prime factor setting off each new crisis of overproduction and contraction.

SUMMARY

There are at least three types of inflation. First, there is normal cyclical inflation. Prices usually rise a little during every business expansion but fall during recessions or depressions. Second, there is wartime inflation. In every war period—from the Revolutionary War to the Vietnam War—there was extreme inflationary pressure. Wartime inflation is caused by demand for war production, which forces governments to attempt to buy more equipment, raw materials, and labor than are actually available. The third type of inflation, sometimes called stagflation, is inflation in the midst of unemployment and stagnation.

The new phenomenon of inflation in the midst of unemployment has not been caused by trade unions, whose membership (as a percentage of all U.S. workers) and power have been slipping. One major cause of the new type of inflation has been the vast increase of monopoly power in the United States. Because of the high level of monopoly power, prices in the monopoly sector actually rose in the four recessions of 1954, 1958, 1961, and 1970, whereas competitive prices fell in those four recessions. In the depressions of 1974–1975 and 1980–1982, prices rose in both sectors, but they rose much faster in the monopoly sector than in the competitive sector.

Monopolies find it more profitable in the long run to raise their prices in the face of declining demands. Their success is shown by the fact that their profit rates fall far less than do profit rates in the competitive sector. Monopolies maintain or raise their high prices by restricting production, thereby also increasing unemployment.

SUGGESTED READINGS

Two interesting books on the unemployment and inflation of the 1970s are John Blair, *Roots of Inflation* (1975), and David Mermelstein, *The Economic Crisis Reader* (1975).

REFERENCES

Akhdar, Farouk. Multinational Firms and Developing Countries. Ph.D. Dissertation, University of California, Riverside, 1975.

Blair, John. *Economic Concentration.* New York: Harcourt Brace Jovanovich, 1972.

———, ed. *The Roots of Inflation* New York: Franklin, 1975.

Edwards, Richard. "The Impact of Industrial Concentration on the Economic Crisis." In Mermelstein, pp. 215–230.

Eichner, Alfred. "A Theory of the Determination of the Mark-up Under Oligopoly." *Economic Journal* 83 (Dec. 1973), pp. 1184–1199.

Harrison, Bennett. "Inflation by Oligopoly: Two Case Histories," *The Nation*, August 30, 1975, pp. 145–148.

Means, Gardiner. "Inflation and Unemployment." In John Blair, ed., *The Roots of Inflation*, pp. 1–15.

Mermelstein, David, ed. *The Economic Crisis Reader.* New York: Random House, 1975.

Mills, Frederick. *Price-Quantity Interaction in Business Cycles.* New York: National Bureau of Economic Research, 1946.

Roberts, Markley. "The Interlock of Corporate Power." *AFL-CIO American Federationist,* August 1978, pp. 5–8.

Robbins, William. "The American Food Scandal." In Mermelstein, pp. 320–331.

Sherman, Howard J. *Profits in the United States.* Ithaca, N.Y.: Cornell University Press, 1968, p. 171.

U.S. Small Business Administration. *Annual Report on Small Business and Competition.* Washington, D.C.: GPO, 1982.

Wachtel, Howard, and Peter Adelsheim. "The Inflationary Impact of Unemployment: Price Markups During Postwar Recessions, 1947–1970." U.S. Congress Joint Economic Committee, *Hearings.* Washington, D.C.: GPO, November 1976.

Chapter
38

Inflation and Government Controls

We have explained that since the Great Depression, the total spending of federal, state, and local governments has risen to equal about one-third of GNP. Total taxes amount to almost as much. We have also discovered that the Federal Reserve System can and does take many measures to increase or decrease the money supply, to lower or raise interest rates.

In a time of recession or depression, with high unemployment, the government often tries to increase demand by increasing spending (both military and civilian), decreasing taxes (to increase consumer and investor demand), and increasing the supply of money for lending (to reduce interest rates and increase investment). If the private economy has reached the point in the business cycle where it is ripe for a new upturn, then these policies may trigger an economic expansion. In the expansion, not only does unemployment decline, but also—unfortunately—there seems to be an increase in the rate of inflation.

Near the peak of the expansion, and especially in wartime expansion, there is a further increase in the rate of inflation. To combat rising prices—and especially to combat rising wages—many U.S. administrations have increased taxes, reduced government spending, and reduced the money supply. These policies, undertaken when the private economy is already reaching a peak and is ripe for a downturn, have often acted as a catalyst to begin a recession or depression. This certainly increases unemployment; it is also supposed to reduce inflation, but that did not happen in the 1973–1975 depression. In the 1981–1982 depression, inflation was finally reduced to 4 or 5 percent, but the cost in terms of the human misery of unemployment was very high.

Various government policies have thus reinforced the private-sector business cycle by setting off some depressions as well as some recoveries. Furthermore, policies that were supposed to reduce inflation have usually caused unemployment, while policies that were supposed to reduce unemployment have usually increased inflation.

Massive government intervention also appears to have had another effect. It has changed people's expectations. No one expects government to allow another Great Depression. So no one expects government anti-inflation policy to actually reduce inflation by much—it appears that only extreme unemployment and depression would do that. Therefore, most people expect inflation to continue. Because of this expectation, consumers tend to make inflation worse by rushing to buy before prices go up further. Because of the same expectation, business leaders tend to worsen inflation by refusing to reduce their prices in a recession (expecting that government will help stimulate demand). Thus government policy itself is partly responsible for the continuing inflation in the midst of unemployment—yet it surely would be unthinkable to cause the misery of extreme unemployment just to end the expectation of continuing inflation.

In the 1970s, after some early signs in the 1950s and 1960s, the American economy experienced a first in the nation's history: simultaneous high unemployment and high inflation. This situation appears impossible, according to elementary Keynesian analysis, because inflation implies an excess of demand over supply. Part of the answer to the riddle, as demonstrated earlier, lies in the monopoly power of American capitalism. In spite of a certain amount of unemployment, the largest corporations actually still have the power to continue to raise their prices, in what may be called profit-push inflation. Government policy itself has been a second factor causing continued inflation in the midst of unemployment.

No aggregate monetary or fiscal policy can remedy or prevent both inflation and unemployment in these circumstances. To end unemployment by increasing aggregate demand sufficiently to affect output in all sectors allows the monopoly sector to set off another inflation spiral. To end inflation by reducing aggregate demand sufficiently to affect monopoly prices causes catastrophic unemployment in the whole economy. The capitalist governments of the United States and Europe have generally chosen to combat inflation at the expense of more unemployment. Yet even high levels of unemployment have failed to end inflation; only truly catastrophic levels of unemployment would end inflation given (1) the present monopoly structure of the economy and (2) the expectation of further inflation.

WAGE-PRICE CONTROLS

Since neither monetary nor fiscal policy does much good against stagflation, in the early 1970s some liberal economists—especially John Kenneth Galbraith—began to call for direct wage-price controls over the economy. Knowing that the conservative President Nixon would never use such controls, the liberal Democrats in Congress gave the president power to use controls just to embarrass him politically before the 1972 election. Nixon, however, wanted to win the election and knew that he might lose it if he did nothing to end unemployment and inflation. Therefore, despite the conservative ideology against controlling the economy, on August 15, 1971, Nixon imposed wage and price controls to reduce inflation. He also increased military spending to reduce unemployment. He won the election.

Why should this ancient history concern us? Because this is the only case of wage and price controls in America in peacetime (the Vietnam War was at least winding down). We can learn much from studying it. Of course, in the late 1970s President Carter imposed voluntary controls. But all we can say about voluntary controls is that they have no appreciable impact on inflation.

Phase 1 of Nixon's controls ran for 90 days from August to November 1971. All wages, prices, and rents were frozen. Profits were not frozen. Nixon explained that the controls were necessary because we had combined inflation and unemployment, and all other monetary and fiscal policies had failed.

Phase 2 lasted from November 1971 until January 1973. The freeze was ended, but there were mandatory controls over wages, prices, and rents—though, again, not of profits. Under this system inflation continued, though at a reduced rate of "only" about 4 percent per year. Unemployment fell from its highest level (in the official data) of about 6 percent in the 1971 recession down to about 5 percent. Wages were successfully kept to a very, very slow increase in this period, but profit rates rose. Profit rates on investor's equity before taxes were "only" 16.5 percent in 1971, but rose to 18.4 percent in 1972.

Phase 3 was supposed to "phase out the economic stabilization program back to the free market, since the price target was being achieved," according to administration spokespersons. It removed all controls over prices in all industries except food, health, and construction, and substituted voluntary controls. The voluntary controls were no controls at all because they had no enforcement procedure; therefore business paid no attention to them, so prices skyrocketed, rising at about 8 percent a year. In the end even the administration admitted failure in holding down prices and had to institute a new freeze. Phase 3 lasted only from January to June 1973. A striking feature of it was the pressure kept on the unions to abide by voluntary controls and the extent to which the unions did restrain workers from asking for wage raises. Thus there was a very, very slight rise in money wages, and a drastic decline in the earning power of workers. Again there were no controls on profits, which continued to soar. The profit rate on equity rose to 21.6 percent in 1973.

Phase 3½ was a second freeze. All prices were frozen, but there were no controls on unprocessed food or on rents. Neither wages nor profits were frozen, but wages remained under Phase 3 controls. This phase lasted only 60 days, from June to August 1973.

Phase 4 began in August 1973 and ended in April 1974. It was again a mandatory system of controls over prices, wages, and rents, but not over profits. It was very effective in holding down wages, but prices continued to rise at about 10 percent per year. The lack of enforcement on the price side was apparent in the case of the oil industry. The Cost of Living Council allowed the price of "old oil" (from existing wells, averaging less than $1 a barrel to produce) to rise from $4.25 to $5.25 a barrel. The council allowed the price of "new oil" (which cost no more than $2 a barrel to produce) to rise to $10.50. Then during the shortage in the winter of 1974, the Federal Energy Office allowed the retailers' profit margin to rise from 7.25 cents a gallon to 11 cents—and this increase was not rescinded in the later period of surplus (see Harrison, p. 147). The profit rate on stockholder's equity for all of manufacturing rose to 23.4 percent in 1974, while real wages declined.

Controls, Inefficiency, and Corruption

Economists of all ideological views criticized the controls of 1971–1974 but for different reasons. Conservatives, such as Milton Friedman, were horrified at the violation of the First Commandment of laissez-faire economics: Thou shalt not interfere with the market process of setting wages and prices (see Friedman, p. 45). They have always argued that resources, including capital and labor, cannot be efficiently allocated if prices are not set by competition in the market. If the government arbitrarily sets prices, how can a businessperson calculate most efficiently what to produce or what technology to use? If a business calculates rationally on the basis of the arbitrary prices set by the government, then it will not choose the inputs that would be cheapest in a purely competitive market, so it will not produce in the cheapest possible way in the light of available resources. Thus, wage-price controls doom a capitalist economy to inefficiency.

Other economists go further along these lines to point out that a huge bureaucracy would be needed to really enforce these controls. Not only would that bureaucracy have enormous repressive power, but it would also be wide open to corruption. After all, if businesspeople cannot freely raise their prices when opportunity arises, then they are better off spending their time and money bribing bureaucrats to raise their prices than worrying about producing a better-quality product. At the same time, the controls do not end the money-grubbing aspect of capitalism. If capitalists cannot freely raise prices, then they will either bribe the bureaucrats or else evade the controls by selling illegally (that is, on a black market, the way much gasoline was sold during the crisis). In this sense comprehensive wage-price controls in a capitalist system combine the worst aspects of capitalism and Soviet-style socialism: a huge and inefficient bureaucracy plus private greed.

CONTROLS AND INCOME DISTRIBUTION

When the conservatives such as Friedman argued against the controls, their own solution was an unregulated private capitalism. Liberals such as Paul Samuelson pointed out politely that Nixon had already tried that solution and that it was an unregulated private capitalism that had resulted in our present unpleasant mixture of inflation and unemployment. Moreover, they pointed out that even the usual monetary and fiscal policies could not cope with inflation and unemployment at the same time. In fact, it was the liberals who first advocated the controls; they expected controls to hold down prices, while welfare spending would increase demand to eliminate unemployment. At first the liberals applauded Nixon's controls. Even in their naiveté, though, their initial reactions were a little doubtful on two points: Would Nixon actually hold down prices or just wages? And would he actually spend enough on welfare programs to end unemployment?

They were right to worry and wrong to applaud at all. Nixon actually (1) held down wages, (2) allowed prices to continue to rise, and (3) did nothing to cure unemployment, except some military spending. The important thing to understand is that this was not accidental, nor would Nixon be the only president to attempt such a policy. It was shown above that all U.S. governments have been strongly probusiness, for the very good reason that business money elects them (and many other reasons). Any wage-price controls under a business-dominated government can be expected to favor business.

President Nixon was much more blunt about his probusiness biases than most presidents have been. For example, in his speech announcing the wage-price controls, Nixon said, "All Americans will benefit from more profits. More profits fuel the expansion. . . . More profits means more investment. . . . And more profits mean there will be more tax revenues. . . . That's why higher profits in the American economy would be good for every person in America" (Nixon, television speech). Vice-President Agnew repeated the theory, saying: "Rising corporate profits are needed more than ever by the poor" (Agnew, speech). Can you think of some things the poor might need more than rising corporate profits?

Nixon and Agnew succeeded quite well in their objectives of limiting wages and raising profits. Thus in all of Phase 1 and Phase $3\frac{1}{2}$ wages didn't rise at all. During all of the longer phases 2 and 3, average hourly earnings rose only 5.9 percent a year. At the same time, the cost of living rose by about 4 percent yearly in Phase 2, 8 percent yearly in Phase 3, and about 10 percent yearly in Phase 4. Since the cost of living rose faster than wages in 1973, for the first time on record in a year of economic expansion, the buying power of workers declined. In 1973, during Phases 3 and 4, wages rose by about 5 percent and retail prices by about 9 percent, so real wages (that is, what the worker can buy) declined by 4 percent. While real wages were declining, profit rates were rising. The only peacetime expansions in US history in which real wages declined were those under presidents Nixon and Reagan.

One way Nixon achieved these results was by appointing a probusiness Pay Board to make wage decisions. The big unions first joined it, hoping to salvage some crumbs, then withdrew when they found they were to be allowed nothing. The AFL-CIO said: "We joined the Pay Board in good faith, desiring—despite our misgivings—to give it a fair chance. . . . The so-called public members are neither neutral nor independent. They are tools of the Administration, and inbued with its viewpoint that all of the nation's economic ills are caused by high wages. As a result, the Pay Board has been completely dominated and run, from the very start, by a coalition of the business and so-called public members. . . . The trade union movement's representatives on the board have been treated as outsiders— merely as a facade to maintain the pretense of a tripartite body" (AFL-CIO Executive Committee, p. 7).

One must conclude that the inevitable results of wage-price controls under a capitalist government are additional corruption and inefficiency, as well as a shift in income distribution away from wages and toward profits. The meaning of the *political* business cycle is also clarified. At the peak of expansion, when workers are pushing for higher wages, the U.S. government talks about inflation; and it uses restrictive monetary or fiscal or direct controls to lower wages and even promote a little unemployment. At the bottom of the depression, the U.S. government is moved by corporate pleas to stimulate the economy. The capitalist system would generate boom-and-bust cycles without government interference, but the government does reinforce them and may often serve as the catalyst setting off the downswing as well as the upswing (at such times as the economy was ripe for a change in direction anyway).

STAGFLATION POLICY AND THE IDEOLOGY OF ECONOMISTS

It was noted earlier that most traditional economists see high wages as the cause of economic downturns. According to Leftwich and Sharp: "The general solution to involuntary unemployment is a reduction in real wage rates until the amount of labor demanded equals the amount supplied. In a competitive market, the reduction in real wage rates would take place automatically" (Leftwich and Sharpe, p. 249). In their view, the problem is that unions use monopoly power to prevent workers' wages from falling, since competition among workers would force wages to drop when unemployment exists. So they imply that government should control wages. Of course, it is true that lower labor costs would induce capitalists to hire more workers if demand for products remains the same. But demand is the fly in the ointment. Wage income is the largest component of consumer demand, so lower wages mean less demand for products, which means less demand for workers.

When conservatives tire of discussing unions, they discuss government. Thus Milton Friedman and the monetarist school explain depressions in this way:

> Most of the blame is assigned to misguided policies of the government. . . . For example, a considerable amount of government activity was generated in an effort to combat the (Great) Depression, which is usually blamed on instability of the private sector. However, monetarists contend that the Depression was caused by improper monetary policies. . . . The government is seen as using intervention as a cure for problems which are actually caused by intervention. . . . The (private) economy can restore equilibrium through appropriate changes in prices with relatively little instability in output, employment, or other real factors. (Mitchell, Hand, and Walter, pp. 271–272)

Friedman's monetarist views involve a whole catalog of errors, which can only be briefly listed here. First, as was shown in earlier chapters, the Great Depression and most other depressions were created by the normal workings of the private capitalist system. Government policies may worsen, or sometimes set off, depressions, but they are not the basic cause of capitalist systemic instability and its proclivity to cycles of boom and bust. Second, monetary policy played a very small role in the 1930s, though Roosevelt's fiscal policy did help somewhat in the mid-1930s (but it was too little and too late). Moreover, it was the Republican Hoover who let the depression intensify. How much more conservative and noninterventionist than Hoover could a president be? Earlier in this chapter we saw that the U.S. government is not an independent factor above the battle, but usually follows the desires of private capitalism.

Third, the modern monetarists repeat the ancient advice of Say's law—that the private economy left to itself will automatically restore full employment. As a main mechanism, they rely on prices dropping under competitive pressures as demand drops; this would sell more goods and keep a high level of production and employment. Unfortunately, as shown in this chapter, the competitive process now operates only in one small sector where prices and profits drop drastically. In the larger monopoly sector, prices do not fall and even rise in the recession, while production and employment fall rapidly. Moreover, as shown previously, even if wages and prices moved downward with alacrity, this would more likely result (as it often did in earlier depressions) in a downward spiral of falling demand than in an immediate cure.

Faced with simultaneous inflation and unemployment, the liberal Paul Samuelson saw a dilemma with no obvious way out of it. Milton Friedman and his friends see it simply as a case requiring the sacrifice of heavy unemployment (by workers, not by Friedman) to keep stable prices. He claims that in any given situation there is a natural rate of unemployment, which is the level of unemployment that will prevent further inflation. "This unemployment rate is thus consistent with any rate of inflation, and they argue that attempts to move the unemployment rate permanently below . . . this 'natural rate' by use of aggregate demand policies will result in an acceleration of the rate of inflation" (Ott, Ott, and Yoo, p. 260). Since it is natural, nothing can be done about it, and any attempt to reduce the natural unemployment will only make things worse. Perhaps high unemployment with stable or rising monopoly prices is natural in the monopoly stage of capitalism; but capitalism itself is not a natural phenomenon and can be replaced.

ANTITRUST POLICY

There are many liberal economists, and even many U.S. senators, who agree that monetary and fiscal policy are inadequate to stop an inflation generated by monopoly power. In fact, they perceive monopoly power as the prime cause of many U.S. political and economic problems. Their solution is to break up the monopolies through stronger antitrust laws. For several reasons, the trust-busting solution is not a good one, although any critical economist can sympathize with it.

Liberals see monopoly as an accident, a temporary aberration. It was shown earlier, however, that the monopolies are the very heart of U.S. capitalism. Giant monopoly corporations produce and sell the majority of American goods. Therefore, to break up all the monopolies is not a simple reform but would constitute a major revolution.

It must also be emphasized that breaking up a monopoly into just four or five parts does little good. Most of our so-called monopoly industries are right now technically oligopolies, with four to eight major firms dominating them. They all play follow-the-price-leader, however, so they all act exactly like a single monopoly firm. To achieve something approaching pure competition requires many thousands of small firms in each industry, so each monopoly must be broken into thousands of parts. Would it make technological sense to break up the auto, oil, or steel industries into thousands of tiny firms?

Even if Americans were willing to sacrifice that much efficiency and extra effort in production, is it politically feasible? As long as U.S. capitalism is to be preserved, how could there be the political and economic power to cut up its very heart into thousands of pieces? To make a major revolution without disturbing the basic system is not feasible. At present, as we saw earlier, the antitrust laws are much too mild to be any barrier to increasing economic concentration. But even if stronger laws were passed, that would not be enough because the antitrust laws are never enforced. The antitrust division of the U.S. Justice Department always operates on a shoestring, with a budget far less than the legal department of any of the giant corporations. And if the laws are totally rewritten, and the enforcement budget multiplied a thousand times, the conservative U.S. Supreme Court always narrowly restricts the antitrust laws (and might declare a sweeping one unconstitutional). There is thus no feasible political hope within the capitalist system for substituting millions of competitive firms for the present monopolies.

Suppose, however, such a political revolution within capitalist boundaries were successful. A country of all small, competitive firms would presumably resemble the present competitive sector. This sector is characterized by (1) sweat-shops, low wages, more exploitation of workers; (2) self-exploitation of the small business owner and his or her family, with long hours and little rewards; (3) little or no research and very little efficiency; and (4) violent swings downward in depression, with big losses and thousands of bankruptcies. Is this what one wants as an ideal situation?

OTHER SOLUTIONS

One liberal solution to unemployment and inflation, advocated at times by John Kenneth Galbraith, Senator Edward Kennedy, and the AFL-CIO, is to combine a certain amount of Keynesian stimulation with price controls. A large enough amount of peaceful, constructive government spending will stimulate the economy and will remove unemployment. We have noted earlier that there are many administrative and political barriers to this solution, but it is a feasible solution to unemployment. The major economic problem with this solution is that it tends to lead to inflation.

But inflation can be overcome by price controls. Since wages always follow prices, no wage controls are needed; this will prevent bias against workers. Since the main sector raising prices in the face of recession is the monopoly sector, no controls are needed on small business prices. This reduction in price controls to a relatively small number of giant corporations would make the controls much easier to administrate. Thus, such controls are also feasible in the short run. In the long run, however, most of the problems cited above still will be impossible to overcome. Thus, a policy of stimulation and price controls may be very useful in the short run but cannot succeed in the long run.

If that policy were tried, but eventually ran into problems, then one would either have to return to no controls or try the more radical road of a planned economy. Historical experience in other countries seems to prove that inflation and unemployment can be combatted by outright public ownership of enterprises and a planned economy, but we shall see in Part Four that this solution also presents various problems.

SUMMARY

Since aggregate monetary and fiscal policy will not cure simultaneous inflation and unemployment, the Nixon-Ford administration was forced to try direct wage-price controls to restrict cost-push inflation. The problems of this policy were (1) inefficiency, as prices no longer reflected demand and supply conditions; (2) probusiness bias, allowing for reduction of real wages through price loopholes and little attention to unemployment; and (3) continued monopoly profits based on new loopholes in the regulations and new black markets. For all of these reasons, price controls may be a useful part of a short-run effort to stop inflation under certain circumstances, but very few economists believe that it is a long-run answer.

The ability of public ownership to end unemployment and inflation, as well as the problems of public ownership, are discussed in Part Four of this book.

REFERENCES

AFL-CIO Executive Committee. *The National Economy.* AFL-CIO, 1973.

Agnew, Spiro, Vice-President. Speech at National Governors' Conference, 1971.

Friedman, Milton. *Newsweek,* August 30, 1971.

Harrison, Bennett. "Inflation by Oligopoly." *The Nation.* August 30, 1975.

Leftwich, Richard, and Ansel Sharp. *Economics of Social Issues.* Homewood, Ill.: Irwin, 1974.

Mitchell, William, John Hand, and Ingo Walter. *Readings in Macroeconomics.* New York: McGraw-Hill, 1975.

Nixon, Richard, President. Speech on television, August 15, 1975.

Ott, David, Attiat Ott, and Jang Yoo. *Macroeconomic Theory.* New York: McGraw-Hill, 1975.

Samuelson, Paul. *Newsweek,* August 30, 1971.

Chapter
39

Economic Growth

This chapter is confined to growth in the industrialized capitalist countries, leaving growth in less developed countries to Chapter 42 and growth in planned economies to Part Four. It is assumed here that growth is a good thing, but its undesirable aspects are discussed in the next chapter. We begin with the clash between the classical theory of growth and the critics of that theory. Then we shall turn to practical issues of present concern.

CLASSICAL VIEW OF GROWTH

The classical economists believed in Say's law, which argues that demand always automatically adjusts to supply. Thus, they had no worries about lack of demand, but discussed growth only in terms of supply. In its simplest terms, they visualized the supply of output as equal to the amount of capital times the productivity of capital, according to the classical economists. Productivity of capital is defined here merely as the ratio of the amount of output to the amount of capital. The productivity of capital would be determined by technology, availability of skilled workers, and availability of raw materials. The amount of capital would be determined by the amount of saving from current output, with most saving coming from the profits of capitalists. Thus, more capital would be invested if wages were held down so as to produce more profits. Also, the competition among capitalists to make profits would pressure them into finding and applying new technology in the economy, which would increase the productivity of capital.

The *rate of growth* is defined as the change in output as a percentage of current output. If the current level of output is 100 units and there is an increase in output of 5 units, then the rate of growth is 5/100 equals .05, or 5 percent. According to the classical economists the rate of growth will equal the productivity of capital times the propensity to save. Thus:

Growth rate = productivity of capital × propensity to save

What exactly do these mysterious terms mean? The propensity to save is the ratio of saving (which is nonconsumption) to income or output, so we could represent it as saving/output. The classical economists assumed that all saving is invested, so this term just tells us how much of current output is used for new investment in plant and equipment. New plant and equipment tells us the amount of increase in capital.

Naturally, the next question is what is produced by this increase in capital? The classical economists assumed that technology determines some ratio between increases in capital and increases in output. So if we know how much capital is saved and how much a unit of capital produces, we know the growth rate. A simple equation, reflecting this view, is

Growth rate

= increase in output/increase in capital × saving/output

Notice that "saving" means "increase in capital" in this view. If that is true, these two terms may be canceled, leaving

Growth rate = increase in output/output

which is true by definition.

An example will clarify the equation. Suppose that initial output is 100 units. Suppose we save 9 percent, or 9 units. Then saving to output equals .09. Suppose each 3 units of new capital (or "saving") produce one unit of new output, so that increase of output to increase of capital equals $\frac{1}{3}$. Therefore, the rate of growth is equal to .09 times $\frac{1}{3}$ equals .03, or 3 percent. We may think of this process as saving 9 units of capital, which produce 3 additional units of output. The long-run growth rate of the United States was 3 percent a year for many decades.

SAVING AND GROWTH

There are two quite distinct points of view about saving. Classical economists, concerned as they were about economic growth, called for as much thriftiness and saving as possible. In early nineteenth-century England they observed that the savings of businesspeople were being used to build more capital. They drew the moral that more thrift and saving led to a more rapid increase of capital and, consequently, to more rapid economic growth.

Keynes pointed out that this conclusion is true only if we assume full employment and the rule of Say's law, which claims that demand is always enough for any supply of goods and that all saving is automatically invested. The classicals did make this assumption when they asked how fast the economy would grow if there were always enough demand and if all saving were always invested. This assumption, however, is not true. During each recession or depression it is painfully obvious to all Americans that there is not full employment. In each recession or depression most saving is not being invested; this fact is ignored by supply-side economists and by all those who emphasize the mythical "shortage of capital."

Keynes showed that, with unemployment and lack of investment opportunities, more saving actually leads to less production rather than more. This finding constitutes the *paradox of thrift*, which says that greater thrift and saving may sometimes lead to less investment, not more. If the economy is faced with a lack of effective demand, then a higher propensity to save may simply lower consumer demand still further. The lower consumer demand may then lead to still less output and income and therefore to less aggregate saving and investment than there was before individuals tried to save more of their income. Thrift may always be an individual virtue, as Ben Franklin preached, but it is not always a social virtue when there is a lack of paying customers in a private-enterprise economy.

More saving at a given income level is a benefit to the economy if, and only if, there is an equal increase in investment. In other words, more saving, which could supply more capital to produce more output, is helpful only if businesspeople expect demand to rise by an equal amount. Otherwise they will not invest, but will hoard the increased saving and precipitate a recession or depression.

In the modern world we cannot afford to ignore either side of the problem. The U.S. rate of growth has declined. Setting aside more saving to invest in more capital makes it *possible* to raise the rate of growth. But this possibility cannot become a reality as long as significant numbers of unemployed persons and unused capacity continue. Such conditions show that all of the savings now available are not being invested. More saving would only cause more unemployment in this case. First one must guarantee a solution to the Keynesian problem of finding profitable investment outlets for all existing savings. Then one can worry about the classical problem of generating a higher rate of saving to allow the possibility of more investment.

IS THERE A SHORTAGE OF CAPITAL?

We have noted above that decline in growth is usually traced by the classical economists to a decline in capital investment. New capital is seen as coming from saving, mostly from the profits of business. In the 1970s and 1980s, this viewpoint was brought back to the center of the stage very strongly. Specifically, it was argued that the lack of capital could be traced back to a falling rate of profit. Among supply-side economists and other new clas-

Table 39.1   PROFIT RATES, BEFORE TAXES, ON STOCKHOLDERS' EQUITY
1933–1982 (ALL MANUFACTURING CORPORATIONS)

Cycle	Average Profit Rate (%)	Events
1933–1938	3.8	Great Depression
1938–1945	16.2	World War II
1945–1949	17.8	
1949–1954	24.3	Korean War
1954–1958	21.0	
1956–1961	17.3	
1961–1970	19.3	Vietnam War
1970–1975	19.5	Vietnam War, wage-price controls
1975–1980	22.9	
1980–1982	18.3	Reagan depression

Sources: 1933–1949, annual data from U.S. Internal Revenue Service, Statistics of Income, Corporate Income Tax Returns (Washington, D.C.: GPO, 1935–1951); 1949–1982, quarterly data from U.S. Federal Trade Commission and Securities and Exchange Commission, Quarterly Financial Report of Manufacturing Corporations (Washington, D.C.: GPO, 1950–1988).

sical economists, the low profits were then seen as caused by either the strength of unions and high wages or by high taxes imposed by government.

In the mid-1970s, propaganda from Wall Street contended that the overall profit rate of U.S. corporations had been falling since at least 1965 (editorial in the *Wall Street Journal*, February 20, 1975). A look at the data in Table 39.1, taken from official sources, shows that profit rates have fluctuated enormously but have not indicated any trend. Profit rates were lowest during the Great Depression. Profit rates rose greatly in World War II but were held down somewhat by wartime controls. When the controls were removed, profit rates rose again. They reached their height in the Korean War, when only minimal controls existed. Profit rates then fell for two cycles. They were revived again by the Vietnam War and thus rose in the 1960s and 1970s. Profit rates fell in the Reagan depression of 1981–1982. In general, profit rates rose in wars and fell in depressions. There is no long-run trend in this 50-year period.

Many business economists argued in the 1970s and 1980s that lower amounts of profit led to a "shortage of capital" available for investment for long-run growth. For example, it was written in 1975 that "the total amount of new investment capital that will be needed for continued economic growth between 1974 and 1985 has been set at $4.7 *trillion* by a recent New York Stock Exchange study" (Wycko, p. 16). A very similar estimate by the Commerce Department was cited by the U.S. Treasury Department as a basis for arguing that present levels of corporate profits after taxes are insufficient to fill these immense capital needs. Treasury Secretary William Simon then drew the conclusion (which this argument was leading to) that the corporate tax rate should be lowered, perhaps to zero! (See United Press International.) On the basis of the same argument, he also favored lower tax rates on capital gains.

There are several problems with the argument that lack of profits leads to lack of capital for investment, both in depressions and over the long run. First, it has been shown here that profit rates in the United States have not fallen in the long run. Similarly, a careful British study found that the same conservative propaganda about a profit crisis in their economy is mythical, that in fact the share of profits after taxes in the United Kingdom has been stable (King).

Second, profits do drop in each recession or depression, but that does not mean that there is a lack of capital. In a depression, there is a surplus of capitalist saving with no profitable place to invest it. For example, Treasury Secretary Simon complained about lack of capital for investment in June 1975, a recession period. Yet, according to the government's own figures, in June 1975 fully 25 percent of all U.S. plant and equipment was standing idle (U.S. Department of Commerce, 1975). How can the problem be lack of capital when 25 percent of existing physical capital is not being utilized?

Lastly, it should be apparent that the main purpose of the conservatives' argument is to justify lighter taxes on corporations. A congressional investigation shows, however, that corporations are already paying very little in taxes because of loopholes in the law. Although the corporate rate was supposed to be 48 percent, in 1976 the actual rate paid by all corporations was only 13 percent of profits. Seventeen major corporations (including the United States Steel Company, with $518 million adjusted net income) paid no taxes at all. Representative Charles Vanik, chairman of the congressional investigation, concluded: "If U.S. corporations are already paying little or nothing in federal income taxes, it makes no sense to give them tax relief in an effort to stimulate investment capital" (see Vanik). Since that time (1978), some loopholes have been closed, but tax rates have been drastically lowered.

THE GOLDEN AGE (1950–1969)

The 1950s and 1960s were a golden age of growth in the United States. The GNP grew an average 4.1 percent a year from 1950 through 1969. Real wages, family income, and labor productivity, all grew continuously. There was more income equality and poverty declined. The main reasons for this golden age were (1) U.S. international dominance in both production and trade, (2) plenty of domestic demand, including government economic stimulation, (3) relatively low amounts of debt for both consumers and businesses, (4) fairly strong unions, and (5) relatively healthy small business.

THE DECLINE OF U.S. GROWTH (1970 TO PRESENT)

The growth rate declined drastically in the 1970s and 1980s. The GNP grew only 2.3 percent per year from 1970 to 1983. Family income stagnated. One study found that real family income was the same in 1987 as in 1973 (Mishel and Simon, p. 51). Many families maintained the same level only by having the wife go to work for pay, while those families with no increase in the number at work had reduced income. In 1979 to 1987 (mostly Reagan-Bush years) real hourly wages dropped by 7 percent! Productivity growth declined from 2.9 percent a year in 1950–1969 down to only 0.8 percent in 1970–1983. Inequality has increased under Reagan and Bush, with income from property ownership rising three times faster than income from work in the 1979–1983 period. The percentage of people living in poverty increased.

The declines in growth of GNP, family income, and productivity—as well as the absolute decline in real wages—resulted not only from the policies of the Reagan-Bush administration, but also from a number of structural changes. What are these major structural changes?

First, the 1950s and 1960s were influenced by major wars, including the aftermath of World War II, the Korean War, the Vietnam War, and a continuing cold war. As a result, the United States had a very high level of military spending in those years. The high military spending stimulated the economy and made it possible to have mild recessions and quick recoveries. This military spending declined in the 1970s as a percentage of GNP, but President Reagan increased military spending once more in the 1980s.

A second structural change has been in the international role of the United States. In 1950, the United States was totally dominant in production and trade. There was high demand for U.S. products from the war-devastated countries of Europe and Asia and almost no competition in most industries. Now the U.S. economy faces very serious competition from Japan and Western Europe.

Third, there has been a vast increase in consumer debt and business debt. This has made the economy of the 1970s and 1980s much more fragile and vulnerable to economic crisis than it was in the 1950s and 1960s; for example, some large banks have failed in recent recessions. Fourth, there has been an increase in monopoly power, resulting in price increases in the midst of recession, which makes recovery more difficult. Fifth, there has been a continuous decline in the percentage of workers in unions since 1955, which has lowered workers' bargaining power, lowered wages, and hence lowered consumer demand.

These structural changes have resulted in longer and more intensive recessions in the 1970s and 1980s than in the preceding two decades. For example, in the 1950s and 1960s, real wages and labor productivity continued to grow even in mild recessions, but both real wages and productivity actually fell in the more severe recessions of the 1970s and 1980s. The declining productivity in recessions may be the main reason for the declining average rate of growth of labor productivity. Obviously, if there is lower growth or productivity, this would be one reason for lower growth of GNP.

The increase in recessions also meant an increase in unemployment and a decrease in the utilization of capacity. From 1950 to 1969, unemployment rates averaged 4.5 percent, while capacity utilization averaged 84 percent. From 1970 to 1983, the average unemployment rate rose to 6.8 percent, while the average capacity utilization fell to 74 percent. This means that there were many more millions of unemployed workers and many more idle factories and idle machines in the 1970s and early 1980s than in the preceding decades. Of course, that would mean less growth of GNP.

Thus, it appears that the main reasons for lower growth rates have been related to a lack of effective demand, not to a lack of saving and capital; there has, rather, been an excess of saving and capital relative to the demand for goods and services during most of the period.

POPULATION AND GROWTH

Thomas Malthus compared the need for food for an expected increase in population with the expected returns of output from that increased population. The law of diminishing returns states that each additional worker adds less output than the previously hired worker. It holds true only if capital, natural resources, and technology remain unchanged and after some minimum scale of employment has been reached. Given these assumptions, the law of diminishing returns is a truism; it cannot be other than true. All other things remaining the same, it is obvious that if enough workers are crowded onto a single plot of land or even into the entire world, the crowding alone will eventually cause the product of an additional worker to decline. But many of the classical economists—Malthus, for example—went much further than the truism allowed in the law of diminishing returns. They predicted that diminishing returns per worker in the economy as a whole *would* come about in actual fact. Malthus reached this dismal conclusion on the grounds that population increase would be very rapid and would far outweigh the slow increase of capital, technology, and natural resources.

The gloomy long-run prediction based on this interpretation of the law of diminishing returns has not been borne out by the facts of historical progress. First, it is not even clear that the world population is at the minimum level at which further additions to the working force would bring diminishing returns, even if natural resources, capital, and technology were to remain constant. Second, labor itself improves in quality with advances in scientific and technical education. Third, it was usual to argue that the earth is only so large and that its natural resources are slowly being depleted. The supply of *known* natural resources is instead steadily expanding as a result of continual discoveries of new reserves. Furthermore, there have been important discoveries of new uses for previously neglected materials—for example, coal was once merely a hard black stone of no use for fuel or heating purposes. Moreover, better ways have been found to use available resources—for example, power production by atomic fusion or food production by hydroponic farming. Of course, the last two means of resource expansion are also aspects of technological improvement.

Another reason why there have not been diminishing returns per worker in the economy as a whole is the increasing use of capital per worker, which allows a single worker to produce far more than previously. The final and most important reason for the defeat of diminishing returns is that development of technology in the past century has meant a much more efficient use of the available capital, natural resources, and labor. At the early date Malthus wrote, it was still possible largely to ignore technological progress. Today even the blindest economist is forced to take into account the startling advances continually being made in production techniques.

Empirically the evidence shows that population in the developed countries has not outraced technology, natural resources, and capital, but that, on the contrary, product per person has grown enormously. In U.S. agriculture, increase of output has far outrun increase of employment. In fact, between 1870 and 1940 employment in agriculture rose by only 34 percent while output rose by 279 percent. The United States thus has no problem of lack of food but, rather, a surplus relative to effective cash demand.

There are, of course, periods of very low productivity under capitalism—usually when there is a lack of effective demand. We saw earlier in this chapter that the lower growth rates of the 1970s and 1980s were due primarily to an increased number of years of recession per decade.

It may be concluded that *in the industrialized private enterprise economies slowed progress or retrogression is caused not by natural and technical problems but by economic institutions that give rise to recurrent economic catastrophes.* The advent of atomic and solar energy makes it clear that the natural sciences have given us ample power to obtain in the future fantastic levels of abundance or to blow to pieces the entire world.

How fast is population likely to grow? Many Malthusian theorists mechanically project the present world rate of population growth into the near future and easily arrive at quite astronomical figures for total population. But it was demonstrated earlier that, to date at least, capital and technology have had no trouble keeping ahead of population growth; they probably could even keep pace with massive population growth in the coming years.

The mechanical prognostications of vast population growth, however, do not seem to have taken into account the best present knowledge of population growth patterns. Malthus described people breeding like animals and population exploding with only a few kinds of checks to its expansion. He spoke of "preventive checks" as those that cause lower birth rates. He recognized only abstention from sex or "vice and sexual deviation" and did not consider voluntary birth control through family planning and contraceptive methods. When preventive checks fail, according to Malthus, the result will be "positive checks" to population, where "positive" means a higher death rate. Thus positive checks include wars, famine, and disease.

It is true that in many primitive economies at a low level of productivity, we often find very high birthrates. At this stage, however, population may be constant for centuries because it is held in check by equally high deathrates, caused indeed by wars, disease, and starvation. A second stage of rapid population growth usually follows the beginnings of industrialization and the introduction of modern methods of public health sanitation. With better control of disease and enough food production, deathrates decline. As long as birth rates remain high, the population soars.

At the third stage, however, as the economy matures, we find culture and education spreading to all the population. Knowledge of contraceptive devices for birth control also spreads, as does the desire to use these means in order to keep the family to a manageable size. Thus all of the more industrialized countries have shown some tendency toward lower and lower birth rates during the past 100 years, although there have been some upward spurts in the rate for short periods.

SUMMARY

The classical and neoclassical economists contend that sufficient capital (given labor and raw materials and technology) is the key to economic growth. More capital can be obtained by increasing profits and the income of the wealthy. Keynes argued that there can be no growth without sufficient demand for goods and services. Inequality of income distribution, according to Keynesians and Marxists, may reduce consumer demand and thereby prevent growth.

Recent economists with a classical or neoclassical outlook have contended that low growth has resulted from lack of profits. Keynesians and Marxists have contended that structural changes in the U.S. economy and the world economy have caused more severe recessions, which have been the main cause of lower productivity and lower growth.

We also examined Malthus' contention that population is likely to outrun economic growth. The critics have noted that his gloomy predictions have been proved untrue, primarily because technology has caused rapid growth, while birthrates have declined.

Let us repeat that economic growth is necessary if many social ills are to be solved. With the widespread existence of poverty here and abroad, no one can deny that a larger output of goods and services is needed if everyone is to enjoy a high standard of living. Yet excessive concern with growth for its own sake has often obscured many significant economic and social problems. In Chapter 40 we will see that human welfare could be improved even with no further growth if various kinds of wastes were eliminated—and if more of the product went to the average person than to a minority of rich individuals. It will also be shown that the quality of economic growth (with a minimum of waste and pollution) is at least as important as the quantity of growth.

SUGGESTED READINGS

An excellent and very readable explanation of the structural changes that have lowered U.S. growth is found in Bennett Harrison and Barry Bluestone, *The Great U-Turn* (New York: Basic Books, 1988).

REFERENCES

King, M. A. "The United Kingdom Profits Crisis: Myth or Reality?" *The Economic Journal* 85:1 (March 1975), pp. 33–54.

Mishel, Lawrence, and Jacqueline Simon. "The State of Working America." *Challenge* 12:4 (November–December 1988), pp. 50–51.

United Press International. "Lower Corporate Taxes." *Riverside Press Enterprise*, June 20, 1975, p. A-3.

U.S. Department of Commerce. *Survey of Current Business*, August 1975.

Vanik, Charles. "Annual Corporate Tax Study of House Ways and Means Committee." *Congressional Record*, January 26, 1978.

Wycko, Bill. "The Work Shortage." *Review of Radical Political Economics* 8:2, (Summer 1975), pp. 10–21.

Chapter
40

Waste and Pollution

Growth in the U.S. capitalist economy has involved waste, pollution, and environmental destruction. Wasteful production should not be included in a calculation of social welfare because no social benefit is derived; nevertheless, it is included in the government's accounting of GNP. In fact, the pollution and other harm caused by some products should actually be *subtracted* from GNP as a social cost if we wish to compute the total national welfare from economic growth.

MILITARY PRODUCTION AND WASTE

It was seen earlier that most military "goods and services" (or "evils and disservices") are not needed by the people of the United States. Military spending serves the interests of the big businesses that produce for the military or have investments abroad that the armed forces protect from foreign revolutions. A dollar of military expenditure not only generates demand to that amount but also generates further spending by the workers and profit makers who receive the military spending. In other words, *if the system cannot reach full employment any other way, then military spending can produce full employment.* On the other hand, if military spending takes place when there is already full employment, then it competes with private spending for labor and resources and can only cause inflation.

It is a fact, however, that the U.S. capitalist system normally operates far below full employment. It is also a political fact of life that without military spending no other kind of government spending can possibly be done on the scale needed to produce full employment. Therefore, within the present system's political and economic constraints, it is true that vast military spending is "necessary" to maintain full employment. Moreover, we have noted that such spending not only puts people to work producing military destruction but also has secondary effects of rising consumer and investor spending.

Obviously, however, military spending and wars also result in more taxes, inflation, wounds, deaths, and alienation and deterioration of life for millions. Conservatives believe present military spending is necessary for "defense." Most liberals believe that there is more military spending than is necessary for defense, and that the spending could be used better for constructive projects. Radicals believe most military spending is unnecessary for defense, and is wasteful, but there are obstacles in the capitalist system to more constructive projects, so peaceful full employment spending could be achieved only in a democratic socialist system.

WASTEFUL SALES EXPENSES

In the United States a very large amount of human effort is put into the peculiar occupation of convincing people to buy products they may not want or need. Obviously every society needs to distribute its goods from the factories to the consumers, but the U.S. economy goes far beyond that. It spends billions of dollars and millions of hours of labor time for sales workers to go around from door to door or to stand in a store to persuade other people to buy things. A huge percentage of this effort is not technically necessary and so may be called wasteful (see the excellent analysis in Baran and Sweezy).

A second aspect of selling is advertising. Again, some small amount of advertising is needed in any society to supply useful information to customers. Studies of the U.S. economy, however, indicate that more than 90 percent of all advertising is not information but an attempt to persuade consumers that each of several identical products is better than the others. Therefore $15–20 billion a year (or more) is spent on advertising that can be described as wasteful. A good example of wasteful or even harmful advertising is the advertising for smoking cigarettes, cigars, and other forms of tobacco, despite the U.S. government's well-documented evidence that smoking causes cancer, heart disease, and other illness. Yet the tobacco companies continue to devote huge amounts of money to induce people to continue or begin smoking—*and* the U.S. government still subsidizes tobacco production!

A third aspect of selling is cost estimation. In many industries, such as construction, a tremendous amount of highly skilled effort by highly paid engineers consists in providing estimates their company may use to bid for a new job (e.g., a public school or road or military facility). In each of these cases the buyer of the construction has already had its own engineers furnish an estimate; in addition, another 10 or 12 sets of engineers may do this difficult work of cost estimation all over again.

A fourth aspect of selling reaches back into production. It is the designing of new products or changes in existing products—not to make them better and sometimes even to make them worse—in such a way that they will be more attractive to consumers. One example is women's skirts, in which the hemline is regularly raised or lowered so that women wishing to keep in style will have to buy new skirts or dresses. Another example is the yearly change of automobile models. One year tails were put on cars, another year they were taken off. In some years it has been estimated that these automobile model changes took up to 2.5 percent of the entire GNP in totally wasted effort (see Fisher, Grilliches, and Kaysen, p. 223).

Last but not least, sales efforts take the even more despicable form of "planned obsolescence." This means engineers are put to work designing a product that will fall apart quicker than previous ones so that the consumer will have to buy a new one.

ENVIRONMENTAL DESTRUCTION

One poetic observer writes, "America was once a paradise of timberland and streams but it is dying because of the greed and money lust of a thousand little kings who slashed the timber all to hell and would not be controlled" (Bell, p. 3). It is not, however, just a matter for poets and of far-off forests. Anyone flying to Los Angeles will notice a large, brownish cloud covering much of southern California. And this cloud—called smog— does not merely look bad and cut visibility but is also a menace to the health of the public. Ironically, many people came to southern California in the 1930s and 1940s because they had respiratory problems, and it was a place where the air was crystal clear, warm, dry, and healthy. It seems almost incredible that in such a short time it could become a place where a few minutes of outside work in the afternoon are exhausting and the air itself causes thousands of respiratory diseases among children.

Let us list systematically the major forms of pollution (based on Edel). First, there are visible objects such as cans and wastepaper and smoke. Businesses spew over 25 billion tons of pollutants into the air and water and land every year. This includes about 150 million tons of smoke and fumes that blacken the skies and poison the air, 22 million tons of waste-paper products, and 3 million tons of mill tailings. This is not a new phenomenon, but has increased with economic growth. It is a particular problem in slums in central-city areas that get much of the smoke and act as dumping grounds for garbage, to the extent of blocking some rivers with solid wastes.

Second, there are organic wastes, detergents, and fertilizers, including human and animal wastes, and materials such as nitrates and phosphates that lead to rapid growth of algae. Altogether, about 50 *trillion* gallons of heated and polluted liquids are dumped into our streams, rivers, and lakes each year. This amount has been rapidly increasing in recent years. When the organic wastes and algae cause exhaustion of the oxygen in the water, other life is unable to survive, and septic decay by anaerobic bacteria causes terrible odors and serves as an incubator for many diseases.

Third, there is local air pollution, including smoke, carbon monoxide from auto exhausts, nitrogen and sulfur oxides, and photochemical smog produced by hydrocarbons reacting chemically in the air. Automobiles are the worst offenders, producing 86 million tons of pollutants a year, but industry and power plants produce another 43 million tons. Altogether, all sources in the U.S. economy introduce 72 million tons of carbon monoxide, 26 million tons of sulfur oxides, 13 million tons of nitrogen oxides, 19 million tons of hydrocarbons, and 12 million tons of particular matter into the air each year. This pollution causes property damage, local weather changes, lung disease, and many other diseases; in some temporary emergency situations (caused by local air inversions) even deaths have been caused by pollution.

Fourth, there is worldwide atmospheric pollution, including carbon dioxide and dust clouds, which may affect the climate. Increasing carbon dioxide in the atmosphere tends to trap heat and warm the earth, while dust reflects the sun's rays, so that it tends to cool the earth. If either trend becomes dominant, our climate would change drastically.

Fifth, there are persistent poisonous materials, including DDT and the heavy metals (lead, mercury, and cadmium), that threaten health. DDT remains in each animal until it is eaten by another, right up the food chain to humans, causing various health effects. The heavy metals tend to attack the central nervous system of any animal.

Sixth, there is increasing stray energy, from sonic booms to radioactivity. Of increasing importance is the fact that nuclear power plants produce heat, atomic contamination, and radioactive fallout. Radioactivity not only has a direct harmful effect on one's own body but carries over through genetic defects to the next generation. Nuclear accidents—such as the one at the Three Mile Island plant in Pennsylvania in 1979—can spread radioactivity over an enormous area in a short time. In addition, no one has yet devised a good way to eliminate the increasing piles of radioactive waste, which remain dangerous for thousands of years.

CAUSES OF AND CURES FOR POLLUTION

The diagnosis of what causes pollution leads each different theory to a different prescription for how to cure it. Each of these diagnoses and prescriptions is associated with a general political outlook—conservative, liberal, and radical.

The Conservative View

Many conservatives deny that the picture is as grim as we have painted it. They acknowledge that there is some environmental problem, but give it very low priority. (Profits come first.) The conservative economists who do take the problem seriously begin, as usual, with Adam Smith's analysis—that the "invisible hand" of competitive private enterprise will balance all costs and benefits to consumers and producers and will finally give the optimal social result. They acknowledge that to some extent the market does not seem to be working well enough to prevent pollution. They argue that the reason is that pollution costs constitute a slight exception to Adam Smith's rule (that competition results in an optimal social result).

The reason that Adam Smith's rule is partially violated in this area, they say, is that some costs—like pollution—are costs to all of society but not costs to individual firms. Moreover, the benefits of nonpollution go to all of society rather than to individual firms. Thus, the costs of pollution do not lower their profits, nor do the benefits of nonpollution raise their profits. Therefore, since the behavior of individual firms is determined solely by their expected profits, they ignore the fact of the pollution they create. This is the view of serious conservative economists, although they use slightly different rhetoric to describe the problem.

Since the problem is "merely" that pollution does not affect the competitive market producer, the solution is to make pollution marketable. One conservative approach is to make air and water into private property so owners could sell or rent them. Then we could have competition between those who wish to buy air to pollute and those who wish to buy air to breathe. Of course, if someone got a monopoly of air, we might not be able to afford breathing. And how much a person could breathe or drink would depend on one's income.

To avoid a monopoly on air and water, the slightly less fanatic conservatives suggest that the government could auction off the "right to pollute" certain areas, or firms could pay for pollution damage, or we could all pay firms not to pollute by giving them subsidies from local governments!

During the administration of Ronald Reagan, the fight for the environment lost ground. His first Environmental Protection Agency (EPA) director lost her job because she protected business instead of the environment, held back law enforcement for political reasons, and lied about it to the U.S. Congress. Reagan himself wanted to rewrite the Clean Air Act to get rid of most enforcement because—he claimed—it caused unemployment. He opposed cleaning up industry or automobile pollution because—he claimed—there is worse pollution "from trees and other pollution." Even after experts pointed out that trees do not pollute, Reagan repeated his amazing statement (see Nelson, p. 1). He made this statement on the day of the worst smog in Los Angeles in nine years.

The Liberal View

Liberals argue that it could make capitalism look slightly ridiculous and would be highly inequitable to buy and sell air and water. Mainly they argue that the problem is much broader than the conservatives acknowledge, so much minor patching could not work. They argue that these costs of pollution—which are external to private accounting and are therefore called *externalities*—pervade the whole system. They are not simply a minor exception to Adam Smith's model, but are involved in almost all production of goods and services. Furthermore, they point out that many of the benefits of nonpollution of air or water are collective or public goods by nature; that is, there is no way to divide up clean air for sale to some people but not to others.

Therefore the liberals conclude that private enterprise cannot solve this problem by tinkering with new "property rights" in air and water, but that the government must exercise its power to stop pollution. Thus, the liberal Samuelson says: "Is reliance on spontaneous business efforts futile in the solution of a problem like this? Experience gives a pessimistic answer. . . . Since no one profit maker has the incentive, or, indeed, the power to solve problems involving 'externalities,' here is a clear case for some kind of public intervention" (Samuelson, pp. 816–817). So liberals advocate various laws to control the polluters (see Freeman, Haveman, and Kneese).

Power and Pollution: A Critique of the Liberal View

Liberals assert that the capitalist state can pass and enforce laws controlling pollution while preserving capitalism. They fail to see that the "right to pollute" is deeply embedded in our present economic system and that all efforts to control it will meet the fiercest opposition. Thus, the *New York Times* (in an editorial on February 9, 1971) stated that "a corporate manager has his attention focused on the profit targets and production schedules. He has a *natural resistance* to taking into account environmental costs." The *Times* also admits that the U.S. government proposes many excellent environmental measures, but "often talks the old fashioned language of the profit-first businessman."

We have seen that the entire governmental apparatus always tends to put the interests of private property ahead of human values. Therefore, the "natural resistance" of businesspeople to pollution controls tends to be passed along to the government that it dominates. This is almost as true of liberal as it is of conservative governments. A delicate balance must be maintained—politicians must say enough about the environment to get elected by a public that demands pollution controls, and yet they must also be careful that few such controls are put into effect or they will antagonize the business people who give them their campaign funds.

For these reasons, since the early 1970s, presidents have often emphasized ecology in various State of the Union addresses. But when it came to proposing laws, the administration always argued for the words "taking into account the practicability of compliance." These words mean that no pollution control is "practical" or legal if it reduces profits in any way! Since almost all controls do cut into profits, no controls would be practical in this view. President Carter, for example, argued that energy production is more important than environmental protection. Therefore, he suggested ignoring many environmental laws (and safety laws) in order to license coal and nuclear plants more rapidly.

Many politicians have admitted that clean air is less important than continued profit making in the auto industry because clean air is not important to the U.S. economy. Indeed, the automobile and related industries are very important interests in our economy. When we add together automobile production, plus gas and oil production, plus highway builders, plus tire companies, and so on, we arrive at more than 12 percent of GNP. Needless to say, the political clout of this group is enormous. When we ask why there is not more public investment in rapid transit systems or more public research into alternatives to the internal combustion engine, the answer seems to be the raw political-economic power of the auto, gas, and highway industries. In fact, private opposition and political constraints helped to reduce rides on public transit from 23 billion in 1945 to only 8 billion a year in 1967, though there has been some increase since then.

The automobile industry has always done everything possible to prevent public transportation by rail. In the 1940s and 1950s General Motors set out deliberately to destroy the electric trolley system, which had been in wide use till then. They organized a company that bought out the trolley systems and replaced them with GM buses in New York, Philadelphia, Los Angeles, and many smaller cities (see Commoner).

The highway lobby is probably second in power only to the military-industrial complex. There are lobbyists at Congress from the American Road Builders Association, the Associated General Contractors of America, the National Highway Users Conference, American Trucking Association, the American Association of State Highway Officials, and the American Automobile Association—as well as representatives of many individual firms. So far this lobby has been able to prevent much use of the immense highway funds for public transit. (The same lobbyists have also been successful in preserving the oil depletion tax loophole.)

In addition to preventing the passage of pollution-control laws (or better rapid transit or research for better cars), the same forces have been quite successful in preventing effective use of the laws that have been passed. For example, there are antipollution boards in many states, but most of them are totally dominated by the very polluting firms they are supposed to control. In the 1970s the Federal Power Commission was found to be similarly controlled by the gas and electric power interests. Even newly created commissions suffer the same fate. For example, in California the construction industry spent millions of dollars to defeat a law for the preservation of the seashore; when the law was passed anyway, the governor (Reagan) and local governments appointed representatives of the same polluting interests to the new boards designed to oversee the protection of the seacoast.

Since automobiles are the most important source of smog, we would expect many legal procedures to force the auto companies to institute controls. Their tremendous power, however, has been used to emasculate such law enforcement. For example: "throughout 1969, the Department of Justice in Washington held a secret hearing to discuss with industry lawyers its charge that automobile manufacturers have conspired to stifle the introduction of smog-control devices on automobiles. On September 11, the department announced that it had entered into a consent decree allowing the companies to escape federal sanctions by promising that they would not conspire any more" (Bell, p. 269). Furthermore, in the general atmosphere of big business influence, it was easy for the auto companies to exert pressure on the Environmental Protection Agency. As a result, the EPA has postponed the enforcement of the standards set by the Clean Air Act passed by Congress. Finally, the automobile lobby has forced Congress itself to postpone enforcement of the Clean Air Act.

Even if the laws are enforced, the existence of the capitalist system brings about a clash between the environmental and economic interests of most people. For example, under the Clean Air Act a cement factory in the little town of San Juan Batista has been found guilty of terrible pollution of the air. The company admitted this but said that it will "cost too much"— that is, it will lower profits—to install the proper purification machinery; therefore the entire cement factory closed and moved elsewhere. In this way the burden of environmental protection is made to fall on local workers and on the local populations and governments.

This strategy is known as *divide and rule.* It has been very effectively used by polluting businesses to split the opposition to pollution. Thus in the case of the California shoreline protection law, the construction industry bosses got the construction unions to oppose it as well—for the reason that more of them would be unemployed if there were less construction. Similarly, in the case of funds for highways the Teamsters Union always supports these funds and new road building against community wishes— again because they wish to protect their jobs. "Because America does not guarantee workers jobs in their own communities, people must be concerned that investment take place near where they live" (Edel, p. 130). So the conflict between jobs and ecology is built into our present capitalist system.

Another conflict utilized by the big polluters is that between the interests of different states. Given this conflict, the oil companies wanted the individual states rather than the federal government to control "tidelands oil." Each state by itself is relatively weak compared to the industrial giants, so the firms can always threaten to take their business elsewhere.

Similar threats can be utilized at the national level. Already many small countries have capitulated to the demands of polluters rather than lose business and jobs to other countries. Even the United States is not immune. Since the environmental protection laws have been tightened, many of the most powerful U.S.-based multinational corporations have moved or threatened to move whole enterprises to less well-protected countries.

At the present time, the big corporations have launched a well-financed drive to modify or end antipollution and safety regulations in many industries. The corporations (and many economists) argue that they are forced to spend a great deal of money for safety and to reduce pollution, so that these laws are a major cause of reduced investment, lowered growth, and raised prices. On the other hand, the ecology movement points out that the lack of stricter safety and pollution laws has resulted in the loss of lives.

The fight has come to a head over nuclear regulation. The corporate lobby wants unrestricted construction of new nuclear plants. The accident at the Three Mile Island nuclear plant in 1979, however, alerted millions of Americans to the dangers of nuclear plants. As a result, the ecology movement for very strict safety and antipollution controls on nuclear plants has gained enormous momentum. It has become a major political force. The lines of conflict have been drawn between the profit motive and the preservation of human life.

The Revival of Malthusianism

In the early nineteenth century the Reverend Malthus studied population and poverty. He decided that population always increases geometrically— 2, 4, 8, 16, and so on—because people breed like rabbits. He also decided that production could increase only arithmetically—1, 2, 3, 4, and so on— because of our limited land and resources. From this mechanical exercise he therefore concluded that poverty is caused by too much population and that there is nothing we can do about it. The only alternatives are to abstain from sex altogether or to wait until famine and disease remove the excess population. Malthus overlooked technology, which allows us always to produce more per worker. He also overlooked the fact that after industrialization more educated and sophisticated men and women would decide to have less children per family by practicing birth control. Therefore, instead of ever-decreasing product per person, the developed countries have experienced ever-increasing product per person. Furthermore, we shall see in Chapter 42 that the less developed countries are kept that way not by population pressure but by foreign imperialism and by domestic obstacles.

In recent years many conservatives, some liberals, and even some radicals have brought back to life the old Malthusian argument: They conclude that rising population and rising production together doom us to ecological catastrophe and to eventual poverty as our resources are eventually depleted. The only way out, they tell us, is to have a zero population growth and a zero rate of economic growth under capitalism. Partly they are concerned with the very real problems inherent in growth in capitalism. The well-known liberal economist John K. Galbraith makes this perfectly correct point, saying, "I am not quite sure what the advantage is in having a few more dollars to spend if the air is too dirty to breathe, the water too polluted to drink, the commuters are losing out the struggle to get in and out of the city, the streets are filthy, and the schools are so bad that the young perhaps wisely stay away, and hoodlums roll citizens for some of the dollars they saved in tax" (quoted in Harrington, p. 8).

The problem comes when this correct point is pushed much too far. One commentator in the *New York Times* wrote: "There are, alas, a few 'iron laws'. . . . The hard fact is: growth of production is the basic cause of pollution growth" (Dale, p. 27). Even stronger are the doomsday statements made by the Club of Rome, a group of businessmen and management experts. On the basis of certain arbitrary assumptions about resource and waste disposal variables, they "scientifically prove"—by putting everything into a computer—that in just a certain number of years hundreds of millions of people will die from either pollution or lack of food. On this basis some conservatives conclude that we can do nothing but live—and die—with pollution and poverty. Similarly, some liberals and some radicals argue that the only hope is to limit absolutely to present or lower levels the amount of economic growth and the amount of population.

We certainly agree that there is an enormous problem here. It is not true, however, that nothing can be done or that limiting growth and population are the only or even the best answers. In the first place, the link between pollution and GNP growth is not a simple one-to-one relationship. If we spend $10 to go to the movies, the accountants record $10 GNP growth, but very little pollution has been created. If, on the other hand, we spend $10 for gas for pleasure driving, a great deal of pollution has been created. It turns out that much of the worst pollution is associated with petroleum products, certain heavy industries, and military industry. If we eliminated the automobile and military production, most pollution would be gone.

The problem is not merely the fact that some GNP growth involves much more pollution than other growth; it is also the fact that much of this spending is on unnecessary or even harmful goods that could be eliminated—without reducing food, clothing, and shelter. Furthermore, some activities *should* grow—for example, services to combat pollution—even though these will be treated as GNP growth by the accountants. Finally, much more of the GNP can be recycled.

In the second place, no-growth policies cannot be considered apart from income redistribution policies. Under the present capitalist system, poor people rightly suspect that "no growth" means they would be frozen into poverty forever.

In the third place, international redistribution must be considered. At United Nations conferences, when affluent American delegates have argued for no-growth policies, the poor countries have concluded that this means that their whole countries would be doomed to poverty for all time. Moreover, when birth control is advocated by the U.S. government for these countries, they are rightly suspicious of nationalist and racist motives for reducing their populations but not the U.S. population. It is also a fact that the best way to introduce birth control and reduce population growth is to achieve an urban and industrialized society (which means more growth for these countries), since people then have the knowledge of birth control and the desire to limit the number of children they have.

In the fourth place, the theorists of no growth never consider whether a different political-economic system could achieve much less pollution even with the same growth. Yet we have seen that although some pollution is caused by any massive economic growth under present technology, it is capitalist greed for profits that causes many additional problems. It is a government dominated by capitalist economic power that is slow to legislate and slow to enforce pollution controls. It is a capitalist system that cannot guarantee workers other jobs when some jobs are eliminated because of pollution effects. It is capitalist systems that cannot willingly redistribute to poor people and poor countries the existing goods and services. It is the capitalist system that makes poor people and poor countries suspicious of birth control—though birth control would make very good sense under a non-profit-oriented system. Finally, it is impossible to conceive of a no-growth rule imposed on capitalism; how could private enterprises exist if it is prevented from growing? It would mean monopolies for existing industries, ever-higher prices, and the exclusion of new competitors—plus a very extensive government bureaucracy to give detailed instructions to prevent growth.

The Radical View

Radicals agree that some pollution is likely in any highly industrialized, densely populated economy. For all the reasons given previously, however, a very large part of pollution in the U.S. economy is due to the capitalist economic system. "Look at the values which galvanize energies and allocate resources in the business system: pursuit of money, enrichment of self, the exploitation of man—and of nature—to generate still more money. Is it surprising that a system seeking to turn everything into gold ends up turning everything into garbage?" (Ramparts, p. 2).

Radicals argue that the correct solution is a new economic system, one in which the people decide democratically how to run it, rather than having the decisions being made by a few people. Note that this is a classic definition of "socialism." It excludes the Soviet Union, however, because that country also has an economic system dominated by a few undemocratically selected rulers.

Under a democratically run socialist economy, wasteful goods and services—such as vast military production, oversized private automobiles, and advertising signs by the millions—would be eliminated. Under a de-mocratically run socialist economy, the national income would be shared much more equally than today, so most people could live better at any level of GNP than under our present system of unequal distribution. Under a democratically run socialist economy, there would be no private enter-prises to push frantically for more growth to make more profits. Finally, birth-control information and devices would be freely available to all.

THE NUCLEAR EXPLOSION

Nuclear bombs were first exploded in 1945. The government supported the nuclear industry by (a) giving it all of the government-owned plants for a few pennies on the dollar, (b) giving it a huge amount of research and development money, and (c) passing laws to protect it. In 1957, Con-gress passed the Price-Anderson Act, which provided federal insurance for nuclear accidents up to at least $500 million and limited the liability of a company for a nuclear accident to $560 million—even though a gov-ernment study found that one accident could cause $7 billion property damage and 3400 deaths. The government gave the nuclear industry this support because of its military uses and its promise of self-sufficiency.

In 1963, the first nonsubsidized nuclear reactor was sold. With gov-ernment encouragement, the nuclear industry exploded into an enormous new building program. The reactor manufacturers underestimated costs (by several magnitudes), so they charged low prices—and either rene-gotiated contracts or incurred big losses. By 1967, a total of 75 reactors were ordered by U.S. utilities, an amazing investment in an untested product. Some orders were for nuclear reactors five times the size of any existing one.

The nuclear industry—and humanity—has run into three kinds of problems. First, in spite of studies proving it "impossible," there have been a large number of accidents and some very near disasters. Second, there is a limited amount of uranium, which will soon (a few decades) be used up under present technology. The "breeder" technology would ex-tend the use of uranium for 50 to 60 times as long, but would also create large amounts of plutonium wastes, which are very toxic and can be used to make atomic bombs. Third, how do we get rid of the waste? Nuclear waste has now reached over 7 million cubic feet, and another 11 million cubic feet will be generated by 1999. This waste remains toxic for a quarter of a million years (estimated costs of "safe" disposal are enormous and no clearly safe method has been discovered).

These three problems not only mean dangers for all of us, but much higher costs. So the nuclear construction explosion has fizzled, with many cancellations by the utilities and almost no new contracts for some years now.

SUMMARY

There are various kinds of economic waste—military production, monopoly misallocation, most advertising and sales expenses, planned obsolescence, lack of conservation, and pollution. There is pollution of land, air, and water. Extreme conservatives argue that nonpollution (such as clean air) could be given a price and bought and sold in the market, thus automatically solving the problem. Liberals believe that is insufficient; legal controls are needed to prevent pollution by private enterprise. Radicals don't believe controls will work under capitalism; a democratic socialist society is a necessary condition for an end to waste and pollution.

SUGGESTED READINGS

A powerful little book on pollution and ecological problems is Mathew Edel, *Economics and the Environment* (Englewood Cliffs, N.J.: Prentice Hall, 1973). Three good books on energy are: John Blair, *The Control of Oil* (New York: Pantheon, 1979); Barry Commoner, *The Poverty of Power* (New York: Bantam, 1978); and Michael Tanzer, *The Political Economy of International Oil and the Underdeveloped Countries* (Boston: Beacon Press, 1060).

REFERENCES

Baran, Paul, and Paul Sweezy. *Monopoly Capital.* New York: Monthly Review Press, 1968.

Bell, Garret de, ed. *The Environmental Handbook.* New York: Ballantine, 1970.

Commoner, Barry. *The Poverty of Power: Energy and the Economic Crisis.* New York: Knopf, 1970.

Dale, Edwin. "Viewpoint." *New York Times Magazine*, April 19, 1970.

Edel, Mathew. *Economics and the Environment.* Englewood Cliffs, N.J.: Prentice Hall, 1973.

Fisher, Franklin, Zvi Grilliches, and Carl Kaysen. "The Costs of Automobile Changes Since 1949." *Journal of Political Economy* 59:4 (October 1962), pp. 221–229.

Freeman, A, R. Haveman, and A. Kneese. *The Economics of Environmental Policy.* New York: Wiley, 1973.

Harrington, Michael. "Reactionary Keynesianism." *Encounter* 6:1 (March 1966), pp. 1–11.

Nelson, Jack. "Pollution Curbed, Reagan Says; Attacks Air Cleanup." *Los Angeles Times*, October 9, 1980, p. 1.

Ramparts. Editorial, May 1970.

Samuelson, Paul. *Economics.* 9th ed. New York: McGraw Hill, 1973.

Chapter
41

International Capitalist Trade and Finance

This chapter examines the importance of multinational firms, the rise and decline of U.S. economic power, and the resulting problem of U.S. trade deficits.

CONCENTRATION BY MULTINATIONAL FIRMS

The present degree of economic concentration in the entire capitalist world by a few enormous multinational corporations constitutes a new structural stage for international capitalism. The term *multinational* suggests management from many countries, but this is somewhat misleading. The truth is that each firm is governed mostly by the nationals of one developed capitalist country. These corporations are multinational in the sense that the whole globe is their oyster, that vast profits may be made by control of markets in several countries (so some writers call them *global corporations*).

In pursuit of profit, U.S.-based multinational corporations have been rapidly expanding abroad. In terms of total assets of U.S. industries, by 1974 about 40 percent of all consumer goods industries, about 75 percent of the electrical industry, about 33 percent of the chemical industry, about 33 percent of the pharmaceutical industry, and over 50 percent of the $100 billion petroleum industry were located outside the United States (all data from Barnett and Muller). Moreover, this expansion trend has increased and perhaps accelerated in recent years. In 1957 investment in plant and equipment by U.S. firms abroad was already 9 percent of total U.S. domestic investment in plant and equipment; by 1970 that investment abroad rose to 25 percent of domestic investment. In 1961 sales of U.S. manufacturing abroad were only 7 percent of total sales by all U.S. manufacturing corporations, but by 1970 that figure rose to 13 percent. In 1960 foreign profits were 12 percent of all U.S. corporate profits (after taxes), but by 1980 U.S. corporate profits from abroad rose to 24 percent of all their profits. In 1960 the foreign dollar deposits of the largest U.S. banks were only 8.5 percent of domestic deposits, but by 1970 foreign deposits rose to 65 percent of domestic deposits.

The pattern of ownership by foreign-owned multinational corporations is most striking in the less developed countries. In Chile, before Allende's socialist government, in 1969 multinational corporations controlled at least 51 percent of the 160 largest firms. In Argentina, multinational corporations control more than 50 percent of the total sales of the 50 largest firms. In Mexico, multinational corporations control 100 percent of rubber, electrical machinery, and transportation industries. Moreover, in Mexico, foreign ownership in the metal industry rose from 42 percent in 1962 to 68 percent in 1970, while foreign ownership in tobacco rose from 17 percent in 1962 to 100 percent in 1970. In Brazil, multinational corporations own 100 percent of automobile and tire production, while their share of machinery production rose from 59 percent in 1961 to 67 percent in 1971, and their share of electrical equipment manufacturing rose from 50 percent in 1961 to 68 percent in 1971.

It is also important to note that many transactions within and between capitalist countries are conducted solely between subsidiaries of the same parent corporation. More than 50 percent of total foreign trade transactions in the capitalist world are of this nonmarket intracorporate variety between subsidiaries of the same company. This means that taxes can be shifted to those countries where the rates are lowest. It also means that fiscal policies may not be operative—or may operate mainly to the benefit of the multinational giants. The largest corporations in the United States already absorb a disproportionate part of all government spending and tax reductions designed to stimulate the economy.

The multinational manufacturing corporations are serviced by global banks whose tentacles reach almost everywhere. At their urging, additional credit has been created as a new currency: the $110-billion pool of Eurodollars (and the Special Drawing Rights, which acts as currency). Since there are no reserve-deposit requirements on the Eurodollars, they are particularly unstable and contribute a strong impetus, by further credit creation, to inflationary pressures. This international credit expansion, plus rapid monetary flows between corporate subsidiaries across borders, makes it less possible than ever for any capitalist nation to control its money supply by any conceivable monetary policies.

Similarly, union bargaining power has been weakened by the power of the multinational corporations to shift production rapidly from high-wage areas to low-wage areas. For example, if the United States has high

Table 41.1   LOCATION OF HOME OFFICES OF THE LARGEST
             MULTINATIONAL INDUSTRIAL CORPORATIONS

Country	1963	1971	1979
United States	67	58	47
Germany	13	13	13
United Kingdom	7	7	7
France	4	5	11
Japan	3	8	7
Italy	2	3	3
Netherlands	1	2	3
Netherlands–U.K.	2	2	2
Other	1	4	7

Source: Los Angeles Times, April 8, 1981, Pt. 4, page 1.

wages, multinationals can simply shift production to Mexico, and if even Mexican wages are considered too high, they can shift to Hong Kong.

Where do the multinational firms reside? Their official homes, which may not always reflect reality, are given in Table 41.1. It is evident that U.S. corporations were still dominant in 1987. It is also evident, however, that power was shifting from U.S. corporations to foreign ones. This process has continued.

THE INTERNATIONAL BUSINESS CYCLE

The international concentration of investment decision making in a relatively small number of corporations, plus the very intimate ties of international trade and investment among the capitalist countries, binds these economies closely together. Therefore, a contraction begun in one country or in just a few multinational corporations spreads very rapidly to the others. If investor demand declines in several countries at once, then their import trade in raw materials declines, lowering demand for exports in several other countries. If unemployment rises in several countries at once, then their demand for consumer goods from abroad also declines. Thus the entire capitalist world tends to move in the same direction in its investment decisions as well as its demands from trading partners. This encourages explosive expansion amid spiraling optimistic speculations, or universal contraction amid a downward spiral of lower profits and pessimism.

The close relationship of cycles in industrial production in the three main capitalist areas—the United States, Europe (OECD), and Japan—can be seen in Figure 41.1. The troughs and peaks are the U.S. troughs and peaks, but the cycles of Europe and Japan have very similar dates. All

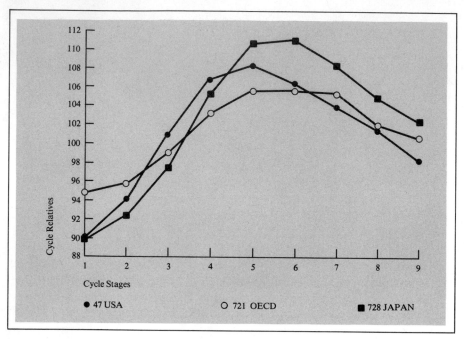

Figure 41.1 Industrial production, three cycles, 1970–1982. *Source:* Series numbers given in the key are from the U.S. Department of Commerce, *Handbook of Cyclical Indicators* (Washington, D.C.: GPO, 1984).

three have the same low points or troughs. Europe reaches a peak at the same stage as the U.S. economy, but then stays at about that level for a while. Japan peaks one stage later than the U.S. economy, but then declines rapidly. Altogether, the conclusion is that capitalist economies move up and down at about the same times, thus reinforcing upward movements, but also reinforcing downward movements.

There is a close relation between a nation's income and its demand for imports. When U.S. income rises, so do our imports from abroad. When Europe's income rises, so does its demand for U.S. exports. But the same is also true on the downward side, so falling European income leads to less demand for U.S. goods.

THE CASE OF CANADIAN-AMERICAN ECONOMIC RELATIONS

Canada invests hundreds of millions of dollars annually in less developed countries. With these investment dollars goes a large measure of Canadian economic power within many of these countries. However, a Canadian government report issued in 1968 showed that foreigners owned a large percentage of Canadian assets (all data from Canadian Privey Council).

The principal owners of these assets were the United States (approximately 80 percent) and the United Kingdom (approximately 12 percent).

The composition of this foreign ownership conformed perfectly with the time-honored explanation of economic expansionism: the securing of sources of raw materials and markets for manufactured goods. Fifty-four percent of all Canadian manufacturing industries were owned directly by foreigners, and 60 percent were controlled by foreigners. Foreign ownership of mining and smelting stood at 62 percent. The petroleum and natural gas industry was 64 percent foreign owned and 74 percent foreign controlled.

Within the manufacturing sector the industries that were oligopolistically organized were almost completely foreign owned: 97 percent of the automobile industry, 97 percent of the rubber industry, 78 percent of the chemical industry, and 77 percent of the electrical appliance industry. These industries were controlled almost exclusively by U.S. interests.

The immense profitability of American subsidiaries in Canada is grossly underestimated if one looks simply at the billions of dollars a year in interest and dividends received from Canadian firms. Payments for management fees, royalties, franchises, advertising, rent, professional services, and so forth, constitute an additional large amount, although accurate statistics on these do not exist.

Very possibly an even larger source of profits (for which no statistics would be available) lies in the buying-and-selling policies of parents and subsidiaries. Thus an American company controlling Canadian natural resources can pay a high price for these resources and show a large profit on the books of the subsidiary—or it may pay a low price and show the profits on its own books. Similarly, an American manufacturing firm that requires its Canadian subsidiary to purchase manufactured components from the parent company can follow pricing policies that can make the profits appear on whichever side of the border it chooses. This permits the company to use an optimum combination of tax loopholes in both countries.

It appears probable, however, that the greatest pressures exist for American corporate managers to maximize the parent company's profits. It is generally the profits of the parent on which these managers' personal careers depend.

The results of this economic takeover have manifested themselves in the decreasing degree of independence both externally and internally in Canada's economic and political policies. In recent years Canada has been under constant pressure to follow the U.S. "line" on foreign policy more closely. For example: U.S. subsidiaries have openly refused employment to U.S. immigrants who appeared to be draft dodgers; Canada has not rejected American nuclear weapons; and by taking orders from the parent company, Canadian subsidiaries follow U.S. State Department guidelines and partially subvert the Canadian government's attempts to increase trade with certain communist states.

Moreover, American control of the composition of Canadian investment results in an industrial structure that is far less than optimally arranged. American firms have literally made a "little America" of Canada's economy. The result in many industries is a large number of units, each producing at a smaller-than-optimum scale. Canada, with a population equivalent to roughly 10 percent of that of the United States, gives its consumers an array of brand names virtually identical to those offered to the American consumer.

Perhaps in the long run the worst evil of American ownership will be the complete elimination of the possibility for Canadians to achieve a more equitable distribution of wealth. Within a capitalist society the primary means of redistributing wealth (if a government wishes to do so) would be the use of death duties, inheritance taxes, taxes on gifts and bequests, and capital gains taxes. Because almost all Canadian assets owned by foreigners are owned by foreign corporations, and because the foreign corporations almost never die or divest themselves of their Canadian holdings, these methods can never be used to redistribute wealth.

RISE AND DECLINE OF THE U.S. EMPIRE

Until the Civil War American capitalism was far behind European capitalism. It had the advantage, however, of having no feudal or semifeudal encumbrances. After the Civil War the United States also abolished slavery and opened the whole country to capitalism. Moreover, the U.S. economy was relatively short of labor, so it was forced to use the most advanced technology. As a result, U.S. industrialization proceeded very rapidly after 1870, and it eventually overtook and surpassed British and other European industry. Finally, the two world wars devastated much of Europe but stimulated the U.S. economy. By 1945 the United States was completely dominant in the capitalist world.

Between 1945 and 1950 the U.S. gross domestic product (GDP) was equal to that of the rest of the world combined. In 1950 the French GDP was only 10 percent of the American, West Germany's only 8 percent, Italy's only 5 percent, Japan's only 4 percent, the United Kingdom's only 13 percent—and all five together only 39 percent of the American GDP. In 1950 the United States produced 82 percent of all the world's passenger vehicles, accounted for 55 percent of the world's steel production, and consumed 50 percent of the world's energy production (see Szymanski, pp. 65–70).

Throughout this period U.S. firms also extended their control over much of European industry. By 1965 American firms or their subsidiaries owned 80 percent of computer production, 24 percent of the motor industry, 15 percent of the synthetic rubber industry, and 10 percent of the production of petrochemicals *within* the entire European Common Market. Furthermore, it should not be forgotten how concentrated this ownership is: About 40 percent of all U.S. direct investment in Britain, France, and

Germany is owned by Ford, General Motors, and Standard Oil of New Jersey (see Mandel, pp. 22–23).

In that period American firms had a relative superiority over western European firms because of (1) greater size of capital assets and (2) greater technological advances. The size advantage of U.S. corporations was reflected by the fact that, of the 100 largest multinational corporations, 67 were based in 1963 in the United States. Because of their greater size and financial power, U.S. firms were able to do more technological research. Furthermore, the continued enormous U.S. military spending subsidized much of the technological research done by U.S. firms. Research spending per capita in the United States was still three to four times that of European research spending. Finally, the United States had lured many of the best brains in Europe (after they were trained in Europe). Between 1959 and 1967 about 100,000 doctors, scientists, and technicians left western Europe for the United States.

In spite of all these initial advantages, the absolute superiority of the U.S. economy in world production has slowly faded away. One reflection of the U.S. decline was the fact that by 1979, U.S.-based multinationals numbered only 47 out of the top 100. The U.S. superiority had been restricted and then reduced primarily by three factors: First, the Soviet Union broke away from the capitalist world in 1917 and has steadily gained on the U.S. economy since the late 1920s. Despite the one awful hiatus of World War II, Soviet production now is very large relative to the U.S. total.

Second, the old colonial empires were overthrown at the end of World War II. The new "independent" neocolonial countries turned to the U.S. economy for aid and investment, which, at first, further expanded U.S. power. Later, however, wars of liberation (as in Vietnam) spread and were focused against the United States, which was engaged in seeing that the world remained safe for imperialism.

Last, as a counterweight to the communist countries and the increasing resistance of the Third World, the United States was forced to give strong support to the rebuilding of the capitalist economies of Japan and western Europe. These economies began in 1945 with a skilled labor force but devastated factories. Their industry was rebuilt from scratch, but it was based on the latest technology. The United States ruled supreme in the early 1950s, but it began to be challenged by the growing power and competition of Japan and western Europe in every market by the early 1970s.

The U.S. economy was still the largest, but it no longer was far larger than the combination of all the rest. Thus, by 1972 the French GDP had risen to 17 percent of American GDP, West Germany's rose to 22 percent, Italy's rose to 10 percent, Japan's rose incredibly to 24 percent, the United Kingdom's to 14 percent—all five of these together now had a GDP equal to 86 percent of American GDP. In specific areas of basic production, the U.S. share of the world total fell between 1950 and 1972 from 82 to 29 percent of passenger vehicles, from 55 to 20 percent of steel production, and from 50 to 33 percent of world energy production. By the 1980s, the U.S. economy faced severe competition in every area and its share of production and trade continued to shrink.

The competitive position of Japan and western Europe was also strengthened by the fact that their productivity per labor-hour, especially Japanese productivity, rose much faster than that of the United States. On the other hand, Japanese and western European wage levels also rose faster than U.S. wage levels, which hurt their competitive position a little, but they are still somewhat lower than U.S. wage levels.

THE TRADE DEFICIT OF THE 1980s

For the first 70 years of the twentieth century, the U.S. economy had a trade surplus—that is, exports were larger than imports. Net exports—which are exports minus imports—were positive. Since exports generate a money flow to the United States while imports generate a money flow away from it, positive net exports means a flow of money demand into the United States. Since 1971, however, the U.S. economy has suffered a trade deficit in all but two years. So in this period, net exports were negative, money flowed out of the United States, and demand for U.S. products decreased by that amount. The extent of this trade deficit is shown in Figure 41.2. It reveals a dramatic decline in the trade balance from a positive trade surplus from 1945 to 1978, dropping to negative levels (or a trade deficit) after 1971. By 1980, the trade deficit was $25 billion. By 1988, the trade deficit grew to $160 billion.

This was also a period in which the overall importance of trade to the U.S. economy increased. Through most of the twentieth century, foreign trade was a small part of the U.S. economy, with exports and imports each averaging only 2 to 4 percent of GNP. In 1970, imports were 3.9 percent of GNP, while exports were 4.2 percent of GNP—thus there was a small positive net export or trade surplus. But by 1980, imports jumped to 9.1 percent of GNP, while exports rose to 8.2 percent of GNP. Thus total trade became more important, but there were negative net exports, or a trade deficit. By 1988, the trade deficit (the difference between imports and exports) had grown to 3.5 percent of GNP, a significant factor decreasing demand for U.S. goods by that net amount.

International payments are not only made for goods and services, but also for returns on investments in the form of interest and profits. Until the 1980s, the United States had far more investment abroad than foreigners had in the United States. Every year large sums of money flowed to the United States in the form of profits and interest, while much smaller sums flowed abroad. In 1981 the net U.S. international investment position—U.S. investments abroad minus foreign investment in the United States—peaked at a healthy $141 billion. By 1987, however, net U.S.

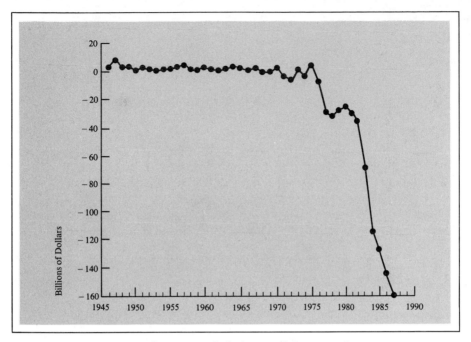

Figure 41.2 Merchandise foreign trade balance of the United States, 1946–1987.
Source: Council of Economic Advisors, *Economic Report of the President, 1988.*

investments were minus $403 billion; that is, foreigners owned $403 billion
more of capital assets in the United States than U.S. firms owned abroad
(see MacEwan). Naturally, this meant that profits and interest flowed more
out of the U.S. economy than into it, hurting our balance of payments.

BALANCE OF PAYMENTS PROBLEMS

Problems with the U.S. balance of payments have arisen largely because
of the resistance of the Third World and the increasing competition of
Japanese and western European capitalists. To demonstrate this we must
understand exactly what the balance of payments is and how it works.

Suppose a U.S. firm exports $1000 worth of Coca-Cola to Germany.
Then the German importer sells the Coca-Cola for deutschemarks (DM),
say, for 4000 DM. If the exchange rate is $1 = 4 DM, then the importer
buys 1000 U.S. dollars with the 4000 DM, and pays the U.S. exporter 1000
dollars. Suppose at the same time a U.S. importer buys beer worth 4000
DM from Germany and sells the beer for 1000 dollars (or more). Then
the U.S. importer buys 4000 DM for 1000 dollars and pays the 4000 DM
to the German beer firm. In this case both sides are satisfied, the trade
between the two countries is in balance, and the monetary exchanges
balance.

Table 41.2 U.S. BALANCE OF PAYMENTS, 1986
In Billions of Dollars

+$224	Exports		
−$368	Imports		
		Net balance of trade	−$144
+$ 88	Investment receipts		
−$ 67	Investment payments		
−$ 4	Net military transactions		
−$ 10	Net travel and transport		
+$ 12	Other services		
−$ 16	Remittances, pensions, and grants to foreigners		
		Net balance on current account	−$141
−$ 96	Net U.S. investments abroad		
+$213	Net foreign investments in U.S.		
		U.S. balance of payments	−$ 24

Source: Council of Economic Advisors, *President's Economic Report for 1988* (Washington, D.C.: GPO, 1988).

There are two reasons why this example worked out so neatly. First, the demand for *foreign exchange* (which is generally what foreign currencies are called) was exactly equal to the supply of foreign exchange. The demand for foreign exchange, it should be noted, arose from the importation of foreign goods, whereas the supply of foreign exchange arose from the exportation of domestic goods. Second, the supply of and demand for foreign exchange were equal because the *exchange rate* at which dollars could be converted was $1 = 4 DM. There are, then, two important considerations in the financing of foreign transactions: (1) the number and magnitude of transactions giving rise to a demand for and supply of foreign exchange and (2) the rate at which dollars can be converted to foreign exchange, or the exchange rate between American dollars and the various foreign currencies. Both of these must be considered. We begin by taking the exchange rate as given and examining the international transactions that give rise to a demand for and supply of foreign exchange.

Table 41.2 shows all of U.S. international transactions, including three kinds of balances: the narrowly defined balance of trade, the broader balance of current accounts, and the most broadly defined balance of payments. Transactions creating money flows to the United States are marked with a plus (+), such as exports of +$224 billion. Transactions creating money flows away from the United States are marked with a minus (−), such as imports at −$368 billion. The net balance of trade, or net flow to the United States, is exports minus imports. In 1986, the net balance of trade was −$144 billion, showing that we paid foreigners $144 billion more for their goods than they paid us for our goods. This is bad news and is called a trade deficit.

There are many other transactions, all given in billions. We must add—

because they are money flows to the United States—receipts of profits and interest from U.S. investments abroad (+$88 billion) and other services by U.S. firms to other countries (+$12 billion). We must subtract—because they are money flows away from the United States—payments to foreigners on their investments in the United States (−$67 billion), net U.S. military spending abroad (−$4 billion), net travel expenses by U.S. tourists and U.S. transport expenses in foreign boats (−$10 billion), as well as remittances sent from the United States by Americans to their families in foreign countries (−$16 billion). When all these are added and subtracted to exports and imports, the result is called the net balance of *current account,* which records all sales of goods and services between Americans and foreigners.

Finally, we record the money spent by Americans to make investments abroad (−$96 billion) and the money spent by foreigners to make investments in the United States (+$213 billion). When these capital movements are added to the current account of goods and services, the grand total is called the U.S. *balance of payments,* or the systematic account and total of all the international transactions for the year. The net U.S. balance of payments for 1986 was −$24 billion. That is bad news. It would be much worse—because the trade deficit was −$144 billion—but for the fact that foreigners invested $213 billion in the United States. That saves the United States this year, but it makes the problem worse in the future years when foreigners get profits paid from those investments.

RISE AND DECLINE OF THE VALUE OF THE DOLLAR

As we have seen, the balance of payments summarizes the country's sources of foreign exchange and the uses to which the foreign exchange is put. Now we must discuss the value or exchange rate of the dollar versus the rate of the other currencies. In the 1950s and 1960s, when the American dollar was widely used as an international currency, people all over the world wanted to hold their cash in American dollars. This unusual demand for the American dollar made it easy to finance a worldwide military network of U.S. bases, but it also made it easy to acquire an enormous private economic empire through American investment abroad.

By the early 1970s, however, other countries began to beat the U.S. economy in economic competition in many fields. The increased competition reduced U.S. exports relative to imports, creating deficits in the balance of trade. At first, these deficits were met by the export of U.S. gold. Soon, however, the large stockpile of U.S. gold was disappearing; as it neared zero, the U.S. government recognized a crisis. In 1971, President Nixon took the U.S. off of a fixed exchange standard of gold for dollars. After a brief return to fixed exchange, the United States finally severed the connection between gold and dollars in 1973. Since then, the value of the American dollar in relation to other currencies has been allowed to fluctuate according to supply and demand.

When the dollar loses value—or is devalued by government manipulation—it is much easier to sell U.S. exports abroad (because our exports appear cheaper to foreigners). Between 1971 and 1980 the Nixon, Ford, and Carter administrations attempted to finance a larger part of the foreign investments of American business and worldwide American military empire by trying to devalue the dollar and hence expand exports and restrict imports. While this policy may have had some limited success, it was grossly insufficient.

Since the very cheap borrowing of the 1950s and 1960s was no longer possible, American businesses and the U.S. government turned increasingly to borrowing from foreigners at the normal rate of interest to finance foreign economic investments of American corporations and to finance militarism. The Reagan-Bush administration financed the federal debt by selling bonds at high interest rates. These high interest rates led to a desire of foreigners to acquire dollars in order to loan them to the U.S. government. In the early 1980s this demand drove the value of the U.S. dollar up to artificially high levels. As a consequence, commodities produced in the U.S. became prohibitively expensive to foreigners, so U.S. exports declined. At the same time, the high value of the dollar made foreign goods cheaper for Americans to buy, so our imports rose. American firms had trouble competing abroad, both because of the high value of the U.S. dollar (and the prices of U.S. goods) and because other countries were raising their productivity faster. For these reasons, the trade deficit rose to unprecedented levels.

By the late 1980s the value of the U.S. dollar had declined considerably from peak levels. This did help reduce the trade deficit somewhat, but low rate of growth in U.S. productivity and competition from other countries kept the U.S. trade deficit at a high level.

INCREASE IN THIRD WORLD DEBT TO U.S. BANKS

At the same time that American businesses and government were borrowing from foreigners, American banks were loaning vast amounts of money (at very lucrative interest rates) to Third World countries. As a consequence, the debt of the Third World countries was increasing at extraordinary and very alarming rates. Table 41.3 shows this growth of debt in third-world, or developing countries, from 1973 to 1983.

This massive expansion of American lending to Third World countries is extremely dangerous. In 1983, Third World countries had to make debt-service and interest payments, for that one year alone, that were nearly 150 percent of the *entire* debt of 1973. As Table 41.3 shows, while the debt of these countries grew by 428 percent, their debt-service payments grew by 500 percent and their annual interest payments grew by 858 percent.

Table 41.3   THIRD WORLD DEBT 1973–1983
In Billions of U.S. Dollars

	1973	1980	1983	Percent increase 1973–1983
All Third World countries' debt	$109	$300	$575	428
Debt service payments	16	71	96	500
Interest payments	4.8	30.6	46.0	858

Source: World Bank, *Debt and the Developing World, Current Trends and Prospects* (Washington, D.C.: World Bank, 1984), p. ix.

The increase of international borrowing by Third World countries greatly increases the chance of an international financial crisis in which the international debt structure would collapse and a general worldwide economic crisis ensue. When A owes B, who owes C, who owes D, and so forth, a bankruptcy on A's part starts a chain reaction of bankruptcies. Given the enormous increase in the debt-servicing costs and the interest costs of Third World countries, as shown in Table 41.3, the danger of this chain reaction of bankruptcies is very great. If this were to happen, it would undoubtedly create a worldwide economic crisis that could be more severe than the Great Depression of the 1930s. Of course, governments are trying to prevent such a collapse, but there is still some danger that events could move faster than government actions at some point.

SUMMARY

International economic transactions differ from those within national boundaries. The two main differences are (1) different currencies are involved and must be exchanged and (2) differing economic and political relations exist among nations, with some dominant, others subordinate, and others intermediate.

The balance of payments is an accounting of all transactions between the residents of one country and the rest of the world. It summarizes the country's sources of foreign exchange and the uses to which the foreign exchange is put. Whereas the U.S. economy was totally dominant in the 1950s, it now faces severe competition. The competition limits U.S. sales abroad and has led to a continuing U.S. trade deficit. The overall balance of payments is made worse by the fact that foreigners now receive more profits and interest from the United States than do US firms from abroad.

APPENDIX A

The Alleged Gains from International Trade

If international trade causes such problems, why does the U.S. engage in it? The most obvious reason why nations engage in foreign trade is that many commodities cannot be grown or produced in certain regions of the world. Without foreign trade Americans would be unable to purchase coffee, cocoa, tea, coconuts, bananas, or any of a large number of commodities that cannot be produced in the United States. In addition to these consumer commodities, the United States depends heavily on imports for many of the most important minerals. In the late 1960s, for example, imports of iron ore were equivalent to 43 percent of the amount mined domestically; for copper, the figure was 18 percent; for lead, 131 percent; for zinc, 140 percent; for bauxite, 638 percent; and for petroleum, 31 percent. This partial listing alone indicates how crucial imports of agricultural products and minerals are to the American economy.

The United States can also gain from importing manufactured commodities if the *relative* costs of producing two commodities differ between the United States and another country. To illustrate this, let us return to the example of beer and Coca-Cola.

Assume that the United States and Germany each produce all the beer and Coca-Cola they consume domestically. Assume further that in the United States the average annual production per worker of beer is 5,000 gallons and of Coca-Cola is 7,500 gallons. Assume further that in Germany the figures are 4,000 gallons (beer) and 3,000 gallons (Coca-Cola). Table 41.4 shows hypothetical prices for the two commodities (German prices are given in dollars for easier comparison) in the two countries. These prices reflect ratios of labor productivity.

From these figures we see that the United States is more efficient in the production of both beer and Coca-Cola. Economists would say that the United States has an *absolute advantage* in the production of both commodities. It might seem that the United States would be better off not to import either beer or Coca-Cola from Germany because it can produce both more efficiently. This is not true, however. It would pay the United States to import beer and export Coca-Cola because the United States has a comparative advantage in the production of Coca-Cola and Germany has a comparative advantage in the production of beer.

The existence of a comparative advantage depends on the *relative* costs of the two commodities, not the absolute efficiency in producing them. In the United

Table 41.4 PRICE PER GALLON OF BEER AND
COCA-COLA IN THE UNITED STATES
AND GERMANY BEFORE TRADE
In Dollars

United States		Germany	
Beer	$0.60	Beer	$0.75
Coca-Cola	0.40	Coca-Cola	1.00

States, beer costs 50 percent more to produce than Coca-Cola, whereas in Germany, beer costs 25 percent less to produce than Coca-Cola. Therefore, relative to the cost of producing Coca-Cola, Germany is more efficient in producing beer. Similarly, in the United States, Coca-Cola costs 33 percent less to produce than beer, whereas in Germany, Coca-Cola costs 33 percent more to produce than beer. Therefore, relative to the cost of producing beer, the United States is more efficient in producing Coca-Cola.

Assume that the United States persuades Germany to exchange beer for American Coca-Cola at the prices prevailing in Germany. Some American workers will be shifted from beer production to Coca-Cola production. For each worker transferred from producing beer to producing Coca-Cola, the United States will lose 5,000 gallons of beer (which the worker will no longer produce) and gain 7,500 gallons of Coca-Cola (which the workers will begin to produce). This Coca-Cola can be sold in Germany for $7500 (because the price of Coca-Cola is $1 per gallon in Germany). Then, paying the German price of 75 cents per gallon for beer, the United States can use the proceeds to purchase ten thousand gallons of beer.

The final result of this series of events will be that for every worker in the United States shifted from beer production to Coca-Cola production, the United States will lose 5,000 gallons of domestically produced beer but gain 10,000 gallons of German-produced beer. Obviously, the United States will be better off after the trade. But the prices at which the two countries traded are identical to the German prices before trade. This means that the United States received all of the gains from trade and Germany received no gains at all.

Assume now that Germany persuades the United States to trade at the prices prevailing in the United States. Then Germany will receive all of the gains from trade. When the Germans shift a worker from production of Coca-Cola to production of beer, the worker will produce 4,000 gallons of beer (rather than 3,000 gallons of Coca-Cola). This beer will be sold in the United States (at 60 cents per gallon) for $2400. With the proceeds of this sale the Germans can purchase 6,000 gallons of Coca-Cola (at the rate of 40 cents per gallon). Thus if trade occurs at the U.S. prices, the Germans will shift workers from production of Coca-Cola to production of beer, which they will export to the United States. In doing so they will lose 3,000 gallons of domestically produced Coca-Cola for every worker so shifted, but they will gain 6,000 gallons of American-produced Coca-Cola. Obviously this situation benefits Germany.

From these examples two conclusions can be drawn: (1) If the relative costs of producing two commodities in two countries differ, then trade can benefit one or both of the countries, and (2) if the prices at which trade takes place are the same as those prevailing in one country before trade began, then that country receives none of the gains from trade and the other receives all of the gains.

We can draw a third conclusion, which is undoubtedly obvious from the preceding discussion. If the ratio of prices at which trade takes place lies somewhere between the price ratios in the two countries, then both countries will share in the gains from trade. If, in the beer and Coca-Cola example, the United States and Germany traded at the rate of 1 gallon of beer equals 1 gallon of Coca-Cola, then both countries would benefit from trade. The reader can calculate the gains in each country as workers are shifted to export production. Such a calculation will verify the fact that both countries would benefit from trade at a price ratio that lies between the two domestic price ratios.

When two countries engage in trade, the one that is able to exert the greater bargaining power will succeed in pushing the trade prices closer to the ratio of prices and production costs of the other country. In doing this the more powerful country will reap most of the gains from trade. Many economists have collected evidence to show that in the trade that takes place between advanced industrialized countries and less developed agricultural countries, the industrialized countries reap nearly all of the benefits (see, e.g.: Prebisch; Singer).

Another problem is that the *law of comparative advantage*—the theory that everyone gains when countries produce what they do best—holds true, if at all, only at a given moment. If the United States had an advantage in producing corn rather than machines in 1776, the "law" would have told us never to switch to producing machines. This rule thus would freeze all the unevenness of development at a given point.

APPENDIX B

The Case for Free Trade and the Case for Tariffs

To what extent should a country engage in international trade? Nearly 200 years ago the classical economists (particularly David Ricardo) developed the analysis of comparative advantage and identified the economic gains that two trading partners can secure. On the basis of this analysis they concluded that as long as anyone in either of the two countries desired to engage in further trade, then it was possible to reap more gains from trade. In practice, they argued that the government ought to place no restrictions on trade. People should be free to trade to any extent they wished. This conclusion was an integral part of the general laissez-faire policy advocated by the classical economists.

Over the past 200 years most orthodox economists have advocated free trade. They have extended and refined their analyses of comparative advantage and the gains from trade, but they have not altered the essential argument. They have consistently contended that any restrictions on international trade will reduce the volume of trade and that any reduction of volume will reduce the gains from trade. Most economists have therefore concluded that restrictions on international trade reduce a nation's economic welfare.

The consistent advocacy of free trade might seem surprising in view of the fact that only rarely during the past 200 years have the governments of the major capitalist countries pursued such a policy. Most of the time they have erected a wall of tariffs to keep out foreign goods. A tariff is a tax on an import that forces the importer to charge a higher price to the general public in order to pay the tariff. Thus the tariff is really a tax paid by the consumer of the import.

Tariffs have usually been imposed for two reasons. First, in the nineteenth century the American government used the tariff as its chief source of tax revenue. Second, industries that must compete with foreign producers for the domestic market have lobbied for tariffs to protect their monopoly power from foreign competition. Because neither of these reasons would be particularly appealing to the general public, many arguments with greater popularity have been put forward. Historically there have been three very common arguments for tariffs in the United States. Economists consider all of them fallacious. We shall examine each.

1. If is often argued that tariffs protect American workers from competition from foreign workers who are paid very low wages. This argument concludes that tariffs maintain higher wage rates for American workers. Although free trade may hurt the workers in industries that are undersold by foreign competitors (the workers will probably have to transfer to new occupations), it should raise the overall wage level. This is because, as we have seen, the total output available for consumption increases after trade. It seems unlikely that workers would not share in this increase.

2. It is sometimes proposed that tariffs are ideal taxes because the foreign exporter pays the tax. As we have already noted, however, the American importer is forced to raise the price that is charged to the American customers. Therefore the American public pays most of the tax in the form of higher prices for the commodities it consumes.

3. Finally, there are the campaigns to "buy American products" to "keep money in the United States." This simplistic argument assumes that when imports are purchased, money leaves the country, and that if they had not been purchased, consumers would have bought American-produced commodities. It is argued that purchasing foreign products deprives American businesses of sales and American workers of jobs. The problem with this argument is that it ignores the fact that when the United States engages in foreign trade, commodities are *exported* as well as imported. The foreign demand for U.S. exports increases the sales of American businesses and creates jobs for American workers.

There are other arguments for tariffs, some not so obviously fallacious as those we have discussed. Most economists agree, however, that in a powerful, industrialized economy like the United States there are really no convincing arguments for tariffs. The few problems that tariffs might help solve (e.g., industrial relocations or regional economic depressions) could certainly be solved more efficaciously by other, more direct government policies.

What is true for industrialized countries, however, is not necessarily true for less developed countries. Many less developed countries have become suppliers of raw materials and agricultural products for industrial countries. They generally receive such low prices for their exports that their standard of living remains abysmally low. If they engage in free trade, small local manufacturing industries cannot hope to compete with foreign giants. As a consequence, industrialization takes place very slowly, if at all. Those countries would certainly be justified in placing some kind of restrictions on imports as an aid to industrialization. The issues involved in the relationship between advanced industrialized countries and less developed countries are considered in Chapter 42.

SUGGESTED READINGS

An excellent general article on current international problems is David Gordon's "The Global Economy: New Edifice or Crumbling Foundations?" *New Left Review* 168 (March-April, 1988), pp. 24–65. A fascinating view of the debt crisis in Latin America is Robert Pollin's "Debt Crisis, Accumulation Crisis, and Economic Restructuring in Latin America," *International Review of Applied Economics* 10 (Spring, 1988), pp. 231–248. An outstanding article on international finance is

Arthur MacEwan's "International Debt and Banking: Rising Instability Within the General Crisis," *Science and Society* 50 (Summer 1986): 177–209. A more popular article stating the issues very clearly is Arthur MacEwan's "International Trade and Economic Instability," *Monthly Review* 40 (Feb. 1989): 10–22.

REFERENCES

Barnett, Richard, and Ronald Muller. *Global Reach.* New York: Simon and Schuster, 1974.

Canadian Privey Council. *Report of the Task Force on the Structure of Canadian Industry.* Ottawa: Queen's Printer, 1968.

MacEwan, Arthur. "International Trade and Economic Instability." *Monthly Review* 40 (February 1989), pp. 10–22.

Mandel, Ernest. *Europe vs. America: Contradictions of Imperialism.* New York: Monthly Review Press, 1970.

Prebisch, Raoul. "The Role of Commercial Policies in Underdeveloped Countries." *American Economic Review* 49 (May 1959), pp. 412–423.

Singer, Hans. "The Distribution of Gains Between Investing and Borrowing Countries." *American Economic Review* 48 (May 1958), pp. 334–342.

Szymanski, Albert. "The Decline and Fall of the U.S. Eagle." In *The Economic Crisis Reader.* Edited by David Mermelstein. New York: Random House, 1975.

Chapter
42

Economic Underdevelopment: Natural Causes or Imperialism?

Earlier, the problems of economic growth in developed industrial economies were considered. In economies that have not industrialized, the problems of economic growth are substantially and qualitatively different from those already examined in this book. Before meaningful growth in per capital output and income can take place in these economies, they must undertake industrialization.

The economic, social, and political obstacles to industrialization in such countries are different from the problems of advanced industrial countries. Economic growth in the developed countries merely means incremental additions to output within an established structure. Development of the less developed countries means basic social, political, and structural economic changes to lay the foundations for growth.

It is therefore necessary to devote an additional chapter to the question of economic development. The countries of the world are commonly divided into three groups: (1) industrially developed capitalist countries, (2) socialist countries, and (3) less developed or underdeveloped capitalist countries, or the *Third World*. It is with this third group that we shall be concerned in this chapter. The terms "underdeveloped" and "less developed" are used interchangeably in the literature, and neither term is perfectly accurate. We shall use the term less developed to emphasize that development is relative, not absolute. A country may be less developed than others or less developed than it could be if certain obstacles had not existed.

FACTS OF ECONOMIC UNDERDEVELOPMENT

There are at least two generally accepted definitions of a less developed country, one based on an economic index and the other based on certain distinguishing characteristics. The economic index generally employed is average income per person: GNP divided by population. According to this criterion, a country with an average income per person of less than some amount—say, $1000 per year—is classified as less developed (but this figure changes over time because it is relative to the more developed countries).

The term *less developed*, it must be emphasized, has misleading sociological connotations. For example, there is no correlation between level of income and level of cultural or social development. Obviously, ancient Greece or Egypt or China had very highly developed cultures and very low average income levels. Further, an average may hide wide disparities in individual incomes. For example, Kuwait has one of the highest levels of average income per person, but most of the income is concentrated in the hands of a few very rich people, and there is an enormous gulf between the very rich and the very poor (despite Kuwait's much-publicized welfare programs). The high average income per Kuwaiti is solely the result of this little country's oil resources, and therefore one cannot assume that it is highly developed in an overall sense.

Dissatisfaction with the use of a single, purely economic measure of development has led some students of the subject to suggest a definition based on several distinguishing characteristics of less developed countries: (1) a relatively low income per person, (2) the existence of a relatively high portion (often 60 percent or more) of the population engaged in agriculture, (3) a relatively low level of techniques used in production, (4) a relatively low level of education, and (5) a relatively low level of capital formation.

According to any definition of developed and less developed, the fact is that more than 50 percent of the population of the capitalist, or private-enterprise, world live in countries that can be classified as less developed. Among private-enterprise, or capitalist, countries in the lowest category, with average income per person of less than $410 per year (and mostly agrarian and lacking in technology, education, or capital) fall India and most Asian and African nations. Lower middle-income economies range from Sudan with a per capita income of $440 to Colombia and Paraguay, with $1,460 and $1,610, respectively. Upper middle-income countries, which are partly developed, include among others Jordan ($1,690), South Korea ($1,910), Brazil ($2,240), Greece ($4,290), and Israel ($5,090). Incomes in the industrial market economies ranged from Ireland's $5,150 per capita to Switzerland's $17,010; the United States stood fourth in 1982 with $13,160. The high-income oil exporters had higher average incomes as a group than the industrial market economies and included the United Arab Emirates, with the world's highest per capita income of

$23,770. The sharp decline in world oil prices since 1982, however, has undoubtedly changed the relative position of various countries.

In the advanced capitalist countries, workers' wages have grown greatly in the past 100 years. But in the less developed capitalist countries improvements in living standards have not always occurred. Even where per capital incomes were rising, the wealthy classes were often the main beneficiaries, so inequality increased while poverty was perpetuated. In a 1977 study of seven Asian countries (Pakistan, India, Bangladesh, Sri Lanka, Malaysia, Indonesia and the Philippines), the International Labour Office found worsening income distribution and declining real income of the rural poor, with the proportion of the population living below the poverty line increasing in each case. This occurred even though all of these countries except Bangladesh had rising per capital incomes.

The deterioration of the situation of the rural poor was even worse in sub-Saharan Africa, where per capita incomes for the entire region actually fell between 1970 and 1983. Starvation in parts of Africa made international headlines in the mid-1980s, but in the low-income capitalist countries as a whole, more than half the population regularly does not get enough to eat.

In 1980, the less developed capitalist countries had an average per capita income of $815 ($222 in the low-income countries), compared to $10,440 in the industrial capitalist economies. Between 1960 and 1983, the less developed countries as a group had growth rates averaging about 1.5 percent higher than the industrial countries, but on a per capita basis the differential is less than 1 percent due to the much higher population growth rates in the less developed countries. Moreover, the performance among countries was quite uneven, and even in those less developed countries that grew rapidly, the wealthiest classes were usually the prime beneficiaries. If we compare India and the United States between 1955 and 1980, for example, average income (in constant 1980 dollars) in the United States rose from $7,030 to $11,560, or an average 2 percent per year, whereas in India it rose from $170 to $260, or an average 1.7 percent per year. Thus America's income increased from 41 to 44 times India's income in this period. But even where incomes grew more rapidly in the less developed countries, poverty tended to persist and the absolute gap between their incomes and those in the industrialized economies tended to widen.

COLONIALISM AND NEOCOLONIALISM

It will help us to understand the current economic, social, and political conditions of less developed countries if we briefly examine some aspects of their history. In particular, we are interested in their relationships with the economically more advanced countries over the last several centuries.

From the fifteenth century onward, the developing capitalist economies of Europe grew economically and militarily at a rate then unparalleled in human history. From the fifteenth to the nineteenth centuries, they slowly came to dominate much of the rest of the world. They plundered, enslaved, and ruled so as to extract the maximum from their subjects.

Such havoc was created that ancient and culturally advanced civilizations disappeared, as in Peru and West Africa, and progress was set back hundreds of years by the destruction of native industries, as in India. On the other side, the plunder was so great that it constituted the main element—along with the exploitation of the European working class—in the formation of European capital and eventual industrialization.

By the end of the nineteenth century, almost all of the present less developed countries were under the colonial rule of the more advanced countries. The imperialist countries reaped astoundingly high profit rates from investments in the colonial countries, primarily because of a cheap labor supply and enforced lack of competition. The capital was invested mainly in extractive industries that exported raw materials to the imperial country. In the imperial country, the cheap raw materials were profitably turned into manufactured goods, part of which were exported back (tariff-free) to the colonial country.

The tariff-free importation of manufactured goods completed through competition the destruction (often begun by plunder) of the colonial country's manufacturing industries. An example of this may be seen in colonial India, especially in its textile industry:

> India, still an exporter of manufactured products at the end of the eighteenth century, becomes an importer. From 1815 to 1832, India's cotton exports dropped by 92 percent. In 1850, India was buying one quarter of Britain's cotton exports. All industrial products shared this fate. The ruin of the traditional trades and crafts was the result of British commercial policy. (Bettleheim, p. 47)

The development of the colonial areas was thus held back by the imperialist countries, while the development of the imperialist countries was greatly speeded by the flow of plunder and profits from the colonies. The exception that proves the rule is Japan. Japan escaped colonialism as a result of several more or less accidental factors. Thus it was able to industrialize independently and develop its own advanced capitalist economy. Japan alone achieved this among the countries of Asia, Africa, and Latin America because the others had all been reduced to colonies or to semi-colonial status, preventing their further development.

The half-century from 1890 to World War II was the peak period of colonialism, when all the world was divided among the western European and North American powers. In the late 1940s and 1950s, a new era began, with formal independence achieved by hundreds of millions of people throughout Asia and Africa as a result of struggles fomented by the impact of two world wars, the Russian and Chinese revolutions, and long-pent-up pressures for liberation. The day of open colonialism is over, but the pattern of the ex-colonial countries exporting food or raw materials usually still holds. Some have succeeded today in producing and exporting light manufactured goods, but still have to import most of their capital goods and technology. Foreign investment often dominates their industries. Because of the continuance of the underlying colonial economic pattern, we are justified in describing this situation as *neocolonialism* in spite of formal political independence.

In fact, formal independence has changed the essential economic relationships very little. On the one side are all the underdeveloped, newly independent countries, still under foreign economic domination, still facing all the old obstacles to development. On the other side are the advanced capitalist countries, still extracting large profits from the dependent Third World. The imperialist group includes all the countries that extract profits by trade and investment—thus most of western Europe, Japan, and the United States. Neocolonial profits from the less developed countries flow even to countries like Switzerland that never held colonial power over any less developed country.

Neocolonial control in the world today comes through economic and monetary penetration, together with political alliances between the neocolonial powers and the ruling classes in the developing countries. This ranges from blatant forms such as subsidies and military supplies to highly complex monetary agreements. It also seems to be characteristic to grant independence to small territories, tiny divisions of former colonial domains. Thus they have no political or economic power with which to resist continued domination.

It should also be noted that the economic control often is not direct but built up in a complex pyramid. For example, some American companies directly invest in northeast Brazil. More control of that area, however, is achieved through American domination of major southern Brazilian companies, which, in turn, buy controlling interests in companies in the Brazilian northeast. Still more control is achieved through American domination of some western European companies, which, in turn, own some major Brazilian firms or directly own some of the local firms in the Brazilian northeast.

OBSTACLES TO DEVELOPMENT

Is overpopulation the primary obstacle to economic development? This view is widely held by the average person in the street, many newspaper reporters, and even some university professors, though little systematic evidence has been presented to substantiate it. Generally proponents merely point to the vast number of poor and starving people in India as an example. Even such an eminent "economist" as Robert S. McNamara (former president of Ford Motor Company and former U.S. secretary of defense) asserts that "the greatest single obstacle to the economic and social advancement of the majority of the peoples in the underdeveloped world is rampant population growth" (quoted in Gray and Tangri).

The important point to note about McNamara's ideology is that it tells the hungry people that the "greatest single obstacle" to their development is their own animal sexual desires. The function of this ideology is thus identical to that of the theory that lack of development is due to racial inferiority, the laziness and/or stupidity of "the natives." It shifts the blame to the victims and makes it unnecessary to admit that their problems are due to antiquated social systems, rapacious ruling classes, and, above all, foreign domination and exploitation. Given its wide acceptance, this "blame the victim" view is quite effective.

If one turns to the facts, there is no evidence that high population density is the prime cause of underdevelopment. More precisely, there is no statistically significant correlation between high population density and low income per person. On the contrary, many countries with high incomes per person also have high population densities. For example, Belgium has 816 people per square mile, West Germany has 624, and the United Kingdom has 588. India has only 406 people per square mile, and most of the less developed countries have much lower population densities.

In fact, we find many cases of concomitant successful development with rapid population increase. The highest recorded rate of population growth over a long period occurred in the United States during the years 1850–1950; but because U.S. production also grew at record rates, America not only became a developed country but also had record growth rates of output *per person*, and thus individual welfare improved.

Of course, if a country is standing still economically, any growth of population is a terrible problem. We do not deny that overpopulation can be a problem; we only maintain that it is always *relative* to growth of output. The basic problems are seen when we try to explain why the problems of poverty and inequality persist in less developed countries. Although population is a problem, it is secondary to these larger problems, and exclusive focus on it tends to hide the more important problems.

Moreover, it turns out that the key to reducing population growth is development of industrialization and urbanization. A rural family with a primitive technology finds young children useful for many tasks. An urban family in an industrialized country sees children as an economic burden until they have undergone a long education. Furthermore, birth-control information is much more effective in an urban setting in which a woman may find cultural interests outside the home and needs family planning to develop her own independent life. Thus all the developed areas from the United States to the Soviet Union have witnessed rapid declines in birthrates as the agrarian sector has shrunk, while education and culture have spread as a result of economic development.

Another theory of underdevelopment claims that the less developed nations are all those that by accident have relatively few natural resources on their territories. Yet the less developed countries in 1965 provided

37.5 percent of the total output of raw materials in the capitalist world, including the bulk of many strategic materials. This is certainly a large enough absolute amount for a solid industrial base. But the less developed countries do not produce anything like 37.5 percent of manufactured goods. In fact, most of their raw materials are taken away to the advanced capitalist countries and are there manufactured into finished goods (some of which are sold back at a high profit to the less developed countries).

It appears, therefore, that the main obstacles to development are *not* natural or biological factors inherent in the less developed countries. The main obstacles are *not* sexual desires and procreation, laziness, low intelligence, or lack of natural resources. The obstacles reside in the present social relationships of human to human: the fact that all of the peasants' and workers' surplus over immediate needs is extracted from them by the landlords, moneylenders, tax collectors, and foreign corporations. We shall show that the native ruling classes use their high incomes for luxury consumption and that most of the foreign corporations' enormous profits are removed from the country.

As a result, there is a lack of capital for investment in development, and what investment does take place is often oriented toward the benefit of the wealthy classes, such as the production of consumer durables that only a few can afford. The lack of capital (and lack of nonhuman power per person) is correlated with low income per person (see Landes). Lack of capital means not only little construction but also little new equipment and little technological improvement. It also means few funds available for education and training, let alone research. Lack of capital also means that millions of workers cannot be employed at a sufficient rate of profit and thus are left unemployed or underemployed. Thus it is the social relationships (and their consequences) that are the real obstacles to development.

As an example, consider the "green revolution" in agriculture that several less developed countries have experienced (see Griffin). In this green revolution, new types of grains have been introduced in countries like India and Pakistan. They have brought much higher yields, and thus one of the technical barriers to feeding the population seems to be falling. To make efficient use of the new processes and output, however, requires considerable investment in irrigation, fertilizer, insecticides, and so forth. The large landowners who can afford this investment find that their profits are enhanced by evicting tenants and mechanizing the production process. Indeed this has been taking place on a growing scale, helping to explain the persisting and often worsening poverty even where growth is taking place. The dispossessed peasants are swelling the ranks of the unemployed in the cities. Thus the social relationships form a barrier aggravating the very problems that development is expected to cure.

It is a mere truism to say growth would be faster if the less developed countries had more capital, more technology, and more education and training. The real question, however, is to identify the social relationships that limit these factors, and to clarify the impact on them of the capitalist world system. In the process of development, moreover, a complete change is needed from a rural, agrarian economy to an urban, industrialized economy. The issue, then, is how to change the social relationships and interaction with the industrial countries in a way that will make possible this sweeping change in economic structure.

We shall argue that the obstacles are mainly institutional: (1) an internal ruling class that spends much of its income on luxuries and government revenues on unnecessary public monuments or military expenditures, (2) a foreign trade conducted on very poor terms, creating an exploitative economic dependence and importing the wrong items for development, and (3) foreign investment directed toward low-priority areas, with resultant high profits sent abroad. Notice that this view is quite opposite to the views of most traditional economists.

INTERNAL OBSTACLES TO DEVELOPMENT

Let us begin with the internal obstacles to development created by the less developed countries' social systems. The typical situation finds millions of peasants engaged in subsistence farming, obligated to pay high rents to landlords, high interest to moneylenders, and high taxes to local and national governments. From their original small net product, peasants usually pay more than half to meet these obligations, thus retaining hardly enough for their bare subsistence and none for major improvement or investment.

The landlords and moneylenders take much of the surplus from the peasant and spend it on conspicuous luxury consumption. If they reinvest any, their extreme conservatism prompts them to invest in more land or to send it to some safe foreign country; little, if any, is invested in industry. The governments are mostly dominated by a small elite of wealthy landlords and merchants (in turn, often dominated by foreign elements), who have little motivation to invest government funds in constructive projects; in fact, the advent of industrial capitalism would undermine their power. Most government revenues are spent on military goods and services for the purpose of internal repression. Governments spend some on showcase projects (e.g., sports arenas) or, as in Venezuela, in beautification of the capital city. The little that is invested constructively is usually for roads or ports to serve the needs of foreign investors.

The reactionary ruling groups in the less developed capitalist countries are generally supported by the advanced capitalist countries, including the U.S. State Department. It is not that the U.S. State Department *wants* backwardness and governments dominated by reactionary landlords and military cliques. On the contrary, it would undoubtedly be happier with rapidly developing liberal capitalist countries (with American firms having most of the development investments). The problem is that these areas have only very few and very weak native capitalists who are linked by blood and marriage to the landlords and militarists. The countries are very much a part of the international commercialized capitalist market, but they have no steam to develop their own dynamic capitalism and thus remain appendages of the advanced capitalist countries.

Not only is there no strong group willing to build a liberal capitalism in these countries, but also the real political alternative is usually a left-leaning socialist government. Plans for rapid development have been an essential part of socialist programs, as with the socialist government of Cuba. But these socialist development programs have been violently attacked by the U.S. State Department. In Brazil and Greece and several other countries, very mild socialist governments (whose practical measures only *helped* native small capitalists and were not yet even contemplating socialism) were overthrown by military coups supported by the CIA. Thus the real choice in the less developed countries has not been one of landlords and militarists versus liberal capitalists but, rather, landlords and militarists (and a few native capitalists) versus socialist movements, composed of workers and peasants and students. In every case so far, the United States has chosen to support reactionary landlords and militarists such as the shah of Iran.

EFFECTS OF FOREIGN TRADE ON LESS DEVELOPED COUNTRIES

The colonial era left the economies of the Third World countries very dependent on foreign demand and consequently highly sensitive to the foreign business cycle of expansion and depression. It is also a fact that international investments and trade in primary products (i.e., raw materials, both agricultural and mineral) show the greatest fluctuations. "It follows that any country whose economy is intimately dependent on foreign investment or whose trade is greatly dependent on primary commodities will be seriously affected by swings of business arising outside its own borders" (United Nations, p. 42).

This dependence has been recognized in the less developed countries. In 1949 the government of what was then Ceylon (now Sri Lanka) acknowledged: "The economy of Ceylon depends almost entirely on its export in tea, rubber and coconut products. . . . About 80 percent of the people are employed directly or indirectly in the production and handling of these exports" (ibid., p. 43). The government of Burma said explicitly that "the most important source of unemployment in Burma is a decline in prices of raw materials caused by the depression generated elsewhere" (ibid., p. 21).

Less developed countries are highly dependent on their exports to the industrial countries, so that cyclical slowdowns in the Western world tend to affect them sharply, a consequence both of lower export volume and falling or depressed export prices. In this context, the impact of the world-wide recession of 1980–1983, the worst since the Great Depression, was especially severe. During this period, per capita incomes fell by 2 to 10 percent a year in less developed countries as diverse as Argentina, Brazil, Chile, Ivory Coast, and Yugoslavia, all of which had raised per capita incomes in the preceding decade.

Although mineral and agricultural products predominate among Third World exports, many countries have developed a modest level of industrial exports and a few have proved highly successful in increasing industrial exports rapidly. Among these are a number of the smaller countries in eastern and Southeastern Asia, including South Korea, Taiwan, Hong Kong, and Singapore; Brazil has also been moderately successful along these lines. It should be emphasized, however, that these "success stories" have usually occurred under highly repressive regimes, and that they do not indicate a pathway open to all. When Third World exports compete too vigorously with manufactured products in the industrial countries, "protectionist" measures to keep them out tend to appear in the form of tariffs, quotas, or the like. The factors limiting Third World industrial exports become clearer when we consider the manner in which such exports affect capitalist interests in the industrial countries.

Other things being equal, the lower the wage rates are, the higher the profit rate for capitalist firms. When the labor movement in the industrial countries became strong enough to raise real wages significantly after World War II, it was natural for firms to look for new means of limiting wages. Setting up manufacturing subsidiaries in low-wage countries was one way of doing this. Perhaps of even greater importance, the very threat of doing so greatly strengthened the bargaining position of the capitalist firms relative to their workers. Finally, to the extent that firms can purchase low-cost supplies overseas, they can increase their profitability. All of these factors created a situation in which some less developed countries could begin to industrialize.

It is important to recognize, however, that many firms in the industrial countries are threatened by competition. When industrial imports from less developed countries increase, that fact in itself generates strong pressures to limit them, pressures that are increased by the inability of industrial capitalist countries to assure displaced workers of new jobs. This means that the very success of a few less developed countries in increasing industrial exports is itself a factor limiting the possibilities for other countries to follow the same course.

Even where less developed countries are able to expand their exports to the industrial economies, the results may not be purely beneficial. Thus Jamaica received about $1 billion in foreign investment from 1953 to 1972, mainly in the mining and refining of bauxite for export, but when a reformist government tried to assert national control over the industry and to divert some of its profits to improving social welfare, the foreign firms cut back production sharply and the investment flows dried up (see Girvan). This created a foreign exchange crisis in which the International Monetary Fund (IMF), as a condition for extending credit, forced the government to cut back on its subsidies to the poor and to cut real wages (by limiting monetary wage gains to a maximum of 15 percent while the price level rose by 40 percent).

The IMF conditions were imposed in the name of stabilization and conservative fiscal policy, but together with the actions of the multinational corporations they led to an acute social crisis and the replacement of the reformist government. The lesson of Jamaica's experience is that once multinational corporations come to play a strategic role in the economy of a less developed country, it is extremely difficult to reassert national control over the economy. Experiences like those of Jamaica have given rise to an extensive literature on "dependency," a situation in which the economic structure and performance of less developed countries is determined largely by the actions of industrial economies, actions over which they have no control.

For most of the twentieth century, the terms of trade for the Third World vis-à-vis the industrial countries worsened, since the price of mineral and agricultural products fell relative to the price of industrial products. This trend was interrupted in the 1970s by the sharp increase in oil prices. For a number of Third World countries this provided a temporary bonanza, but for the even larger number that must import oil, economic difficulties were magnified. When oil prices started falling in the 1980s, even the oil exporters suffered, since many had begun long-term development projects that they were no longer able to fund. Both groups of countries found that involvement in international markets is a two-edged sword, sometimes yielding benefits and sometimes leading to crisis.

In the early and mid-1980s, the crises were magnified by the high levels of debt owed by Third World countries to the capitalist industrial countries. Weak markets and protectionist measures in the industrial countries were a response to the deep recession of the early 1980s, making it difficult for the less developed countries to export enough to meet payments on their foreign debt. At the same time, most of the money borrowed from foreign banks bears a fluctuating interest rate, and when the U.S. Federal Reserve forced up interest rates steeply to fight inflation, the interest payments of the less developed countries were forced up accordingly; it has been estimated that every 1 percent rise in the interest rate they must pay costs the less developed countries $6 billion per year. Their total debt outstanding rose from $68.4 billion in 1970 to $595.8 billion in 1983, and the ratio of debt to GNP rose in the same period from an average of 13.3 percent to 26.7 percent (see World Bank, p. 31).

In the 1980s, a real possibility emerged that some of the Third World countries would be unable to pay their debts. In most cases, the private banks refused to negotiate extended payments unless they agreed to conditions laid down by the International Monetary Fund (IMF), which tied its own extensions to harsh conditions as well. This gave the industrial countries tremendous leverage over the less developed ones. The most typical condition was cutting government spending to balance the budget, and the burden of this adjustment fell most heavily on the poor, whose bare subsistence often depended on government subsidies to keep the cost of food and other essential goods and services within reach. Once again, involvement in the international economy controlled by the industrial economies proved treacherous for the less developed countries, and especially for the poorest within them, as they lost control over their basic economic policies.

While the dependence of the less developed countries on the industrial ones increased further and assumed new forms in the 1980s, trade between the two continued to be vital to the industrial countries as well. When developed capitalist countries import major food products and raw materials, they realize that these imports are very important. The food products are essential to the diets of Westerners, and the raw materials are indispensable for their factories. The manufactured goods that the less developed countries buy are needed desperately because these countries do very little manufacturing themselves. Today, moreover, most of the Third World countries actually import food from the developed capitalist countries—especially Canada, the United States, and Australia.

FOREIGN INVESTMENT

It is often argued that American foreign investment channels American dollars into less developed countries. These dollars, it is claimed, can then be used to finance industrialization in the less developed countries. While this has in fact played a limited role in industrialization, it has also exposed the less developed countries to severe pressures as we have seen. Moreover, the data reveal that the rates of profit of U.S. firms in the Third World are so high that they extract more profit each year than they put into the area in investments.

The multinational, or global, firms are the present instrument whereby enormous profits are extracted from the neocolonial countries and sent back to the imperialist countries. All U.S. firms' profits from abroad are 30 percent of total U.S. corporate profits. The top 298 U.S.-based multinational corporations earn 40 percent of their entire net profits overseas, and their rate of profit from abroad is much higher than their domestic profit rate (see Muller, p. 183). In office equipment, for example, the overseas rate is 26 percent compared to a domestic rate of only 9 percent.

In the neocolonial countries, the multinational corporations skim off a very large percentage of all profits for themselves. For example, in 1971 in Brazil the multinational corporations took 70 percent of the total net profits of the five important sectors of rubber, motor vehicles, machinery, household appliances, and mining. Moreover, much of these corporate investments are not U.S. funds at all, but are provided by local capitalists. In all of the Latin American manufacturing operations of U.S.-based multinational corporations from 1960 to 1970, about 78 percent of the in-

Table 42.1   PROFIT AND DIRECT FOREIGN INVESTMENT, U.S., 1950–1970
In Billions of Dollars

	Western Europe	Canada	Latin America	Asia and Africa
Investment from United States	15.5	10.6	6.0	9.5
Profit to United States	10.4	10.0	17.1	24.6
Net gain of capital in foreign region	5.1	0.6	−11.1	−15.1

Source: U.S. Department of Commerce, *U.S. Business Investments in Foreign Countries* (Washington, D.C.: GPO, 1970), p. 85. Later data from Department of Commerce collected in Linda Majka, *The Military Industrial Complex Reconsidered* (unpublished M.A. thesis, University of California, Santa Barbara, 1973).

vestments were financed by local funds. Yet the same corporations, between 1965 and 1968, sent 52 percent of all their profits to the United States (see Barnett and Muller, pp. 16–17).

As a result of the use of local funds for investment, plus high profit rates and the sending of most profits to the United States, the neocolonial or Third World countries actually have a net outflow of capital to the United States. This surprising fact has been documented by the U.S. Department of Commerce for the period 1950–1970, in which there were striking differences in the flow pattern to and from the less developed Third World.

Table 42.1 shows that U.S. firms invested much more in the advanced capitalist countries of western Europe than they extracted in profits. In Canada the profit and investment flows to and from the U.S. firms were about even. But in Latin America, Asia, and Africa, the United States— acting through multinational firms—extracted $26 billion more in profits than it invested in the same period!

In Latin America alone, in the shorter period 1950–1965, there was a net flow of 7.5 billion U.S. dollars from that area to the United States ($11.3 billion profit minus $3.8 billion new investment). Yet profit rates were so high that at the same time the value of U.S. direct investments in Latin America rose from $4.5 billion to $10.3 billion. In fact, in the period 1957–1964 only 12 percent of direct U.S. investment in Latin America came from the United States; 74 percent was reinvestment of profits or depreciation funds from Latin American operations. Similarly, in Africa and Asia in the period 1950–1965 American corporations invested only $5 billion but transferred to the United States $14 billion in profits, for a net flow of $9 billion to the United States. Yet, enough profit remained for reinvestment that U.S. direct investments in Africa and Asia rose from $1.3 to $4.7 billion.

The situation has changed little since that study was done. In 1981 U.S. investments in all the Third World countries earned a 23.1 percent rate of return. In 1982 the total return was $6.25 billion, of which $3.4

billion was sent back to the United States and $2.9 billion was reinvested (see U.S. Department of Commerce, p. 19).

Two facts are blatantly obvious from these data: (1) The rate of profit in U.S. investments abroad is several times higher in the less developed than in the advanced capitalist countries, and (2) the less developed neocolonial countries generously make a good-sized contribution to U.S. capital accumulation.

IMPERIALISM AND CAPITAL FLOW

What is the impact on the U.S. economy of the extraordinarily high profits that flow in from the neocolonial countries? When each U.S.-based multinational firm finds and grabs a new market, its excess investment funds can now be invested abroad. Moreover, the new investment can be expected to yield high profits year after year. The problem is that for the economy as a whole these new profits pour in from overseas faster than new investment areas can be found for the mounting funds. This capital accumulation is in excess of the investment opportunities domestically or abroad. Therefore, in a depression the situation is worsened by adding to savings when there is already a surplus of saving beyond what can be invested profitably.

For the less developed Third World countries, the outflow of immense amounts of capital (in the form of profits) is disastrous for their growth and feeds their own peculiar type of stagnation. These neocolonial countries have long suffered the odious combination of inflation and unemployment. The rates of unemployment in the less developed capitalist countries have been scandalous for many years, often more than 30 or 40 percent of the urban labor force.

To understand their type of stagnation, it must be stressed that the less developed neocolonial countries suffer from a severe lack of capital— quite unlike the advanced capitalist countries, who usually suffer from a surplus of capital far beyond the profitable investment opportunities. Lack of capital means not only little new factory construction but also little new equipment, meager research funds, and very slow technological improvement. Lack of capital also means few funds for the education and training of human beings, the most important lack in the long run.

The Third World countries lack capital because of the institutional-structural arrangements within most of them and vis-à-vis the capitalist world. First, most have an internal ruling class that spends much of its income on luxuries, expends government revenues on unnecessary public monuments or on vast military establishments, and banks much of its wealth in Switzerland or the United States. Second, most of them have very poor terms of trade for large parts of each business cycle because prices of raw materials from the Third World fall much faster in depressions than prices of finished goods from the advanced capitalist world. Thus in the 1981–

1982 depression, prices of most raw material remained constant or fell, while prices of finished goods soared.

Finally, as shown above, the outflow of profits and interest from the Third World countries is considerably more than the flow of foreign investment into them. For all these reasons there are dire lacks of plant and equipment, technological progress, and highly trained workers.

The lack of plant and equipment means that millions and millions of workers have little or nothing with which to work and therefore cannot be profitably employed. Since the rate of profit would be insufficient, these millions of human beings are left unemployed. Because this unemployment is due to lack of capital, it continues even in the face of demand for products and severe shortages leading to inflation.

Stagnation in the less developed capitalist world is thus characterized by lack of capital, whereas in the advanced capitalist world it is characterized by surplus capital. This difference is reflected in the fact that mass unemployment of workers in the advanced capitalist countries is accompanied by high rates of nonutilization of capital (idle machines and factories). On the contrary, mass unemployment of workers in the less developed capitalist countries may coexist with full utilization of their tiny supply of capital plant and equipment (although there are also cases of underutilization of capital in the industries supplying the luxury export market).

Of course, stagnation in the neocolonial countries is worsened by their dependent position. The multinational corporations generally have little competition and exercise their monopoly power to keep prices of goods within these countries high even during global depressions. Moreover, the multinational corporations often reduce all their investments during a depression (though not as much as competitive firms must do), but they continue to extract and return to their home countries as much profit as possible throughout the depression, thus intensifying the lack of capital. Finally, it is worth repeating that the raw materials of the Third World suffer the greatest price declines or the smallest price rises in depression periods, so they bear a considerable part of the international burden of the slump.

INVESTMENT BY MULTINATIONAL FIRMS

The ways in which multinational firms—American, European, and Japanese—extract profits from less developed countries have changed since World War II. At one time most investment was in the form of loans or stock purchases in existing companies or the creation of brand new companies—with or without local participation. Today such purely financial movements are less important; rather, the capitalist corporation simply establishes branches of its own firm or completely subordinates satellite firms. The day of the multinational firm is here.

Not only does the giant multinational firm operate equally well in the industrial capitalist nation and abroad, but also its board of directors and its sphere of influence usually reflect an inseparable mixture of financial and industrial interests. In the fantastic size and complexity of their structure, which includes both finance and industrial capital, and the multiplicity of their interests, which include both domestic and foreign sales, the giant corporations of today are very different from earlier banking or industrial interests.

The capitalists of all the developed countries together own a large share of the major industrial enterprises of the less developed capitalist countries. "There are no reliable figures for the Third World as a whole which measure the extent of foreign economic intervention, but it is certain that many, perhaps even most of the industrial undertakings of the underdeveloped countries are foreign-owned or controlled" (Jalee, p. 22). A careful investigation of one important neocolony concludes: "Foreign capital can . . . be said to share the control of the Indian economy with domestic capital on what is very nearly a fifty-fifty basis" (Bettleheim, p. 47).

It should also be stressed that most of these multinational firms are among the very largest corporations of industrial countries. In the case of the United States, an official survey by size of firm found that 45 giants (each investing over $100 million abroad) had 57 percent of total American direct foreign investment, that 163 firms had 80 percent, and that 455 firms had 93 percent (see U.S. Department of Commerce, p. 144). Certainly any survey today would show increased concentration.

The concentration of profits is much greater. In 1966 more than half of American profits from abroad went to only 16 firms (all among the top 30 according to the *Fortune* listing). Moreover, these profits were not a small sum, even in terms of total American profits. By 1980, 23.8 percent of total U.S. corporate profits came from investments abroad. As one example, in 1983, Exxon made 54 percent of its profits abroad.

It was also noted in Chapter 41 that foreign sales are growing much more rapidly than domestic sales. Moreover, in 1961 only 460 of the 1000 largest U.S. companies had a subsidiary branch in Europe, but by 1965 more than 700 of them had a branch in Europe. This means, of course, that there is amazing concentration of capital in the few largest American firms, not only the capital of the United States but also that of the entire capitalist world. Japanese and European interests, however, are constantly increasing their percentage of ownership of the largest multinationals— and now control a majority of them.

All of the largest American firms are on the road to being truly global, considering their worldwide investments. Therefore, they are not merely interested, as was the earlier industrialist, in the export of commodities or, as was the earlier banker, in the export of capital. Rather, many have some of their major assembly plants in foreign countries and export a great deal from those subsidiaries. In fact, many foreign subsidiaries are large-scale exporters to the U.S. market. For example, in 1967, sales of all U.S. enterprises abroad totaled $32 billion, of which 11 percent was exported to the United States. That 11 percent constituted a total of $3.5 billion of goods, or 25 percent of total U.S. imports that year.

As noted earlier, this especially means that profits can be transferred around within the corporation, from a subsidiary in one country to a subsidiary in another. Therefore, the reports of total profit remittances from Third World areas to the United States can no longer be trusted as more than a general indicator. An entire corporation's total profits are the crucial point, and they often include hidden profits in one subsidiary by reason of another selling to it more cheaply, or hidden losses in one subsidiary by reason of another selling to it at prices above the market price. For example, it appears that in 1961 bauxite production in Jamaica, Surinam, and Guyana yielded to American corporations a rate of profit of from 26 to 34 percent. Yet this does not really give the total picture. Much of their costs "on materials and services" turn out to be exceedingly high payments to American corporations, also subsidiaries of the same major corporate group. On top of that, between 1939 and 1959 the price of bauxite in the United States almost doubled, but the price of bauxite exported from Surinam and Guyana remained almost the same throughout the whole period. These firms' West Indian subsidiaries thus overpaid greatly for their materials and services and were underpaid for their finished product. (Note that this also means more corporate taxes going to the United States but much less going to the West Indies.)

It follows that the multinational companies may have conflicting interests when it comes to terms, export subsidies, foreign investment, and so forth. They are absolutely united, however, in desiring there be as many nations as possible whose laws and institutions are favorable to the unhampered development of private enterprise. Thus there is much intracorporate conflict over economic details, but there is no conflict over the main political and strategic issues concerning the defense of imperialism.

What are the consequences of multinational firms? On the political side there is an important and expected change. Under the old system, there was conflict, direct and inevitable, between each of the investing countries. Under the new system at least some of the conflict is eliminated; thus a global or multinational firm has the interests of many different countries and many different investment bases to consider. The multinational firms frequently operate contrary to the interests of their home country.

NEOCOLONIAL "AID"

Investment and loans in the Third World constitute only about 1 percent of the national income of the imperialist countries. Furthermore, this is a very generous estimate, using extremely exaggerated figures. Such a small amount could not be considered much of a burden. And also, unfortunately, it is not much of a help.

As we have seen, the private investment is more than offset by the profit and interest return on the investments. The small public aid does not even offset the capital extracted by imperialism. The public aid that is (1) nonmilitary and (2) in the form of official donations or grants may be of some help, but it is not a large total amount. Even this "help" has extreme qualifications in that it is often used to bolster repressive governments, to subsidize foreign investments, "to subsidize foreign imports which compete with national products, to introduce technology not adapted to the needs of less developed countries, and to invest in low-priority sectors of the national economies" (Dos Santos, p. 233). The long-term public loans for nonmilitary purposes may also be some help, but the necessity to return principal and interest is rapidly becoming a main worry of the less developed areas. Thus for all of the less developed countries other than China and India, the foreign public debt averaged 28.7 percent of GNP in 1982, and interest payments alone used up 26.2 percent of new loans (World Bank, p. 248).

It is the declared policy of all of the American agencies, such as the Agency for International Development, that the countries receiving aid shall use it primarily to beef up the private enterprise sectors of their economies and not for public investment, which is often the most necessary investment needed in these countries for rapid development. Obviously it goes without saying that the aid of the United States is directed to shoring up these countries against communism and is not given for any pure idealistic reason. In fact, the American aid agencies often point out: "(1) Foreign aid stimulates the development of new overseas markets for U.S. goods and services. (2) Foreign aid stimulates the development of new overseas markets for U.S. companies. (3) Foreign aid orients national economies toward a free-enterprise system in which U.S. firms can prosper" (Magdoff, 1969, p. 13).

The U.S. Agency for International Development boasts: "Private enterprise has greater opportunities in India than it did a few years ago . . . fertilizer is an example of a field which is now open to the private sector, and was not in the past. This is largely a result of the efforts which we have made, the persuasion that we along with other members of the consortium have exerted on the Indian government" (U.S. Congress, p. 185). A more blatant case of political pressure occurred in Brazil, where American aid fell from $81.8 million to $15.1 million from 1962 to 1964 because the United States disliked the Goulart government. When "good" reactionary military officers overthrew Goulart, American aid jumped to $122.1 million in 1965 and $129.3 million in 1966.

Nor are all the rewards of foreign aid purely ideological and in overseas areas. Just as the aid agencies claim, large parts of U.S. business benefit directly from the foreign-aid program. Thus 24.4 percent of U.S. exports of iron and steel products are financed by the U.S. Agency for International

Development. Similarly financed are 30.4 percent of the fertilizer exports, 29.5 percent of railroad equipment exports, 11.5 percent of nonferrous metal exports, and 5–10 percent of the U.S. exports of machinery and equipment, chemicals, motor vehicles and parts, rubber and rubber products, and textiles.

IMPACT OF IMPERIALISM ON THE UNITED STATES

The impact of military spending on the United States was seen in an earlier chapter. Most U.S. military expenditures at home and abroad serve goals of imperialism: protecting raw materials, foreign markets, commercial routes, spheres of influence of U.S. business, and U.S. investment opportunities (as well as capitalism in general). The profits from U.S. foreign trade and U.S. foreign investment and from the military production to defend U.S. interests amount to about 25 to 30 percent of all profits. And recalling that most military and foreign profits go to the same few giant corporations, we begin to have some idea of the importance of American imperialism.

Conservative economists would object to lumping military profits with the profits from imperialism, but we believe it is impossible to separate the two. By 1969 the United States had a total of 1,517,000 military personnel in 1,400 foreign bases of all types, in 70 or 80 foreign countries (not including Korea and Vietnam). The major reason for this multibillion-dollar allocation of resources is the need to maintain control over the vast American overseas investment empire. Note also that the decision to fight for a given area depends not only on the profits to be made from that area but even more on its military-strategic importance to the structure of imperialism in a wider area.

> Understood in these terms, the killing and destruction in Vietnam and the expenditure of vast sums of money are not balanced in the eyes of U.S. policymakers against profitable business opportunities in Vietnam; rather they are weighed according to the judgment of military and political leaders on what is necessary to control and influence Asia, and especially Southeast Asia, in order to keep the entire area within the imperialist system in general, and within the United States sphere of influence in particular. (Magdoff, 1970, pp. 14–15)

We may now make an evaluation of the costs and benefits of imperialism and militarism to the United States. On the benefit side, military production and military service do increase employment, assuming that the nation begins from a position of major unemployment. On the harmful side, the flow of capital to the United States (profits and interest from foreign investment less current investment) must have a negative effect on domestic profit rates and employment through the competition of more capital. Still, the net effect on employment is probably positive.

The public at large—the taxpayers—pays the direct costs, including $115 billion for six years of fighting in Vietnam. Non-Vietnam military expenditures continued throughout the period at about $50 billion a year. Because America entered the war with a low level of unemployment, unemployment was not reduced (although *perhaps* a major depression was avoided at some point); but employment and demand remained high enough that monopoly power brought about price inflation, which lowered the public's real income.

More than 50,000 Americans were killed in Indochina and more than five times that many wounded. (About 3 million Indochinese civilians were killed, but that was presumably not a cost to America.)

The necessary climate of racism against the "inferior" Indochinese also worsened racism at home as racism, learned and practiced by the U.S. soldiers in Vietnam, was brought back to the United States. The need to limit opposition to the war increased repression and denial of civil liberties and especially undermined academic freedom in the colleges. The attempt to curb inflation by cutting all welfare spending increased the costs to the poor. For the public as a whole, therefore, the costs in blood and money were vast and outweighed any slight employment benefits.

For the largest corporations, however, the balance was very different. They did pay some added taxes for war, but they were able to pass on most of these to consumers and workers. They did have some higher costs from inflation, but their own prices rose faster. We speak here of the whole military-imperialism effort, not just the war in Vietnam. Some sections of big business found that the Vietnam War overheated the economy too much or was a tactically "bad" (that is, losing) war, and so opposed it. Aside from that specific tactical situation, their interests are clear: Profits from military production and from foreign investment represent about 25 to 30 percent of all corporate profits.

Furthermore, the largest 100 corporations receive more than half of that very large amount, or the difference between depression and very high profit rates. Therefore, for the giant corporations the benefits of the military-imperialist effort clearly outweigh the costs. Whether or not some of these benefits dribble down to the very top strata of labor in order to keep labor content is still highly controversial. Because the same corporate interests are dominant in the capitalist state, it is no wonder that militarism and imperialism (as in El Salvador) continue to be American policy, regardless of the tremendous cost to the American people.

SUMMARY

The less developed capitalist countries are not only poor, but are growing unevenly. When growth does take place, its benefits are distributed very unequally among their people. Although too much population is obviously a problem for less developed countries, the most important barriers to their development are: (1) reactionary ruling classes that waste much of the product in unproductive ways, (2) a trade pattern in which the less developed countries export mainly raw materials and import most of their finished goods, and (3) imperialist investment at such high profit rates that the profit outflow is greater than the current investment inflow.

Imperialism and militarism have both benefits and costs for the United States. Imperialist wars and military spending for them do create some jobs, but they also create inflation, high taxation, reduction in welfare services, increased racism, and thousands of dead and wounded Americans (and there are more rational and constructive ways of creating employment). On the other side, there are vast benefits for a small number of giant corporations that make very high profit rates on foreign investment and on military production.

SUGGESTED READINGS

A pioneering work in the area of underdevelopment was Paul Baran, *The Political Economy of Growth* (New York: Monthly Review Press, 1958). Another classic work is Harry Magdoff's *The Age of Imperialism* (New York: Monthly Review Press, 1969). On foreign aid, see Teresa Hayter, *Imperialism as Aid* (New York: Monthly Review Press, 1974). The best survey of theories in this area is by Keith Griffin and John Gurley, "Radical Analysis of Imperialism, the Third World, and the Transition to Socialism," *Journal of Economic Literature* 23 (Sept. 1985): 1089–1143.

REFERENCES

Barnett, Richard, and Ronald Muller. *Global Reach.* New York: Simon and Schuster, 1974.

Bettleheim, Charles. *India Independent.* New York: Monthly Review Press, 1968.

Dos Santos, Theotino. "The Structure of Dependence." *American Economic Review* (May) 1970.

Girvan, Normal. "Swallowing the IMF Medicine in the Seventies." In Charles Wilber, ed. *The Political Economy of Development and Underdevelopment.* 2d ed. Edited by Charles Wilber. New York: Random House, 1984.

Gray, H., and Shanti Tangri. *Economic Development and Population Growth.* Lexington, Mass.: D. C. Heath, 1970.

Griffin, Keith. *The Green Revolution.* New York: UNRIFD, 1972.

International Labor Office. *Poverty and Landlessness in Rural Asia.* Geneva: ILO, 1977.

Jalee, Pierre. *Pillage of the Third World.* New York: Monthly Review Press, 1965.

Landes, David. *The Unbound Prometheus.* Cambridge, England: Cambridge University Press, 1969.

Magdoff, Harry. *The Age of Imperialism.* New York: Monthly Review Press, 1969.

———. "Militarism and Imperialism." *American Economic Review* 22:2 (May 1970).

Muller, Ronald. "Global Corporations and National Stabilization Policy." *Journal of Economic Issues* 9 (June 1975), pp. 181–196.

United Nations, Department of Economic Affairs. *National and International Measures for Full Employment.* New York: United Nations, 1949.

U.S. Congress, House Committee on Foreign Affairs. *Hearing on Foreign Assistance Act of 1968.* Washington, D.C.: GPO, 1968. Government Printing Office.

U.S. Department of Commerce. *United States Business Investments in Foreign Countries.* Washington, D.C.: GPO, 1960.

———. *Survey of Current Business.* Washington, D.C.: GPO, August 1983.

World Bank. *World Development Report 1984.* New York: Oxford University Press, 1984.

PART Four

SOCIALIST ECONOMIC SYSTEMS

An Introduction to Comparative Economics

Chapter
43

Varieties of Socialism

The word *socialism* has been used to mean a great many different things. To begin with, it refers to (1) a system of ideas, (2) a political movement, and (3) an economic system of actual institutions. As a system of ideas, socialism was discussed in earlier chapters on utopian socialist ideologies and the Marxist socialist theories. To complicate matters, there are now many varieties of Marxist socialist ideas alone, not to speak of other socialist ideas. Different views within the general framework of Marxist ideas are currently expressed by the Russians, the Chinese Maoists, Cuba's Castro, and many others. We shall not develop each of these, but we shall refer to them from time to time when relevant.

In the second category, political movements, there is also a wide variety. In fact, most systems of socialist thought have generated socialist political movements. Today there are many parties calling themselves socialist or labor parties. Many of these, such as the Social Democratic party of West Germany, specifically do *not* advocate a fully socialized economy but urge a mixture of capitalist and socialist economic forms (mostly the status quo, as it now exists in West Germany). The other main political branch of the socialist movement is occupied by the parties calling themselves communist. These parties do claim to advocate socialist economic systems. Finally, there are many radicals in the United States and elsewhere who advocate socialism but do not belong to any of the socialist or communist parties.

Socialist *ideas* are those put forth by the various socialist movements. Socialist *movements* include all the socialist, communist, and radical parties and individuals who favor some variety of socialist system. What is a socialist economic *system?* A capitalist economic system is one in which there is private ownership for private profit of all the means of production (factories, equipment, land). *A socialist economic system is one in which there is public (or social) ownership for the public good of all the means of production.*

The words "public ownership," however, are very ambiguous. We must ask three very basic questions to clarify this definition: (1) What is the political form (or system) of public decision making? (2) At what level, national or factory or other, are decisions made by the "public"? (3) Who owns the product of this "public" production?

DEMOCRACY, SOCIALISM, AND GLASNOST

Who is the "public"? The classical socialist vision assumed that public ownership meant extension of political democracy into the economic sphere. Under capitalism, a few powerful individuals own and control the economy. Under socialism, the public, through its democratically elected representatives, would own and control the economy. This control by the masses of the people—by the multitudes of working men and women rather than the few plutocrats—was seen as the heart of socialism.

Unfortunately, the end of private ownership of productive facilities came first in the less developed countries of eastern Europe, the Soviet Union, and China. In these countries there were few democratic traditions or institutions; their socialist governments were born in the midst of civil and world wars; and survival and rapid growth were their main problems. Therefore, contrary to every socialist dream, they emerged as one-party dictatorships. Political and economic power were held by tiny, self-appointed elites.

Can this be called socialism? There is, by law, only "public" and no private ownership of the productive facilities. But the "public" decisions are made by a small, nonelective elite. In Chapter 44 we shall discuss the development and functioning of the Soviet Union as an example of an economy with government ownership and decisions made by a one-party political dictatorship. For convenience we shall call this economy socialist, but readers must decide for themselves whether it really meets the definition of socialism as public or social control of the economy. The Soviet leader Mikhail Gorbachev now argues for more democracy or "openness," for which the Soviet term is *glasnost*; this issue will be discussed in Chapter 46.

CENTRAL PLANNING, SOCIALISM, AND PERESTROIKA

As we shall see, during the period of Stalin's control of the Soviet Union, it was taken for granted by most people that socialism meant central planning. Indeed, in the Soviet Union, Stalin and a small elite around him decided on the economic direction, while a small group of economic planners in Moscow developed a plan to carry out his decisions. That plan was law, and it governed all Soviet enterprises in considerable detail. Even in the Soviet Union, however, the exclusive use of planning has been challenged. Gorbachev now calls for "restructuring," or *perestroika*, which means a drastic reform to use both the market and planning under socialism. Gorbachev's perestroika is discussed in Chapter 45.

In eastern Europe this process has been carried much further, with individual enterprises acting as independent units in the market in several countries. It has gone furthest in Yugoslavia, where the manager of the enterprise is no longer appointed by the government but by a council elected by all the workers in the enterprise. The Yugoslavs claim that this is an essential feature of "real" socialism, but others claim that this is a retreat from public or national ownership back toward capitalism. Again, the reader will have to decide. The Yugoslav market socialist economy is discussed in Chapter 45.

SOCIALISM AND COMMUNISM

Political ideology aside, what is the difference between a socialist economic system and a communist economic system? As a matter of definition it is generally agreed that *socialism* means public ownership plus the payment of wages according to work done, where wages are used to buy consumer goods and services. A pure *communist* economy, however, would be one in which there was public ownership plus distribution according to need. In other words, there would be no wages or prices, and people would take goods and services without paying as they needed them.

No present government or major political party advocates complete and immediate communism. The Soviet Union continues to have a very wide range of wages, but it does have a considerable sector of free goods and services; mainly, all medical and educational services are free to the public. Even the United States has a few free goods and services, such as our public parks and highways.

SUMMARY

Socialism refers to a set of ideas, a political movement, or an economic system. A socialist economic system is usually defined as having "public" ownership of the means of production. But several questions about this definition are very controversial. Is it socialism if decisions are made by a small group rather than democratically by all the people in a free election process? Does socialism mean central planning by the federal government, or does it mean decentralized decision making by each local group of workers? Socialism does mean continuing differential prices and wages according to ability, but communism means communal ownership of the product with individuals taking what they need.

Chapter
44

The Soviet Union: A Centrally Planned Economy

World War I so weakened the economic and political structure of Russia that the tsarist government collapsed in 1917. It was replaced by a provisional government, which also proved unable to cope with the chaotic situation.

A socialist revolution overtook the fallen giant, and in October 1917 the Bolsheviks led by Lenin seized power, in the name of Marxism in an almost bloodless coup. For the first time socialists had the reins of power and could attempt to create a society without the many evils of capitalism they had consistently denounced. The problems that had overcome the tsar and the provisional government, however, were of an overwhelming magnitude, and the Bolsheviks, who were mostly political activists without experience in governing, had enormous difficulties confronting them when they first assumed power.

The new government found itself in the midst of a war that had devastated the foundations of the economy, slowed transportation and communication almost to a half, and created something approximating social anarchy. One of the chief sources of Bolshevik power was the support of the mass of peasants who were revolting against centuries of ruthless exploitation. In an initial revolutionary thrust, the peasants seized the holdings of wealthy landlords and rich peasants. They divided the land up into millions of tiny plots. When, as one of their first acts after taking power, the Bolsheviks announced a land reform, they were merely putting an official stamp of approval on an event that was a fait accompli, about which they could have done nothing even if they so desired. Nevertheless, the new, small and inefficient peasant holding made it exceedingly difficult for the Bolsheviks to secure food for their armies and for urban dwellers. Moreover, the newly independent peasants wanted to save the little they produced for their own consumption.

In the cities, most important enterprises and industries were in the hands of capitalists who were hostile to and distrusted the Bolsheviks. A very large percentage of the physical capital of these enterprises had been destroyed, and the allocation of raw materials and supplies had been severely disrupted. The Soviets had hardly begun to extricate themselves from the war with Germany when a group of reactionary tsarist and pro-capitalist generals launched a military drive to destroy the new government.

The reactionary forces were supported by the major capitalist powers. Not only did their army, called the *White Army,* receive financial and material aid, but most of the major capitalist governments also sent armed troops to destroy the Soviet government. Few Americans realized it at the time, but President Wilson sent thousands of American soldiers and spent millions of tax dollars on a war that, like the Vietnam War nearly a half century later, was undeclared. The army of the Bolsheviks, called the Red Army, eventually won the war, but only after three years of hard fighting.

WAR COMMUNISM

Thus in a period of bitter and extensive warfare, while the economy and whole society were approaching a state of total anarchy, the Bolsheviks were forced to adopt extreme measures in order to survive. The policies followed during the period 1918–1921 were called *war communism.* The Communist government was driven under the exigencies of war, hunger, and chaos to attempt to impose centralized control on all economic processes. (The Bolshevik party changed its name to the Communist party at this time.)

Being unable directly to secure sufficient resources to keep the economy going and fight the civil war, the government printed large sums of money with which to purchase resources in the market. The result was an inflation so drastic that money became almost worthless. Many state enterprises ceased using money in transactions among themselves. In 1919 and 1920 most workers' wages were no longer paid in money but rather in products or services. Many essential commodities, including municipal services such as public trains and tramcars, were free to workers.

The government was forced to nationalize almost all industry, from the largest factories down to enterprises employing only a few people. This was the only way in which they could gain the necessary control over industry. It was made necessary not only because of the confusion but also because most capitalists and managers had a deeply ingrained hostility toward their efforts. The nationalization drive ultimately became an attempt to eliminate all privately owned manufacturing enterprises.

There was also a drive to ban all private trade. Middlemen and tradespeople were declared to be parasites who exploited both producers and consumers for their profits. All trade and selling was to be transacted by governmental agencies. The government was never very effective at enforcing this ban, especially in a number of critical areas in which severe shortages existed. The government also requisitioned food directly from the peasants without paying for it. By 1920, when it became obvious that the White Army would be defeated, many peasants began to resist the government's confiscation of their surpluses. Other pressures against the total regimentation of economic life began to assert themselves. In early 1921 the sailors at the Kronstadt naval station revolted against the miserable conditions of their life. (Ironically it had been a revolt of the sailors at the same naval station that had helped the Bolsheviks seize power three and a half years earlier.)

THE NEW ECONOMIC POLICY

Under these pressures the government abruptly abandoned many of the policies of war communism and inaugurated what was called the *New Economic Policy*. The government continued to own and operate heavy industry, power, transportation, banking, and some wholesale trade, but most government enterprises were decentralized and made independent of central planning. Moreover, many small businesses and most retail and wholesale trade were returned to private ownership and private profit making. Peasants were allowed to sell their goods in the market, and confiscation was ended.

The economy responded very rapidly to the New Economic Policy. By 1928 the crises were over and the economy had been restored to its prewar levels of output in most industries. But the prewar levels were woefully inadequate. The USSR was still primitive and backward by Western standards. Furthermore, given the earlier armed intervention by the Western powers and the continuing barrage of anticommunist pronouncements and propaganda from Western governments, the Communists felt threatened. Believing that the USSR would eventually be attacked by hostile Western powers unless it achieved sufficient strength to discourage such an attack, the Communists accepted the fact that rapid industrialization would be absolutely necessary. Moreover, their socialist goals also required an industrialized economy.

THE INDUSTRIALIZATION DEBATE

Although all Communists accepted the necessity of rapid industrialization, a debate raged in the late 1920s over the most efficient method of financing this industrialization. In order to feed and clothe the workers producing capital goods and to spare the material resources necessary for the construction of factories and machinery, large surpluses had to be appropriated by the government. Foreign capital goods could also be purchased if the surpluses could be marketed in the West. With the overwhelming majority of the Soviet work force employed in agriculture (a large percent of these in subsistence agriculture), it was obvious that most of the surplus would have to come from agriculture. But Soviet economists and political leaders were divided on the question of how best to appropriate this agricultural surplus.

One group of conservative Communists (or *right-wing deviationists,* as Stalin called them) was led by the economist Nikolai Bukharin. He believed that industrial planning should emphasize increased production of agricultural machinery and consumer goods to be sold to the peasants. The peasants should be paid high prices for their grain and should be offered consumer goods and agricultural machinery at low prices to induce them to expand output and market a continually larger surplus. Industrial development, Bukharin believed, was limited by the rate of expansion of agricultural production.

A second group, consisting of more radical Communists (or *left-wing deviationists,* according to Stalin) was led by Leon Trotsky, ex-commander of the Red Army and Lenin's chief lieutenant during the civil war, and Eugene Preobrazhensky, the leading Marxist economist of the period. They favored extracting a maximum surplus from agriculture by paying peasants low prices for farm produce, charging them high prices for manufactured goods, and putting heavy taxes on farm profits. Agriculture should be more efficiently organized, they believed, by consolidating private plots of land into large-scale collective farms. Many sectors of the economy should be purposely neglected or shortchanged in order to devote a maximum of resources and labor power to the rapid expansion of heavy industry, which, when fully operational, would efficiently produce the capital necessary to catch up in the industries neglected in the initial phases of industrialization.

Joseph Stalin used the antagonisms created in the debates as a means of achieving power for himself. At first he aligned himself with the conservatives to form a coalition that ousted Trotsky and his left-wing sympathizers. He then turned on Bukharin and his followers and successfully stripped them of their power, leaving himself in full control. Having thus gained power, he began to move along lines that had been advocated by Trotsky and Preobrazhensky, although he moved more rapidly and more harshly than they had ever advised.

COLLECTIVIZATION

In November 1929 the government announced a policy of promoting collectives as a means of increasing agricultural production. At first the collectivization was to have been voluntary. Suddenly, however, in early 1930 the government decided to force collectivization as widely as possible and eliminate the richer peasants *as a class* by turning their holdings over to collectives. The resulting change was so profound that a careful expert could say: "The events of 1929–34 constitute one of the great dramas of history" (Nove, 1969, p. 160).

Only the poor peasants could be persuaded to join the collectives voluntarily; but they owned so few animals and so little capital that collectives could not succeed with them alone. The middle-income and rich peasants resisted forced collectivization with bitterness and ferocity. At times this resistance was so widespread as to constitute what could almost be called a second civil war. When the richer peasants realized they could not defeat the government directly, they began to burn buildings, destroy equipment, and slaughter animals. By 1931 one-third of Russia's cattle, half of its sheep and goats, and one-fourth of its horses had been slaughtered.

The drama of the battle over collectivization was one about which many books have been written. Here it will suffice to say that an immense social cost was incurred but that it did bring about the revolution in Soviet agriculture that made industrialization possible. Collectivization succeeded in drastically increasing the government's collections of grain. The 22.1 million tons from the 1930–1931 harvest amounted to more than twice the tonnage collected by the government in 1928–1929.

INDUSTRIALIZATION

When collectivization placed a large economic surplus in government hands, Soviet industrialization proceeded at a striking rate on the basis of successive five-year plans during the 1930s. Industrial growth at such a rapid pace was unprecedented in history. Official Soviet figures for the 1930s show an average annual growth rate in industrial production of about 16 percent. Studies by Western economists using different methods of arriving at indexes of industrial production show somewhat lower rates (ranging from about 9 percent to about 14 percent), but by any of these estimates the performance was without historical precedent.

The major Soviet achievement was not simply a higher rate of industrial growth; it was a significant transformation of the whole society so that industrial growth could begin and continue. Before 1928 the USSR was mostly rural; by 1938 the urban population had tripled—there was a constant flow of people from country to city and a flow of ideas from city to country. Before 1928 there was 80 percent illiteracy; by 1938 over 90 percent could do some reading and writing, there was a very large adult education movement, and all young people were in school. In other words, the Soviet Union changed from a less developed country in 1928 to one of the main developed countries in 1938. This spectacular rate of growth was interrupted by World War II, during which the Soviet Union suffered unparalleled losses. Estimates of the number of Soviet citizens killed in World War II are generally around 20 million, although some experts place the figure as high as 30 million. Early in the war, Hitler rapidly conquered an area that contained more than half of the USSR's prewar productive capacity. The German-occupied territory had accounted for 70 percent of Soviet coal mining, 60 percent of iron ore production, 50 percent of steel capacity, and 33 percent of the area sown in grain.

When the Soviet army retreated, it destroyed many productive facilities to prevent their use by the Germans. When the Germans were subsequently pushed back, they also pursued a scorched-earth policy, destroying everything of value as they retreated. Especially hard hit were factories and houses. In addition to killing more than 20 million Soviet people, the Germans destroyed the homes of another 25 million, totally razing about 2,000 towns and 70,000 villages.

The destruction of these millions of people, homes, factories, untold millions of animals, and railroad, transportation, and communications systems left the USSR an almost totally devastated "victor" in World War II. The economic progress of the 1930s, purchased at high social and human cost, was in large measure erased by the Nazi attempt to conquer the Soviet Union.

Despite these losses, however, the Soviets retained their economic organization and general skills, and with their experience with economic planning during the 1930s, they recovered with miraculous speed. By 1950, gross industrial production was much higher than prewar and agriculture had recovered the prewar level.

THE STALINIST DICTATORSHIP

The Soviet Union achieved the overthrow of capitalism, development from a backward agricultural to an advanced industrial economy, striking advances in health and education, and very rapid economic growth. It must also be said that the Soviet people have suffered from dictatorship that has deprived them of democratic rights. After a struggle lasting from 1924 to 1928, Stalin won undivided power. His main opponent, Leon Trotsky, was exiled in 1928 and murdered in Mexico in 1940. The other old Bolshevik leaders continued to work under Stalin's direction until most were killed in the purge trials of 1936–1938. During the Stalin era, many hundreds of thousands of possible (or even rumored) opponents were jailed and thousands were killed. Stalin eliminated three-fourths of the men who were on the Party Central Committee in 1934, 90 percent of the Soviet army's generals, and 75 percent of delegates to the Party Congress of 1937. In all, perhaps a half-million people were imprisoned or executed, not including those peasants sent to forced-labor camps in the collectivization drive. In the meantime, the Soviet Union was rapidly industrializing. The industrialization was carried out on the basis of restricted consumption enforced by extreme repression.

After 1928, Stalin ruled alone until his death in 1953. Soon after he took power, Stalin transformed Marxism-Leninism into a "divinely given" rigid doctrine. Only Stalin could make new interpretations, which he did to suit his needs, with little regard for theoretical niceties. Dissent was met with prison or death, and silence descended on the Marxist theoretical stage. Through his hold on foreign Communist parties, and through their position in each country, Stalin dominated international Marxist thought from about 1926 till his death in 1953. This was a period of sterility in Soviet Marxist thought, with few major contributions, and a dogmatic adherence to a vulgar form of Marxism. No serious attention was paid to Western social science, except to criticize it.

WHY THE STALINIST DICTATORSHIP?

Socialist economists have always argued that the government under capitalism is dominated by the capitalist class to an extent that diminishes democratic political forms. On the other hand, conservative economists have long argued that central planning and bureaucracy under socialism must inevitably lead to a dictatorship of a small group of people. Their favorite case in point has been the dictatorship of the Soviet Union that grew up under Stalin. There is no question that the Soviet Union under Stalin was a harsh dictatorship (and that under subsequent regimes it has become a more moderate dictatorship with some elements of democracy). The question is *Why?* We contend that Soviet dictatorship was established *in spite* of public ownership and planning, not because of them. Other factors seem to bear the primary responsibility. These factors are:

1. The antidemocratic tradition of tsarist Russia
2. The underground training of the Bolshevik leaders
3. The effect of the Russian civil war
4. The effect of foreign intervention
5. The overwhelming realities of economic backwardness and illiteracy, combined with the industrialization drive to end backwardness

Tsarist Russia

Prerevolutionary Russia, headed by the tsar, was an absolute autocracy for most of its history; it was strongly militarist and imperialist in nature, and was supported by a feudal landowning nobility. Ideas of political democracy came very late in Russia, and for some time after the French Revolution they influenced only the small intelligentsia. After the abortive revolution of 1905, a small degree of parliamentary political democracy was practiced from 1906 to 1917. But even then the Russian Duma (that is, parliament) was neither very popular nor very effective. There was thus very little consciousness of democracy or practical experience with democracy among the Russian people.

The Underground Viewpoint

The Russian Marxists were forced to peruse an illegal conspiracy by the repressive laws of the tsarist government. Therefore, they instituted a very strict discipline within the party, did not always hold elections for top officers, and enforced orders from the top down. In theory, Lenin argued for "democratic centralism," which meant democratic election of central officers plus strict obedience to orders from the elected officers. Tsarist repression made fully democratic election impossible, but the Communist leaders still demanded obedience to orders. The tradition by which the party led the masses, and the top leaders directed the party, was probably necessary for political and military action and was not too detrimental before the 1917 Revolution. Since anyone could leave the party without harm, the party could ask for only voluntary self-discipline. Few revolutionaries thought about what might happen if the party became the all-powerful ruler of the nation. They could not foresee persuasion giving way to censorship and coercion and voluntary discipline being replaced by external compulsion.

Civil War

The Revolution of October 1917 resulted in a government of "Soviets," that is, councils of workers, peasants, and soldiers, led by the Communist party. Within a month after the Revolution, the first step against Western-style political democracy was taken when all the parties (and all the newspapers) advocating capitalism or monarchism were banned. This was partly explained as a temporary measure against the violence of the Revolution and attempts at counterrevolution. But it was also given a more ominous meaning as a "natural act of proletarian dictatorship."

Nevertheless, there were free elections to the Constituent Assembly (which was to write a constitution), in which the biggest winner was the Socialist Revolutionary party—and the Communists ran a poor second. Then two months later the Constituent Assembly was dispersed because, it was said, the attitude of the people had greatly changed and the Socialist Revolutionary party had split. Thus elections to the assembly were now outdated. This was a reasonable democratic argument, except that new elections to the assembly were not called then or ever. A further argument was that the Soviets (meaning councils) were more democratic in nature than a parliamentary assembly because the Soviets represented soldiers, industrial workers, and farmers. Since the owning classes were to be dispossessed, they would eventually also be part of the working classes, so eventually everyone could vote in elections to the Soviets. Furthermore, in 1917–1918 all the various socialist parties still participated in the Soviets. Therefore, except for the exclusion of the capitalist and monarchist parties, the Soviets, it was said, would eventually turn out to be a democratic instrument like the Constituent Assembly.

Within a few more months, however, as the civil war grew in intensity and bitterness, the other socialist parties were also prohibited, to a large extent, from political participation. Even this further measure of political restriction might have been defended in view of the terrible conditions of the time—a single, poor, and exhausted workers' state standing alone against formidable domestic enemies and massive foreign intervention. The problem was that under Stalin this "temporary" emergency measure became a permanent policy.

Many democratic forms tend to fall by the wayside during any violent conflict. After the bitterness of a civil war, it is not difficult to understand the victor's reluctance to let the opposition immediately reenter politics. The long and bloody civil war in the Soviet Union, worsened by foreign intervention, made immediate initiation of widespread political democracy very unlikely. The civil war killed off or dispersed much of the old working class. In fact, the number of workers shrank from a small 2.6 million in 1917 to an even smaller 1.2 million in 1920. Furthermore, the unpopular measures necessary for warfare alienated many former supporters. As a result, the few surviving old Bolsheviks felt as if they were a tiny remnant defending a besieged fortress; but no one has ever heard of a besieged fortress being ruled democratically.

Foreign Intervention

A large number of foreign capitalist countries intervened militarily against the Soviet communists in the years 1918–1921, including the United States, England, France, and Japan. Furthermore, the economic blockade of the Soviet Union was continued for many years. Foreign threats never ceased and culminated in the devastating Nazi invasion in 1941. This was followed by the cold war in the 1950s, the threat of the nuclear bomb, and the renewal of attempts at economic blockade by the United States.

These circumstances did partly make political democracy objectively more difficult. They are also used, however, as a rationale for continued repression by some of the ruling elements in the Soviet Union, in the same way that Senator Joseph McCarthy used the Korean War as an excuse for repression in America. Moreover, each side pointed to repression in the other country as a reason for its own repression.

Economic Backwardness

A great many of the less developed countries, from the Soviet Union to Somalia, have tended toward both "socialist" government ownership of the means of production *and* dictatorial one-party control of political life. Why should economic backwardness generate both government ownership *and* dictatorship? These are countries filled mostly with an intensely felt need for rapid economic growth. Yet they are also largely poor, agrarian countries with little modern industry and few buildings, equipment, skilled workers, or experienced managers. Socialism is viewed as a useful instrument of industrialization in the less developed countries. For one thing, there are few educated and experienced planners; thus the central government can best make use of the ones that exist, whereas many decades might be required for the voluntary emergence of bold, private entrepreneurs. Furthermore, the extreme lack of capital in the less developed countries can most easily be remedied by government control of resources. The government can tax the rich, gather the small savings of the poor, and expropriate foreign profits in order to invest by itself in new factories and equipment.

It is thus clear why socialist state ownership may be chosen as an instrument to overcome backwardness; but why does backwardness also generate one-party dictatorship? The reason lies within exactly the same set of circumstances.

The Soviet people may have been convinced of the desirability of rapid economic growth. Yet the Soviet leadership and their economic planners soon found that there was a conflict between rapid long-run growth and immediate consumption. They discovered that to gather the resources required to build up basic industry, it was necessary to take food from the farm population in order to feed the new industrial working class. In addition, food, as well as raw materials, had to be exported in order to raise the capital needed to import the machinery required by basic industry. Thus, the surplus from agriculture was the only feasible source of capital.

Stalin "solved" the resource problem by forcefully putting the peasantry into collective farms from which the entire surplus could be taken. For the peasantry, this resulted in a long stagnation or drop in living standards and was naturally accompanied by strong resistance to the regime among much of the farm population. For several years Stalin succeeded in putting heavy investments into basic industrial capital and the education of a whole new working class. Such a sudden and unpopular transformation (unpopular to the peasant majority) probably could not have been accomplished without a dictatorship. The main historical issue is whether the Soviet industrial transformation could have been made somewhat more slowly and with more democratic consent.

We conclude that political dictatorship in the Soviet Union resulted from the Russian autocratic tradition, the underground political tradition, civil war, foreign wars and intervention, and from economic backwardness. It was *not* caused by socialism, but arose in spite of socialism. *In an advanced economy*, such as the United States, we believe that a socialist system would provide a better environment for political democracy than does capitalism. The only countries with advanced economies that have a socialist economic structure are Czechoslovakia and East Germany, but they are totally dominated by the Soviet Union. Both have had strong movements for political democracy within socialism that in both instances were ended by Soviet tanks.

CLASS AND STRATIFICATION IN THE SOVIET UNION

Soviet economists deny that there is any ruling class in the Soviet Union, although they are quick to speak of an exploitive ruling class in the United States. This is exactly the same stance as that of the traditional American economists, who deny any ruling class in the United States, but are quick to find one in the Soviet Union. Earlier we described the ruling capitalist class of the United States. Here we examine the ruling class of the Soviet Union, which (although it does exist) is quite different from the American ruling class in many ways. A study by Sweezy and Huberman concludes that the Soviet Union is still "a stratified society, with a deep chasm between the ruling stratum of political bureaucrats and economic managers on the one side and the mass of working people on the other . . ." (p. 11).

There are four main groups in the Soviet ruling class. The first and most powerful is the top level of the Communist party apparatus, including 10 or 15 people in the highest body, the Politbureau, and a few hundred more in the next highest body, the Central Committee. A second group consists of the top levels of the government bureaucracy, such as the Council of Ministers, though most of this group also hold top positions in the party. Third, there are the top officers of the Soviet military establishment. Fourth, there are the top levels of economic management, including the central planners.

Each of these four groups merges and intertwines at the top, and individuals often move from one hierarchy to another at all levels. This merger at the top is why we can speak of one ruling class—or ruling group or ruling stratum—in the Soviet Union. Yet the party leaders, whose abilities are political and not technical, are still dominant. The government bureaucrats, even the very top ones, are still subordinate to the party, although they have shown somewhat more independence and initiative in recent decades. The power and influence of the economic managers have risen with the increase of technology and industrial complexity, but there has been no technocratic challenge to the clear supremacy of the party apparatus. The military is steadily becoming more professional and independent, for example, pushing for higher levels of military spending. The party, however, exercises its control of the military through several channels: Almost all officers are party members, there is intensive indoctrination at all levels, and there is direct interference from party representatives in individual units.

One way in which the Soviet elite differs from the American elite is in relative size. Whereas the very wealthy and powerful of the American ruling class comprises a million or so individuals, the similar group in the Soviet Union is far smaller, less than a hundred thousand. "Only the upper strata of the bureaucracy, of the party hierarchy, the managerial groups, and the military personnel, live in conditions comparable to those enjoyed by the rich and the *nouveaux riches* in the capitalist society" (Deutscher, 1967, p. 55). From an economic equalitarian standpoint, this is quite good in the sense that the Soviet rulers take a very much smaller amount of the total national income for their own use than do the American rulers—as we shall see when we compare the income distribution of the two countries. On the other hand, it means that political power is much more concentrated than in the United States.

This difference in the size of the two ruling classes results from the fact that all of the middle level of the Soviet elite—such as middle-level managers, local party bosses, majors in the army, and middle-level government bureaucrats—actually live on salaries derived from their own labor. They are paid relatively high amounts compared with ordinary workers, but a large part of these salaries probably represents differences according to actual ability and the quality of the work they do. Only at the top of the Soviet hierarchy are the salaries of the leadership a complete secret, classified for "security" reasons. These top leaders receive undeclared salaries and fringe benefits far beyond their own contribution of labor. Thus some large part of their income comes from the value created by the working class of the Soviet Union. So, "their incomes are at least partially derived from the 'surplus value' produced by the workers" (Deutscher, 1969, p. 56).

Yet, unlike the American ruling class, these groups own neither land nor factories, nor can they expand their incomes by investments. The ruling groups have not as yet tried to vest their controlling privileges in their children by legal means. They do, however, give their children a head start through an intellectual home atmosphere and, sometimes, by use of legal and illegal means to get them admitted to college or placed in a job.

Because the Soviet ruling class has no legal ownership of the means of production, as does the capitalist ruling class, their need for direct repressive controls is even greater than that of the capitalists. "The power of property having been destroyed, only the State, that is, the bureaucracy, dominates society; and its domination is based solely on the suppression of the people's liberty to criticize and oppose!" (ibid., p. 109). Suppression plus manipulation (and increasing material prosperity) are the means of political domination used by the Soviet leadership to control the means of production. Income distribution in the Soviet Union is far more equal than in the United States because the Soviet ruling class is so much smaller than the American ruling class and because it appropriates a much smaller share of national income from its working class. This is clear when we compare the official figures on income distribution from both countries (even though both contain several kinds of biases and distortions in them). In the Soviet Union in 1960 the top 10 percent of families had a total income that was 4.8 times the income received by the bottom 10 percent of families (see Yanowitch, 1966, p. 237). In the United States, on the other hand, in 1960 the top 10 percent of families had 30 times the total income of the lowest 10 percent of families! The greater inequality in the United States is almost completely the result of private profits, private rent, and private interest income, almost all of which go to the top income group. The Soviets, on the other hand, have only wage and salary income even in the top group.

It is striking that there is very little difference between the range of inequality of *just* wage and salary income between the United States and the Soviet Union. However, this is very different from *overall income distribution* because that includes American profit, rent, and interest incomes, which do not exist in the Soviet Union. Immediately after the 1917 Revolution, wage and salary income in the Soviet Union was equalized to a very great extent. In the 1930s, however, Stalin decided that the rapid industrialization drive demanded high wage differentials between workers in order to promote incentives. Since there was little money to pay workers, wages of unskilled workers were kept very low. At the same time, those who had the skills to produce more, or to do important jobs, were paid very high wages. Therefore, in the 1930s the ratio of most skilled wage rates to unskilled wage rates stood at 3.5 to 1 in the officially prescribed wage scales, and piece-rate bonuses undoubtedly increased this ratio in practice. This was a much higher wage differential than prevails currently in the United States. On the other hand, the United States had much higher wage differentials—of just about that magnitude—during our own period of rapid industrialization.

In the late 1950s, when a more relaxed climate prevailed in the Soviet Union, the leaders came to realize that such wide wage differentials were no longer necessary and might make the mass of unskilled workers angry at the leadership. Therefore, a number of measures were taken to raise the minimum wages of the unskilled, while holding down the wages of the most skilled. As a result, by 1958 the official differential between the wages of the unskilled and the most skilled had fallen to the ratio of 2.8 to 1. Since that time, the range of wages has been somewhat further narrowed; the degree of wage inequality in the Soviet Union had fallen considerably by the 1980s (see Nove, 1982, pp. 286–288). Soviet wage inequality is now probably less than U.S. wage inequality. Of course, Soviet *overall* income distribution—including profit, rent, and interest—is *far less* unequal than the United States distribution. A comprehensive review of all the research on Soviet inequality by traditional American and western European sociologists concludes: "These studies suggest that the extreme economic inequality of the late Stalinist period has been reduced appreciably in recent years; along with a reduction in interoccupational variation in industrial wages . . . there has been a general leveling and a rise in per capita income" (Dobson, p. 302).

Soviet social scientists have presented quite a bit of data on the inequality and stratification within the working class (see Yanowitch and Wisher). They argue that such inequality is absolutely necessary for the proper functioning of the Soviet Union. This apologia has the same basic cause as in the United States, namely the dominance of a ruling-class ideology, although it parades as Marxism in the Soviet Union. The only difference made by the Marxist approach is that the Soviet authors contend that the present inequality is proper only at the current level of development, but that some day in the distant future, under communism, this inequality will disappear.

All Soviet economists recognize only two classes in the Soviet Union. These are the nonantagonistic classes of collective farmers and workers. The working class includes manual and mental, rural and urban, male and female, Russian and non-Russian workers. These two classes are distinguished by their different relations to the means of production, but it is pointed out—quite correctly—that neither of these two classes exploits the other.

Soviet surveys do show the degree of various forms of inequality between strata *within* the working class, as well as some discussion of the difficulties of advancing from lower to higher strata. For example, they show concretely that unskilled workers have less education, lower wages, fewer cultural activities, and less political participation than more skilled workers, who in turn have less of all of these characteristics than do the intellectual workers (including engineers) and the supervisors and managers. One study of the machine building industry in Leningrad finds, for example, "It is typical that almost 60 percent of unskilled workers in manual, hand labor have no more than a six-year education, and their average educational level is 6.5 grades of school" (quoted in U.S. Congress, Joint Economic Committee, p. 20). The study also found that 26 percent of the unskilled workers do not read books at all; perhaps it is more remarkable that 20 percent did read one or more books a week. A study of three different Soviet cities found that participation in "community activities" (political to some extent) was very low among unskilled workers and very high among intellectuals and managerial personnel. Other studies of mobility reveal that families with highly educated parents tend to have the most highly educated children, so that the inequality is reproducing itself in the Soviet as in the American educational system.

In the years of rapid industrialization there was far more upward mobility in the Soviet Union that in the United States. Sons and daughters of poor peasants could and did emigrate to the cities, to become workers—often very skilled workers—and more rarely rising to be technicians and professionals. This vast inflow from the rural areas has been reduced, so spectacular upward mobility is less frequent than in the earlier period. Upward mobility is still probably greater than in the United States, since there is no private ownership of factories and land, and no inheritance of income-producing property. *If* one can get a higher education in the Soviet Union, the doors are open to advancement to the highest levels of the society. On the other hand, it is clear that the children of educated families (technicians, professionals, and managers) more often succeed in getting a higher education than the children of ordinary manual workers.

SOVIET ECONOMIC PERFORMANCE AFTER 1950

The Soviet economy grew more rapidly than the U.S. economy beginning in the 1950s and through the early 1980s. In the industrial sphere, U.S. production grew an average of 3.4 percent per year between 1951 and 1978 according to official U.S. data. Soviet industrial production grew an average of 9.1 percent per year in the same period according to official Soviet data—or 7.4 percent per year according to U.S. Central Intelligence Agency (CIA) data. Similarly, between 1951 and 1979, U.S. gross national product (GNP) grew by 3.4 percent a year according to official U.S. data, compared to a Soviet GNP growth rate of 7 percent a year according to official Soviet data and 4.9 percent a year according to CIA data (see Zimbalist, Sherman, and Brown, chap. 5).

Why did Soviet production grow more rapidly than U.S. production between 1950 and 1980? First, the Soviet economy is planned, so it does not have unemployment. The U.S. capitalist economy has suffered from unemployment of workers, which reached 11 percent in 1982; while unutilized industrial capacity reached as high as 32 percent in 1982. Second, a planned economy can gather and focus resources, so that the Soviets invest about 30 percent of national income while the United States invests only 15 percent of national income. Third, the Soviets are investing more in education and research. In 1950, the Soviets had fewer people in research and development than the United States. By 1979, Soviet specialists in research and development had increased to 957,000, compared to the U.S. total of only 610,000.

Although the Soviet economy grew faster than the U.S. economy, the Soviet economy does have severe problems, as shown by the fact that its *rate* of growth has been declining. Official Soviet data show the following decline in industrial growth rates per year: 13 percent in 1951–1955, 10 percent in 1955–1960, 9 percent in 1961–1965, 9 percent in 1966–1970, 8 percent in 1971–1975, and 5 percent in 1976–1978. If one can believe the CIA estimates, then real GNP in the USSR grew only 1.9 percent per year in 1981–1985, while it grew 2.4 percent per year in the United States. We can certainly conclude that both U.S. and Soviet growth rates were very low in the early 1980s. Reasons for the decline in Soviet growth rates include (1) higher defense spending; (2) higher spending for consumer goods production; (3) resistance by Soviet managers to the risk of technological innovation, though such innovation has become increasingly important; (4) greater difficulty of central planning as economic complexity increases; and (5) the increasing contradiction between a narrow, self-selected, nondemocratic group of leaders and the need for free and open scientific discussion, flexible and independent leadership at the enterprise level, and enthusiastic participation by workers.

SOVIET ECONOMIC PLANNING

In the capitalist United States most farmland and factories are privately owned. In the socialist Soviet Union, most farmland and factories are publicly owned, with the government claiming to represent the public in their ownership and operation. The Soviet government sells consumer goods, which are then privately owned. Public ownership, of course, tends to mean public direction and, therefore, usually means planning. The principal type of household income in the Soviet Union is wage income for labor, paid by the Soviet government. In the United States, income consists not only of wages but also of profits, rent, dividends, and interest. The latter incomes are derived basically from private property; thus most U.S. planning is necessarily limited in scope to the confines of single enterprises in which decisions reflect the search for private profit.

In the Soviet Union the only exceptions to public ownership are a small percentage of cooperative industrial enterprises, composed mainly of handicraft workers. Many collective farms are supposed to be cooperatives but are subject to considerable central control (and yet each farmer also has a small private plot of land).

In the publicly owned enterprises, the Soviet government, or some agency of the government, appoints a manager, who is solely responsible for the performance of the factory and whose bonus is based on how well the factory performs. The manager's performance and conduct are checked by numerous agencies, and he or she may be promoted, transferred, or fired at any time. In turn, the manager hires and fires all the other workers at the enterprise.

The government grants the enterprise its plant and equipment and initial working capital, although it is now beginning to charge interest on capital. After the initial grant of capital, however, the enterprise is expected to be financially independent. It must meet all costs of wages and materials out of revenue from sales and must also replace or repair depreciated and broken-down capital out of revenues from sales. And it is normally expected to show a profit above all of its costs.

The Soviet economy is centrally planned. The most important economic orders originate from the USSR Council of Ministers, but additional orders to the enterprise may come from regional or local governmental bodies. Further orders may originate or be transmitted through the agency directly supervising the enterprise, whether that agency is associated with a regional governing body or with the ministry directing some industrial area. Finally, all of these orders from government supervisory bodies are supposed to be in accord with the plan, which emanates from the Central Planning Commission or its subordinate agencies. The enterprise manager is solely responsible for the performance of the factory, then, only in the sense that all orders received must be executed within the constraint of the resources allocated.

The Central Planning Commission first collects information up the ladder, beginning with the enterprise and continuing through the various agencies, in order to evaluate the last year's performance and the present conditions and possibilities. Then the Commission is told by the Council of Ministers what goals it must strive to meet. On these bases it draws up a general plan for the whole economy, although production and allocation details are provided for only, say, 2000 commodities. The draft plan is then shown to all agencies on down the ladder to the enterprise. After all these units have added their detailed modifications and suggestions, the Central Planning Commission prepares the final draft.

The plan is supposed to provide sufficient investment for the desired rate of growth, guarantee balance among all the industrial needs and outputs, and select the best assortment of goods. The Central Planning Commission hands the plan over to appropriate government bodies to enact into law. It is then passed on with detailed commands and expanded at each intermediate level, until, finally, the enterprise receives a formidable document that is supposed to tell it exactly what to produce for a year (or some other period), how to produce it, what prices to charge, and what funds it may use. Again, the manager is judged on how well these commands are followed, though he or she has always had some decision-making power over details. The economic reforms of 1965 augmented the manager's decision-making power, which will be discussed later.

AGGREGATE BALANCE VERSUS INFLATION

The problem of aggregate balance in the Soviet economy is mostly a reflection of their attempt to grow very rapidly. Basically the resources supplied for investment must just equal the amount required or demanded for investment, while the amount supplied to consumers must just equal the amount they will demand at present incomes and prices. The capitalist economy of the United States has frequently been plagued by lack of adequate demand for the products of private enterprise. In the planned economy of the USSR, there has always been sufficient aggregate demand since the planning period began in 1928, and there has never been general or aggregate unemployment. The problem in the USSR has usually been that the government has demanded much more for investment than could be supplied and has failed to provide enough consumer goods to satisfy household demand.

Because aggregate demand has always more than equaled the amount of available resources and manpower, aggregate unemployment has been nonexistent since 1928. Of course, the Soviet Union does have a considerable amount of frictional unemployment. *Frictional* unemployment occurs when the structure of industry and technology changes, so that millions of workers must change jobs from one place to another, from one industry to another, or from one skill to another. These changes require large amounts of retraining and moving expenses. Many observers recently have reported significant unemployment from this source. The Soviet Union may also have some seasonal unemployment, which occurs because in certain industries, especially agriculture, demand for labor varies during the year. It may not be profitable for a society to transfer these workers to another job for only a few months, although the Chinese now use the seasonally unemployed to build dams and roads.

The main problem of aggregate balance in the Soviet economy has not been unemployment created by lack of demand but rather inflation caused by excessive demand for labor and all goods. The main reason for the inflation of the 1930s and 1940s was the excessive increase in government demand for investment goods, military supplies, and free, or nonpriced, welfare services, which created an excess demand for all inputs, including labor. The excess demand for labor pushed up wage rates much faster than productivity, and thus workers' demand for consumer goods rose faster than total production and much faster than the output of consumer goods.

The excessive wage payments (which resulted in inflation) occurred as a result of decisions at both the national and individual firm level. In the initial industrialization and wartime periods, the planners called for much larger increases in investment and military goods than in consumer goods; the discrepancy was usually even greater in the fulfillment of plans. Related to the high level of investment and military spending was the practice of "over–full-employment" planning. At the enterprise level, this meant that managers were given output targets that, for most firms, were essentially unachievable with the amount of labor and other inputs legally available to them.

In order to meet their production plans, therefore, Soviet managers found themselves competing strenuously for materials and labor. Prices of material goods going to enterprises were effectively controlled, and most deliveries of goods were ordered by direct central priorities and rationing. Workers, however, could move from job to job according to the incentive of higher wages, and thus this was the path followed by managers competing for labor inputs. In the 1930s and 1940s managers were able to overspend their payrolls with few if any penalties but were under extreme pressure to meet output targets. They would offer notoriously high wages to obtain the scarce supply of workers, and even hoarded unneeded workers against future needs.

As a final result of this process, the workers attempted to spend their rapidly increasing wages on the much smaller increase in consumer goods. The consequence was too much money chasing too few goods in the consumer goods market and steadily rising prices until 1947. This is the basic pattern of prewar and wartime inflation: excess demand for labor as a joint result of the high rate of investment and over–full-employment planning, with excess demand for consumer goods as a result of wages rising faster than productivity and faster than the output of consumer goods.

In the face of these extreme inflationary pressures, Soviet policy was always to maintain constant or declining prices by administrative fiat. In

Table 44.1   IRON INDUSTRY

Total sources	Total uses
1. Imports	1. Exports
2. Reductions in inventory	2. Increase in inventory
+3. Production listed by plants or regions, e.g.:	+3. Uses by other industries, usually listed by region, e.g.:
a. Iron from Ukraine	a. Iron needed in Ukraine
b. Iron from Latvia	b. Iron needed in Latvia

practice, the pressures forced them to raise prices over long periods in the 1930s and 1940s. These reluctantly imposed increases were not sufficient to satisfy all of the demand, however, and the result was *repressed inflation*, or regulation of prices below the free-market level. Repressed inflation showed up in shortages and long lines for many goods. Because their wages often could not be spent for any goods (because none were available at any price), workers' incentives to labor declined.

Only since 1947 has the problem been brought under some control (although a smaller degree of repressed inflation still exists). Since that time, (1) the State Bank allows enterprises to pay wages above the planned amount *only* to the extent that they increase output above plan, and (2) the degree of over–full-employment planning appears to have been sharply reduced (because the most urgent investment and military demands have lessened).

RELATIONS BETWEEN INDUSTRIES: MICROBALANCES

We have examined the aggregate, or macro-, balances between the major parts of the economy, such as consumption and wages or saving and investment. Now we turn to an analysis of the individual, or micro, balances required between different industries. In this context each *industry* is defined as a collection of enterprises producing a single product for which no close substitute exists.

Soviet planners have been using a fairly simple approach called the *method of balances* to determine industrial balances. The following example at least roughly approximates how they would record all the sources from which one product—say, iron—is obtained, and all the uses to which it is put—that is, the total need for iron in the economy.

The balance of sources (or intake) and uses (or outgo) for the iron industry would appear as in Table 44.1. Of course it is only the totals that must balance. But somehow enough iron must be available to meet each use or need in each area of the country.

This method encounters many problems. It is very difficult to achieve such a balance among all the conflicting needs and available materials in any single industry. Moreover, the balances are interrelated because each industry relies on others for supplies. For example, more steel is needed to produce more blast furnaces, but more blast furnaces are needed to make more steel. Recently consideration has been given to adopting the input-output method developed in the West, by which a computer can estimate all the balances *if* it is given the correct information.

PRICES AND ECONOMIC PLANNING

One of the most important issues in Soviet planning is the question of how the planners are to decide which outputs society should produce. A related question is which technology is the cheapest for society to use in production.

Under capitalism, the search for profits dictates what is produced. Socialists have been persistent in pointing out that this method of deciding what to produce gives a higher social priority to trinkets, useless gadgets, and other trivia for the wealthy than it does to the necessities of life for the poor. Socialists have always rejected the notion that market prices reflect meaningful social values.

Yet price offers a convenient basis for comparing goods and services that are not directly comparable. If capitalists determined that they could produce several alternative "bundles" of commodities with, say, the $1 million of resources at their disposal, deciding which bundle to produce would be relatively simple for them. Given the resources at their disposal, they would produce the bundle of commodities that had the highest dollar value. They do not claim to be making a philosophical or moral judgment. They are merely maximizing their profits.

But when socialist planners are faced with the same situation—a fixed group of resources from which several possible combinations of outputs can be attained—theirs is a far more difficult task. They are not attempting to maximize private profits. It is the general social welfare that they wish to maximize. In order to choose the combination of commodities that maximizes social welfare, the prices used for calculations must perfectly reflect the goals of a socialist society.

Until the 1950s this was not a terribly important problem for Soviet planners. The USSR was still a backward economy in the 1930s, and rapid industrialization could therefore be achieved simply by copying the product mix and technologies of the most advanced capitalist countries.

By the mid-1950s, however, the Soviet Union had achieved an advanced industrial economy with immense productive capacity. Many more possibilities were technologically available. Furthermore, although rapid growth was still important, it had lost much of its urgency, and the goal of providing more comforts for consumers had assumed much more importance. Under these circumstances the question of how to evaluate the different possible commodity mixes became a central issue of socialist controversy in the Soviet Union. In the next chapter, we shall examine how Soviet managers and Soviet planners are attempting to change their ways of choosing the best technology and the best product mix.

SUMMARY

The Soviet Union was born in the midst of world war and civil war with a backward economy. These conditions plus the drive to industrialize led to a repressive dictatorship. Its use of central planning did allow it to industrialize, and it is now the world's second largest economy. The Soviet economy has full employment, which has allowed it to grow faster than the U.S. economy. Its overcentralization, however, causes inefficiency and a declining growth rate. The Soviet ruling class consists of the party leadership, government bureaucracy, military leaders, and economic planners and managers. In the next chapter we shall see how the Soviet ruling class is trying to overcome the problems of inefficiency and slow growth.

SUGGESTED READINGS

The history and operation of the Soviet economy is discussed in detail in Andrew Zimbalist, Howard Sherman, and Stuart Brown, *Comparing Economic Systems: A Political-Economic Approach*, 2d ed. (San Diego, Calif.: Harcourt Brace Jovanovich, 1989).

REFERENCES

Deutscher, Isaac. *The Unfinished Revolution.* New York: Oxford University Press, 1967.

———. "Roots of Bureaucracy." In *The Socialist Register, 1969.* Edited by R. Miliband and J. Saville. New York: Monthly Review Press, 1969.

Dobson, Richard. "Mobility and Stratification in the Soviet Union," *Annual Review of Sociology.* 3 (1977), pp. 297–329.

Nove, Alec. *An Economic History of the USSR.* Baltimore, Md.: Penguin, 1969.

———. "Income Distribution in the USSR." *Soviet Studies* 34 (April, 1982), pp. 286–288.

Sweezy, Paul, and Leo Huberman. "50 Years of Soviet Power," *Monthly Review* 19 (Nov. 1967), pp. 1–27.

U.S. Congress, Joint Economic Committee. *USSR: Measure of Economic Development.* Washington, D.C.: GPO, 1982.

Yanowitch, Murray. "The Soviet Income Revolution." In *The Soviet Economy*. Edited by M. Bornstein and D. R. Fusfeld. Homewood: Irwin, 1966.

————, and Wesley Wisher. *Social Stratification and Mobility in the USSR*. White Plains, N.Y.: M. E. Sharpe, 1973.

Zimbalist, Andrew, Howard Sherman, and Stuart Brown. *Comparing Economic Systems: A Political-Economic Approach*. 2d ed. San Diego, Calif.: Harcourt Brace Jovanovich, 1989.

Chapter
45

Market Socialism
and Perestroika

The Soviet economy is extremely centralized, and this has caused increasing problems. Mikhail Gorbachev, the leader of the Soviet Union, has recognized these problems and has called for *perestroika*, which means roughly a drastic restructuring of the Soviet economy toward less central control. This chapter begins with a systematic look at Soviet economic problems—mostly recognized by Gorbachev—followed by an examination of Gorbachev's proposed reforms. Finally, we look briefly at the Yugoslav economy, which has moved from centralized planning to a market form of socialism.

PROBLEMS OF CENTRAL PLANNING

The Soviet economy is faced with enormous problems, but it must be emphasized that these problems are very different from the problems of capitalism. In describing the U.S. capitalist economy, it has been shown that one of the most important problems is the lack of demand, which leads to massive unemployment. American stores are full of goods, but not enough people have the money to buy the goods. Since U.S. production is for private profit, employers fire workers when there is insufficient demand.

The Soviet economy, on the contrary, always has plenty of demand for goods because the planners can always order more goods for the government or can issue additional wages to workers. So the Soviet economy is always at full employment; every Soviet worker assumes that he or she will always have a job, and every Soviet citizen assumes that full employment is the major benefit of socialism.

This great strength, however, is also a major cause of Soviet problems. There is usually too much demand for goods and too much demand for labor; the reason is that planners try to produce more than is possible. One result of this excess demand is shortages. There are not enough goods in the stores, so Soviet consumers must accept low-quality goods or use the black market or not buy what they need. Similarly, Soviet firms are faced with shortages of skilled labor and shortages of essential goods, so that they are forced to hire unskilled workers and cannot afford to fire a poor worker. Moreover, Soviet firms must beg, borrow, or steal essential supplies—of which there are shortages—from other firms.

Shortages also result in inflationary pressures. Since Soviet planners set all prices as well as outputs, they can resist inflationary pressures and keep prices artificially low. But there is a cost to this lid on prices. If prices are set too low, there is more demand than supply at stores, so Soviet consumers wait in long lines and sometimes get nothing.

PRICES AND PLANNING

Since Soviet prices are set arbitrarily, they do not reflect the relative value of goods. How can Soviet planners decide, in a rational way, what to produce or how to produce it if all prices are arbitrary? In theory, planners do not need market-generated prices; to make a correct plan they merely need three types of information. First, they must know the relative preferences of individual consumers, industrial units, and government units. Second, they must know what resources are available, including capital goods, raw materials, and all types of labor. Third, at the present level of technology, they must know what combinations of resources will produce what outputs.

With this information, planners can in theory calculate a rational, efficient, and optimal plan for the economy. In practice, however, it is a very difficult task. It would take an army of planners to collect all of the necessary information on millions of individual preferences, available resources and technology. Since there are millions of products, another army of planners is needed to calculate all of the equations describing an optimal economic solution (though high-speed computers may help).

In practice, Soviet planners have collected some of the information, have made some of the calculations, and have produced partially correct plans. When the economy was relatively simple in the 1930s (and technology could be borrowed from more advanced countries), central planning produced full employment and a high rate of growth. Central planning also allowed the USSR to recover rapidly from the devastation of World War II; it put all workers to work and set clear priorities. As the Soviet economy has become more complex, however, and must develop new technology of its own, central planning has become more and more inefficient. This fact has been one cause of the declining Soviet growth rate.

CENTRAL PLANNING AND MANAGERIAL INCENTIVES

Under full employment and central planning, with large bonuses for fulfilling or overfulfilling a plan, managers have strong incentive to appear to produce a lot of goods, but they have no worry about quality because anything can be sold. Managers also have few worries about efficiency because incentives to produce far outweigh disincentives of high costs. The following problems have been noted with respect to Soviet managerial efficiency (for details, see Zimbalist, Sherman, and Brown).

1. *Withholding or slanting information.* Soviet managers cannot submit absolutely false figures because there are many lines of control from above. They can and do, however, withhold some information and slant information, such as what month something was actually produced. Thus, planners are led astray.
2. *Easy plans.* The manager slants the information about capacity and bargains for an easier plan than the plant can actually accomplish. Thus, the plan appears to be overfulfilled, but it is not optimal.
3. *Poor quality.* The temptation is to produce as much as possible by ignoring any controls for quality.
4. *Few styles.* Since Soviet managers can sell almost anything, they have an incentive to produce as few styles of a good as possible because that makes production easier.
5. *Easiest mix.* Similarly, among different types of goods, the Soviet manager will choose the easiest kind to produce, regardless of consumer desire. In the shortage economy, consumers will grumble, but they will buy anything.
6. *Illegal means of supply.* Given the shortages, Soviet managers use every means—including bribes and persons known as "pushers"—to obtain supplies. These illegal or semilegal purchases must disrupt central planning.
7. *Hoarding supplies.* Given the shortages, a rational Soviet manager will hoard supplies for the future, thus aggravating the shortages.
8. *Hoarding labor.* The same argument applies to the hoarding of skilled labor.
9. *Resistance to innovation.* All of the above are ways in which the system of centrally planned statism seriously reduces efficiency at any given time. But the system also reduces dynamic efficiency—that is, economic innovations that would increase efficiency. One reason is that Soviet managers view innovations as risky because innovations may reduce output for some months during the transition. Soviet managers often have a short time horizon because their bonuses are based on monthly production figures and because they are frequently transferred to new jobs.

REFORMING THE SOVIET ECONOMY

By the mid-1960s, the Soviet leadership understood many of the problems of the Soviet economy and wanted to reform it. They sincerely wanted to decentralize most economic decision making down to the enterprise level so that managers could exercise individual initiative in useful directions based on local condition. But there are two major obstacles to Soviet reforms.

One obstacle is the desire of Soviet leaders to continue to determine the overall direction of the economy through an economic plan. Suppose there is a detailed plan, however, telling a manager that she must produce at least 12,625 red, two-door automobiles, that she must employ no more than 1,985 workers, and she can use no more than 1,308,000 rubles of capital. How much local initiative can be exercised?

A second obstacle to reform is that power in the Soviet Union flows from control over production. Millions of middle-level government and party bureaucrats (called the apparatus in the Soviet Union) oppose any reforms that will deprive them of power over enterprises.

In 1962, Soviet leaders allowed an open debate on economic reforms. A Kharkov professor, Evsei G. Liberman, published an article in *Pravda* that initiated a debate on decentralization. The *Kharkov incentive system,* which was what Liberman named his plan, called for important changes in the planning process only at the level of the firm, leaving most of central planning in place. Liberman proposed that enterprises be assigned only their final output mix. The appropriate technology was to be determined by each firm. The more efficiently a firm used its inputs, the lower would be its costs. The lower its costs, the higher would be its net revenue, or profits (total sales revenues minus total costs). Therefore, the size of a firm's profits would be an index of its efficiency. Bonus payments were to be given to firms that made profits above some profitability norm established for the industrial sector of which the firm was a part.

From 1962 to 1965 the Kharkov system was supported and attacked in a lively and penetrating debate. Critics pointed out that cost and profit calculations do not mean a thing if prices and costs do not accurately reflect a reasonable evaluation of social benefits and social costs. The Liberman proposal did not contain any new insights into the solution of this problem. Supporters argued that giving the individual firms more autonomy and responsibility would result in greater economic maneuverability and stronger individual initiatives. These, they asserted, would lead to greater efficiency regardless of whether prices accurately reflected social values. The greater individual freedom in making production decisions and the lure of profit bonuses would lead to more enthusiastic and conscientious application of productive effort.

Critics countered by pointing out the long socialist tradition that rejects, on moral grounds, any economic system that depends on acquisitive, greedy, pecuniary motives. They insisted that Marx's analysis of alienation proved that the root cause of alienation was the use of human beings by other human beings as mere objects to be utilized in the quest for more profits. What, these critics wondered, would differentiate a socialist factory manager, who hired laborers solely to maximize the factory's profits, from his capitalist counterparts? Liberman's answer was that the profits of Soviet industry would still go not to private capitalists but to the Soviet public.

OFFICIAL REFORMS OF 1967

In September 1967 the government responded with a major organizational reform in industry, which moved somewhat in the direction of the Liberman proposals. The stipulations of the 1967 Reform were conservative and tentative, yet they did begin the process of reform. The section pertaining to the individual enterprise contains four significant new policies. First and most important, managers' bonuses are paid for fulfillment of planned targets for sales, profit, or profitability, and physical output. The scale of bonuses was designed to provide relatively higher rewards for fulfillment of targets. Moreover, to evaluate the amount of sales, the *gross value of output* indicator was replaced by *output sold*, which implies the necessity to produce what consumers desire. Numerous detailed target directives were eliminated, including the norms for labor productivity, number of workers and employees, and average wages.

The new economic system, however, continued to maintain the method of direct material allocation of all supplies to enterprises. The reformed system also kept the central limits on total payrolls and allowed managers to choose the labor mix only within those limits.

Even these limited reforms ran into bureaucratic obstruction and sabotage. Thus there were numerous reports of continued extralegal interference by government and party organs in the day-to-day operations of enterprises, including those on the new system. The undoubted difficulties of the new system were resolved in each crisis by renewed centralization. By 1983 the continued resistance of party and government bureaucrats to any change had resulted in the system returning to almost its prereform level of centralized direction.

THE GORBACHEV REFORMS

When Gorbachev became the Soviet leader, he found a declining growth rate and an economy in trouble. He concluded that a comprehensive reform was necessary to overcome the economic problems. First, the enterprise is to be the basic unit of the system. Enterprises will be largely independent of the government ministries, whose powers will be reduced. Moreover, enterprises will also be responsible for their own profits and losses, without government subsidies, and making use of their own self-financing. Second, enterprises must ensure profitability by cutting costs and paying attention to consumer demand. Unprofitable enterprises will go bankrupt, causing temporary unemployment.

Third, the State Planning Commission and the ministries will provide general guidelines for the economy, but will not attempt to micromanage enterprises. Beginning in 1991, enterprises will write their own one-year and five-year plans! They will be judged on how well they fulfill their planned contractual obligations.

Fourth, rather than using administrative commands in planning, the state will use monetary and financial incentives for firms and for workers. For example, skilled or hard-working workers will get higher salaries relative to other workers than at present.

Fifth, in order to ensure that there are good services on which to spend wages, individuals and cooperatives are allowed to provide services, such as clothes cleaning or restaurants, previously run inefficiently by the state.

Sixth, to ensure rational decision making, many prices will be set freely in the market, while some will be set by the state, but as close as possible to actual social value.

Finally, the present rigid system of supplies, in which materials and equipment are given to firms by suppliers only according to the central plan, will be abolished. The present cumbersome system is something like the U.S. system in World War II, when a firm needed not only money, but also a ration allocation to buy a ton of steel. If all of the firm's inputs are fixed in this way, the firm can exercise little independence or initiative. Under the new system, Soviet state enterprises will buy goods and services from other enterprises on the open market. They will thus be constrained by prices but not by bureaucrats.

These are far-reaching reforms if all of them go into effect. That depends on Gorbachev staying in power and on his ability to overcome bureaucratic resistance. If these reforms do go into effect, the Soviet Union will move closer to a market-based socialism rather than a centrally planned socialism. The optimum mix of central planning and use of the market remains to be seen and can only be discovered by trial and error.

The new mix is likely to be more efficient than the old overcentralized system, but it will generate its own new problems. For a look at one socialist system that has switched from planning to the market and from state control to local workers' control, let us examine the evolution of the small but interesting country of Yugoslavia.

YUGOSLAV MARKET SOCIALISM

The Yugoslav experience revealed to the world that a socialist economy could be largely decentralized and directed mainly by the market. In 1948 Yugoslavia broke with the USSR and advocated complete independence and equality for all socialist nations. The Yugoslavs had begun to decentralize their economy and create their own socialist democracy focused on *worker's councils* in each factory. During this period the Yugoslavs advanced the economic theory that central or administrative planning may at first greatly help the progress of a less developed or war-torn socialist economy. As the economy becomes more built up, complex, and interrelated, however, such extreme central direction becomes a barrier to further progress. Some variant of this theory has become the basis for reforms in much of eastern Europe and even the Soviet Union.

After 1950, farming in Yugoslavia reverted to private ownership. There is also a private business sector, mostly in the areas of trade and handicrafts. Private businesses and farms may hire up to five people, but this limit apparently has been exceeded in practice. Farmers may acquire up to 10 hectares of land. The private sector thus plays a very small role in industry but constitutes almost the whole of the farming sector. Private enterprise also plays an increasing role in the catering and service sector.

In the socialist sector of industry each factory is run as a producers' cooperative under the control of its own workers' council. The workers' councils are a feature unique to Yugoslav socialism.

How does the system of workers' councils operate? The workers elect a council. The manager is then appointed by the local government, but the workers' council has veto power over the appointment of the manager. The council can also fire the manager; set wages, within limits established by the central government; set prices, also within limits defined by the central agencies; set production targets and determine technology; and dispose of its profits after taxes through additions to wages, collective welfare projects, or reinvestment. Taxes collected by the national government are used to finance major investment projects as well as defense and welfare.

In practice, there does seem to be worker participation in decision making on personnel, income, and welfare. Some worker participation has occurred in production decisions, but it is less frequent there than in other decision-making areas. Furthermore, there is fairly high attendance at worker assemblies and workers' caucuses.

Because all firms compete in the market, the prices set will reflect supply and demand, provided that there is pure and perfect competition. Nevertheless, because a large percentage of investment is still under central control, capital cannot freely flow to areas of higher profits. This constitutes a barrier to entry of other firms. It may allow monopoly or oligopoly to arise in any area in which the firm size must be very high to achieve optimum production and minimum costs. Because Yugoslavia is a relatively small country and the total market for many commodities is limited, there are many industries in which optimum firm size requires only one or a few producers. As a result of such monopolies, (1) price relationships are distorted away from the socially rational price, (2) resources are therefore allocated wrongly from the social viewpoint, and (3) consumers are exploited in the sense of paying higher prices to these particular firms.

There is also something new in this system with respect to the question of aggregate investment. What makes investment grow in this system? When will a workers' council decide in favor of growth? What is to keep a particular firm's workers from deciding that all of their profits should go into current wages or welfare projects rather than reinvestment and expansion of the productive base? Legally the only constraint is that the firm must first pay its taxes to the central government. The central government does take a very large tax bite, and much of this revenue has been used for investment.

Yugoslavs also claim that the workers are generally very unwilling to make many large reinvestments, supposedly being content to wait for the large future returns. The Communist party group within each enterprise also strongly encourages collective welfare projects and reinvestment for expansion of the productive base. And the manager of the enterprise exerts a somewhat independent pressure, in most cases advocating expansion of the enterprise's capital. Actually it appears that the balance of power over the distribution of income between workers and managers and higher authorities varies from plant to plant as well as from year to year.

ADVANTAGES OF YUGOSLAV SELF-MANAGEMENT

Yugoslavia claims that it has the best of both worlds, both competition and socialism. Because it is decentralized and practices market competition, its economy should be much more efficient than the overcentralized Soviet economy—and the virtues of competition are praised in Yugoslavia along the lines argued by Adam Smith. It is certainly true that the Yugoslav economy has far less bureaucratic interference than the USSR. The Communist party of Yugoslavia still runs a one-party government, but the central government is relatively weak. Thus most of the economic problems caused by excessive central planning in the USSR are absent in Yugoslavia.

On the other hand, Yugoslavia claims that it has socialism with democratic workers' control at the firm level. Thus Yugoslav theorists claim that they have reached the socialist goal of economic power residing with the workers, while both private capitalists and government bureaucrats have been eliminated from economic decision making. There are periodic elections in every Yugoslav enterprise, in which the workers elect the ruling council that appoints the management.

Any profits are divided as the workers' council decides. Thus the socialist goal of no private profit has been reached. The council may decide to reinvest the profits (beyond taxes) or may decide to distribute the profits as bonuses to the workers. Income distribution is therefore fair, and exploitation has been abolished in the official view.

Moreover, since the workers have full control of the profits, workers should be more highly motivated than in a capitalist-run firm or in a centrally planned firm. Workers have the incentive, not only of their wages, but also of contributing to enterprise profits, which are also theirs. Thus they claim that the incentive problems of centrally planned economies have been eliminated.

PROBLEMS OF YUGOSLAV SELF-MANAGEMENT

It has been argued by some critics that Yugoslavia has the worst of both worlds—the evils that accompany the market as well as the evils of statism. The first problem is that workers' participation in the self-management process is limited. Some workers do not vote for their representatives, many are bored with meetings, and many do not see themselves as really affecting the process. As a result, some elections may be dominated by the organized activities of the trade union or Communist party leaders (like organized groups in all countries). Also due to levels of participation, blue-collar workers are very much underrepresented on the workers' councils, while white-collar and technocratic workers are overrepresented.

Monopoly

A second problem is that a high level of economic concentration drastically limits competition (though there is foreign competition). In 1977 the 130 largest firms in manufacturing and mining had 70 percent of all sales and 48 percent of all employment (see Zimbalist, Sherman, and Brown). Some economists from "socialist" Yugoslavia have even come to the United States to study U.S. antitrust laws, though the U.S. laws have been very ineffectual. Even neoclassical economists do not claim that the market can perform wonders if the industrial structure is mostly oligopolistic. Firms using monopoly power may put local firm's interests above the general social interest.

Income Inequality

Third, the use of the market by each enterprise in competition with all other firms means that some firms are much wealthier than others. More-over, the intensely competitive environment tends to lead to inequality of salaries within the firm. Thus, by rewarding the control that some firms have of resources or of the market, and by rewarding skills within the firm, Yugoslavia has witnessed a growing degree of inequality. Often, within firms the highest paid skilled workers earn 20 times the wages of the least skilled workers; by contrast, the Soviet ratio is only about 3.5 to 1. Of course, U.S. salaries range up to $1,000,000 for some managers, so the ratio is far more unequal. Nevertheless, the overall income distribution of Yugoslavia comes remarkably close to that of the United States. For ex-ample, in 1981, the top 10 percent of U.S. income receivers earned 27 percent of all income, while the top 10 percent in Yugoslavia received 23 percent of all income.

Inflation

Fourth, in practice, the continued increase of the market in Yugoslavia has been one factor leading to more and more inflation under present conditions. From 1956 to 1964, Yugoslavia had 1.5 percent inflation per year. Inflation rose to 10.4 percent per year in 1965 to 1970. Inflation rose still further to 14.5 percent per year from 1976 to 1980. Finally, in 1981 to 1983 inflation was 35 percent per year. Such rates of inflation are very disruptive to the economy as well as to the lives of ordinary people.

Instability and Unemployment

Fifth, another problem that socialism was supposed to have avoided, but that is found in Yugoslavia today, is a certain degree of job insecurity and unemployment. The possibility of unemployment exists because Yugoslavia has a market system and is not subject to central planning of output, savings, and investment—or at least not more central planning than in most capitalist countries. At first this problem was overcome by a sufficient amount of central investment and by exportation of about 400,000 workers, mostly to West Germany. Now West Germany has its own unemployment problems, so many of the Yugoslav workers have been sent back to Yugoslavia.

As the use of the market has grown in Yugoslavia, so has production instability and periodic unemployment. Average unemployment was 5.5 percent from 1960 to 1965, but grew to 7.5 percent from 1965 to 1976, and to 12 percent from 1977 to 1980.

Capitalist-Like Motivations

Finally, the system of competition among firms, decentralization, and use of the market, with growing inequality of income, means that people's psychological motivations are changing in Yugoslavia. Workers and managers are coming to show every sign of capitalist-like greed for income and profits. This is a problem if Yugoslavia wishes to maintain its socialist goals.

SUMMARY

The centrally planned economies of the USSR and eastern Europe have had increasing problems because of too much centralization. The results have been inefficiency, distortions of managerial incentives, and declining growth rates. A new view of socialism has emerged that wishes to overcome these problems by combining some central planning with considerable decentralization and more use of the market while maintaining social or collective ownership. The Soviet leadership is taking bold steps in this direction, but is meeting some resistance, so that the final result is still unknown. Yugoslavia has gone far down this road, with each firm run by a workers' collective management, with most prices and outputs set by the market. Yugoslavia has increased enterprise efficiency and has no shortage of goods in the stores, but it is afflicted with the typical market capitalist diseases of monopoly, inequality, inflation, and unemployment. Obviously, more trial and error will be needed to find an optimum combination of planning and markets under socialism.

SUGGESTED READINGS

These issues of planning and markets under socialism in the Soviet Union, China, eastern Europe, and Cuba are covered in great detail in Andrew Zimbalist, Howard Sherman, and Stuart Brown, *Comparing Economic Systems: A Political-Economic Approach* (San Diego, Calif.: Harcourt Brace Jovanovich, 1989), chaps. 4–15. The political and economic arguments and differing views on these issues are presented more fully in Howard Sherman, *Foundations of Radical Political Economy* (Armonk, N.Y.: M. E. Sharpe, 1987), chaps 10–17. A fascinating book from the Soviet point of view is Mikhail Gorbachev, *Perestroika* (New York: Harper & Row, 1987).

REFERENCE

Zimbalist, Andrew, Howard Sherman, and Stuart Brown. *Comparing Economic Systems: A Political-Economic Approach*, 2d ed. San Diego, Calif.: Harcourt Brace Jovanovich, 1989.

Chapter
46

Socialism, Democracy, and Glasnost

This chapter discusses the democratic vision of socialism held by most American radicals, then contrasts it with the Soviet situation and Gorbachev's promise of *glasnost* (or openness).

THE SOCIALIST VISION

For the last 150 years, millions of people have committed their lives to the fight for socialism. In this struggle many have lost their jobs or gone to jail, and many have been killed (for example, thousands of socialists were killed in Hitler's Germany). Why were all these people willing to give so much for the goal of socialism? Socialists have a vision. It is a vision of a world without poverty, without unemployment, without discrimination, and without war. To achieve such a world they believe it is necessary to end private capitalist ownership of the economy, and to have the economy owned collectively by all the people. Socialism is a world with jobs for all at decent wages under pleasant working conditions, with equality and freedom for all, and peace in a unified world community. It is a world in which there is no bitter and vicious economic competition for survival. It is a world in which all people will cooperate and the people will run the economy in a democratic manner. There will be no more rich employers and poor workers. Socialists believe that this can be achieved with a socialist economy.

Socialism means the democratic control of the economy by the entire working class. The working class is now over 90 percent of the American people. Under socialism, the capitalists would be deprived of their monopolistic private ownership of industry, and the working class would eventually become 100 percent of all Americans. So socialism in the long run means ownership and control of the economy by all the people and for all the people. It means an economy no longer run for profit but with the goal of a maximum social well-being for everyone, black or white, male or female, young or old.

This goal of democratic control of the economy has obviously not been met by the Soviet Union. The Soviet economy is run by the government, but until now that government was run by a small self-appointed group.

ECONOMIC DEMOCRACY

American critical economists have followed the Soviet experience with dismay because of its undemocratic character and overcentralized economy. They have had some interest in the Yugoslav economy because of the worker control exercised in each plant, in spite of the continued undemocratic running of the federal government—but they have also noted the problems generated by Yugoslavia's use of the market. Finally, they have also watched some western European experiments, in which democratic governments do some planning, appoint managers to run some enterprises in the public interest, and have extensive social welfare.

None of these experiments, nor any other foreign country's performance, have been good enough that American critical economists wish to follow any of them blindly. The vision of American critics has always been *economic democracy*, which means the extension of the sovereignty of the people from the political sphere into the economic sphere. Critical economists see it as ethically wrong and economically inefficient in performance to have a few capitalists run enormous corporations for their own benefit. All of the giant monopoly corporations should be run democratically of, by, and for the people. That would include the thousand largest corporations that control two-thirds of the U.S. economy.

Exactly how would economic democracy work? There are many different views among critical economists and no one dominating view. Basically, there are two main possibilities. One is to run the giant firms as government enterprises, just as the post office or the national parks are. The democratically elected U.S. government could then appoint the managers to the enterprises. Many enterprises do not need national management but are local or regional. The regional ones can be run by one state or by several states. The local enterprises can be run by cities, as many now are, including electricity, buses, cable television, and the like.

The second way to have economic democracy is to give workers direct control over their own enterprise. Each worker would have a vote in controlling the enterprise. A few U.S. enterprises are run this way right now. It would be possible to nationalize plants and then turn them over to the workers in them. Many other possibilities exist. Some proponents of economic democracy would slowly extend workers' participation in existing corporations, but this tends to take forever without giving workers any significant control.

Obviously, all of these are far-reaching proposals. Some of the consequences would appear to be very positive, such as reduction of inequality or elimination of business cycles (by democratic planning). There are, however, many problems discussed by the critics, ranging from fear of dictatorial big government if central planning is used, to the problems of the market mechanism apparent in Yugoslav market socialism. Nevertheless, there is a strong movement toward economic democracy evident in much of the world, including the United States to an extent.

SOVIET GLASNOST

For many decades, the Soviet Union has stood as a decisive argument against socialism because it has been so undemocratic and oppressive while claiming to be socialist. During Stalin's rule of the Soviet Union, when he used unpopular methods and ruthless oppression to support a rapid industrialization drive, thousands of people were executed for their political opinions. After Stalin died in 1953, the industrialization drive was relaxed and the most severe repression ended.

No one has been executed in the USSR for political reasons since 1953. When Khrushchev was leader of the Soviet Union in the late 1950s, he criticized Stalin and dictatorship. Khrushchev instituted a few democratic reforms and allowed much open discussion in the Soviet Union for a while. After Khrushchev was overthrown, there was a long period of dull bureaucrats as Soviet leaders; during that time repression increased again, though it never approached the levels under Stalin. Free speech was restricted and some people went to jail; but there was no resumption of wholesale imprisonment for thousands of people (and no one was executed).

Then, in the late 1980s Mikhail Gorbachev became the leader of the Soviet Union. He instituted a policy of *glasnost*, or "openness," which has already resulted in a remarkable transformation of the Soviet Union. One reason for democratic openness is that the Soviet leaders are convinced that lack of free speech has hindered economic development and prevented economic reform. Thus, economic crisis has helped to open the door to democratization.

The drive for openness has meant that Soviet people feel free to speak their minds. There is an intensive debate in many areas, particularly in the discussion of economic reform. Soviet newspapers—once so dull that no one wanted to read them—now are full of political arguments and people wait in line to buy them. In February 1989, there appeared the first letter in a Soviet newspaper criticizing Gorbachev by name. If the Soviet Union is really to be democratized to any great extent, it will be a revolutionary event affecting world history in our time. A Soviet Union practicing democracy with an efficient socialist economy would clearly make socialism more attractive around the world.

In December 1988, the Soviet congress, called the Supreme Soviet, under Gorbachev's leadership decided to make drastic changes in the Soviet constitution, completely revamping their political process. Under glasnost, there has been some endorsement of these proposals, but there have also been widespread criticisms that the proposals do not go far enough in democratization.

It was proposed that all elections should be by secret ballot, that anyone can be nominated, and that there must be at least two candidates for each office. On the other hand, an electoral commission can reduce the candidates if more than two are nominated. Moreover, many seats are reserved without election to the Communist Party and organizations controlled by it.

Under the new constitution, in May 1989 the Soviets elected a new congress of 2500 members, which met and passed some major reforms. It then elected a smaller body of 450 members to be Supreme Soviet. The Supreme Soviet elected Mikhail Gorbachev to be president and then began to work on the details of the reform legislation.

Critics of the new constitution were worried that the Communist Party apparatus would dominate the elections and the new Supreme Soviet, but that has not happened. In the congressional elections, about 25 percent of all official Communist Party candidates were defeated. In the new Supreme Soviet, the legislators have proven to be quite independent. They have rejected some government nominees for high positions and they have even subjected the head of the secret police to a rigorous interrogation.

There is also a Committee of Constitutional Oversight, which cannot declare anything unconstitutional by itself, but it can suspend legislation and attempt to persuade the legislature or president that the law is unconstitutional. Critics are unhappy because they wanted a supreme court that could invalidate a law completely if it is unconstitutional.

All of these steps are progressive, with some greater democratization, but Gorbachev's reforms leave a long way to go. It will require experience over many years to see how much democracy is actually produced by these reforms.

The Gorbachev political reforms resemble the political reforms of Alexander Dubchek in Czechoslovakia in 1968, when he tried to lead the Czech Communist party toward "socialism with a human face," a completely democratic and socialist society. Dubchek was overthrown by an invasion of Soviet soldiers and tanks. He dropped out of sight, but has recently resurfaced and spoken in favor of Gorbachev's reforms. Dubchek said that violations of civil and human rights "are in complete contrast with the ideals of socialism. . . . Socialism and democracy are two matching terms. If democracy weakens, if its ties with socialism are not respected, socialism itself is diminished, thus leading to crisis" (Dubchek, p. 47).

When Dubchek was asked about the power of Gorbachev to reform the Soviet Union, Dubchek replied that it will be a long, hard road with much opposition: "But . . . [Gorbachev] has one advantage: there is no danger of the tanks that rolled over us in 1968" (ibid., p. 49).

Its military might is indeed the difference between the USSR and eastern Europe. Thus Soviet repression often leads to eastern European repression, whereas Soviet reforms (perestroika and glasnost) are leading toward eastern European reforms. If both the USSR and eastern Europe are democratized, then most Communist parties will change their tune and democratic socialist movements will grow in western Europe, Japan, and the United States.

SUMMARY

Socialists define *socialism* to mean economic democracy, the extension of democratic control by the people from the political process to the economic process. Democratic control of the economy means the end of enormous private fortunes; it means that the economy is controlled of, by, and for those who work for a living (the vast majority of the U.S. population—85 or 90 percent of the people). There would be democratic control both through the government and through local control of enterprises.

Although the Soviet Union claims to be socialist, until recently it had nothing in common with this vision. It was controlled over most of its history by a small, dictatorial group exercising repressive powers. Whenever democratic socialism looked as if it might liberate an eastern European country (Hungary in 1957, Czechoslovakia in 1968, or Poland in 1980), the Soviet Union smashed these movements. Now, however, the Soviet leader, Gorbachev, is himself promising democratic reforms. Some of these reforms have been put into practice, but how far they will go is still completely unpredictable.

SUGGESTED READINGS

Issues of socialism and democracy are covered extensively in Howard Sherman, *Foundations of Radical Political Economy* (Armonk, N.Y.: M. E. Sharpe, 1987), pts. 3 and 4. Also see the fascinating book by Mikhail Gorbachev, *Perestroika* (New York: Harper & Row, 1987).

REFERENCE

Dubchek, Alexander. "Time as a Gentleman." *New Perspectives Quarterly* 5 (Winter 1989), pp. 46–49.

Index